HUMAN DEVELOPMENT REPORT 2002

Deepening democracy in a fragmented world

Published
for the United Nations
Development Programme
(UNDP)

New York   Oxford
Oxford University Press
2002

Oxford University Press
Oxford   New York
Athens   Auckland   Bangkok   Calcutta
Cape Town   Chennai   Dar es Salaam   Delhi
Florence   Hong Kong   Istanbul   Karachi
Kuala Lumpur   Madrid   Melbourne
Mexico City   Mumbai   Nairobi   Paris
Singapore   Taipei   Tokyo   Toronto

and associated companies in
Berlin   Ibadan

Copyright ©2002
by the United Nations Development Programme
1 UN Plaza, New York, New York, 10017, USA

Published by Oxford University Press, Inc.
198 Madison Avenue, New York, New York, 10016

Oxford is a registered trademark of Oxford University Press

ISBN 0-19-521915-5

9 8 7 6 5 4 3 2 1
Printed in by Phønix-Trykkeriet A/S, Aarhus, Denmark on acid-free, recycled paper. ISO 14001 certified and EMAS-approved.

Cover and design: Gerald Quinn, Quinn Information Design, Cabin John, Maryland

Editing, desktop composition and production management: Communications Development Incorporated,
Washington, DC

TEAM FOR THE PREPARATION OF
Human Development Report 2002

Director and Lead Author
Sakiko Fukuda-Parr

Lead Consultant
Ngaire Woods

Special Adviser
Nancy Birdsall

Core team
Omar Noman (Deputy Director), Haishan Fu (Chief of Statistics), Silva Bonacito, Emmanuel Boudard, Claes Johansson, Petra Mezzetti, Tanni Mukhopadhyay, Richard Ponzio, Paul Segal, David Stewart and Aisha Talib

Statistical adviser: Tom Griffin

Principal consultants
Isabella Bakker, Nicole Ball, Christian Barry, Michael Brzoska, Richard Falk, Ann-Marie Goetz, Robert Jenkins, Mary Kaldor, Adeel Malik, Malini Mehra, Santosh Mehrotra, Pippa Norris, Siddiqur Osmani, Paul Streeten and Ashutosh Varshney

Editors: Stephanie Flanders and Bruce Ross-Larson
Design: Gerald Quinn

Foreword

This *Human Development Report* is first and foremost about the idea that politics is as important to successful development as economics. Sustained poverty reduction requires equitable growth—but it also requires that poor people have political power. And the best way to achieve that in a manner consistent with human development objectives is by building strong and deep forms of democratic governance at all levels of society.

That assertion remains controversial. Many detractors suggest that, particularly in developing countries, democracy tends to be too messy, uncontrolled and prone to manipulation and abuse to provide the stability and continuity needed for sustained social and economic reform. But as the Report makes clear, such arguments are wrong on two grounds.

First, while there is clearly scope for legitimate and lively debate on what policies and practices are best for securing economic growth, democracies are on balance no worse than other forms of government in boosting economic performance. And democracies are notably better in meeting the most pressing social needs of citizens, particularly at moments of crisis or displacement that most affect poor people. Second—and just as important—democratic participation is a critical end of human development, not just a means of achieving it.

Nevertheless, whether we are talking about global governance systems confronting the myriad challenges of an increasingly interconnected world, national governments struggling to meet the needs of their citizens or the corporate and private forces in national and global life thrown up by the economic, social and technological changes of recent decades, it is clear that effective democratic governance is not yet a reality.

As the Report also shows, at current trends a significant portion of the world's states are unlikely to achieve the Millennium Development Goals, including the overarching target of halving extreme poverty by 2015. Many countries are poorer than 10, 20 and in some cases 30 years ago. Just as troubling, the flush of euphoria that saw the number of countries embracing many of the hallmarks of democracy—particularly multiparty elections—soar to 140 over the past 15 years is starting to turn into frustration and despair.

While there are some welcome and notable exceptions, in many of these countries governments have failed to provide the jobs, services and personal security their citizens so badly need and want. A growing number of this new wave of democratic governments—and even some longer-established ones—have slipped back into increasingly undemocratic practices, with leaders altering constitutions, bullying weak legislatures and judiciaries, and openly manipulating elections, often with a devastating effect on human development.

Further, in countries where majority rule through the ballot-box is established, it is often at the expense of minority rights: too often the absence of a democratic culture means that those who lose elections are either persecuted by the winners or refuse to accept legitimate electoral outcomes. Democracies require not just legitimate governments but legitimate oppositions too.

In some of these countries—and in many others that have yet to take even timid steps towards democracy—the result is an increasingly alienated and angry population, especially young people. That hostility is triggering a backlash against both existing regimes and the impersonal forces of globalization. In the most extreme cases radical or fundamentalist groups are embracing violent solutions to their grievances, as tragically illustrated by the terrorist attacks of September 11, 2001, and their global repercussions.

When combined with growing transnational threats, from HIV/AIDS to climate change, and exacerbated by a global economic system that on most measures remains firmly tilted in favour of industrial countries, the result is a growing crisis in governance in many parts of the world. From the streets of Seattle, Washington, and Genoa, Italy, to the factories and fields of large parts of Asia, Africa and Latin America, citizens everywhere have been losing faith in the ability and commitment of their political leaders to tackle these pressing challenges.

How should we respond?

It has become common in recent years to hear policy-makers and development experts describe good governance as the "missing link" to successful growth and economic reform in developing countries. But attention has focused almost exclusively on economic processes and administrative efficiency.

The central message of this Report is that effective governance is central to human development, and lasting solutions need to go beyond such narrow issues and be firmly grounded in democratic politics in the broadest sense. In other words, not democracy as practiced by any particular country or group of countries—but rather a set of principles and core values that allow poor people to gain power through participation while protecting them from arbitrary, unaccountable actions in their lives by governments, multinational corporations and other forces.

That means ensuring that institutions and power are structured and distributed in a way that gives real voice and space to poor people and creates mechanisms through which the powerful—whether political leaders, corporations or other influential actors—can be held accountable for their actions.

At the national level such a deepening of democracy requires a focus on strengthening the democratic state institutions that form the necessary foundation for achieving any broader objectives. And at the global level it highlights the urgency of forging a much more democratic space in which international institutions and transnational coalitions operate with the highest degree of transparency and give developing countries both a seat at the table and a meaningful say in decisions that affect them.

More practically, for the work of agencies like UNDP, it also highlights the importance of devoting resources and expertise to the difficult question of how to give these ideas practical form by identifying and helping countries implement policies and practices—in areas ranging from strengthening parliaments to building accountable police forces to decentralizing power to the local level—that will best achieve these overarching objectives.

Like all *Human Development Reports*, this is an unapologetically independent analysis aimed at advancing the debate on human development. As such it is not a formal statement of UNDP or UN policy. Nevertheless, I believe that its central message is very relevant for the broader work of UNDP and its partners. The Millennium Development Goals are still achievable. But we will only succeed in meeting them if national and global leaders have the vision and courage to first confront these critical issues of democratic governance.

Mark Malloch Brown
Administrator, UNDP

The analysis and policy recommendations of this Report do not necessarily reflect the views of the United Nations Development Programme, its Executive Board or its Member States. The Report is an independent publication commissioned by UNDP. It is the fruit of a collaborative effort by a team of eminent consultants and advisers and the *Human Development Report* team. Sakiko Fukuda-Parr, Director of the Human Development Report Office, led the effort, with extensive advice and collaboration from Nancy Birdsall, Special Adviser to the Administrator.

Acknowledgements

This Report could not have been prepared without the generous contributions of many individuals and organizations.

The Report team is particularly grateful to Amartya Sen for his advice and insights on the important role of democracy for human development and for his continued participation in the annual *Human Development Reports*.

CONTRIBUTORS

Background research commissioned for the Report was contributed by Isabella Bakker, Nicole Ball, Christian Barry, Michael Brzoska, Lynn Carter, Richard Falk, Ann-Marie Goetz and Robert Jenkins, Mary Kaldor, Kees Kingma and Herbert Wulf, Linda Maguire, Adeel Malik, Malini Mehra, Santosh Mehrotra, Shandana Khan Mohmand, Pippa Norris and Dieter Zinnbauer, Siddiqur Osmani, Paul Streeten, Ashutosh Varshney and Ngaire Woods.

Regional studies on selected themes commissioned for the Report were contributed by Marek Dabrovski and Radzislawa Gortat, Mohammad Fajrul Falaakh, Takashi Inoguchi, Wojciech Marchlewski, Lincoln Mitchell and Leo Glickman, Ahmed Mohiddin, Nazih Richani, Naomi Sakr, Catalina Smulovitz and Enrique Peruzzotti, Sergio Spoerer, Katarina Subasic, Wisdom Tettey and Raimo Vayrynen.

Several organizations generously shared their data and other research materials: the Carbon Dioxide Information Analysis Center, Center for International and Interarea Comparisons (University of Pennsylvania), Food and Agriculture Organization, Freedom House, International Institute for Strategic Studies, International Labour Organization, International Telecommunication Union, Inter-Parliamentary Union, Joint United Nations Programme on HIV/AIDS, Luxembourg Income Study, Organisation for Economic Co-operation and Development, PRS Group, Stockholm International Peace Research Institute, Transparency International, UNDP Oslo Governance Centre, United Nations Children's Fund, United Nations Conference on Trade and Development, United Nations Department for Disarmament Affairs, United Nations Department of Economic and Social Affairs, United Nations Educational, Scientific and Cultural Organization, United Nations High Commissioner for Refugees, United Nations Interregional Crime and Justice Research Institute, United Nations Population Division, United Nations Statistics Division, University of Maryland Polity IV Project, World Bank, World Health Organization, World Intellectual Property Organization and World Trade Organization.

ADVISORY PANELS

The Report benefited greatly from intellectual advice and guidance provided by an external advisory panel of eminent experts on democracy, human rights, global economic policies and governance. The panel included Charles Abugre, Tunku Abdul Aziz, Kwesi Botchwey, Diane Elson, Richard Goldstone, Rima Khalaf Hunaidi, Asma Jahangir, Devaki Jain, Anders B. Johnsson, Devesh Kapur, Martin Khor, Klaus M. Leisinger, Juan J. Linz, Mahmood Mamdani, Olawuyi Omitoogun, Hafiz Pasha, Ann Pettifor, Sonia S. Picado, Sandra Pralong, Bengt Säve-Söderberg, Paul Streeten, Mark Suzman and Emmanuel Tumusiime-Mutebile. An advisory panel on statistics included Sudhir Anand, Lidia Barreiros, Jean-Louis Bodin, William de Vries, Lamine Diop, Carmen Feijo, Andrew Flatt, Paolo Garonna, Leo Goldstone, Irina Krizman, Nora Lustig, Shavitri Singh, Tim

Smeedling, Sudardi Surbakti, Alain Tranap and Michael Ward.

CONSULTATIONS

The Report benefited from the inputs provided at a series of regional meetings. These meetings, organized with the help of UNDP's regional bureaus, were conducted to solicit regional perspectives on the themes of the Report for Africa, Latin America and the Caribbean, the Arab States, Asia and the Pacific, South Asia and Central and Eastern Europe and the Commonwealth of Independent States (CIS). The meetings were hosted by the country offices of Bangladesh, Costa Rica, Indonesia, Japan, Morocco and Poland. The success of these meetings owed much to their hosts, particularly Bo Asplund, Marc Destanne de Bernis, Bouna Sémou Diouf, Ligia Elizondo, Sukehiro Hasegawa and Jorgen Lissner. The Report team is also grateful to the organizers in the country offices, including Latifa Bakhiyi, Mohamed Boussami, Jeanne Felix, Akiko Fuji, Charaf-e Gharbaoui, Shamim Hamid, Andre Klap, Karolina Myzk, Edward Newman, Olivier Ranaivondrambola, Bona Siahaan, Alek Siwinski and Cathy Stevulak.

The Report team also thanks all those who participated in the consultations. In Dhaka (Bangladesh): Muzzamel Huq, Akmal Hussain, Javed Jabbar, Abdur Rob Khan, Prakash Chandra Lohani, Neelabh Mishra, Saeed Quereshi, Mohan Man Sainju, Bhabani Sen Gupta, Rehman Sobhan and Asha Swarup.

In San Jose (Costa Rica): Manuel Alcántara, Dante Caputo, Thomas Carothers, Michael Coppedge, Pablo Da Silveira, Miguel Gutiérrez, Osvaldo Iazzetta, Gabriela Ippólito, Marta Lagos, Nobert Lechner, Sebastián Mazzuca, Juan Mendez, Cerdas Rodolfo, Juan Manuel Salazar, María Herminia Tavares, Jorge Vargas Cullell, Evelyn Villarreal and Laurence Whitehead.

In Jakarta (Indonesia): Dewi Fortuna Anwar, Antonio Assuncao, Ernesto Bautista, G. Bayasgalan, Binny Buchori, Edimon Ginting, Bambang Harymurty, Vu Quoc Huy, Dita Indahsari, Yuli Ismartono, Ryaas Rasjid, Bong-Scuk Sohn, Phonesaly Souksavath, R. Sudarshan, Wilfrido V. Villacorta, Erna Witoelar and Roya Tabatabaei Yazdi.

In Tokyo (Japan): Julius Court, Wakako Hironaka, Ryokichi Hirono, Yukiko Kawahashi, Katsuhide Kitatani, Yoko Kitazawa, Yoko Komiyama, Kyoko Kuwajima, Kazumoto Momose, Kimihide Mushakoji, Shuzo Nakamura, Deepak Nayyar, John O'Shea, Yasuaki Onuma, Yasutami Shimomura, Makoto Taniguchi, Ramesh Thakur, Chizuko Ueno and Yozo Yokota.

In Tangier (Morocco): Rachid Belkahia, Benacer El Baz, Mostapha Faïk, Nader Fergany, Ahmed Gouitâa, Carol Hakim, Ahmed Ibrahimi, Moncef Kouidhi, Amina Lemrini, Camille Mansour, Achille Mbembe and Sandra Pepera.

In Warsaw (Poland): Viatsheslav Bakhmin, Dagmara Baraniewska, Andrzej Brzozowski, Janusz Czamarski, Wojciech Gasparski, Miroslawa Grabowska, Pawel Grzesik, Barbara Imiolczyk, Antoni Kamiński, Lena Kolarska-Bobińská, Ilko Kucheriv, Lidia Kuczmierowska, Barbara Mrówka, Krzysztof Mroziewicz, Ewa Poplawska, Jerzy Regulski, Janusz Reykowski, Anna Rozicka, Andrzej Rychard, Talis Tisenkopfs, Irena Wóycicka, Sabit Zhusupov and Andrzej Zoll.

Many individuals consulted during the preparation of the Report provided invaluable advice, information and material, and attended other consultation meetings. The Report team thanks Yasmin Ahmad, Alessandra Alfieri, Bettina Aten, Yusuf Bangura, Benjamin Barber, Grace Bediako, Eric Bertherat, Claude Jean Bertrand, Ana-Pilar Betrán, Yonas Biru, Dana Blumin, Barbara Boland, Françoise Bravard, Sharon Capeling-Alakija, Edelisa Carandang, Marc Cassidy, Shiu-Kee Chu, Marc Copin, Patrick Cornu, Marlo Corrao, Marie-France Croisier, Sam Dawes, Michael Doyle, Michael Edwards, Elisabeth Feller-Dansokho, Mariona Ferrer, Rodolfo Roque Fuentes, Maria Gratschew, Emmanuel Guindon, Messaoud Hammouya, Andrew Harvey, Eivind Hoffmann, Bela Hovy, José Augusto Hueb, Jens Johansen, Lawrence Jeffrey Johnson, Ian Johnstone, Gareth Jones, Harriet Kabagenyi, Tapio Kanninen, Karin Karlekar, Daniel Kaufmann, Jim Ketterer, Richard Kohl, Karoly Kovacs, Murat Küpcu, Olivier Labe, Georges LeMaitre, Xiaobo Lu, Nyein Nyein Lwin, Douglas Lynd, Esperanza Magpantay, Monty G. Marshall, Adriana Mata-Greenwood, Jorge Matter, Caralee McLiesh, Farhad Mehran, Maria Helena Capelli Miguel, Branko Milanovic, Mick

viii

Moore, Caroline Moser, Sumie Nakaya, Andrew J. Nathan, Rachel Neild, Guillermo O'Donnell, Paul Oquist, Enrique Ordaz, Jude Padayachy, Rosario Pardo, Christine Pintat, William Prince, Agnes Puymoyen, Jonathan Quick, Hanta Rafalimanana, Asenaca Ravuvu, Mireille Razafindrakoto, Matthias Reister, Horacio Santamaria, Akilagpa Sawyerr, Bernhard Schwartlander, Andrei Shleifer, Joseph Siegle, Petter Stålenheim, Leonard R. Sussman, Karen Taswell, Viviene Taylor, Gordon Telesford, Ramesh Thakur, Maja Tjernström, John van Kesteren, Antonio Viegas, Neff Walker, Tessa Wardlaw, Siemon Wezeman, Abiodun Williams, Yuxue Xue, Sylvester A. Young and Hania Zlotnik.

UNDP READERS

A Readers Group, made up of colleagues in UNDP, provided extremely useful comments, suggestions and inputs during the writing of the Report. The Report team is especially grateful to Neil Buhne, Fernando Calderon, John Hendra, Zahir Jamal, Abdoulie Janneh, Bruce Jenks, Sirkka Korpela, Robert Leigh, Justin Leites, Carlos Lopes, Linda Maguire, Kamal Malhotra, Khalid Malik, Lamin Manneh, Elena Martinez, Saraswathi Menon, Kalman Mizsei, K. Seeta Prabhu, Tore Rose, Andrew Russell, Julia Taft, Pauline Tamesis, Gulden Turkoz-Cosslett, Antonio Vigilante, Gita Welch, Caitlin Wiesen and Kanni Wignaraja

The Report team also benefited from collaboration with colleagues in UNDP's Bureau for Crisis Prevention and Recovery, Bureau for Development Policy, and Institutional Development Group, and in the UN Development Fund for Women.

STAFF SUPPORT

Administrative support for the Report's preparation was provided by Oscar Bernal, Renuka Corea-Lloyd and Mamaye Gebretsadik. Other colleagues from the Human Development Report Office provided invaluable inputs: Sarah Burd-Sharps, Mary Ann Mwangi, Shahrbanou Tadjbakhsh, Frederik Teboul, Nena Terrell and Anne Louise Winsløv. The Report also benefited from the dedicated work of interns: Jenny Berg, Michael G. Bober, Natalia Caruso, Nina Hoas, Eva Kamau, Halima-Noor Khan and Thomas Pave Sohnesen. Linda Cheng and Emily White made valuable contributions to the statistical team.

Liliana Izquierdo, Juan Luis Larrabure and Natalia Palgova of the UN Office for Project Services provided critical administrative support and management services.

EDITING, PRODUCTION AND TRANSLATION

As in previous years, the Report benefited from the editors of Communications Development Incorporated—Meta de Coquereaumont, Paul Holtz, Bruce Ross-Larson, Stephanie Rostron and Alison Strong. The Report was designed by Gerald Quinn and laid out by Damon Iacovelli and Jason Osder.

The Report also benefited from the translation, design and distribution work of Elizabeth Scott Andrews, Maureen Lynch and Hilda Paqui.

* * *

The team expresses sincere appreciation to the Report's peer reviewers—John Cavanagh, Mary Kaldor, Terry Lynn Karl and Adam Przeworski—who carefully reviewed drafts and shared their most recent research and insights. The team is also grateful to Irena Krizman, Lene Mikkelsen and Darryl Rhoades, the statistical peer reviewers who scrutinized the use of data in the Report and lent their statistical expertise.

Finally, the authors are especially grateful to Mark Malloch Brown, UNDP's Administrator, for his leadership and vision. Although thankful for all the support they have received, the authors assume full responsibility for the opinions expressed in the Report.

Sakiko Fukuda-Parr
Director
Human Development Report 2002

Contents

OVERVIEW
Deepening democracy in a fragmented world   1

HUMAN DEVELOPMENT BALANCE SHEET   10

CHAPTER 1
The state and progress of human development   13
Trends in political participation and democracy around the world   14
The Millennium Development Goals: commitments and prospects   16
Appendix 1.1 Gauging governance: measures of democracy and political and civil rights   36

CHAPTER 2
Democratic governance for human development   51
The role of political freedom and participation in human development   52
Democracy and human development   54

CHAPTER 3
Deepening democracy by tackling democratic deficits   63
Public accountability of democratic institutions   65
Strengthening formal democratic institutions   69
Promoting democratic politics to deepen democratic practice   79
Deepening democracy for human development   83

CHAPTER 4
Democratizing security to prevent conflict and build peace   85
Securing peace and public accountability   86
Core priorities for more democratic governance of the security sector   90
Democratic peacebuilding in wartorn societies   94
Democratizing security in a fragmented world   99

CHAPTER 5
Deepening democracy at the global level   101
Pluralism and global democracy: the role of civil society campaigns and multistakeholder processes   102
Building more democratic international institutions   112
Deepening democracy—global and national imperatives   121

Notes   123

Bibliographic note   126

Bibliography   128

SPECIAL CONTRIBUTIONS

The sanctity of human life *Kofi Annan*   14

Human development and human dignity *Aung San Suu Kyi*   52

The world's future belongs to democracy *Seyyed Mohammad Khatami*   64

Democratic governance in Africa *Abdoulaye Wade*   86

Eliminating landmines in wartorn societies *Jody Williams*   103

The role of Jubilee 2000 in debt relief *Bono*   104

BOXES

1.1   Global inequality—grotesque levels, ambiguous trends   19

1.2   Poverty's relative   20

1.3   Achieving the Millennium Development Goals—country by country   31

1.4   National human development reports—innovations in national policy   32

2.1   Good governance—for what?   51

2.2   Human development—the concept is larger than the index   53

2.3   Key principles of democracy—the Inter-Parliamentary Union's Universal Declaration on Democracy   55

2.4   Democracy and economic growth—a review of the literature   56

3.1   Poor people, poor justice   66

3.2   Gender bias subverts legal process   66

3.3   Corporate influence on politics   68

3.4   Quotas make a difference in women's political participation   70

3.5   India's judiciary—independence and activism defending democratic institutions and practices   72

3.6   Judicial activism kept the flag of democracy flying—limply—in apartheid South Africa   73

3.7   The role of independent oversight bodies: Mexico's Federal Election Commission   73

3.8   South Africa's Human Rights Commission—promoting democratic values and practices by investigating racism in the media   74

3.9   China's reform process—expanding participation and accountability   74

3.10   Watchdog media make democratic institutions work   76

3.11   Internet media—overcoming restrictions   77

3.12   Gender-responsive budget initiatives—an increasingly popular tool   80

3.13   Technology and the power of e-governance   81

3.14   Participatory democracy at work—drafting Thailand's new constitution   82

3.15   Costa Rica—citizens audit the quality of democracy   83

4.1   Who's who in the security sector   87

4.2   Old habits die hard—the long legacy of military rule   88

4.3   Principles of democratic governance in the security sector   90

4.4   Democracy and security sector reform: South Africa's experience in the 1990s   91

4.5   Higher regard for police through community policing   94

4.6   Building affordable, ethnically balanced security forces in Bosnia and Herzegovina   95

4.7 Reducing small arms through democratic peacebuilding 97

4.8 Clearing landmines requires civilian and community empowerment 97

4.9 Bringing women to the negotiating table 98

4.10 Building peace through truth commissions 99

4.11 Lessons for long-term peacebuilding in Afghanistan 100

5.1 Access to essential HIV/AIDS medicines—what made the campaign successful? From the campaign diary of CPTech 106

5.2 Making rape an act of genocide and a crime against humanity—the Rwanda tribunal 107

5.3 Should large dams be built? 109

5.4 Pressure from non-governmental organizations for corporate social responsibility 111

5.5 Revisiting the question of an Economic Security Council 118

5.6 United Nations or United Five? Reforming the UN Security Council 120

5.7 The Biosafety Protocol—a model for inclusive global governance? 122

TABLES

1.1 Most people can now vote in multiparty elections, 1999 15

1.2 Worldwide, the number of people living on less than $1 a day barely changed in the 1990s 18

1.3 Maternal mortality is much higher in some regions 27

1.4 Exports and debt service dominate resource flows to and from developing countries 31

A1.1 Subjective indicators of governance 38

A1.2 Objective indicators of governance 42

A1.3 Progress towards Millennium Development Goals 46

3.1 Falling membership in political parties 69

4.1 Who's guarding the guards? Countries experiencing armed interventions in the 1990s 87

4.2 During the 20th century democides were far more common under totalitarian and authoritarian rule 87

4.3 In the United States poor people are more likely to be victims of violent crime, 1999 88

4.4 During 1996–2001 a few countries dominated global exports of conventional weapons 89

5.1 International NGOs grew quickly in the 1990s 103

5.2 Use of the veto has become rare on the UN Security Council 119

5.3 Vetoes on the UN Security Council apply to a small range of subjects, 1990–2001 119

5.4 Africa lacks representatives at World Trade Organization headquarters 121

FIGURES

1.1 The world is becoming more democratic 15

1.2 Ratification of human rights treaties 16

1.3 The press becomes freer 16

1.4 Womens' participation lags everywhere 17

1.5 The poorest have suffered the most from conflict 17

1.6 Countries on track to meet the Millennium Development Goals 18

1.7 Failing to grow out of poverty 18

1.8 Varying performance within regions 20

1.9 No automatic link between HDI and HPI-1 21

1.10 Rich countries show little variation in HDI, but big differences in HPI 21

1.11 Global disparities in literacy 22

1.12 Global disparities in under-five mortality   26

1.13 Global disparities in life expectancy   27

1.14 Devastation from HIV/AIDS—life expectancy in Sub-Saharan Africa plummets   27

1.15 Carbon dioxide emissions originate disproportionately in high-income countries   28

1.16 Official development assistance must double to meet the Millennium Development Goals   30

1.17 Aid has decreased from most DAC member countries, 1990–2000   30

2.1 Mutually reinforcing capabilities   53

2.2 Democracy is no obstacle to high income   57

2.3 Low income is no obstacle to democracy   57

2.4 Probability of regime change—higher income means greater stability   58

2.5 Democracy and human development—the links   58

2.6 South Africa's public health spending used to belie huge ethnic and regional disparities   59

2.7 Public health spending neglects poor people and favours the wealthy, while education spending shows even greater disparity   59

2.8 No automatic link between democracy and equity   60

2.9 No automatic link between democracy and human development   60

3.1 Inequality is worsening in many transition countries   63

3.2 Trust in institutions   69

3.3 Developing countries' spectacular media growth   77

3.4 Who owns the media?   78

3.5 Public service broadcasting's shifting focus from news to entertainment   79

5.1 Development funds increasingly flow through non-governmental organizations   102

5.2 Whose voice counts at the IMF and World Bank?   113

5.3 Women on the boards of directors of international financial institutions   115

5.4 Whose voices are heard in international negotiations?   121

FEATURES

1.1 Progress towards the Millennium Development Goals—how many countries are on track?   24

1.2 Measuring human development: the human development indices   34

HUMAN DEVELOPMENT INDICATORS

Note on statistics in the Human Development Report   141

MONITORING HUMAN DEVELOPMENT: ENLARGING PEOPLE'S CHOICES . . .

1 Human development index   149

2 Human development index trends   153

3 Human and income poverty: developing countries   157

4 Human and income poverty: OECD, Central & Eastern Europe & CIS   160

. . . TO LEAD A LONG AND HEALTHY LIFE . . .

5 Demographic trends   162

6 Commitment to health: access, services and resources   166

7 Leading global health crises and challenges   170

8 Survival: progress and setbacks   174

. . . TO ACQUIRE KNOWLEDGE . . .

9 Commitment to education: public spending   178

10 Literacy and enrolment   182

11 Technology: diffusion and creation   186

... TO HAVE ACCESS TO THE RESOURCES NEEDED FOR A DECENT STANDARD OF LIVING ...

12 Economic performance   190

13 Inequality in income or consumption   194

14 The structure of trade   198

15 Flows of aid from DAC member countries   202

16 Flows of aid, private capital and debt   203

17 Priorities in public spending   207

18 Unemployment in OECD countries   211

... WHILE PRESERVING IT FOR FUTURE GENERATIONS ...

19 Energy and the environment   212

... PROTECTING PERSONAL SECURITY ...

20 Refugees and armaments   216

21 Victims of crime   220

... AND ACHIEVING EQUALITY FOR ALL WOMEN AND MEN

22 Gender-related development index   222

23 Gender empowerment measure   226

24 Gender inequality in education   230

25 Gender inequality in economic activity   234

26 Gender, work burden and time allocation   238

27 Women's political participation   239

HUMAN AND LABOUR RIGHTS INSTRUMENTS

28 Status of major international human rights instruments   243

29 Status of fundamental labour rights conventions   247

30 BASIC INDICATORS FOR OTHER UN MEMBER COUNTRIES   251

Technical notes

1 Calculating the human development indices   252

2 Assessing progress towards the Millennium Development Goals   259

Statistical references   260

Definitions of statistical terms   262

Classification of countries   269

Index to indicators   273

Countries and regions that have produced human development reports   276

Deepening democracy in a fragmented world

This Report is about politics and human development. It is about how political power and institutions—formal and informal, national and international—shape human progress. And it is about what it will take for countries to establish democratic governance systems that advance the human development of all people—in a world where so many are left behind.

Politics matter for human development because people everywhere want to be free to determine their destinies, express their views and participate in the decisions that shape their lives. These capabilities are just as important for human development—for expanding people's choices—as being able to read or enjoy good health.

In the 1980s and 1990s the world made dramatic progress in opening up political systems and expanding political freedoms. Some 81 countries took significant steps towards democracy, and today 140 of the world's nearly 200 countries hold multiparty elections—more than ever before. But the euphoria of the cold war's end has given way to the sombre realities of 21st century politics.

Developing countries pursued democratization in the face of massive poverty and pervasive social and economic tensions. Several that took steps towards democracy after 1980 have since returned to more authoritarian rule: either military, as in Pakistan since 1999, or pseudo-democratic, as in Zimbabwe in recent years. Many others have stalled between democracy and authoritarianism, with limited political freedoms and closed or dysfunctional politics. Others, including such failed states as Afghanistan and Somalia, have become breeding grounds for extremism and violent conflict.

Even where democratic institutions are firmly established, citizens often feel powerless to influence national policies. They and their governments also feel more subject to international forces that they have little capacity to control. In 1999 Gallup International's Millennium Survey asked more than 50,000 people in 60 countries if their country was governed by the will of the people. Less than a third of the respondents said yes. And only 1 in 10 said that their government responded to the people's will.

Globalization is forging greater interdependence, yet the world seems more fragmented—between rich and poor, between the powerful and the powerless, and between those who welcome the new global economy and those who demand a different course. The September 11, 2001, terrorist attacks on the United States cast new light on these divisions, returning strategic military alliances to the centre of national policy-making and inspiring heated debates on the danger of compromising human rights for national security.

For politics and political institutions to promote human development and safeguard the freedom and dignity of all people, democracy must widen and deepen. That is the subject of this Report.

Economically, politically and technologically, the world has never seemed more free—or more unjust

At the March 2002 UN Conference on Financing for Development in Monterrey, Mexico, world leaders and policy-makers assessed progress towards the development and poverty eradication goals set at the UN Millennium Summit in 2000. They also pledged an unprecedented global effort to achieve those goals by 2015.

For politics and political institutions to promote human development and safeguard the freedom and dignity of all people, democracy must widen and deepen

Many developing countries are making progress on several fronts, particularly in achieving universal primary education and gender equality in access to education. But for much of the world the prospects are bleak. At current trends, 33 countries with more than a quarter of the world's people will achieve fewer than half the goals by 2015. If global progress continues at such a snail's pace, it will take more than 130 years to rid the world of hunger.

Two problems seem intractable. The first is income poverty. To halve the share of people living on $1 a day, optimistic estimates suggest that 3.7% annual growth in per capita incomes is needed in developing countries. But over the past 10 years only 24 countries have grown this fast. Among them are China and India, the most populous developing countries. But 127 countries, with 34% of the world's people, have not grown at this rate. Indeed, many have suffered negative growth in recent years, and the share of their people in poverty has almost certainly increased.

The second major problem is child mortality. Although 85 countries are on track to reduce under-five mortality rates by two-thirds from 1990 levels or have already done so, they contain less than a quarter of the world's people. Meanwhile, 81 countries with more than 60% of the world's people are not on track to achieve this goal by 2015.

Most troubling, many of the countries least likely to achieve the goals are the world's poorest: the least developed countries. And most are in Sub-Saharan Africa: 23 of the region's 44 countries are failing in most areas, and another 11, such as Angola and Rwanda, have too little data to make a judgement. South Africa is the only country in the region where less than 10% of children are malnourished. In six countries—including Eritrea, Ethiopia and Niger—the share is more than 40%. Without a dramatic turnaround there is a real possibility that a generation from now, world leaders will be setting the same targets again.

These mixed prospects highlight a troubling paradox. The spread of democracy, the integration of national economies, revolutions in technology—all point to greater human freedom and greater potential for improving people's lives. But in too many countries, freedom seems to be under ever-greater threat.

Democracy. The world is more democratic than ever before. But of the 140 countries that hold multiparty elections, only 80—with 55% of the world's people—are fully democratic by one measure. And 106 countries still limit important civil and political freedoms.

Peace. The number of wars between countries has dropped considerably. In the 1990s conflicts between countries killed about 220,000 people, a drop of nearly two-thirds from the 1980s. But civil conflicts are more damaging than ever. In the 1990s about 3.6 million people died in wars within states, and the number of refugees and internally displaced persons increased 50%.

Opportunity: New technology and increasing economic integration are paving the way for truly global markets. But amid the wealth of new economic opportunities, 2.8 billion people still live on less than $2 a day. The richest 1% of the world's people receive as much income each year as the poorest 57%. And in many parts of Sub-Saharan Africa the lives of the poorest people are getting worse.

Some argue that bridging the gulf between potential and reality is a matter of time and political will. For others the slow pace of change is not the problem—it is the basic direction. But on one point there is broad agreement: in a more interdependent world, politics and political institutions are even more central to human development. Around the world, discussions on development are placing more emphasis on institutions and governance. These debates have focused on the effectiveness of public institutions and the rules for making markets work and promoting economic growth—from the professionalism and transparency of tax systems to the capacity of judicial systems to enforce commercial contracts.

Such issues are important for human development. When institutions function badly, poor and vulnerable people tend to suffer most. But just as human development requires much more than raising incomes, governance for human development requires much more than having effective public institutions. Good governance also requires fostering fair, accountable institutions that protect human rights and basic freedoms. It is not only about whether judges are trained, but whether they observe due

Just as human development requires much more than raising incomes, governance for human development requires much more than having effective public institutions

process and are blind to differences of race and class. It is not only about whether schools are built, but whether students in poor districts are as well-equipped as students in affluent areas.

This remains relatively new territory for serious research, and the links between political institutions and economic and social outcomes are not fully understood. This Report explores those links from the standpoint of advancing human development. It argues that countries can promote human development for all only when they have governance systems that are fully accountable to all people—and when all people can participate in the debates and decisions that shape their lives.

Advancing human development requires governance that is democratic in both form and substance—for the people and by the people

Democratic governance is valuable in its own right. But it can also advance human development, for three reasons. First, enjoying political freedom and participating in the decisions that shape one's life are fundamental human rights: they are part of human development in their own right. In Brunei Darussalam, Kuwait, Oman, Qatar, Saudi Arabia and the United Arab Emirates women's right to vote has never been recognized. Regardless of their income, this significantly restricts their choices in life. Democracy is the only political regime that guarantees political and civil freedoms and the right to participate—making democratic rule a good in itself.

Second, democracy helps protect people from economic and political catastrophes such as famines and descents into chaos. This is no small achievement. Indeed, it can mean the difference between life and death. Nobel Prize–winner Amartya Sen has shown how elections and a free press give politicians in democracies much stronger incentives to avert famines.

Since 1995 an estimated 2 million people—a staggering 10% of the population—have died of famine in the Democratic People's Republic of Korea. In 1958–61 nearly 30 million people died of famine in China. But since achieving independence in 1947, India has not had a single famine, even in the face of severe crop failures. Food production was hit hard during the 1973

drought in Maharashtra. But elected politicians responded with public works programmes for 5 million people and averted a famine.

Democracies also contribute to political stability, providing open space for political opposition and handovers of power. Between 1950 and 1990 riots and demonstrations were more common in democracies but were much more destabilizing in dictatorships. Moreover, wars were more frequent in non-democratic regimes and had much higher economic costs.

Third, democratic governance can trigger a virtuous cycle of development—as political freedom empowers people to press for policies that expand social and economic opportunities, and as open debates help communities shape their priorities. From Indonesia to Mexico to Poland, moves towards democratization and political opening have helped produce this kind of virtuous cycle, with a free press and civil society activism giving people new ways to participate in policy decisions and debates.

Two prominent examples are participatory budgeting and gender-responsive budgeting. In Porto Alegre, Brazil, citizen participation in preparing municipal budgets has helped reallocate spending to critical human development priorities. During the first seven years of this experiment the share of households with access to water services increased (from 80% to 98%), and the percentage of the population with access to sanitation almost doubled (from 46% to 85%).

Gender-responsive budgeting, which examines the implications for gender equity of national and local budgets, has been pursued in at least 40 countries. In South Africa such efforts have trained parliamentarians in scrutinizing budget proposals and led to the inclusion of gender-sensitive analysis in policy papers and to more effective targeting of public spending.

The links between democracy and human development are not automatic: when a small elite dominates economic and political decisions, the link between democracy and equity can be broken

In recent years people around the world have fought for and won democracy in hopes of gain-

Countries can promote human development for all only when they have governance systems that are fully accountable to all people—and when all people can participate in the debates and decisions that shape their lives

ing political freedom—and social and economic opportunities. But many now feel that democracy has not delivered. During the 1990s income inequality and poverty rose sharply in Central and Eastern Europe and the Commonwealth of Independent States (CIS), sometimes at unprecedented rates. And despite more widespread democracy, the number of poor people in Sub-Saharan Africa continued to increase.

When democratic governments do not respond to the needs of poor people, the public becomes more inclined to support authoritarian or populist leaders who claim that limiting civil liberties and political freedoms will accelerate economic growth and promote social progress and stability. In Latin America high income inequality and poverty go hand in hand with low public trust in political institutions and greater willingness to accept authoritarian rule and violations of human rights.

Authoritarian leaders promise better outcomes and argue that democracy must be sacrificed for economic growth and social progress. But there is no evidence of such a trade-off. Statistical studies find that neither authoritarianism nor democracy is a factor in determining either the rate of economic growth or how it is distributed. Experiences around the world support these findings. Costa Rica, Latin America's most stable democracy, achieved 1.1% annual growth in per capita income between 1975 and 2000, faster than the regional average of 0.7%, and boasts the region's most equitable distribution of income, education and health. But in Brazil democracy coexists with economic and social inequalities that are among the world's largest. More authoritarian Paraguay achieved the region's average per capita income growth rate but has also failed to expand social and economic opportunities.

Democracy that empowers people must be built—it cannot be imported

In many countries a central challenge for deepening democracy is building the key institutions of democratic governance:
• A system of representation, with well-functioning political parties and interest associations.

• An electoral system that guarantees free and fair elections as well as universal suffrage.
• A system of checks and balances based on the separation of powers, with independent judicial and legislative branches.
• A vibrant civil society, able to monitor government and private business—and provide alternative forms of political participation.
• A free, independent media.
• Effective civilian control over the military and other security forces.

These institutions come in many shapes and forms. Because the democracy a nation chooses to develop depends on its history and circumstances, countries will necessarily be "differently democratic". But in all countries democracy is about much more than a single decision or hastily organized election. It requires a deeper process of political development to embed democratic values and culture in all parts of society—a process never formally completed.

Building democratic institutions while achieving equitable social and economic development poses tensions. Granting all people formal political equality does not create an equal desire or capacity to participate in political processes—or an equal capacity to influence outcomes. Imbalances in resources and political power often subvert the principle of one person, one voice, and the purpose of democratic institutions. And judicial proceedings and regulatory institutions are undermined if elites dominate them at the expense of women, minorities and the powerless.

One critical problem is money in politics, which subverts democratic institutions when it exerts undue influence on who gets elected and what legislators vote for. Recent U.S. debates on campaign finance reform and the financial links between Enron and leading politicians from the country's two major parties show that this is a serious concern in long-standing democracies as well as new ones.

Presidential candidates in the 2000 U.S. election spent $343 million on their campaigns, up from $92 million in 1980. Including spending by political parties, more than $1 billion was probably spent on the 2000 campaigns. In 2001 Michael Bloomberg spent a record $74 million to become New York City's mayor, the

The democracy a nation chooses to develop depends on its history and circumstances—countries will necessarily be "differently democratic"

equivalent of $99 a vote. His main opponent spent $17 million.

As campaign costs rise, so does the risk that politicians will be disproportionately influenced by business interests. In the 2000 U.S. election cycle, corporations gave $1.2 billion in political contributions—about 14 times the already considerable amount contributed by labour unions and 16 times the contributions of other interest groups. Although many European countries have more stringent limits on corporate funding, similar patterns emerge in many other countries. In India large corporations provided 80% of the funding for the major parties in 1996.

At the same time, political parties are in decline in many parts of the world. In France, Italy, Norway and the United States the membership of established political parties is half what it was 20 years ago, sometimes less. And recent surveys in Latin America and Central and Eastern Europe found that people have more confidence in television than they do in political parties.

Triggering a virtuous cycle for human development requires promoting democratic politics

Promoting democratic politics means expanding capabilities such as education, to enable people to play a more effective role in such politics, and fostering the development of civil society groups and other informal institutions to help democratic institutions better represent the people.

Over the past two decades there have been many new ways for people to participate in public debates and activities. Though membership has fallen in political parties, trade unions and other traditional vehicles for collective action, there has been an explosion in support for non-governmental organizations (NGOs) and other new civil society groups. In 1914 there were 1,083 international NGOs. By 2000 there were more than 37,000—nearly one-fifth of them formed in the 1990s. Most developing countries have seen an even sharper increase in the number of domestic NGOs and non-profits: in 1996 India had more than 1 million non-profits, and Brazil had 210,000.

More than $7 billion in aid to developing countries now flows through international NGOs, reflecting and supporting a dramatic expansion in the scope and nature of NGO activities. In addition to advocating for and engaging in development projects, NGOs are taking more direct roles in local decision-making and monitoring and are developing new, collaborative forms of governance. The Forest Stewardship Council brings together environmental groups, the timber industry, forest workers, indigenous people and community groups in certifying sustainably harvested timber for export. In Porto Alegre, Brazil, and elsewhere, budgeting processes now involve consultations with civil society groups. In the United Kingdom the Women's Budget Group has been invited to review government budget proposals.

Volunteerism is also flourishing. In the Netherlands work by volunteers is estimated to equal 445,000 full-time jobs, equivalent to $13.6 billion. In the Republic of Korea nearly 3.9 million people volunteer more than 451 million hours, with a value exceeding $2 billion. In Brazil at least 16% of adults volunteer their time. Consumer action is another way for ordinary people to engage in public debates about policy issues—say, by boycotting rugs made by child labour or purchasing products that help small coffee growers. The threat of such action can hold corporations accountable to public expectations of corporate social responsibility.

These and other examples hold enormous scope for broadening participation in governance and promoting more equitable outcomes for people. By and large, civil society works to strengthen democratic institutions, not undermine them.

Civil society groups do not fit easily into traditional models of governance and accountability—which is part of their value to democracies. But when such groups spring from agendas or use tactics that are contrary to democratic values, they can be both civil and "uncivil". The rise of such groups poses challenges for truly democratic political engagement.

There are no simple solutions to this problem. But many civil society groups recognize that they must be publicly accountable for their ac-

Over the past two decades there have been many new ways for people to participate in public debates and activities

tions. In Ethiopia domestic NGOs have adopted codes of conduct to promote effective self-regulation. The codes emphasize the importance of transparency and accountability—and the need for the NGOs to ensure that they truly represent the people whose lives they affect.

A free, independent media is another crucial pillar of democracy. Around the world, restrictions remain on basic civil liberties—such as the rights to free speech, assembly and information. Few countries have freedom of information laws, for example. But in many countries new press freedoms and technologies are enabling the media to contribute more to democratic politics by opening public debates and exposing corruption and abuse. The transparency of Ghana's 2000 election results was helped by the efforts of the country's many private radio stations. The stations made it difficult to rig voting, bringing credibility to the announced results.

Especially in developing countries, most ordinary citizens have many more sources of information to turn to than they did 10 years ago. And less of that information is subject to rigid state control. But to be plural and independent, the media must be free not only from state control but also from corporate and political pressures. Although market reforms and economic integration have reduced state ownership of the media, it has increased concentration in private ownership. Four private media groups own 85% of U.K. daily newspapers, accounting for two-thirds of circulation. And in the United States, six companies control most of the media.

Commercial and political pressures will always skew the playing field in the marketplace for ideas. But the answer to excessive corporate or political influence is not a return to strict regulation by the state. The media need to be free as well as accountable—which is why greater emphasis is being placed on high standards of professionalism and ethics. Journalists and the media are free only when they serve the public first, and the government or private shareholders second. A range of mechanisms can promote these goals without resorting to government controls, including self-regulation through independent bodies, professional codes of ethics

To be plural and independent, the media must be free not only from state control but also from corporate and political pressures

and the use of official ombudspersons, as well as training and raising awareness of journalists.

Establishing democratic control over security forces is another priority—otherwise, far from ensuring personal security and peace, security forces can actively undermine them

Popular disillusionment is not the only problem facing the world's democracies. In many an even greater obstacle is the extensive power of the military, police and intelligence services—not to mention warlords, paramilitary groups and private security companies.

In the second half of the 20th century 46 elected governments were forcibly overturned by authoritarian rule. And since 1989 national armies have directly intervened in the political affairs of 13 Sub-Saharan countries, or about one in four of the region's countries. In some countries—Nigeria in 1993, Myanmar in 1990—military leaders have wrested control from (or failed to cede power to) elected governments under the guise of maintaining civil peace. In others, like Zimbabwe in 2000–02, elected governments have undermined democracy and personal security by using parts of the security sector for their own ends. In still other countries the risk of a failed state—where the security sector is fragmented or even privatized—is as great as the risk of returning to brutal authoritarian rule.

When order breaks down in a country, poor people usually suffer first and most. All too often, violence against civilians emanates from forces under government control. During the 20th century governments killed about 170 million people, far more than died in wars between countries.

Undemocratic governance of security forces can also distort security priorities. Many governments continue to militarize their police forces, blurring their distinction with the military, or seriously underfund them. Without democratic civil control over security forces—including an effective, even-handed national police force—governments cannot guarantee people's safety and security, and human development is severely held back.

Relations between civilians and security forces rarely measure up to the ideal even in long-standing democracies. But encouraging examples in some new democracies, including South Africa, several Eastern European countries and previously coup-prone Latin American countries, show that progress is possible. Success in this area can contribute to the broader process of strengthening democratic institutions and politics. It can also promote external peace and stability, because wars between democratic countries are quite rare.

In wartorn societies, regaining control over the armed forces is a basic condition for progress. Otherwise, peacemaking efforts face the constant risk of reversal, especially moves to share power and expand political representation. Lack of control can also generate rampant lawlessness and provide the conditions in which violent extremists can flourish—as in Afghanistan and Somalia in the 1990s.

Even in these circumstances solutions are possible. But they require political leaders committed to inclusive, fair processes—especially in demobilizing and reintegrating former combatants and building ethnically balanced, professional security forces—and to investments in a just and enduring peace, including recent innovations such as truth commissions. Creating political space for broadly based reconciliation and promoting dynamic local leaders, including women and young people, are critical to national recovery. In some cases, as in Afghanistan and East Timor, countries also need large-scale international help to maintain peace and order, bring human rights violators to account and build democratic institutions that can resolve deep-seated disputes without resorting to violence.

Global interdependence also calls for more participation and accountability in global decision-making

Empowering people to influence decisions that affect their lives and hold their rulers accountable is no longer just a national issue. In an integrated world these democratic principles have a global dimension because global rules and actors often affect people's lives as much as national ones.

This new reality has been reflected in recent antiglobalization protests in both industrial and developing countries. Though these protests take different forms and are driven by diverse agendas, they are often united by the demand that global actors and institutions be more inclusive and responsive to the problems of the world's poorest people. The protestors are not alone in considering this an urgent problem.

In 2001 a global health fund was launched to address an imbalance in health research. Malaria, for example, kills at least 1 million people a year, nearly all of them in the poorest countries. In the 1950s the World Health Organization aimed to eradicate the disease. But over the decades it has attracted little public funding for research or treatment. In 1992 less than 10% of global spending on health research addressed 90% of the global disease burden.

International trade rules have also worked against the economic interests of developing countries and failed to restrain protectionism in industrial countries, especially through antidumping rules and other nontariff barriers. On average, industrial country tariffs on imports from developing countries are four times those on imports from other industrial countries. In addition, countries that belong to the Organisation for Economic Co-operation and Development (OECD) provide about $1 billion a day in domestic agricultural subsidies—more than six times what they spend on official development assistance for developing countries.

Efforts to build more inclusive, accountable global governance face two main challenges. The first is increasing pluralism: expanding the space for groups outside formal state institutions to participate in global decision-making, particularly in developing mechanisms to change the behaviour of private corporations. The second is increasing participation and accountability in multilateral institutions to give developing countries a larger role.

Increasing pluralism in global decision-making. Through a series of high-profile campaigns, civil society movements have been promoting pluralism at the global level. Some tactics have been dramatic and effective, such as the human chain that the Jubilee 2000 debt relief campaign formed around the leaders of G-8 countries in Birmingham, the United Kingdom, in 1998. Similar activism has put the

In an integrated world democratic principles have a global dimension because global rules and actors often affect people's lives as much as national ones

spotlight on other issues—from the role of "blood diamonds" in financing guerrilla warfare in Africa to the way that the World Trade Organization (WTO) agreement on Trade-Related Intellectual Property Rights (TRIPS) risked depriving poor people of access to essential medicines.

Increased pluralism in global politics has also been aided by new forms of collaboration between governments and global civil society groups. Perhaps the most successful example is the 1998 treaty seeking to establish the International Criminal Court. Despite the opposition of several major countries, the treaty was recently ratified—reflecting the support mobilized by hundreds of human rights organizations around the world.

Greater pluralism is also being built into international mechanisms and systems, as with the World Commission on Dams, the International Monetary Fund (IMF) and World Bank's new consultative approach to national poverty reduction strategies and the recently launched UN Global Compact on corporate social responsibility.

Increasing participation and accountability in multilateral institutions. Though the emergence of a global civil society has created opportunities to deepen democracy at the international level, existing international institutions need reform. Developing countries should be given a stronger voice in their operations. Given their enormous—and growing—influence, these institutions should also be held more accountable for their policies and actions.

Consider the World Trade Organization. Every member country has a seat and a vote, which is very democratic. But actual decision-making occurs by consensus, heavily influenced by the largest and richest countries. The imbalance in developing country participation is also evident in global civil society movements. Of the 738 NGOs accredited to the WTO's 1999 ministerial conference in Seattle, Washington, 87% were from industrial countries.

The democratic deficit in international organizations is unavoidable because people do not directly elect their representatives to the WTO, IMF, World Bank or UN Security Council.

Many argue that the imbalances of global political and economic power also make unrepresentative decision-making inevitable at the intergovernmental level. This argument has considerable force. Notably, the influence of the United States over institutions such as the IMF and WTO has little to do with formal voting power—and much to do with the global standing of the United States.

It is perhaps no coincidence that the more representative international institutions, such as the UN Economic and Social Council and the UN General Assembly, are also considered the least powerful. The reality is that powerful countries—crucial to the success of any international institution—tend to gravitate towards institutions that give them the most influence. And they take their power with them: whether it is to the WTO's "green room" meetings or the meetings of the IMF executive board. Efforts to enhance the representation of developing countries must take into account these basic realities.

Still, there is considerable room for making global institutions more democratic. Many proposals have been made to remove such patently undemocratic practices as the veto on the UN Security Council and the way the leaders of the IMF and World Bank are selected. Various commissions, think tanks and civil society organizations have also recommended increasing transparency by, for example, publishing decisions made by the executive boards of the major international financial institutions and making WTO decision-making more inclusive and transparent.

In recent years the IMF, World Bank and United Nations have made important efforts to become more open and transparent. Progress on many of the more ambitious proposals for democratic reform—such as at the UN Security Council—has stalled. But there continues to be strong pressure to extend democratic principles to such organizations, particularly since many have recently become so much more deeply involved in national economic, political and social policies. The deeper is their intervention in sensitive governance reforms in developing countries, the greater is the need for international organizations to be open and accountable.

The traditional argument against such reforms is that they would make decision-making clumsy and unworkable. But against this must be set the realities of a more integrated world. Whether the goal is peace, economic growth or environmental sustainability, international efforts to promote change do not work if national actors feel excluded. Around the world, the United Nations, IMF, World Bank and WTO are coming up against the fact that ownership matters. Increasingly, the leading global powers may recognize that a widespread sense of exclusion and powerlessness in developing countries can threaten economic growth and security in industrial countries as well as developing.

*   *   *

An abiding lesson of the past decade is that national political institutions are not keeping pace with the governance challenges of a more interdependent world. As new democracies struggle to lay the foundations of democratic governance, new forces and institutions are exerting powerful influences on people's lives. And new types of conflicts are proliferating within and between countries.

Many hoped that the September 11 terrorist attacks would inspire global unity in confronting the challenges of national and international governance. And there have been encouraging signs in that direction, such as the increased aid committed at the March 2002 Conference on Financing for Development. But there is an equally strong possibility that the attacks and their aftermath will further weaken global institutions, undermine human rights and exacerbate social and economic fragmentation.

The need to act is clear. Still needed is the will to act in ways that cultivate democracy, advance development and expand human freedoms around the world.

International efforts to promote change do not work if national actors feel excluded

Human development balance sheet

<table>
<tr><th>GLOBAL PROGRESS</th><th>GLOBAL FRAGMENTATION</th></tr>
</table>

DEMOCRACY AND PARTICIPATION

GLOBAL PROGRESS	GLOBAL FRAGMENTATION
• Since 1980, 81 countries have taken significant steps towards democracy,[1] with 33 military regimes replaced by civilian governments[2] • 140 of the world's nearly 200 countries now hold multiparty elections, more than at any time in history[3]	• Of the 81 new democracies, only 47 are fully democratic. Many others do not seem to be in transition to democracy or have lapsed back into authoritarianism or conflict[4] • Only 82 countries, with 57% of the world's people, are fully democratic[5]
• In 2000 there were 37,000 registered international NGOs, one-fifth more than in 1990. More than 2,150 NGOs have consultative status with the UN Economic and Social Council, and 1,550 are associated with the UN Department of Public Information[6]	• 51 countries have not ratified the International Labour Organization's Convention on Freedom of Association, and 39 have not ratified its Convention on Collective Bargaining[7] • NGOs still do not have consultative status with the UN Security Council or General Assembly. Only 251 of the 1,550 NGOs associated with the UN Department of Public Information are based in developing countries[8]
• 125 countries, with 62% of the world population, have a free or partly free press[9] • Between 1970 and 1996 the number of daily newspapers in developing countries more than doubled, from 29 to 60 copies per 1,000 people, and the number of televisions increased 16-fold[10]	• 61 countries, with 38% of the world's population, still do not have a free press[11] • In 2001, 37 journalists died in the line of duty, 118 were imprisoned and more than 600 journalists or news organization were physically attacked or intimidated[12]
• The number of countries ratifying the six main human rights conventions and covenants has increased dramatically since 1990. Ratifications of the International Covenant on Economic, Social and Cultural Rights (ICESCR) and the International Covenant on Civil and Political Rights (ICCPR) grew from around 90 to nearly 150[13]	• 106 countries still restrict important civil and political freedoms[14] • 38 countries have not ratified or signed the ICCPR, and 41 have not ratified or signed the ICESCR[15]
• In 10 countries more than 30% of parliamentarians are women[16]	• Worldwide, only 14% of parliamentarians are women—and in 10 countries none are women[17]
• Only 6 vetoes were cast in the UN Security Council between 1996 and 2001—compared with 243 between 1946 and 1995, an average of 50 a decade[18]	• The World Trade Organization operates on a one-country, one-vote basis, but most key decisions are made by the leading economic powers in "green room" meetings • The executive directors representing France, Germany, Japan, the Russian Federation, Saudi Arabia, the United Kingdom and the United States account for 46% of the voting rights in the World Bank and 48% in the International Monetary Fund[19]

ECONOMIC JUSTICE

GLOBAL PROGRESS	GLOBAL FRAGMENTATION
• The proportion of the world's people living in extreme poverty fell from 29% in 1990 to 23% in 1999[20] • During the 1990s extreme poverty was halved in East Asia and the Pacific and fell by 7 percentage points in South Asia[21]	• The richest 5% of the world's people have incomes 114 times those of the poorest 5%[22] • During the 1990s the number of people in extreme poverty in Sub-Saharan Africa rose from 242 million to 300 million[23]
• East Asia and the Pacific achieved 5.7% annual growth in per capita income in the 1990s; South Asia, 3.3%[24]	• In Central and Eastern Europe and the CIS per capita income shrank 2.4% a year in the 1990s; in Sub-Saharan Africa, 0.3%[25] • 20 countries in Sub-Saharan Africa, with more than half of the region's people, are poorer now than in 1990—and 23 are poorer than in 1975[26]
• The more than 500 million Internet users today are expected to grow to nearly 1 billion by 2005[27]	• 72% of Internet users live in high-income OECD countries, with 14% of the world's population. 164 million reside in the United States[28]

Human development balance sheet

GLOBAL PROGRESS	GLOBAL FRAGMENTATION

HEALTH AND EDUCATION

• Since 1990, 800 million people have gained access to improved water supplies, and 750 million to improved sanitation[29] • 57 countries, with half of the world's people, have halved hunger or are on track to do so by 2015[30]	• Child immunization rates in Sub-Saharan Africa have fallen below 50%[31] • At the current rate it would take more than 130 years to rid the world of hunger[32]
• Some developing countries have made progress in tackling HIV/AIDS. Uganda reduced HIV prevalence from 14% in the early 1990s to around 8% by the end of the 1990s[33]	• By the end of 2000 almost 22 million people had died from AIDS, 13 million children had lost their mother or both parents to the disease and more than 40 million people were living with HIV. Of those, 90% were in developing countries and 75% were in Sub-Saharan Africa[34]
• Between 1970 and 2000 the under-five mortality rate worldwide fell from 96 to 56 per 1,000 live births[35]	• Every day more than 30,000 children around the world die of preventable diseases[36] • Around the world there are 100 million "missing" women who would be alive but for infanticide, neglect and sex-selective abortion[37] • Every year more than 500,000 women die as a result of pregnancy and childbirth[38]
• Worldwide, primary school enrolments rose from 80% in 1990 to 84% in 1998[39] • 51 countries, with 41% of the world's people, have achieved or are on track to achieve universal primary enrolment[40]	• 113 million school-age children are not in school—97% of them in developing countries[41] • 93 countries, with 39% of the world's people, do not have data on trends in primary enrolment[42]
• 90 countries, with more than 60% of the world's people, have achieved or are on track to achieve gender equality in primary education by 2015—and more than 80 in secondary education[43]	• 60% of children not in primary school worldwide are girls[44] • Of the world's estimated 854 million illiterate adults, 544 million are women[45]

PEACE AND PERSONAL SECURITY

• 38 peacekeeping operations have been set up since 1990—compared with just 16 between 1946 and 1989[46] • The International Criminal Court's 60th country ratification, in April 2002, established a permanent structure for adjudicating crimes against humanity	• Genocide occurred in Europe and Africa, with 200,000 people killed in Bosnia in 1992–95 and 500,000 killed in Rwanda in 1994[47] • New forms of international terrorism have emerged, with 3,000 people from more than 80 countries killed in the September 2001 attacks on the World Trade Center in New York City[48]
• The 1990s saw a large decline in deaths from interstate conflicts, to 220,000 people over the decade—down from nearly three times that in the 1980s[49]	• Nearly 3.6 million people were killed in wars within states in the 1990s[50] • During the 1990s the number of refugees and internally displaced persons grew by 50%[51] • Half of all civilian war casualties are children,[52] and there are an estimated 300,000 child soldiers worldwide[53]
• Reflecting pressure from some 1,400 civil society groups in 90 countries, the 1997 Mine Ban Treaty has been ratified by 123 states[54]	• Major countries such as China, the Russian Federation and the United States have not signed the Mine Ban Treaty • 90 countries are still heavily affected by landmines and unexploded ordinance, with 15,000–20,000 mine victims a year[55]

Note: The notes to this balance sheet appear in the Notes section of the Report.

CHAPTER 1

 The state and progress of human development

Human development is about people, about expanding their choices to lead lives they value. Economic growth, increased international trade and investment, technological advance—all are very important. But they are means, not ends. Whether they contribute to human development in the 21st century will depend on whether they expand people's choices, whether they help create an environment for people to develop their full potential and lead productive, creative lives.

Fundamental to enlarging human choices is building human capabilities: the range of things that people can do or be. The most basic capabilities for human development are leading a long and healthy life, being educated, having access to the resources needed for a decent standard of living and being able to participate in the life of one's community. As this Report emphasizes, assuring people's dignity also requires that they be free—and able—to participate in the formation and stewardship of the rules and institutions that govern them. A poor man who cannot afford to send his children to school, but must send them to work in the fields, is lacking in human development. So is a wealthy educated woman whose gender excludes her from voting in elections.

In today's new era of global integration, is human development moving forward? There has been clear progress in some areas. The share of the world's people living in extreme poverty is slowly but steadily declining, from 29% in 1990 to 23% in 1999.[1] Primary school enrolments have risen worldwide, from 80% in 1990 to 84% in 1998.[2] Since 1990, 800 million people have gained access to improved water supplies, and 750 million to improved sanitation.[3] There have also been great improvements in political and civil rights: since 1980, 81 countries have taken significant steps in democratization,[4] with 33 military regimes replaced by civilian governments.[5]

But in a globalizing world the increasing interconnectedness of nations and peoples has made the differences between them more glaring. A girl born in Japan today may have a 50% chance of seeing the 22nd century[6]—while a newborn in Afghanistan has a 1 in 4 chance of dying before age 5. And the richest 5% of the world's people have incomes 114 times those of the poorest 5%.[7] Every day more than 30,000 children around the world die of preventable diseases,[8] and nearly 14,000 people are infected with HIV/AIDS.[9] In Botswana more than a third of adults have the disease; in Swaziland and Zimbabwe more than a quarter. If tuberculosis control does not improve, 1 billion people will contract it by 2020—and 35 million will die from it.[10]

In Sub-Saharan Africa human development has actually regressed in recent years, and the lives of its very poor people are getting worse. The share of people living on $1 a day was about the same at the end of the 1990s—47%—as at the start.[11] Thus, because of population growth, the number of poor people in the region has increased. And while most of the world has increased the share of children who are immunized against the leading diseases, since 1990 immunization rates in Sub-Saharan Africa have fallen below 50%.[12]

Global progress on political freedoms has also been uneven. The spread of democratization appears to have stalled, with many countries failing to consolidate and deepen the first steps towards democracy and several slipping back into authoritarianism. Some 73 countries—with 42% of the world's people—still do not hold free and fair elections,[13] and 106 governments still restrict many civil and political freedoms.[14] In addition, conflict continues to blight the lives of millions: since 1990, 3.6 million peo-

The spread of democratization appears to have stalled, with many countries failing to consolidate and deepen the first steps towards democracy

SPECIAL CONTRIBUTION

In the 21st century I believe that the mission of the United Nations will be defined by a new, more profound awareness of the sanctity and dignity of every human life, regardless of race or religion. This will require us to look beyond the framework of states and beneath the surface of nations and communities. We must focus, as never before, on improving the conditions of the individual men and women who give the state or nation its richness and character.

A genocide begins with the killing of one man—not for what he has done, but because of who he is. A campaign of "ethnic cleansing" begins with one neighbour turning on another. Poverty begins when even one child is denied his or her fundamental right to education. What begins as a failure to uphold the dignity of one life, all too often ends as a calamity for entire nations.

In this new century we must start from the understanding that peace belongs not just to states and peoples, but to every member of those communities. The sovereignty of states can no longer be used as a shield for gross violations of human rights. Peace must be made real and tangible in the daily existence of every person in need. Peace must be sought, above all, because it is required so that every human being can live a life of dignity and security.

Indeed, one lesson of the 20th century is that where the dignity of the individual is trampled or threatened—where citizens do not enjoy the basic right to choose their government, or the right to change it regularly—conflict too often follows, with innocent civilians paying the price in lives cut short and communities destroyed.

Obstacles to democracy have little to do with culture or religion, and much more to do with the desire of those in power to maintain their position at any cost. This is neither a new phenomenon nor one confined to any particular part of the world. People of all cultures value their freedom of choice, and feel the need to have a say in decisions affecting their lives.

Kofi Annan
United Nations Secretary-General

"We will spare no effort to promote democracy and strengthen the rule of law, as well as respect for all internationally recognized human rights and fundamental freedoms."
—Millennium Declaration

Political participation and freedom are fundamental parts of human development. The world has more democratic countries and more political participation than ever, with 140 countries holding multiparty elections (table 1.1). Of 147 countries with data, 121—with 68% of the world's people—had some or all of the elements of formal democracy in 2000 (figure 1.1).[16] This compares with only 54 countries, with 46% of the world's people, in 1980. Since then 81 countries have taken significant steps in democratization, while 6 have regressed.[17] Scores of authoritarian regimes have been replaced by governments more accountable to the people—a real achievement for human development. But true democratization means more than elections. It requires the consolidation of democratic institutions and the strengthening of democratic practices, with democratic values and norms embedded in all parts of society (see chapters 2 and 3).

The last two decades of the 20th century have been dubbed the "third wave" of democratization, as dictatorial regimes fell in scores of countries.[18] Like history's other movements for liberation, these democratic revolutions were propelled by people. In the 1980s growing pressures against the excesses of military dictatorships in Latin America caused them to topple one after another, starting with Ecuador and Peru. In Central and Eastern Europe and what is now the Commonwealth of Independent States (CIS), the fall of the Berlin Wall in 1989 was the turning point. In Africa rising opposition through the 1980s and 1990s tossed out many long-standing dictators, including Mali's Moussa Traoré in 1991 and Malawi's Kamuzu Banda in 1994. People's power in the Philippines removed Ferdinand Marcos in 1986.

For some countries the transition has been less dramatic, as with the move to civilian rule in the Republic of Korea and Thailand and the

---

ple have died in civil wars and ethnic violence, more than 16 times the number killed in wars between states.[15]

There is growing recognition that all countries pay a price for these global injustices. And there is greater acceptance of the need for action to narrow the gap between global potential and reality—and to advance global human development in its deepest sense (see the special contribution by UN Secretary-General Kofi Annan).

In surveying the progress of countries towards human development in its many dimensions, this chapter highlights the directions for change in the years ahead—and how far it will need to go. The chapter begins by looking at global trends in political participation and democracy, the subjects of this Report. It then considers the Millennium Development Goals, set by the global community to monitor development along a number of dimensions. It assesses progress towards the goals, showing that many countries are on track but that many others are lagging and unlikely to achieve the goals.

introduction of elections in Nepal. Perhaps most striking was the advent of full democracy in South Africa in 1994—the result of long negotiations. Democratic reforms have been relatively modest in the Arab States, with a few cases of democratic ferment. But monarchies such as Jordan and Morocco have increased space for people's participation in the political life of the community, and Tunisia has taken steps to expand political participation. Still, the region has been slower to democratize than other parts of the world, and only 4 of 17 countries have multiparty electoral systems.[19]

The global shift from authoritarian to democratic regimes shows up in various indicators of governance (appendix 1.1). According to Polity IV's democracy indicator, the number of authoritarian countries fell from almost 70 in 1980 to fewer than 30 in 2000.[20] Over the same period the number of democratic regimes doubled, from 41 to 82. The breakup of the Soviet Union contributed to the jump in country coverage. Overall, the former Soviet Union and the rest of Eastern Europe have become more democratic.

General indicators do not capture the complexity of political transitions. Most attempts at democratization are fragmented, involving small steps and large, forward and back. Take Peru. In 1980, after 12 years of military rule, it shifted to a democratic regime. But the situation slowly deteriorated, with President Alberto Fujimori's regime becoming increasingly authoritarian. Despite irregularities that led international observers to withdraw, Fujimori was proclaimed the winner of the 2000 elections. But public outrage over political scandals ultimately forced him to flee the country. Alejandro Toledo was elected president after elections in 2001.

While the long-term and recent trends have been impressive, the slight drop in measured democracy in Sub-Saharan Africa and South Asia in the second half of the 1990s reflects the fact that the "third wave" of democratization seems to have stalled. Of the 81 countries that have taken steps in democratization, only 47 are considered full democracies.[21] Many others do not seem to be in transition to anything or have lapsed back into authoritarianism—or conflict, as in the Democratic Republic of Congo, Sierra Leone and others. This has

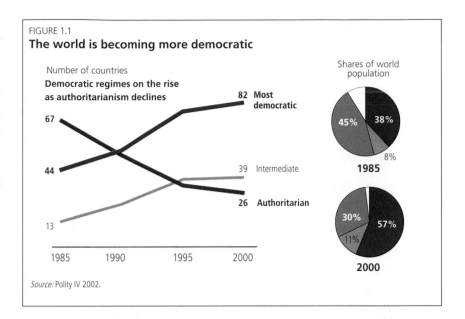

FIGURE 1.1

The world is becoming more democratic

Source: Polity IV 2002.

TABLE 1.1

Most people can now vote in multiparty elections, 1999

Region or country group	Number of countries with multiparty electoral systems (countries with data)	Population of countries with multiparty electoral systems (millions)	Share of regional population living in countries with multiparty electoral systems (percent)
Sub-Saharan Africa	29 (42)	464	77.2
Arab States	4 (17)	115	48.5
East Asia and the Pacific	9 (16)	401	22.0
South Asia	4 (8)	1,170	85.5
Latin America and the Caribbean	25 (26)	468	94.9
Central and Eastern Europe and CIS	21 (25)	350	88.0
OECD	30 (30)	1,120	100.0
Low human development	23 (36)	527	64.4
World	140 (189)	3,923	65.8

Note: Low human development countries are also included in their respective regional groups. Regional data do not sum to the world total because some countries included in the world total are not included in a regional group.
Source: Human Development Report Office calculations based on Alvarez and others 2002.

been especially common in Sub-Saharan Africa and Central Asia. In Belarus, Cameroon, Togo, Uzbekistan and elsewhere, one-party states have allowed elections but ended up permitting only limited opening for political competition. Most of these "limited" democracies suffer from shallow political participation, where citizens have little trust in their governments and are disaffected from politics, or the countries are dominated by a single powerful party or group despite formal elections.[22]

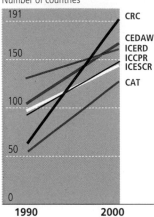

FIGURE 1.2
Ratification of human rights treaties

Number of countries

Note: See indicator table 28 for definitions.
Source: Human Development Report Office calculations based on UNOHCHR 2002.

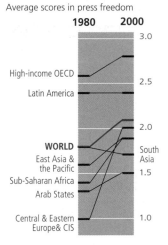

FIGURE 1.3
The press becomes freer

Average scores in press freedom

Source: Human Development Report Office calculations based on Freedom House 2000.

Democratic political participation requires more than elections for governments—truly democratic politics requires civil and political rights to provide the space for effective participation. Illustrating the greater importance attached to human rights worldwide, the number of countries ratifying the six main human rights conventions and covenants has increased dramatically since 1990 (figure 1.2). Upholding human rights is crucial for guaranteeing people's well-being and securing a humane and non-discriminatory society—and for enabling an active and engaged citizenry. Freedoms of association and assembly, of expression and conscience, as laid out in the International Covenant on Civil and Political Rights, are fundamental to political participation.

A free and active press is particularly important for the creation and consolidation of democracy. Freedom House's Freedom of the Press Index indicates levels and trends worldwide, showing that press freedom has also been increasing (figure 1.3).

In addition to civil and political rights, equitable opportunities for participation are crucial to democratic politics. But around the world, women are seriously underrepresented in domestic politics, accounting for only 14% of national parliamentarians. There is little difference between industrial and developing countries. In most industrial countries—including France, Japan and the United States—women account for 10–20% of parliamentarians.[23] Positive exceptions worldwide include both developing and industrial countries (figure 1.4). Nordic countries do particularly well, but in Argentina, Mozambique and South Africa about 30% of parliamentarians are women. Meanwhile, a number of Arab states have no female representation.

THE PROLIFERATION OF CIVIL CONFLICT

The stalling of democratic transitions highlights the fragility of democracies. The proliferation of conflicts, particularly internal conflicts, highlights the fragility of states (figure 1.5). Internal conflicts today vastly outnumber wars between states. Since 1990 an estimated 220,000 people have died in wars between states—compared with nearly 3.6 million in wars within states.[24]

Particularly tragic is the fact that civilians, not soldiers, are increasingly the victims of conflicts. Civilians have accounted for more than 90% of the casualties—either injured or killed—in post–cold war conflicts.[25] Moreover, internal conflicts are usually fought with small weapons, and combatants use strategies that have the strongest impact on the vulnerable. Children account for half of all civilian casualties in wars,[26] and worldwide there are an estimated 300,000 child soldiers—in Sierra Leone, Sudan and elsewhere.[27]

Civil wars also have grave effects on economic growth and food production, as revealed by such human development indicators as infant mortality rates and school enrolments.[28] Seven of the ten countries with the lowest human development indices have recently suffered major civil wars. During Mozambique's 16-year civil war more than 40% of schools were destroyed or forced to close, and more than 40% of health centres were destroyed. Industries were so damaged that postwar production was only 20–40% of prewar capacity, with economic losses estimated at $15 billion—several times Mozambique's prewar GDP.[29]

Fighting between and within states also causes massive refugee flows and displaced populations. At the end of 2000 more than 12 million people were refugees, 6 million were internally displaced and nearly 4 million were returning refugees, asylum-seekers or people otherwise of concern to the UN High Commissioner for Refugees[30]—in all, 50% more than in 1990.[31] The increase in refugees and displaced populations indicates that today's armed conflicts are more intense.

THE MILLENNIUM DEVELOPMENT GOALS: COMMITMENTS AND PROSPECTS

At the UN General Assembly in 2000, heads of state and government took stock of the gross inequalities in human development worldwide and recognized "their collective responsibility to uphold the principles of human dignity, equality and equity at the global level."[32] In addition to declaring their support for freedom, democracy and human rights, they set eight goals for development and poverty eradication, to be achieved by 2015:

- Eradicate extreme poverty and hunger.
- Achieve universal primary education.
- Promote gender equality and empower women.
- Reduce child mortality.
- Improve maternal health.
- Combat HIV/AIDS, malaria and other diseases.
- Ensure environmental sustainability.
- Develop a global partnership for development.[33]

Most of the Millennium Development Goals have quantifiable, monitorable targets to measure progress against standards set by the international community. This Report assesses how likely countries are to achieve the goals by 2015 if recent trends continue, classifying them as achieved, on track, lagging, far behind or slipping back (appendix table A1.1 and technical note). The analysis assumes that trends over the next decade will be the same as over the past decade. Whether countries fall behind or surpass this expectation will depend on their actions and those of the global community between now and 2015.

Many countries have made progress (feature 1.1). But much of the world, generally the poorest countries, seems unlikely to achieve the goals. Although 55 countries, with 23% of the world's people, are on track to achieve at least three-quarters of the goals, 33 countries with 26% of the world's people are failing on more than half (figure 1.6). Especially extraordinary efforts will be needed in Sub-Saharan Africa, where 23 countries are failing and 11 others do not have enough data to be assessed—a possible indication that they are even further behind. That leaves just 10 Sub-Saharan countries on track to meet at least half of the goals.

Lack of data makes it difficult to assess progress on the goal of halving income poverty. But slow growth in average incomes indicates that many countries will have to struggle to achieve the goal. Optimistic estimates suggest that 3.7% annual growth in per capita GDP will be needed, yet in the 1990s only 24 countries achieved such growth (figure 1.7).[34] China and India, the most populous countries, are in

this group. But incomes in nearly 130 countries, with 40% of the world's people, are not growing fast enough—including 52 countries that actually had negative growth in the 1990s. Again, progress is most elusive in the poorest countries: 40 of 44 Sub-Saharan countries, with 93% of the region's people, grew too slowly. Half of those 40 countries, with more than half of the region's people, are poorer now than in 1990. These include 11 of the world's 20 poorest countries.

Countries have come closer to some goals than others. Many developing countries have already achieved or are on track to achieve universal primary education and gender equity in education. Given the importance of education to so many other areas of development, this bodes well for accelerating progress towards the other goals. Most developing countries have also achieved or are on track to achieve the targets for eradicating hunger and improving water supplies (part of the environmental goal). But more than 40 countries, with 28% of the world's people, are not on track to halve hunger by 2015. And 25 countries, with 32% of the world's people, may not halve the share of people lacking access to an improved water source. Most pressing, however, is child mortality: 85 countries with more than 60% of the world's people are not on track to achieve the goal (see feature 1.1).

A goal that cannot be monitored cannot be met or missed—and one of the most startling conclusions is the lack of data. The targets for poverty, HIV/AIDS and maternal mortality cannot be monitored directly with current international data. Even targets that can be monitored have many gaps in the data. Complicating matters, countries lacking data may have the worst performance, giving an inflated impression of the proportion of countries that are progressing.

GOAL 1—ERADICATING EXTREME POVERTY AND HUNGER

Target 1a: Halve the proportion of people living on less than $1 a day

In 1999, 2.8 billion people lived on less than $2 a day, with 1.2 billion of them barely surviving at the margins of subsistence on less than $1 a

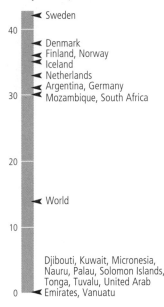

FIGURE 1.4

Womens' participation lags everywhere

Percentage of parliament seats held by women, 2000

Source: IPU 2002c and indicator table 23.

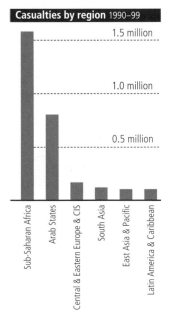

FIGURE 1.5

The poorest have suffered the most from conflict

Source: Human Development Report Office calculations based on Marshall 2000.

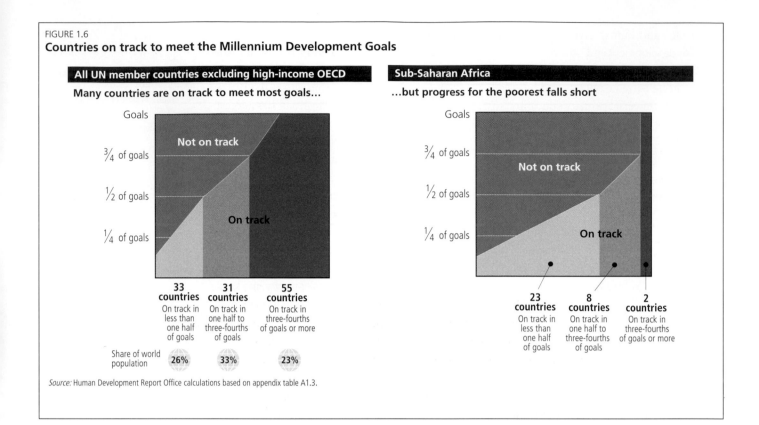

FIGURE 1.6

Countries on track to meet the Millennium Development Goals

All UN member countries excluding high-income OECD

Many countries are on track to meet most goals...

Goals

¾ of goals

½ of goals

¼ of goals

Not on track

On track

33 countries On track in less than one half of goals

31 countries On track in one half to three-fourths of goals

55 countries On track in three-fourths of goals or more

Share of world population | 26% | 33% | 23%

Sub-Saharan Africa

...but progress for the poorest falls short

Goals

¾ of goals

½ of goals

¼ of goals

Not on track

On track

23 countries On track in less than one half of goals

8 countries On track in one half to three-fourths of goals

2 countries On track in three-fourths of goals or more

Source: Human Development Report Office calculations based on appendix table A1.3.

FIGURE 1.7

Failing to grow out of poverty

Number of countries by GDP per capita growth rate (Average annual percentage, 1990–2000)

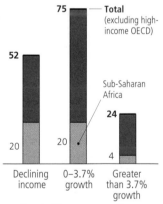

75 — **Total** (excluding high-income OECD)

Sub-Saharan Africa

52

20 | 20 | 24

20 | 4

Declining income | 0–3.7% growth | Greater than 3.7% growth

Level of income growth

Source: Human Development Report Office calculations based on indicator table 12.

TABLE 1.2

Worldwide, the number of people living on less than $1 a day barely changed in the 1990s

| | Share (percent) | | Number (millions) | |
Region	1990	1999	1990	1999
Sub-Saharan Africa	47.7	46.7	242	300
East Asia and the Pacific	27.6	14.2	452	260
Excluding China	18.5	7.9	92	46
South Asia	44.0	36.9	495	490
Latin America and the Caribbean	16.8	15.1	74	77
Eastern Europe and Central Asia	1.6	3.6	7	17
Middle East and North Africa	2.4	2.3	6	7
Total	29.0	22.7	1,276	1,151
Excluding China	28.1	24.5	916	936

Note: $1 a day is $1.08 in 1993 purchasing power parity (PPP) prices.
Source: World Bank 2002c.

day (table 1.2). During the 1990s the number of extremely poor people dropped only slightly. But because of population growth, the share of the world's people living in extreme poverty fell from 29% in 1990 to 23% in 1999.

The declining share of people in extreme poverty is hopeful, but the level remains disturbingly high. And the failure to reduce poverty in Sub-Saharan Africa, the world's poorest region, is a grave concern.

Per capita income. A country's income poverty rate is determined by its per capita income and by the distribution of that income. Though there is no guarantee that poor people

will benefit from an increase in their country's average per capita income, aggregate growth typically does increase their incomes.[35]

Since the mid-1970s growth in per capita income has varied dramatically across regions (box 1.1). East Asia and the Pacific's impressive poverty reduction is primarily due to a quadrupling in its per capita GDP between 1975 and 2000. But Sub-Saharan Africa ended the millennium 5% poorer than in 1990.

Central and Eastern Europe and the CIS was the only other region to suffer a decline in per capita income during the 1990s. Growth in the region is picking up, and a few countries have

BOX 1.1

Global inequality—grotesque levels, ambiguous trends

The level of inequality worldwide is grotesque. But trends over recent decades are ambiguous. The range of economic performance across countries and regions means that inequality has increased between some regions and decreased between others. Between 1975 and 2000 impressive growth in East Asia and the Pacific increased its per capita income—in purchasing power parity (PPP) terms—from about 1/14th of the average per capita income in OECD countries to better than 1/6th. Over the same period Sub-Saharan Africa suffered the reverse, with its per capita income dropping from 1/6th of that in OECD countries to only 1/14th, owing both to its own drop in income and to consistent growth in OECD countries. The worst-off Sub-Saharan countries now have incomes 1/40th or less of those in OECD countries. Latin America and the Caribbean suffered a slight deterioration relative to OECD countries, with its average per capita income dropping from a bit less than half to a bit less than a third, while Arab States dropped from a quarter to a fifth.

Rapid growth in the two largest countries—China since the 1970s and India since the late 1980s—has enabled them to catch up to some extent with rich countries. Since 1975 China has improved its per capita income relative to OECD countries from 1/21st to 1/6th, while India has improved from 1/14th in 1980 to 1/10th.

These aggregate comparisons give an incomplete picture. When considering human development, within-country inequality must be taken into account because simple comparisons of per capita GDP assume that everyone in a country has the same income. Data on within-country inequality, based on household surveys, are often not comparable across countries or over time, so conclusions must be tentative. Still, reasonable estimates can be made, and studies have found interesting results.

Long-term trends in interpersonal inequality, using PPP exchange rates, show that the world has become much more unequal. Between 1970 and the 1990s the world was more unequal than at any time before 1950 (according to any inequality measure in Bourguignon and Morrison 2001)—the legacy of the industrial revolutions that occurred in a few parts of the world. But the trend in inequality since 1970 is ambiguous, depending on the data and the inequality measure. The trend in the well-known Gini measure of inequality varies between studies, with one showing it

increasing to the 1980s and then leveling off and another showing it peaking around 1970. In the first the Theil inequality index increases steadily to the 1990s; in both the variance of the logarithm of incomes peaks around 1980. Other studies find slightly different trends. But in all studies and all measures, changes since 1970 are relatively small and not statistically significant. For instance, most estimates of the Gini coefficient from 1970 to the most recent lie within the range of 0.63 to 0.66, which are not statistically distinguishable. (Bourguignon and Morrison 2001 estimate the 90% confidence interval to be about 0.04.)

The most important factors increasing global inequality in the second half of the 20th century were:
- Rapid economic growth in already rich countries in Western Europe, North America and Oceania relative to most of the rest of the world.
- Slow growth on the Indian subcontinent until the late 20th century, and consistently slow growth in Africa.

Factors decreasing inequality were:
- Rapid growth in China since the 1970s and India since the late 1980s.
- Catching-up between European countries and the United States until the 1990s.

Rapid growth in South-East Asia, while impressive, had little effect on global inequality owing to the relatively small populations involved.

Although it may be difficult to distinguish clear trends in global inequality in recent decades, its level is extremely high—a cause for considerable concern. Milanovic (2001) finds some startling statistics, taking into account inequality within countries and using PPP exchange rates. The most recent available estimates are for 1993, but stagnation in the poorest countries and robust growth in many of the richest imply that these are unlikely to have improved.
- The world's richest 1% of people receive as much income as the poorest 57%.
- The richest 10% of the U.S. population has an income equal to that of the poorest 43% of the world. Put differently, the income of the richest 25 million Americans is equal to that of almost 2 billion people.
- The income of the world's richest 5% is 114 times that of the poorest 5%.

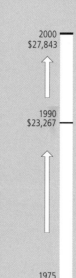

2000 $27,843

1990 $23,267

1975 $16,048

Global disparities in income: are regions closing the gap?

GDP per capita (2000 purchasing power parity U.S. dollars, thousands)

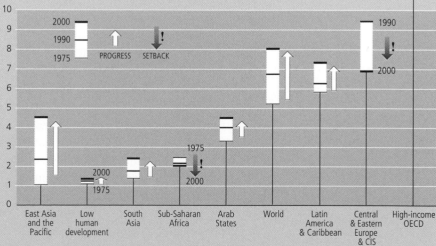

Source: Human Development Report Office calculations based on World Bank 2002e.

Source: Bourguignon and Morrisson 2001; Schultz 1998; Milanovic 2001.

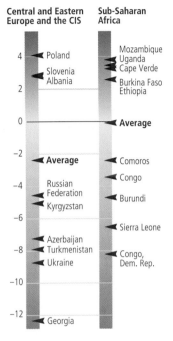

BOX 1.2

Poverty's relative

Even the poorest people in rich countries generally have much higher incomes than poor people in developing countries—but they still suffer severe deprivation. The reason? As a country gets richer, its inhabitants require more expensive goods and services to take part in normal life. Children may be unable to join in classroom conversations if their parents do not own a television; a construction worker may be unable to get work without a car. Such goods, once luxuries, become necessities as they proliferate throughout society. So, even in a rich country with no absolute income poverty, relative income poverty may lead to absolute poverty in important dimensions of human development—such as education, self-respect or the ability to get decent work.

OECD countries have increased their incomes over the past two decades, but most have seen rising income inequality—most consistently and dramatically in the United Kingdom and the United States. Between 1979 and 1997 U.S. real GDP per capita grew 38%, but the income of a family with median earnings grew only 9%. So most of the gain was captured by the very richest people, with the incomes of the richest 1% of families growing 140%, three times the average. The income of the top 1% of families was 10 times that of the median family in 1979—and 23 times in 1997.

Canada and Denmark have bucked the OECD trend, registering stable or slightly reduced inequality. This was achieved primarily through fiscal policy and social transfers—indicating that with political will, nothing is inevitable about inequality increasing with rising incomes.

Source: Smeeding and Grodner 2000; Atkinson 1999; Human Development Report Office calculations based on World Bank 2001e; Krugman 2002.

done quite well. But in many countries incomes remain far lower than in the past (figure 1.8).

Income inequality within countries. The amount of growth required to reduce poverty depends on a country's level of inequality—the more unequal is the distribution of income, the fewer are the benefits of growth to poor people. Studies of inequality trends within countries suffer from a lack of reliable, comparable data (see box 1.1). The limited available evidence indicates that worldwide, within-country income inequality has been increasing for the past 30 years.[36] Among the 73 countries with data (and 80% of the world's people), 48 have seen inequality increase since the 1950s, 16 have experienced no change and only 9—with just 4% of the world's people—have seen inequality fall.[37] The increase in inequality has impeded poverty reduction. Given current inequality levels, most countries are not growing fast enough to meet the poverty target. Thus efforts must focus on making growth more pro-poor.[38]

Inequalities beyond income. This Report's human development index (HDI), when calculated for regions and for groups within countries, can provide summary information on inequalities in several aspects of human development within countries (feature 1.2). This information can spotlight stark contrasts that in many coun-

tries have fuelled national debates and helped policy-makers assess differences in human development between regions, between rural and urban areas and between ethnic and income groups. In South Africa in 1996 the HDI for the Northern Province was just 0.531, compared with 0.712 for Gauteng.[39] In Guatemala in 1998 the rural HDI, at 0.536, was well below the urban HDI, at 0.672.[40] In 1996 the HDI for "untouchables" in Nepal, at 0.239, was almost half that for Brahmins, at 0.439.[41]

Another way to look at the distribution of human development achievements within countries is to estimate the human poverty index (HPI), a measure introduced in *Human Development Report 1997* to go beyond income and consider poverty in the same multiple dimensions as the HDI: health, education and a decent standard of living. The United Republic of Tanzania and Uganda, for example, have similar HDI rankings (140 and 141), but Uganda has higher human poverty (figure 1.9; indicator table 3).

Poverty is not just an issue for developing countries (box 1.2). The HPI-2, calculated for certain countries that belong to the Organisation for Economic Co-operation and Development (OECD), can be particularly revealing (see feature 1.2). Its focus on deprivations differentiates industrial countries more clearly, using such indicators as poverty rates, functional literacy and long-term unemployment (see technical note). Estimated for 17 OECD countries—with nearly identical HDIs—the HPI-2s range from 6.8% in Sweden to 15.8% in the United States (figure 1.10; indicator table 4).

Target 1b: Halve the proportion of people suffering from hunger

Children suffer doubly from hunger: it affects their daily lives and has devastating consequences for their future mental and physical health. In 50 countries with almost 40% of the world's people, more than one-fifth of children under the age of five are underweight.[42] That 17 of those countries are in the medium human development category underscores hunger's pervasiveness. Still, the problem is worst among the world's poorest countries. In Sub-Saharan Africa only South Africa has less than a 10% incidence of child malnourishment. In six Sub-Saharan countries that figure is more than 40%.

A rough indication of how countries are moving towards halving hunger by 2015 comes from changes in the number of malnourished people—a less precise indicator of hunger than child malnutrition rates, based on national food availability and estimated distribution. In 1997–99 an estimated 815 million people were undernourished: 777 million in developing

countries, 27 million in transition economies and 11 million in industrial countries.[43]

There are some reasons for optimism. Fifty-seven countries, with half of the world's people, have halved hunger or are on track to do so by 2015 (see feature 1.1). But progress is far from universal. Twenty-four countries are far behind in achieving the target. And in 15 more—6 from Sub-Saharan Africa—the situation worsened in the 1990s.

While the proportion of hungry people has been declining, the world's booming population means that the number of malnourished people has not been falling fast enough. During the 1990s it declined by just 6 million people a year.[44] At this rate it would take more than 130 years to rid the world of hunger.

GOAL 2—ACHIEVING UNIVERSAL PRIMARY EDUCATION

Target 2a: Ensure that children everywhere—boys and girls alike—complete a full course of primary education

Education is important in its own right and has strong spillover benefits to mortality rates, income and even social cohesion. Worldwide, primary enrollments have been improving, rising from 80% in 1990 to 84% in 1998. But that still means that of the 680 million children of primary school age, 113 million are not in school—97% of them in developing countries.[45]

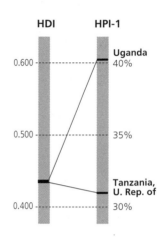

FIGURE 1.9
No automatic link between HDI and HPI-1

Source: Indicator tables 1 and 3.

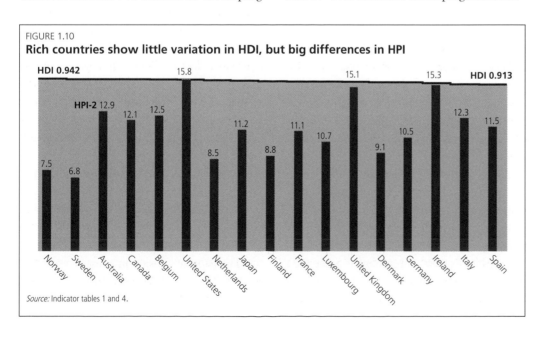

FIGURE 1.10
Rich countries show little variation in HDI, but big differences in HPI

Source: Indicator tables 1 and 4.

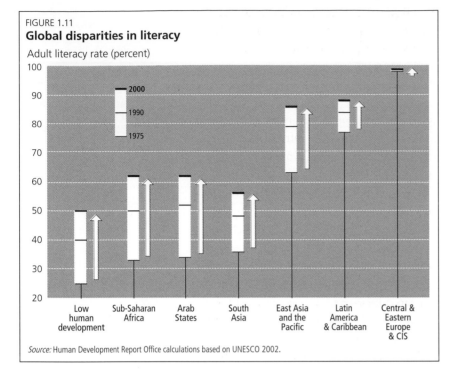

FIGURE 1.11
Global disparities in literacy

Adult literacy rate (percent)

Legend: 2000, 1990, 1975

Categories: Low human development; Sub-Saharan Africa; Arab States; South Asia; East Asia and the Pacific; Latin America & Caribbean; Central & Eastern Europe & CIS

Source: Human Development Report Office calculations based on UNESCO 2002.

Many countries have good prospects for achieving universal primary education. But there is little middle ground: most of those not on track to achieve the goal are far behind or have worsening primary enrollments (see feature 1.1). Sub-Saharan Africa fares worst—of the 21 countries with data, 14 are far behind the target or have deteriorating enrollments. Furthermore, 93 countries with 39% of the world's people do not have sufficient data to make a judgement.

Enrolling children in primary school is only half the battle, because it is meaningful only if they complete it—which requires that they and their families be able to resist the pressures of forgone income and work in the home. Of the few countries with data on primary school completion, most seem to be on track (appendix table A1.1). But again the news is worse for Sub-Saharan Africa, where 6 countries are on track and 5 are far behind or slipping back—and the 33 countries without data are likely to be among the poor performers.

Literacy. One of the most important outcomes of primary education is literacy. And literacy rates are slow to change, reflecting the education of previous generations of children and the history of school enrolment. Since 1975 literacy rates have increased substantially in all developing regions (figure 1.11). East Asia and

the Pacific and Latin America and the Caribbean seem to be converging, with close to 90% adult literacy. But Sub-Saharan Africa, South Asia and Arab States, despite significant progress, are much further behind, with adult literacy rates of about 60%. In the past 25 years literacy rates in low human development countries have doubled—though only to 50%.

Functional literacy. Among OECD countries, literacy rates are often assumed to be close to 100%. But the truth is very different. The concept of functional illiteracy describes the inability to understand and use common channels of communication and information in an everyday context, from newspapers and books to pamphlets and instructions on medicine bottles. Based on this measure, in most OECD countries an incredible 10–20% of people are functionally illiterate, with Sweden and Norway doing relatively well at 8% and 9% while Ireland, the United Kingdom and the United States have levels over 20% (indicator table 4).

GOAL 3—*PROMOTING GENDER EQUALITY AND EMPOWERING WOMEN*

Target 3a: Eliminate gender disparities in primary and secondary education, preferably by 2005, and in all levels of education by 2015

The Millennium Development Goal for gender equality in education responds to dramatic gender disparities in many parts of the world, particularly South Asia and West, Central and North Africa. In India the enrolment ratio of boys aged 6–14 is 17 percentage points higher than that of girls the same age, in Benin 21 percentage points. Yet in many developing countries, mostly in Latin America, girls have no disadvantage or even a small advantage.[46] Still, of the world's estimated 854 million illiterate adults, 544 million are women—and of the 113 million children not in primary school, 60% are girls.[46] The world is still a long way from achieving equal rights and opportunities between females and males.

The gaps are closing in primary and, to a lesser extent, secondary enrollments: 90 countries, with more than 60% of the world's people, have achieved or are on track to achieving gender equality in primary education by 2015—and more than 80 in secondary education (see feature 1.1; appendix table A1.1).

Perhaps most surprising is the performance of Arab States—countries generally associated with high gender inequality. All but one of those with data are on track to meet the target for primary enrollments. Again, Sub-Saharan Africa is making the least progress, but even there most countries have achieved or are on track to achieve gender equality in primary enrolment.

Education is just one aspect of human development in which there is discrimination between the sexes. Around the world, women still earn only around 75% as much as men. Domestic violence against women is common in many societies. And around the world there are an estimated 100 million "missing" women—50 million in India alone—who would be alive but for infanticide, neglect or sex-selective abortions. A recent survey in India found 10,000 cases of female infanticide a year, and a study of a clinic in Bombay found that 7,999 of 8,000 aborted foetuses were female.[48]

The gender-related development index (GDI) adjusts the HDI for inequalities in the achievements of men and women (see feature 1.2 and indicator table 21). With gender equality in human development, the GDI and the HDI would be the same. But for all countries the GDI is lower than the HDI, indicating gender inequality everywhere. The extent of the inequality varies significantly. Although many countries have similar male and female literacy rates, 43 countries—including India, Mozambique and Yemen—have male rates at least 15 percentage points higher than female rates.

Worse outcomes for women in many aspects of human development result from the fact that their voices have less impact than men's in the decisions that shape their lives. This inequality in empowerment is partly captured by the gender empowerment measure (GEM), introduced in *Human Development Report 1995* to help assess gender inequality in economic and political opportunities. This year the GEM has been estimated for 66 countries (indicator table 23). Some observations:

- GEM values range from less than 0.300 to more than 0.800—indicating enormous variation around the world in empowering women.
- Only 5 of the 66 countries—Denmark, Finland, Iceland, Norway and Sweden—have a GEM above 0.800, while 22 have a GEM below 0.500.
- Some developing countries outperform much richer industrial countries. The Bahamas and Trinidad and Tobago are ahead of Italy and Japan. Barbados's GEM is 25% higher than Greece's. The message: high income is not a prerequisite to creating opportunities for women.

Inequalities beyond gender. The Millennium Development Goals consider gender inequality in education—but this is only one aspect of unfair access to schooling. While gender gaps in education are large in some countries and nonexistent in others, wealth gaps exist the world over. Extreme examples include Senegal, where the enrolment ratio for 6–14-year-olds from the poorest households is 52 percentage points lower than for those from the richest households, and Zambia, with a 36 point difference. Such wealth gaps perpetuate the cycle of poverty: those born poor are likely to die poor. Furthermore, in some countries (Egypt, India, Morocco, Niger, Pakistan) the gender gap in education is much larger for poor households. In India the gender gap in enrolment is only 3 percentage points in the richest households, but 34 points in the poorest.[49]

One cause of such gaps is that in many countries, public spending on education is skewed towards the rich. In Ecuador the poorest 20% of households receive only 11% of public education spending, while the richest 20% receive 26%—more than twice as much.[50] Even when public spending is distributed more equitably, rich parents can buy a far better education for their children at private schools. In Chile, Peru, the Philippines and Thailand private spending accounts for more than 40% of education spending.[51]

Education inequality is also a serious problem in some industrial countries. In the United States race is a significant factor: minorities have lower schooling levels and less access to high-quality schooling. Controlling for parental education and immigrant status, young African

Worse outcomes for women in many aspects of human development result from the fact that their voices have less impact than men's in the decisions that shape their lives

PROGRESS TOWARDS THE MILLENNIUM DEVELOPMENT GOALS—HOW MANY COUNTRIES ARE ON TRACK?

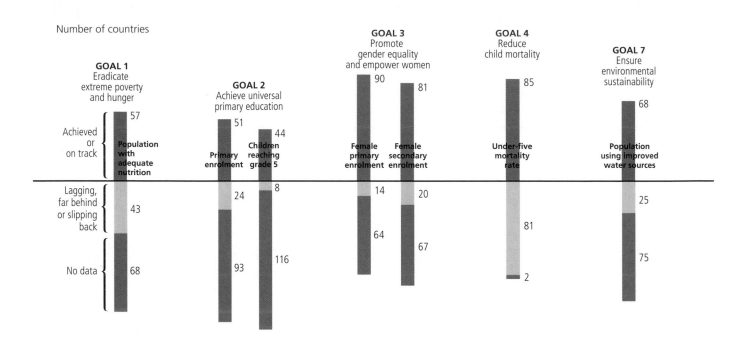

Number of countries

Millennium Development Goal 1—halving hunger

Number of countries

	Achieved	On track	Lagging	Far behind	Slipping back	No data
Sub-Saharan Africa	2	14	2	11	6	9
Arab States	1	5	0	1	0	10
East Asia and the Pacific	0	6	0	3	1	9
South Asia	0	3	0	3	0	2
Latin America and the Caribbean	3	10	2	5	3	10
Central and E. Europe and the CIS	0	11	0	0	1	13
Total	**6**	**51**	**4**	**24**	**15**	**68**

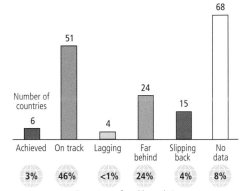

Number of countries

Achieved	On track	Lagging	Far behind	Slipping back	No data
6	51	4	24	15	68
3%	46%	<1%	24%	4%	8%

Percentage of world population

Millennium Development Goal 2—achieving universal primary education

Number of countries

	Achieved	On track	Lagging	Far behind	Slipping back	No data
Sub-Saharan Africa	0	7	0	9	5	23
Arab States	1	6	0	4	0	6
East Asia and the Pacific	3	7	0	0	0	9
South Asia	0	0	0	0	1	7
Latin America and the Caribbean	2	11	0	2	1	17
Central and E. Europe and the CIS	1	11	0	0	1	12
Total	**8**	**43**	**0**	**15**	**9**	**93**

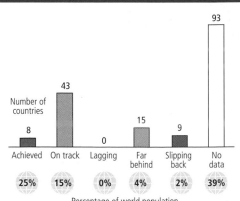

Number of countries

Achieved	On track	Lagging	Far behind	Slipping back	No data
8	43	0	15	9	93
25%	15%	0%	4%	2%	39%

Percentage of world population

Millennium Development Goal 3—achieving gender equality in primary education

Number of countries

	Achieved	On track	Lagging	Far behind	Slipping back	No data
Sub-Saharan Africa	5	15	0	8	1	15
Arab States	1	12	0	1	0	3
East Asia and the Pacific	5	7	0	1	0	6
South Asia	0	5	0	0	0	3
Latin America and the Caribbean	3	13	0	1	0	16
Central and E. Europe and the CIS	4	16	0	0	0	5
Total	**20**	**70**	**0**	**13**	**1**	**64**

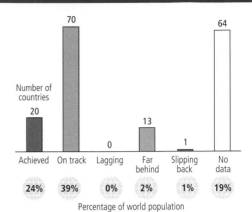

Millennium Development Goal 4—reducing under-five mortality by two-thirds

Number of countries

	Achieved	On track	Lagging	Far behind	Slipping back	No data
Sub-Saharan Africa	0	7	3	24	10	0
Arab States	0	11	1	4	1	0
East Asia and the Pacific	0	13	1	3	1	1
South Asia	0	6	1	1	0	0
Latin America and the Caribbean	0	25	0	8	0	0
Central and E. Europe and the CIS	0	10	0	13	2	0
Total	**0**	**85**	**7**	**59**	**15**	**2**

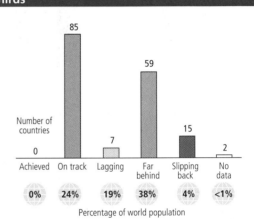

Millennium Development Goal 7—halving the proportion of people without sustainable, safe drinking water

Number of countries

	Achieved	On track	Lagging	Far behind	Slipping back	No data
Sub-Saharan Africa	1	9	4	9	0	21
Arab States	0	8	0	3	0	6
East Asia and the Pacific	0	6	1	4	0	8
South Asia	3	4	0	0	0	1
Latin America and the Caribbean	1	21	1	2	0	8
Central and E. Europe and the CIS	0	8	0	0	0	17
Total	**5**	**63**	**7**	**18**	**0**	**75**

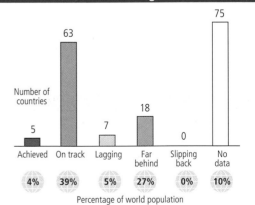

Note: Regions include only HDI countries while the total includes all UN member countries excluding high-income OECD members.
Source: Human Development Report Office calculations based on appendix table A1.3.

Americans perform worse in functional literacy tests than do young white Americans—on average, by the equivalent of four to five years of schooling. The gap for Hispanic Americans is one and a half to two years.[52]

GOAL 4—REDUCING CHILD MORTALITY

Target 4a: Reduce infant and under-five mortality rates by two-thirds

Every year about 11 million children die of preventable causes, often for want of simple and easily provided improvements in nutrition, sanitation and maternal health and education. Some developing regions have made rapid improvements in this area—especially Arab States, where 6% of children die before age five, down from 20% in 1970 (figure 1.12).

Although Latin America and the Caribbean is doing well as a whole, eight countries are far from achieving the infant mortality target. In East Asia and the Pacific 13 countries are on track but 3, including China, are far behind—and in Cambodia under-five mortality rates are increasing (see feature 1.1). Central and Eastern Europe and the CIS, doing badly as a whole, combines good performance from the European countries and worse performance from the more populous CIS countries. In Sub-Saharan Africa 34 of 44 countries are far behind or slipping back.

Immunizations against leading diseases are a vital element in improving child survival. After soaring in the 1980s, immunizations in developing countries levelled off at about 75% in the 1990s. And in recent years the proportion of children immunized in Sub-Saharan Africa has fallen below 50%.[53]

Child mortality has a dramatic effect on a country's life expectancy, which is part of the HDI and is an excellent indicator of a country's overall health. Between 1975 and 2000 East Asia and the Pacific increased life expectancy by about 8 years, to almost 70 (figure 1.13). South Asia, Latin America and the Caribbean and Arab States also achieved consistent increases. But high-income OECD countries are still head and shoulders above the rest, with a life expectancy of 77 years—7 years more than the next-highest region.

Sub-Saharan Africa, ravaged by HIV/AIDS and conflict, saw life expectancy reverse in the 1990s from already tragically low levels. Eastern Europe and the CIS also suffered a decline, and is the only other region where life expectancy is lower now than in 1990.

GOAL 5—IMPROVING MATERNAL HEALTH

Target 5a: Reduce maternal mortality ratios by three-quarters

Every year more than 500,000 women die as a result of pregnancy and childbirth,[54] with huge regional disparities (table 1.3). The situation is worst in Sub-Saharan Africa, where a woman has a 1 in 13 chance of dying in pregnancy or childbirth.

Increasing the number of births attended by skilled health personnel is key to reducing maternal mortality ratios, and again there is wide variation—with as few as 29% of births attended by skilled personnel in South Asia and 37% in Sub-Saharan Africa.[55]

There are not enough data on maternal mortality or births attended by skilled health personnel to assess how countries are progressing towards this important goal, indicating an urgent need for more complete, comparable data on this vital issue.

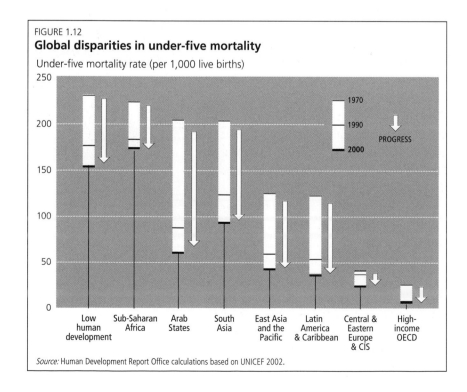

FIGURE 1.12
Global disparities in under-five mortality

Under-five mortality rate (per 1,000 live births)

1970
1990
2000
PROGRESS

Low human development · Sub-Saharan Africa · Arab States · South Asia · East Asia and the Pacific · Latin America & Caribbean · Central & Eastern Europe & CIS · High-income OECD

Source: Human Development Report Office calculations based on UNICEF 2002.

TABLE 1.3 **Maternal mortality is much higher in some regions**	
Region	Lifetime chance of dying in pregnancy or childbirth
Sub-Saharan Africa	1 in 13
South Asia	1 in 54
Middle East and North Africa	1 in 55
Latin America and the Caribbean	1 in 157
East Asia and the Pacific	1 in 283
Central and Eastern Europe and CIS	1 in 797
OECD	1 in 4,085

Note: Data refer to most recent year available.
Source: UNICEF 2002.

GOAL 6—COMBATING *HIV/AIDS, MALARIA AND OTHER DISEASES*

Target 6a: Halt and begin to reverse the spread of HIV/AIDS

By the end of 2000 almost 22 million people had died from AIDS, 13 million children had lost their mother or both parents to the disease and more than 40 million people were living with the HIV virus—90% of them in developing countries, 75% in Sub-Saharan Africa.[56]

In Botswana, the most affected country, more than a third of adults have HIV/AIDS and a child born today can expect to live only 36 years—about half as long as if the disease did not exist (figure 1.14). In Burkina Faso, the 20th most affected country, 330,000 adults are living with HIV/AIDS, and life expectancy has fallen by 8 years.[57]

The toll on life expectancy is only the beginning. In Thailand one-third of AIDS-affected rural families saw their incomes fall by half because the time of farmers, and those caring for them, was taken from the fields.[58] At the same time, medical expenses shoot up. In Côte d'Ivoire caring for a male AIDS patient costs an average of $300 a year, a quarter to half of the net annual income of most small farms.[59] The effect on poor households, with little or no savings to cope with such shocks, is devastating. In urban Côte d'Ivoire food consumption dropped 41% per capita, and school outlays halved.[60]

HIV/AIDS is also a concern in the Caribbean, the region with the second highest infection rate. In Latin America 1.3 million people have HIV/AIDS. Central and Eastern Europe and the CIS has fast-rising infection rates—240,000 people are now infected in Ukraine.[61] And there are warnings that Asia is on the verge of an epidemic. In Ho Chi Minh City, Vietnam, one sex worker in five is HIV positive, up from almost none in the mid-1990s. And nearly 4 million people are now infected in India, second only to South Africa.[62] Without strong preventative measures, as in Thailand, the epidemic could rage out of control.

There are no comparable trend data for assessing how well countries are fighting the disease. But it is clear that policies can make a difference and that contraceptive prevalence and reproductive rights for women are vital. Through preventive measures, Uganda reduced HIV rates from 14% in the early 1990s to around 8% by the end of the 1990s.[63]

Also vital is providing treatment and care to those already affected. But at a cost of $300 per year per patient—well over half the GDP per capita of Sub-Saharan Africa—antiretroviral drugs that can prolong life expectancy are out of reach for the average African HIV patient. As homes to the leading pharmaceutical companies, some industrial countries have pressured developing countries not to manufacture generic alternatives of these patented drugs. But in No-

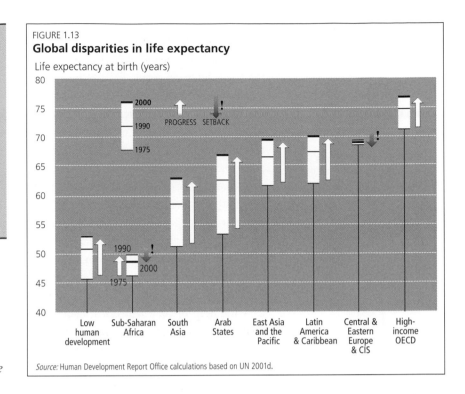

FIGURE 1.13
Global disparities in life expectancy

Life expectancy at birth (years)

Source: Human Development Report Office calculations based on UN 2001d.

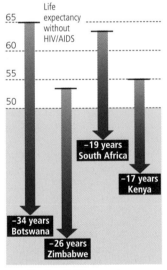

FIGURE 1.14
Devastation from HIV/AIDS— life expectancy in Sub-Saharan Africa plummets

Decline in life expectancy by 2000–2005

Source: UNDESA 2001.

Carbon dioxide emissions originate disproportionately in high-income countries

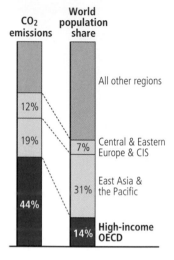

vember 2001 the World Trade Organization ministerial conference in Doha, Qatar, adopted the Declaration on Trade-Related Intellectual Property Rights and Public Health, affirming the sovereign right of governments to protect public health. The legal status of this declaration is not yet clear, but it indicates that rulings on disputes may now favour public health. One issue that remains uncertain is whether countries can override patents and produce generic drugs for export to other developing countries—a crucial question for all developing countries with no pharmaceutical industry of their own. Goal 8, developing a global partnership for development, includes the aspiration of resolving this problem with the help of pharmaceutical companies. Whether this proves to be possible, in the wake of the Doha declaration it is clear that international law must put global public health first.

Target 6b: Halt and begin to reverse the incidence of malaria and other major diseases

Every year there are more than 300 million cases of malaria, 90% of them in Sub-Saharan Africa.[64] And every year 60 million people are infected with tuberculosis.[65] Current medical technologies can prevent these diseases from being fatal, but lack of access means that tuberculosis kills 2 million people a year[66] and malaria 1 million.[67] The poorest people typically suffer most.

Without much more effective control, by 2020 nearly 1 billion people will be infected and 35 million will die from tuberculosis.[68] In addition to its human costs, disease takes a heavy economic toll: for instance, high malaria prevalence can lower economic growth by 1% or more a year.[69] Work is under way to strengthen national health systems and increase international support, and there are some encouraging signs: the World Health Organization, for example, has struck a deal with the Swiss firm Novartis on the drug Coartem, an extremely effective malaria treatment. The price of this drug, which can reduce infection and fatality rates by 75%, has fallen to less than $2.50 a treatment.[70] But this is still far more than many people can afford—and only the beginning of efforts to overcome these diseases.

GOAL 7—ENSURING ENVIRONMENTAL SUSTAINABILITY

The diversity of environmental issues across countries and regions makes it extremely difficult to set global targets, so this goal sets out general principles for achieving sustainability and reducing the human costs of environmental degradation.

Target 7a: Integrate the principles of sustainable development into country policies and programmes and reverse the loss of environmental resources

Global warming is a universal concern—and carbon dioxide emissions are one of its main causes. Such emissions have increased dramatically, to more than 6.6 billion tons in 1998, up from 5.3 billion in 1980.[71] High-income countries generate a far higher proportion than their share of the world's population (figure 1.15).

Around the world, goods production has generally become more energy-efficient in the past few decades. But the increased volume of global production means that such improvements are far from sufficient to reduce world carbon dioxide emissions. So the Kyoto Protocol to the Framework Convention on Climate Change aims to reduce emissions, mainly through controls on industrial pollution. The protocol could be a big step towards controlling emissions. But 165 countries, responsible for 89% of global carbon dioxide emissions, have yet to ratify it (indicator table 19). The key missing player is the United States, responsible for almost one-quarter of the world's carbon dioxide emissions.

The ratification of international treaties can be a useful means of measuring a country's formal commitment to key environmental issues that are not globally monitorable. Deforestation, risks to endangered species and the state of the world's fisheries are broadly covered by the 1992 Convention on Biological Diversity, ratified by 168 countries (indicator table 19). But such treaties are no guarantee of action. What is needed is detailed understanding of the situation in each country, with plans to ensure that people's enjoyment of the Earth is not at the expense of others—today or in the future.

To that end Agenda 21, adopted in 1992 by governments at the United Nations Conference on Environment and Development (UNCED) in Rio de Janeiro, establishes principles for achieving sustainable development based on the need to manage the economy, the environment and social issues in a coherent, coordinated fashion. By March 2002, 73 countries had signed Agenda 21 and 33 countries had ratified it.[72]

One major topic addressed by Agenda 21 is desertification. Dryland ecosystems—covering more than a third of the world's land area—are extremely vulnerable to overexploitation and inappropriate land use. Poverty, political instability, deforestation, overgrazing and bad irrigation practices can all undermine the land's productivity.

The human cost is enormous. More than 250 million people living off the land are directly affected by desertification. In addition, the livelihoods of 1 billion people in more than a hundred countries are at risk. These include many of the world's poorest, most marginalized and politically powerless people.

The United Nations Convention to Combat Desertification—ratified by 115 countries—aims to combat desertification and mitigate the effects of drought, particularly in Africa. This requires long-term integrated strategies that focus on increasing the productivity of land and on rehabilitating, conserving and sustainably managing land and water resources.[73]

Target 7b: Halve the proportion of people without sustainable safe drinking water

Target 7c: Achieve, by 2020, a significant improvement in the lives of at least 100 million slum dwellers

Environmental conditions particularly affect the health of poor people. Traditional hazards such as lack of safe drinking water, sanitation and waste disposal lead to major outbreaks of diarrhoea, malaria and cholera. Modern hazards such as urban and indoor air pollution can lead to respiratory infections, while exposure to agroindustrial chemicals and waste also causes harm.

The Millennium Declaration separates the goals for safe water and sanitation, using sanitation as an indicator of improving the lives of slum dwellers. In 2000, 1.1 billion people lacked access to safe water, and 2.4 billion did not have access to any form of improved sanitation services.[74]

The health consequences are significant. About 4 billion cases of diarrhoea occur each year, leading to 2.2 million deaths, predominantly among children—representing 15% of child deaths in developing countries. Other concerns include intestinal worms, which infect about 10% of people in the developing world, and trachoma, which has left 6 million people blind and another 500 million at risk.[75]

Human dignity is also at stake. A survey in the Philippines found that among the reasons given for wanting latrines, rural households cited the desire for privacy, cleaner surroundings, lack of flies and lack of embarrassment ahead of health benefits.[76]

There was progress in the 1990s: 800 million more people now have access to improved water than in 1990, and 750 million more to improved sanitation.[77] Most countries with data are on track to halving the proportion of people without access to improved water sources (see feature 1.1). But the challenge remains enormous, with 27% of the world's people living in countries that are far behind the target.

GOAL 8—*DEVELOPING A GLOBAL PARTNERSHIP FOR DEVELOPMENT*

The implications of goal 8 are clear: global action must create an environment in which all people and countries have the chance to realize their potential.

International aid for the Millennium Development Goals

A key responsibility is finance. Aid from official and new sources is essential to kickstart the performance of countries failing to achieve the goals—as well as to keep on track those doing well. But how much aid is needed? Accurately estimating the costs of achieving the millennium goals is almost impossible—but it is important for understanding the size of the responsibility of richer nations. Detailed coun-

More than 250 million people living off the land are directly affected by desertification

FIGURE 1.16

Official development assistance must double to meet the Millennium Development Goals

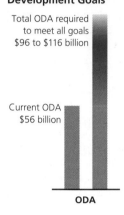

Total ODA required to meet all goals $96 to $116 billion

Current ODA $56 billion

ODA

Source: World Bank and IMF 2001.

FIGURE 1.17

Aid has decreased from most DAC member countries, 1990–2000

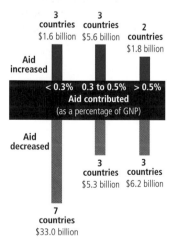

3 countries $1.6 billion

3 countries $5.6 billion

2 countries $1.8 billion

Aid increased

< 0.3%   0.3 to 0.5%   > 0.5%
Aid contributed
(as a percentage of GNP)

Aid decreased

3 countries $5.3 billion

3 countries $6.2 billion

7 countries $33.0 billion

Source: Human Development Report Office calculations based on indicator table 15.

try assessments should be the basis of global estimates. These would allow thorough investigations of how countries are progressing towards the goals, better understanding of the areas for policies to focus on and a much more accurate estimate of the costs of these policies and possible sources of finance. Currently, there are too few country studies of this type to paint a global picture (boxes 1.3 and 1.4).

Calculating an overall estimate of the cost of achieving all the goals using less direct means is tricky because it must take into account the positive side effects of achieving success in different areas. Some consensus is being reached on a figure that takes these synergies into account—giving a rough total of $40–60 billion a year in addition to the current $56 billion (figure 1.16).

While approximate, these numbers give an idea of what is required. When compared with current official development assistance from industrial countries, around $56 billion a year, it is clear that aid needs to double. That would amount to about 0.5% of GNP of the countries on the Development Assistance Committee (DAC) of the Organisation for Economic Co-operation and Development—substantially less than the 0.7% agreed at the UN General Assembly in 1970.

The Millennium Declaration set no specific targets for aid, but if it had most OECD countries would be performing badly. Of the 22 countries on the DAC, 17 give less than 0.5% of their GNP in foreign aid, and 11 give less than 0.3%—and most gave less in 2000 than in 1990 (figure 1.17).[78] Countries with big economies give the most in absolute terms but not as a percentage of GNP. At $13.5 billion, Japan gives the most aid of all countries, though as a share of its GNP it is in the middle of the range. The United States gives the second highest amount but the lowest proportion (indicator table 15).

Aid has fallen substantially in recent years, but announcements in March 2002—at the UN's International Conference on Financing for Development—suggest that this trend may be reversing. The Bush administration proposed increasing aid over the next three fiscal years so that from the third year onwards the United States would give an additional $5 billion a year

over the current level—representing a 50% increase, to about 0.15% of GNP.[79] EU heads of state and government announced a new target of 0.39% of GNP, to be achieved by 2006, representing an additional $7 billion a year.[80] Though short of doubling aid, and the 0.5% of GNP needed, the proposed increases are a step in the right direction.

Some countries, generally smaller, have bucked the recent trend of diminishing aid. During the 1990s Ireland doubled its aid from 0.16% of GNP to 0.30%, and Luxembourg tripled its from 0.21% to 0.71%.

Alternative forms of financing have become more important but fall far short of substituting for increased official aid. Though small relative to official development assistance, resources generated by non-governmental organizations (NGOs) are substantial (table 1.4). The same is true of contributions by philanthropists. The George Soros Foundation Network gives about $500 million a year, most of it in developing and transition countries, with a focus on human rights, culture and economic and social development.[81] And the Bill and Melinda Gates Foundation has given more than $4 billion since the beginning of 2000, with half of it spent on global health initiatives.[82]

Many developing countries still pay enormous sums in debt. Not all debt is bad: borrowing today to provide returns tomorrow is often prudent. But in many countries debt strangles the public purse—and is often for money spent unproductively long ago, by authoritarian regimes.

The most recent move to reduce debt is the Heavily Indebted Poor Countries (HIPC) initiative, launched by the World Bank and the International Monetary Fund (IMF) in 1996 to provide comprehensive debt relief to the world's poorest, most heavily indebted countries.[83] For low human development countries, 28 of them part of the initiative, debt service fell from 5.1% of GDP in 1990 to 3.6% in 2000 (indicator table 16). But there have been calls, led by Jubilee 2000, that the relief is not enough—and that too many countries desperately in need are not included. Recent new commitments by the World Bank and the IMF to deepen and broaden debt relief are positive developments.[84]

TABLE 1.4

Exports and debt service dominate resource flows to and from developing countries

Type of flows	Percentage of developing countries' GDP, 2000
Exports	26.0
Debt service	6.3
Net foreign direct investment	2.5
Aid	0.5
Net grants from NGOs	0.1

Source: Human Development Report Office calculations based on indicator tables 14, 15 and 16.

Better aid

More aid may be needed to achieve the goals, but there is no guarantee it will have the right impact in the right places. For transfers to hit the targets laid out in the Millennium Declaration, there needs to be not only more aid, but better aid.

Who should receive it? Donors are concentrating aid in countries with a demonstrated ability to monitor and use it effectively.[85] While understandable, this approach also bears great risks. It means that the countries falling behind in achieving the goals, and in greatest need of resources, are least likely to receive aid.

Not only does aid need to be directed to the countries that need it most, it must also go to the right sectors. Only $2 billion of the annual aid from DAC countries is directed towards education.[86] To achieve the goals for education, this will have to increase by $9–12 billion, from about 3.5% of aid to well over 10%. Similarly, a larger proportion of aid will need to go to other basic social services to achieve the goals. But that raises tough issues of setting priorities and reaching an understanding of how best to distribute aid among competing areas.

Trade and foreign direct investment

One-way financial transfers will not be enough to build a global partnership, nor should they be. Developing countries need to compete and prosper in the world economy to drive their own development. The financial flows that developing countries receive from exports dwarf

---

BOX 1.3

Achieving the Millennium Development Goals—country by country

Examining the Millennium Development Goals at the global level provides only so much understanding of how much progress is being made, how far there is to go and what needs to be done—to achieve the goals or to move on to further challenges. These questions need to be investigated at the country level, and national Millennium Development Goal reports are being produced to fill this gap. Reports have been published for Bolivia, Cambodia, Cameroon, Chad, Madagascar, Nepal, the United Republic of Tanzania and Viet Nam, and more are on the way. The reports provide a deeper, more detailed story than the global analysis—and sometimes contradict it.

Providing access to safe water in Uganda

Over the past decade Uganda's water services have expanded considerably, with national data showing the proportion of people without access to safe water falling from 82% in 1991 to 46% in 2001—placing the country well within reach of the Millennium Development Goal target. Yet international data indicate that Uganda is far behind achieving the target (appendix table A1.3). To truly understand a country's progress, it is important to reach consensus on definitions, sources and standardization procedures. Uganda has also gone a step further and set a national target of universal access to safe water. This will require further protecting water sources to counter the receding water table—which will require community participation and ownership.

Combating HIV/AIDS in Malawi

Malawi's government recognizes that its HIV/AIDS problem has grown well beyond the realm of the traditional public health sector and that, if not contained, the pandemic will become the greatest danger to national development. Policy is now focused on raising awareness and improving information, aggressively promoting behaviour change and increasing condom use—particularly among high-risk groups. The government has established a network of decentralized public-private partnerships charged with implementing a multisectoral campaign against HIV/AIDS.

Primary education in the Philippines

For better-off countries, achieving the goals is not a sufficient target for development—further challenges remain, specific to each country, and should not be overlooked. The Philippines has already achieved the goal of universal primary enrolment. But to further improve education levels, policy is now focused on raising completion rates and schooling quality. National targets have been set to increase the number of teachers by 70% between now and 2015, the number of classrooms by 60% and the stock of textbooks by 130%.

Source: UNDP 2002e.

---

those from other sources, indicating how integrated many of these countries already are (see table 1.4). And during the 1990s foreign direct investment grew faster than other financial flows to developing countries, from 0.9% of their GDP to 2.5% (indicator table 16). Developing countries—especially the poorest countries—still receive only a tiny fraction of total foreign direct investment, but that inflow is now greater than official development assistance.

In principle, participating in the global market offers the same benefits as a flourishing market economy within a country. But global trade is highly regulated, with the powerful holding sway and the playing field far from level. The average poor person in a developing

BOX 1.4

National human development reports—innovations in national policy

Published every year or two, national human development reports build on the analytical framework of the global *Human Development Report* by examining countries' most pressing development issues and exploring ways to place human development at the forefront of the national political agenda.

National human development reports are unique country-owned products, written by leading national experts and intellectuals and often containing data not published elsewhere. Through a country-led process of consultation, research and report writing, they bring together diverse voices, put difficult issues on the table and help mobilize action for human development policy-making. The reports are also a tool for policy analysis and planning that contribute to progress towards the Millennium Development Goals and provide a unique, valuable resource in analysing global issues.

Six fundamental principles underpin the creation of successful national human development reports and form the UNDP's corporate

policy on them:
• National ownership.
• Independent analysis.
• High-quality analysis.
• Participatory, inclusive preparation.
• Flexible, creative presentation.
• Sustained follow-up.

Since 1992 more than 400 regional and national human development reports have been produced in more than 135 countries.

All national human development reports emphasize key human development concepts. In addition, each national team addresses specific themes tied to the country's most urgent development issues. Reports have addressed human development approaches to governance, poverty, economic growth, gender, peace and security, survival and health, the environment, education and information and communications technology. Although 299 national reports have been on general human development, most have addressed other pressing issues facing the nation at the time of publication—including 263 that have

analysed governance-related topics such as civil society, youth, human rights, the role of the state, decentralization, social cohesion and exclusion, participation, inequity and democracy (see tables). The reports offer concrete policy recommendations on how to tackle these thematic areas through the human development prism.

National human development reports published since 1992

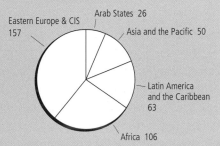

National human development reports by theme

Theme	Africa	Arab States	Asia and the Pacific	Eastern Europe and the CIS	Latin America and the Caribbean	Total
General human development	86	18	32	100	63	299
Governance	41	14	20	145	43	263
Poverty, incomes and economic growth	54	15	35	123	39	266
Gender	12	8	11	27	5	63
Peace and security	7	1	3	28	9	48
Survival and health	11	5	13	34	6	69
Environment	18	4	12	39	8	81
Knowledge	11	10	11	45	8	85

National human development reports with analysis of governance related topics

	Africa	Arab States	Asia and the Pacific	Eastern Europe and the CIS	Latin America and the Caribbean	Total
Governance	19	1	4	30	11	65
Civil society	8	0	1	12	0	21
Youth	0	3	4	7	2	16
Human rights	3	0	1	11	2	17
Role of the state	3	2	3	21	15	44
Decentralization	2	1	2	11	5	21
Social cohesion and exclusion	0	0	3	25	2	30
Participation	4	5	1	18	1	29
Inequity	0	0	0	2	1	3
Democracy	2	2	1	8	4	17

Note: Reports can cover more than one theme.

Source: National Human Development Report Unit calculations based on UNDP 2002d.

country selling into global markets confronts barriers twice as high as the typical worker in industrial countries,[87] where agricultural subsidies alone are about $1 billion a day—more than six times total aid. These barriers and subsidies cost developing countries more in lost export opportunities than the $56 billion in aid they receive each year.[88]

If there were a levelling of the global playing field, many of the gains would come in low-income, low-skill areas such as agriculture, textiles and clothing. So in many cases both the poorest countries and the poorest people would benefit.[89] Eliminating trade barriers and subsidies in industrial countries that inhibit imports from developing countries is therefore an urgent priority, and potentially a route to greatly accelerated development.

The Millennium Declaration's call for a non-discriminatory trading system places a clear responsibility on the world's richer countries, but it is a small step towards changing the system. And while liberalizing trade will bring substantial gains overall, it is not universally a win-win situation—some sectors in some countries will lose out, and they are likely to voice opposition.

But the losers must be seen as more than lobbying groups to overcome. They are individuals, families and communities whose lives change immediately and for the worse because of globalization and foreign competition. People across the globe share this despair, and as trade continues to liberalize, their numbers will grow.

Although the question remains a subject of vigorous debate, a number of recent studies have suggested that increased international trade was a factor in the sharp increase in inequality in industrial countries in the 1980s and 1990s.[91] But holding trade back is most likely to hurt those who are even poorer in developing countries.

Since trade increases overall income, the answer to this moral dilemma—which appears to pit poor workers in industrial countries against even poorer workers in developing countries—is to redistribute some of the overall gain to those who directly lose out. That means providing greater social security and more help in finding alternative employment for people who lose their jobs. Canada and Denmark have successfully used fiscal transfers and social security to counter rising inequality in before-tax market wages (see box 1.2), showing that the inevitable sectoral losses from increased trade can be distributed fairly within each economy.

To ensure that the gains from globalization are more widely distributed, industrial countries need to eliminate trade barriers against developing countries. The 2001 World Trade Organization meeting in Doha produced a framework for lowering trade barriers worldwide, but there is concern that reductions in the most important areas—barriers against textiles and subsidies for agriculture—may stall when the formal rules are developed. Industrial countries must also ensure that domestic workers in sectors hit by global competition do not shoulder the full burden of the adjustments that global innovation and integration can bring.

The new era of global integration offers enormous potential benefits. But they will not be realized unless more of the world's people are included. This has important implications for national and international policies in industrial as well as developing countries. Perhaps the most important is the need to include more people in the decisions that shape their lives in the modern world—and to include more people in the economic and social gains. The challenge of achieving these goals and finally making democratic governance work for human development in its fullest sense is the focus of this Report.

The average poor person in a developing country selling into global markets confronts barriers twice as high as the typical worker in industrial countries

MEASURING HUMAN DEVELOPMENT: THE HUMAN DEVELOPMENT INDICES

Human development index

The human development index (HDI) is a simple summary measure of three dimensions of the human development concept: living a long and healthy life, being educated and having a decent standard of living (see technical note). Thus it combines measures of life expectancy, school enrolment, literacy and income to allow a broader view of a country's development than using income alone—which is too often equated with well-being. Since the creation of the HDI in 1990 three supplementary indices have been developed to highlight particular aspects of human development: the human poverty index (HPI), gender-related development index (GDI) and gender empowerment measure (GEM).

The HDI can highlight the successes of some countries and the slower progress of others. Venezuela started with a higher HDI than Brazil in 1975, but Brazil has made much faster progress. Finland had a lower HDI than Switzerland in 1975 but today is slightly ahead. Rankings by HDI and by GDP per capita can also differ, showing that high levels of human development can be achieved without high incomes—and that high incomes do not guarantee high levels of human development (see indicator table 1). Pakistan and Viet Nam have similar incomes, but Viet Nam has done much more to translate that income into human development. Similarly, Jamaica has achieved a much better HDI than Morocco with about the same income.

Swaziland achieves the same HDI as Botswana with less than two-thirds of the income, and the same is true of the Philippines and Thailand. So with the right policies, countries can advance human development even with low incomes.

Most regions have seen steady progress in HDI over the past 20 years, with East Asia and the Pacific performing particularly well in the 1990s. Arab States have also seen substantial growth, exceeding the average increase for developing countries. Sub-Saharan Africa, by contrast, has been almost stagnant—on par with South Asia in 1985, it has fallen far behind. Two groups of countries have suffered such setbacks: CIS countries going through what has become for many a long, painful transition to market economies, and poor African countries whose development has been hindered or reversed for a variety of reasons—including HIV/AIDS and internal and external conflicts.

Although the HDI is a useful starting point, it omits vital aspects of human development, notably the ability to participate in the decisions that affect one's life. A person can be rich, healthy and well-educated, but without this ability human development is held back.

The omission of dimensions of freedoms from the HDI has been highlighted since the first *Human Development Reports*—and drove the creation of a human freedom index (HFI) in 1991 and a political freedom index (PFI) in 1992. Neither measure survived past its first year, testament to the difficulty of adequately capturing in a single index such complex aspects of human development. But that does not mean that indicators of political and civil freedoms can be ignored entirely in considering the state of a country's human development.

When indicators of democracy and participation are considered alongside the HDI, some different stories emerge. Greece and Singapore rank closely on the HDI, but when democratic participation is also considered Greece does considerably better. The same applies to Belarus and the Russian Federation, with the Russian Federation receiving better democracy scores—measuring its democratic achievements (see indicator table 1 and appendix table A1.1).

There is no simple relationship between the HDI and democracy, although the countries with the highest levels of democracy also have relatively high HDIs. Chapter 2 examines the relationship in detail and finds

Different paths in HDI

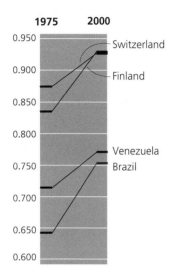

Source: Indicator table 2.

HDI, HPI-1, HPI-2, GDI—same components, different measurements

Index	Longevity	Knowledge	Decent standard of living	Participation or exclusion
HDI	Life expectancy at birth	1. Adult literacy rate 2. Combined enrolment ratio	GDP per capita (PPP US$)	—
HPI-1	Probability at birth of not surviving to age 40	Adult illiteracy rate	Deprivation in economic provisioning, measured by: 1. Percentage of people not using improved water sources 2. Percentage of children under five who are underweight	—
HPI-2	Probability at birth of not surviving to age 60	Percentage of adults lacking functional literacy skills	Percentage of people living below the income poverty line (50% of median disposable household income)	Long-term unemployment rate (12 months or more)
GDI	Female and male life expectancy at birth	1. Female and male adult literacy rates 2. Female and male combined primary, secondary and tertiary enrolment ratios	Estimated female and male earned income, reflecting women's and men's command over resources	—

that there is no automatic link between democracy and development.

Human poverty index

While the HDI measures overall progress in a country in achieving human development, the human poverty index (HPI) reflects the distribution of progress and measures the backlog of deprivations that still exists. The HPI measures deprivation in the same dimensions of basic human development as the HDI.

HPI-1

The HPI-1 measures poverty in developing countries. It focuses on deprivations in three dimensions: longevity, as measured by the probability at birth of not surviving to age 40; knowledge, as measured by the adult illiteracy rate; and overall economic provisioning, public and private, as measured by the percentage of people not using improved water sources and the percentage of children under five who are underweight.

HPI-2

Because human deprivation varies with the social and economic conditions of a community, a separate index, the HPI-2, has been devised to measure human poverty in selected OECD countries, drawing on the greater availability of data. The HPI-2 focuses on deprivation in the same three dimensions as the HPI-1 and one additional one, social exclusion. The indicators are the probability at birth of not surviving to age 60, the adult functional illiteracy rate, the percentage of people living below the income poverty line (with disposable household income less than 50% of the median) and the long-term unemployment rate (12 months or more).

Gender-related development index

The gender-related development index (GDI) measures achievements in the same dimensions and using the same indicators as the HDI, but captures inequalities in achievement between women and men. It is simply the HDI adjusted downward for gender inequality. The greater is the gender disparity in basic human development, the lower is a country's GDI compared with its HDI.

Gender empowerment measure

The gender empowerment measure (GEM) reveals whether women can take active part in economic and political life. It focuses on participation, measuring gender inequality in key areas of economic and political participation and decision-making. It tracks the percentages of women in parliament, among legislators, senior officials and managers and among professional and technical workers—and the gender disparity in earned income, reflecting economic independence. Differing from the GDI, it exposes inequality in opportunities in selected areas.

Same income, different HDI

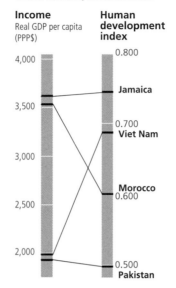

Source: Indicator table 1.

Same HDI, different income

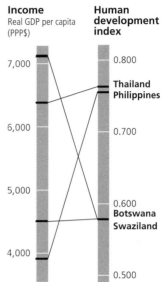

Source: Indicator table 1.

Global disparities in HDI

Human development index

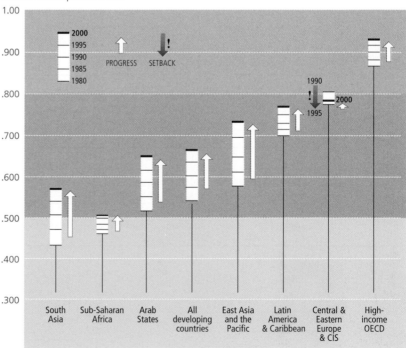

Source: Human Development Report Office calculations based on indicator table 2.

GAUGING GOVERNANCE: MEASURES OF DEMOCRACY AND POLITICAL AND CIVIL RIGHTS

Many indicators aim to show the extent of democracy or political and civil rights in countries. But—unlike for income, health and education—there is no unambiguous, uncontroversial measure. Researchers have two options, both with drawbacks. They can use objective measures, such as voter turnout or the existence of competitive elections, or subjective measures based on expert opinions about a country's degree of democracy (see tables below for summaries of some objective and subjective governance indicators, and appendix tables A1.1 and A1.2 for comprehensive country data).

Objective measures may not reflect all aspects of democracy. In some cases a country may hold elections without their ever resulting in a change in power. In others there are changes in power, but civil liberties such as press freedoms may be curtailed. Truly democratic governance requires widespread, substantive participation—and accountability of people holding power. Objective measures fail to capture such concepts. Subjective measures should, in principle, capture more of what is meant by the concept of democracy. But being subjective, they are open to disagreement and perception biases.

Several subjective indices cover a large portion of the world's countries; this Report mainly relies on three. Though useful for summarizing general trends, they are subjective and open to dispute.

They therefore should not be taken as authoritative but as giving a general indication of progress.

The Polity IV dataset, developed at the University of Maryland's Center for International Development and Conflict Management, compiles annual information on regime and authority characteristics for most of the world's independent states. Autocracy is defined as a political system where citizens' participation is sharply restricted, chief executives are selected from the political elite and there are few institutional constraints on the exercise of power. Democracy is defined as a system with institutionalized procedures for open and competitive political participation, competitively elected chief executives and substantial limits on the powers of the chief executive. Each country's polity score is based on a linear scale from autocracy to democracy. This indicator measures the institutional factors necessary for democracy—whether laws and institutions allow democratic participation—but not the actual extent of political participation. The database includes scores going back to 1975 and is therefore useful for mapping trends over time.

Freedom House surveys political rights and civil liberties around the world. It defines political rights as the freedoms that enable people to participate freely in the political process, and civil liberties as the freedom to develop views, institutions and personal autonomy apart from the

state. In 1997 Freedom House published an assessment of freedom of the press, taking into account freedoms in law and in practice, freedom from political and economic influences on media content and violations of freedoms such as arrests or murders of journalists. Its surveys rely on a wide range of sources—including foreign and domestic news reports, publications by nongovernmental organizations, think tank and academic analyses and professional contacts. Wide country coverage and data for many countries going back to 1980 and earlier makes this the only database able to provide global trends on press freedom.

A World Bank team has constructed six aggregate indices based on numerous indicators from more than a dozen sources. The indicators are combined in different groupings to create aggregate indices for democracy (titled "voice and accountability"), political instability and violence, rule of law, graft (corruption), government effectiveness and regulatory burden. The voice and accountability index, used in chapter 2, combines several indicators of the political process, including the selection of governments, with indicators of civil liberties and political rights, and press freedom and independence. This index does not include long time trends but it is better at distinguishing between developing countries than are other measures.

Objective indicators of governance

Indicator	Source
Date of most recent election	Inter-Parliamentary Union
Voter turnout	Inter-Parliamentary Union
Year women received right to vote	Inter-Parliamentary Union
Seats in parliament held by women	Inter-Parliamentary Union
Trade union membership	Inter-Parliamentary Union
Non-governmental organizations	Yearbook of International Organizations
Ratification of the International Covenant on Civil and Political Rights • Recognizing that, in accordance with the Universal Declaration of Human Rights, the ideal of free human beings enjoying civil and political freedom and freedom from fear and want can be achieved only if conditions allow all people to enjoy their civil, political, economic, social and cultural rights	UN Treaty Section
Ratification of Freedom of Association and Collective Bargaining Convention 87 • The International Labour Organization declares "recognition of the principle of freedom of association" to be a means of improving conditions for workers and establishing peace	UN Treaty Section

Subjective indicators of governance

Indicator	Source	Concept measured	Methodology	Range
Polity score	Polity IV dataset University Of Maryland	• Competitiveness of chief executive recruitment • Openness of chief executive recruitment • Constraints on chief executive • Regulation of participation • Regulation of executive recruitment • Competitiveness of participation	In-house expert opinion	−10 (less democratic) to 10 (most democratic)
Civil liberties	Freedom House	• Freedom of expression and belief • Freedom of association and organizational rights • Rule of law and human rights • Personal autonomy and economic rights	In-house expert opinion	1.0–2.5 free 3.0–5.0 partly free 6.0–7.0 not free
Political rights	Freedom House	• Free and fair elections for offices with real power • Freedom of political organization • Significant opposition • Freedom from domination by powerful groups • Autonomy or political inclusion of minority groups	In-house expert opinion	1.0–2.5 free 3.0–5.0 partly free 6.0–7.0 not free
Press freedom	Freedom House	• Media objectivity • Freedom of expression	In-house expert opinion	0–30 free 31–60 partly free 61–100 not free
Voice and accountability	World Bank Governance Indicators Dataset	• Free and fair elections • Freedom of the press • Civil liberties • Political rights • Military in politics • Change in government • Transparency • Business is kept informed of developments in laws and policies • Business can express its concerns over changes in laws and policies	Aggregate of a variety of sources including Freedom House and International Country Risk Guide	−2.5 to 2.5; higher is better
Political stability and lack of violence	World Bank Governance Indicators Dataset	• Perceptions of the likelihood of destabilization (ethnic tensions, armed conflict, social unrest, terrorist threat, internal conflict, fractionalization of the political spectrum, constitutional changes, military coups)	Aggregate of a variety of sources including the Economist Intelligence Unit, PRS Group and Business Environment Risk Intelligence	−2.5 to 2.5; higher is better
Law and order	International Country Risk Guide	• Legal impartiality • Popular observance of the law	In-house expert opinion	0–6; higher is better
Rule of law	World Bank Governance Indicators Dataset	• Black markets • Enforceability of private and government contracts • Corruption in banking • Crime and theft as obstacles to businesses • Losses from and costs of crime • Unpredictability of the judiciary	Aggregate of a variety of sources including PRS Group and Economist Intelligence Unit	−2.5 to 2.5; higher is better
Government effectiveness	World Bank Governance Indicators Dataset	• Bureaucratic quality • Transactions costs • Quality of public health care • Government stability	Aggregate of a variety of sources including PRS Group, Freedom House, and Business Environment Risk Intelligence	−2.5 to 2.5; higher is better
Corruption Perceptions Index	Transparency International	• Official corruption as perceived by businesspeople, academics and risk analysts	In-country surveys of experts	0–10; higher is better
Graft (corruption)	World Bank Governance Indicators Dataset	• Corruption among public officials • Corruption as an obstacle to business • Frequency of "irregular payments" to officials and judiciary • Perceptions of corruption in civil service. Business interest payment	Aggregate of a variety of sources including Freedom House, Economist Intelligence Unit and Business Environment Risk Intelligence	−2.5 to 2.5; higher is better

Source: Marshall and Jaggers 2000; Freedom House 2000, 2002; Kaufmann, Kraay and Zoido-Lobatón 2002; PRS Group 2001; Transparency International 2001; IPU 1995, 2002; ILO 1997; UIA 2000; UN 2002a.

HDI rank		Polity score [a] 2000 (−10 to 10)	Civil liberties [b] 2000 (7 to 1)	Political rights [b] 2000 (7 to 1)	Press freedom [c] 2000 (100 to 0)	Voice and account-ability [d,e] 2000–01 (−2.50 to 2.50)	Political stability and lack of violence [d] 2000–01 (−2.50 to 2.50)	Law and order [f] 2001 (0 to 6)	Rule of law [d] 2000–01 (−2.50 to 2.50)	Government effec-tiveness [d] 2000–01 (−2.50 to 2.50)	Corruption Perceptions Index [g] 2001 (0 to 10)	Graft (corruption) [d] 2000–01 (−2.50 to 2.50)
	Democracy						Rule of law and government effectiveness				Corruption	
High human development												
1	Norway	10	1	1	5	1.58	1.32	6.0	1.70	1.35	8.6	1.76
2	Sweden	10	1	1	10	1.65	1.38	6.0	1.70	1.51	9.0	2.21
3	Canada	10	1	1	15	1.33	1.24	6.0	1.70	1.71	8.9	2.05
4	Belgium	10	2	1	9	1.24	0.87	5.0	1.34	1.29	6.6	1.05
5	Australia	10	1	1	10	1.70	1.26	6.0	1.69	1.58	8.5	1.75
6	United States	10	1	1	15	1.24	1.18	6.0	1.58	1.58	7.6	1.45
7	Iceland	10	1	1	12	1.53	1.57	6.0	1.77	1.93	9.2	2.16
8	Netherlands	10	1	1	15	1.61	1.48	6.0	1.67	1.84	8.8	2.09
9	Japan	10	2	1	23	1.03	1.20	5.0	1.59	0.93	7.1	1.20
10	Finland	10	1	1	14	1.69	1.61	6.0	1.83	1.67	9.9	2.25
11	Switzerland	10	1	1	8	1.73	1.61	5.0	1.91	1.93	8.4	1.91
12	France	9	2	1	21	1.11	1.04	5.0	1.22	1.24	6.7	1.15
13	United Kingdom	10	2	1	17	1.46	1.10	6.0	1.61	1.77	8.3	1.86
14	Denmark	10	1	1	9	1.60	1.34	6.0	1.71	1.62	9.5	2.09
15	Austria	10	1	1	14	1.34	1.27	6.0	1.86	1.51	7.8	1.56
16	Luxembourg	10	1	1	10	1.41	1.48	6.0	1.86	1.86	8.7	1.78
17	Germany	10	2	1	13	1.42	1.21	5.0	1.57	1.67	7.4	1.38
18	Ireland	10	1	1	18	1.57	1.24	6.0	1.54	1.79	7.5	1.16
19	New Zealand	10	1	1	8	1.59	1.21	6.0	1.71	1.27	9.4	2.09
20	Italy	10	2	1	27	1.10	0.82	6.0	0.72	0.68	5.5	0.63
21	Spain	10	2	1	20	1.15	1.01	4.0	1.12	1.57	7.0	1.45
22	Israel	10	3	1	30	0.98	−0.54	5.0	0.94	0.87	7.6	1.12
23	Hong Kong, China (SAR)	..	3	5	..	−0.33	1.13	4.0	1.37	1.10	7.9	1.16
24	Greece	10	3	1	30	1.12	0.79	3.0	0.62	0.65	4.2	0.73
25	Singapore	−2	5	5	68	0.11	1.44	6.0	1.85	2.16	9.2	2.13
26	Cyprus	10	1	1	18	1.28	0.48	5.0	0.96	0.91	..	1.24
27	Korea, Rep. of	8	2	2	27	0.98	0.50	4.0	0.55	0.44	4.2	0.37
28	Portugal	10	1	1	17	1.42	1.41	5.0	0.94	0.91	6.3	1.21
29	Slovenia	10	2	1	21	1.07	0.87	5.0	0.89	0.70	5.2	1.09
30	Malta	..	1	1	14	1.43	1.05	5.0	0.68	0.73	..	0.13
31	Barbados	..	1	1	16	1.27	..	..	1.16	..	..	..
32	Brunei Darussalam	..	5	7	74	−0.93	0.86	6.0	1.29	0.88	..	−0.17
33	Czech Republic	10	2	1	24	1.04	0.74	5.0	0.64	0.58	3.9	0.31
34	Argentina	8	2	1	33	0.57	0.55	4.0	0.22	0.18	3.5	−0.36
35	Hungary	10	2	1	28	1.19	0.75	4.0	0.76	0.60	5.3	0.65
36	Slovakia	9	2	1	26	0.99	0.62	4.0	0.36	0.23	3.7	0.23
37	Poland	9	2	1	19	1.21	0.69	4.0	0.55	0.27	4.1	0.43
38	Chile	9	2	2	27	0.63	0.87	5.0	1.19	1.13	7.5	1.40
39	Bahrain	−9	6	7	75	−0.96	−0.04	5.0	0.42	0.62	..	0.04
40	Uruguay	10	1	1	30	1.08	1.05	2.5	0.63	0.61	5.1	0.71
41	Bahamas	..	1	1	7	1.15	0.68	4.0	0.85	1.04	..	0.74
42	Estonia	6	2	1	20	0.94	0.73	4.0	0.78	0.86	5.6	0.73
43	Costa Rica	10	2	1	16	1.37	1.08	4.0	0.61	0.74	4.5	0.87
44	Saint Kitts and Nevis	..	2	1	18	..	..	..	..	..	..	..
45	Kuwait	−7	5	4	48	0.08	0.64	5.0	1.10	0.13	..	0.59
46	United Arab Emirates	−8	5	6	76	−0.51	1.09	4.0	1.12	0.60	..	0.13
47	Seychelles	..	3	3	51	..	..	..	..	..	..	..
48	Croatia	7	3	2	50	0.48	0.18	5.0	0.29	0.10	3.9	0.02
49	Lithuania	10	2	1	20	1.00	0.29	4.0	0.29	0.26	4.8	0.20
50	Trinidad and Tobago	10	2	2	28	0.61	0.27	4.0	0.41	0.62	5.3	0.49

		Democracy				Rule of law and government effectiveness					Corruption	
HDI rank		Polity score [a] 2000 (−10 to 10)	Civil liberties [h] 2000 (7 to 1)	Political rights [h] 2000 (7 to 1)	Press freedom [r] 2000 (100 to 0)	Voice and account- ability [d, e] 2000–01 (−2.50 to 2.50)	Political stability and lack of violence [d] 2000–01 (−2.50 to 2.50)	Law and order [f] 2001 (0 to 6)	Rule of law [d] 2000–01 (−2.50 to 2.50)	Government effec- tiveness [d] 2000–01 (−2.50 to 2.50)	Corruption Perceptions Index [g] 2001 (0 to 10)	Graft (corruption) [d] 2000–01 (−2.50 to 2.50)
51	Qatar	−10	6	6	62	−0.54	1.40	6.0	1.00	0.82	..	0.57
52	Antigua and Barbuda	..	2	4	46	..	..	..	..	..	..	..
53	Latvia	8	2	1	24	0.81	0.50	5.0	0.36	0.22	3.4	−0.03
Medium human development												
54	Mexico	8	3	2	46	0.12	0.06	2.0	−0.41	0.28	3.7	−0.28
55	Cuba	−7	7	7	94	−1.49	0.07	4.0	−0.32	−0.22	..	−0.12
56	Belarus	−7	6	6	80	−1.04	0.04	4.0	−0.81	−0.99	..	−0.06
57	Panama	9	2	1	30	0.77	0.57	3.0	−0.12	−0.14	3.7	−0.45
58	Belize	..	1	1	25	1.01	0.32	..	0.74	0.55	..	0.48
59	Malaysia	3	5	5	70	−0.13	0.31	3.0	0.34	0.53	5.0	0.13
60	Russian Federation	7	5	5	60	−0.35	−0.41	3.0	−0.87	−0.57	2.3	−1.01
61	Dominica	..	1	1	16	..	..	..	..	..	..	..
62	Bulgaria	8	3	2	26	0.59	0.37	4.0	0.02	−0.26	3.9	−0.16
63	Romania	8	2	2	44	0.50	−0.08	4.0	−0.02	−0.54	2.8	−0.51
64	Libyan Arab Jamahiriya	−7	7	7	90	−1.35	−0.38	4.0	−0.89	−1.12	..	−0.90
65	Macedonia, TFYR	6	3	4	44	0.03	−1.45	..	−0.33	−0.63	..	−0.51
66	Saint Lucia	..	2	1	13	..	..	..	..	..	..	..
67	Mauritius	10	2	1	17	1.27	1.12	..	1.00	0.76	4.5	0.49
68	Colombia	7	4	4	60	−0.41	−1.36	1.0	−0.77	−0.38	3.8	−0.39
69	Venezuela	7	5	3	34	−0.34	−0.33	2.0	−0.81	−0.81	2.8	−0.59
70	Thailand	9	3	2	29	0.37	0.21	5.0	0.44	0.10	3.2	−0.46
71	Saudi Arabia	−10	7	7	92	−1.07	0.51	5.0	0.19	0.00	..	−0.35
72	Fiji	.. [h]	3	6	44	0.05	0.39	..	−0.52	0.38	..	1.01
73	Brazil	8	3	3	31	0.53	0.47	2.0	−0.26	−0.27	4.0	−0.02
74	Suriname	..	2	1	28	0.63	0.12	3.0	−0.59	0.10	..	0.13
75	Lebanon	.. [i]	5	6	61	−0.32	−0.55	4.0	−0.05	−0.02	..	−0.63
76	Armenia	5	4	4	59	−0.22	−0.84	3.0	−0.35	−1.03	..	−0.80
77	Philippines	8	3	2	30	0.53	−0.21	2.0	−0.49	0.03	2.9	−0.49
78	Oman	−9	5	6	71	−0.50	1.00	5.0	1.06	0.85	..	0.44
79	Kazakhstan	−4	5	6	70	−0.80	0.29	4.0	−0.60	−0.61	2.7	−0.83
80	Ukraine	7	4	4	60	−0.31	−0.59	4.0	−0.63	−0.75	2.1	−0.90
81	Georgia	5	4	4	53	−0.07	−1.00	..	−0.43	−0.72	..	−0.69
82	Peru	.. [h]	3	3	54	0.15	−0.23	3.0	−0.53	−0.35	4.1	−0.04
83	Grenada	..	2	1	20	..	..	..	..	..	..	..
84	Maldives	..	5	6	65	−0.81	..	..	..	..	..	..
85	Turkey	7	5	4	58	−0.55	−0.75	4.0	−0.16	−0.15	3.6	−0.48
86	Jamaica	9	2	2	11	0.78	0.35	2.0	−0.38	−0.30	..	−0.06
87	Turkmenistan	−9	7	7	89	−1.42	0.11	..	−1.02	−1.23	..	−1.12
88	Azerbaijan	−7	5	6	76	−0.70	−0.70	4.0	−0.78	−0.95	2.0	−1.05
89	Sri Lanka	5	4	3	74	−0.23	−1.63	3.0	−0.31	−0.44	..	0.00
90	Paraguay	7	3	4	51	−0.70	−0.87	3.0	−0.83	−1.20	..	−0.97
91	St. Vincent & the Grenadines	..	1	2	16	..	..	..	..	..	..	..
92	Albania	5	5	4	56	0.01	−0.60	2.0	−0.71	−0.89	..	−0.60
93	Ecuador	6	3	3	40	−0.14	−0.80	3.0	−0.76	−0.94	2.3	−0.98
94	Dominican Republic	8	2	2	30	0.42	0.46	2.0	0.01	−0.24	3.1	−0.20
95	Uzbekistan	−9	6	7	84	−1.18	−1.17	..	−0.71	−0.86	2.7	−0.66
96	China	−7	6	7	80	−1.11	0.39	4.0	−0.19	0.14	3.5	−0.30
97	Tunisia	−3	5	6	74	−0.61	0.82	5.0	0.81	1.30	5.3	0.86
98	Iran, Islamic Rep. of	3	6	6	72	−0.36	0.02	4.0	−0.39	−0.21	..	−0.64
99	Jordan	−2	4	4	60	0.10	0.13	4.0	0.66	0.42	4.9	0.09
100	Cape Verde	..	2	1	32	0.92	..	..	0.15	..	..	..

A1.1 Subjective indicators of governance

		Democracy				Rule of law and government effectiveness				Corruption	
HDI rank	Polity score[a] 2000 (-10 to 10)	Civil liberties[b] 2000 (7 to 1)	Political rights[b] 2000 (7 to 1)	Press freedom[c] 2000 (100 to 0)	Voice and account-ability[d,e] 2000-01 (-2.50 to 2.50)	Political stability and lack of violence[d] 2000-01 (-2.50 to 2.50)	Law and order[f] 2001 (0 to 6)	Rule of law[d] 2000-01 (-2.50 to 2.50)	Government effec-tiveness[d] 2000-01 (-2.50 to 2.50)	Corruption Perceptions Index[g] 2001 (0 to 10)	Graft (corruption)[d] 2000-01 (-2.50 to 2.50)
101 Samoa (Western)	..	2	2	21	..	..	..	0.49	..	..	..
102 Kyrgyzstan	-3	5	6	61	-0.57	-0.32	..	-0.72	-0.61	..	-0.85
103 Guyana	6	2	2	22	0.94	-0.70	4.0	0.13	0.02	..	-0.45
104 El Salvador	7	3	2	37	0.21	0.62	3.0	-0.65	-0.25	3.6	-0.33
105 Moldova, Rep. of	7	4	2	59	0.12	-0.29	5.0	-0.42	-1.10	3.1	-0.83
106 Algeria	-3	5	6	74	-1.19	-1.27	2.0	-0.97	-0.81	..	-0.62
107 South Africa	9	2	1	23	1.17	0.07	2.0	-0.05	0.25	4.8	0.35
108 Syrian Arab Republic	-7	7	7	71	-1.40	-0.28	5.0	-0.52	-0.81	..	-0.83
109 Viet Nam	-7	6	7	80	-1.29	0.44	4.0	-0.57	-0.30	2.6	-0.76
110 Indonesia	7	4	3	47	-0.40	-1.56	2.0	-0.87	-0.50	1.9	-1.01
111 Equatorial Guinea	-5	7	7	79	-1.30	..	..	-1.20	..	..	..
112 Tajikistan	-1	6	6	79	-0.69	-1.77	..	-1.25	-1.31	..	-1.08
113 Mongolia	10	3	2	28	0.73	0.72	4.0	0.42	0.39	..	-0.19
114 Bolivia	9	3	1	22	0.27	-0.61	3.0	-0.41	-0.47	2.0	-0.72
115 Egypt	-6	5	6	69	-0.65	0.21	4.0	0.21	0.27	3.6	-0.16
116 Honduras	7	3	3	45	-0.04	0.25	1.0	-1.06	-0.58	2.7	-0.63
117 Gabon	-4	4	5	55	-0.40	-0.44	3.0	-0.44	-0.45	..	-0.58
118 Nicaragua	8	3	3	40	-0.06	0.31	4.0	-0.79	-0.73	2.4	-0.80
119 São Tomé and Principe	..	2	1	25	1.00	..	..	..	..	..	..
120 Guatemala	8	4	3	49	-0.33	-0.77	2.0	-1.00	-0.63	2.9	-0.69
121 Solomon Islands	..	4	4	22	0.16	..	..	..	..	..	..
122 Namibia	6	3	2	34	0.32	-0.52	6.0	1.24	0.60	5.4	1.25
123 Morocco	-6	4	5	53	-0.23	0.16	6.0	0.46	0.10	..	0.44
124 India	9	3	2	42	0.66	-0.05	4.0	0.23	-0.17	2.7	-0.39
125 Swaziland	-9	5	6	77	-0.93	..	..	0.15	..	..	..
126 Botswana	9	2	2	27	0.80	0.71	3.5	0.68	0.83	6.0	0.89
127 Myanmar	-7	7	7	100	-1.93	-1.20	3.0	-1.02	-1.25	..	-1.18
128 Zimbabwe	-5	5	6	69	-0.90	-1.25	0.5	-0.94	-1.03	2.9	-1.08
129 Ghana	2	3	2	55	0.02	-0.11	2.0	-0.08	-0.06	3.4	-0.28
130 Cambodia	2	6	6	61	-0.77	-0.13	..	-0.38	0.34	..	0.34
131 Vanuatu	..	3	1	37	..	..	..	..	..	..	..
132 Lesotho	..[h]	4	4	52	-0.15	..	..	-0.19	..	..	..
133 Papua New Guinea	10	3	2	29	-0.03	-0.48	2.0	-0.28	-0.67	..	-1.21
134 Kenya	-2	5	6	70	-0.68	-0.83	2.0	-1.21	-0.76	2.0	-1.11
135 Cameroon	-4	6	7	71	-0.82	-0.13	2.0	-1.02	-0.40	2.0	-1.11
136 Congo	-6	4	6	71	-1.38	-1.36	2.0	-1.11	-1.58	..	-0.49
137 Comoros	-1	4	6	38	-0.35	..	..	..	..	..	..
Low human development											
138 Pakistan	-6	5	6	57	-1.43	-0.39	3.0	-0.74	-0.48	2.3	-0.79
139 Sudan	-7	7	7	85	-1.53	-2.01	2.0	-1.04	-1.34	..	-1.24
140 Bhutan	-8	6	7	76	-1.27	..	..	..	..	..	..
141 Togo	-2	5	5	72	-1.06	-0.62	3.0	-0.82	-1.32	..	-0.48
142 Nepal	6	4	3	57	-0.06	-0.26	..	-0.65	-1.04	..	-0.31
143 Lao People's Dem. Rep.	-7	6	7	69	-1.05	0.00	..	-0.72	-0.39	..	-0.31
144 Yemen	-2	6	5	69	-0.63	-1.07	2.0	-1.12	-0.77	..	-0.70
145 Bangladesh	6	4	3	60	-0.20	-0.57	2.0	-0.76	-0.54	0.4	-0.64
146 Haiti	-2	5	6	59	-0.80	-0.38	2.0	-1.45	-1.32	..	-0.84
147 Madagascar	7	4	2	32	0.28	-0.34	3.0	-0.68	-0.35	..	-0.93
148 Nigeria	4	4	4	55	-0.44	-1.36	2.0	-1.13	-1.00	1.0	-1.05
149 Djibouti	2	5	4	63	-0.44	..	..	-0.19	..	..	..
150 Uganda	-4	5	6	40	-0.79	-1.31	4.0	-0.65	-0.32	1.9	-0.92

HDI rank		Democracy				Voice and account-ability [d, e] 2000–01 (−2.50 to 2.50)	Rule of law and government effectiveness				Corruption	
		Polity score [a] 2000 (−10 to 10)	Civil liberties [b] 2000 (7 to 1)	Political rights [b] 2000 (7 to 1)	Press freedom [c] 2000 (100 to 0)		Political stability and lack of violence [d] 2000–01 (−2.50 to 2.50)	Law and order [f] 2001 (0 to 6)	Rule of law [d] 2000–01 (−2.50 to 2.50)	Government effec-tiveness [d] 2000–01 (−2.50 to 2.50)	Corruption Perceptions Index [g] 2001 (0 to 10)	Graft (corruption) [d] 2000–01 (−2.50 to 2.50)
151	Tanzania, U. Rep. of	2	4	4	49	−0.07	−0.34	5.0	0.16	−0.43	2.2	−0.92
152	Mauritania	−6	5	6	67	−0.59	−0.87	..	−0.57	−0.66	..	−0.97
153	Zambia	1	4	5	62	−0.17	−0.42	4.0	−0.39	−0.75	2.6	−0.87
154	Senegal	8	4	3	34	0.12	−0.68	3.0	−0.13	0.16	2.9	−0.39
155	Congo, Dem. Rep. of the	.. [j]	6	7	83	−1.70	−2.59 [k]	1.0	−2.09	−1.38	..	−1.24
156	Côte d'Ivoire	4	5	6	77	−1.19	−0.95	2.5	−0.54	−0.81	2.4	−0.71
157	Eritrea	−6	5	7	68	−1.04	−0.38	..	−0.43	..	..	−0.97
158	Benin	6	2	2	30	0.47	−0.72	..	−0.57	0.12	..	..
159	Guinea	−1	5	6	71	−0.98	−0.99	3.0	−0.59	0.41	..	0.13
160	Gambia	−5	5	7	70	−0.73	0.49	5.0	0.00	0.41	..	0.13
161	Angola	−3	6	6	80	−1.26	−1.98	3.0	−1.49	−1.31	..	−1.14
162	Rwanda	−4	6	7	72	−1.42	−1.16	..	−1.17	..	..	0.35
163	Malawi	7	3	3	52	−0.14	0.03	3.5	−0.36	−0.77	3.2	0.10
164	Mali	6	3	2	22	0.32	−0.13	3.0	−0.66	−1.44	..	−0.41
165	Central African Republic	6	4	3	61	−0.59	..	..	..	..	..	..
166	Chad	−2	5	6	72	−0.88	..	..	−0.86	..	..	..
167	Guinea-Bissau	6	5	4	56	−0.87	−1.21	1.0	−1.50	−1.48	..	0.10
168	Ethiopia	1	5	5	64	−0.85	−0.55	5.0	−0.24	−1.01	..	−0.40
169	Burkina Faso	−3	4	4	39	−0.26	−0.54	4.0	−0.79	−0.02	..	−0.93
170	Mozambique	6	4	3	48	−0.22	0.20	3.0	−0.32	−0.49	..	0.10
171	Burundi	−1	6	6	80	−1.35	−1.54	..	−1.07	−1.14	..	−1.40
172	Niger	4	4	4	62	0.11	−0.61	2.0	−1.17	−1.16	..	−1.09
173	Sierra Leone	.. [j]	5	4	75	−1.35	−1.26	3.0	−0.38	−1.60	..	−0.45

Note: The data in this table are subjective measures of governance and thus are open to dispute and should not be taken as authoritative. The measures are from a variety of institutions and are based on different methodologies and scoring systems. Thus higher numbers may reflect better or worse scores, depending on the measure. The range of scores for each measure is shown in the column heading, with the first number representing the worst score. The indicators in no way reflect the official position of UNDP. For more details on definitions and methodologies see appendix A1.1. Data for a range of years were collected in both years shown.

a. Developed by the University of Maryland's Polity IV project, this measure reflects the presence of institutional factors necessary for democracy—whether laws and institutions allow democratic participation—but not the extent of political participation. Scores range from −10 (authoritarian) to 10 (democratic).

b. Freedom House designates countries with an average score for civil liberties and political rights between 1 and 2.5 as free, those with a score between 3 and 5 as partly free and those with a score between 6 and 7 as not free. Countries with an average score of 5.5 could be classified as either partly free or not free, depending on the underlying data used to determine their civil liberties and political rights scores.

c. Freedom House designates countries with a score between 0 and 30 as having a free press, those with a score between 31 and 60 as having a press that is partly free and and those with a score between 61 and 100 as having a press that is not free.

d. This indicator, developed in World Bank research, is based on a statistical compilation of perceptions of the quality of governance. The data are from a survey covering a large number of respondents in industrial and developing countries as well as non-governmental organizations, commercial risk rating agencies and think tanks. The measures in no way reflect the official position of the World Bank, the supplier of these data. Estimates are subject to a large margin of error. For further details on methodology see appendix A1.1 and Kaufmann, Kraay and Zoido-Lobatón (2002). The index ranges from around −2.50 to around 2.50 (higher is better).

e. The voice and accountability index combines several indicators of the political process (including the selection of governments) with indicators of civil liberties, political rights and press freedom and independence.

f. The law and order measure, from the *International Country Risk Guide*, ranges from 0 to 6 (higher is better).

g. Transparency International's Corruption Perceptions Index ranges from 0 to 10 (higher is better).

h. Country is in a transitional period in which new institutions are being planned, legally constituted and put into effect.

i. Country is occupied by a foreign power.

j. Country has had a complete collapse of its central political authority.

k. Score falls outside the approximate range specified in the column heading.

Source: Column 1: Polity IV 2002; *columns 2 and 3:* Freedom House 2001; *column 4:* Freedom House 2000; *columns 5, 6, 8, 9 and 11:* World Bank 2001c; *column 7:* PRS Group 2001; *column 10:* Transparency International 2001.

HDI rank	Participation				Civil society		Ratification of rights instruments [e]	
	Latest election for lower or single house [a]		Year women received right to vote [b]	Seats in parliament held by women (as % of total) [c]	Trade union membership (as % of non-agricultural labour force) [d] 1995	Non-governmental organizations 2000	International Convention on Civil and Political Rights	Freedom of association and collective bargaining convention 87
	Year	Voter turnout (%)						
High human development								
1 Norway	2001	74	1907, 1913	36.4	52	2,571	●	●
2 Sweden	1998	81	1861, 1921	42.7	77 [f]	2,975	●	●
3 Canada	2000	61	1917, 1950	23.6	31 [f]	2,329	●	●
4 Belgium	1999	91	1919, 1948	24.9	38	3,162	●	●
5 Australia	2001	95	1902, 1962	26.5	29	2,171	●	●
6 United States	2000	51	1920, 1960	13.8	13	2,685	●	●
7 Iceland	1999	84	1915	34.9	71 [f]	1,072	●	●
8 Netherlands	1998	73	1919	32.9	22	3,203	●	●
9 Japan	2000	62	1945, 1947	10.0	19	2,122	●	●
10 Finland	1999	65	1906	36.5	60	2,647	●	●
11 Switzerland	1999	43	1971	22.4	20 [f]	2,966	●	●
12 France	1997	71	1944	10.9	6	3,551	●	●
13 United Kingdom	2001	59	1918, 1928	17.1	26	3,388	●	●
14 Denmark	2001	87	1915	38.0	68 [f]	2,806	●	●
15 Austria	1999	80	1918	25.1	37	2,684	●	●
16 Luxembourg	1999	86	1919	16.7	40	1,175	●	●
17 Germany	1998	82	1918	31.0	30	3,505	●	●
18 Ireland	1997	66	1918, 1928	13.7	36 [f]	1,996	●	●
19 New Zealand	1999	90	1893	30.8	23	1,478	●	
20 Italy	2001	81	1945	9.1	31 [f]	3,257	●	●
21 Spain	2000	71	1931	26.6	11 [f]	3,116	●	●
22 Israel	1999	79	1948	13.3	23	1,800	●	●
23 Hong Kong, China (SAR)	..	..	..	..	18 [f]	1,130	–	–
24 Greece	2000	76	1927, 1952	8.7	15	2,137	●	●
25 Singapore	2001	95	1947	11.8	14	1,039		
26 Cyprus	2001	91	1960	10.7	54	783	●	●
27 Korea, Rep. of	2000	57	1948	5.9	9	1,315	●	
28 Portugal	1999	62	1931, 1976	18.7	19	2,289	●	●
29 Slovenia	2000	70	1945	12.2	..	1,197	●	●
30 Malta	1998	95	1947	9.2	58 [f]	636	●	●
31 Barbados	1999	63	1950	20.4	..	346	●	●
32 Brunei Darussalam	– [g]	– [g]	– [g, h]	– [g]	..	184		
33 Czech Republic	1998	74	1920	14.2	36	1,891	●	●
34 Argentina	2001	75	1947	31.3	25	1,666	●	●
35 Hungary	1998	56	1918	8.3	52	2,050	●	●
36 Slovakia	1998	84	1920	14.0	52	1,259	●	●
37 Poland	2001	46	1918	20.7	27	2,084	●	●
38 Chile	2001	87	1931, 1949	10.1	16 [f]	1,262	●	●
39 Bahrain	1973 [i]	..	1973 [i, j]	– [i]	..	288		
40 Uruguay	1999	92	1932	11.5	12 [f]	923	●	●
41 Bahamas	1997	68 [k]	1961, 1964	19.6	..	269		●
42 Estonia	1999	57	1918	17.8	26	897	●	●
43 Costa Rica	2002	70	1949	19.3 [l]	13	772	●	●
44 Saint Kitts and Nevis	2000	64	1951	13.3	..	130		●
45 Kuwait	1999	80	– [h]	0.0	..	499	●	
46 United Arab Emirates	1997	..	– [h]	0.0	..	452		
47 Seychelles	1998	87	1948	23.5	..	195	●	●
48 Croatia	2000	69	1945	16.2	..	1,148	●	●
49 Lithuania	2000	59	1921	10.6	..	848	●	●
50 Trinidad and Tobago	2001	62	1946	20.9 [l]	..	468	●	●

HDI rank		Participation				Civil society		Ratification of rights instruments [e]	
		Latest election for lower or single house [a]		Year women received right to vote [b]	Seats in parliament held by women (as % of total) [c]	Trade union membership (as % of non-agricultural labour force) [d] 1995	Non-governmental organizations 2000	International Convention on Civil and Political Rights	Freedom of association and collective bargaining convention 87
		Year	Voter turnout (%)						
51	Qatar	− [g]	− [g]	− [g, h]	− [g]	..	220		
52	Antigua and Barbuda	1999	64	1951	8.3	..	171		●
53	Latvia	1998	72	1918	17.0	..	774	●	●
Medium human development									
54	Mexico	2000	64	1947	15.9	31 [f]	1,566	●	●
55	Cuba	1998	98	1934	27.6	..	647		●
56	Belarus	2000	61	1919	18.4	96	474	●	●
57	Panama	1999	76	1941, 1946	9.9	14 [f]	591	●	●
58	Belize	1998	90	1954	13.5	..	212	●	●
59	Malaysia	1999	..	1957	14.5	12	1,065		
60	Russian Federation	1999	62	1918	6.4	75 [f]	1,752	●	●
61	Dominica	2000	60	1951	18.8	..	167	●	●
62	Bulgaria	2001	67	1944	26.2	51 [f]	1,277	●	●
63	Romania	2000	65	1929, 1946	9.3	41 [f]	1,390	●	●
64	Libyan Arab Jamahiriya	1997	..	1964	..	..	306	●	●
65	Macedonia, TFYR	1998	73	1946	6.7	..	383	●	●
66	Saint Lucia	2001	53	1924	13.8	..	186		●
67	Mauritius	2000	81	1956	5.7	26	444	●	
68	Colombia	1998	45	1954	12.2	7	1,122	●	●
69	Venezuela	2000	56	1946	9.7	15	1,115	●	●
70	Thailand	2001	70	1932	9.6	3	1,028	●	
71	Saudi Arabia	− [g]	− [g]	− [g, h]	− [g]	..	688		
72	Fiji	2001	78	1963	..	..	343		
73	Brazil	..	..	1934	6.7	32 [f]	1,830	●	
74	Suriname	2000	70	1948	17.6	..	203	●	●
75	Lebanon	2000	51	1952	2.3	..	577	●	
76	Armenia	1999	52	1921	3.1	..	287	●	
77	Philippines	2001	79	1937	17.2	23	1,071	●	●
78	Oman	− [g]	− [g]	− [g, h]	− [g]	..	232		
79	Kazakhstan	1999	63	1924, 1993	11.2	..	274		●
80	Ukraine	1998	70	1919	7.8	..	890	●	●
81	Georgia	1999	68	1918, 1921	7.2	..	397	●	●
82	Peru	2001	63	1955	18.3	8 [f]	996	●	●
83	Grenada	1999	57	1951	17.9	..	150	●	●
84	Maldives	1999	74	1932	6.0	..	82		
85	Turkey	1999	87	1930	4.2	22	1,420	○	●
86	Jamaica	1997	65	1944	16.0	..	499	●	●
87	Turkmenistan	1999	99	1927	26.0	..	101	●	
88	Azerbaijan	2000	68	1921	10.5	75	223	●	●
89	Sri Lanka	2001	80	1931	4.4	..	707	●	●
90	Paraguay	1998	80	1961	8.0	9	563	●	●
91	St. Vincent & the Grenadines	2001	69	1951	22.7	..	153	●	●
92	Albania	2001	60	1920	5.7	..	389	●	●
93	Ecuador	1998	..	1929, 1967	14.6	10	728	●	●
94	Dominican Republic	1998	66	1942	14.5	17	519	●	●
95	Uzbekistan	1999	93	1938	7.2	..	216	●	
96	China	1998	..	1949	21.8	55	1,275	○	
97	Tunisia	1999	92	1957, 1959	11.5	10 [f]	748	●	
98	Iran, Islamic Rep. of	2000	83	1963	3.4	..	1	●	
99	Jordan	1997	47	1974	3.3	..	537	●	
100	Cape Verde	2001	54	1975	11.1	17	120	●	●

HDI rank	Participation: Latest election for lower or single house [a] Year	Voter turnout (%)	Year women received right to vote [b]	Seats in parliament held by women (as % of total) [c]	Civil society: Trade union membership (as % of non-agricultural labour force) [d] 1995	Non-governmental organizations 2000	Ratification of rights instruments [e]: International Convention on Civil and Political Rights	Freedom of association and collective bargaining convention 87
101 Samoa (Western)	2001	86	1990	6.1	..	165		
102 Kyrgyzstan	2000	64	1918	6.7	..	130	●	●
103 Guyana	2001	89	1953	20.0	25 [m]	284	●	●
104 El Salvador	2000	38	1939	9.5	7	460	●	●
105 Moldova, Rep. of	2001	70	1978, 1993	12.9	..	276	●	●
106 Algeria	1997	66	1962	4.0	..	663	●	●
107 South Africa	1999	89	1930, 1994	29.8 [n]	22	1,590	●	●
108 Syrian Arab Republic	1998	82	1949, 1953	10.4	..	361	●	●
109 Viet Nam	1997	100	1946	26.0	..	437	●	
110 Indonesia	1999	93	1945	8.0	3	1,033		●
111 Equatorial Guinea	1999	95	1963	5.0	..	80	●	●
112 Tajikistan	2000	94	1924	12.4	..	90	●	●
113 Mongolia	2000	82	1924	10.5	..	232	●	●
114 Bolivia	1997	70	1938, 1952	10.2	16 [f]	658	●	●
115 Egypt	2000	48 [l]	1956	2.4	30	1,148	●	●
116 Honduras	2001	73 [k]	1955	5.5	4 [f]	438	●	●
117 Gabon	2001	44	1956	11.0	2	287	●	●
118 Nicaragua	2001	75	1955	20.7	23	408	●	●
119 São Tomé and Principe	1998	65	1975	9.1	..	64	○	●
120 Guatemala	1999	54	1946	8.8	4 [f]	587	●	●
121 Solomon Islands	2001	62	1974	0.0	..	..		
122 Namibia	1999	63	1989	20.4	22	356	●	●
123 Morocco	1997	58	1963	0.5	5 [f]	817	●	
124 India	1999	60	1950	8.9	5 [f]	1,718	●	
125 Swaziland	1998	..	1968	6.3	19	264		●
126 Botswana	1999	77	1965	17.0	12	356	●	●
127 Myanmar	1990 [o]	..	1935	– [o]	..	207		●
128 Zimbabwe	2000	49	1957	10.0	14	714	●	●
129 Ghana	2000	62	1954	9.0	26 [f]	625	●	●
130 Cambodia	1998	..	1955	9.3	..	136	●	●
131 Vanuatu	1998	75	1975, 1980	0.0	..	..		
132 Lesotho	1998	74	1965	10.7	..	268	●	●
133 Papua New Guinea	1997	81 [k]	1964	1.8	..	397		●
134 Kenya	1997	65	1919, 1963	3.6	17	822	●	
135 Cameroon	1997	76	1946	5.6	15	567	●	●
136 Congo	1998 [p]	–	1963	12.0	..	303	●	●
137 Comoros	1996 [q]	20 [q]	1956	– [q]	..	84		●
Low human development								
138 Pakistan	1997 [q]	35 [q]	1947	– [q]	6 [f]	873		●
139 Sudan	2000	55 [l]	1964	9.7	..	414	●	
140 Bhutan	– [r]	..	1953	9.3	..	64		
141 Togo	1999	..	1945	4.9	..	364	●	●
142 Nepal	1999	66	1951	7.9 [l]	..	398	●	
143 Lao People's Dem. Rep.	2002	99 [l]	1958	21.2 [l]	..	107	○	
144 Yemen	1997	61	1967 [s]	0.7	..	205	●	●
145 Bangladesh	2001	75	1972	2.0	4	593	●	●
146 Haiti	2000	60	1950	9.1	..	308	●	●
147 Madagascar	1998	..	1959	8.0 [l]	..	369	●	●
148 Nigeria	1999	41	1958	3.3	17 [f]	894	●	●
149 Djibouti	1997	57	1946	0.0	..	130		●
150 Uganda	2001	70	1962	24.7	4	487	●	

A1.2 Objective indicators of governance

		Participation				Civil society		Ratification of rights instruments [e]	
		Latest election for lower or single house [a]		Year women received right to vote [b]	Seats in parliament held by women (as % of total) [c]	Trade union membership (as % of non-agricultural labour force) [d] 1995	Non-governmental organizations 2000	International Convention on Civil and Political Rights	Freedom of association and collective bargaining convention 87
HDI rank		Year	Voter turnout (%)						
151	Tanzania, U. Rep. of	2000	84	1959	22.3	17	554	●	●
152	Mauritania	2001	54	1961	3.0 [l]	3	225		●
153	Zambia	2001	68	1962	12.0	12	489	●	●
154	Senegal	2001	67	1945	19.2	22	565	●	●
155	Congo, Dem. Rep. of the	1993 [q]	..	1967	– [q]	..	480	●	●
156	Côte d'Ivoire	2000	32	1952	8.5	13	556	●	●
157	Eritrea	1994	..	1955	14.7	7	78	●	●
158	Benin	1999	70	1956	6.0	..	371	●	●
159	Guinea	1995	62	1958	8.8	2	249	●	●
160	Gambia	2002	69 [l]	1960	2.0 [l]	..	237	●	●
161	Angola	1992	91	1975	15.5	..	235	●	●
162	Rwanda	1994 [p]	–	1961	25.7	..	241	●	●
163	Malawi	1999	92	1961	9.3	..	318	●	●
164	Mali	1997	22	1956	12.2	14	298	●	●
165	Central African Republic	1998	..	1986	7.3	..	207	●	●
166	Chad	1997	49	1958	2.4	..	190	●	●
167	Guinea-Bissau	1999	80	1977	7.8	..	118	○	●
168	Ethiopia	2000	90	1955	7.8	4	380	●	●
169	Burkina Faso	1997	45	1958	11.0	..	340	●	●
170	Mozambique	1999	80	1975	30.0	..	311	●	●
171	Burundi	1993	91	1961	14.4 [l]	..	226	●	●
172	Niger	1999	..	1948	1.2	..	253	●	●
173	Sierra Leone	1996	50	1961	8.8	..	328	●	●

● Ratification, accession or succession.

○ Signature not yet followed by ratification.

a. Data are as of 8 March 2002.

b. Data refer to the year in which the right to vote on a universal and equal basis was recognized. Where two years are shown, the first refers to the first partial recognition of the right to vote.

c. Data are as of 18 March 2002. Where there are lower and upper houses, data refer to the weighted average of women's shares of seats in both houses.

d. Data are derived from various national sources using different methodologies for data collection. For further information see ILO (1997).

e. The International Convention on Civil and Political Rights was adopted in 1966, and the Freedom of Association and Protection of the Right to Organize Convention in 1948.

f. Data refer to a year other than that specified.

g. The country has never had a parliament.

h. Women's right to vote has not been recognized.

i. The first legislature of Bahrain was dissolved by decree of the emir on 26 August 1975.

j. According to the constitution in force (1973), all citizens are equal before the law; however, women were not able to exercise electoral rights in the only legislative elections held in Bahrain, in 1973. Women were allowed to vote in the referendum of 14–15 February 2001, however, which approved the National Action Charter.

k. Data refer to average turnout in the 1990s. No official data are available. The figures are from International IDEA (1997).

l. Information for the most recent elections was not available in time for publication; data refer to previous elections.

m. Data refer to union membership as a percentage of the economically active population.

n. Calculated on the basis of the 54 permanent seats (that is, excluding the 36 special rotating delegates appointed on an ad hoc basis).

o. The parliament elected in 1990 has never been convened nor authorized to sit, and many of its members were detained or forced into exile.

p. Transitional appointed unicameral parliament created by decree.

q. Parliament has been dissolved or suspended for an indefinite period.

r. The elected members of the Tshogdu (chamber of parliament) come from single-member constituencies. The timing of their election varies depending on the expiration of members' terms.

s. Refers to the former People's Democratic Republic of Yemen.

Source: Columns 1 and 2: IPU 2002a; *column 3:* IPU 1995; *column 4:* Human Development Report Office calculations based on data on parliamentary seats from IPU 2002b; *column 5:* ILO 1997; *column 6:* UIA 2000; *columns 7 and 8:* UN 2002a.

HDI rank	Goal 1 Eradicate extreme poverty and hunger — Target Halve the proportion of people suffering from hunger — Undernourished people (as % of total population)[b]	Goal 2 Achieve universal primary education — Target Ensure that all children can complete primary education		Goal 3 Promote gender equality and empower women — Target Eliminate gender disparity in all levels of education [a]		Goal 4 Reduce child mortality — Target Reduce under-five and infant mortality rates by two-thirds — Under-five mortality rate (per 1,000 live births)	Goal 7 Ensure environmental sustainability — Target Halve the proportion of people without access to improved water sources — Population using improved water sources (%)
		Net primary enrolment ratio (%)	Children reaching grade 5 (%)	Female gross primary enrolment ratio as % of male ratio	Female gross secondary enrolment ratio as % of male ratio		
High human development							
22 Israel	..	..	..	..	On track	On track	..
23 Hong Kong, China (SAR)	..	..	..	Achieved	Achieved	..	..
25 Singapore	..	On track	..	On track	..	On track	On track
26 Cyprus	..	Slipping back	Achieved	Achieved	Achieved	On track	On track
27 Korea, Rep. of	..	On track	On track	Achieved	Achieved	On track	On track
29 Slovenia	..	On track	Achieved	Achieved	Achieved	On track	On track
30 Malta	..	Achieved	Achieved	On track	On track	On track	On track
31 Barbados	..	..	..	..	..	On track	On track
32 Brunei Darussalam	..	On track	..	On track	Achieved	On track	..
33 Czech Republic	..	..	..	On track	Achieved	On track	..
34 Argentina	..	Achieved	..	On track	Achieved	On track	..
35 Hungary	..	Slipping back	..	On track	Achieved	On track	On track
36 Slovakia	..	..	Achieved	Achieved	Achieved	On track	On track
37 Poland	..	On track	..	On track	On track	On track	..
38 Chile	Achieved	On track	Achieved	On track	Achieved	On track	On track
39 Bahrain	..	On track	On track	Achieved	Achieved	On track	..
40 Uruguay	Achieved	On track	On track	On track	Achieved	On track	On track
41 Bahamas	..	..	..	..	..	On track	On track
42 Estonia	On track	On track	..	On track	Achieved	Far behind	..
43 Costa Rica	On track	On track	On track	On track	Achieved	On track	On track
44 Seychelles	..	..	On track	..	..	On track	..
45 Saint Kitts and Nevis	..	..	..	..	..	On track	On track
46 Kuwait	Achieved	On track	Achieved	On track	Achieved	On track	..
47 United Arab Emirates	..	..	..	On track	Achieved	On track	..
48 Croatia	..	On track	Achieved	On track	Achieved	On track	..
49 Lithuania	On track	On track	Achieved	On track	Achieved	Far behind	..
50 Trinidad and Tobago	Far behind	Far behind	On track	On track	Achieved	On track	..
51 Qatar	..	Far behind	..	On track	On track	On track	..
52 Antigua and Barbuda	..	..	..	..	..	On track	On track
53 Latvia	On track	On track	Achieved	On track	Achieved	Far behind	..
Medium human development							
54 Mexico	On track	Achieved	On track	On track	Achieved	On track	On track
55 Cuba	Slipping back	On track	..	On track	Achieved	On track	On track
56 Belarus	..	..	Achieved	On track	Achieved	Far behind	On track
57 Panama	On track	..	..	..	..	On track	..
58 Belize	..	..	..	..	..	Far behind	..
59 Malaysia	..	Achieved	..	Achieved	Achieved	On track	..
60 Russian Federation	On track	On track	..	..	..	Far behind	On track
61 Dominica	..	..	..	..	..	On track	On track
62 Bulgaria	Slipping back	On track	..	On track	On track	Far behind	On track
63 Romania	..	On track	Achieved	On track	On track	On track	..
64 Libyan Arab Jamahiriya	..	..	..	..	..	On track	Far behind
65 Macedonia, TFYR	On track	On track	On track	On track	On track	On track	..
66 Saint Lucia	..	..	..	..	..	On track	On track
67 Mauritius	On track	On track	On track	Achieved	Achieved	On track	On track
68 Colombia	On track	On track	On track	On track	Achieved	Far behind	On track

A1.3 Progress towards Millennium Development Goals	Goal 1 Eradicate extreme poverty and hunger	Goal 2 Achieve universal primary education		Goal 3 Promote gender equality and empower women		Goal 4 Reduce child mortality	Goal 7 Ensure environmental sustainability
	Target Halve the proportion of people suffering from hunger	**Target** Ensure that all children can complete primary education		**Target** Eliminate gender disparity in all levels of education [a]		**Target** Reduce under-five and infant mortality rates by two-thirds	**Target** Halve the proportion of people without access to improved water sources
	Undernourished people (as % of total population) [b]	Net primary enrolment ratio (%)	Children reaching grade 5 (%)	Female gross primary enrolment ratio as % of male ratio	Female gross secondary enrolment ratio as % of male ratio	Under-five mortality rate (per 1,000 live births)	Population using improved water sources (%)
HDI rank							
69 Venezuela	Slipping back	Far behind	On track	Achieved	Achieved	Far behind	..
70 Thailand	On track	..	..	..	..	On track	On track
71 Saudi Arabia	..	Far behind	On track	On track	On track	On track	On track
72 Fiji	..	..	..	..	..	On track	..
73 Brazil	On track	..	..	..	..	On track	On track
74 Suriname	On track	..	..	..	..	On track	On track
75 Lebanon	..	..	..	On track	Achieved	Far behind	On track
76 Armenia	..	..	Achieved	..	..	Far behind	..
77 Philippines	Far behind	Achieved	..	On track	Achieved	On track	Far behind
78 Oman	..	Far behind	On track	On track	On track	On track	Far behind
79 Kazakhstan	..	..	Achieved	Achieved	Achieved	Slipping back	On track
80 Ukraine	On track	..	..	..	..	Far behind	..
81 Georgia	..	..	Achieved	On track	On track	Far behind	..
82 Peru	Achieved	On track	..	On track	On track	On track	Lagging
83 Grenada	..	..	..	..	..	On track	On track
84 Maldives	..	..	..	On track	Achieved	On track	On track
85 Turkey	..	On track	..	On track	Far behind	On track	Lagging
86 Jamaica	On track	..	..	On track	..	Far behind	..
87 Turkmenistan	On track	..	..	..	..	Far behind	..
88 Azerbaijan	..	..	Achieved	On track	On track	Far behind	..
89 Sri Lanka	On track	..	..	On track	Achieved	On track	Achieved
90 Paraguay	On track	On track	On track	On track	Achieved	Far behind	On track
91 St. Vincent & the Grenadines	..	..	..	..	..	Far behind	On track
92 Albania	On track	Achieved	..	Achieved	Achieved	On track	..
93 Ecuador	On track	On track	..	..	..	On track	..
94 Dominican Republic	Far behind	..	..	Achieved	Achieved	On track	Far behind
95 Uzbekistan	On track	..	..	..	..	Slipping back	..
96 China	On track	Achieved	On track	Achieved	On track	Far behind	Far behind
97 Tunisia	..	Achieved	On track	On track	On track	On track	..
98 Iran, Islamic Rep. of	On track	Slipping back	..	On track	On track	On track	Achieved
99 Jordan	On track	..	..	..	..	Lagging	On track
100 Cape Verde	..	..	..	On track	Achieved	On track	..
101 Samoa (Western)	..	On track	..	On track	Achieved	On track	On track
102 Kyrgyzstan	On track	On track	..	On track	Achieved	On track	..
103 Guyana	On track	Slipping back	On track	On track	Achieved	Far behind	On track
104 El Salvador	Far behind	On track	..	On track	Achieved	On track	..
105 Moldova, Rep. of	On track	..	Achieved	On track	Achieved	Far behind	On track
106 Algeria	On track	On track	On track	On track	On track	Slipping back	On track
107 South Africa	..	On track	..	On track	Achieved	Slipping back	..
108 Syrian Arab Republic	..	On track	On track	On track	On track	On track	..
109 Viet Nam	On track	..	..	On track	On track	Lagging	Lagging
110 Indonesia	On track	On track	On track	On track	On track	On track	On track
111 Equatorial Guinea	..	..	..	..	..	On track	..
112 Tajikistan	..	..	..	On track	..	Far behind	..
113 Mongolia	Slipping back	..	Achieved	Achieved	Achieved	On track	..

A1.3 Progress towards Millennium Development Goals

HDI rank	Goal 1 — Target Halve the proportion of people suffering from hunger — Undernourished people (as % of total population)[b]	Goal 2 — Target Ensure that all children can complete primary education — Net primary enrolment ratio (%)	Children reaching grade 5 (%)	Goal 3 — Target Eliminate gender disparity in all levels of education[a] — Female gross primary enrolment ratio as % of male ratio	Female gross secondary enrolment ratio as % of male ratio	Goal 4 — Target Reduce under-five and infant mortality rates by two-thirds — Under-five mortality rate (per 1,000 live births)	Goal 7 — Target Halve the proportion of people without access to improved water sources — Population using improved water sources (%)
114 Bolivia	Lagging	..	..	..	..	On track	On track
115 Egypt	On track	On track	..	On track	On track	On track	On track
116 Honduras	Far behind	..	..	..	..	On track	On track
117 Gabon	On track	..	..	..	..	Far behind	..
118 Nicaragua	Far behind	On track	Far behind	Achieved	Achieved	On track	On track
119 São Tomé and Principe	..	..	..	..	..	Far behind	..
120 Guatemala	Slipping back	..	..	Far behind	On track	On track	Achieved
121 Solomon Islands	..	..	..	..	..	On track	..
122 Namibia	Far behind	On track	..	Achieved	Achieved	Far behind	Lagging
123 Morocco	On track	On track	Far behind	On track	On track	On track	On track
124 India	Far behind	..	..	On track	Far behind	Lagging	On track
125 Swaziland	Far behind	On track	Far behind	On track	On track	Slipping back	..
126 Botswana	Slipping back	Slipping back	On track	Achieved	Achieved	Slipping back	..
127 Myanmar	On track	..	..	..	..	Far behind	Far behind
128 Zimbabwe	Far behind	..	..	On track	Far behind	Slipping back	On track
129 Ghana	Achieved	..	..	..	..	Lagging	On track
130 Cambodia	On track	On track	..	..	Lagging	Slipping back	..
131 Vanuatu	..	..	..	..	..	On track	..
132 Lesotho	Lagging	Slipping back	..	Achieved	Achieved	Far behind	On track
133 Papua New Guinea	Far behind	..	..	Far behind	Far behind	Far behind	Far behind
134 Kenya	Far behind	..	..	Achieved	On track	Slipping back	Lagging
135 Cameroon	On track	..	..	..	..	Slipping back	On track
136 Congo	Far behind	..	..	On track	Far behind	Far behind	..
137 Comoros	..	..	..	..	On track	On track	Achieved
Low human development							
138 Pakistan	On track	..	..	..	..	Far behind	On track
139 Sudan	On track	..	..	On track	On track	Far behind	On track
140 Bhutan	..	..	..	..	..	On track	..
141 Togo	On track	On track	..	Far behind	Far behind	Far behind	Far behind
142 Nepal	Far behind	..	..	On track	On track	On track	On track
143 Lao People's Dem. Rep.	Far behind	On track	..	On track	Far behind	On track	On track
144 Yemen	Far behind	..	..	..	..	Far behind	Far behind
145 Bangladesh	Far behind	..	..	..	..	On track	Achieved
146 Haiti	Lagging	On track	..	..	..	Far behind	Far behind
147 Madagascar	Slipping back	Slipping back	..	On track	Achieved	Far behind	Far behind
148 Nigeria	Achieved	..	..	..	..	Far behind	Lagging
149 Djibouti	..	Far behind	Slipping back	Far behind	On track	Far behind	On track
150 Uganda	Far behind	..	..	On track	Far behind	Lagging	Far behind
151 Tanzania, U. Rep. of	Slipping back	Far behind	Far behind	On track	On track	Far behind	Far behind
152 Mauritania	On track	..	Slipping back	On track	Far behind	Far behind	Far behind
153 Zambia	Far behind	Slipping back	..	On track	..	Slipping back	On track
154 Senegal	Far behind	On track	On track	On track	Far behind	Far behind	On track
155 Congo, Dem. Rep. of the	Slipping back	..	..	..	..	Far behind	..
156 Côte d'Ivoire	On track	Far behind	Far behind	Far behind	Far behind	Slipping back	On track
157 Eritrea	..	Far behind	..	..	..	On track	..

HDI rank	Goal 1 Eradicate extreme poverty and hunger **Target** Halve the proportion of people suffering from hunger Undernourished people (as % of total population)[b]	Goal 2 Achieve universal primary education **Target** Ensure that all children can complete primary education Net primary enrolment ratio (%)	Children reaching grade 5 (%)	Goal 3 Promote gender equality and empower women **Target** Eliminate gender disparity in all levels of education[a] Female gross primary enrolment ratio as % of male ratio	Female gross secondary enrolment ratio as % of male ratio	Goal 4 Reduce child mortality **Target** Reduce under-five and infant mortality rates by two-thirds Under-five mortality rate (per 1,000 live births)	Goal 7 Ensure environmental sustainability **Target** Halve the proportion of people without access to improved water sources Population using improved water sources (%)
158 Benin	On track	On track	..	Far behind	Far behind	Far behind	..
159 Guinea	On track	Far behind	..	On track	Far behind	On track	Far behind
160 Gambia	On track	..	..	On track	On track	Far behind	..
161 Angola	On track	..	..	..	..	Slipping back	..
162 Rwanda	Slipping back	..	..	..	..	Slipping back	..
163 Malawi	On track	..	..	On track	On track	Lagging	Lagging
164 Mali	Far behind	Far behind	On track	On track	Slipping back	Far behind	On track
165 Central African Republic	Far behind	..	..	..	..	Far behind	Far behind
166 Chad	On track	Far behind	Far behind	Far behind	Far behind	Far behind	..
167 Guinea-Bissau	..	..	..	..	..	Far behind	..
168 Ethiopia	..	Far behind	..	Slipping back	Slipping back	Far behind	Far behind
169 Burkina Faso	On track	Far behind	..	Far behind	..	Far behind	..
170 Mozambique	On track	Slipping back	..	Far behind	Far behind	Far behind	..
171 Burundi	Slipping back	..	..	Far behind	..	Far behind	..
172 Niger	Far behind	Far behind	On track	Far behind	On track	Far behind	Far behind
173 Sierra Leone	Lagging	..	..	..	..	Far behind	..
Others							
Afghanistan	Far behind	..	..	Far behind	Slipping back	Far behind	..
Andorra	..	..	..	..	..	On track	On track
Bosnia and Herzegovina	On track	..	..	..	..	On track	..
Iraq	Slipping back	..	..	Far behind	Far behind	Slipping back	..
Kiribati	..	..	On track	..	..	Lagging	..
Korea, Dem. Rep. of	Slipping back	..	..	..	..	Far behind	On track
Liberia	Slipping back	..	..	..	..	Far behind	..
Liechtenstein	..	..	..	..	..	On track	..
Marshall Islands	..	..	..	..	..	On track	..
Micronesia, Fed. Sts.	..	..	..	..	..	On track	..
Monaco	..	..	..	..	..	On track	On track
Nauru	..	..	..	..	..	..	..
Palau	..	..	..	..	..	Far behind	..
San Marino	..	..	Achieved	..	..	On track	..
Somalia	Slipping back	..	..	..	..	Far behind	..
Tonga	..	..	..	..	..	On track	On track
Tuvalu	..	..	..	..	..	Far behind	On track
Yugoslavia	On track	..	Achieved	Achieved	Achieved	On track	..
Number of countries in category (% of world population)[c]							
Achieved or on track	57 (49.2)	51 (40.6)	44 (32.2)	90 (63.3)	81 (44.4)	85 (24.4)	68 (43.4)
Lagging, far behind or slipping back	43 (28.0)	24 (5.7)	8 (1.6)	14 (3.4)	20 (22.0)	81 (61.2)	25 (32.1)
No data	68 (8.5)	93 (39.4)	116 (51.9)	64 (19.0)	67 (19.4)	2 (0.1)	75 (10.3)

Note: The table shows the results of analysis assessing progress towards goals for 2015 based on linear interpolation of trends in the 1990s. Each of the Millennium Development Goals is accompanied by multiple targets. The selection of goals and targets in the table is based principally on data availability. The trend assessment uses two data points at least five years apart. For further details see technical note 2. The table includes all UN member countries except high-income OECD countries; it also includes Hong Kong, China (SAR).

a. The goals for gender equality in primary and secondary education are preferably to be achieved by 2005, and by the latest by 2015. Progress towards the goals is assessed here based on a 2015 target.

b. A complementary indicator for monitoring hunger is the prevalence of underweight children, but very limited trend data are available for that indicator.

c. Population shares do not sum to 100% because the analysis excludes high-income OECD countries.

Source: Column 1: FAO 2001; *column 2:* UNESCO 2001; *column 3:* UNESCO 1999b; *columns 4 and 5:* UNESCO 1999a; *column 6:* UNICEF 2002; *column 7:* WHO, UNICEF and WSSCC 2000.

CHAPTER 2

Democratic governance for human development

Good governance is perhaps the single most important factor in eradicating poverty and promoting development.
—UN Secretary-General Kofi Annan[1]

Around the world, more people are recognizing that governance matters for development—that institutions, rules and political processes play a big role in whether economies grow, whether children go to school, whether human development moves forward or back. So, promoting human development is not just a social, economic and technological challenge: it is also an institutional and political challenge.

Accompanying this new consensus is a growing conviction that many persistent development problems reflect failures of governance. Studies in a range of countries and regions hold weak governance responsible for persistent poverty and lagging development. The governance crisis is evident in widespread corruption, inefficient public services and a host of other failures. These studies have also shown what poor governance means for ordinary citizens—schools without teachers, courts without justice, local bureaucrats demanding bribes at every turn.[2]

What does it mean to promote good governance? There is no single answer. But much of the recent debate has focused on what makes institutions and rules more effective, including transparency, participation, responsiveness, accountability and the rule of law. All are important for human development—especially since ineffective institutions usually cause the most harm to poor and vulnerable people.

But just as human development is about much more than growth in national incomes, governance for human development is about much more than effective institutions and rules (box 2.1). For three reasons, it must also be concerned with whether institutions and rules are fair—and whether all people have a say in how they operate:

- Participating in the rules and institutions that shape one's community is a basic human right and part of human development.
- More inclusive governance can be more effective. When local people are consulted about the location of a new health clinic, for example, there is a better chance it will be built in the right place.
- More participatory governance also can be more equitable. Much is known about the economic and social policies that help eradicate poverty and promote more inclusive growth. But few countries pursue such policies vigorously, often because the potential beneficiaries lack political power and their interests are not fully represented in policy decisions.

Governance for human development is partly about having efficient institutions and rules that promote development by making markets work and ensuring that public services

---

BOX 2.1

Good governance—for what?

From the human development perspective, good governance is democratic governance. Democratic governance means that:
- People's human rights and fundamental freedoms are respected, allowing them to live with dignity.
- People have a say in decisions that affect their lives.
- People can hold decision-makers accountable.
- Inclusive and fair rules, institutions and practices govern social interactions.
- Women are equal partners with men in private and public spheres of life and decision-making.
- People are free from discrimination based on race, ethnicity, class, gender or any other attribute.
- The needs of future generations are reflected in current policies.
- Economic and social policies are responsive to people's needs and aspirations.
- Economic and social policies aim at eradicating poverty and expanding the choices that all people have in their lives.

Source: Human Development Report Office.

Political freedom and
participation are part of
human development,
both as development
goals in their own right
and as means for
advancing human
development

live up to their name. But it is also about protecting human rights, promoting wider participation in the institutions and rules that affect people's lives and achieving more equitable economic and social outcomes. Thus governance for human development is concerned not just with efficient, equitable outcomes but also with fair processes. Governance for human development must be democratic in substance and in form—by the people and for the people (see the special contribution by Nobel Prize–winner Aung San Suu Kyi).

THE ROLE OF POLITICAL FREEDOM AND PARTICIPATION IN HUMAN DEVELOPMENT

Political freedom and participation are part of human development, both as development goals in their own right and as means for advancing human development.

POLITICAL FREEDOM AND PARTICIPATION ARE ESSENTIAL GOALS OF HUMAN DEVELOPMENT

Political freedom and the ability to participate in the life of one's community are capabilities that are as important for human development as being able to read and write and being in good health. People without political freedom—such as being able to join associations and to form and express opinions—have far fewer choices in life. And being able to participate in the life of one's community—commanding the respect of others and having a say in communal decisions—is fundamental to human existence.

That political freedom and participation are crucial to human development is not always well understood. Indeed, there is a widespread misperception that human development is only about economic and social outcomes such as reducing

---

SPECIAL CONTRIBUTION

Human development and human dignity

Respect for human dignity implies commitment to creating conditions under which individuals can develop a sense of self-worth and security. True dignity comes with an assurance of one's ability to rise to the challenges of the human situation. Such assurance is unlikely to be fostered in people who have to live with the threat of violence and injustice, with bad governance and instability or with poverty and disease. Eradicating these threats must be the aim of those who recognize the sanctity of human dignity and of those who strive to promote human development. Development as growth, advancement and the realization of potential depends on available resources—and no resource is more potent than people empowered by confidence in their value as human beings.

The concept of human development is no longer new. But some analysts still consider its aspirations bold and daring—some might say overwhelming and foolhardy. The problems are innumerable, forever changing and forever the same—a complex, fluid spectrum of social, economic and political issues that is impossible to grasp entirely. That it defies delimitation is the core of the challenge posed by the task of human development. It demands constant effort and capacity for rethinking, flexibility and fast reactions. The process of human development calls for human resolve and ingenuity. Hopeless, helpless people stripped of their dignity are hardly capable of such activities. And so we return to the link between human development and human dignity.

Human development encompasses all aspects of human existence. It is generally accepted that its scope includes political and social rights as well as economic ones—but the different rights are not always given the same weight. For example, some people still claim that humanitarian aid and economic assistance cannot wait for political and social progress. This insidious idea creates dissonance between complementary requirements. If the people that aid targets are not empowered, it cannot achieve more than a very limited, very short-term alleviation of problems rooted in long-standing social and political ills. After all, human development is not intended to produce impotent objects of charity.

At this time when the world is preoccupied with the menace of terrorism, it is worth considering that people who feel deprived of control over their lives—necessary for a dignified life—are liable to search for fulfilment along the path of violence. Merely providing them with a certain material sufficiency is not enough to win them over to peace and unity. Their potential for human development has to be realized and their human dignity respected so that they can gain the skills and confidence to build a world strong and prosperous in harmonious diversity.

Aung San Suu Kyi

Aung San Suu Kyi
Winner of the Nobel Peace Prize, 1991

---

income poverty and improving health and education. Though these are important for human development, its aim is much broader—to promote the freedom, well-being and dignity of people everywhere. Economic growth is a means to these broader ends. The success of the human development index (HDI)—itself only a partial measure of the economic and social dimensions of human development—has contributed to this misperception because it leaves out so many aspects of human development (box 2.2).

THEY ARE ALSO IMPORTANT FOR MAKING HUMAN DEVELOPMENT HAPPEN

As the first *Human Development Report* said in 1990, "People are the real wealth of a nation."[3] People are not only the beneficiaries of economic and social progress, they are also its agents, both as individuals and by making common causes with others. That is one reason strategies for promoting human development have traditionally emphasized investing in education and health and promoting equitable economic growth. These are two pillars of development because they mobilize individual agency by strengthening productive capacities.

But this Report highlights a third pillar of a 21st century human development strategy: promoting participation through democratic governance. Participation promotes collective agency as well as individual agency—important because collective action through social and political movements has often been a motor of progress for issues central to human development: protecting the environment, promoting gender equality, fostering human rights. In addition, participation and other human development gains can be mutually reinforcing. Political freedom empowers people to claim their economic and social rights, while education increases their ability to demand economic and social policies that respond to their priorities (figure 2.1).[4]

BROADENING THE SCOPE OF HUMAN DEVELOPMENT: WHY PARTICIPATION, AND WHY NOW?

Putting participation at the heart of human development strategies raises a question about the scope of human development: which capabilities are part of human development? Human development is certainly broader than education and health. Many other capabilities are also important in expanding human choices. But public policy is about setting priorities. And the human development approach requires deciding which capabilities are most important for public policy.[5]

There can be no single answer: societies and people value capabilities differently depending on their situation. *Human Development Reports* have applied two criteria in identifying an important capability. First, it

---

BOX 2.2

Human development—the concept is larger than the index

Ironically, the human development approach to development has fallen victim to the success of its human development index (HDI). The HDI has reinforced the narrow, oversimplified interpretation of the human development concept as being only about expanding education, health and decent living standards. This has obscured the broader, more complex concept of human development as the expansion of capabilities that widen people's choices to lead lives that they value.

Despite careful efforts to explain that the concept is broader than the measure,

human development continues to be identified with the HDI—while political freedoms, participating in the life of one's community and physical security are often overlooked. But such capabilities are as universal and fundamental as being able to read or to enjoy good health. They are valued by all people—and without them, other choices are foreclosed. They are not included in the HDI because they are difficult to measure appropriately, not because they are any less important to human development.

Source: Fukuda-Parr 2002.

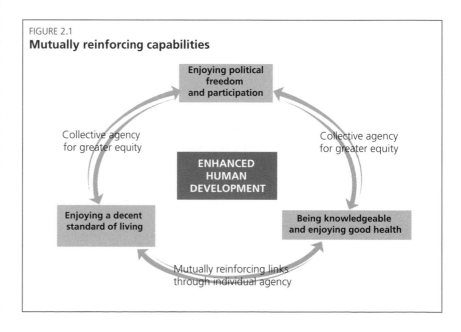

FIGURE 2.1
Mutually reinforcing capabilities

must be universally valued by people the world over. Second, it must be fundamental in the sense that the lack of it would close off many options in life. Other than that, the basic concept of human development has remained open-ended. Different capabilities may be considered important over time and in different parts of the world.

In the decade since the first *Human Development Report,* political freedom and participation have become much more prominent in public policy debates. The political shifts of the 1990s built greater consensus on the value of political freedom and human rights—consensus reflected in recent intergovernmental declarations such as the Millennium Declaration of the UN General Assembly and the consensus document of the March 2002 UN Conference on Financing for Development.

In an era of rapid globalization, markets and political liberalization—not government planning—are often the main drivers of economic and social change. But a decade ago, with the legacy of the cold war still alive, the world was divided on the importance of political freedom and participation. And 1990 was the tail end of the planning era of development, with the state as the primary actor. As a result human development strategies emphasized the need to reallocate public investments in favour of human development priorities, especially the two pillars of expanding primary health care and education and promoting pro-poor growth.

Changes in the world have shifted human development priorities and made political freedom, participation and collective action much more important as public policy issues. Alongside the economic entrepreneurship that drives markets, social entrepreneurship now drives policy debates on issues that matter for people. In addition, consensus is emerging on the importance of collective action by people and civil society groups in shaping the course of human development.

Other capabilities might be considered important today—such as personal security or the capability to be free from physical danger or violence. Chapter 4 highlights the importance of democratic governance of security forces.

Democratic principles follow naturally and inescapably from this vision of human development. The word *democracy,* from the Greek, means "rule by the people". It sums up well the human development approach to governance because it expresses the idea that people come first: governance must conform to the needs of people, not vice versa. Whether there can be such a thing as "will of the people" in a world with disparate and competing interests, the basic democratic principle—of the equal concern for all people in the formation of governance structures—captures a key part of what human development should be about.

The democratic system of voting in elections adds another crucial element of governance from a human development standpoint, because elections are the paradigm of enforceable accountability. When a government fails to live up to the needs and desires of the people, the people can throw it out of office. No form of accountability is more direct. There is also no more egalitarian form of participation. The principle of "one person, one vote" gives every individual an equal say in the choice of government—in theory if not in practice. Other forms of participation can also be important for ensuring the accountability of state and non-state actors when, for one reason or another, the ballot box fails to do the job. But there is always the risk that particular groups and interests will wield undue influence, as those with more resources, or simply more determination, impose their views.

It would be a mistake to equate democracy with regular elections and to fall into the fallacy of "electoralism".[6] Some analysts consider the mere fact of elections a sufficient condition for the existence of democracy, assuming that once fair and free elections are regularly held, all other democratic institutions and practice will naturally follow.

But democracy also requires functioning institutions. It requires a legislature that represents the people, not one controlled by the president, prime minister, bureaucrats or the military. It requires an independent judiciary that enforces the rule of law with equal concern for all people. It

Alongside the economic entrepreneurship that drives markets, social entrepreneurship now drives policy debates on issues that matter for people

requires well-functioning political parties and electoral systems. It requires security forces that are professional, politically neutral and serve the needs of people. It requires an accessible media that is free, independent and unbiased, not one controlled by the state or by corporate interests. And it requires a vibrant civil society, one that can play a watchdog role on government and interest groups—and provide alternative forms of political participation. These institutions, underpinned by democratic values and respect for human rights, provide checks and balances against the risks of tyranny—and of populism, because in democracies populist politicians can mobilize support by using propaganda and appeals to racism and other forms of intolerance.

In democratic societies people participate in the public sphere in many ways—debating issues with friends and neighbours, writing to newspapers on the rights and wrongs of government policies, marching in protests, becoming members of political parties or trade unions—giving them a say in the decisions that affect their lives. Participation involves engaging in deliberative processes that can bring people's concerns to the fore. Open space for free political debate and the diverse ways in which people can express their views are the essence of democratic life and are what make decision-making work in democracies. In representative systems of government, decision-making is delegated to officials. But informed decisions require input from the people affected by them and cannot rely solely on "expert knowledge".

Democracies take different shapes and forms—because political systems vary, they may be "differently democratic" on many fronts.[7] For the world's parliamentarians the essence of democracy lies in its basic principles (box 2.3). It is the only political regime compatible with human development in its deepest sense, because in democracy political power is authorized and controlled by the people over whom it is exercised. The most benign dictatorship imaginable would not be compatible with human development because human development has to be fully owned. It cannot be granted from above. As *Human Development Report 2000* explained, democracy is also the only political regime that respects open contests for power and

is consistent with the respect and promotion of all human rights—civil, cultural, economic, political and social.

IS THERE A TRADE-OFF BETWEEN DEMOCRACY AND DEVELOPMENT?

In many countries questions linger about compatibilities and trade-offs between democracy and development. Military takeovers are most often justified on the grounds that democratically elected governments are incompetent in man-

---

BOX 2.3

Key principles of democracy—the Inter-Parliamentary Union's Universal Declaration on Democracy

In 1995 the Inter-Parliamentary Union assembled experts from various regions and disciplines to develop an international standard on democracy. Building on this work, the Universal Declaration on Democracy was adopted in 1997.

The declaration starts with basic principles. Democracy is a universally recognized ideal, based on values common to people everywhere regardless of cultural, political, social or economic differences. As an ideal, democracy aims to protect and promote the dignity and fundamental rights of the individual, instil social justice and foster economic and social development. Democracy is a political system that enables people to freely choose an effective, honest, transparent and accountable government.

Democracy is based on two core principles: participation and accountability. Everyone has the right to participate in the management of public affairs. Likewise, everyone has the right to access information on government activities, to petition government and to seek redress through impartial administrative and judicial mechanisms.

Genuine democracy presupposes a genuine partnership between men and women in conducting the affairs of society. Democracy is also inseparable from human rights and founded on the primacy of the law, for which judicial institutions and independent, impartial, effective oversight mechanisms are the guarantors.

The declaration sets out the prerequisites for democratic government, empha-

sizing the need for properly structured, well-functioning institutions. These institutions must mediate tensions and preserve the equilibrium between society's competing claims.

A parliament representing all parts of society is essential. It must be endowed with institutional powers and practical means to express the will of the people by legislating and overseeing government action. A key feature of the exercise of democracy is holding free, fair, regular elections based on universal, equal, secret suffrage.

An active civil society is also essential. The capacity and willingness of citizens to influence the governance of their societies should not be taken for granted, and is necessary to develop conditions conducive to the genuine exercise of participatory rights.

Society must be committed to meeting the basic needs of the most disadvantaged groups to ensure their participation in the workings of the democracy. Indeed, the institutions and processes essential to any democracy must include the participation of all members of society. They must defend diversity, pluralism and the right to be different within a tolerant society.

Democracy must also be recognized as an international principle, applicable to international organizations and to states in their international relations.

Democracy is always a work in progress, a state or condition constantly perfectible. Sustaining democracy means nurturing and reinforcing a democratic culture through all the means that education has at its disposal.

Source: Johnsson, IPU 2002.

aging economic and social life. Authoritarian regimes often argue that they have an advantage in building strong states that can make tough decisions in the interests of the people. They also argue that democratic processes create disorder and impede efficient management—that countries must choose between democracy and development, between extending political freedom and expanding incomes.

These arguments are not supported by empirical evidence. Rather, there are good reasons to believe that democracy and growth are compatible. With just two exceptions, all of the world's richest countries—those with per capita incomes above $20,000 (in 2000 purchasing power parity)—have the world's most democratic regimes (figure 2.2). In addition, 42 of the 48 high human development countries are democracies.[8] These outcomes do not mean that there is a causal relationship—that democracy leads to economic growth or higher income. Indeed, the correlation between democracy and income weakens or disappears when only low-income countries are considered (figure 2.3). In fact, the literature finds no causal relationship between democracy and economic performance, in either direction. A systematic study by Adam Przeworski and others of 135 countries from 1950–90 discredits the notion of a trade-off between democracy and development.[9] Similarly, studies of sources of economic growth find no strong evidence that democracy is an explanatory factor (box 2.4).[10]

DEMOCRACY CONTRIBUTES TO STABILITY AND EQUITABLE ECONOMIC AND SOCIAL DEVELOPMENT

Democracy expands political freedom, a desirable outcome in itself. But democratic institutions and processes can also contribute to development, especially human development. Competition for political power—through elections and other features of democracy—makes politicians more likely to respond to people's needs and aspirations. It can also help manage conflict and promote stability.

In democracies people have a voice—underpinned by freedom of speech and thought, freedom of information, free and independent media and open political debate—that allows

---

BOX 2.4

Democracy and economic growth—a review of the literature

Why should a positive relationship be expected between democracy and economic growth, and why might richer countries be more likely to be democratic? Some researchers argue that democracies are better guarantors of property rights than non-democracies (see, for example, Clague and others 1996) and that enforcing property rights and contracts is essential for investment and growth. Democracies also appear to be better at managing and consolidating economic reforms, because democracies are better at winning the support of groups that lose out from reforms (Haggard 1997).

But there is little consensus on these points—because there are also arguments that democracy is bad for growth. Take the claim that dictators are less open to pressure from self-interested pressure groups and so are better able, should they so choose, to focus on the nation's well-being.

Empirical studies of democracy and growth are equally inconclusive. Borner, Brunetti and Weder (1995) found that 3 empirical studies identified a positive association between democracy and growth, 3 a negative association and 10 no conclusive relationship. In another influential study Barro (1996) tested a non-linear relationship and found that at low levels of democracy, more democracy is better for growth—but at high levels, more democracy is harmful to growth.

Other research also finds conflicting effects. According to Tavares and Waczairg (2001), democracy increases human capital accumulation and lowers income inequality, increasing growth—but it also lowers physical capital accumulation and raises government consumption, lowering growth. One striking finding: fertility rates are significantly lower in democracies at all income levels, and they go up and down as countries transition between dictatorships and democracies. This has strong implications for women's well-being. And as Przeworski and others (2000) find, it also means that even if democracy has no effect on aggregate GDP growth, it may affect per capita GDP growth.

Another robust finding is that while the economic performance of dictatorships varies from terrible to excellent, democracies tend to cluster in the middle. The fastest-growing countries have typically been dictatorships, but no democracy has ever performed as badly as the worst dictatorships (Przeworski and others 2000). The same is true for poverty reduction (Varshney 2002). Thus democracy appears to prevent the worst outcomes, even if it does not guarantee the best ones.

Does economic development increase the likelihood of a country being democratic? Modernization theory holds that the conversion to democracy is an inevitable result of economic development, making richer countries more likely to transition to democracy. But the evidence does not support this: middle-income countries have been more likely than poor or rich countries to move from dictatorships to democracies, according to Przeworski and others (2000). In Latin America, Landman (1999) finds that the level of economic development has no significant effect on the rate of change to democracy for any of seven measures of democracy. The rate of economic growth also has little impact: dictatorships can fall during periods of expansion or contraction.

Even so, high-income countries are more likely to be democratic once other factors are taken into account (Londregran and Poole 1996; Barro 1997). The explanation is that democratic regimes are much more likely to survive in high-income countries, though they are not more likely to emerge. Between 1951 and 1990 none of the 31 democratic regimes with per capita incomes above $6,055 (1985 purchasing power parity dollars) fell, while 38 poor democracies collapsed (Przeworski and others 2000). There is also evidence that reversions to authoritarianism are likely in economic downturns, but it is not clear, argue Londregan and Poole (1996), whether bad economic performance causes democracies to fall or whether democracies about to fall exhibit bad performance.

Several studies have considered the relationship between democracy and income inequality, but poor data make findings tenuous. Data incomparability between countries and within countries over time precludes clear conclusions.

Source: Clague and others 1996; Haggard 1997; Borner, Brunetti and Weder 1995; Barro 1996, 1997; Tavares and Waczairg 2001; Przeworski and others 2000; Varshney 2002; Landman 1999; Londregan and Poole 1996.

---

them to be heard in public policy-making. Public pressure can influence the decisions and actions of public officials as well as private agents, as with environmental pollution or abusive labour practices. These democratic processes are clearly related to three aspects of development.

First, democracies are better than authoritarian regimes at managing conflicts, because the political space and the institutions that provide for open contests give opponents hope that change is possible without destroying the system. Some politicians argue that democracy leads to political instability, undermining development. But empirical studies show that the reverse is true. Socio-political unrest and handovers of power occur more often in democracies than in dictatorships, but they do not disrupt development. Between 1950 and 1990 democracies experienced twice as many riots and demonstrations and three times as many labour strikes. But such events—as well as changes in government—did not slow economic growth in democracies. Under dictatorships they did. Dictatorships were also more prone to violent political upheavals, experiencing a war, on average, every 12 years, compared with every 21 years in democracies. And wars caused greater economic hardship in dictatorships than in democracies.[11] Democracies can mitigate internal conflicts so that they do not develop into political crises and economic turmoil.

The same relationship holds in the opposite direction—that is, higher incomes help democracies survive once they emerge, and the likelihood of reverting to authoritarianism declines as incomes increase (figure 2.4).[12] Higher incomes also contribute to political stability.[13]

Second, democracies are better at avoiding catastrophes and at managing sudden downturns that threaten human survival. As Amartya Sen has argued, democratic institutions and processes provide strong incentives for governments to prevent famines. Without opposition parties, uncensored public criticism and the threat of being thrown out of office, rulers can act with impunity. Without a free press, the suffering from famine in isolated rural areas can be invisible to rulers and to the public. "Famines kill millions of people in different countries of the world, but they don't kill the

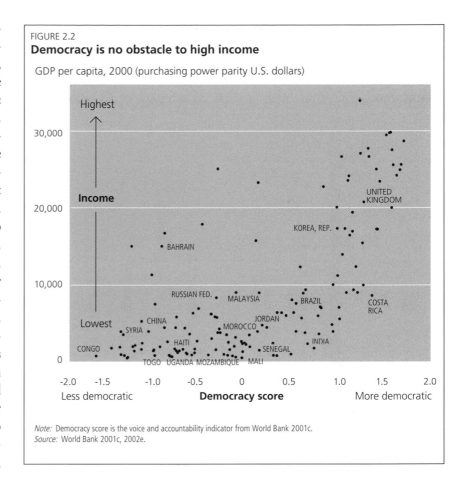

FIGURE 2.2
Democracy is no obstacle to high income

GDP per capita, 2000 (purchasing power parity U.S. dollars)

Note: Democracy score is the voice and accountability indicator from World Bank 2001c.
Source: World Bank 2001c, 2002e.

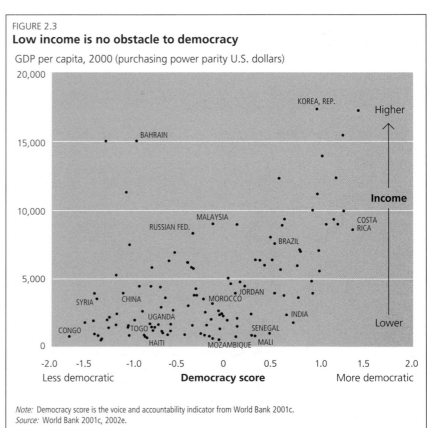

FIGURE 2.3
Low income is no obstacle to democracy

GDP per capita, 2000 (purchasing power parity U.S. dollars)

Note: Democracy score is the voice and accountability indicator from World Bank 2001c.
Source: World Bank 2001c, 2002e.

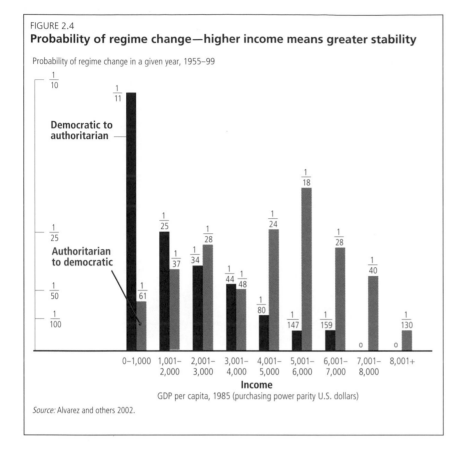

FIGURE 2.4
Probability of regime change—higher income means greater stability

Probability of regime change in a given year, 1955–99

Income
GDP per capita, 1985 (purchasing power parity U.S. dollars)

Source: Alvarez and others 2002.

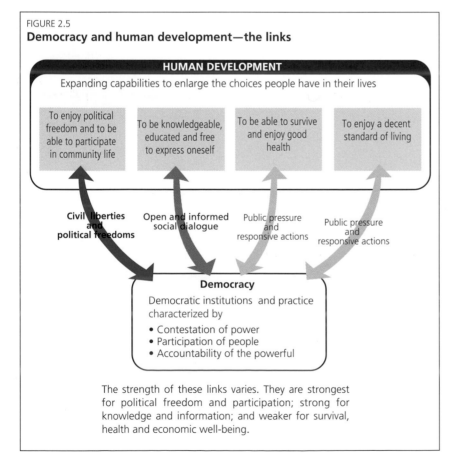

FIGURE 2.5
Democracy and human development—the links

HUMAN DEVELOPMENT
Expanding capabilities to enlarge the choices people have in their lives

To enjoy political freedom and to be able to participate in community life

To be knowledgeable, educated and free to express oneself

To be able to survive and enjoy good health

To enjoy a decent standard of living

Civil liberties and political freedoms

Open and informed social dialogue

Public pressure and responsive actions

Public pressure and responsive actions

Democracy
Democratic institutions and practice characterized by
• Contestation of power
• Participation of people
• Accountability of the powerful

The strength of these links varies. They are strongest for political freedom and participation; strong for knowledge and information; and weaker for survival, health and economic well-being.

rulers. The kings and the presidents, the bureaucrats and the bosses, the military leaders and the commanders never are famine victims."[14]

Consider China, India and the Democratic People's Republic of Korea. In India famines were common under colonial rule—for example, 2–3 million people died in the 1943 Bengal famine. But since independence and the establishment of democratic rule, there has been no recurrence of famine—despite severe crop failures and massive losses of purchasing power for large segments of the population, as in 1968, 1973, 1979 and 1987. Each time the government acted to avoid famine. For example, food production fell sharply during the 1973 drought in Maharashtra, but famine was averted, partly because 5 million people were quickly put to work in public works projects. In contrast, during 1958–61, famines in China killed nearly 30 million people. And one of the worst famines in history continues in the Democratic People's Republic of Korea, having already killed an estimated 1 in 10 citizens.

Political incentives in democracies also seem to help societies avoid other disasters, especially economic ruin and the collapse of development. The worst economic crises in democracies have been much less severe than the worst under dictatorships. True, some of the highest economic growth has been achieved under non-democratic rule, notably in the East Asian tigers between the 1960s and 1990s. But authoritarian regimes have also taken countries to economic ruin—as in Mobutu Sese Seko's Congo, Papa and Bebe Doc's Haiti and Idi Amin's Uganda. Only 1 of the 10 countries with less than 1% annual growth for at least 10 years between 1950 and 1990 was a democracy.

Third, democracies help spread the word about critical health issues, such as the negative implications for women of a large number of births, the benefits of breast feeding and the dangers of unprotected sex in the context of HIV/AIDS. In these areas open dialogue and public debate can disseminate information and influence behaviour. Sharp declines in fertility in highly literate Indian states such as Kerala were due not only to high literacy but also to its interaction with public debates on the benefits of small families.[15] Free, open public debates are the cornerstone of what Amartya Sen calls the "constructive role" that democracies can play in promoting development. And among countries with similar incomes, people live longer, fewer children die and women have fewer children in democratic regimes.[16] This hugely important result has strong implications for human development given the importance of lower fertility for women's lives and choices and for the health of future generations. Understanding what lies behind this result and identifying the policies that made a difference are research priorities.

STILL, THE LINKS BETWEEN DEMOCRACY AND EQUITABLE DEVELOPMENT NEED TO BE STRENGTHENED

When more than growth is considered, democratic institutions and processes contribute to development (figure 2.5). But the links are by no means automatic. Social injustices are widespread in democratic and authoritarian regimes alike, whether deliberate or otherwise in the allocation of public services or in discrimination against squatters, street children, migrants and other socially marginal groups. Discrimination against ethnic minorities, women, the elderly and others continues even in long-established democracies, as the Commission for Racial Equality recently reported in the United Kingdom.[17] Political incentives to respond to the needs of ordinary people may be offset by incentives to respond to the demands of the powerful or the wealthy.

Much is known about how to promote equitable development that benefits poor people: widening access to credit, reforming land ownership, investing in basic social services for all, promoting the informal sector, following sound macroeconomic policies. But too often such policies are not adopted because of systematic biases that protect the interests of elites. Around the world, public spending is often skewed in favour of rich people in such critical areas as basic health and education (figures 2.6 and 2.7).[18] Moreover, taxation and spending policies are not more progressive in the countries with the highest income inequalities. According to one study covering more than 50 countries, countries

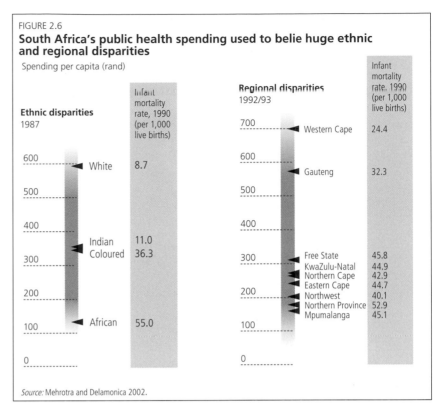

FIGURE 2.6
South Africa's public health spending used to belie huge ethnic and regional disparities

Source: Mehrotra and Delamonica 2002.

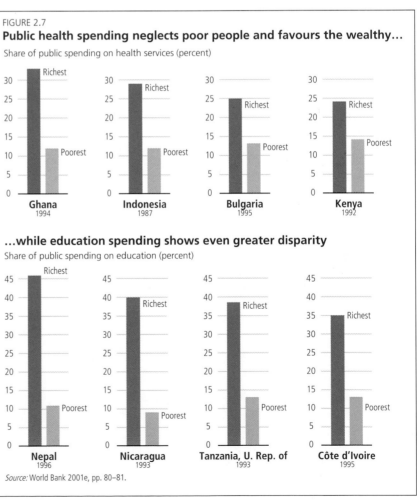

FIGURE 2.7
Public health spending neglects poor people and favours the wealthy...
Share of public spending on health services (percent)

...while education spending shows even greater disparity
Share of public spending on education (percent)

Source: World Bank 2001e, pp. 80–81.

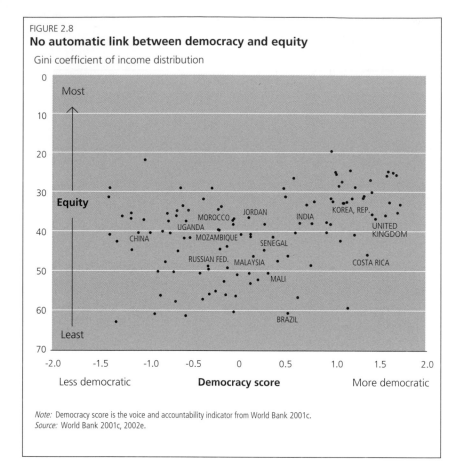

FIGURE 2.8

No automatic link between democracy and equity

Gini coefficient of income distribution

Note: Democracy score is the voice and accountability indicator from World Bank 2001c.
Source: World Bank 2001c, 2002e.

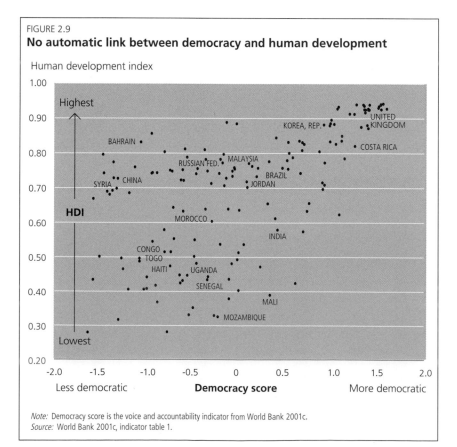

FIGURE 2.9

No automatic link between democracy and human development

Human development index

Note: Democracy score is the voice and accountability indicator from World Bank 2001c.
Source: World Bank 2001c, indicator table 1.

with higher income disparities have lower tax revenues and government spending than countries with more evenly distributed incomes.[19]

Such biases occur in both authoritarian and democratic regimes. Democracies range from those with highly uneven income distributions to those that are more egalitarian. The same is true for less democratic regimes (figure 2.8). Similarly, there is a wide range of achievements in key human development indicators such as the under-five mortality rate or the net primary enrolment ratio. Mali has progressed further than Togo in stabilizing its democratic structures but has done no better in spreading primary schooling, raising literacy or reducing infant mortality. Bahrain and Syria have done as much to spread primary education as more democratic Jordan—and more than Morocco (figure 2.9).

Some democracies have huge, often growing inequalities in income, wealth, social advantage and power. Consider Brazil and the Russian Federation, with some of the world's widest income disparities. In many Latin American countries disparities in income and education rose in the 1990s after democratic rule was restored in the 1980s.[20] Income inequalities also jumped in the former Soviet Union, Central and Eastern Europe and the Baltics. By contrast, Indonesia, the Republic of Korea and Malaysia achieved solid economic growth and reduced income inequalities under non-democratic rule in the 1970s.[21]

So, while democracy can promote equitable development, the goals of democracy and equity should be considered largely independent—with both requiring dedicated effort and political will. Democracy may not automatically secure equitable social and economic development, but poverty does not prevent democracy from taking root: Costa Rica, Jordan, Mozambique and Senegal have expanded people's freedoms and participation much more than their less democratic neighbours with similar incomes. The lesson is that democracy is not a luxury for developing countries. On the contrary, democracy has intrinsic value for human development because it has strong links to political and civil freedoms and can contribute to social and economic development.

But these links are not automatic, and strengthening them is the challenge of democratic governance—making democratic institutions serve human development.

TODAY'S GOVERNANCE CHALLENGE

Democracy and human development have something else in common. They are both more a journey than a destination—a promise rather than a list. Societies can be more or less democratic, just as people can have broader or more constrained choices to lead lives they value. But there is no defined end point. No society is ever completely democratic or fully developed. What matters is moving forward, and not slipping back.

People everywhere want to determine their destiny. The kind of democracy they choose need not follow a particular model—the North American or the Western European, for example. The model must be adapted to local circumstances and history. But everywhere, democracy requires a long process of political development. It needs basic institutions, formal and informal, of the state and outside it. It will not thrive without the spread of democratic culture—of values and principles that guide the behaviour of individuals and groups. Threats to democracy come not only from political parties that are personalized and unable to represent people, but also from intolerance, extremism and a lack of respect for human rights and human dignity.

The implication is that priorities for advancing democratic principles vary according to the social context, just as priorities for human development vary over time and across communities. Promoting the equal concern for all people in the formation of governance structures meant something different in an era of state-owned industry and the transistor radio than it does in an era of transnational corporations and the Internet.

It follows that fulfilling the promise of democratic governance in a 21st century world cannot depend simply on making state institutions function better. It must also take into account the fact that global economic integration and political liberalization are reshaping the environment in which state institutions operate—often fundamentally changing what it means for people to have a say in how they are governed.

To be sure, the nation-state is still a powerful force shaping individual lives, and in most cases it is the most important one. But new actors are also becoming important, from the World Trade Organization to national and international corporations, to new groups in civil society and the media, both local and international. As the actors change, so do the rules: from participatory local budgeting to regional trade rules to international protection of human rights. And as people's lives become more interdependent, democratic principles of participation and equal concern for all must be reflected in the way that these new actors structure their institutions and in the way that rules are formulated and implemented.

Democratic governance in this fast-changing environment is about more than people having the right to vote. It must be about strengthening democratic institutions so that they keep pace with the changing distribution of economic and political power. And it must be about promoting democratic politics that make participation and public accountability possible even when the relevant power and processes lie outside the formal institutions of the state. What this two-part strategy implies for governance is the subject of the rest of this Report.

People everywhere want to determine their destiny. The kind of democracy they choose need not follow a particular model

CHAPTER 3

Deepening democracy by tackling democratic deficits

In earlier times there were lengthy discussions on whether one country or another was yet "fit for democracy". That changed only recently, with the recognition that the question was itself wrong-headed: a country does not have to be judged fit for democracy, rather it has to become fit through democracy. This is a truly momentous change.

—Amartya Sen[1]

The last two decades of the 20th century saw a historic shift in the global spread of democracy. Some 81 countries—29 in Sub-Saharan Africa, 23 in Europe, 14 in Latin America, 10 in Asia and 5 in the Arab states—took steps towards democratization.[2] Often this meant the overthrow of an authoritarian one-party regime, the introduction of multiparty elections or both—a major advance. But the recent mixed experience with democracy in these countries—and around the world—shows that the process of deepening democracy and making it work for people has barely begun.

Why is there less optimism about democracy today than in the euphoric period just after the cold war? One reason is that many countries that embraced democracy have suffered reversals, while many others have limited political competition and continuing abuse of political and civil rights. Today 47 of the 81 countries are considered functioning democracies.[3] Then there's the disturbing spread of "illiberal" democracies, as in Kyrgyzstan and Zimbabwe, where elected governments act the same as their authoritarian predecessors, depriving citizens of human rights and ignoring constitutional limits on power.[4] So, why call them "transitional"? They do not seem to be transitioning anywhere.[5]

Even where democracy is more firmly established, people are disappointed by the economic and social results. Many fought for—and won—democracy in the hope of greater social justice, broader political participation and peaceful resolution of violent conflicts. Rightly or wrongly, they expected democracy to bring more effective development. Just since 2000 in Latin America alone, presidents have been pressured to resign in Argentina (twice), Ecuador, Peru and Venezuela.

Now, 10 to 20 years later, democracy has not produced dividends in the lives of ordinary people in too many countries. Income inequality and poverty have risen sharply in Eastern Europe and the former Soviet Union, sometimes at unprecedented rates (figure 3.1). Poverty has continued to increase in a more democratic Sub-Saharan Africa. And many newly democratic regimes in Latin America seem no better equipped to tackle the region's high poverty and inequality than their authoritarian predecessors. Political instability and violence have also marred democratic transitions in Indonesia, Nigeria, the former Yugoslavia and elsewhere.

Perhaps most serious, people around the world seem to have lost confidence in the effectiveness of their governments—and often seem to be losing faith in democracy. More than 70% of survey respondents in Latin America complain of increasing poverty, crime, corruption and drug trafficking and addiction.[6] Nor is reduced faith in governments and politics limited to new democracies. Gallup International's Millennium Survey asked more than 50,000 people in 60 countries, "Would you say that your country is governed by the will of the people?" Fewer than a third said yes. The survey also asked, "Does government respond to the will of the people?" Only 10% said that it did.[7]

The last two decades of the 20th century saw a historic shift in the global spread of democracy

FIGURE 3.1

Inequality is worsening in many transition countries

Gini coefficient of per capita income

Kyrgyzstan
Russian Federation
All transition countries
Czech Republic

1978–88   1993–95

Source: Milanovic 1998, p. 41.

For some people these disappointments mean that democracy is incompatible with economic and social development. History and evidence, as outlined in chapter 2, argue that this is not the case. But history also teaches that democracy, in itself, does not guarantee greater social justice, faster economic growth or increased social and political stability. The links between democracy and human development can be strong—but they are not automatic. And in almost every country those links need to be strengthened. The best way to achieve this is by strengthening democratic institutions and promoting democratic politics, the focus of this chapter (see the special contribution by President of Iran Seyyed Mohammad Khatami).

The links between democracy and human development can be strong—but they are not automatic

SPECIAL CONTRIBUTION

The world's future belongs to democracy

In the name of God

Humanity, anguished by its journey through the 20th century, marred by bloodshed, calamities and discriminations, is eager for a better future in the new century—a future guided by justice illuminating the gloomy skies of the past and present and based on the dignity and rights of all human beings.

Much has been said about the pains and sufferings of humankind. Too often have victims of all ages paid the price for the power, wealth and deceptions of a privileged few. In one corner of the world people may have attained acceptable living conditions. Yet the rupture between form and content and the ensuing spiritual anguish have tormented their lives. In other, far more populous parts of the world people struggle with a multitude of afflictions—ranging from poverty, ignorance and exclusion to undemocratic rulers who are often subservient to the world's major powers.

Over the past century democracy evolved as a value, inspiring new models of governance. In an age of awakening for people and nations, rulers must come to terms with this value—and allow human beings to realize liberty, spirituality and dignity.

The main features of democracy—which should be clearly distinguished from its various manifestations—include people's right to determine their destinies; the emanation of authority, particularly political authority, from the free will and choice of the people and its submission to their continued scrutiny; and the institutionalization of such accountability. No single form of democracy can be prescribed as the one and final version. Hence unfolding efforts to formulate democracy in the context of spirituality and morality may usher in yet another model of democratic life.

Democratic principles have become the criteria for good governance domestically. They deserve to become the new norm governing global interactions. Thus the exigencies of a few power holders should not supersede the interests of humanity through now-familiar practices of endorsing undemocratic governments, unresponsive to the will and needs of their people, and applying double and multiple standards in response to incidents around the globe.

The structure of power in our contemporary world must be reformed. In a global society whose constituents are nations with equal rights and dignity—much like equal individuals within nations—diverse cultures and civilizations should work together to build a moral, humane world with liberty and progress for all.

The global community ultimately requires the emergence of a responsive moral society, avoiding the use of force and coercion in national and international disputes. Values and norms that are not codified into laws, and laws that lack enforcement mechanisms, will have no tangible effect. Thus globalization is intertwined with the articulation of new collective rights and ethics, and the ensuing impact on national and international norms and institutions.

The world's future belongs to democracy at all levels of governance, advancing ethical, legal and political values based on dialogue and the free exchange of ideas and cultures. Let us advance the United Nations to promote the equitable participation of all nations and civilizations in tomorrow's global governance.

S. M. Khatami

Seyyed Mohammad Khatami
President of the
Islamic Republic of Iran

PUBLIC ACCOUNTABILITY OF DEMOCRATIC INSTITUTIONS

If democracies are not always responsive to the needs and concerns of ordinary people, how can they be made to work better? The answer turns on whether people can go beyond simply expressing their views and preferences to check the power of rulers and influence decisions.

Accountability is about power—about people having not just a say in official decisions but also the right to hold their rulers to account. They can demand answers to questions about decisions and actions. And they can sanction public officials or bodies that do not live up to their responsibilities. Today the insistence that public officials be held accountable is extending to corporations, multinational organizations and others who have more power in public decision-making. Because of their influence over the lives of people and communities, they are holders of the public trust—and so answerable for their actions to national legislatures and to the public.

Accountability means different things in different contexts. To whom, for what and by which standards is accountability judged? Often the concern is with sanctions against legal wrongdoing: when a corporation violates environmental pollution standards, for example. If a company can pollute its environment with impunity, there is no accountability because national laws and regulations are weak or poorly enforced. In other cases the concern may be to sanction teachers, doctors and others who are not meeting minimum professional standards. All these kinds of accountability are central to democratic governance—to ensuring that the holders of the public trust are acting effectively and fairly.

In democracies, people can demand accountability in two ways: through action by civil society and through structures of representation and delegation. But apart from elections, most formal mechanisms of accountability are delegated. The most important are the checks and balances between the judiciary, legislature and executive—and specialized and independent oversight entities such as human rights commissions, electoral commissions, public service commissions, ombudspersons, auditors general and anticorruption bodies.

The problem is, democratic institutions in many countries—especially newer democracies—are overburdened and lack the means to do their jobs. Political parties are disorganized. Representatives cannot keep in close contact with their constituents. Oversight and regulatory agencies lack well-trained staff. And bureaucrats are underpaid, overworked or both. Many countries that held multiparty presidential elections for the first time in the 1980s and 1990s did so with political parties created just months before.

Resource constraints are not the only institutional weakness. Sometimes national institutions are ineffective because real power lies elsewhere. In a more integrated world, weak and indebted states face vast areas of policy-making over which they share control with international actors—if they share it at all. Decisions at the global level can bind states, and national elections and checks and balances lack the reach to hold powerful global actors to account. Or states may have little real authority because subversive groups have taken over: guerrilla movements, international drug traffickers and crime syndicates, powerful rural landowners, slumland gangs.[8]

Even where arrangements for accountability exist, they do not function well in many democracies. They do not promote the interests of most people. And they do an even poorer job of protecting the interests of minorities, women and poor people. There are two main reasons:
- Democratic institutions are subverted by corruption and elite capture.
- Democratic institutions have inadequate reach, and there are gaps in democratic practice.

SUBVERSION OF INSTITUTIONS BY CORRUPTION OR MONEYED INTERESTS

Corruption, abuses of power, intimidations by criminal elements—all weaken democratic accountability. Oversight and regulatory agencies may also fail to act when they have been captured by political or special interests. For example, in the late 1990s South-East Asia suffered from a persistent atmospheric haze—creating

Accountability is about power—about people having not just a say in official decisions but also the right to hold their rulers to account

Poor people, poor justice

Judicial systems often seem more diligent in prosecuting crimes committed by poor people than crimes against them. According to its Pastoral Land Commission, between 1964 and 1992 Brazil experienced 1,730 politically motivated killings of peasants, rural workers, trade union leaders, religious workers and human rights lawyers. By 1992 only 30 of these cases had been brought to trial, and just 18 resulted in convictions.

Surveys of poor people find that at best, the police and judiciary are considered unresponsive—at worst, as aggressive abusers of judicial rights. A recent World Bank survey found that around the world, poor people often view police as:

• Unresponsive—absent when needed, coming only when someone has been killed.
• Corrupt—making false arrests, accusations and imprisonments, with release conditioned on large bribes; stealing money from children; threatening, blackmailing and extorting citizens; using illegal drugs; conniving with criminals.
• Brutal—harassing street vendors; confiscating identification documents; raping women who register complaints; beating up innocent people; torturing and killing homeless boys.

Judicial systems reinforce these biases by failing to punish police abuses. Corruption can also subvert oversight—by police complaint authorities, ombudspersons, independent judicial commissions and national human rights commissions. When the president of Mexico's Human Rights Commission was murdered in 1990, a police commander was accused of the killing. In the course of his trial, six prosecution witnesses were murdered. In 1992 El Salvador established a human rights ombudsperson. But in 1998 the national assembly replaced the activist who had held the position with a man who had nine outstanding complaints filed against him by the same human rights office—including charges of corruption, obstructing justice and violating legal principles. The office was later discredited further by high staff turnover, apparent mismanagement of funds and a reduced emphasis on investigating human rights complaints.

Source: Narayan, Chambers, Shaha and Petesh 2000, pp. 163–64; Goetz and Jenkins 2002; Pinheiro 1999, p. 55.

Gender bias subverts legal process

A study of land disputes in Uganda's Kabale District found that gender bias and corruption routinely lead local tribunals to fail to uphold women's land rights in disputes with male relatives over the sale of family and homestead land. These disputes often involve adult sons or male relatives harassing elderly widows to relinquish the land they have inherited from their husbands, or husbands selling family land without consulting their wives. Routinely faced with officials' demands for "informal" payments, women who tried to pursue their cases were generally unable to outbribe their male relatives. In some cases land sellers colluded with members of the village councils.

The gender bias and corruption are not checked by any type of accountability. The electoral system is particularly inadequate because women face many obstacles to winning seats on local village councils.

Source: Goetz and Jenkins 2002.

would not penalize junior officers for failing to enforce regulations. Subordinates returned the favour by not blowing the whistle on those higher up. Only when the haze from the fires began spreading over Malaysia and Singapore in 1997 did international embarrassment catalyse a crackdown.[9]

Transparency International Bangladesh, in a 2000 study of the nation's banking industry, found that people getting credit from the formal banking sector had to pay a direct bribe equal to 2–20% of the loan value. The higher percentages were extorted from uneducated rural applicants, partly because the bribes were being shared with government officials reviewing the loans.[10] Worse, borrowers often paid up to half of a loan's value to secure a promise from branch managers that the loan would not have to be repaid, a promise often breached. When the supposed beneficiaries are left with little choice but to collude in bribery, it undermines their willingness to protest—and corruption becomes harder to expose.

Judicial proceedings can also be undermined, providing little protection to ordinary people, especially poor people. Judicial systems are often inaccessible. They use official language that many people cannot speak or write. And too often they are open to bribes. Where victims have no judicial recourse, their abusers often go unpunished—especially when they are members of the police. Studies in Latin America have shown that minorities, poor people and other marginalized groups (such as homosexuals and street children) are disproportionately the victims of physical abuse and other mistreatment by the police (box 3.1). Gender bias in judicial proceedings is another problem. Male-dominated village councils systematically fail to uphold the rights of women, as in land disputes in Uganda (box 3.2).

Electoral processes can be subverted by fraud. Numerous elections have been contested by opposition candidates charging fraud and irregularities. In 1997 Cameroonian President Paul Biya was re-elected with 93% of the vote—but the three main opposition parties had boycotted the election, and the government had dismissed demands for an independent electoral commission.[11] Too many other recent elec-

serious health hazards—because plantation owners bribed Indonesian officials to turn a blind eye to illegal forest fires. Burning land was much cheaper than clearing it manually. Payoffs flowed into all levels of the administrative hierarchy, almost guaranteeing that supervisors

tions have been similarly marred: among others, Haiti in 2000,[12] Chad in 2001, Zimbabwe in 2002, Madagascar in 2002.

Money in politics is especially serious because it can distort democratic institutions at every level. It can distort the election process and the extent to which elected leaders represent their constituents. And it can distort parliamentary politics and the functioning of the judiciary and the executive. This problem has recently reached the top of the political agenda in many countries, often as a result of scandals at the highest levels of government. In several countries politicians have been charged with accepting money from criminals, for their private benefit or for campaign purposes. The downfall of the Christian Democrats in Italy in the 1990s owed much to accusations that the party was "financially connected to the mafia".[13] And in Germany in the early 1980s the "Flick Affair" severely shook the nation as it uncovered illegal contributions from the Flick Company.[14] Senior politicians from all the main political parties allegedly disregarded campaign financing laws.[15] The scandal prompted the passage of campaign contribution laws meant to prevent political financing abuse. Yet in 1999 Helmut Kohl, the former chancellor, resigned as honorary chairman of his party after acknowledging having run a network of secret accounts and receiving clandestine donations equal to $6.5 million.[16] This scandal later ensnared other members of the Christian Democratic Union.

Electoral processes cannot operate without financing. But where money plays a decisive role in politics, it turns unequal economic power into unequal political advantage and undermines the principle of "one person, one vote". The problem is not new. But the soaring cost of elections has almost certainly made the situation worse. In 1980 U.S. presidential candidates spent $92 million—but that rose to $211 million in 1988 and $343 million in 2000.[17] Including spending by political parties, the total cost in 2000 was more than $1 billion.[18] Though a large campaign budget does not guarantee success, it is important in many contests: one study of U.S. campaigns in the 1970s showed that candidates challenging incumbent members of Congress won an extra 1 percentage point of votes for every $10,000 spent.[19]

Such costs make for an uneven playing field in political contests because they make it almost impossible for an underfunded candidate to enter a race. These costs also increases politicians' dependence on certain sources of financing, leaving the democratic system vulnerable to the undue influence of special interest groups—particularly corporate interests (box 3.3)

INADEQUATE REACH AND GAPS IN DEMOCRATIC PRACTICE

Even well-functioning formal structures of participation and accountability are at best only blunt instruments. Elections and other formal checks enable citizens only to end the tenure of politicians who abuse their mandates. And joining political parties, seeking to influence their agendas and voting in elections have rarely been enough to safeguard the rights of women, minorities and poor people.

Nor do these mechanisms have the reach to tackle injustices that affect people's daily lives. For example, a recent World Bank review of the weak impact of Colombia's land reforms concluded that even repeated parliamentary questioning had not gone to the heart of the problem, which was that elites had captured the program and distorted it to their own ends. There was collusion between sellers and buyers to overstate land prices, divide the surplus and let the government foot the bill.[20]

One solution to such problems is to decentralize power to lower levels of government—bringing it closer to the people. But local officials are no more immune to elite capture than officials in central government. Indeed, far from strengthening local democracy, decentralization can actually reinforce the power and influence of local elites.[21] In these circumstances citizens may have more luck with officials who are farther away. A recent survey of 12 countries found that in only half was there any evidence—some quite limited—that decentralization empowers more people, reduces poverty, enhances social progress or mitigates spatial inequality.[22] Decentralization helps poor people most when local politics are democratic, with strong structures and

Where money plays a decisive role in politics, it turns unequal economic power into unequal political advantage and undermines the principle of "one person, one vote"

BOX 3.3

Corporate influence on politics

Why do business interests influence public policy in democracies? Sometimes it is a matter of corrupt public officials seeking personal gain. But two other factors are also at work. First, governments serve the public interest by promoting businesses, which create jobs and generate economic growth. Policies that discouraged the success of businesses could not only undermine national economies but could also drive businesses overseas. Second, businesses tend to command resources and access unmatched by other groups—whether representing workers, consumers or environmental causes.

Corporate cash and political patronage

In many countries corporate contributions and lobbying are prominent features of the political landscape. The passage of historic campaign finance reform legislation in the United States in early 2002 owed much to public outrage at the dramatic expansion of corporate campaign contributions, much of it "soft money". Corporations gave $1.2 billion in political contributions during the 2000 elections—about 14 times the already enormous amount contributed by labour unions and 16 times the contributions of other interest groups. Although many European countries have tighter limits on corporate funding, similar patterns emerge elsewhere. And in India big businesses provided an estimated 80% of the financing for major parties in 1996.

Corporate donations and lobbies often drown out the voices of workers, consumers, women, environmentalists and other interest and citizen groups. For example, agroindustries have exerted considerable influence on national positions in international trade negotiations. And highly publicized cases—such as Enron's $3 billion Dabhol power project in India and the Aguas del Tunari water corporation project in Bolivia—show how the concerns of local people, intellectuals, environmentalists and other groups are often ignored until they develop into protests and major confrontations. In Bolivia hundreds of workers went on a general strike, bringing transportation to a standstill and evoking a violent police response in which a demonstrator was shot. Martial law was declared shortly thereafter.

Cases like these feed public scepticism about corporate accountability, and not just within the antiglobalization movement. Concerns about corporate influence resonate with broader international public opinion. In its 1999 Millennium Survey, Gallup International interviewed 57,000 people in 60 countries—and found widespread suspicion and scorn of corporate conduct and higher expectations of corporations' social responsibility. Almost four out of five respondents held companies responsible for public health and safety. Two-thirds said that companies are responsible for bribery and corruption. In 12 European countries more than half the people surveyed said that business did not pay enough attention to its social responsibilities.

People are increasingly concerned that corporations are not held accountable for their actions, either because laws are weak or are weakly enforced. Indeed, even when domestic legislation is adequate, it is often not implemented. In the United States white-collar crime receives much less attention from law enforcement than other types of crime. Between 1992 and 2001 the Securities and Exchange Commission referred 609 white-collar cases to U.S. attorneys for criminal charges. But only 187 were prosecuted, with 142 defendants found guilty and 87 going to jail.

Multiple approaches to influencing policy processes

Donations to politicians and political parties are only one way for businesses to influence policies. Corporations engage in a broad range of activities to ensure that their views get a hearing and influence policy. Corporations draft and submit legislation, offer testimony and participate in consultations. They also influence how policies are applied—by negotiating implementation schedules, supporting certain nominees for official appointments and influencing the judiciary through briefing seminars. A recent study of three U.S. trade advisory committees found that of 111 members, only 2 represented labour unions—and none represented consumers (the seat reserved for an environmental advocacy organization had not been filled). But corporations were well represented, with 92 members from individual companies and 16 from trade associations.

U.S. policy debates on climate change illustrate these trends. The U.S. Global Climate Coalition, an industry group that coordinates business participation in international policy debates, has lobbied aggressively to this end, vigorously challenging scientific arguments on climate change. And while most top scientists agree that greenhouse gas emissions have to be reduced, the coalition has argued forcefully that the targets set by the Kyoto Protocol are "unrealistic".

What can be done?

Asymmetries in resources and access cannot be wished away. So how can undue corporate influence be tackled? Reforming political financing is crucial, and should include:
- Increasing transparency and disclosure of the sources of all election, party and candidate financing.
- Setting clear limits on spending as well as on contributions—by level and by source.
- Providing public funding for candidates and parties.

Many countries are pursuing such measures. Indonesia, the Republic of Korea and Thailand have introduced comprehensive legislation requiring transparency and setting limits on spending and contributions. In 2000 the United Kingdom began requiring all parties to disclose the sources of donations above 5,000 pounds at the national level and 1,000 pounds at the local level. Public funding can take different forms—from a "maximalist" approach, where public funding is the main source of party and election finance (as in Germany, Korea and Sweden), to a "minimalist" approach, where only elections are partly subsidized (as in Australia, Canada and Ireland). The United Kingdom does not provide direct state funding, but candidates receive free broadcasting opportunities and free postal service.

Initiatives can also address the flip side of the coin, by introducing norms for socially responsible corporate behaviour in political activity. More responsible political activity includes:
- *Transparency,* with corporations making clear their political activities. Novartis publishes position papers on biosafety protocols, and Astra Zeneca discloses its funding of lobbyist groups.
- *Accountability,* with corporations making an effort to respond to public concerns. Scottish Power invites external comments on its policies.
- *Consistency,* with corporations making their positions consistent with those of groups that advocate on their behalf, such as industry associations or "front groups".

The most effective—and ambitious—approach would be for corporations to get out of politics altogether. In all likelihood this would require legislation because all businesses would need to act simultaneously. But some businesses are taking steps in this direction. Shell, for example, has stopped making political contributions.

Source: Center for Responsive Politics 2001; Mahbub ul Haq Human Development Centre 1999; Madeley 1999; Human Rights Watch 2002; Parry 2001; Grunwald 2002; Zadek 2001; Leaf 2002.; Korten 1995; SustainAbility 2001, p.14; Global Climate Coalition 2002; Sridharan 2001.

open participatory practices. Only if accompanied by strong support to community groups can decentralization empower ordinary people.[23]

Thus formal structures of accountability in democracy are strong in theory but are often undermined by self-perpetuating concentrations of power and influence. In some countries the same prime ministers have alternated at the helm for decades, and dynastic politics continues. In Mexico the same party was in power for more than 70 years until the 2000 elections ended its rule. Despite democratic upheavals and some inroads into politics by underrepresented groups, elites hold on to state power, and unequal power structures prevail.[24]

Breaking such vicious circles will require strengthening democratic institutions and state capacities. But that is only part of the solution. Political pressure also has to come from outside formal structures, through the emergence of a more vibrant democratic politics.

STRENGTHENING FORMAL DEMOCRATIC INSTITUTIONS

Most of the 81 countries that recently took steps towards democratization have yet to shake off the legacies of authoritarian pasts, and democratic institutions and practices have yet to take root. Representative processes appear to be in crisis even in well-established democracies. In the United States the turnout of registered voters in presidential elections fell from 96% in 1960 to 51% in 2000, and in the United Kingdom from 78% in 1992 to 59% in 2001. Though these trends are not universal—voter turnout has been rising in some countries, especially in Latin America—large drops have been seen in eight other OECD countries.[25] In France, Italy, Norway and the United States party membership is half (or less) of what it was 20 years ago (table 3.1). According to recent surveys in Latin America and Central and Eastern Europe, far fewer people have confidence in political parties than in the church, the armed forces or television (figure 3.2).[26]

Countries can start to restore public trust in representative structures and reduce the concentration of political power by:

• Developing stronger vehicles for formal po-

litical participation and representation through political parties and electoral systems.

• Strengthening checks on arbitrary power by separating powers among the executive, judiciary and legislature, and by creating effective independent entities.

• Decentralizing democratically: devolving power from the central government to provinces and villages, underpinned by stronger local democratic institutions and practices.

• Developing free and independent media.

DEVELOPING STRONGER VEHICLES FOR FORMAL POLITICAL PARTICIPATION AND REPRESENTATION

A well-functioning democracy depends on well-functioning political parties responsive to people, but new democracies mean new parties. These parties are not yet able to fulfil their traditional functions of political education, mobilization and representation of diverse interests. In many African countries opposition parties disappear between elections, while ruling parties behave like they used to under single-party systems. A dearth of public funding and limits on fundraising leave parties dependent on a few wealthy individuals to finance their activities and campaigns. And with perks and patronage flowing from ruling parties, politicians are increas-

TABLE 3.1

Falling membership in political parties

Country	Period	Change in members	
		Number	Percentage
France	1978–99	–1,122,000	–64.6
Italy	1980–98	–2,092,000	–51.5
United States	1980–98	–853,000	–50.4
Norway	1980–97	–219,000	–47.5
Czech Republic	1993–99	–225,000	–41.3
Finland	1980–98	–207,000	–34.0
Netherlands	1980–2000	–136,000	–31.7
Austria	1980–99	–446,000	–30.2
Switzerland	1977–97	–119,000	–28.9
Sweden	1980–98	–143,000	–28.0
Denmark	1980–98	–70,000	–25.5
Ireland	1980–98	–28,000	–24.5
Belgium	1980–99	–136,000	–22.1
Germany	1980–99	–175,000	–9.0
Hungary	1990–99	8,000	5.0
Portugal	1980–2000	50,000	17.0
Slovakia	1994–2000	38,000	29.6
Greece	1980–98	375,000	166.7
Spain	1980–2000	809,000	250.7

Source: Mair and van Biezen 2001, p. 12.

FIGURE 3.2

Trust in institutions

Percentage of people expressing "a lot" or "some" confidence

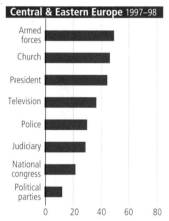

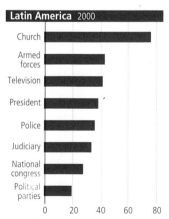

Source: Lagos 2001; Rose and Haerpfer 1999.

BOX 3.4

Quotas make a difference in women's political participation

Worldwide, women account for less than 14% of the lower houses of parliaments, a share that is growing at a snail's pace. To accelerate this trend, many countries have introduced quotas. They are in use in all 11 countries that have achieved more than 30% representation by women, from Sweden and other Nordic countries to Argentina—the first Latin American country to introduce a quota, in 1991—to Mozambique. Quotas can be legislated percentages in parliaments or voluntary targets adopted by political parties.

Legislated quotas in legislatures

In India one-third of the seats in local governments (*panchayats*) have been reserved for women since 1993. Local parties and interest groups have had to seek out female candidates to represent them and win their support. In 1998 women won as many as 40% of seats in panchayat elections.

Progress and setbacks of women in national parliaments, 1995–2000

103 countries where women's representation grew

17 countries where women's representation did not change

40 countries where women's representation declined

In France a 1999 constitutional amendment required that at least half the candidates for municipal elections be women. As a result women won 48% of elections in 2001, up from 22% in 1995. In national elections, where there is no such requirement, the share of women elected increased from 7% in 1998 to just 9% in 2001.

Voluntary quotas in political parties

In 1994 South Africa's African National Congress introduced a one-third quota for women, triggering impressive gains. With 120 women in the 400-member National Assembly, the country now ranks 8th in the number of women in national parliaments, up from 141st in 1994.

In the United Kingdom the Labour Party introduced all-women shortlists for open seats from 1993 until the 1997 general election. In 2000 the British House of Commons had 121 female members, nearly twice as many as in 1995.

But quotas are not a silver bullet

Quotas are designed to facilitate women's access to elected office. But increasing women's political participation requires a long-term strategy for changing long-standing practices that keep women out of politics. Such change cannot be legislated overnight. Not everyone—including some women's rights activists—considers quotas a sustainable strategy. But without such radical measures it would be difficult to achieve the critical mass of women's representation needed to foster a new culture—one that should culminate in the balanced presence of women both in parliaments and in the governing bodies of political parties. Quotas are primarily a temporary remedial

measure, and are no substitute for raising awareness, increasing political education, mobilizing citizens and removing procedural obstacles to women getting nominated and elected. And being voted into office is merely the beginning of women's struggles for full participation—it does not mean that they acquire a real political base, and inexperience is a handicap for new legislators.

So, improving the quality of women's participation in policy-making is as important as increasing the number of women elected, and many initiatives are under way to support women once elected. In the Philippines the Center for Legislative Development, a non-governmental organization (NGO), provides training in such areas as legislative agenda setting, proposal development, advocacy and participation in committee and floor deliberations. This training has helped female legislators in three provinces pass gender-related ordinances, such as the creation of crisis centres for women, and promoted gender-responsive policy decisions on issues such as violence against women. Forging links between female politicians and women's groups sustains advocacy initiatives to pass laws that promote women's rights.

In Trinidad and Tobago a network of NGOs called Working to Get the Balance Right trained 300 women to run in local government elections in 1999. The goal was to sensitize the women to gender-specific concerns and to how these concerns can be addressed through their participation as advocates or public officials. The number of female candidates nominated to run was 91—an almost 100% increase over 1996. And 28 won seats—a 50% increase.

Source: International IDEA 2002b; IPU 2000a, 2001, 2002b; Reyes 2000.

---

ingly switching party affiliation—"crossing the carpet"—to join the winning party. This practice has become so common in West Africa that some governments, as in Benin and Niger, have made it illegal.[27]

Too often the organizational structure of parties is anything but participatory. Parties that are not open and transparent are unlikely to be democratic in their policy commitments. Without internal democracy, parties become individual fiefdoms. Charismatic leadership, more than party platform, often drives party

loyalty. Creating a culture of democracy in political parties is thus vital. At the very least this should involve open, competitive elections for party leadership. Such a requirement would be useful to include in any agenda for political reform—as in Panama's new electoral code, established in 1995.

Elections are complex processes requiring systematic organization. Improving voter registration and rolls and setting up independent electoral commissions are cornerstones of a free and fair system. The inclusion of parties and candidates as stakeholders, monitors and defenders of elections, and not just as contenders, can help ensure stability—as in Mozambique in 1994, where party representatives were included in every aspect in the run-up to the elections.[28] The media can also contribute to this effort—diffusing information, focusing public debate and increasing civic and voter education (see below). So can civil society. In Indonesia nongovernmental organizations (NGOs) played a central role in voter education, explaining to citizens their rights and duties to vote according to their free will and conscience, the value of voting in a democracy and the nature of new election laws. These campaigns also helped convince citizens of the fairness of the system, its new transparency and the new parties and personalities entering into the political life of the country.

Many countries are trying to strengthen systems of representation. Whether in established or new democracies, these efforts tend to have common elements:

• *Improving governance in political parties,* with ethical standards, training, discipline and better financial management. The Democrat Party of Thailand, for example, has embarked on a process to professionalize party management. The Labang Demokratikong Pilipino Party of the Philippines is working on the problem of patronage, establishing a research institute and conducting seminars and policy discussions.[29]

• *Promoting the participation of minorities and women.* Political parties have been a major institutional factor behind the chronic underrepresentation of minorities and women. The situation is improving, but at a snail's pace. In 103 countries the proportion of women in parliament increased between 1995 and 2000, but around the world it still averages just 14%. Affirmative action is often needed to overcome entrenched obstacles. Quotas, either in legislatures or in parties, have been instrumental in raising representation. They have been used in the countries with the highest representation of women in parliament and are making changes in countries where female participation in politics has historically been lower, such as France and South Africa (box 3.4).

• *Building electoral systems.* Many countries, both long-established and new democracies, are reforming their electoral systems. The success of the 2000 Mexican elections largely rested on the 1996 reform of electoral and political frameworks, as well as the complete reform of the electoral commission, the Instituto Federal Electoral.

• *Limiting the distorting influence of money in politics.* Reform of political finance is under active debate in many countries, aiming to improve transparency, level the playing field (by setting limits on spending and contributions), encourage public subsidies and grass-roots contributions and manage undue corporate and business influences on public policy. In the wake of allegations of political corruption a common response has been new laws—already introduced in some countries such as France and the United States and hotly debated in others such as India. Elements of these initiatives include disclosure laws, spending limits, contribution limits, bans on certain types of donations, direct and indirect public subsidies for parties and candidates and subsidies for political broadcasting (see box 3.3). But a study of 60 countries by the International Institute for Democracy and Electoral Assistance shows that stricter laws are only a first step—and that when political financing laws are accompanied by silence, indifference and lack of technical training, abuses are best able to flourish.[30]

STRENGTHENING CHECKS ON ARBITRARY POWER BY SEPARATING POWERS

Democracies suffer reversals when elected governments are overturned. But many elected governments have turned authoritarian, increasingly behaving like their autocratic predecessors. The keys to preventing such abuses of power are strengthening the separation of powers and the independence of the legislature and judiciary—and professionalizing the bureaucracy and the military.

Whether the judiciary can maintain its independence is often the litmus test for whether democratically elected rule can avoid turning autocratic. The fierce independence of India's judiciary is a cornerstone of the country's democracy. Indeed, the tug of war between a ju-

Whether the judiciary can maintain its independence is often the litmus test for whether democratically elected rule can avoid turning autocratic

India's judiciary—independence and activism defending democratic institutions and practices

India's judiciary—its Supreme Court and state high courts—has been a cornerstone of the country's democracy since independence. Over the decades the judiciary has rebuffed continued encroachments on its independence. In recent years renewed judicial activism has vigorously defended citizens' fundamental rights. It has also safeguarded environmental and other public goods. And it has tackled issues of democratic accountability and charges of corruption in the executive.

In the 1970s the courts encountered several challenges to their independence. In a celebrated case in 1976, the prime minister at the time tried to eliminate the use of judicial review to limit parliament's powers. The attempt was defeated and the courts ruled that the basic framework of the constitution could not be altered.

In the 1980s the courts started to hear public interest litigation involving the human rights of poor and powerless people, especially in cases of police brutality and torture, custodial rape and inhumane treatment in jails. These cases also protected such public goods as clean air and water and uncontaminated blood supplies. This judicial activism coincided with the rise of civil society organizations and social movements dedicated to social justice and human rights goals. The synergy built among civil society, reform-minded members of the middle classes and several supreme and high court justices like Justices P. N. Bhagwati and Krishna Iyer helped advance these causes. Legal reforms provided for class action suits on behalf of poor, oppressed and victimized citizens.

In the 1990s the courts sought to uphold the principle of separation of powers and delink the intelligence services from the control of the political executive. They did so to restore the accountability of the Central Bureau of Investigations, the government's main investigative agency. A series of scandals had revealed an unhealthy relationship between the bureau, the prime minister's office and other political elites. The courts restructured authority over the bureau and set its director's tenure to a minimum of two years. There were countermoves in parliament, which alleged that the judiciary was encroaching on legislative and administrative functions beyond its authority, and that judges were exploiting recent corruption trials. A lively debate continues about these institutions, their development and their contribution to the vitality of democratic politics in India.

Source: Kohli 2001; Rudolph and Rudolph 2001.

diciary fighting to stay autonomous and political parties and the executive is a continuing feature of Indian political life. From the efforts to eliminate judicial review of legislation in the 1970s to the judicial activism of the 1990s in taking up cases of political corruption, the judiciary has vigorously defended the separation of powers and ensured that checks and balances are a reality (box 3.5).[31] In Egypt the Constitutional Court played a key role in imposing judicial supervision of polling stations in the 1987 and 2001 elections.[32] In 1997 Mali's Constitutional Court annulled the first round of legislative elections and ordered new balloting in response to a petition from opposition parties. And in 2001 Gabon's Constitutional Court quashed a presidential decree appointing all the members of the country's Economic and Social Council, saying that the decree violated a constitutional requirement that 85% of the council's members be elected by their peers from throughout the country.[33]

During apartheid South Africa's government used the law and the courts to implement—and defend—its policies, causing the oppressed majority to view the judicial system as a tool of white oppression. But human rights lawyers and a few sympathetic judges kept the judicial process from losing all credibility, which proved crucial to the establishment of a democratic constitution. Today strong measures guarantee an independent judiciary, and the Constitutional Court ensures an appropriate separation of powers between the three branches of government. In addition, the Constitutional Court and the independent Judicial Services Commission have made courts more representative—of 199 superior court judges, 45 are black and 26 are women. In 1994, when apartheid ended, there were no more than one or two of either (box 3.6).[34]

In many new democracies, however, domination by the executive branch—and excessive influence of security forces, especially the military—remain stubborn legacies. Shifting to a more balanced system, with an independent judiciary and legislature, does not happen overnight. The legislature often plays a limited role in policy-making—for example, with budgets discussed only at their final stage in many parliaments. In South Africa parliamentarians have no power to amend budgets, only to approve what is presented or reject it outright. But rejection is not a realistic option, because it would immobilize the business of government.[35] In other countries the controlling majority often amends constitutions without broad debate. As political pressure mounts to challenge their power, rulers may try to maintain their hold on it through, for example, constitutional amendments that reinforce the power of the executive. In Cameroon military tribunals can exercise jurisdiction over civilians in cases involving civil unrest. Establishing civilian control of the military and the police is an enormous challenge in many new democracies (see chapter 4).

In many countries bureaucratic rule continues as well, often conflicting with democratic reforms even in long-established democracies such as Japan. Civil servants may not readily adjust to the role of holder of public trust. Jurisdictional conflicts between electoral commissions and ministries of the interior highlight the difficulties of overcoming bureaucratic rule. So does the reluctance of presidential appointees and auxiliaries to tolerate the emergence of political parties and civil society organizations.

Often the legislature and the judiciary simply lack technical capacity, office space and access to information. A 1993 study of Argentina, Bolivia, Brazil, Chile and Honduras found that parliamentary committees lacked skilled staff. Parliamentarians in El Salvador and Mexico are also bereft of professional assistance, staffed only by secretaries. Fewer than a dozen of Nepal's 205 members of parliament have any training in economics.[36]

Many countries are trying to confront these problems, with mixed success. In addition to providing parliaments and judiciaries with equipment, procedures and adequately trained professional staff, they are introducing innovations and structural reforms to reinforce checks on abuses of power. And they are strengthening parliamentary committees to foster more effective decision-making and to monitor the executive. In 1983 Ireland established a committee system that conducts research for members of parliament.[37] In Portugal, Romania and elsewhere, opposition leaders are appointed to lead powerful legislative committees, including the finance committee.[38] And in Morocco the 1996 constitution introduced a bicameral legislature to promote more pluralistic representation.[39]

Another approach is to strengthen independent entities—especially ombudspersons, electoral commissions and human rights commissions. All can promote and defend critical reforms and democratic practices in countries with imbalances of power between the executive and the other branches. Independent electoral commissions play a critical role in ensuring free and fair elections (box 3.7). An important condition for their independence is budgetary independence, best secured by legal arrangements—and with budgets not only for elections but also for preparatory processes, then audited.

BOX 3.6

Judicial activism kept the flag of democracy flying—limply— in apartheid South Africa

Until 1994 South Africa essentially had no written constitution and certainly no bill of rights. Parliament was supreme, and no court had the power to strike down its laws—no matter how unjust or unfair. But courts did have the power to interpret legislation, which they used to blunt some of the more notorious apartheid laws.

The Legal Resources Centre, a public interest law firm, was active in using the courts to fight apartheid laws. The centre won rulings from the country's highest courts, bringing relief to hundreds of thousands of black South Africans—such as the court reversal of policies that had prevented the wives and children of urban workers from joining their husbands and fathers in "white" cities. In another case the centre prevented the eviction of black South Africans from areas legally reserved for white South Africans. Another human rights organiza-

tion, Lawyers for Human Rights, provided free defence counsel for hundreds of cases prosecuting illiterate victims of the apartheid system for transgressing oppressive laws.

Without the efforts of these organizations, the lawyers who worked for them and their supporters in other countries, South Africa's courts would have lost all legitimacy in the eyes of black South Africans. That the black majority retained some trust was crucial to the establishment of a democratic constitution. Otherwise the judicial system's credibility in safeguarding the constitutional values of equality and protection of all people's dignity would have been fatally undermined.

In hindsight such efforts might appear to have been obvious. But at the time there was little if any light at the end of the tunnel. The justice and fairness achieved are a credit to the many activists who fought for them.

Source: Goldstone 2002.

BOX 3.7

The role of independent oversight bodies: Mexico's Federal Election Commission

Mexico's 2000 presidential elections marked a major step forward for the country's democracy. This positive outcome has been widely attributed to 1996 constitutional reforms of electoral and political systems—and to the efforts and growing credibility of the Federal Election Commission (Instituto Federal Electoral). These changes were driven by pressure from civil society, the opposition and the international community resulting from the controversial presidential election of 1988 and lingering questions about process in the 1994 election.

In 1990 constitutional reforms established the Federal Election Commission as an independent entity fully responsible for federal elections and an Electoral Court that handles appeals of election-related disputes. Reforms in the early and mid-1990s strengthened the commission's independence and authority. The 1996 constitutional reforms, in particular, eliminated executive oversight by the Ministry of Internal Affairs and created a non-partisan

General Council of nine independent "electoral counsellors".

Mexico's other electoral innovations include creating observer committees, including judges as members of the election commission and establishing a professional service for supervising elections that is responsible for updating voter lists every year. The election commission has also instituted campaign finance reforms, though critics argue that Congress approved a much higher ceiling than was initially proposed to benefit the wealthy PRI—the party that had been in power for more than 70 years.

These improvements contributed to the opposition winning a majority in the Chamber of Deputies in the watershed 1997 legislative elections—for the first time in Mexico's modern history—and to the 2000 presidential elections bringing an opposition candidate, Vicente Fox, to power. Electoral reforms have considerably strengthened direct democratic participation by all Mexican citizens in government institutions and processes.

Source: Lopez-Pintor 2000; Instituto Federal Electoral 2002; Grayson 2000; Washington Office on Latin America 2000; Maguire 2002; Di Rosa 2002.

South Africa's Human Rights Commission—promoting democratic values and practices by investigating racism in the media

South Africa's Human Rights Commission—an independent institution created by the country's 1994 constitution—has turned its attention to racism in the media. Its investigations began with a 1998 complaint from the Black Lawyers Association and the Association of Black Accountants of South Africa, accusing two newspapers of racism in reports involving black people.

The commission later decided to broaden its inquiry to racism in the media generally. Racial discrimination at every level of society had featured heavily in complaints brought to the commission since its creation, posing risks to a peaceful and integrated South Africa. In broadening its investigation, the commission was not seeking to make a scapegoat of the media. Rather, it was recognizing the media's immense power to shape public opinions and perceptions.

The outcry accompanying the announcement of the inquiry was significant in itself. Critics argued that the inquiry violated the media's right to freedom of expression, undermining the commission's role as protector of all the rights granted in South Africa's constitution and bill of rights.

In its report the commission shared its understanding and interpretation of racism, particularly "subliminal racism". But the commission had already achieved an important objective: it generated a broad public discussion on an issue that threatened to be a major obstacle to building democracy and respect for human rights across South Africa. In doing so, it enhanced the prospect of a popular consensus.

Source: Pityana 2000.

China's reform process—expanding participation and accountability

As reform unfolds in China, and the government and the Communist Party retreat from governing all aspects of society and the economy, the country's leaders have taken steps to increase participation and accountability in local government. The first efforts came in the 1980s, with elections for village committees under the 1987 Organic Law of Village Committees, following a series of grass-roots initiatives by villagers.

The law has had mixed results, leading to lively debate among scholars about whether village elections can serve as the basis for more fundamental political reform. According to unofficial central government sources, only 60% of elections meet all the relevant legal requirements. Once elected, village leaders' activities can be constrained by preexisting power structures. Still, most analysts agree that the elections are increasing the accountability, legitimacy and efficiency of grass-roots administration.

The elections are giving greater voice to the people in formulating national reform policies and programmes. This new form of political interaction will be tested in the coming years by fundamental agricultural reforms. Will the reforms help avoid major hardships for rural populations? And will they enable people to stay in rural areas rather than migrate to cities and towns?

There have also been important changes at the national level, with the party and the government becoming less closely intertwined. Several high-ranking government officials are not party members. In addition, much of the public service system is being professionalized. And there have been ambitious efforts to combat corruption. At all levels of government—central, provincial and below—the state is being downsized and rationalized. The government has also voiced its commitment to strengthening the rule of law and to throwing off the remnants of the old-style "rule by man". In all, major reform of all aspects of Chinese governance has been set in motion, at least with the potential to alter the relationship between the state and its citizens.

Source: UNDP China Country Office 2002; UNDP 1999a.

Independent commissions have been critical to protecting and promoting human rights. By 1998, 40% of the world's parliaments had formal human rights bodies.[40] South Africa's commission actively monitors the application of constitutionally guaranteed rights. It has tackled a wide range of issues, including the provision of social services, human rights in farming communities and racism in the media. The commission is making the vision of a nation founded on human rights a reality (box 3.8).

DECENTRALIZING DEMOCRATICALLY

In principle, decentralizing power from the centre to provinces, districts or villages enables people to participate in decision-making more directly. But in reality it can simply transfer power from one set of elites to another. Democratic decentralization—truly giving voice to the people—requires more than just decentralizing and devolving power. It also requires widening participation—especially by people who are often marginalized, such as women, minorities and the poor—and increasing the accountability of public officials at local levels.

India's *panchayati raj* illustrate this process. Despite democracy's success at the national and state levels, India's constitutionally mandated local governments—the panchayati raj—used to be prone to capture by elites and to subversion by central political authority. The 1992 and 1993 constitutional amendments revitalized the panchayats by giving them constitutional status, providing for regular elections and reserving one-third of seats for women and proportional representation for marginalized social groups.

In many parts of India this change dramatically increased the visibility and extent of popular participation. It also enabled marginalized groups to enter political debates—infusing new political resources into the system, enhancing the legitimacy of state institutions and bringing a measure of uniformity to the institutional structure of local governments all over the country. In Madhya Pradesh and Rajasthan, two states with low incomes and some of the country's worst schooling and literacy rates, literacy jumped 20 percentage points between 1991 and 2001. Community involvement in mapping households and identifying children out of school was a major factor in voicing need. Although 80,000 schools had opened in the 50 years since independence, 30,000 more were created within three years of the scheme's announcement in 1997.[41] In addition, enrolments of girls and tribal children increased enormously.

Not all panchayati raj institutions have been affected the same way. Political authorities in several states—Kerala, Madhya Pradesh, Maharashtra, Rajasthan, West Bengal—have supported decentralization through the panchayats and effectively decentralized decision-making to local levels. In some states progress has been slower in the absence of resource transfers. And in others, such as Bihar, the reform has exacerbated social divisions and violence, further weakening these institutions.[42] The successes have been most pronounced in states where democratic principles permeate local political parties and other institutions and processes and are reflected in the strong trust people have in them.[43] Where local hierarchies are more deeply entrenched, the reform has made less headway.

Bolivia provides another interesting example of democratic decentralization. Its 1994 Popular Participation Law broadened political participation and decentralized fiscal decision-making. The law created municipalities in rural areas with no previous state presence. It officially recognized local grass-roots organizations. It reduced inequality by redistributing fiscal resources based on population density. And it gave more power to local governments by decentralizing physical infrastructure for health care, education, local roads, irrigation systems and cultural activities. The grass-roots organizations play a key role: the law establishes procedures for them to make proposals to satisfy municipal needs and to oversee municipal government services and projects.

Bolivia's law led to very positive empowerment in some communities but not others. Some critics say that the local organizations are too heterogeneous and disorganized—and that they undermine other civil society organizations, such as labour unions, that represent people's interests.

Others say that elites can still hijack the process. They say that the impact of the law would have been greater had it been accompanied by measures to restructure local party politics and crack down on local corruption. They attribute the law's limited results to the continuing hold of patronage-based political systems and processes in which decisions are made without systematic consultation. Still, this innovative initiative brings civil society groups more clearly into local governance and deepens democratic practice.[44]

Democratic decentralization is also spreading in industrial countries, with moves to devolve power to Scotland and Wales in the United Kingdom and to the regions in Italy and Spain. But perhaps one of the most interesting developments in decentralization over the past decade has been the expansion of people's participation and public officials' accountability at the local level in China and Viet Nam.

In 1998 Viet Nam issued the Grass-roots Democracy Decree, partly in response to some farmers' dissatisfaction with the lack of transparency in local budget allocations. The decree defines areas of policy where local people need to be kept informed, including administrative procedures and budget planning and spending. It also outlines areas where local people should discuss and comment on government decisions before they are made. Meanwhile, China has introduced elections in villages and in some townships (box 3.9).

DEVELOPING FREE AND INDEPENDENT MEDIA

Perhaps no reform can be as significant for making democratic institutions work as reform of the media: building diverse and pluralistic media that are free and independent, that achieve mass access and diffusion, that present accurate and unbiased information. Informed debate is the lifeblood of democracies. Without it, citizens and decision-makers are disempowered, lacking the basic tools for informed participation and representation.

Free media play three crucial roles in promoting democratic governance:
• As a civic forum, giving voice to different parts of society and enabling debate from all viewpoints.

Informed debate is the lifeblood of democracies

Watchdog media make democratic institutions work

A free press is probably never more important to democratic governance than when acting as a public watchdog. Watchdog and investigative journalism, no longer the preserve of alternative publications, are moving into the mainstream in all corners of the world.

• *Stimulating debates on economic policy.* In Mozambique Carlos Cardoso used his daily fax news sheet, Metical, to offer an opposing view of the policy prescriptions contained in the government's agreements with the World Bank and International Monetary Fund (IMF). His efforts helped spark national and international debates on World Bank and IMF programmes and on the Mozambican government's accountability to its people.

• *Monitoring elections.* In Ghana the transparency of the 2000 election results was partly due to the large number of private radio stations around the country. The stations made it difficult to rig voting and brought credibility to the declared results. Radio personnel monitored the polls and reported irregularities, and ordinary citizens used the stations to report suspicious activities. In the past, citizens could learn about poll results only through official channels, and suspicion was rife that the official results did not always reflect votes cast.

• *Exposing human rights abuses.* A dogged investigation by Daniel Bekoutou, a Chad-born reporter collaborating with human rights groups, led to the arrest and indictment of Chad's former dictator Hissène Habré by Senegalese authorities in February 2000. Bekoutou's investigations revealed evidence of political killings, torture and "disappearances" in Chad when Habre was president. This indictment, unprecedented in Africa, shows how the media can help hold even heads of state accountable for their crimes.

• *Exposing political corruption.* In Peru newsweeklies such as *Caretas, Oiga* and *Si* and newspapers such as *La Republica* and *El Comercio* published investigations critical of then-President Alberto Fujimori. The investigations revealed death squads, military involvement in corruption and links between drug lords and the political establishment. Most spectacularly, in 2000 Peru cable television broadcast videos of bribes made in exchange for votes, secretly taped by Peru's head of security. Fujimori resigned immediately after the broadcast.

• *Empowering women.* The Palestinian coalition for women, the Women's Affairs Technical Committee, has raised awareness of women's rights through an active partnership with the media. In the runup to the 1996 elections for the Legislative Council, a biweekly newsletter, *Women and Elections,* advocated for a 30% quota for women. Though the quota did not emerge, the effort raised awareness and helped establish the committee's legitimacy. It has kept women's issues at the fore of national debate by providing speakers for radio, briefing local and foreign journalists and introducing newspaper supplements and radio and television programmes.

Source: Tettey 2002; Smulovitz and Peruzzotti 2002b; Sakr 2002.

• As a mobilizing agent, facilitating civic engagement among all sectors of society and strengthening channels of public participation.

• As a watchdog, checking abuses of power, increasing government transparency and holding public officials accountable for their actions in the court of public opinion (box 3.10).

The past two decades have seen major advances in the spread of independent media. Economic and political reforms have loosened restrictions on the media—including censorship and ownership controls—and strengthened constitutional and legal guarantees of freedom of speech and information.

Many countries, from Indonesia to Qatar, have abolished restrictive press laws.[45] And deregulation and privatization of media markets have made them more competitive and often more diverse and pluralistic—notably through the increased penetration of global and regional multimedia companies, such as CNN and Al-Jazeera, into national markets. Information technology and the Internet have also greatly broadened the scope for mass communications, making it possible for even small media organizations to reach large audiences. The Internet can also break the barriers of state control (box 3.11).

These changes have dramatically expanded the media's nature and scale. Between 1970 and 1996 the number of daily newspapers in developing countries more than doubled, from 29 to 60 copies per 1,000 people (figure 3.3).

In many countries political, economic and technological forces are levelling the playing field in the market for ideas, enabling new voices and viewpoints to be heard. Most people have many more sources of information—both in quantity and diversity—than they did just 10 years ago. Widely available information is crucial to democratic governance because it helps challenge government authorities and provokes more balanced debate on problems and policies. Freedom and diversity are reinforcing the media's roles as mobilizing agents and watchdogs.

Still, many countries are a long way from having a genuinely free and independent media that can serve democratic purposes. State-owned media monopolies persist: for example, Lebanon is the only Arab state that allows private broadcasting. Few countries have freedom of information laws, and journalists often work under strict constraints. According to Freedom House, in only a handful of new democracies is press freedom comparable to that in most established democracies. Making the list are most countries in Central and Eastern Europe and the Baltics, several in Latin America and the Caribbean (such as Costa Rica, Jamaica and Trinidad and Tobago) and a few in Africa (Mauritius, Senegal, South Africa) and Asia (Mongolia, the Philippines, Thailand).[46]

Even where press freedoms are constitutionally guaranteed, governments have invented new ways to rein in the press. In many countries in Central and Eastern Europe and elsewhere, libel laws are used to silence critics.[47] In Chile "contempt of authority" is a crime against state security, and despite the 2001 Press Law, restrictions on freedom of expression still pervade Chilean legislation—where the defamation laws that Augusto Pinochet's regime used to great effect are still in force.[48] In several countries the vague crime of "dangerousness" has been used to curtail independent journalism. The Democratic Republic of Congo outlaws reporting that might "demoralize" the public. In Zimbabwe, with a history of a vigorous and independent media, the president has forced through legislation that severely constrains press freedoms.

Journalism also remains a hazardous occupation. In 2001, 37 journalists died in the line of duty. Another 118 were imprisoned.[49] Worldwide, more than 600 journalists or their news organizations were intimidated or physically attacked—mostly because some people did not agree with what they reported.[50]

In 1944 writer Albert Camus said, "The press is free when it does not depend on either the power of government or the power of money."[51] To be free and independent and to produce factual, unbiased information, the media must be free not just from state control—but also from corporate and political pres-

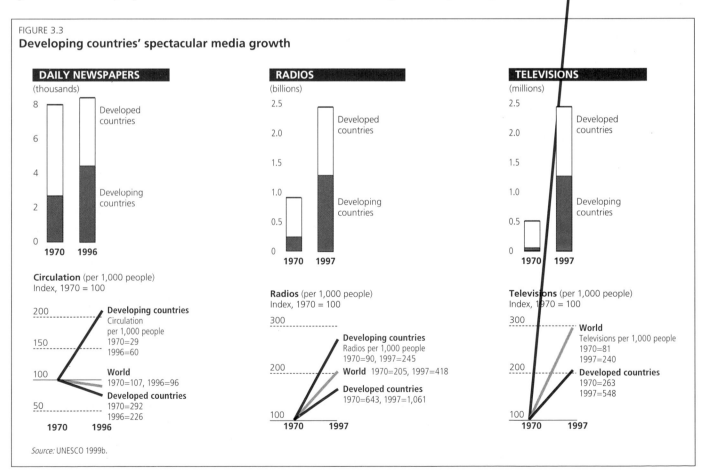

FIGURE 3.3
Developing countries' spectacular media growth

DAILY NEWSPAPERS
(thousands)

Developed countries
Developing countries
1970   1996

Circulation (per 1,000 people)
Index, 1970 = 100

Developing countries
Circulation per 1,000 people
1970=29
1996=60

World
1970=107, 1996=96

Developed countries
1970=292
1996=226

1970   1996

RADIOS
(billions)

Developed countries
Developing countries
1970   1997

Radios (per 1,000 people)
Index, 1970 = 100

Developing countries
Radios per 1,000 people
1970=90, 1997=245

World 1970=205, 1997=418

Developed countries
1970=643, 1997=1,061

1970   1997

TELEVISIONS
(millions)

Developed countries
Developing countries
1970   1997

Televisions (per 1,000 people)
Index, 1970 = 100

Developing countries
Televisions per 1,000 people
1970=10
1997=157

World
Televisions per 1,000 people
1970=81
1997=240

Developed countries
1970=263
1997=548

1970   1997

Source: UNESCO 1999b.

FIGURE 3.4
Who owns the media?

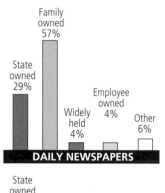

Family
owned
57%

State
owned
29%

Employee
owned
4%

Widely
held
4%

Other
6%

DAILY NEWSPAPERS

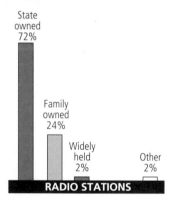

State
owned
72%

Family
owned
24%

Widely
held
2%

Other
2%

RADIO STATIONS

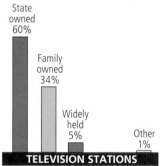

State
owned
60%

Family
owned
34%

Widely
held
5%

Other
1%

TELEVISION STATIONS

Note: Percentages are average shares of ownership for 97 countries' top five newspaper and broadcast enterprises.

Source: Djankov and others 2001.

sures. With greater media pluralism comes an expectation of greater political pluralism in the media and greater potential for broader, better-informed debate. But commercial and political pressures still skew the market for ideas.

Liberalization, privatization and new technology have taken the media out of government hands and into private hands. Most of the world's publishing media are privately owned, although the public sector still accounts for 60% of television station ownership worldwide (figure 3.4).[52] However, private ownership of the media is highly concentrated, often by families. In the United Kingdom four groups own 85% of the daily press (accounting for two-thirds of total circulation). In the United States six companies control most of the media: AOL Time Warner, General Electric, Viacom, Disney, Bertelsmann, News Corporation. In Australia Rupert Murdoch's media empire controls 60% of the circulation of daily newspapers.[53] In a few countries families of influential politicians are major owners of the media; the most well-known case is Silvio Berlusconi and his family in Italy. Mexico's Televisa and Brazil's Globo are two of the world's greatest media monopolies controlled by individuals and their families, encompassing all aspects of production and distribution of television, radio, film, video and much of the advertising industries in their countries. In Venezuela two large family-owned companies dominate the market: Grupo Phelps and Grupo Cisneros.[54]

From Bolivia to France to the United States, citizens, politicians and journalists are engaging in lively debates about how the media's politicization and poor professional standards contribute to the deterioration of democratic life.[55] The media can be subjected to overtly political aims, compromising basic professional ethics of providing unbiased, accurate information. Truth is the first casualty of war, but the media are usually the victims, not the aggressors. But not in Rwanda in 1994, when radio—the country's most common media—was used to incite genocide. The journalists involved now face charges of crimes against humanity before the International Criminal Tribunal for Rwanda.

Media companies are businesses and can be expected to behave as such. Hence the increasing trend towards "infotainment"—the merging of information and entertainment—also viewed as a threat by many (figure 3.5). Media companies also have a civic role as providers of news and information. The tensions between these two roles will never be eliminated—and the answer to excessive corporate influence over the news cannot be a return to excessive control by the state. Solutions must combine the need to hold the media accountable and responsible with the need to keep it free. The media can be free of both corporate and state control if it serves the public first and foremost and follows higher standards of professionalism and ethics.

A range of mechanisms for promoting higher standards of professionalism and responsibility do not depend on restrictive state controls:

• *Independent media commissions.* Among the handful of independent media commissions is the Ghana Media Commission, which is authorized "to take all appropriate measures to ensure the establishment and maintenance of the highest journalistic standards in the mass media".[56] Using a combination of moral suasion and professional goodwill, the commission has often ruled against the abuse of power by newspapers and directed them to issue apologies and retractions. So far it has taken on more than 50 cases, and has resolved 28 amicably.

• *Market sanctions—voting with the pocketbook.* The public can always withdraw its support for an offending newspaper or medium by refusing to buy or view it. Zimbabwe's state-owned newspaper *The Herald* lost more than 40% of its readers, from 744,000 in 2000 to 430,000 in 2001, partly because people lost faith in its credibility. By contrast, the private *Daily News* saw its readership grow from 512,000 in 2000 to 582,000 in 2001.[57]

• *Self-regulation.* Self-regulation includes professional standards and internal guidelines by newspapers and news agencies. Press councils that examine complaints about media performance are another key element. Ombudspersons, maintained by newspapers in Brazil, Canada, Japan, Spain and the United States, also belong to this category.[58] There is greater attention to the need to raise professional standards through codes of ethics, training, education and a broader emphasis on quality.

Many of the above elements come together in Claude Jean Bertrand's Media Accountability System (also known as M*A*S), which emphasizes greater efforts by the media to develop ethical standards, especially through open debates with the public. The system also makes clear that media responsibility does not derive solely from institutional efforts. It starts with the consciences of individual journalists and must be based on socially accepted norms and standards of fair conduct. In recent years there have been positive developments in this regard: the news media are more willing to publicly examine press ethics and performance, and journalism courses are addressing ethics more often.

PROMOTING DEMOCRATIC POLITICS TO DEEPEN DEMOCRATIC PRACTICE

Though strengthening democratic institutions is essential, it is not enough to promote more effective participation by people and more responsive decision-making by those in power. An alert citizenry is what makes democratic institutions and processes work. Political pressure from below is usually the most effective trigger of change. Major advances in human development over the past two centuries—the abolition of slavery, the recognition of equal rights of women, the advance of democracy itself—would not have been granted from above. They had to be fought for.

While much has been written about the challenges of creating democratic institutions, there has been much less analysis of democratic politics: the struggles of poor and marginalized people to claim their rights and to overcome institutionalized obstacles. These struggles depend as much on strengthening civil liberties, civil society institutions and a free media as on strengthening political liberties and political institutions. "It is quite possible to have accountability in…the high politics of the state, honest rulers and free elections, and yet profound injustice or irresponsibility in the deep politics of society, that is, the relations between rich and poor, powerful and weak."[59]

A trend of the past decade is the expansion of democratic politics, with a groundswell of civic activism around the world demanding greater accountability of government authorities

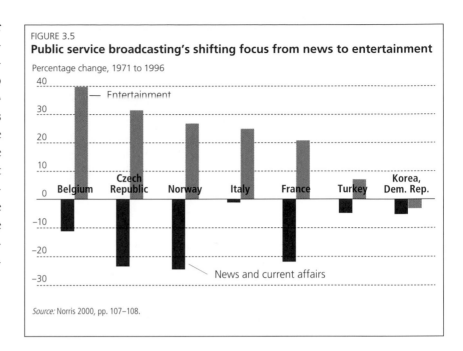

FIGURE 3.5

Public service broadcasting's shifting focus from news to entertainment

Percentage change, 1971 to 1996

— Entertainment

News and current affairs

Source: Norris 2000, pp. 107–108.

and of private business and multilateral organizations. These civil society actors are using new and innovative approaches to get their messages heard, and expanding their role from watchdogs that monitor to active participants in setting agendas.

One of the more significant examples is the rise of participatory and accountable budgeting: civil society initiatives to scrutinize public spending and in some cases participate in the development of official budgets. Few government decisions mean as much for ordinary people as those made during the writing of public budgets—especially for poor people who rely on "public incomes" such as schooling, health care, roads, water supply and electricity. Yet ordinary people typically have little say in budget formulation. In most countries the budget process is almost exclusively the prerogative of bureaucrats and the executive branch. Parliaments also participate, but often only at the end. And much of the process is usually shrouded in secrecy unmatched by any other part of government decision-making aside from national security.

But recent initiatives by citizen groups to examine local and central budgets are helping to open this process to the voices of ordinary people. Many of these initiatives start with social audits or impact evaluations—analyses that elicit concerns about spending priorities and the mis-

BOX 3.12

Gender-responsive budget initiatives—an increasingly popular tool

Gender-responsive budgets are an innovative new tool that empower women's organizations and civil society to hold public spending accountable to international and national commitments for promoting gender equality. In recent years such initiatives have spread to more than 40 countries. They are globally networked with the support of agencies such as the Commonwealth Secretariat, United Nations Development Fund for Women and Organisation for Economic Co-operation and Development. Still experimental, the initiatives will take time to develop and bear fruit.

What are gender-responsive budgets?

Gender-responsive budgets are not separate budgets for women and girls. Rather, they are analyses of public spending through the lens of gender. They are a way of ensuring consistency between social commitments to achieve gender equality goals—such as in education or work—and the resources being allocated. The key question is, what impact does fiscal policy have on gender equality? Does it reduce gender inequality, increase it or leave it unchanged?

Gender-responsive budgets were started by Australian activists who pushed the government to assess the impact on gender equity of all elements of the national budget between the mid-1980s and mid-1990s. Many other countries later adopted the concept to expand participation and accountability in budgeting, especially in light of international commitments to promote gender equality.

Diverse country initiatives

Over the past decade advocates for gender equality began using gender-responsive budgets in a multitude of ways. Some were initiated by government, as in Australia. Others were initiated by civil society groups, as in the Philippines and South Africa. And yet others were initiated by parliamentarians, as in Uganda. Most focus on monitoring, while some engage in preparatory phases, as in Brazil and the United Kingdom. Most work at the national level, but some—as in Uganda—focus on local levels, where traditional and oppressive gender relations are stronger. All point to the effect of this new tool in stimulating a new participatory politics challenging the "power of the purse".

In *South Africa* the Women's Budget Initiative empowers parliamentarians and others with analysis and information to oversee and critique government budgets. It has been a collaborative venture of the Gender and Economic Policy Group (part of the parliamentary Committee on Finance) and two non-governmental organizations (NGOs) focused on policy research. By linking researchers and members of parliament, the researchers could be assured that their work would be taken forward into advocacy, while the parliamentarians would have a solid basis for their advocacy. From the start the core members of the initiative were also expected to draw in others as researchers and reference people. The initiative published a series of books and, more recently, a series of papers called *Money Matters,* written to be accessible to a broad range of readers. South Africa's government has also introduced gender budget analysis within the government, led by the Ministry of Finance. This and the above initiative have had some positive effects. For example, all sectoral budget reviews now include gender-sensitive analysis.

In *Tanzania* gender budgeting drew inspiration from Australia and South Africa. Initiated by the Tanzanian Gender Networking Programme, an NGO, the programme's main strengths are the alliances created with government, especially its gender equality activists. Teaming up an NGO researcher with a government officer, the initiative has commissioned research on four sectoral ministries (education, health, agriculture, industry and commerce), on the Ministry of Finance and Planning Commission and on the budget process. It has also done research in selected districts.

In *Mexico* the NGO Equidad de Genero (Gender Equality) and the Fundar Center for Analysis and Research, a policy research NGO, have undertaken gender budgeting projects within their states and municipalities, evaluating them in light of decentralization experiences and the transfer of resources for local budgets. They have tried to do so by involving civil society organizations, public servants and statistical institutions, and have encouraged public debate on local budget decisions.

In the *Philippines* the gender machinery—in the form of the National Commission on the Role of Filipino Women—provides technical assistance to government agencies in devising gender and development plans and budgets, and

monitors the stipulated 5% budget allocations of government agencies for such activities.

Uganda's initiative has been spearheaded by the Forum for Women in Democracy, an NGO that was established by female parliamentarians and has strong links with the special interest groups caucus in parliament. It brings together women occupying seats reserved for them, people with disabilities, youth and workers as well as women who have won "open" seats, to go beyond the monitoring of budget allocations and processes to examine the impact of all spending and revenue, and increase inclusiveness and transparency in official processes.

In the *United Kingdom* the Women's Budget Group, an extragovernmental group of activists, has since 1990 formally submitted a prebudget consultation paper in November of each year, outlining the main policies and proposed changes to the treasury. The group focuses on taxes and benefits rather than on spending because these affect a far larger portion of the population than they do in developing countries.

In *Porto Alegre, Brazil*, the gender budget initiative is part of the broader process of participatory budgeting. NGOs such as Centro de Assessoria e Estudos Urbanos (CIDADE) backstop this process, with CIDADE monitoring and analysing council meetings, holding workshops and training courses for delegates, council members and community leaders, researching participants' perception of these processes and disseminating information through papers, the monthly journal *De Olho No Orçamento* and its Website. Citizens participate in two annual meetings organized by the local government where they rank 5 priority sectors from a list of 14 (sewerage, housing, pavement, education, social assistance, health, transportation, city organization, sports, leisure, economic development, culture, environmental sanitation, street lighting), revising regional or thematic demands and budget allocations. Environmental sanitation and street lighting were added to the list in 2000–01 through this participatory process. Between 1991 and 2001 the number of citizens participating in the budget process quintupled. Although this initiative is not specifically targeting gender issues, the participatory process and the research and advocacy work accompanying it have highlighted several gender-related concerns and provide insights for other gender budget initiatives.

Source: Budlender, Sharp and Allen 1999; Byanyima 2000; Cagatay and others 2000; Esim 2000; Himmelweit 2000; Budlender and others 2002; Sharp 2000; Bakker 2002; Osmani 2002a; Caruso 2002; Hewitt and Mukhopadhyay 2001.

use of funds. These efforts sometimes help reverse official decisions. In Israel the government proposed deep cuts in social spending in 1998. The Adva Centre, a non-partisan, action-oriented policy analysis organization, assessed the potential impact of these cuts. As a result a wide coalition lobbied the government—and cuts in child care and pensions were withdrawn, universal health care was preserved and cutbacks in teaching hours and housing assistance were reduced.

In Rajasthan, India, a grass-roots organization called Mazdoor Kisan Shakti Sangathan (MKSS, or Workers and Farmers Power Association) launched a campaign in 1988 to secure minimum wages for government drought-relief workers. It soon became clear that corruption was at the root of low wages. The MKSS analysed government accounts and discovered that local authorities were billing the central and state governments for wage costs far above what workers were being paid. To combat this and other fraud—including inflated estimates for public works projects and the use of shoddy materials—the MKSS investigations catalysed state agencies to monitor spending and require all village accounts to be scrutinized at village meetings open to all.

These new types of popular participation are spreading across the globe as civil society groups go beyond whistle-blowing and protests to take on oversight functions that are normally the responsibility of state institutions. Argentina's Poder Cuidadano movement monitors the internal workings of political parties—a function previously performed solely by state agencies. Moreover, the movement is forcing change through better enforcement of existing rules and regulations, institutional reform and enhanced transparency and monitoring.

Such initiatives have led to participatory budgeting—more systematic, institutionalized public participation in the preparation of budgets. In 1989 Porto Alegre, Brazil, introduced a process that enables citizens to participate in preparing municipal budgets. In its first seven years the process resulted in remarkable gains in human development spending for poor people: the share of households with access to water services rose from 80% to 98%, the portion of

---

BOX 3.13

Technology and the power of e-governance

From Asia to Europe to Latin America to Africa, governments are adopting more innovative ways of interacting with citizens by adapting many practices of electronic commerce. Whether it's the 2 million subscribers to the Japanese prime minister's email list or government-sponsored online consultations throughout Europe and Australia, the Internet is encouraging more direct citizen engagement with elected representatives.

The benefits of e-governance for public service delivery have also begun to extend to developing countries. In the Indian state of Karnataka, farmers can download land records and related information from nearby RTC (Record of Right, Tenancy and Cultivation) information kiosks. In the United Arab Emirates the Dubai Courts Project has established a complete online system for tracking and monitoring court cases, from the first filing to the final decision. In Chile an e-government project enables poor people to apply online for housing vouchers and subsidies—avoiding the time, cost and red tape of applying in person at Ministry of Housing offices located only in major cities.

The Internet has also improved transparency and exposed corruption in government departments. Anticorruption Websites are proliferating in and out of government, inspired by efforts such as Latin America's Respondanet (www.respondanet.com), which links professionals, government officials and citizens concerned about the proper use of public funds.

With today's 0.5 billion Internet users expected to grow to nearly 1.0 billion by 2005, governments should expand e-governance for the benefit of all citizens—at least where the required time and financing are not prohibitive:
• Announce all public meetings online in a systematic, reliable way.
• Use comment forms, online surveys and focus groups to obtain the input required for genuine e-government. In South Africa citizens can review policy proposals online and submit comments even before a policy issue reaches the Green Paper and draft law stage.
• Hold government-citizen online consultations. To have a real impact on policymaking, such consultations should be highly structured.

Source: UNPAN 2002; Nua Publish 2002; Clift 2002; Working Group on E-Government in the Developing World 2002.

---

people with access to sewage facilities jumped from 46% to 85% and the number of children enrolled in public school doubled.[60] This approach has been replicated in about 100 other municipalities in Brazil. In addition, more than 40 countries have used participatory budgeting to promote gender-responsive public spending (box 3.12).

Participatory budgeting shows that even the veil of technical complexity that has protected budgets from open questioning can be lifted once citizen groups have time, skills and access to information. These new forms of people's participation—from influencing agendas through protests to increasing collaboration in decision-making—are reinforcing democratic institutions. E-governance is another emerging avenue for people's participation in politics, encouraging more direct citizen engagement with elected representatives (box 3.13).

Participatory democracy at work—drafting Thailand's new constitution

In drafting Thailand's new constitution, civil society organizations insisted on and were given the opportunity to make substantive inputs. The Constitutional Drafting Assembly was itself a participatory body, with 99 members—76 representing the country's different provinces.

Civil society organizations offered suggestions to the assembly on two occasions. In addition, 28 organizations active in democracy met regularly in early 1997 to formulate draft resolutions on the new constitution. Another set of recommendations was published jointly by the main networks of non-governmental organizations (NGOs), private organizations, the Coordinating Committee on Rural Development (with 300 members), the 28 democratic organizations, the Political Reform and Civil Society Group, the Women and Constitution Network, the Labour Organization of Thailand and the Regional People's Forum for the Constitution.

These initiatives were complemented by others that broadened the debate on the new constitution through mass media campaigns, and by public hearings organized in Bangkok and all the provinces.

Source: UNDP 1999d.

Popular demands for greater accountability no longer stop at the state or at national boundaries. As discussed in chapter 5, global economic integration has reinforced the power and influence of global actors—intergovernmental organizations such as the World Bank, International Monetary Fund, World Trade Organization and global corporations. These global institutions and their rules govern important aspects of national economic policies and have enormous impacts on people's lives—creating a global-national gap in democratic participation and accountability.

Global civil society networks are working to redress such gaps, with varying success. They are being aided in their efforts by the Internet, which makes it possible to create formal networks of non-governmental organizations (NGOs) as well as much looser networks of individuals and organizations that can quickly mobilize collective action. For example, a campaign by Rain Forest Action Network and Greenpeace led Home Depot, the world's largest lumber retailer, to stop buying timber from endangered forests and from suppliers that engaged in unsustainable harvesting. The key feature of this initiative was that it mobilized hundreds of environmental organizations and grass-roots groups.[61]

Many such actions abound. If not for the Internet, these organizations and grass-roots groups would have remained isolated, engaged in dispersed efforts. Chapter 5 discusses in greater detail how such global public action has become a real force in global governance, providing checks and balances on corporations, governments and intergovernmental organizations—and achieving important breakthroughs for human development.

These autonomous efforts offer enormous promise because they offer a more direct channel of accountability—defying conventional constraints on social action, which typically require going through established institutions of accountability. But that disregard for convention also raises difficult questions for accountability and democratic governance. In particular, the ability of these global networks to inflict large and immediate costs on the reputations of public and private actors tends to work against the notion of due process. Criteria for weighing information are usually vague and subject to change without notice, and the scope for malicious misinformation is enormous.

These and other concerns about the proper roles and responsibilities of civil society actors have created demand for these groups to be more publicly accountable for their activities: a demand that many are working to meet. Ethiopian NGOs have adopted codes of conduct for effective self-regulation. The codes emphasize the importance of transparency and accountability and the need to ensure that the NGOs are truly representative of the people whose lives they affect.

Expanding political and civic space for popular social engagement is critical for deepening democracy and building democratic governance. Responsibilities for expanding this space lie both with the state, which must protect civil and political freedoms, and with the members of society who engage in and invigorate this exercise. Over the past decade 68 countries signed the International Covenant on Civil and Political rights, nearly twice the number that signed in the preceding 25 years. But as of February 2002, 39 countries still had not.[62] And while guaranteeing basic political and civil freedoms is a crucial first step, many countries restrict the activities of trade unions, professional organizations and NGOs. In some countries NGOs can be banned for having political aims. And as noted, in many countries the media are restricted from voicing dissent or have inadequate dissemination.

Civic activism cannot be said to have failed just because some actions do not lead to change. Some initiatives are bound to fail, just as all but one candidate will necessarily lose an election. What is important in democracies is the spread of democratic practice, where people can voice their views, influence decisions and monitor performance against commitments—both national and international. Thailand's unique approach to drafting its constitution is an example of this kind of participatory democracy (box 3.14).

DEEPENING DEMOCRACY FOR HUMAN DEVELOPMENT

Strengthening accountability is central to a larger process of embedding democratic values, practices and principles in every aspect of society—to build strong, durable and inclusive democracies more responsive and accountable to ordinary people. But the gap between democratic aspiration and practice is wide in long-standing democracies as well as new ones. The chronic underrepresentation of women, the neglect of minority interests and the unaccountable and untransparent military and civil service are common issues. Costa Rica's remarkable experiment in public consultations on the state of democracy illustrates this well (box 3.15).

Democratic deficits can mean hollow citizenship. People do not have fully equal rights and entitlements because constitutions fail to guarantee them or because administrative institutions fail to enforce them. And when there is a lag between norms and entitlements, rights are not respected—as is often the case with discrimination against women.

Democratic realists say that this is to be expected of representative democracy, which above all is a system of political competition, not one intended exclusively to empower citizens, generate high or direct participation in gov-

---

BOX 3.15

Costa Rica—citizens audit the quality of democracy

The Citizens Audit on the Quality of Democracy was a systematic process of public deliberation and analysis conducted in Costa Rica in 1998–2001. It mapped out how democracy works in everyday life for average citizens, identifying where life comes close to their democratic aspirations—and where there are shortfalls.

The process first defined standards for assessing the quality of democracy—a set of shared democratic aspirations. A panel of prominent Costa Ricans—politicians, academics, business leaders and others—was established for this purpose, augmented by surveys and focus group consultations. This was followed by field research involving more than 50 researchers collecting empirical evidence, which panels of citizens then assessed against the standards using an objective methodology.

The audit found that people do not evaluate the quality of democracy as a whole. Instead, using the metaphor of Costa Rica's rugged territory, they emphasized glaring contrasts between different parts of democratic life. Among the peaks are the quality of the electoral system and the constitutional review of public policies. Among the valleys are local governments. The hot spots are the lack of citizen participation in social and political organizations and in public policies, extensive clientelistic practices in social policy programmes and poor treatment of citizens by bureaucrats.

By investigating democratic aspirations, the audit brought home an important insight. For Costa Ricans, democracy is more than a democratic regime. Although elections and freedom lie at the democratic core, most people also believe that democracy is a way of exercising political power in daily life. In other words, democracy is a political regime requiring a particular kind of state—one that protects human rights, ensures accountability and the rule of law and treats people with fairness and respect. Citizens view democracy as a way of organizing society so that people do not suffer extreme inequalities that impede the exercise of their citizenship.

The audit also found stark subnational differences in the quality of democratic life, underscoring the importance of going beyond conventional nation-state approaches to democracy. These insights call new attention to the importance of social and economic inequalities and political participation.

The audit has already left its mark. The government's proposal for administrative reform includes a chapter on the rights of citizens, based largely on the audit's findings on widespread poor treatment by public officials. The audit has also helped entrepreneurial chambers and trade unions launch fresh exchanges on the divisive issue of freedom of organization in private firms. Moreover, the audit is inspiring other countries to perform similar exercises.

Source: Vargas Cullell 2002; O'Donnell 1999; 2001; Proyecto Estado de la Nación 2001.

---

ernment affairs or produce economic and social justice. And certainly, democratization does not guarantee social justice any more than it guarantees economic growth, social peace, administrative efficiency, political harmony, free markets or the end of ideology. But the institutions, practices and ideals of democracy have the capacity to challenge the concentration of political power and prevent the emergence of tyranny. Thus they play a crucial role in building governance that is by the people as well as for the people.

CHAPTER 4

 Democratizing security to prevent conflict and build peace

When we were in the military regime, we didn't get anything from the government, but we had peace. Now we are in a democracy, we don't get anything from the government, and we don't have peace.

—Muhammad Umaru, a tailor in Nigeria[1]

Human development in its fullest sense requires democratic governance—with all people able to participate in the institutions and decisions that shape their lives and all those who hold power held accountable for their actions. Achieving human development also depends on peace and personal security.

In places where governments have not delivered civic peace—including, in recent years, Afghanistan, Liberia, Sierra Leone and Somalia—people begin to question whether there is a trade-off between securing peace and establishing democratic governance. With 53 major armed internal conflicts in the 1990s resulting in an estimated 3.6 million deaths (mostly civilians), it is easy to understand why some people may favour a despotic peace over no peace at all.[2]

The challenge of sustaining peace looms large in many other countries, including many that triumphantly embraced democracy in the 1980s and 1990s. Since 1989 national armies have intervened in the political affairs of 13 Sub-Saharan states: about one in four countries in the region.[3] In Pakistan in 1999, military leaders resumed control of democratic institutions under the banner of maintaining civil peace. In Zimbabwe in 2000–02, the elected government has undermined democracy and personal security by using the country's security forces to pursue its ends. In other countries the risk of a "failed state"—where security is fragmented, even privatized—is at least as

great as the risk of returning to brutal authoritarian rule.

Does that mean that civil order is incompatible with genuine democracy in these countries? Many would say yes, arguing that people need governments to focus on peace and state building first, and democracy building after. Others would draw the opposite conclusion: that people in these countries will never see enduring public peace and personal security until the police, military and other security forces are under firm democratic control.

Recent evidence supports the second argument, showing that established democracies are unlikely to experience civil war[4]—and that less rooted democracies are still better able than authoritarian regimes to cope with political unrest. Why? Probably because democracies, unlike dictatorships, offer non-violent ways of resolving political conflicts, and opposition groups have reason to hope that their turn will come. In the international realm research has also shown the near absence of war between democracies that supports the notion of *democratic peace.*[5] That democratic countries seem to enjoy a permanent peace among themselves challenges the widely held view that nation-states are doomed to exist in a state of war.

Yet history also shows that the early years of building a democratic state tend to be the most perilous: both for democracy and for civil peace. Between 1951 and 1999, 46 elected governments were forcibly overturned by authoritarian rule.[6] And nearly all of today's most stable democracies—including the United States—suffered a civil war early in their history. Most took several generations to develop a professional army under democratic civil control. This should give pause to any who would argue that the goals of building democracy and se-

Democracies, unlike dictatorships, offer non-violent ways of resolving political conflicts, and opposition groups have reason to hope that their turn will come

curing public order are perfectly aligned. Democratic governance is easier to start than to institutionalize (see the special contribution by President of Senegal Abdoulaye Wade).

This chapter considers the importance for human development of personal security and public order, underpinned by state security forces under firm democratic control. It asks why these things are so hard to achieve, even in well-established democracies. It then briefly assesses the implications for advancing the kind of democratic governance outlined in this Report—in all the world's democracies, but especially its newest ones, and in post-conflict situations such as Afghanistan, where the foundations of government and public order have to be rebuilt.

SECURING PEACE AND PUBLIC ACCOUNTABILITY

Building a functioning state requires a basic level of security. And by being responsive to the need for security, democratic governance can help lay the foundations for maintaining order and managing development. It follows that human development will be held back in any country where the military, police and other security-related institutions hold sway over democratic institutions or are not democratically accountable for much of their power or are fragmented and anarchic (box 4.1). Yet that is the situation in most developing countries today.

In the second half of the 20th century 50 countries moved from authoritarian military rule to democratically elected governments.[7] But armed interventions in the political affairs of the state remain too common (table 4.1). In many other developing democracies the military continues to exert profound political and economic influence (box 4.2). Moreover, security forces are often largely responsible for formulating security policy in new and old democracies alike.

In both democratic and non-democratic countries, parts of the security sector can become the tools of extremist politicians or parties. Or they may actually rest in private hands—with warlords, paramilitary groups or private security companies. Moreover, legitimate security services are often unable to deal with rising crime,

In the second half of the 20th century 50 countries moved from authoritarian military rule to democratically elected governments

---

SPECIAL CONTRIBUTION

Democratic governance in Africa

In the long, sombre history of Africa—including recurring periods of autocratic and military rule—it is no exaggeration to proclaim that at the beginning of the third millennium, many signs affirm that our continent is finally on the right path.

Stepping beyond the many plans forged since independence 40 years ago, African heads of state have for the first time conceived a long-term vision that outlines Africa's main priorities and the means to implement them in partnership with rich countries. The New Partnership for Africa's Development, adopted at the Lusaka Summit of July 2001, emphasizes three main principles as parameters for transforming Africa—enabling the continent to make up for lost time relative to developed countries:
• First, recognizing that good governance is indispensable for Africa's development.
• Second, accepting regional development as the approach chosen by African states.
• Finally, for the first time, opening Africa to private capital.

Within this framework the New Partnership for Africa's Development focuses on eight priority areas: infrastructure development in a broad sense, education,

health, agriculture, the environment, new information and communications technology, energy and access to the markets of developed countries. Building national capacity to meet these commitments will require administrative and civil service reforms, strong parliamentary oversight, more participatory decision-making at all levels, effective measures to combat corruption and comprehensive judicial reform.

New and courageous forms of democratic governance are sweeping across Africa. By encouraging political pluralism, free and open elections, civilian control of the military, a thriving private sector and the protection of labour unions and other civil society groups, Africa's leaders are bringing new hope and opportunities to their people.

Abdoulaye Wade
President of Senegal

TABLE 4.1

Who's guarding the guards? Countries experiencing armed interventions in the 1990s

Algeria, 1992
Burundi, 1993
Central African Republic, 1996
Comoros, 1998
Congo, 1993 and 1997
Congo, Dem. Rep., 1997
Côte d'Ivoire, 1999
Ethiopia, 1991
The Gambia, 1994
Guinea-Bissau, 1999
Haiti, 1991
Lesotho, 1994 and 1998
Myanmar, 1990
Niger, 1995
Nigeria, 1993
Pakistan, 1999
Rwanda, 1993
Sierra Leone, 1997
Somalia, 1991

Source: Chege 2001; Economist Intelligence Unit 2002; Eldis 2002; World Bank 2002a.

BOX 4.1

Who's who in the security sector

A country's security community can include a range of actors:

• *Organizations authorized to use force:* armed forces, police, paramilitary forces, gendarmeries, intelligence services (military and civilian), secret services, coast guards, border guards, customs authorities, reserve and local security units (civil defence forces, national guards, presidential guards, militias).

• *Civil management and oversight bodies:* president and prime minister, national security advisory bodies, legislature and legislative select committees, ministries of defence, internal affairs and foreign affairs, customary and traditional authorities, financial management bodies (finance ministries, budget offices, financial audit and planning units), civil society organizations (civilian review boards, public complaints commissions).

• *Justice and law enforcement institutions:* judiciary, justice ministries, prisons, criminal investigation and prosecution services, human rights commissions and ombudspersons, correctional services, customary and traditional justice systems.

• *Non-statutory security forces:* liberation armies, guerrilla armies, private bodyguard units, private security companies, political party militias.

• *Non-statutory civil society groups:* professional groups, the media, research organizations, advocacy organizations, religious organizations, non-governmental organizations, community groups.

Source: Ball and others forthcoming.

human rights violations or ethnic violence. In all these cases personal security and democratic governance are at risk, because the means for the legitimate use of force are not subject to democratic control.

THE HUMAN DEVELOPMENT CASE FOR DEMOCRATIC CIVIL CONTROL OF THE SECURITY SECTOR

Throughout history and in many developing countries today, authoritarian governments have resisted or overturned moves towards democracy—arguing that democracy is incompatible with public order and personal security. But the record suggests that the opposite is true: democratic civil control over state security forces, far from opposing personal security, is essential to it. Without that control the supposed guarantors of personal security can be its greatest threat.

During the 20th century "deaths by government" or "democides"—through direct violence or gross negligence in major disasters—were estimated at 170 million people, far higher than the number of deaths in wars (table 4.2).[8] The democides include millions of deaths in China, Germany and the Soviet Union, and many more on a smaller scale. None of this would have been possible without the support and efforts of police, intelligence services, the military and official and unofficial paramilitary forces. Where governments rely on security for their power base, security forces are often the main cause of insecurity for their citizens and neighbouring states.

Unchecked and unaccountable, security institutions often prey on the most vulnerable members of society, hampering daily struggles for survival and other basic freedoms. Throughout much of Africa there is widespread torture, intimidation and harassment of civilians by police on behalf of ruling regimes.[9] And worldwide, too many police forces are absent where needed, fail to respond to calls for help or arrive on the scene only when someone has been killed.

Despite all this, people desperately need the police to provide basic physical security in

TABLE 4.2

During the 20th century democides were far more common under totalitarian and authoritarian rule

Type of government	Number of unarmed people intentionally killed by government (millions)	Number of people killed in wars (millions)
Democratic	2	4
Authoritarian	29	15
Totalitarian	138	14

Source: Rummel 1997, table 4.

Old habits die hard—the long legacy of military rule

Normally hidden after the handover of power to elected governments, the military's political and economic influence remains strong and unaccountable in most young democracies—and in many older ones as well. From significant formal and informal business dealings to constitutional powers to dissolve elected governments to veiled threats to elected leaders who challenge military interests, the military remains an immensely powerful public institution. Its vast political and economic interests in many countries require democratic leaders to proceed cautiously, sometimes acceding to military demands to protect democratic imperatives. Well-known examples of strong military influence after direct rule by the armed forces include:

Nigeria. The role of Nigeria's armed forces in first overturning (1993) then restoring democratically elected leaders (1999) shows its position at the heart of government. The winner of the 1999 elections, President Olusegun Obasanjo, is a former military leader. And individuals in the military—especially retired officers—continue to exert political influence, providing substantial funds to political parties. Many former soldiers are now members of the National Assembly. Retired military officers also maintain pervasive influence in major sectors of the economy, including farming, banking, oil and air transport.

Chile. In 1989 constitutional reform brought parity between civilian and military representatives in government. But the ruling coalition, Concertacion, has struggled to eliminate seats for "designated" senators

(eight are appointed, and two former presidents serve for life), redefine the role of the National Security Council and review military funding. For instance, the armed forces receive 10% of the export earnings of Codelco, the state-owned copper company.

Indonesia. More than three years after the restoration of democratic rule, the military and police still maintain effective control over security policies and practices. They also continue to hold 38 appointed seats in the national legislature, though this is much lower than a few years ago, and several retired generals serve in the president's cabinet. About two-thirds of military spending is funded by military business interests outside the central government's control.

Turkey. Democratic rule in Turkey was interrupted by the armed forces in 1960–61, 1971–73 and 1980–83. The military has a constitutional and traditional role as the ultimate guardian of the constitution, and especially of the state's secular character. The 1982 constitution created a high-level National Security Council, with half its members drawn from the armed forces. The council's influence on national policy has grown in response to regional security concerns.

Argentina. Argentina's National Commission of the Disappeared scrutinized three military juntas that governed the country between 1976 and 1982, and sentenced several powerful figures. But pressure from the armed forces later led to presidential pardons for the convicted officers.

Source: Human Development Report Office; Ball and others 2002 ; Chege 2001; Omitoogun 2002; *The Economist* 2002.

In the United States poor people are more likely to be victims of violent crime, 1999

Family income of victims	Victimization rate (crimes per 1,000 people aged 12 and older)
Less than $7,500	59.5
$7,500–$14,999	45.6
$15,000–$24,999	36.1
$25,000–$34,999	39.1
$35,000–$49,999	30.8
$50,000–$74,999	33.7
$75,000 and above	24.1

Source: U.S. Bureau of Justice Statistics 1999, table 14.

their neighbourhoods. Participatory poverty assessments often find that lack of physical security is one of poor people's main concerns.[10] The irony is that those most in need of professional, well-functioning security forces—poor and socially excluded people—are generally the most suspicious of the services these public institutions provide, and not without reason. They recognize that, all too often, security forces are behind the proliferation of civil conflict.

Undemocratic governance of security forces can also distort security priorities. In many countries a bias towards military security has led governments to militarize police forces (further blurring their distinction with the military) or to seriously underfund them, undermining their capacity to guarantee people's safety and security. Especially in low-income countries, the police and other security forces have barely subsistence wages, limited or no training, corrupt management and high illiteracy levels. So, economic and social inequalities translate into large inequalities in personal security. In response, poor communities feel that they must create local militias or even resort to less organized forms of delivering "justice". Even in the United States poor people are much more likely than rich people to fall victim to violent crime (table 4.3). Moreover, in industrial countries businesses and individuals increasingly contribute to the $100 billion a year private global security industry—a direct consequence of weak public security.[11]

A POWER UNTO ITSELF: THE DIFFICULTY OF HOLDING SECURITY FORCES ACCOUNTABLE

Why has it been so difficult for democratic regimes—especially new ones—to rein in security forces and make them more responsive to people's security needs? Because history casts a long shadow. Elected leaders in fledgling democracies often depend on security forces, including military units, to stay in office because those forces are the most powerful in society. For the same reason, leaders may actively resist greater accountability and openness for the military, because they depend on its power for their own ends.

Another reason is the natural tendency towards secrecy and lack of transparency in security affairs. Security policies—both internal and external—are at the centre of power relations within and among societies. Yet they are also usually the area where civil society, the government and its oversight institutions have the least say. The lack of transparency and accountability is particularly problematic in budgeting, where a select few individuals in the executive branch make decisions on security policies and resources. Key officials in the ministry of finance and other parts of the executive are often excluded from decision-making—or find their decisions circumvented. Parliamentary bodies—which may even have oversight authority in the national constitution—and the media and civil society are routinely kept in the dark.

Making matters worse in many countries is that the military has income sources outside the formal budget. In Nigeria under General Sani Abacha, a large part of the Petroleum Fund went to the armed forces. Or the military has sizable business activities. The Chinese People's Liberation Army had an extensive business empire. This began to be dismantled by the central government in 1998, causing the official defence budget to increase.[12] Such extra-budgetary activities tend to be almost impossible to oversee and control, giving armed forces considerable leeway to run their affairs independently of any democratic control.

And given the secrecy that often shrouds arms purchases, the procurement of expensive weapons by unaccountable military leaders is prone to corruption even when direct military rule has ended. Procurement decisions are often based on foreign policy, not just technical criteria. That allows military decision-makers, and their civilian counterparts in the executive branch, to hide personal financial interests behind poorly defined claims of "national security".

Strict military hierarchies and a lack of parliamentary and auditing control in security matters further limit careful scrutiny of arms contracts. According to one U.S. government study, about half the known bribes since the mid-1990s were for defence contracts—and those are just the known bribes.[13] Arms dealers from both industrial and developing countries conduct their dealings in private and often route arms and payments through intermediate countries that do not cooperate in corruption cases (table 4.4). The global arms bazaar, underpinned by powerful economic interests, reinforces excessive secrecy and corruption in many countries' security sectors.

Governments and their security forces have an obligation to protect the security of their borders and their people. This perhaps justifies more confidentiality than applies to other parts of government. But in democratic systems there should also be an obligation for policy-makers and security forces to be accountable to the public for their decisions and for their use of public resources. Minor adjustments can accommodate legitimate needs for confidentiality without violating the principles of sound public management.

Effective accountability in security matters will never materialize if oversight institutions lack the capacity to assess security activities. Without that capacity, a cycle of ignorance will persist. When legitimate civilian actors are denied participation or a monitoring role over security policy-making, they lack detailed knowledge of security issues. This limited knowledge then enables security forces to argue that decision-making should rest with those with relevant knowledge—with the security forces.

Core principles for democratic governance of the security sector can help governments bal-

In democratic systems there should also be an obligation for policy-makers and security forces to be accountable to the public for their decisions and for their use of public resources

TABLE 4.4
During 1996–2001 a few countries dominated global exports of conventional weapons

Exporter	Exports (billions of U.S. dollars)	Share of world total (percent)
United States	54	45
Russian Federation	21	17
France	11	9
United Kingdom	8	7
Germany	6	5
Other	20	17
Total	121	100

Note: Data are trend indicator values, which indicate only the volume of international arms transfers, not their actual financial value. Published reports of arms transfers provide only partial information because not all transfers are fully reported. These estimates are conservative and may understate actual transfers of conventional weapons.

Source: SIPRI 2002.

BOX 4.3

Principles of democratic governance in the security sector

- Ultimate authority on key security matters must rest with elected representatives.
- Security organizations should operate in accord with international and constitutional law and respect human rights.
- Information about security planning and resources must be widely available, both within government and to the public. Security must be managed using a comprehensive, disciplined approach. This means that security forces should be subject to the same principles of public sector management as other parts of government, with small adjustments for confidentiality appropriate to national security.
- Civil-military relations must be based on a well-articulated hierarchy of authority between civil authorities and defence forces, on the mutual rights and obligations of civil authorities and defence forces, and on a relationship with civil society based on transparency and respect for human rights.
- Civil authorities need to have the capacity to exercise political control over the operations and financing of security forces.
- Civil society must have the means and capacity to monitor security forces and provide constructive input into the political debate on security policy.
- Security personnel must be trained to discharge their duties professionally and should reflect the diversity of their societies—including women and minorities.
- Policy-makers must place a high priority on fostering regional and local peace.

Holding the military and the police accountable

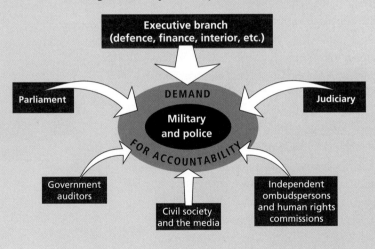

Source: Based on U.K. Department for International Development 2000; see also Nathan 1994; Bland 1999; and Legault 2001.

---

ance the need for secrecy with the need for greater democratic control (box 4.3). But few countries approach this ideal, and democratic governance is being held back by a systematic failure to transform the role of the military and the police.

CORE PRIORITIES FOR MORE DEMOCRATIC GOVERNANCE OF THE SECURITY SECTOR

Countries attempting to achieve democratic governance of security forces face three challenges. The first is establishing direct leadership of security forces by executive departments, fiscal oversight by parliament and specialized auditing bodies and monitoring by the media and civil society. The second challenge is developing a culture of professionalism and political neutrality within security forces. The third is clearly separating an effective police force from the military and encouraging community policing.

Even in long-standing democracies the relationships between civilians and their security forces rarely measure up to the ideal. But encouraging examples in several new democracies—in South Africa, Eastern Europe and previously coup-prone nations in Latin America—show that progress is possible. They also show that success can give added momentum to the broader challenge of strengthening democratic institutions and promoting democratic politics.

STRENGTHENING DEMOCRATIC CONTROL OVER SECURITY INSTITUTIONS BY THE STATE AND CIVIL SOCIETY

With the move to democracy, formal control of security forces is supposed to be transferred to civil authorities. But real control and public accountability often lag far behind. In many countries the military has a highly privileged position in the allocation of national resources. Similarly, spending on security forces does not compete on an equal footing with spending to meet the basic needs of all people, particularly the vulnerable. Democratic governance requires that decisions about the size, structure and operations of security forces rest on solid legal foundations, exercised with political responsibility. Civil authorities need to be in control, but they also need to give clear guidance to security forces, working with them and respecting their expertise.

The budget process is the main instrument for transparency and accountability. Budgets provide a detailed statement of plans to which people can hold parliament accountable, and to whose proper execution parliament can hold security forces accountable. Managing security spending has four related elements:
- Identifying the needs and key objectives of the security sector as a whole and the specific

missions that different security forces will be asked to undertake.

- Determining what is affordable.
- Allocating resources based on priorities within and between different security agencies.
- Ensuring the efficient, effective use of resources.

Executive departments—including the chief executive and ministries of defence, finance and interior—must play the central role in governing and regulating the fiscal accountability of security institutions. Strengthening the capacity of civilians to manage and monitor the budgets of security forces is therefore a high priority, especially where military elites dominate decision-making because of unequal power and knowledge.

All spending on different security forces—their personnel, operations and equipment—should be included in their budgets. Those budgets should also indicate how this spending is financed. Yet most security budgets meet neither condition. Intrabudgetary allocations are opaque, and total spending—which may include funds from a number of departments—remains unclear. In countries with extensive off-budget activities, governments themselves often lack accurate information. That is why a primary yardstick for accountability—comparing plans and execution—cannot be used. Officials in the ministry of defence and other parts of the executive branch need defence-specific technical knowledge to make appropriate decisions on defence policy, budgeting and procurement.

Addressing the off-budget problem is often highly political, requiring fundamental long-term changes in civil-military relations.[14] The quality of leadership in the executive branch is critical in determining the extent to which legal and cultural norms for democratic governance find acceptance. Efforts to create a security force that follows democratic principles and sound public spending will succeed only if a country's political and administrative leadership is committed to creating effective, accountable institutions and ensuring that they function well (box 4.4).

Mature democracies suggest that a wide range of formal oversight bodies can strengthen

---

BOX 4.4

Democracy and security sector reform: South Africa's experience in the 1990s

Under apartheid South Africa was a highly militarized society, with defence spending accounting for 19% of government spending in fiscal 1978. In the late 1980s military spending accounted for 4% of GDP, making South Africa the continent's largest military spender. The power of the apartheid-era military—the South African Defence Force—penetrated deeply into the lives of South Africans and directly influenced political decision-making.

The dismantling of apartheid and the transition to democracy between 1990 and 1994 coincided with efforts to restructure the armed forces. Between 1989 and 1998 the military budget fell by more than half (in real terms), and the Department of Defence retired or transferred thousands of military personnel as part of demobilization and rationalization programmes. In addition, defence policy now emphasizes regional cooperation rather than destabilization. Other changes have included dismantling the nuclear weapons industry, closing military bases around the country, destroying vast quantities of surplus weapons, abolishing conscription for white males and overall downsizing to develop an affordable and professional "core force". The defence department's current programme aims to reduce force levels from 86,000 to 65,000 personnel.

The progress in reforming South Africa's security sector is largely due to high-level political engagement and efforts to put the military firmly under civilian control. A 1996 review process involving government representatives, civilian specialists and non-governmental organizations reoriented the mission, roles and tasks of the post-apartheid armed forces—the South African National Defence Force (SANDF)—making them defensive rather than offensive. The armed forces are now subordinate and fully accountable to parliament and the executive, and are to respect human rights and the democratic political process.

Still, the legacy of 30 years of militarization has been difficult to eradicate, and the armed forces still wield considerable political, economic and ideological power. Sometimes deployed to contain violent crime, the National Defence Force has also started to re-emerge as an instrument of foreign policy. These expanded roles may jeopardize the military's political neutrality and professionalism, impeding its ability to perform its primary role of safeguarding citizens against external threats.

Source: Batchelor, Cock and McKenzie 2000; Nathan 2000.

---

and enforce democratic civil control of the security sector, particularly by providing fiscal transparency. These include specialized parliamentary oversight committees and independent audit boards. But such bodies are effective only to the extent that they have the information and expertise needed to do their jobs. Many legislatures are not equipped to play even a limited role in oversight, partly because of decades—and sometimes centuries—of executive supremacy and partly because of the culture of secrecy. Confidentiality should not be the rule—it should be the well-justified exception. A culture of secrecy and unaccountable authority can undermine civil oversight from day one.

The lesson for governance reform is that even modest injections of transparency can yield benefits. When security budgeting and other aspects of security policy move closer to the ideals of transparency (see box 4.3), chances are they will also move closer to true democratic civil control. Increased transparency strengthens the hand of formal democratic institutions such as parliament and the judiciary. It also unleashes the potential for civil society and the media to strengthen civil accountability and control by scrutinizing security budgets, providing technical input and opening security policies to public debate.

Citizens can help shape security policy even in the poorest countries. In Sierra Leone in 1998, shortly after the restoration of the elected government that had been overthrown by the army and Revolutionary United Front rebels, the executive branch began developing plans for reconstituting the armed forces. In response, civil society organizations held multistakeholder consultations and offered the government a range of reform proposals—including widely circulating photographs of all recruits so that civilians could vet them for human rights abuses. The government responded favourably to many of these suggestions.

Central and Eastern Europe also show that win-win solutions are possible when democratic institutions are combined with new forms of participatory democracy. Popular participation promotes public trust and boosts the morale of security forces even as it helps hold security actors accountable. These efforts are leading to new thinking about democracy and security.

Since the early 1990s many Central and Eastern European countries—the Czech Republic, Estonia, Hungary, Latvia, Lithuania, Poland, Slovenia and to a lesser extent Bulgaria and Romania—have been democratizing civil-military relations.[15] With few exceptions, there is little threat of direct military intervention in domestic politics. New legal and institutional mechanisms for civilian oversight of military affairs have created opportunities for greater transparency and for participation in security policy by parliaments, media, academics and civil society organizations. In forging a more holistic approach to civil-military relations, these democratic reforms have buttressed steps in many countries to establish civilian mechanisms

for making defence policy and managing the security sector.

But when interior ministry troops, paramilitary police and intelligence services are drawn into domestic political struggles, efforts to improve democratic civil control are often jeopardized. In the Russian Federation and Ukraine interior ministries have 100,000 troops and heavy equipment to manage internal political dissent.[16] So it is tempting for elected officials (especially extremist politicians) to manipulate security forces for party purposes—or worse, to create non-statutory armed groups such as the Ogoni militia in Nigeria. Dealing with these and other issues of building state capacity is essential for consolidating effective democratic control.

BUILDING PROFESSIONALISM AND POLITICAL NEUTRALITY

Efforts to transform security institutions must also force change from within. This requires a shift in internal culture and new incentives for members to respect democratic civil authority and promote the public interest. Senior officers need to take a firm stand against corruption. They also need to make clear that they do not tolerate the diversion of state resources in other ways—such as using military and police vehicles for private purposes.

Achieving these goals can be a matter of professional training. Indeed, in the long run there is probably no substitute for military training and broadly based education that teaches soldiers to respect human rights and abide by principles of democratic governance. National military academies do this, but they need to be tied to high professional standards for recruitment, instruction and promotion that are less prone to political interference and corruption. Perhaps even more urgent is professional training of police officers, which can do much for accountability and public trust. Induction programmes for police officers should focus on what it means to be a police officer in a democratic society, with special emphasis on policing by consent.[17]

Achieving these goals also requires sufficient public revenue. Without appropriate

Citizens can help shape security policy even in the poorest countries

equipment and decent wages, security forces will suffer from poor discipline and corruption. For police, public resources can sometimes be supplemented by innovative public-private partnerships. Since 1990 the Citizen's Police Liaison Committee of Karachi, Pakistan, has provided free health care to police officers injured in the line of duty. Financed by businesses, the committee also recently provided gas connections to flats occupied by police officers and their families, as well as water lines, furniture, lighting and a children's park. Such public-private initiatives raise the morale of police officers—another element in building a more effective, corruption-free police force.

In addition to pursuing these crucial long-term goals, democratic leaders must work to change the behaviour of security forces today—especially by punishing human rights violations and unprofessional conduct. Professional codes of police, military and intelligence conduct and review tribunals within security services can help in this regard. So can civilian commissions that investigate possible excesses. Postwar investigations of human rights violations during civil wars in El Salvador, Guatemala and Sierra Leone, often launched by governments and civil society organizations, have been important steps towards greater accountability in the security sector. They helped expose human rights violations committed covertly—or even openly—by security forces.

Over the medium and long term, judicial reform is also critical in enforcing accountability in security forces. Police action against crime cannot promote personal security if judges can be bribed easily or if there are no prisons for convicted criminals. When judicial systems are controlled by privileged individuals whose appointments are merely political rewards, law enforcement is likely to be partial—and rule is more likely to be *by law* (which may permit manipulation of the courts) than *of law*.[18] When judicial systems fail to perform basic tasks, including issuing warrants and other legal orders, police officers often must resort to illegal actions to perform regular functions.[19] Corrupt judicial and penitentiary systems also undermine the professionalism and credibility of the security sector if they allow crimes by soldiers or police officers to go unpunished.

SEPARATING THE POLICE FROM THE MILITARY AND PROMOTING COMMUNITY OUTREACH

In many countries the accountability and behaviour of security forces also suffer from a failure to clearly demarcate between the military (as the guardian of external security) and the police (as the guardian of domestic law and order). Mixing the functions and firepower of the police with those of the military risks "overkill" and unnecessary violence, as in Haiti and parts of Central America. It also raises the prospect of politicians turning the police into an instrument of arbitrary power—as in Zimbabwe in 2000–02.

In Botswana, Ghana, Mauritius, Senegal and South Africa a clear division of labour between the military and the police has encouraged professionalism in both.[20] Other Latin American governments with long histories of military control, including El Salvador and Guatemala, have also been separating the military from the police.[21]

Such reforms need to be combined with efforts to enhance the standing and capacity of the police. Even in communities where physical abuse and corruption by the police have been the norm, efforts to build trust and confidence can foster a new relationship between the police and the people. One way is for the police to get involved in the lives of young people, ethnic minorities and low-income groups. Another is to support community policing (box 4.5).

Police forces with officers from diverse backgrounds tend to respond better to the challenges of diverse communities. Appointing and training female police officers in the state of Para, Brazil, increased reports of violence against women and girls to police and hospitals. In Bosnia and Herzegovina and the Former Yugoslav Republic of Macedonia more ethnically balanced police forces are fostering trust and respect for the police. In addition, police forces should not give special treatment to certain units, such as criminal investigation and narcotics. Doing so can create serious internal tensions.

In many countries the accountability and behaviour of security forces suffer from a failure to clearly demarcate between the military and the police

Such reforms take time and deep political commitment. For change to be sustained, democratic leaders must ensure that security institutions feel ownership in the process. Such reforms pose unique challenges but also yield unique benefits—for the security of citizens and the credibility of democratization. South Africa's police reforms are a notable example. After the 1994 elections, members of government and parliament acquired expertise in oversight and leadership through self-education and collaboration with unions, churches and research institutions. Despite many challenges, strong political leadership and partnerships with civil society are leading to a less militarized, more professional police force.

CONDITIONS FOR CHANGE IN THE SECURITY SECTOR

Substantive security sector reform involves so many deep-rooted aspects of local and national governance that it can seem like a hopeless task. It has a political dimension (civil control of security forces), an economic dimension (consumption of resources by security forces), a social dimension (guaranteeing citizens' security) and a strong institutional dimension (professionalizaton of the security sector and institutional separation of the various actors).[22] But a number of developments can help trigger major security sector reforms:

- *Economic constraints:* reforms result from financial pressures to downsize the military—as in Uganda and other African countries.
- *Civilian control:* a power shift occurs and the military steps down by choice or by force—as in Indonesia and many Latin American countries.
- *Western mainstreaming:* the armed forces are modernized as part of efforts to join the European Union or North Atlantic Treaty Organization (NATO)—as in many Central and Eastern European countries.
- *New armies:* often funded and initially trained by foreign donors and influenced by civil society to respect human rights—as in Bosnia and Herzegovina, East Timor, El Salvador, Estonia, Latvia and Lithuania.
- *Scandals:* often media-driven and influential in reforming the police, intelligence agencies and civil-military relations—as in many industrial countries.

When such developments are combined with committed leadership and an engaged civil society, conditions are ripe for significant democratic reforms of security forces that can reinforce broader political change—especially in countries recovering from violent armed conflict.

DEMOCRATIC PEACEBUILDING IN WARTORN SOCIETIES

In wartorn societies, establishing effective control over the use of armed force is the foundation for all other progress. Without it, peacebuilders face the constant risk of reversal in building a functioning state. At the extreme, as in Afghanistan and Somalia, the result will be rampant lawlessness and a fertile environment for violent extremism.

Timely international intervention can mitigate the tension between building civil peace and establishing democratic control. How? By establishing an environment of civic peace for national democratic institutions to develop. In the early 1990s alone, more peacekeeping missions were undertaken than during the UN's first four and one-half decades. But while this new generation of peace operations may help end violence, they alone cannot promote durable, democratic peace. Internal tensions will never be

---

BOX 4.5

Higher regard for police through community policing

Police reforms, especially those creating new forces, must foster new relationships with local communities. Community policing can overcome mistrust and advance collaboration between communities and police by giving people a substantial role in defining and guiding the performance of policing.

In 1997 a community policing pilot in Hatillo, Costa Rica, a neighbourhood in the capital, engaged the community in the fight against crime through four local police stations and a citizens advisory committee to the precinct commander. The police stations provided regular patrol services, while the committee identified security problems and possible solutions. A year after the project began, crime in the area had fallen by 10%, perceptions of insecurity by 17% and fear of being robbed at home by 32%. Although 71% of the people surveyed in Hatillo believed that crime had increased in the country, only 38% thought that was true for Hatillo. Moreover, only 8% of those polled claimed never to have seen police in the neighbourhood, down from 35% before the project. The project helped improve the image of the police force in Hatillo, and its success led to its expansion in other communities.

Source: Neild 1998.

easily eliminated when conflict and poor governance have fractured the foundations of the state. This strengthens the case for pre-emptive democratic peacebuilding, to promote peaceful resolution of simmering conflicts before they turn into wars.

Where basic order has broken down, the pressures of limited time and resources produce tension between restoring civil peace and establishing democratic control. Cambodia in the early 1990s suggests that holding national and local elections in an atmosphere of widespread violence and mistrust can unravel the peace process or legitimize the warring parties, as they did in Bosnia and Herzegovina after the Dayton Peace Accords. But experiences in East Timor, El Salvador, Mozambique and other post-conflict settings suggest that marked progress is possible in three key areas:

• Reforming or creating a professional military and police.

• Managing the demobilization and reintegration of combatants.

• Creating political space for broadly based reconciliation.

REFORMING OR CREATING A PROFESSIONAL MILITARY AND POLICE

As noted, the military and the police have blurred roles in many developing countries. During wars the distinction breaks down altogether, with the armed forces taking responsibility for both the external and internal security of the state. This suggests a need to identify the main security threats in wartorn societies and to devise appropriate policies for the armed forces, the police, intelligence services and other security forces. Among the main tasks include making the armed forces more manageable, affordable and professional, and clearly separated from the police.

After armed conflicts, many countries in West and Southern Africa and Central America have overhauled the composition and role of their militaries. Sierra Leone and South Africa absorbed former combatants into their armed forces while reforming their militaries' missions and orientations. In Afghanistan it is hoped that a multiethnic army will resolve factional

fighting among ethnic Tajiks, Pashtuns, Hazaras and others. A similar experiment in Bosnia and Herzegovina offers lessons for other wartorn countries (box 4.6).

Developing a civil (apolitical) police force—in some cases from scratch—is generally a priority in peace agreements. It is especially important for promoting civil peace after war, when organized crime, weapon smuggling and violence are rampant—and likely to surge as communities are flooded with unemployed combatants. From El Salvador and Gaza to Bosnia and Herzegovina, Mozambique and Rwanda, the transition from civil war to civil society has been linked to broadly based police forces that are democratically accountable, impartial, depoliticized and composed of different political contingents and ethnic groups.[23] Such forces can emerge only through effective training—particularly in the skills of community policing and other specialized training—and through better ethnic and gender balance. It may be tempting to convert soldiers to police officers, but this should be handled with care. Soldiers, especially those with human rights

BOX 4.6

Building affordable, ethnically balanced security forces in Bosnia and Herzegovina

With the signing of the Dayton Peace Accords in 1995, the international community sought to deal with the three belligerent wartime armies that had caused so much damage in Bosnia and Herzegovina—the Bosnian-Muslim forces, the Bosnian-Croat Croatian Defense Council and the Bosnian-Serb Army. But assistance soon broadened to establish standards for democratic governance across the country's spectrum of security and non-security agencies (military, police, customs and border service, judicial, corrections, intelligence). Not since the end of World War II has the international community committed such resources to reform a country's security sector.

Various initiatives have sought to build confidence between the former armies and create conditions for appropriate, common, cost-effective, durable security. High military spending, consuming as much as 40% of the public budget, remains a major concern. But with the slow demobilization of 370,000 soldiers, out of an estimated 400,000 in 1995, the military budget has become more manageable. Even so, substantial resources are needed to create jobs for, educate and counsel former soldiers.

More challenging than creating affordable security forces has been reducing mistrust among former combatants. And until the problem of three armies in one state is resolved, everything achieved in implementing democratic civil control and professionalizing the armed forces will remain fragile and uncertain. International planners hope that defence policies will converge by 2005, allowing a common state-level approach. There has been consensus-building among the Bosnian armies, with joint training exercises, stringent selection criteria for new police officers and the January 2001 inauguration of the first multiethnic Bosnian contingent to serve as UN military observers abroad—a good example of peacebuilding in action.

Source: King, Dorn and Hodes forthcoming.

violations, may have methods and experience poorly suited to the police.

The international community can help build accountable, effective police forces in post-conflict environments. Until 1989 only three peace-keeping operations included UN Civilian Police units. With the end of the cold war, space opened for international assistance to provide more police aid. Besides regional and bilateral assistance, the UN Civilian Police is now a common presence in a new generation of peace-keeping, although many argue that its role requires further development.

In Cambodia the UN Civilian Police provided public security and arrested suspects. In El Salvador and Haiti it helped design and train a new civilian police force—experiences recently replicated in East Timor and Kosovo. As the United Nations assumes more complicated peacebuilding tasks involving public security, its Civilian Police and the broader development community require well-funded international police officers who are not only good cops, but experts in building institutions— police with experience setting up police academies, organizing and restructuring police organizations and fostering community policing that serves citizens rather than entrenching the power of ruling regimes (see box 4.5).[24] To succeed, such interventions require support for domestic constituencies for police reform. They also require collecting accurate, credible data on domestic crime—and convincing leaders of wartorn countries that repressive policing is part of the problem, not part of the solution.

MANAGING THE DEMOBILIZATION AND REINTEGRATION OF COMBATANTS

Demobilizing combatants and reintegrating them into normal life is one of the most challenging priorities in post-conflict situations. Since 1990 major post-war demobilizations have occurred in a wide range of countries: Bosnia and Herzegovina, El Salvador, Eritrea, Ethiopia, Guatemala, Haiti, Mozambique, Nicaragua, Sierra Leone and Uganda. In addition, smaller-scale demobilizations have taken place in Chad, Lebanon, Mali, Panama, Rwanda and South Africa. Such efforts require as much participation as possible so that affected groups will take ownership of reform.

Many actors have a stake in the outcomes. They include demobilized combatants—male and female former child soldiers, government soldiers and guerrillas. They also include families of former combatants, communities where former combatants resettle and other groups trying to reintegrate—such as returned refugees and internally displaced people. And they include local security forces, government agencies, local and international non-governmental organizations, the United Nations and its agencies and other official donors. But because of time pressures and the vast number of people and groups involved, many of these actors have had little voice in the design of demobilization and reintegration programmes. Indeed, the process has often been led by outside agencies, muting the voices of local people.

Limited participation may be inevitable in the immediate aftermath of conflict. But demobilization and reintegration programmes should be structured so that they can be adjusted over time, through inclusive dialogue with former combatants, their families, affected communities and others. In Uganda, to test the feasibility of their reintegration, some soldiers were allowed to visit their home areas before demobilization. And interactions between former soldiers and veteran field officers helped the demobilization in Rwanda in the late 1990s.

Unsurprisingly, targeted assistance to former combatants has generated heated debate, raising issues of fairness and accountability. There are humanitarian arguments for giving former combatants special support: after demobilization, they are unemployed and far from home. In some cases they have given years of their lives to fight for what they considered the good of their country. But they may also have been forcibly recruited into the armed forces (as with the Derg army in Ethiopia and Renamo, the Mozambican National Resistance). And they may have great difficulty re-establishing themselves in civilian life, perhaps threatening the peace process by getting involved in criminal activity or violent political opposition.

Support for former combatants can also reduce illicit trade in small arms and light weapons.

Demobilizing combatants and reintegrating them into normal life is one of the most challenging priorities in post-conflict situations

Such trade—valued at $4–6 billion a year—is an attractive source of revenue for former combatants in poor, conflict-ridden societies (box 4.7). In Sierra Leone these issues were taken into account when disarming and demobilizing more than 75,000 combatants since 1998, including roughly 7,000 child combatants.[25]

In most cases former combatants are far outnumbered by returning refugees and other people displaced by war who need to be readily equipped for myriad post-conflict challenges, such as landmines (box 4.8). Given scarce resources, demobilization support programmes will thus have to balance helping former combatants too much and too little. Consensus seems to have developed that special efforts for former combatants are generally necessary and justified during demobilization and resettlement—but that support in the reintegration phase should, as much as possible, be community- and area-based and part of broader development programmes. Indeed, support from communities is often crucial for the reintegration of former combatants. These findings underscore the need for inclusive processes that promote reconciliation and peacebuilding by promoting day-to-day cooperation on the ground.

CREATING POLITICAL SPACE FOR BROADLY BASED RECONCILIATION

Armed conflict is not conducive to political openness and participation. In fact, it often shuts them down. Armed conflict is also the worst enemy of human rights, poor people, minority rights and freedom of information. The period before a cease-fire (or sometimes military victory) and immediately after a war are thus critical to establishing more open, inclusive politics. Ending a war can be as destabilizing as war itself, and it is impossible to democratize political decision-making immediately. But there needs to be as much openness and participation as possible for peace and true reconciliation to take root—and for strengthening civil society and democratically minded parts of the population.

To be specific, if the termination of a war is based on a peace agreement, the leading

---

BOX 4.7

Reducing small arms through democratic peacebuilding

Worldwide, the uncontrolled proliferation of an estimated 550 million small arms—including 100 million assault rifles—contributes to some 500,000 firearm-related deaths each year. Their availability and use are not confined to conflicts alone, but also fuel violent crime, economic exploitation and illicit trafficking in goods and people. One remarkable effort to collect and curb the flow of small arms is in Albania, where hundreds of thousands of military weapons and explosives are still circulating. Nearly a third of the weapons looted from government arsenals in 1997 have been retrieved, and more than 100,000 weapons have been destroyed.

The programme's success can largely be attributed to extensive public awareness and advocacy highlighting the socio-economic impact of small arms, and to comprehensive data on small arms for a regional early warning system. Besides increasing transparency, direct community participation has been invaluable in the exchange of looted weapons for public works support such as road construction, school rehabilitation and installation of street lights and public telephones.

Building government capacity—within a broader security reform effort—is critical to implementing a comprehensive small arms reduction strategy, including legislative and regulatory development, law enforcement, tracing and marking, stockpile management and security, and destroying small arms and light weapons retrieved. Cooperation among customs, police, intelligence and arms control officials at the national and international levels is another important aspect of the UN action programme to combat the spread of small arms and light weapons. An International Code of Conduct on Arms Transfers, recently proposed by Nobel Peace Prize Laureate and former President of Costa Rica Dr. Oscar Arias, would further restrict the flow of deadly weapons—both small and large are used to kill or injure thousands of civilians every year.

Source: Arias Foundation, BASIC and Saferworld 1997; Muggah and Berman 2001; UN 2001b; UNDP 2001a, 2002a.

BOX 4.8

Clearing landmines requires civilian and community empowerment

Ninety countries are affected by landmines and unexploded ordinance, with rough estimates of 15,000–20,000 mine victims each year. To destroy landmines, humanitarian mine action programmes empower civilian authorities, not just the military, to set priorities and assume leadership of long-term demining programmes. If left to the military alone, demining activities might serve only narrow strategic interests, ignoring areas where mine clearance could benefit civilians. In Thailand the military has cooperated with civil society groups in clearance based on results of the Landmines Impact Survey. In Afghanistan, through a range of partnerships, 24 million square metres of mined and suspected land were cleared in 2000. Other recent success stories come from Azerbaijan, Mozambique and Tajikistan.

During 2000 and early 2001 mine clearance operations were carried out in 76 countries and regions. Successful mine action programmes—which include mine awareness, capacity building, victim assistance, socio-economic assistance and advocacy in addition to mine removal and destruction—encourage the return of refugees and internally displaced persons. They also help in the economic and social rehabilitation of communities, particularly in food security.

Broad, high-level political commitment sustains these multifaceted programmes, which cost an estimated $200 million a year. Clearing a small field that might contain only one mine can cost thousands of dollars, and undoing global landmine contamination will cost billions. In heavily mined countries, mine action programmes are a peacebuilding priority, essential for helping humanitarian and development organizations operate effectively and reducing the threat of renewed violent conflict.

Source: ICBL 2001; Canada, Department of Foreign Affairs and International Trade 2001, United Nations 2001a.

voices in shaping the country's future will be the negotiating parties and their teams. Civilians, particularly women, are usually heavily underrepresented in peace talks (box 4.9). The overwhelming predominance of combatants in negotiations can seriously constrain the democratic development of these societies and reduce the long-term stability of peace. But the inter-Congolese dialogue and the greater involvement of women in peacemaking elsewhere suggest that this problem is slowly gaining wider recognition.

Peacemakers must also recognize that long, deadly civil conflicts completely transform societies—whether through the displacement of local populations, destruction of infrastructure or upheaval of traditional family and social networks. In wartorn societies such as Sri Lanka, male combatants are recruited from poor communities. For their survival, women in these communities have often transcended their traditional gender roles in terms of family, work and community. Peace negotiations and local leaders must take these radically changed realities

into account when designing programmes for recovery and reconciliation. Giving a greater voice to previously marginalized groups is not only morally right, it is also practical.

A growing number of peace processes address the need for strengthening democratic institutions and protecting human rights, including provisions for creating or fortifying national human rights institutions. In 1992 a UN-sponsored peace agreement in El Salvador created the Procurador para la Defensa de los Derechos Humanos to prevent human rights violations in areas such as police conduct, prison conditions, children's rights and violence against women.[26] Bosnia and Herzegovina`s Human Rights Ombudsman, established by the 1995 Dayton Peace Accords, has extensive powers to investigate, report, initiate and intervene in court proceedings.[27] Given the severe human rights problems and pressures facing the judicial branch in most wartorn societies, human rights institutions are often essential in the transition to democracy by promoting international human rights commitments and providing key administrative oversight—especially in the security sector. Other recent examples in East Timor, Guatemala and Kosovo underscore their importance to democratic peacebuilding in states emerging from civil and other complex conflicts.

To build a more stable and inclusive future, states in post-conflict situations need to deal with the past. Many countries recovering from wars are exploring avenues for justice, such as community trials in East Timor and the *gacaca* process in Rwanda, that may help build public support.[28] In addition, war crimes tribunals— and in the future, a permanent International Criminal Court—are redressing past injustices (see chapter 5). Truth commissions have also provided a way for people to voice grievances about past atrocities—and give them a feeling that justice has been done (box 4.10). Since 1974 more than 20 such commissions have sought to set straight countries' historical records, with varying objectives, structures and results. Such processes face the challenge of managing the tension between justice (retribution) and reconciliation (forgiveness). They do not always strike the best balance. But in many societies emerging from brutal conflict, such

---

BOX 4.9

Bringing women to the negotiating table

In most post-war circumstances it is not easy to broaden participation in the formal peace process. Peace negotiations and the design and implementation of peacebuilding and reconstruction efforts—including security sector reform—usually involve only a small group of people. In many cases they are men, especially those who had taken up weapons. Rewarded with a place at the negotiation table, they obtain a strong say in post-war policies and institutions, including the military and police.

In most cases women are almost completely excluded from post-war decisionmaking. Only recently has their role in the various aspects and phases of peacemaking and peacebuilding been recognized internationally. Women bring to peace talks a practical understanding of real life security concerns. And their commitment to peace is often critical to ensure the sustainability of peace agreements. From Burundi to Guatemala to Northern Ireland, their involvement in peace

processes has shown real benefits for vulnerable groups. In Somalia 100 women, representing six clans, participated in the Somali National Peace Conference in May 2000. As a result 25 seats were allocated to women in the 245-member Transitional National Assembly.

Among initiatives to correct ongoing biases, the UN Security Council adopted a resolution in October 2000 to urge UN member states to increase representation of women at all decision-making levels in institutions and mechanisms for preventing, managing and resolving conflict. It calls on all actors negotiating and implementing peace agreements to adopt a gender perspective and include women in implementing mechanisms of the peace agreement. The decision to include four women in the Bonn, Germany, talks on the future of Afghanistan in December 2001 and two women to serve at senior levels in the interim government of Afghanistan show that progress in this area is possible.

Source: UN Information Centre Bonn 2001; Human Development Report Office; Anderlini 2000; Ball and others 2002.

mechanisms may be the best—and only—option available.

DEMOCRATIZING SECURITY IN A FRAGMENTED WORLD

Conflict is part of every society. The question is, how can societies give expression to conflict and provide open political space for all groups without generating violence and war? Democracies are supposed to provide the answer, with open political debate and open competition for power. But many well-established democracies have not eliminated violent conflicts—as illustrated by recent violence in Gujarat, India, and by long-standing conflicts in Northern Ireland and Sri Lanka. Elsewhere, democratic processes have been ruthlessly undermined by authoritarian, often military, rule that squeezes the space for civil society and democratic politics. Peace and personal security are the losers, especially when the accountability and effectiveness of security forces are eroded.

The alarming number of conflict-prone countries underscores the need for a broader approach to conflict prevention—one that avoids artificial segmentation between pre-conflict, crisis and post-conflict. It also indicates the need for an appropriate mix of political, security, humanitarian and developmental responses. Securing a just, sustainable peace in conflict-prone situations means building strong, transparent states with professional, civilian-led military and police. It means developing a democratic framework that tolerates diversity. It means building an open civil society that promotes democratic governance and personal security. And it means instilling in all state institutions—but especially the security forces—a culture of democracy rooted in respect for the rule of law and individual rights and dignity. This is the essence of democratic peacebuilding.

In countries recovering from violent armed conflict—such as Afghanistan (box 4.11) and Sierra Leone—the human costs of failing to achieve democratic governance of the security forces are clear. But these are just extreme examples of the security dilemmas that all countries face in deciding how to confront internal

and external security threats such as widespread violent crime or domestic and international terrorism.

In the United States and elsewhere, heightened concerns about terrorism have triggered debates on the dangers of compromising human rights for national security reasons. Antiterrorist measures taken in response to these and other new security threats often risk violating human rights or at least make it easier for them to be violated—including the prohibition of torture and other inhumane treatment, freedom from arbitrary arrest, the presumption of innocence, the right to a fair trial and rights to freedom of opinion, expression and assembly.[29] On Human Rights Day 2001, 17 independent experts from the UN Commission on Human Rights issued a statement denouncing human rights violations and measures that have targeted groups such as migrants, the media, political activists, human rights defenders, asylum-seekers and refugees, and religious and ethnic minorities.[30]

Democracies face difficult challenges in devising legitimate ways to prevent terrorist attacks and bring the perpetrators to justice. There are few

---

BOX 4.11

Lessons for long-term peacebuilding in Afghanistan

Devastated by two decades of civil war, compounded by a three-year drought and omnipresent landmines and kalashnikovs (assault rifles), Afghanistan faces unprecedented challenges in providing peace and hope to its 23 million people. In addressing potential "conflict triggers" in the current phase of recovery, UN organizations recognize the need to connect short-term humanitarian responses to long-term recovery. They also recognize that the key to securing a just and lasting peace in Afghanistan will depend on the leadership and commitment of the Afghans.

The successes and failures of multibillion-dollar UN peace operations in the 1990s offer the following lessons for a long-term peacebuilding strategy in Afghanistan:
- Sequence reconstruction phases skilfully so that security imperatives are balanced with the need to slowly open governance processes and aid the most vulnerable.
- Fund and staff reintegration programmes for Afghanistan's 4.8 million refugees and internally displaced (80% of them women and children), as well as former combatants.
- Build strong local governance to address interethnic and intertribal conflict, discrimination against minorities and weaknesses of the central government.
- Design ethnically balanced and professional security institutions, under clear civilian control and guided by democratic principles, to protect the physical security of all citizens (as in Bosnia and Herzegovina and South Africa in the 1990s).
- Strengthen grass-roots institutions for conflict resolution and management: the police, the judiciary and alternative dispute settlement mechanisms such as shuras.
- Empower civilian leaders to oversee comprehensive landmine action programmes, and strengthen capacity in communities to provide incentives for having weapons destroyed.
- Build respect for the rule of law and a commitment to national reconciliation.
- Promote dynamic local leaders, including women and youth.
- Ensure a sustained political and financial commitment by the international community—always a problem in the second and third years of the programme, when the global spotlight has turned elsewhere.

Source: Ottaway and Lieven 2002; UNDP 2001d, 2002b.

simple solutions. But respect for human rights lies at the heart of what it is to be a democracy and at the heart of democratic civil control of the security sector. In addressing legitimate concerns about public safety, free societies cannot afford to lose sight of protecting core human freedoms.

CHAPTER 5

 Deepening democracy at the global level

One illusion has been shattered on September 11: that we can have the good life of the West irrespective of the state of the rest of the world...The dragon's teeth are planted in the fertile soil of wrongs unrighted, of disputes left to fester for years, of failed states, of poverty and deprivation.

—U.K. Prime Minister Tony Blair[1]

It has been said that the terrorist attacks of September 11 marked the end of the post-cold war era. Overnight, a broad range of simmering global challenges came to the surface, and the international community found itself in new and unfamiliar territory.

In the first few months after the attacks the hope was that the shared tragedy would bring the world together. And in several ways it has. The March 2002 UN Conference on Financing for Development, in Monterrey, Mexico, reversed the post-cold war decline in aid to developing countries. An agreement at the World Trade Organization (WTO) ministerial conference in Doha, Qatar, a few months earlier gave mutlilateral trade negotiations a new lease on life, avoiding the impasse that closed the previous ministerial meeting in Seattle, Washington.

These developments offer hope that the coming years will mark a new era for global decision-making. But there are also reasons to fear even greater global fragmentation and even greater weakening of international institutions. The war against terrorism and escalating violence in the Middle East risk creating new global fault lines. The most powerful states in the international system are not consistently seeking multilateral approaches to international security issues. And unrelated events—the collapse of Enron in the United States, the instability in Argentina—add to global unease about the rules

and institutions underlying global commerce. Economically and politically, frustration in developing countries about the skewed distribution of global power has seldom been greater.

This challenging global environment comes after a remarkable period of change and contrasting fortune. The 1990s began with great promise, with the end of the cold war heralding a new era. A world riven by the divisions of ideology was to be integrated by markets and technology. There was a wave of new democracies, unprecedented prosperity in North America and Western Europe and exceptional technological dynamism—most evident in the information and communications technology and human genome revolutions. Development also progressed notably in the world's two largest developing countries, China and India.

But while some developing countries did fairly well—both economically and in expanding political freedoms—the past decade has also seen severe reversals: The worst plague in human history as the death toll from AIDS surpassed that from the bubonic plague in Europe during the Middle Ages.[2] One of the worst famines ever, in the Democratic People's Republic of Korea. Serious conflicts in more than 50 countries.[3] Bouts of severe instability in the financial systems of emerging markets. And sharp increases in social and economic inequalities, including rapid surges in poverty in countries such as Afghanistan and Pakistan.

Trade rules consistently work against products from developing countries, such as agriculture and textiles, and fail to restrain protectionist abuses in industrial countries. On average, industrial country tariffs on imports from developing countries are four times those on imports from other industrial countries. And industrial countries provide about $1 billion a

Economically and politically, frustration in developing countries about the skewed distribution of global power has seldom been greater

day in domestic agricultural subsidies—more than six times what they spend on official development assistance for developing countries.[4]

In the face of these challenges, protests and cries of frustration have hit the streets in both industrial and developing countries, reflecting concerns that marginalized and less powerful people and states are losing out because of how global security and economic affairs are managed. These protests spring from different interests and have diverse agendas. But they are symptomatic of an almost universal belief that global cooperation must do a better job of preventing and managing a host of issues—especially those affecting people in developing countries. Such criticism spotlights global institutions and decision-making—and the need to make them more inclusive, democratic and effective.

There is no world government that can be made more democratic. But two elements could make global arrangements more effective and more reflective of democratic ideals:

• First, greater pluralism—expanding the space for non-state actors to influence policies and hold powerful actors accountable.

• Second, more democratic international organizations—increasing representation, transparency and accountability in decision-making.

PLURALISM AND GLOBAL DEMOCRACY: THE ROLE OF CIVIL SOCIETY CAMPAIGNS AND MULTISTAKEHOLDER PROCESSES

Over the past 20 years there has been an explosion in transnational civil society networks. The first registered international non-governmental organization (NGO), the Anti-Slavery Society, was formed in 1839, and by 1874 there were 32. But there was an astonishing increase in the 20th century, with the number of international NGOs growing from 1,083 in 1914 to more than 37,000 in 2000. Nearly a fifth of today's international NGOs were formed after 1990 (table 5.1).[5] And around the world, there are more than 20,000 transnational NGO networks. In many ways this revolution parallels the rapid growth of global business over the same period.

According to the Union of International Associations, membership in international

NGOs in low- and middle-income regions has increased faster than in high-income regions, with the biggest increases in Asia and Eastern Europe.[6] In Nepal the number of registered NGOs grew from 220 in 1990 to 1,210 in 1993, in Tunisia from 1,886 in 1988 to 5,186 in 1991. In 1996 the largest-ever survey of non-profits found more than 1 million such groups in India and 210,000 in Brazil.[7] The flow of resources through international NGOs has also risen substantially, increasing more than sevenfold in the past three decades (figure 5.1).

As a result a new global politics is emerging with the potential to catalyse change and innovation. A significant feature of these new movements is the pressure they exert on politicians and corporations in industrial countries to respond to the needs of developing countries. In 1992 an international campaign was launched to ban landmines. Few people predicted its success. Yet by 1997 some 1,400 NGOs in about 90 countries had succeeded in getting a Mine Ban Treaty signed prohibiting the use, production, trade and stockpiling of antipersonnel landmines.[8] The landmine campaign has raised consciousness and helped monitor compliance, and was awarded a Nobel Prize (see the special contribution by Campaign Ambassador Jody Williams).

JUBILEE 2000

The growing debt of very poor countries has provoked moral outrage around the world—outrage channelled into an effective movement for debt relief by the Jubilee 2000 campaign. The campaign put pressure on politicians in industrial countries through civic activism and protests in African, Asian and Latin American countries on the devastating effects of mounting debt on their development prospects. The global campaign thus magnified the voices of diverse groups across the world—and coordinated them in a global movement.

Jubilee 2000 had its beginnings at Keele University (in Staffordshire, United Kingdom) in 1990, when a campaign on the growing problem of developing country debt was proposed. Jubilee 2000 was launched in 1996.

In 1997 the International Confederation of

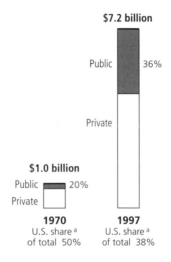

FIGURE 5.1

Development funds increasingly flow through non-governmental organizations

NGO funding to developing countries

$7.2 billion

Public — 36%

Private

$1.0 billion

Public — 20%

Private

1970
U.S. share [a] of total 50%

1997
U.S. share [a] of total 38%

Note: Includes official development assistance contributions to NGOs and official development assistance grants through NGOs.
a. Average of public and private contributions.
Source: Lindenberg and Bryant 2001

Free Trade Unions—representing 137 countries and 124 million workers—endorsed the Jubilee 2000 charter after the World Bank announced that in just one year the debt of developing countries had increased by more than 7%.[9] The International Union of Physicians—a powerful international organization formed by eminent professors of medicine—joined the confederation in its support of the Jubilee campaign. The two organizations eventually worked for the launch of Jubilee 2000 in Spain, coordinating Spanish NGO efforts.

National campaigns started to flourish worldwide. During the same year organizations

TABLE 5.1

International NGOs grew quickly in the 1990s

Purpose	1990	2000	Growth (percent)
Culture and recreation	2,169	2,733	26.0
Education	1,485	1,839	23.8
Research	7,675	8,467	10.3
Health	1,357	2,036	50.0
Social services	2,361	4,215	78.5
Environment	979	1,170	19.5
Economic development, infrastructure	9,582	9,614	0.3
Law, policy and advocacy	2,712	3,864	42.5
Religion	1,407	1,869	32.8
Defence	244	234	–4.1
Politics	1,275	1,240	–2.7
Total	31,246	37,281	19.3

Source: Anheier, Glasius and Kaldor 2001.

SPECIAL CONTRIBUTION

Eliminating landmines in wartorn societies

International social movements have grown tremendously in recent years and are increasingly influencing global policies. This trend is evident in the dramatic, largely unexpected success of the International Campaign to Ban Landmines between its 1992 creation and the 1997 signing of the Mine Ban Treaty prohibiting the use, production, trade and stockpiling of antipersonnel landmines.

In its short life the treaty—signed by 143 nations and ratified by 123—has had significant impact all over the world. More than 25 million stockpiled mines have been destroyed. Landmine production has fallen dramatically, and trade in the weapon has all but disappeared. Resources for mine clearance and victim assistance have increased. Most important, the number of new mine victims is falling in many countries. Moreover, the ban movement continues to gain momentum.

Global civil society—some 1,400 non-governmental organizations from about 90 countries that form the International Campaign to Ban Landmines—was responsible for raising public consciousness and drove the movement that resulted in the Mine Ban Treaty. Working with governments, the campaign stepped outside the normal diplomatic framework, formulating the treaty in just one year.

The campaign recognized the signing of the 1997 treaty as the beginning of the real work to eliminate landmines. It knew that for the treaty to be fully implemented and complied with, innovative strategies would continue to be needed to sustain its partnerships and maintain the momentum. In addition to continuing its global advocacy on banning landmines, the campaign created another powerful tool to advance its efforts—the Landmine Monitor, which uses 120 researchers around the world to monitor the treaty and other aspects of the landmine problem. The annual *Landmine Monitor Report* provides the baseline against which progress towards eliminating landmines is measured.

The International Campaign to Ban Landmines and its Landmine Monitor have shown the critical role that civil society can play in changing global policies and monitoring compliance with agreed policies. The campaign recognizes that civil society does not replace government. But true democratic governance must provide a place for civil society to advocate change and ensure accountability in achieving that change.

Jody Williams,
Campaign Ambassador,
International Campaign to Ban Landmines

such as Friends of the Earth, Witness for Peace, Bread for the World, the Catholic Bishops Conference, the Methodist, Mennonite and Presbyterian churches, the Fifty Years Is Enough campaign and the Sojourners launched Jubilee 2000 in the United States and strongly pushed the U.S. Congress to back debt relief. By 1999 there were 31 national campaigns.[10]

In lobbying influential decision-makers, international financial institutions and others, Jubilee 2000 found allies such as the rock star Bono (see the special contribution by the lead singer of U2). These efforts played a big role in winning debt relief concessions from G-7 countries, including an expanded heavily indebted poor countries (HIPC) initiative and bilateral commitments to write off debt from countries such as the United States. The NGO campaign was facilitated by growing recognition at the International Monetary Fund (IMF) and World Bank that debt relief was critical to reviving development in many countries.

In lobbying influential decision-makers, international financial institutions and others, Jubilee 2000 found allies such as the rock star Bono

THE ESSENTIAL DRUGS CAMPAIGN

By 1996 protease inhibitors and triple therapy for AIDS patients were sharply reducing deaths in countries where patients could afford the $10,000–$15,000 a year needed for treatment.[11] At the same time, a number of international NGOs became concerned about the impact that the WTO's accord on Trade-Related Intellectual Property Rights (TRIPS) would have on prices and access to vital medicines. In October 1996 Health Action International, a network of public health workers with members in more than 70 countries, led the first major NGO meeting on the issue. Soon Health Action In-

---

SPECIAL CONTRIBUTION
The role of Jubilee 2000 in debt relief

Many things about the 21st century are bizarre. That people listen to rock stars talking about politics. That if your daughter is born in Malawi, chances are she may not reach her 5th birthday—but if she is born in the United States, she'll probably still be around at 80.

The facts that shock us must also anger us and inspire us to be bold. If everybody, whether born in Accra or Albuquerque, is to be able to achieve their full potential, the immense structural inequalities that define our world need to be broken down.

The Jubilee 2000 movement showed what can happen when forces join together. Millions blazed a path that we all must follow. Ordinary people from around the world articulated their concerns about a global economic injustice—unpayable, unjust debts—thereby altering rich country policy towards poor countries.

People in rich countries said that they didn't want the money back; people in poor countries said that the benefits must be used to reduce poverty. Student unions and mothers unions teamed up with nuns in Zambia and priests in Peru. Twenty-four million people from more than 60 countries signed the world's largest petition using pens, pencils, thumbs and computers. Where these people led, politicians began to follow.

The movement made history—though not actually in terms of getting enough debt cancelled. This we are still working on. But in terms of the sheer force of people coming together to put pressure on governments—rich and poor—to be more responsive and more responsible.

We need to empower with information and listen to those who are most in need about how they can be supported. In Uganda schools using money freed by debt relief have blackboards on their walls detailing how the cash is being spent—for pupils and parents to monitor. The Uganda Debt Network in turn receives official funding to ensure that debt relief money is well spent on a national scale. This best practice needs to be copied much more widely, and shows how accountability and transparency can strengthen democracy.

People's movements in rich countries need to help give voice to the democratically elected leaders of poor countries and to civil society groups. Rich countries cannot be allowed to dictate just because they have the power. Some of us are well placed to develop and amplify the melody line—for greater democracy, accountability and transparency—but the chorus needs to be stronger. Individuals, communities and corporations need to step up. Too much is at stake for silence to be anybody's option.

Bono
U2

---

ternational and the U.S.-based lobbying group CPTech formed a coalition and began campaigning for early access to medicines, with a core goal being to recast trade agreements to support public health goals. Médecins Sans Frontières joined the coalition shortly thereafter.

South Africa became a focus of the campaign when in July 1997 its new Medicines Act was challenged by U.S. pharmaceutical companies. South Africa wanted to proceed with a bill designed to accomplish rather modest goals: authorizing parallel imports of medicines and generic drug substitution. But large U.S. drug companies bitterly opposed the parallel trade provisions and claimed that the generic drug substitution provisions violated provisions of the TRIPS agreement. Adding weight to the threats of the drug companies, the U.S. government began putting considerable pressure on South Africa's government to repeal or modify the bill.

In 1998 the World Health Organization (WHO) also became a focus, when Zimbabwe's minister of health took a resolution to its executive board asking members to pass a revised drug strategy. The intent was to ensure that public health rather than commercial interests would have primacy in pharmaceutical and health policies and to review options under the TRIPS agreement to safeguard access to essential drugs. The resolution had been drafted with significant input from the NGO campaign group.

The WHO resolution created a furore in the pharmaceutical industry. Within a few weeks 37 pharmaceutical companies sued the South African government over its new Medicines Act, and at the same time pressed their governments (the United States and EU countries) to oppose the new WHO resolution. Though the WHO eventually adopted a revised drug strategy, in January 2001 the pharmaceutical companies reactivated their lawsuit against the South African government—invigorating a wider campaign by NGOs to preserve access to essential drugs. For example, Oxfam announced a campaign calling for Glaxo to withdraw from the South Africa case and lower its prices. Adverse publicity and government pressure eventually forced the drug companies to withdraw their case and compensate the South African government for its legal bills (box 5.1).

In the meantime the campaign began seeking generic suppliers of crucial HIV/AIDS drugs. A pharmaceutical company in India, CIPLA, agreed with Médecins Sans Frontières to provide African countries with the medicines for $350 a year per patient. This move transformed the immorality of withholding life-saving medicines into a real choice—putting enormous pressure on politicians in Europe and North America as well as on the major pharmaceutical companies and the TRIPS regime.

In November 2001 the WTO ministerial conference in Doha adopted a declaration on the TRIPS agreement asking member countries to implement it in a way that protects public health and promotes access to medicines for all people. The declaration gives countries the freedom to choose the grounds for granting compulsory licenses and the right to determine what constitutes a national emergency or urgent circumstances. The declaration also gives least developed country members until 2016 to implement the TRIPS agreement for pharmaceuticals, and allows for the possibility of further extensions. Though this was an important step in facilitating access to essential medicines, the campaign continues in full swing. The declaration did not resolve many issues, notably measures to help countries with no manufacturing capacity achieve access to medicines produced as generics in other countries.

The campaign for international human rights and an International Criminal Court

International relations have long been based on state sovereignty and sovereign immunity—protecting states and state leaders from outside interference. Yet crimes against humanity in the 20th century led to a powerful and universal belief that there are certain acts for which individuals have to be held accountable by the international community. Tragically, the last decade of the 20th century provided several cases where the consensus against war criminals was put to the test in countries such as Bosnia

Crimes against humanity in the 20th century led to a powerful and universal belief that there are certain acts for which individuals have to be held accountable by the international community

BOX 5.1

Access to essential HIV/AIDS medicines—what made the campaign successful?
From the campaign diary of CPTech

The campaign worked closely with governments. Non-governmental organizations (NGOs) helped developing country governments frame policies and initiatives while also lobbying policy-makers in the European Union and the United States, where major pharmaceutical companies are based. For example, activists advised South Africa's government on its Medicines Act and helped Zimbabwe draft the resolution asking the World Health Organization (WHO) to pass a revised drug strategy. In February 1999 U.S. campaign members proposed adding a provision to African trade legislation to cut off funding to agencies that pressed African countries to adopt intellectual property laws exceeding the requirements of the World Trade Organization agreement on Trade-Related Intellectual Property Rights (TRIPS). In March 1999 CPTech, Health Action International and Médecins Sans Frontières organized a workshop on compulsory licensing in Geneva. The information presented at the workshop shocked developing country delegations, inspiring an increasingly well-informed, determined coalition of NGOs and developing country delegates to challenge U.S. and EU trade policies on medicines.

Developing country negotiators were expert and well-briefed. NGOs worked closely with Southern African countries, which considered a new essential medicines strategy essential to counter U.S. and EU trade pressures on patent issues. Dr. Olive Shisana, the key ne-

gotiator for African countries, was tough and well informed—often reading sections of the TRIPS agreement and U.S. compulsory licensing decisions to poorly briefed U.S. and EU negotiators. The final strategy was an almost complete victory for developing countries and NGOs.

Local NGOs played an important role. In September 1998 NGOs from Thailand organized the first demonstration demanding compulsory licenses for HIV drugs. The Thai efforts were partly successful: Thai regulators permitted competition for fluconazole, and in nine months its price fell from 200 baht to 6.5 baht. Similarly, in late 1998 the Treatment Access Campaign was formed in South Africa.

Industrial country activists were mobilized. In 1999 CPTech began meeting with AIDS activists to discuss patent and trade issues—focusing on the growing disparities between industrial and developing countries in access to medicines. Few of the activists were aware of compulsory licensing or U.S. trade pressures on South Africa, Thailand and other countries.

Generics manufacturers made the difference. Pharmaceutical companies in developing countries played a critical role in the process. India's CIPLA offered generic substitutes of HIV drugs for $350 a year per treatment—a small fraction of the price charged by the Western firms that held the patents on the drugs. The pressure exerted by generic substitutes from developing countries transformed the debate.

The U.S. government changed its position. At the chaotic 1999 WTO ministerial con-

ference in Seattle, Washington, U.S. President Bill Clinton announced a shift in policy, stating that U.S. health care and trade policies would ensure access to needed medicines for people in developing countries. And after President George W. Bush took office in January 2001, the new U.S. trade negotiator shocked the country's pharmaceutical industry by declaring that the government would not overturn Clinton's executive order and would continue to consider public health in matters concerning trade and intellectual property rights. Increasing media coverage focused on the moral imperative of protecting public health in developing countries.

The European Commission played a constructive role. In 2000 the European Commission launched an extensive review of its trade policy on access to medicines. A series of consultations with NGOs and drug companies addressed both general and technical issues, allowing EC trade officials to clarify issues and evaluate different arguments. These discussions fostered the environment that in 2001 led to the WTO's supportive declaration on public health, essential drugs and the TRIPS agreement.

Adverse publicity forced drug companies to withdraw their case. In March 2001 the court case pitting U.S. and EU drug companies against the South African government began with massive global publicity. Médecins Sans Frontières' Internet petition asking the companies to drop the suit received about 250,000 signatures—about the same number of South Africans who died of AIDS the previous year.

Source: Love 2002.

and Herzegovina and Rwanda. Global judicial mechanisms faced an unprecedented challenge because the overwhelming majority of conflicts occurred within states.

As international intervention in these conflicts increased, there was an inevitable demand for judicial mechanisms to hold accountable the perpetrators of injustices. Several ad hoc tribunals had a major impact on international law, including the recognition of rape as an act of genocide and a prosecutable crime against humanity (box 5.2).

Campaigns for international human rights have owed their unexpected success to voluntary associations of citizens acting on the basis of transnational values and goals. Amnesty In-

ternational and Human Rights Watch, particularly for civil and political rights, have developed extremely effective ways of influencing governments. Links have been established among transnational NGOs, local activists and individuals and groups that were targets of government abuse. Information became an instrument of "soft power" because most governments were reluctant to have their images tarnished by objective reports that could not be dismissed as hostile propaganda.

The emergence of such networks has evolved to the point where it is plausible to posit the emergence of "global civil society" as a constituency of networks committed to attaining global justice on a range of issues. The strength of this new dimension of world politics has been augmented by a flexible capacity to enter collaborative relationships with governments in the pursuit of shared goals. The most successful expression of this collaborative process led to the establishment of an International Criminal Court.

As early as 1948 the UN General Assembly instructed the International Law Commission to study the issue of an international criminal court. But the initiative went nowhere for several decades as a result of the cold war. Then in the aftermath of the establishment of ad hoc tribunals for Rwanda and the former Yugoslavia, the General Assembly asked the commission to submit a draft statute for an International Criminal Court. In 1996 the General Assembly carried the process a step further, mandating a diplomatic conference that would seek intergovernmental agreement on the establishment of such a tribunal.

This conference, held in Rome in 1998, led to the adoption in treaty form of the Rome Statute of the International Criminal Court. Civil society human rights organizations across the world mobilized support for the court, campaigning nationally and internationally for ratification. The court passed a key milestone in April 2002 when the 60th ratification was received by the United Nations—the critical mass needed to establish the court.

The International Criminal Court has the authority to prosecute genocide, crimes against humanity, war crimes and the crime of aggression (if an agreed definition of this crime can be reached along with conditions for its application). The exercise of criminal jurisdiction is limited by acceptance of the complementarity principle: the court can act only if systems of national justice fail to indict and prosecute those alleged to be guilty of such criminality. In this sense the international court is a second line of protection, with primary reliance being placed on national judicial systems.

Formidable obstacles remain for the International Criminal Court, including opposition from powerful countries such as the United States and several countries in Asia. The United States, which "un-signed" the treaty and withdrew in May 2002, objects to the court because

---

BOX 5.2

Making rape an act of genocide and a crime against humanity— the Rwanda tribunal

In 1998 the testimony of a Rwandan woman, identified simply as JJ, made legal history leading to the first case of a court holding rape to be an act of genocide and a crime against humanity. Jean-Paul Akayesu, mayor of Taba, Rwanda, was found guilty of ordering, instigating, aiding and abetting acts of sexual violence in a case brought before the International Criminal Tribunal for Rwanda.

The first person ever prosecuted for war crimes by an international military tribunal was Sir Peter von Hagenbach, in 1474. Rape was included among the charges only because von Hagenbach had failed to inform the city in which he and his men committed the rapes that it was officially occupied. It took a long time for rape to become a central charge in international trials against war criminals. The Geneva Conventions dedicate only two articles specifically to rape and only implicitly condemn it in others as "outrages upon personal dignity" or "inhuman treat-

ment". The conventions do not make rape a war crime, but a "grave breach".

Rape was first defined as a crime against humanity in 1996, in the statutes of the Yugoslav war crimes tribunal. This definition made it a prosecutable offence, considered quite revolutionary. But human rights activists and women's groups complained that the category of "crime against humanity" involved difficult questions of proof. So, after months of debate, rape was also listed in the category of "genocide"—a less limiting concept. In that sense the Yugoslav tribunal paved the way for the Rwandan trial against Akayesu, who was first arrested in 1995 on charges that did not include sex crimes. Akayesu's conviction represents a fundamental step in the evolution of international law and sent an important message not only to the international community but also to a country where, as the UN Special Rapporteur on Rwanda put it, "rape was the rule and its absence the exception".

Source: Neuffer 2001.

---

of fears that U.S. nationals will be brought to trial through a process that it finds questionable. These controversies affect issues such as funding and judicial independence. There are also practical difficulties of determining whether justice has been rendered at the national level. Further, as litigation over former Chilean dictator Augusto Pinochet highlighted, there is evolving support for the exercise of universal jurisdiction by national courts: for holding an individual subject to indictment and prosecution for crimes of state wherever and whenever they took place. In theory, this could downplay the role of the International Criminal Court.

Even so, the establishment of a widely ratified international court is a promising innovation. The court provides a measure of legal protection against the worst abuses of state power directed at people. It limits territorial sovereignty by making leaders accountable to external standards. Such accountability may have a deterrent effect, as well as provide those victimized by the crimes with vindication and punitive relief. And it extends the rule of law to the behaviour of the highest officials—and to those who act under the cloak of their authority. For all these reasons the international court is an important achievement for a campaign in which NGOs provided vociferous support to the United Nations.

A rise in transnational civil society campaigns has come alongside the emergence of new multistakeholder processes as an important new feature of global power and decision-making. In part this is due to the recognition that participation, public support and ownership by local actors and governments is vital for international cooperation to work. But it also reflects a rise in the aspirations of civil society, academics and business groups to become involved in policy at the global level.

These new processes challenge the traditional intergovernmental model of international relations. They reach inside states to involve local communities and affected people. They also reach beyond governments to transnational groups, alliances and experts. Equally important, the new multistakeholder processes stretch beyond mere consultations to a more active role for non-state actors in setting agendas and formulating and monitoring policy.

A rise in transnational civil society campaigns has come alongside the emergence of new multistakeholder processes as an important new feature of global power and decision-making

THE WORLD COMMISSION ON DAMS

The World Commission on Dams, which began its work in 1998, has been described as a watershed in new global processes. The commission is an experiment in multistakeholder negotiations, with four commissioners from governments, four from private industry and four from NGOs. It reviewed the development effectiveness of large dams and developed internationally acceptable criteria, guidelines and standards for the planning, design, appraisal, construction, operation, monitoring and decommissioning of dams. Its findings have been published as a major report.

The commission's process represents a complex, innovative new approach to an important global problem (box 5.3). The commission has established significant benchmarks and norms for incorporating environmental considerations. China, India and other large countries have criticized some results out of fear that opposition to dam construction will handicap their efforts to meet national energy needs. But the commission has promoted a rich, nuanced debate on environmental considerations.

This underscores the lesson of the campaign for the International Criminal Court: that new process does not always create new consensus. As with the court, a key challenge for supporters of the commission is to find ways to engage in constructive dialogue with their opponents.

POVERTY REDUCTION STRATEGIES

The IMF and World Bank have adopted a new multistakeholder process for forging poverty reduction strategies in the context of debt relief programmes. All countries requesting debt relief under the latest phase of the heavily indebted poor countries (HIPC) initiative must adopt a Poverty Reduction Strategy or an interim strategy developed through a broad participatory process. The IMF and World Bank describe the process as one in which the borrowing country and its people take the lead, with Poverty Reduction Strategy Papers being prepared by the government with the active participation of civil society, donors and international institutions. The international institutions hope the process will generate fresh ideas about strategies to achieve shared growth and poverty reduction goals—and to help develop a sense of ownership and national commitment to reaching those objectives.

The new process attempts to ensure that a wider range of stakeholders get influence and share control over priority setting, policy-making, resource allocations and access to public goods and services. But the kind of participation envisaged by the process holds mixed implications for democratic governance. Most notably, the term *participation* tends to refer to a wide range of interactions with stakeholders at the governmental, national and local levels. An intragovernmental meeting in a ministry of finance counts as participation, as does a village-level participatory poverty assessment. Some interactions involve disseminating information. Others involve consultation. In rare cases does interaction involve the kind of collaborative planning and decision-making envisaged in the

BOX 5.3

Should large dams be built?

In 2000 the World Commission on Dams released its comprehensive report, *Dams and Development*, to address the acrimonious debate over building large dams. Supporters of large dams believe that they are an efficient, effective way of meeting a society's water and energy needs, arguing that opponents overestimate the capacity of alternatives to meet growing needs. Supporters also contend that more transparent, participatory and publicly accountable decision-making on dams could be prohibitively expensive. And they believe that decisions about dams' broader social and environmental effects are political—and should be resolved through the political process, not through a specific project's decision-making process.

Opponents of large dams argue that governments build them without full recognizing their social and environmental costs. They also contend that pro-dam groups undervalue alternatives means of meeting a society's water and energy needs. And they believe that the decision-making and operations of proposed dams are non-transparent and offer no opportunities for participation to people affected by the projects.

The report by the World Commission on Dams addresses these and other issues and offers a framework for decision-making based on seven strategic priorities: gaining public acceptance, assessing all available options, addressing existing dams, sustaining rivers and livelihoods, recognizing entitlements and sharing benefits, ensuring compliance and sharing rivers for peace, development and security. The report proposes the adoption of a rights-based approach, in consonance with the UN Charter, Universal Declaration of Human Rights, UN Declaration on the Right to Development and Rio Declaration on Environment and Development.

The debate on dams reflects deeper divisions in the development community on the nature of legitimate, viable decision-making—divisions illustrated by recent conflicts on corporate relocation decisions and by protests against the World Trade Organization in Seattle, Washington, in 1999 and against the World Bank and International Monetary Fund in Prague, Czech Republic, in 2000. On one side is a technocratic view of executing economic policies and projects that have already been sanctioned by the mandated authorities. On the other are increasingly loud calls for these policies to take better account of the broader human and environmental costs for people and communities.

In the past there was fairly broad consensus that social and political issues could be separated from economic and technocratic issues. This tidy demarcation made conventional decision-making easier, with environmental and social issues resolved through political processes and economic and technical issues resolved through program-specific decision-making. But as the debate on dams has highlighted, this separation is now much more hotly contested.

The World Commission on Dams report shows that the conventional model of development decision-making—isolated from social, environmental, cultural and political implications—is no longer feasible. But it recognizes that there are still considerable arguments over what constitutes an alternative. Although the report has received much acclaim, it has also been subject to serious criticisms and reservations—particularly from the dam-building lobby, which finds itself split between those willing to accept the report's recommendations and other major players who remain implacably opposed. In addition, some large developing countries have complained that the report's recommended approach threatens their sovereignty.

That said, the contents of the report and the way it was produced set a useful precedent for the international community. By bringing accountability and participation to an issue previously considered technocratic and beyond public scrutiny, the World Commission on Dams extended the debate and broadened the scope for similar innovations in other contested areas.

Source: American University International Law Review 2001.

---

description of shared control over decisions and resources.

The problems are perhaps not accidental, because the desire of international institutions to build a participatory capacity-building and policy-making process has clashed with the need to disburse debt relief as rapidly as possible. Indeed, these institutions have often been under intense pressure to disburse debt relief from the same civil society groups that are pressing for deeper popular participation.

Take Burkina Faso, where participation in the HIPC/Poverty Reduction Strategy process took the form of a one and a half hour meeting of donors and civil society.[12] Where participation has been limited to ad hoc consultations, workshops and meetings, there is little evidence that it has affected decision-making or accountability.

These and other experiences with the Poverty Reduction Strategy process have underscored that more genuinely inclusive decision-making requires the full sharing of information and tasks, multistakeholder involvement in assessing and monitoring progress and institutional reforms that embed new participants in processes of priority setting, policy-making, implementation and monitoring in an ongoing and continuous way. These are the common elements in two successful Poverty Reduction Strategy experiences in Uganda and Viet Nam,[13] though in developing their strategies both countries were also able to draw on existing policies and institutions. In their poverty reduction activities both governments have been held accountable by institutionalized transparency, consultation and participation in planning and monitoring.

THE UN GLOBAL COMPACT AND OTHER INITIATIVES FOR CORPORATE SOCIAL RESPONSIBILITY

The UN Global Compact, since its formal launch in July 2000, has grown to encompass several hundred participating companies as well as international labour groups and more than a dozen international civil society organizations. Its aim is to bring such players together to advocate and promulgate nine core principles drawn from the Universal Declaration of Human Rights, the International Labour Organization's Fundamental Principles on Rights at Work and the Rio Declaration on Environment and Development. In signing the compact, companies are asked to commit to these principles in their corporate domains. The compact has been taken up in more than 30 countries, including Brazil and India.[14]

Of the 400 companies that have expressed interest in supporting the compact's core principles, only 70 have provided examples of how they have put these principles into effect.[15] Such practical examples are necessary for inclusion on the compact's Website, after which a company is more open to public scrutiny on its commitment to social responsibility.

Clearly, the compact is not a regulatory regime—or even a code of conduct. The United Nations describes it as "a value-based platform designed to promote institutional learning. It utilizes the power of transparency and dialogue to identify and disseminate good practices based on universal principles."[16] That said, the compact reflects how international organizations and large multinational private actors perceive a need to respond not just to global markets but also to global social and political pressures. As markets have gone global, so too must the idea of corporate citizenship and the practice of corporate social responsibility.

Several NGOs support the Global Compact but would like it to have more regulatory teeth—something for which it has neither the capacity nor the mandate. In New York the compact's secretariat employs just four professionals. And no member country has given the compact the mandate to "name and shame" or to take legal action.

While recognizing that the Global Compact is an important innovation, many civil society organizations are wary that it could be used in public relations. Accordingly, several of them—including Corpwatch—have started scrutinizing the activities of firms that sign the compact. Such pressure helps corporations be more conscious of the public spotlight on their environmental and labour records. Indeed, much of the current movement towards corporate social responsibility has been due to the pressure exerted by NGOs, consumers and the media (box 5.4).

NEXT STEPS IN DEEPENING THE ROLE OF CIVIL SOCIETY

NGOs are helping reshape global politics by playing two distinct roles. One is to put pressure on decision-makers through campaigns. This role provides voice to different groups but does not place any responsibility on these organizations to engage with formal processes of change. Any group or individual is entitled to a voice. This is a legitimate part of democratic pluralism. As long as this voice does not infringe on the rights and liberties of others, it does not require channelling or control.

But the second role of NGOs is distinctly different—involving them directly in global negotiations. Furthering this role requires formal arrangements that involve responsibilities for both international NGOs and intergovernmental agencies. This suggests a need to give some formal structure to their role in decision-making.

NGOs participating in global forums are trying to address this issue in three ways. The first has been to aggregate the views and demands of various NGOs and present a coherent case for negotiations. For example, umbrella groups such as the Women's Environment and Development Organization have often tried to play a constructive role in aggregating demands and negotiating proposals. Similarly, the Conference of Nongovernmental Organizations is trying to provide a platform for joint discussion of issues and procedures, such as accreditation to intergovernmental organizations.

A second form of structured dialogue involves formulating common codes of conduct

As markets have gone global, so too must the idea of corporate citizenship and the practice of corporate social responsibility

Pressure from non-governmental organizations for corporate social responsibility

The 1990s saw a considerable increase in non-governmental organization (NGO) activism on corporate responsibility. This was partly a response to the perception that governments were not effective at controlling large corporations following the extensive deregulation of the 1980s. NGO activists also became more aware of the power and influence of transnational corporations, and became concerned that unregulated globalization would have negative social and environmental consequences in developing countries.

NGO campaigns have focused on three major areas involving the impact of transnational corporations. The first, labour rights, has been taken up by international development NGOs such as Oxfam, Christian Aid and the Catholic Institute for International Relations. Some have focused on specific issues within their area of expertise—for example, Save the Children Fund has focused on child labour. In addition, new NGOs and coalitions of NGOs have emerged, such as the Clean Clothes Campaign in Europe and the Coalition for Justice in the Maquiladoras in the Americas.

A second prominent area involves human rights, particularly relative to the actions of security forces and the rights of indigenous populations. Mining and oil companies, developing new sources of natural resources in developing countries, have often found themselves in conflict with indigenous groups in the areas where they operate. Yet many governments, interested in increasing exports, tax revenues and extractive royalties, have repressed local opposition. As a result some transnational corporations have found themselves conniving, at least tacitly, in the suppression of indigenous populations. The most prominent example was Shell's involvement in Nigeria's repression of the Ogoni people. Organizations such as Human Rights Watch and Amnesty International have raised questions about the impact of transnational corporations on human rights.

NGOs have also been active in highlighting the effects of corporate actions on the environment. Shell was also the target of a Greenpeace campaign against the dumping of the Brent Spar oil platform in the North Sea. Other examples include campaigns against the environmental impacts of transnational corporations engaged in mining—as with BHP in Papua New Guinea. In 1997 Friends of the Earth drafted a model code of conduct for mining projects.

Without an intergovernmental system for regulating global business, many NGOs see comprehensive codes of conduct for transnational corporations—if effectively monitored and independently verified—as a means of constraining corporate power. But there is broad agreement that such codes should complement government regulation, not substitute for it.

The variety of organizations makes generalizations difficult. For example, environmental NGOs focus on environmental codes, while development NGOs tend to emphasize labour rights. Whatever the cause, targeted campaigns by NGOs can threaten the reputations of corporations—forcing them to respond. In mining, companies long attacked for corruption and lack of concern for the environment and indigenous communities have responded by forming the Global Mining Initiative. Other NGO campaigns include those that led to the (U.S.) White House Apparel Code condemning sweatshops in developing countries and the OECD Convention to Outlaw Foreign Commercial Bribery.

Many corporations have responded to such activism by establishing codes of conduct and changing business practices. Some have also set standards for domestic firms on labour, environmental and human rights issues. Little of this activity would have occurred without the high-profile efforts of NGOs.

Source: Jenkins 2001.

---

for members. This derives from the need for many NGOs to distance themselves from violent, nihilistic groups, evident in many protests against globalization. Accordingly, groups such as Friends of the Earth Europe have launched codes emphasizing peaceful protest and proposals advocating positions, rather than simply reacting negatively. Similar codes on advocacy, non-violence and tolerance have been adopted by the U.K. New Economics Foundation.

The third set of measures relates to the increased involvement of NGOs from developing countries, to increase the representativeness of groups based in industrial countries. Only 251 of the 1,550 NGOs associated with the UN Department of Public Information come from developing countries, and developing country NGOs account for an even smaller share of those in consultative status with the UN Economic and Social Council.[17] But coalitions are being built, and national NGOs are participating in global networks on issues of relevance to them. In the Jubilee 2000 campaign a frequently cited example comes from Uganda, where industrial country NGOs such as Oxfam provided technical assistance to local organizations so that they could develop proposals for their dialogue on debt relief with their government. The results were then incorporated in the global campaign. A similar process was evident in the essential drugs campaign.

Official intergovernmental bodies are also responding to the need to structure NGO participation in global governance. In some cases, particularly involving human rights, UN treaty bodies allow "alternative" reports, prepared by NGOs, to accompany official reports. In other cases, such as the committee process for the Organisation for Economic Co-operation and Development (OECD), discussions are organized between official delegations and NGOs prior to formal deliberations. International organizations have also formulated policies for NGOs, outlining criteria for their accreditation and mechanisms for engagement.

Moves by NGOs and intergovernmental bodies to structure the role of NGOs are part of a natural evolution that has the potential to add a fresh voice to global decision-making. But these new multistakeholder processes are only a partial step towards more inclusive global governance—since they address only a few distinct issues.

Civil society groups have also brought their energies to bear on international institutions more broadly, lobbying for greater voice and deeper participation. These efforts can often bring new insight, expertise and energy to policy-making. But easier access to international institutions and businesses—through revolutions in communications technology and global coalitions—can also magnify the voice of obscure, unrepresentative or antidemocratic organizations. And it can undermine formal accountability.

These concerns have come to the fore at the global level in recent debates about NGO access to international institutions such as the WTO. International NGOs have fought a long campaign for greater access to such institutions, but progress has been limited. The UN General Assembly, for example, still does not allow NGOs to participate in formal decision-making. On one side, developing country officials complain that their sovereign rights are being undermined by NGOs that lack the legitimacy of elected governments. On the other, NGOs counter that they are interested only in having a voice, not a vote, and that national institutions often offer little scope for citizens' voices to be heard.

There are no simple solutions to these dilemmas, especially in countries where all the elements of governance crucial to human development—economic, social and political— are undergoing dramatic change. But there is growing awareness that accountability, where NGOs are concerned, must be a two-way street. To genuinely contribute to stronger democratic institutions and more democratic politics, civil society groups are recognizing that they too must be accountable for their actions. Otherwise, they risk losing public confidence and the legitimacy that enables them to engage in civic life.

There is growing awareness that accountability, where NGOs are concerned, must be a two-way street

BUILDING MORE DEMOCRATIC INTERNATIONAL INSTITUTIONS

Multilateral organizations face two distinct problems in the contemporary world: the inadequate commitment of powerful member governments and the disillusionment of weaker states. In the face of these challenges, policymakers are all too aware that international institutions have to be made more effective and more accountable.

This concern has been expressed in proposals for new institutions to deal with the problems of globalization. In a series of high-level commissions appointed by politicians, international organizations and private foundations, proposals have been made for a new global environment organization, a global bankruptcy mechanism, a global financial regulator and an international tax organization.

Creating such new institutions would require tremendous political will from powerful states: political will that so far is not very apparent. More profoundly, however, the structure and workings of any such new institutions would need to take into account some of the emerging lessons about how and why international organizations need to be made more representative and more accountable.

Although globalization has vastly expanded the demands on global institutions, it has also heightened a crisis of legitimacy and effectiveness. Large parts of the public no longer believe that their interests are represented in institutions such as the IMF, World Bank, UN Security Council and WTO—or that the institutions are adequately accountable for what they do. Representation and accountability have always been weak in these multilateral institutions. But today the weaknesses are glaring because the institutions are being called on by their powerful members to intrude much more deeply into areas previously the preserve of national governments—especially in developing countries. Over the past two decades these institutions have increasingly prescribed and required structural and institutional reforms. For example, in the 1980s countries that borrowed from the IMF and World Bank were required to meet 6–10 performance criteria—and in the 1990s, some 26.[18]

Efforts to deepen democracy in international institutions must confront the realities of global power. Powerful countries will inevitably invest more energy and political capital in institutions that enable their power to be exercised. Once they are members of an elite club, countries are reluctant to lose that power or see it diluted by opening to new members. This explains why proposals for reform always encounter stiff resistance. And that is why broad acceptance of the principle of democratization has translated into so little progress at the level of specific proposals.

PROMOTING DEMOCRATIC PRINCIPLES IN INTERNATIONAL FINANCIAL INSTITUTIONS

Although developing countries are deeply affected by the decisions of institutions such as the IMF, World Bank and WTO, they have little power in their decision-making. There is an unavoidable democratic deficit in international organizations because people do not get to directly elect (or throw out) their representatives. This would be true even if all member countries of international organizations were flourishing democracies. Under present arrangements, even if they so wished, citizens could not use their votes to influence, restrain or hold accountable their government in its actions in an international organization. Nor can citizens rely on their parliaments and politicians to hold international organizations accountable. That said, however, the democratic deficit does not rule out improving the representativeness of international organizations.

The role of developing country governments in global governance needs to be bolstered through changes in formal representation. This is a necessary (albeit insufficient) condition to redress the existing bias in international organizations. Although many organizations work by "consensus" and say that this diminishes the importance of formal voting power and seats, consensus decisions are always underpinned by the realities of power and a knowledge of which actors can veto or push final decisions. In reality, consensus decision-making seldom gives voice to marginalized actors.

What is needed is to rewrite the way seats and votes are allocated within international or-

ganizations, to better recognize the increased stake of developing countries. Their cooperation and commitment to international agreements is vital if any international organization is to succeed in managing globalization.

For this reason the old rules about representation are no longer viable or desirable. Put bluntly, the IMF and World Bank will not be able to do their jobs effectively if they remain tied to structures that reflect the balance of power at the end of the Second World War. In the past 55 years their roles and duties have changed beyond recognition, as have the expectations of their vastly increased membership.

Nearly half of the voting power in the World Bank and IMF rests in the hands of seven countries (figure 5.2). This voting power is exercised in the formal decision-making bodies—the executive boards—of each institution.

Equally important are the informal influences and traditions that shape the work of these organizations. These informal processes further weight the scales in favour of industrial countries. For example, the heads of the World Bank and IMF are chosen according to a political convention whereby the United States and Europe nominate their candidate for each, respectively. Other countries and critics rightly brand the process as undemocratic and insufficiently accountable.

Yet more profoundly, the institutions are often criticized by academics, industrial country NGOs and developing country analysts for basing their economic advice and policy conditionality on a narrow world view that reflects the interests of their most powerful members. In particular, they are widely perceived as being overly accountable to their largest shareholder, largely through informal influences such as the location and staffing of the organizations and their susceptibility to pressure on select issues.[19]

These concerns about who the IMF and World Bank represent have been heightened as the institutions have begun to prescribe policies over an ever broader range of issues. Concerns about corruption and other aspects of politics affecting macroeconomic imbalances in IMF member states have led that organization to join the World Bank in paying more attention

FIGURE 5.2

Whose voice counts at the IMF and World Bank?

Voting power at the IMF

52% 48%

U.S., Japan, France, U.K., Saudi Arabia, China, Russian Federation

Rest of the world

Voting power at the World Bank

54% 46%

U.S., Japan, France, U.K., Saudi Arabia, China, Russian Federation

Rest of the world

Source: IMF 2002a; World Bank 2001b.

The new role of the IMF and World Bank highlights the need for deeper participation by their borrowers: developing countries

to governance issues in its policy prescriptions and programmes. These shifts have increased scrutiny of the institution's internal governance—specifically the representation of countries, the way policy advice is formulated and the uneven risks associated with policy advice. The new role of the IMF and World Bank highlights the need for deeper participation by their borrowers: developing countries.

A primary source of contention relates to the shares of developing and industrial countries in decision-making. Members of the IMF do not have equal voting power. Voting weights are based on two components. Each member has a set of 250 basic votes that come with membership.[20] The second component is determined by economic power. Votes accompany country quotas that reflect the economic strength of countries. Since the formation of the IMF there has been a major imbalance in the evolution of the two sources of voting power. Basic votes have declined dramatically as quotas have increased. The share of basic votes in voting power has declined from 12.4 % to 2.1%.[21] At the same time, an additional 135 countries have become members, including many transition economies.[22]

During this period the basic nature of the IMF and World Bank has changed. They were created at the end of the Second World War as institutions of mutual assistance. The IMF would provide resources to any country facing temporary balance of payments difficulties. The World Bank would help channel investment to countries for postwar reconstruction and development. This sense of mutual assistance has changed in the intervening years.

Today the IMF and World Bank lend exclusively to developing and emerging economies. Furthermore, their loans are linked to conditions that increasingly impinge on the domestic policies of the state. The result is a new kind of division between creditor countries on one hand, who enjoy increased decision-making power and have used it to expand conditionality, and borrowing countries on the other, who view conditionality as externally imposed. This can be particularly worrisome when there is considerable division of opinion on that policy advice, and when the risks associated with the

policy advice are borne almost exclusively by the people of the borrowing country.

Consider full capital account convertibility, suggested by the IMF in recent years. Many analysts claim that this advice contributed to greater instability in East Asia, the Russian Federation and elsewhere. The IMF came under sharp criticism for such advice, as well as for the way it handled various crises. This debate is complex, and the IMF has vigorously defended its role. The point here is not to debate the technical merits of the policy advice. It is to see what can be done to make decision-making more transparent and accountable—and to increase the voice of developing countries in shaping those decisions.

There is now greater recognition of the need for the World Bank and the IMF to increase the representation of developing countries. They could do so in a number of ways.

First, by increasing the proportion of basic votes allocated to each member. When the IMF was created, each member was given an equal number of basic votes as well as a percentage of votes that reflected its economic size. As noted, basic votes have been neglected and now account for less than 3% of total votes.[23] Restoring a degree of parity in voting strength for developing countries requires increasing basic votes to an agreed proportion of voting rights.

Second, by enhancing the voice of developing countries within the institutions. Formally, all members of the IMF and World Bank executive boards are supposed to appoint the institutions' presidents. But by convention, Europeans select a candidate for director of IMF and the U.S. government selects the head of the World Bank. The adverse symbolism of a closed, secretive selection process based on privilege in institutions committed to greater accountability and transparency is obvious. The selection process needs to be opened and perhaps made somewhat more substantive regarding the candidates' views on the vision for the organizations. A selection committee for such a post would enable broader participation and transparency.

Another step would be increasing the number of seats for developing countries on the executive boards. At present executive directors from developing countries represent large constituencies and have minimal input on policy formation. The number of developing country executive directors could easily be increased, along with more input from technical staff that could better help them prepare for serious policy discussions. Moreover, as in many other institutions, female representation at the highest levels remains low (figure 5.3).

The democratic character of these institutions could be enhanced by revising the role of quotas, improving the gender balance in high-level decision-making and strengthening the executive directors of developing countries and involving them in the selection of the institutions' presidents. These reforms would also change perceptions of international financial institutions—away from a continuing suspicion of external domination to one where developing countries feel greater ownership and responsibility for decision-making.

Third, by making the institutions more accountable for their actions, not just to their board members but also to the people affected by their decisions. Governments are held accountable through a variety of social, political and legal institutions. These institutions must also be used to make global financial institutions more accountable. Specifically, this means ensuring transparency and monitoring and evaluating their rules, decisions, policies and actions.

Transparency. Although it is a cornerstone of accountability, international financial institutions long argued that they had to limit transparency to protect proprietary or confidential information and to not adversely affect full and frank discussion in their decision-making processes. But this revolution has occurred in many international organizations, such as the IMF and World Bank.

The World Bank adopted an information disclosure policy in 1993, leading the way for other institutions. By 2001 the Bank had expanded the policy's scope to include the release of documents on the Heavily Indebted Poor Countries initiative and Poverty Reduction Strategy Papers, including summaries of board discussions of these documents, and papers by International Development Association deputies

on replenishment negotiations. A revision of this diclosure policy in September 2001 further extended the information available to the public to include a greater number of project-related documents and the chairman's summaries of board discussions of Country Assistance Strategies and Sector Strategy Papers. A more systematic approach to accessing Bank archives was also developed.

At the IMF, where most information was previously inaccessible to anyone outside the walls of the institution, research is now published on the organization's Website along with considerable documentation on work with individual countries. The IMF is also pressing governments to permit greater disclosure and publication of policies and agreements with the IMF (these must be kept confidential if a government so wishes).

But serious gaps in transparency remain. For democratic accountability the most noticeable are decisions by the Bank and IMF executive boards. The minutes of board meetings are not published. Votes are not taken and so cannot be recorded or publicized. This means that citizens of member countries (or interested outsiders) cannot hold executive directors or their governments accountable for their policies in the IMF or World Bank.

The secrecy of board deliberations and members' positions is often defended on the grounds that it reinforces the collegiality of the executive board, the frankness of discussion and its capacity to make decisions by consensus. Interestingly, the Monetary Policy Committee of the Bank of England once made a similar argument—debunked by the subsequent experience of that agency, whose minutes and votes have been recorded and published shortly after meetings since 1998.

Monitoring and evaluation. Like most institutions, global organizations are under constant pressure from shareholders, members, NGOs and critics to evaluate their operations and effectiveness in a more thorough, effective and public way. This includes subjecting themselves to outside, independent scrutiny and to constant internal monitoring. The new expectation that institutions conduct and publish critical independent evaluations of themselves

FIGURE 5.3

Women on the boards of directors of international financial institutions

IMF

100% Male

World Bank

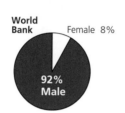

Female 8%

92% Male

Source: Women's Environment and Development Organization 2002.

was highlighted by the UN's publication of a critical independent examination of its policy in Rwanda, commissioned by the Secretary General in May 1999.[24]

Similarly, the IMF's executive board has published independent evaluations of the Fund's Enhanced Structural Adjustment Facility, its surveillance and its research. More recently, the IMF created a semi-independent Office of Independent Evaluation. More extensive evaluations are undertaken in the World Bank Operations Evaluation Department. This department is part of the Bank and reports directly to the executive board, rating the development impact and performance of the Bank's policies, processes and lending operations.

To be effective, the results of all of these evaluations must be published, followed up and investigated, and necessary changes undertaken. This is particularly important for large organizations suffering from considerable inertia.

Without publication of independent assessments of what organizations are doing, it is not only difficult for the public to judge how well or poorly an organization is undertaking its responsibilities, it is also impossible for outsiders to offer support to insiders who recognize the need for change. By publishing critical reports, institutions can catalyse public attention and external pressure for change, helping to overcome inertia or vested interests within the organization. For these reasons the IMF may want to re-evaluate its policy of not publishing the work of the Office of Internal Audit and Inspection or of internal evaluations by operational staff. Similarly, the World Bank may want to consider publishing all the work of the Operations Evaluation Department (since 1993 its *Annual Review of Development Effectiveness* has been published along with summaries of evaluation reports for selected projects).

Judicial-style accountability. The newest form of accountability in international organizations goes beyond transparency and evaluations and offers a more active, participatory form—best described as judicial-style accountability. Just as tribunals, ombudspersons and other processes of redress permit citizens to hold governments accountable in national settings, international counterparts are emerging to hold international organizations accountable. This form of accountability is intended to ensure that organizations act within their powers—and in keeping with their operational rules. Specific actions or decisions are examined, and attention is drawn to any breach of rules. Judicial-style accountability does not correct bad decisions. But it can publicize wrong-doing and encourage organizations to reconsider decisions.

The most notable recent steps in this direction are the World Bank's Inspection Panel, created in 1993 to deal with loans, and the Compliance Adviser/Ombudsman's Office, created in 1999 to deal with the work of the International Finance Corporation and Multilateral Investment Guarantee Agency. The Inspection Panel investigates complaints from any group of people able to show that:

• They live in a project area (or represent people who do) and are likely to be adversely affected by project activities.

• They believe that the actual or likely harm they have suffered results from failure by the Bank to follow its policies and procedures.

• Their concerns have been discussed with Bank management and they are not satisfied with the outcome.

The Inspection Panel makes preliminary assessments of the complaints, taking into account Bank management's responses to the allegations. The panel can then recommend to the Bank's executive board that the panel proceed with a full investigation. The board retains the power to launch full investigations and to make final decisions based on the findings of the panel and the recommendations of Bank management.

The Compliance Adviser/Ombudsman's Office—set up after consultations with shareholders, NGOs and members of the business community—aims to find workable, constructive approaches to dealing with environmental and social concerns and complaints of people directly affected by projects financed by the International Finance Corporation and Multilateral Investment Guarantee Agency. The office's work focuses on dialogue, mediation and conciliation. The office has the power to make rec-

The newest form of accountability in international organizations goes beyond transparency and evaluations and offers a more active, participatory form— best described as judicial-style accountability

ommendations but not to act as judge, court or police officer.

Both these experiments have resulted in the development and publication of detailed operating principles and procedures—standards to which the institutions can be held accountable. In this respect they have increased transparency and opportunities for monitoring and evaluation.

That said, there are several limits to judicial-style accountability, particularly for developing countries. First, not everyone is in an equal position to use the procedures—not just in lodging formal complaints but also in ensuring that the threat of such actions makes officials mindful of their powers and their organizations' rules. In many cases people in developing countries have relied on industrial country NGOs to help fund and present their cases. Critics allege that the role of NGOs risks skewing the work of accountability tribunals towards issues and areas of most concern to people in industrial countries, as expressed through their NGOs. That would leave unserviced people in the developing world who have not attracted the attention of such NGOs. A further risk is that the outcomes of a formal process, such as that of the Bank's Inspection Panel, may end up being shaped more by the desire of industrial country NGOs to garner publicity through confrontations and showdowns, not by quiet measures that more modestly improve the lives of people directly affected by projects.

Second, judicial-style accountability can be used to attack good decisions that suffer only a minor technical flaw relative to the rules. It can also be long, costly and time-consuming—diverting resources from the institution's central purposes. For this reason the threshold for a complaint to spark a full inspection is crucial.

Third, judicial-style accountability examines whether an institution has adhered to its policies and operational rules. It does not examine or adjudicate the quality or purposes of those policies and rules. Nor does it substitute for or offer recourse against the responsibility of decision-makers to make good policies and rules. It cannot prevent or call to account bad decisions made within the rules—which means that accountability for the quality of the rules has to be achieved through other means.

Fourth, judicial-style accountability does not resolve problems of unrepresentative or poor decision-making. But new institutions of scrutiny and monitoring can promulgate greater transparency and monitoring of global institutions. They also offer people within states some measure of redress in the institutions that affect their lives—yet in which they have little or no voice.

PROMOTING DEMOCRATIC PRINCIPLES IN THE UNITED NATIONS

The call for greater inclusion and democracy at the United Nations has led to calls for widening the organization's representative base. Reform proposals focus on three areas. The first involves expanding representation in the UN system—increasing the plurality of voices so that the institution is not seen as being solely for governments and bureaucrats. There have been proposals for a People's Assembly—something similar to an elected European parliament, with citizens around the world electing representatives. In addition, proposals have been made to allow civil society organizations to participate in the discussions of the General Assembly, Economic and Social Council and Security Council.

A second set of reform proposals focus on shifting power in international organizations towards those with more democratic decision-making procedures. Such reforms would redress the imbalance in power weighted towards organizations in which a few countries dominate decision-making. Ironically, the more representative parts of the United Nations—the General Assembly and the Economic and Social Council—are usually considered the least effective. Especially for economic and social issues, much of the power and influence has shifted to the better-funded World Bank and IMF.

In part this is because the powerful industrial countries that are the main contributors to the United Nations are loath to endow the General Assembly or Economic and Social Council with real powers because these bodies are dominated by developing countries. Global governance ultimately has to balance power and principles, effectiveness and legitimacy. Recognizing this, proposals have been made to bol-

Critics allege that the role of NGOs risks skewing the work of accountability tribunals towards issues and areas of most concern to people in industrial countries, as expressed through their NGOs

ster the UN role in the economic and social arena. The proposal for an Economic Security Council tries to strengthen the role of the United Nations while recognizing that any such proposal will require the support of the world's major powers (box 5.5).

The third set of reform proposals seek to remove or reduce UN procedures seen as fundamentally undemocratic. Among these the use of the veto at the Security Council has attracted much attention—on the grounds that giving this power to the council's five permanent members divides countries into first- and second-class citizens. In recent years the rapid growth of peacekeeping operations has focused more at-

tention on the Security Council (see chapter 4). Vetoes have not impeded its recent activism because there have been few disputes among the five permanent members (table 5.2). And on the rare occasions when the veto is used, it applies to a limited number of issues (table 5.3).

Nonetheless, the Security Council's secretive processes and the veto power of its five permanent members have come under repeated criticism. Though progress has been made on making some processes more transparent, proposals for wider reform remain unaddressed (box 5.6). Pressure for reform will likely increase.

PROMOTING DEMOCRATIC PRINCIPLES IN THE WORLD TRADE ORGANIZATION

Few people deny the enormous advantages of increased global trade. Over the past year the WTO's conference in Doha and its extension of membership to China have highlighted the organization's vast potential for improving the lives of the world's poorest people. Most developing countries support the principle of multilateral negotiations to open global markets for the benefit of all. But many countries have widespread concerns about WTO agreements—particularly the way they are negotiated.

Although all countries have a seat and a vote in the WTO, actual decision-making occurs in the "green room"—the small group meetings convened by the director-general and heavily influenced by Canada, the European Union, Japan and the United States. Most developing countries are usually excluded.

Until a few years ago the general public was also in the dark. Most people knew little about the negotiations under way at the WTO and even less about their implications. Even today many parliamentarians and politicians seem ignorant of important WTO negotiations, even though as WTO members their countries are compelled to change their policies—sometimes substantially—based on the agreements that result.

Recently, however, civil society groups from both developing and industrial countries have become heavily involved in WTO issues. Labour

---

BOX 5.5

Revisiting the question of an Economic Security Council

Human Development Report 1994 proposed creating a UN Economic Security Council. Several others have also put forward the idea, including the Commission on Global Governance in 1995, Stewart and Daws in 2000 and, more recently, the United Nations University in 2001. *Human Development Report 1994* proposed that:

A further step in strengthening the UN role in sustainable human development would be the creation of an Economic Security Council (ESC)—a decision-making forum at the highest level to review the threats to global human security and agree on required actions. The council must be kept small and manageable. Its membership could consist of 11 permanent members from the main industrial and more populous developing countries. Another 11 members could be added on a rotating basis from geographical and political constituencies.

The voting system in an Economic Security Council should not include a veto. But to reassure all constituencies that their legitimate interests would be protected, the voting system should be to have all decisions ratified not just by a majority of all members but also by majorities of the industrial and developing countries.

As well as coordinating the activities of the UN agencies, the Economic

Security Council would act as a watchdog over the policy direction of all international and regional financial institutions. To implement its decisions effectively, the council should have access to a global human security fund. The council would need to be backed by a professional secretariat to prepare policy options for its consideration.

An intermediate alternative to the Economic Security Council would be to extend the mandate of the present Security Council so that it could consider not just military threats but also threats to peace from economic and social crises.

Since then there has been some progress in this regard, as the UN Security Council met for a session on HIV/AIDS in 2000, a recognition of wider threats to human security. But like other proposals seeking to re-energize the original intent of making the United Nations a major influence on socio-economic development, progress on the Economic Security Council has been painfully slow. These and other proposals aim to reverse the shift in power on economic and social policy to the World Bank and International Monetary Fund, with UN agencies relegated to a fairly minor role. A body such as the Economic Security Council is also intended to improve coordination among diverse UN agencies that, over the years, have often been in conflict.

Source: Commission on Global Governance 1995; Nayyar 2001; Stewart and Daws 2000; UNDP 1994, p.84.

TABLE 5.2
Use of the veto has become rare on the UN Security Council

Period	China[a]	France	Soviet Union/ Russian Federation	United Kingdom	United States	Total
Total	5	18	120	32	74	249
2001	–	–	–	–	2	2
2000	–	–	–	–	–	0
1999	1	–	–	–	–	1
1998	–	–	–	–	–	0
1997	1	–	–	–	2	3
1996	–	–	–	–	–	0
1986–95	–	3	2	8	24	37
1976–85	–	9	6	11	34	60
1966–75	2	2	7	10	12	33
1956–65	–	2	26	3	–	31
1946–55	1	2	79	–	–	82

a. Between 1946 and 1971 the Chinese seat on the Security Council was occupied by the Republic of China (Taiwan).

Source: Global Policy Forum 2002a.

TABLE 5.3
Vetoes on the UN Security Council apply to a small range of subjects, 1990–2001

Date of vote	Vetoing member	Vote (yes–veto –no or abstain)	Subject
14 December 2001	United States	12-1-2	On the withdrawal of Israeli forces from Palestinian-controlled territory and condemning acts of terror against civilians
27 March 2001	United States	9-1-5	On establishing a UN observer force to protect Palestinian civilians
25 February 1999	China	13-1-1	On the extension of UN peacekeeping in the former Yugoslav Republic of Macedonia
21 March 1997	United States	13-1-1	Demanding Israel's immediate cessation of construction at Jabal Abu Ghneim in East Jerusalem
7 March 1997	United States	14-1-0	Calling on Israel to refrain from East Jerusalem settlement activities
10 January 1997	China	14-1-0	Authorization of 155 observers to verify the agreement on the ceasefire in Guatemala
17 May 1995	United States	14-1-0	On the Occupied Arab Territories (East Jerusalem)
2 December 1994	Russian Federation	13-1-1	On transport of goods between Bosnia and Herzegovina and the former Yugoslavia
11 May 1993	Russian Federation	14-1-0	On Cyprus (finances)
31 May 1990	United States	Not available	On the Occupied Arab Territories
17 January 1990	United States	Not available	On the violation of diplomatic immunities in Panama

Source: Global Policy Forum 2002d.

BOX 5.6

United Nations or United Five? Reforming the UN Security Council

Reform of the UN Security Council has been on the agenda of the General Assembly since 1979. But it has gained much greater salience in the post–cold war period as the council has become better able to act. In 1988 the council passed only 13 resolutions—in 1992 it passed 93. This renewed activism, particularly in peacemaking and peacekeeping, have strengthened calls from both industrial and developing countries for a more representative, accountable and open Security Council.

When the UN Secretary-General invited member states to submit comments on council reform in 1992, 80 states responded. The General Assembly has since established an open-ended working group to consider all aspects of the question of increasing Security Council membership and other proposals. Reform proposals have come from state entities and civil society: for example, from the NGO Working Group on the Security Council and from independent think-tanks such as the Commission on Global Governance. All the proposals focus on two issues: expanding the council and taming its veto.

Lack of consensus, with the council's five permanent members supporting the status quo, thwarts progress on either issue. Several proposals have suggested enlarging the council by increasing both permanent and non-permanent seats. In addition, Germany, India and Japan have joined forces to win permanent membership.

But several countries have opposed increasing the number of permanent seats. Many others support increasing council membership, but on a rotating basis through periodic elections and with a quota of seats assigned to every region. But though it is broadly agreed that African, Asian, Eastern European and Latin American states should be guaranteed representation, the question of which countries should represent each region raises thorny questions: how to choose between Argentina and Brazil, for example, or between India and Pakistan.

Steps to reform the power of veto are also controversial. Among others, the Commission on Global Governance and the Canadian Committee for the 50th Anniversary of the United Nations have strongly argued that new permanent members should be denied the veto. But many see this as a new form of discrimination between first- and second-class members within the council. The Canadian committee also raised the possibility of requiring a double or triple veto to halt a resolution, and suggested limiting the issues that can be vetoed to charter amendments and the appointment of the Secretary-General.

As an alternative, the Ford Foundation has suggested that peacekeeping and enforcement measures be the only measures susceptible to veto power. The Commission on Global Governance envisaged a two-phase reform process. Initially, the five permanent members would agree to forgo the use of the veto while new, non-veto-holding members were added. In the second phase the five permanent members would have grown accustomed to not having veto power and be willing to let it die. This suggestion is based on the fact that in recent years countries have been making much greater efforts to avoid a veto.

Debate over the veto is symbolic of much wider concern about the UN role in the world. In a more unipolar world, many critics allege that the institution has become an instrument of foreign policy for a few major powers. There is related concern that the will of the international community should be based on procedures that make the United Nations more democratic. Given global power imbalances, such efforts can only go so far. But in a world where international agencies are actively promoting democracy for the first time, there is much greater scrutiny of decision-making in international organizations. In response to strong pressure from Australia, Canada and Sweden the Security Council has become more open and transparent. Information is less restricted—for example, an agenda is now published in advance of council meetings to allow non-members to lobby on specific issues. The flow of information to the General Assembly has also improved. But the Security Council is still widely perceived as an outdated legacy of the Second World War, functioning primarily as an instrument of a few major powers. With little or no progress on the broader reform agenda, such as elimination of the veto, this perception will persist.

Source: Paul 1995, 2001; UNAC 1995; Global Policy Forum 2002c; Commission on Global Governance 1995; Thakur and Newman 2000.

unions and groups focused on development, poverty and the environment have sought to use the WTO to further their causes. And the WTO is feeling their influence, not so much as a result of NGO activity within the WTO but because of the highly public criticism they have levelled against it.

In 1993 in Bangalore, India, a rally of 500,000 farmers pledged to defy the WTO's Uruguay Round agreements.[25] Farmers groups in France have also held large protests against the WTO's agriculture agreement. And environmental and consumer groups have highlighted threats to environmental and food safety standards from WTO agreements. As a result of these and other efforts, the WTO secretariat and many WTO members have begun to work with civil society organizations more directly, contributing to the policy dialogue and negotiating process within the WTO.

In principle, the WTO's consensus procedure gives every member country the power of veto. The decision-making process and the power it confers on developing countries enabled many to resist the inclusion of labour standards on the agenda of the 1999 ministerial summit in Seattle, Washington (United States). But the backroom deals among powerful states that underpin "consensus" decision-making have led to frequent complaints.

The WTO is accused of being one of the least transparent international organizations,

TABLE 5.4
Africa lacks representatives at World Trade Organization headquarters

Number of countries	Number of representatives
15	0
16	1 to 3
6	4 to 6

Note: As of August 2001.
Source: CUTS-ARC 2001.

largely because few developing country members are able to participate effectively in negotiations and decision-making. Decisions are based on "one country, one vote" and made by consensus, giving the WTO the appearance of democratic decision-making. Decisions are made by the General Council or by representatives in subsidiary bodies (such as the TRIPS Council or Agriculture Committee). Major decisions are also made or endorsed by WTO ministers at ministerial conferences, usually held every two years.

But in practice, the WTO is dominated by a few major industrial countries—while the poorest developing countries have little or no representation or negotiation capacity. In 2000 as many as 15 African countries did not have a representative at WTO headquarters in Geneva (table 5.4)—while Mauritius, a very small country, had five. The WTO has responded to these disparities by seeking to establish a technical assistance unit to help developing countries with negotiations.

Demands for greater voice in the WTO echo a recent history of underrepresentation in international negotiations. Relative to their share of the world's population, low and medium human development countries have poor representation in negotiations on international conventions, such as the one on plant genetic resources (figure 5.4). Deeper reform of WTO decision-making will require consideration of proposals for improving transparency and participation in the WTO system.

First, WTO consultations, discussions, negotiations and decision-making have to be made truly transparent, participatory and democratic. Discussions and negotiations being planned and taking place at the WTO must be

made known, and all members must be allowed to participate. To facilitate fair representation of members' various positions, consideration should be given to a negotiation system that combines full participation by all members with the efficiency of a representational mechanism. The Cartegena Protocol on Biosafety offers an interesting model for such a system (box 5.7).

Second, the WTO should be impartial and be seen as impartial. In particular, it should not be seen as taking sides with more powerful countries at the expense of developing countries. The system should reflect the fact that most WTO members are developing and transition economies, which have at least as great a stake as industrial countries in a fair and balanced multilateral system. Procedures should enable developing countries to voice their interests and exercise their rights. In addition, developing countries should be better represented in the WTO secretariat, especially in senior positions.

Third, there should be much greater transparency in the WTO—and other international organizations—in relation to national democratic processes. Parliamentarians should be kept constantly informed of developments at the WTO and other international organizations. And given the potential effects of these developments on national policies and practices, they should be debated. Open debate may be opposed by adversely affected groups, but the process can create political legitimacy for trade liberalization. Such is the case in India, where some groups remain opposed to trade liberalization but open debate has created a substantial constituency of support across the main political parties.

DEEPENING DEMOCRACY—GLOBAL AND NATIONAL IMPERATIVES

Many reforms have been proposed in this chapter, covering a variety of ways that democratic processes could be advanced globally. These include ways of increasing representation, transparency and accountability to promote specific reforms in international institutions.

The traditional argument against greater participation and representation is that they render decision-making clumsy and unworkable.

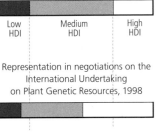

FIGURE 5.4
Whose voices are heard in international negotiations?

Countries in the world

| Low HDI | Medium HDI | High HDI |

Representation in negotiations on the International Undertaking on Plant Genetic Resources, 1998

Source: UNDP 2000a.

The Biosafety Protocol—a model for inclusive global governance?

Global negotiations have proliferated in recent years—and taken on much greater significance. This has led people to compare the many kinds of negotiations under way and to search for more transparent, democratic models. In particular, many forums have been looking for ways to give all participating countries a fairer say. The Cartagena Biosafety Protocol, established under the Convention on Biological Diversity, is a case in point.

Negotiations for the protocol started in 1996 and concluded in 2000. At one stage, as the target date for concluding the negotiations neared and the differences among the contending parties still looked wide, there were fears that the talks would break down. But a combination of transparent, innovative methods and an active, impartial chairperson allowed the successful conclusion of one of the most contentious negotiations in international law.

Juan Mayr Maldonado, Colombia's minister of environment, introduced the new methods when he became chair of the Extraordinary Meeting of the Conference of Parties to the Convention on Biological Diversity, held in Cartagena in February 1999. He continued to use these methods at an informal consultation of the members in Vienna in September 1999, until the conclusion of the negotiations at a resumed Extraordinary Meeting of the Conference of Parties in Montreal in January 2000.

The main features of the methods involved:
• Grouping country participants by their interests and positions, rather than by geography or income. A significant innovation was the formation of the like-minded group, which enabled most of the developing countries to caucus while the few that held a different position could join another group.

This was a departure from the norm, in which developing countries come under the single umbrella of "the Group of 77 and China".
• Selecting representatives from each group to act as spokespersons, with the number of spokespersons depending on the number of members in the group. This approach allowed for a more equitable representation of views.
• Allowing all member countries to be present during negotiations, even though the negotiations were carried out among the group spokespersons. Thus the meetings were transparent and open to the participation of all members.
• Encouraging the participation of non-governmental organizations (NGOs). In Vienna the chairperson met separately with NGOs and industry. In response to NGO requests for access to the negotiations, instantaneous audio reception was provided in a "spillover" room next to the government consultation room. Thus NGOs and representatives of international organizations were able to follow the discussions. And in Montreal all observers, including the media, were able to sit in on the plenary sessions.

These new arrangements brought the complicated, often contentious negotiations over the protocol to a successful conclusion. They helped strike an effective balance between three sometimes competing priorities: allowing all members to participate, enabling negotiations among so many countries to flow within time constraints and ensuring transparency and openness so that members could have the information needed to follow the discussions. The new approach also improved the flow of information to NGOs and increased NGO involvement.

Source: Ling 2000; Khor 2002.

But this view must be set against a new reality. The United Nations, IMF, World Bank and WTO have all found that without greater participation and representation, progress is often not possible.

International organizations are expected to provide a wide range of global public goods that demand deep compliance the world over. These organizations require people in both industrial and developing countries to commit to global goals—and to act accordingly. Such commitment and action can be achieved only if international organizations are considered legitimate. This does not mean that international institutions must—or could—reflect the interests of every group in the world. But it does mean that these institutions must take into account a diversity of interests and adjudicate among them in a fair, just way.

Achieving deeper democracy globally will require expanding political space for a range of civil society actors and including developing countries more deeply in the decision-making of international institutions. Efforts to achieve these goals must confront the realities of global power. But they hold out the possibility that both industrial and developing countries will be better served by more inclusive global cooperation that gives excluded and marginalized people a stronger voice.

Whether this can be realized will largely depend on citizens and governments in more powerful countries recognizing that reform is in their interest. But in a more interdependent world, that interest is becoming more apparent. International institutions are promoting democracy and democratic principles in developing and transition economies—a very positive development. But they will not succeed without the natural corollary: greater democracy, transparency and accountability in the institutions themselves. This dual process—deepening democracy at the national and global levels—has the potential to transform the lives of the world's people.

Notes

Human development balance sheet

1. Human Development Report Office calculations based on Polity IV 2002. Following Marshall and Jaggers 2000, p.12, a change of 3 or more in the polity score is considered significant. Countries that were members of the Soviet Union in 1980 are given its score.
2. Human Development Report Office calculations based on Alvarez and others 2002.
3. Human Development Report Office calculations based on Alvarez and others 2002.
4. Human Development Report Office calculations based on Polity IV 2002.
5. Human Development Report Office calculations based on Polity IV 2002.
6. Anheier, Glasius and Kaldor 2001.
7. Indicator table 29.
8. Kendig 1999.
9. Freedom House 2000.
10. UNESCO 1999b.
11. Freedom House 2000.
12. Cooper 2002 and CPJ 2002.
13. Human Development Report Office calculations based on UNOHCHR 2002.
14. Freedom House 2002. Figure refers to the number of countries described as "not free" or "partly free".
15. Human Development Report Office calculations based on UNOHCHR 2002.
16. Indicator table 23.
17. Indicator table 23.
18. Human Development Report Office calculations based on Global Policy Forum 2002.
19. Human Development Report Office calculations based on IMF 2002 and World Bank 2001b.
20. World Bank 2002c.
21. World Bank 2002c.
22. Milanovic 2001.
23. World Bank 2002c.
24. Indicator table 12.
25. Indicator table 12.
26. Indicator table 12.
27. Nua Publish 2002.
28. Nua Publish 2002.
29. WHO, UNICEF and WSSCC 2000.
30. Appendix table A1.3.
31. UNICEF 2002.
32. FAO 2001.
33. UNAIDS 2000a.
34. UNAIDS 2001.
35. Indicator table 8.
36. WHO 1997.
37. Hunger Project 2002.
38. UNICEF 2002.
39. UNESCO 2000.
40. Appendix table A1.3.
41. UNESCO 2000.
42. Appendix table A1.3.
43. Appendix table A1.3.
44. UNESCO 2000.
45. Filmer 1999.
46. Human Development Report Office calculations based on UN 2002.
47. Marshall 2000.
48. Laurenti 2002.
49. Human Development Report Office calculations based on Marshall 2000.
50. Human Development Report Office calculations based on Marshall 2000.
51. Human Development Report Office calculations based on indicator table 20 and UNHCR 2001.
52. UNICEF 1996.
53. UNHCR 2001a.
54. ICBL 2001.
55. ICBL 2001.

Chapter 1

1. World Bank 2002c.
2. UNESCO 2000, p. 9.
3. WHO, UNICEF and WSSCC 2000, p. v.
4. Human Development Report Office calculations based on Polity IV 2002. Following Marshall and Jaggers 2000, p. 12, a change of 3 or more in the polity score is considered significant. Countries that were members of the Soviet Union in 1980 are given its score.
5. Human Development Report Office calculations based on Alvarez and others 2002.
6. Oeppen and Vaupel 2002.
7. Milanovic 2001.
8. WHO 1997.
9. Human Development Report Office calculations based on WHO 2001.
10. WHO 2002a.
11. World Bank 2002c.
12. UNICEF 2002, p. 10.
13. Freedom House 2002.
14. Freedom House 2002. Figure refers to number of countries described as "not free" or "partly free".
15. Human Development Report Office calculations based on Marshall 2000.
16. Human Development Report Office calculations based on Polity IV 2002.
17. Human Development Report Office calculations based on Polity IV 2002. Following Marshall and Jaggers 2000, p. 12, a change of 3 or more in the polity score is considered significant. Countries that were members of the Soviet Union in 1980 are given its score.
18. Huntington 1991.
19. Human Development Report Office calculations based on Alvarez and others 2002.
20. Human Development Report Office calculations based on Polity IV 2002.
21. Human Development Report Office calculations based on Polity IV 2002, where a polity score of 6 or higher denotes full

democracy.

22. Carothers 2002.
23. Indicator table 23.
24. Human Development Report Office calculations based on Marshall 2000.
25. UNHCR 2000.
26. UNICEF 1996.
27. UNHCR 2001a, p. 2.
28. Stewart and Fitzgerald 2000.
29. Carnegie Commission on Preventing Deadly Conflict 1997, p. 20.
30. Human Development Report Office calculations based on UNHCR 2002. Besides returning refugees and asylum-seekers, people otherwise of concern to the UN High Commissioner for Refugees include forced migrants, stateless persons and others.
31. Human Development Report Office calculations based on indicator table 20 and UNHCR 2001, p. 4.
32. UN 2001c, paragraph 2.
33. UN 2000b, pp. 56–58.
34. Hanmer and Naschold 2000.
35. Dollar and Kraay 2001.
36. Dikhanov and Ward 2001. The authors find that the worldwide within-country Theil index of inequality increased steadily, from 0.211 in 1970 to 0.267 in 1999.
37. Cornia and Kiiski 2001.
38. Cornia and Court 2001.
39. UNDP 2000b.
40. UNDP 1999b.
41. UNDP 1998.
42. Human Development Report Office calculations based on indicator table 3.
43. FAO 2001.
44. FAO 2001.
45. UNESCO 2000, pp. 8–9.
46. Filmer 1999.
47. UNESCO 2000.
48. Hunger Project 2002.
49. Filmer 1999.
50. World Bank 2001e, p. 80.
51. OECD and UNESCO Institute for Statistics 2001.
52. Willms 1999.
53. UNICEF 2002.
54. UNICEF 2002, p. 11.
55. UNICEF 2002, p. 12.
56. UNAIDS 2001.
57. UNDESA 2001.
58. UNAIDS 2000b.
59. UNAIDS 2000b, p. 32.
60. UNAIDS 2000b, p. 27.
61. UNAIDS 2000b.
62. UNAIDS 2001.
63. UNAIDS 2000a.
64. WHO 2000a.
65. WHO 2000a.
66. WHO 2000a.
67. WHO 2001.
68. WHO 2000a.
69. Sachs 2001, p. 25.
70. WHO 2001.
71. CDIAC 2001.
72. UNCCD 2002.
73. UNCCD 2002.
74. WHO, UNICEF and WSSCC 2000, p. v.
75. WHO, UNICEF and WSSCC 2000.
76. WHO, UNICEF and WSSCC 2000, p. 34.
77. WHO, UNICEF and WSSCC 2000, p. v.
78. Greece lacks 1990 data and so is not included in figure 1.17.
79. Larson 2002.
80. EU 2002.
81. Open Society Institute 2001, p. 9.
82. Bill and Melinda Gates Foundation 2002.
83. World Bank 2002d.
84. World Bank 2002d.
85. Morrisey 2002.
86. Naschold 2002.
87. World Bank 2002c.
88. Mehrotra 2001.
89. World Bank 2002c.
90. See discussion in Atkinson 1999, pp. 6–7.

Chapter 2
1. UN 1998.
2. Court and Hyden 2000, 2001; Mahbub ul Haq Human Development Centre 1999; UNDP 2001e, 2002c; Kaufmann, Kraay and Zoido-Lobatón 1999, 2002.
3. UNDP 1990, p. 9.
4. UNDP 2000a.
5. The capabilities approach to development—and human development, its application—leaves open the final definition of valuable ends to social and individual values. According to Sen, democracy is an essential condition for identifying priorities in a society (Nussbaum and Sen 1993).
6. Schmitter and Karl 1991.
7. Schmitter and Karl 1991.
8. Polity IV 2002.
9. Przeworski and others 2000; Alvarez and others 2002.
10. Barro 1997.
11. Przeworski and others 2000.
12. Przeworski 2000.
13. Barro 1991.
14. Sen 2000, p. 181.
15. Sen 2000.
16. Przeworski and others 2000.
17. Commission for Racial Equality 2001.
18. World Bank 2001e.
19. Przeworski 1998.
20. Karl forthcoming.
21. Quibria 2002.

Chapter 3
1. Tanzi, Chu and Gupta 1999, p. 1.
2. Human Development Report Office calculation based on Polity IV 2002. Following Marshall and Jaggers 2000, p. 12, a change of 3 or more in the Polity score is considered significant. Countries that were members of the Soviet Union in 1980 are given its score.
3. Based on Polity IV 2002.
4. Zakaria 1997.
5. Carothers 1999.
6. Latinobarómetro 2002. Data are from interviews of 1,000–1,200 urban residents in each of 17 Latin American countries—for a total of 18.000 interviews—conducted by Corporación Latinobarómetro, a non-profit Chilean NGO, each year since 1995.
7. Gallup International 1999.
8. UNDP 1999c.
9. Goetz and Jenkins 2002.
10. Goetz and Jenkins 2002.
11. Freedom House 2001, p. 123.
12. Freedom House 2001, p. 244.
13. ACE Project 2001a.
14. von Alemann 2000.
15. ACE Project 2001a.
16. International IDEA forthcoming; *Business Week* 2000; Hooper 2000.
17. Mitchell and Glickman 2002.
18. Center for Responsive Politics 2002.
19. ACE Project 2001a.

20. Deininger 1998.
21. UNDP 2001b, p. 45.
22. UNDP 2001b.
23. Mehrotra 2002.
24. Mahbub ul Haq Human Development Centre 1999.
25. International IDEA 2002a.
26. Marta Lagos 2001.
27. Fomunyoh 2001 p. 48.
28. ACE Project 2001b.
29. NDI 2001.
30. International IDEA forthcoming.
31. Kohli 2001; Rudolph and Rudolph 2001.
32. Richani 2002.
33. Fomunyoh 2001, p. 45.
34. Goldstone 2002.
35. Bakker 2002; Budlender, Sharp and Allen 1999.
36. Mahbub ul Haq Human Development Centre 1999.
37. Whaley 2000.
38. Davis 2002.
39. Ketterer 2001, pp. 135–50.
40. IPU 1998.
41. Mehrotra 2002.
42. Mitra 2001.
43. In 1996 the New Delhi–based Centre for Study of Developing Societies interviewed 10,000 people in 104 of India's parliamentary constituencies on their attitudes towards social, political and economic issues. The survey found varying degrees of trust in political institutions and processes (Mitra 2001).
44. Calderón 2002; UNDP 2002c.
45. Sakr 2002.
46. Freedom House 2000.
47. Pralong 2002b.
48. Human Rights Watch 2001.
49. Cooper 2002.
50. CPJ 2002.
51. International Federation of Journalists 1999.
52. Data on media ownership are from a survey in 97 countries of who owns the five largest newspapers, radio stations and television channels; see Djankov and others 2001.
53. Data on media concentration are from Bertrand 2001, p. 7.
54. Smulovitz and Peruzzotti 2002b.
55. Bertrand 2002; UNDP 2002c.
56. Tettey 2002.
57. Tettey 2002.
58. Bertrand 2002.
59. Lonsdale 1986, cited in Luckham and others 2000.
60. de Sousa Santos 1998; Osmani 2002a.
61. Hammond and Lash 2000.
62. UNOHCHR 2002.

Chapter 4
1. Onishi 2002.
2. SIPRI 2001; SIPRI refers to armed conflicts with more than 1,000 registered deaths in any single year. Human Development Report Office estimates of people killed in the 1990s are based on data from Marshall 2000.
3. Chege 2001.
4. Hegre and others 2001.
5. Brown, Lynn-Jones and Miller 1996.
6. Human Development Report Office calculations based on Alvarez and others 2002.
7. Human Development Report Office calculations based on Alvarez and others 2002.

8. Rummell 1997; Leitenberg 2001.
9. Hills 2000.
10. Narayan and others 2000.
11. Security Industry Association 2000.
12. Mulvenon 2001.
13. U.S. Government 2000, chapter 2
14. Hendrickson and Ball 2002, p. 13.
15. Edmunds, Cottey and Forster forthcoming; Edmunds 2002.
16. Edmunds, Cottey and Forster forthcoming.
17. Neild 1998.
18. Hills 2000.
19. Neild 2001a.
20. Chege 2001.
21. Neild 2001a.
22. Wulf 2000.
23. Call and Barnett 1999.
24. Call and Barnett 1999.
25. Lecoq 2002.
26. Reif 2000.
27. Reif 2000.
28. Gacaca is a traditional justice system where people gather at the invitation of village elders to resolve community disputes. Those indicted for a crime in this process are returned to prison, while those perceived as innocent are declared free. Gacaca is helping Rwanda deal with the more than 100,000 suspects in jail awaiting trial on genocide-related charges.
29. Amnesty International, Cairo Institute for Human Rights Studies, Federation International des Ligues des Droits de l'Homme, Human Rights Watch and International Commission of Jurists 2002.
30. UNOHCHR 2001.

Chapter 5
1. Ford 2001.
2. WHO 2000b.
3. SIPRI 2001, p. 52.
4. World Bank 2001c.
5. Anheier, Glasius and Kaldor 2001, p. 4.
6. Anheier, Glasius and Kaldor 2001, p. 6.
7. Edwards 2000, pp. 9–10.
8. ICBL 2002.
9. Jubilee Australia 1999.
10. Jubilee Australia 1999.
11. Love 2002.
12. Woods 2002.
13. Woods 2002.
14. Global Compact 2001.
15. Korpela 2002.
16. Global Compact 2001.
17. Kendig 1999 in Edwards and Gaventa 2001, p. 9.
18. Kapur 2001.
19. Woods 2002.
20. Stewart and Daws 2000.
21. Buira 2000.
22. Buira 2000.
23. Buira 2000.
24. Woods 2002.
25. Khor 2002.

Bibliographic note

Human development balance sheet draws on Alvarez and others 2002; Anheier, Glasius and Kaldor 2001; Cooper 2002; CPJ 2002; FAO 2002; Filmer 1999; Freedom House 2000, 2002; Global Policy Forum 2002; Hunger Project 2002; ICBL 2001; IMF 2002a; IPU 2002; Kendig 1999; Laurenti 2002; Marshall 2000; Marshall and Jaggers 2000; Milanovic 2001; Nua Publish 2002; Polity IV 2002; UN 2002; UNAIDS 2000a, 2001; UNESCO 1999b, 2000; UNHCR 2001a; UNICEF 1996, 2002; UNOHCHR 2002; WHO 1997; WHO, UNICEF and WSSCC 2000; World Bank 2001b, 2002c.

Chapter 1 draws on Carter and others 2002; Court 2002; Alvarez and others 2002; Atkinson 1999; Atkinson and Brandolini 2001; Bill and Melinda Gates Foundation 2002; Bourguignon and Morrison 2001; Carnegie Commission on Preventing Deadly Conflict 1997; Carothers 2002; CDIAC 2001; Cornia and Court 2001; Cornia and Kiiski 2001; Court and Hyden 2000; 2001; Dikhanov and Ward 2001; Dollar and Kraay 2001; EU 2002; FAO 2001; Filmer 1999; Freedom House 1999, 2000, 2002; Hanmer and Naschold 2000; Hunger Project 2002; Huntington 1991; ILO 1997; International IDEA 1997; IPU 2002a, 2002b, 2002c; Kaufmann, Kraay and Zoido-Lobatón 1999, 2002; Krugman 2002; Larson 2002; Machel 1996; Malik 2002; Marshall 2000; Marshall and Jaggers 2000; Mehrotra 2001; Milanovic 2001; Morrisey 2002; Naschold 2002; OECD 2001; OECD and UNESCO 2001; Oeppen and Vaupel 2002; Open Society Institute 2001; Polity IV 2002; PRS Group 2001; Sachs 2001; Schultz 1998; Smeeding and Grodner 2000; Stewart and Fitzgerald 2000; Transparency International 2001; UIA 2000; UN 2000a, 2000b, 2001c, 2002a; UNAIDS 2000a, 2000b, 2001; UNCCD 2002; UNDESA 2001; UNDP 1998, 1999b, 1999d, 2000b, 2002d, 2002e; UNESCO 1999a, 2000, 2001, 2002; UNHCR 2000, 2001a, 2001b, 2001c, 2002; UNICEF 1996, 2002; UNOHCHR 2001, 2002 ; U.S. Bureau of Census 1999; WHO 1997, 1998, 2000a, 2000b, 2001; WHO, UNICEF and WSSCC 2000; Willms 1999; World Bank 2001c, 2001d, 2001e, 2002c, 2002d, 2002e; World Bank and IMF 2001.

Chapter 2 draws on Alvarez and others 2002; Atkinson and Brandolini 2001; Barro 1991, 1996, 1997; Barro and Lee 2000; Barry 2002; Balgescu and others 2001; Borner, Brunetti and Weder 1995; Clague and others 1996; Commission for Racial Equality 2001; Court and Hyden 2000, 2001; Fukuda-Parr 2002; Haggard 1997; Hyden and Court 2001; Johnson, IPU 2002; Karl forthcoming; Kaufmann, Kraay and Zoido-Lobatón 1999, 2002; Landman 1999; Lijphart 1999; Linz and Stepan 1978, 1996; Linz and Valenzuela 1994; Londregan and Poole 1996; Mahbub ul Haq Human Development Centre 1999, 2000, 2001; Mehrotra and Delamonica 2002; Milanovic 1998; Nussbaum and Sen 1993; Osmani 2002b; Przeworski 1998, 2000; Przeworski and others 2000; Quibria 2002; Schmitter and Karl 1991; Sen 1989, 2000; Streeten 2002; Tavares and Waczairg 2001; UN 1998; UNDP 1997b, 1997c, 2000a, 2001e, 2002c; UNESCO 2002; Varshney 2002; Waczairg 2000; World Bank 2001c, 2001e, 2002b.

Chapter 3 draws on ACE Project 2001a, 2001b; Adejumobi 2000; Atkinson and Brandolini 2001; Ayee 2000; Bakker 2002; Bertrand 2001, 2002; Borner, Brunetti and Weder 1995; Budlender, Sharp and Allen 1999; Budlender and others 2002; Business Week 2000; Byanyima 2000; Çagatay and others 2000; Calderón

2002; Carothers 2002; Caruso 2001; Center for Responsive Politics 2001; Chege 2001; Clift 2002; Common Cause 2001; Cooper 2002; CPJ 2002; Davis 2002; de Sousa Santos 1998; Deccan 2002; Deininger 1998; Di Rosa 2002; Djankov and others 2001; Esim 2000; Falaakh 2002; Fomunyoh 2001; Franco 2000; Freedom House 2000, 2001; Gallup International 1999; Global Climate Coalition 2002; Goetz and Jenkins 2002; Goldstone 2002; Grayson 2000; Grunwald 2002; Haggard 1997; Hammond and Lash 2000; HCCI 2001; Hewitt and Mukhopadhyay 2001; Himmelweit 2000; Hooper 2000; Human Rights Watch 2001, 2002; Inoguchi 2002; International Federation of Journalists 1999; International IDEA 2000a, 2000b, 2000c, 2001, 2002a, 2002b, forthcoming; Instituto Federal Electoral 2002; IPU 1998, 2000a, 2000b, 2001, 2002a, 2002b; Kaldor 2002; Kamal 2000; Karam 1998; Karl forthcoming; Ketterer 2001; Kohli 2001; Korten 1995; Lagos 2001;Latinobarómetro 2002; Leaf 2002; Lijphart 1999; Linz and Stepan 1978, 1996; Linz and Valenzuela 1994; Loada 2001; Lonsdale 1986; Lopez-Pintor 2000; Luckham and others 2000; Madeley 1999; Maguire 2002; Mahbub ul Haq Human Development Centre 1999; Mair and van Biezen 2001; Marshall and Jaggers 2000; McChesney 1999; Mehrotra 2002; Mehrotra and Delamonica 2002; Méndez and Pinheiro 1999; Mezzetti 2002; Milanovic 1998; Mitchell and Glickman 2002; Mitra 2001; Narayan, Chambers, Kaul Shaha and Petesh 2000; Narayan, Patel, Schafft, Rademacher and Koch-Schulte 2000; NDI 2001; Norris 2000, 2002; Norris and Zinnbauer 2002; Nua Publish 2002; O'Donnell 1999, 2000, 2002; Osmani 2002a; Parry 2001; Pinheiro 1999; Pityana 2000; Polity IV 2002; Pralong 2002b; Proyecto Estado de la Nación 2001; Rana 2000; Reyes 2000; Richani 2002; Rose and Haerpfer 1999; Rudolph and Rudolph 2001; Sakr 2002; Sandbrook 2000; Sen 2000; Sen and Drèze 2002; Sharp 2000; Shell 2002; Smulovitz and Peruzzotti 2002a, 2002b; Sridharan 2001; Streeten 2002; Subasic 2002; SustainAbility 2001; Tanzi, Chu and Gupta 1999; Tettey 2002; Tokman and O'Donnell 1998; UNDP 1993, 1997a, 1997b, 1997c, 1999a, 1999b, 1999c, 1999d, 2000a, 2001b, 2001c, 2001e; UNDP China Country Office 2002; UNDP Viet Nam Country Office 2002; UNESCO 1999b; UNOHCHR 2002; UNPAN 2002; Vargas Cullell 2002; Varshney 2002; von Alemann 2000; Waczairg 2000; Washington Office on Latin America 2000; Whaley 2000; World Bank 2001c, 2001e; Working Group on E-Government in the Developing World 2002; Zadek 2001; Zakaria 1997.

Chapter 4 draws on Alvarez and others 2002; Amnesty International, Cairo Institute for Human Rights Studies, Federation International des Ligues des Droits de l'Homme, Human Rights Watch and International Commission of Jurists 2002; Anderlini 2000; Annan 1999; Arias Foundation, BASIC and Saferworld 1997; Ball 1988; 1997, 1998, 2000, 2001; Ball and Spies 1998; Ball and others 2002; Ball and others forthcoming; Batchelor, Cock and McKenzie 2000; Bendaña 1999; BICC 2001; Bland 1999; Brömmelhörster and Paes forthcoming; Brown and Miller 1996; Brzoska 1981, 1992, 1995; Buzan 1991; Call and Barnett 1999; Canada, Department of Foreign Affairs and International Trade 2001; Chege 2001; Collier and Hoeffler 2001; The Economist 2002; Economist Intelligence Unit 2002; Edmunds 2002; Edmunds, Cottey and Forster forthcoming; Eldis 2002; GENIE 2001; Gurr, Marshall and Khosla 2001; Hayner 2001; Hegre and others 2001; Hendrickson and Ball 2002; Hills 2000; ICBL 2001; Jubb 2001; Kaldor 2001; King, Dorn and Hodes forthcoming; Kingma 2000, 2001; Krause 1997; Lecoq 2002; Legault 2001; Leitenberg 2001; Londono and Guerrero 1999; McCulloch 2000, forthcoming; Muggah and Berman 2001; Mulvenon 2001; Narayan, Chambers, Kaul Shaha and Petesh 2000; Nathan 1994, 2000; Neild 1998, 2001a, 2001b; Nübler 2000; OECD DAC 1997; Omitoogun 2002; Onichi 2002; Ottaway and Lieven 2002; Pauwels 2000; Reif 2000; Rummel 1997; Security Industry Association 2000; SIPRI 2001, 2002; Sköns and others 2001; Stewart 1998, 2000; Stewart and Fitzgerald 2001; Summers 2000; Tepperman 2002; U.K. Department for International Development 2000; UN 1999, 2001a, 2001b; UN Information Centre Bonn 2001; UNDP 1994, 2001a, 2001d, 2002a, 2002b; UNOHCHR 2001; U.S. Bureau of Justice Statistics 1999; U.S. Department of State Bureau of Arms Control 2000; U.S. Government 2000; U.S. Institute of Peace 2002; Wallensteen and Sollenberg 2000; World Bank 2002a; Wulf 2000.

Chapter 5 draws American University International Law Review 2001; Albin 1999, 2001; Anheier, Glasius and Kaldor 2001; Broad and Cavanagh 1998; Buira 2000; Commission on Global Governance 1995; CUTS-ARC 2001; Edwards 1999, 2000; Edwards and Gaventa 2001; Edwards and Hulme 1995; Feldstein 1998; Ford 2001; Global Compact 2001; Global Policy Forum 1997, 2002a, 2002b, 2002c, 2002d; Held 1995, 2001; ICBL 2002; IMF 2002a, 2002b; Imhof, Wong and Bosshard 2002; Jenkins 2001; Jubilee Australia 1999; Kaldor 2002; Kapur 2001; Kapur, Lewis and Webb 1997; Kendig 1999; Kennedy, Messner and Nuscheler 2002; Khor 2002; Korpela 2002; Krueger 1997; Lindenberg and Bryant 2001; Ling 2000; Love 2001, 2002; Mehrotra 2001; Mikesell 1994; Nayyar 2001; Neuffer 2001; Paul 1995, 2001; SIPRI 2001; Stewart and Daws 2000; Thakur and Newman 2000; UN 2000b; UNAC 1995; UNDP 1994, 1999c, 2000a; WHO 2000b, 2001; Woods 2002; Women's Environment and Development Organization 2002; World Bank 1998, 2001a, 2001b.

Bibliography

Background papers, regional studies and background notes are available from the Human Development Report Office.

Background papers

Bakker, Isabella. 2002. "Fiscal Policy, Accountability and Voice: The Example of Gender Responsive Budget Initiatives."

Ball, Nicole, and Michael Brzoska, with Kees Kingma and Herbert Wulf. 2002. "Voice and Accountability in the Security Sector."

Barry, Christian. 2002. "Towards Social Justice in Governance."

Falk, Richard. 2002. "Trends towards Transnational Justice: Innovations and Institutions."

Goetz, Ann Marie, and Robert Jenkins. 2002. "Voice, Accountability and Human Development: The Emergence of a New Agenda."

Kaldor, Mary. 2002. "Civil Society and Accountability."

Khor, Martin. 2002. "Some Aspects of Global Governance and Decision-Making Processes."

Malik, Adeel. 2002. "State of the Art in Governance Indicators."

Mehra, Malini. 2002. "Corporate Accountability—Breakdown, Reforms and Innovations."

Mehrotra, Santosh. 2002. "Basic Social Services for All? Ensuring Accountability through Deep Democratic Decentralisation."

Mezzetti, Petra. 2002. "The Impact of Corruption on Human Development: The Economic, Social and Moral Costs."

Norris, Pippa, and Dieter Zinnbauer. 2002. "Giving Voice to the Voiceless. Good Governance, Human Development and Mass Communications."

Osmani, Siddiq. 2002a. "Expanding Voice and Accountability through the Budgetary Process."

———. 2002b. "Governance for Social Justice."

Streeten, Paul. 2002. "Empowerment, Participation and the Poor."

Varshney, Ashutosh. 2002. "Poverty Eradication and Democracy in the Developing World."

Woods, Ngaire. 2002. "Accountability in Global Governance."

Regional studies

Dabrowski, Marek, and Radzislawa Gortat. 2002. "Political and Economic Institutions, Growth and Poverty—Experience of Transition Countries."

Falaakh, Mohammad Fajrul. 2002. "Enhancing Accountable Governance to Support Poverty Eradication: The Role of Civil Society in Southeast Asia."

Inoguchi, Takashi. 2002. "-Voice and Accountability: The Media and the Internet in Democratic Development."

Marchlewski, Wojciech. 2002. "Regional Study of the Role of Civil Society Organizations in Promoting Accountability among the Poor and Disadvantaged Groups: Poland."

Mitchell, Lincoln, and Leo Glickman. 2002. "Mixing Money and Politics: How Campaign Finance Affects Democratic Governance in the U.S."

Mohiddin, Ahmed. 2002. "Regional Overview of the Impact of the Failures of Accountability on Poor People."

Richani, Nazih. 2002. "Political Parties, Justice Systems and the Poor: The Experience of the Arab States."

Sakr, Naomi. 2002. "Civil Society, Media and Accountability in the Arab Region."

Smulovitz, Catalina, and Enrique Peruzzotti. 2002a. "Civil Society, the Media and Internet as Tools for Creating Accountability to Poor and Disadvantaged Groups."

Spoerer, Sergio. 2002. "Failures of Political and Judicial Accountability for Poor People in Latin America."

Subasic, Katarina. 2002. "Role of the Media and the Internet as Tools for Creating Accountability to Poor and Disadvantaged Groups in the Former Yugoslavia."

Tettey, Wisdom. 2002. "The Media, Accountability and Civic Engagement in Africa."

Vayrynen, Raimo. 2002. "Human Development, Accountability and the European Union."

Background notes

Calderón, Fernando. 2002. "Governance Reform In Bolivia."

Carter, Lynn, Zeric Smith and Joseph Siegal. 2002. "Memorandum on Measuring Voice and Accountability"

Caruso, Natalia. 2002. "Budget Initiatives in Developing Countries."

Court, Julius. 2002. "Input for Trends in Political Participation and Democracy around the World."

Goldstone, Richard. 2002. "The Role of the Judiciary in Apartheid South Africa."

International Institute for Environment and Development. 2002a. "National Strategies for Sustainable Development: New Thinking and Time for Action."

———. 2002b. "Transforming Organisations for Deliberative Democracy and Citizen Empowerment."

Johnsson, Anders, IPU (Inter-Parliamentary Union). 2002. "The Inter-Parliamentary Union—Universal Declaration of Democracy."

Leigh, Robert. 2002. "Broadening the Governance Agenda: The Role of Volunteerism."

Maguire, Linda. 2002. "Voice and Accountability: Literature Review for *Human Development Report 2002*."

Mohmand, Shandana Khan. 2002. "Contemporary Perspectives on Voice."

Pralong, Sandra. 2002a. "Media Accountability Practices I—Western Europe."

———. 2002b. "Media Accountability Practices II—Eastern Europe."

Sakr, Naomi. 2002a. " Media and Accountability in the Arab Region"

Smulovitz, Catalina, and Enrique Peruzzotti. 2002b. "How Can the Media Be Held More Accountable?"

UNDP (United Nations Development Programme) China Country Office. 2002. "China Democratization: Reform, Development and Stability."

UNDP (United Nations Development Programme) Viet Nam Country Office. 2002. "The Grassroots Democracy in Viet Nam: Context and Main Issues."

Vargas Cullell, Jorge . 2002. "The Citizen's Audit on the Quality of Democracy in Costa Rica: Understanding and Improving the Level of Democracy in Political Life."

Villacorta, Wilfrido. 2002. "Civil Society Organizations and Philippine Democracy."

References

ACE (Administration and Cost of Elections) Project. 2001a. "Party and Candidate Financing." [http://www.aceproject.org/main/english/pc/pcd.htm]. April 2002.

———. 2001b. "Political Parties and the Electoral Process." [http://www.aceproject.org/main/english/pc/pcb.htm]. April 2002

Adejumobi, Said. 2000. "Engendering Accountable Governance in Africa." Paper commissioned for the regional workshops of the International Institute for Democracy and Electoral Assistance's Democracy Forum 2000. [http://www.idea.int/2000df/commissioned_papers_5.htm]. March 2002.

Albin, Cecilia. 1999. "Can NGOs Enhance the Effectiveness of International Negotiations?" *International Negotiation* 4 (3): 371–87.

———. 2001. Justice and Fairness in International Negotiation. Cambridge: Cambridge University Press.

Alvarez, Michael, Jose Antonio Cheibub, Jennifer Gandhi, Fernando Limongi, Adam Przeworski and Sebastian Saiegh. 2002. "D&D2000." Dataset provided in correspondence. March.

American University International Law Review. 2001. "Reactions to the Report of the World Commission on Dams." *American University Journal of International Law and Policy Review* 16 (6).

Amnesty International, Cairo Institute for Human Rights Studies, Federation International des Ligues des Droits de l'Homme, Human Rights Watch and International Commission of Jurists. 2002. "A Human Rights Framework for Responding to Terrorism." Open statement to the UN Office of the High Commissioner for Human Rights, London.

Anderlini, Sanam Naraghi. 2000. *Women at the Peace Table: Making a Difference.* New York: UN Development Fund for Women.

Anheier, Helmut, Marlies Glasius and Mary Kaldor, eds. 2001. *Global Civil Society 2001.* New York: Oxford University Press.

Annan, Kofi. 1999. "Peace and Development—One Struggle, Two Fronts." Address to World Bank staff, October 19. [http://www.worldbank.org/html/extdr/extme/kasp101999.htm]. March 2002.

Arias Foundation, BASIC (British American Security Information Council) and Saferworld. 1997. "Nobel Peace Laureates' International Code of Conduct on Arms Transfers." [basicint.org/code_itl.htm]. March 2002.

Atkinson, Anthony B. 1999. "Is Rising Income Inequality Inevitable? A Critique of the Transatlantic Consensus." Annual Lecture 3. United Nations University and World Institute for Development Economics Research, Helsinki, Finland. [http://www.wider.unu.edu/events/annuel1999a.pdf].

Atkinson, Anthony B., and Andrea Brandolini. 2001. "Promise and Pitfalls in the Use of 'Secondary' Datasets: Income Inequality in OECD Countries." *Journal of Economic Literature* 39 (3): 771–99.

Ayee, Joseph R.A.. 2000. "Participation." Paper commissioned for the regional workshops of the International Institute for Democracy and Electoral Assistance's Democracy Forum 2000. [http://www.idea.int/2000df/commissioned_papers_6.htm]. March 2002.

Balgescu, Monica, Julius Court, Goran Hyden, Ken Mease and Keiko Suzuki. 2001. "Assessing and Analyzing Governance: Lessons from the World Governance Assessment Pilot Phase." World Governance Assessment Working Paper 2. United Nations University, Tokyo. [http://www.unu.edu/p%26g/wgs/pdf/assessinggovernance.pdf]. April 2002.

Ball, Nicole. 1988. *Security and Economy in the Third World.* Princeton, N.J.: Princeton University Press.

———. 1997. "Demobilizing and Reintegrating Soldiers: Lessons from Africa." In Krishna Kumar, ed., *Rebuilding Societies after Civil War: Critical Roles for International Assistance.* Boulder, Colo., and London: Lynne Rienner.

———. 1998. "The International Development Community's Response to Demobilization." In Kiflemariam Gebrewold, ed., *Converting Defense Resources to Human Development.* Bonn, Germany: Bonn International Center for Conversion.

———. 2000. "Transforming Security Sectors: The IMF and World Bank Approaches." *Conflict, Security and Development* 1 (1).

———. 2001. "Report of a Conference Organized by the Programme for Strategic and International Studies, Graduate Institute of International Studies, Geneva." [www.humansecuritynetwork.org/report_may2001_3-e.asp]. March 2002.

Ball, Nicole, and Chris Spies. 1998. *Managing Conflict: Lessons from the South African Peace Committees.* PN-ACA-910. Washington, D.C.: U.S. Agency for International Development, Center for Development Information and Evaluation.

Ball, Nicole, J. Kayode Fayemi, Funmi Olonisakin and Rocklyn Williams with Martin Rupiya. Forthcoming. *Security Sector Governance.*

Barro, Robert. 1991. "Economic Growth in a Cross-Section of Countries." *Quarterly Journal of Economics* 106 (2): 407–43.

———. 1996. "Democracy and Growth." *Journal of Economic Growth* 1 (1): 1–27.

———. 1997. *Determinants of Economic Growth: A Cross-Country Empirical Study.* Cambridge, Mass.: MIT Press.

Barro, Robert, and Jong-Wha Lee. 2000. "International Data on Educational Attainment: Updates and Implications." NBER Working Paper 7911. National Bureau of Economic Research, Cambridge, Mass. [http://www.nber.org/papers/w7911]. March 2002.

Batchelor, Peter, Jacklyn Cock and Penny McKenzie. 2000. "Conversion in South Africa in the 1990s: Defense Downsizing and Human Development Challenges" Brief 18. Bonn International Center for Conversion, Bonn, Germany.

Bendaña, Alejandro. 1999. *Demobilization and Reintegration in Central America: Peace-building Challenges and Responses.* Managua, Nicaragua: Centro de Estudios Internacionales.

Bertrand, Claude Jean. 2001. "A Strategy For Democracy." University of Paris, Institut Français de Presse, Paris.

———. 2002. *An Arsenal for Democracy: Media Accountability Systems.* Cresskill, N.J.: Hampton Press.

BICC (Bonn International Center for Conversion). 2001. *Conversion Survey 2001: Global Disarmament, Demobilization and Demilitarization.* Baden-Baden, Germany: Nomos.

Bill and Melinda Gates Foundation. 2002. "Grant Highlights." [http://www.gatesfoundation.org/grants/default.htm]. April 2002.

Bland, Douglas. 1999. "A Unified Theory of Civil-Military Relations." *Armed Forces and Society* 26 (1).

Borner, Silvio, Aymo Brunetti and Beatrice Weder. 1995. *Political Credibility and Economic Development.* New York: Macmillan.

Bourguignon, Francois, and Christian Morrison. 2001. "Inequality among World Citizens: 1820–1992." [http://www.delta.ens.fr/XIX/paper_WD19.pdf]. May 2002.

Broad, Robin, and John Cavanagh. 1998. "The Corporate Accountability Movement: Lessons and Opportunities." [http://www.umass.edu/peri/pdfs/broad.pdf]. May 2002.

Brömmelhörster, Jörn, and Wolf Paes, eds. Forthcoming. *Soldiers in Business: The Military as an Economic Player.* London: Ashgate.

Brown, Michael, Sean Lynn-Jones and Steven Miller. 1996. *Debating the Democratic Peace.* Cambridge, Mass.: MIT Press.

Brzoska, Michael. 1981. "The Reporting of Military Expenditures." *Journal of Peace Research* 18 (4).

———. 1992. "Military Trade, Aid and Debt." In Geoffrey Lamb and Valeria Kallab, eds., *Military Expenditure and Economic Development: A Symposium on Research Issues.* World Bank Discussion Paper 185. Washington, D.C.

———. 1995. "World Military Expenditures." In Keith Hartley and Todd Sandler, eds., *Handbook of Defense Economics.* Vol. 1. Amsterdam: Elsevier.

Budlender, Debbie, Rhonda Sharp and Kerri Allen. 1999. "How To Do a Gender-Sensitive Budget Analysis: Contemporary Research and Analysis." Australian Agency for International Development and Commonwealth Secretariat, Canberra and London.

Budlender, Debbie, Diane Elson, Guy Hewitt and Tanni Mukhopadhyay 2002. *Gender Budgets Make Cents: Understanding Gender-Responsive Budgets.* London: Commonwealth Secretariat.

Buira, Ariel. 2000. "The Governance of the International Monetary Fund." Paper presented at the Group of 24 meeting, 29–30 September, Vienna.

Business Week. 2000. "Kohl's Shame Could Be His Party's Salvation." 17 January. [http://www.businessweek.com/2000/00_03/b3664153.htm]. April 2002.

Buzan, Barry. 1991. *People, States and Fear.* Second ed. Boulder, Colo.: Lynne Rienner.

Byanyima, Winnie. 2000. "Strengthening Parliamentary Governance through Gender Budgeting: The Experience of Three African Countries." Paper presented at the Commissione Pari Opportunita workshop on Gender Auditing of Government Budgets, Presidenza del Consiglio dei Ministri, 15–16 September, Rome.

Çagatay, Nilüfer, Mümtaz Keklik, Rhadika Lal and James Lang. 2000. "Budgets as if People Mattered: Democratizing Macroeconomic Policies." Conference Paper Series 4. United Nations Development Programme, Social Development and Poverty Eradication Division, New York. [http://www.undp.org/seped/publications/budgets.pdf]. March 2002.

Calderón, Fernando. 2002. *La reforma de la política: Deliberación y Desarrollo.* Caracas-Venezuela: Nueva Sociedad.

Call, Chuck, and Michael Barnett. 1999. "Looking for a Few Good Cops: Peacekeeping, Peacebuilding and CIVPOL." *International Peacekeeping* 6 (4).

Canada, Department of Foreign Affairs and International Trade. 2001. "Landmines and Development." [http://www.mines.gc.ca/I_F-e.asp]. March 2002.

Carnegie Commission on Preventing Deadly Conflict. 1997. *Preventing Deadly Conflict: Final Report.* New York: Carnegie Corporation of New York. [http://www.ccpdc.org/pubs/rept97/finfr.htm]. April 2002.

Carothers, Thomas. 1999. Aiding Democracy Abroad: The Learning Curve. Washington, D.C.: Carnegie Endowment for International Peace.

———. 2002. "The End of the Transition Paradigm." *Journal of Democracy* 13 (1). [http://muse.jhu.edu/demo/jod/13.1carothers.html]. March 2002.

CDIAC (Carbon Dioxide Information Analysis Center). 2001. "Trends: A Compendium of Data on Global Change." [http://cdiac.esd.ornl.gov/trends/trends.html]. April 2002.

Center for Responsive Politics. 2001. "Election Overview, 2000 Cycle: Business-Labor-Ideology Split in PAC, Soft & Individual Donations to Candidates and Parties." [http://www.opensecrets.org/pubs/whospay00/blio.asp]. April 2002.

Chege, Michael. 2001. "Civil-Military Relations in the Transition to Democracy: Patterns and Policy Alternatives." Working Paper. University of Florida, Center for African Studies, Gainesville.

Clague, Christopher, Philip Keefer, Stephen Knack and Mancur Olson. 1996. "Property and Contract Rights in Autocracies and Democracies." *Journal of Economic Growth* 1 (2): 243–76.

Clift, Steven. 2002. "The Future of E-Democracy." [http://www.publicus.net/articles/future.html]. April 2002.

Collier, Paul, and Anke Hoeffler. 2001. "Greed and Grievance in Civil War." World Bank, Development Research Group, Washington, D.C. [http://www.worldbank.org/research/conflict/papers/qjejanuary4ver2.pdf]. April 2002.

Commission for Racial Equality, "Disadvantage & Discrimination in Britain Today—The Facts." [http://www.cre.gov.uk/duty/duty_facts.html]. March 2002.

Commission on Global Governance. 1995. *A Call to Action: Summary of Our Global Neighbourhood.* Geneva.

Common Cause. 2001. "National Parties Raise Record $463 Million in Soft Money during 1999–2000 Election Cycle." [http://commoncause.org/publications/feb01/020701st.htm]. April 2002

Cooper, Ann. 2002. "Daniel Pearl's Essential Work." *The New York Times*, 23 February. [http://college3.nytimes.com/guests/articles/2002/02/23/902281.xml]. May 2002.

Cornia, Andrea, and Julius Court. 2001. "Inequality, Growth and Poverty in the Era of Liberalization and Globalization." Policy Brief 4. United Nations University and World Institute for Development Economics Research, Helsinki, Finland. [http://www.wider.unu.edu/publications/publications.htm]. April 2002.

Cornia, Andrea, and Sampsa Kiiski. 2001. "Trends in Income Distribution in the Post–World War II Period: Evidence and Interpretation." Discussion Paper 2001/89. United Nations University and World Institute for Development Economics Research, Helsinki, Finland. [http://www.wider.unu.edu/publications/dps/dp2001-89.pdf]. April 2002.

Court, Julius, and Goran Hyden. 2000. "A World Governance Survey: Pilot Phase." United Nations University, Tokyo. [http://www.unu.edu/p%26g/wgs/index.htm]. April 2002.

———. 2001. "Towards a World Governance Assessment: Preliminary Findings from the Pilot Phase." World Governance Assessment Working Paper 3. United Nations University, Tokyo. [http://www.unu.edu/p&g/wgs/pdf/worldgov-assessment.pdf]. April 2002.

CPJ (Committee to Protect Journalists). 2002. "Attacks on the Press in 2001." [http://www.cpj.org/attacks01/pages_att01/attacks01.html]. May 2002.

CUTS–ARC (Consumer Unity and Trust Society–Africa Resource Centre). 2001. "Capacity Building for WTO Participation: African Perspectives." Policy Brief 3. Harare, Zimbabwe. [http://cuts.org/arc%202001-3.pdf]. March 2002.

Davis, Randi. 2002. Correspondence on parliamentary strengthening. United Nations Development Programme, Bureau for Development Policy, Institutional Development Group. 11 April. New York.

de Sousa Santos, Boaventura. 1998. "Participatory Budgeting in Porto Alegre: Towards a Redistributive Democracy." *Politics and Society* 26 (4): 461–510.

Deccan, Herald. 2002. "IT Should Reach Rural Masses: CM" DH News Service, Bangalore, India. 17 January. [http://www.deccanherald.com/deccanherald/jan17/ietapal.htm]. March 2002.

Deininger, Klaus. 1998 "Making Negotiated Land Reform Work: Initial Experience from Colombia, Brazil and South Africa." Working paper. World Bank, Land Policy Network, Washington, D.C.

Di Rosa, Lisa. 2002. Correspondence on Mexico's Electoral Commission. Council of the Americas. 18 April. New York.

Dikhanov, Yuri, and Michael Ward. 2001 "Evolution of the Global Distribution of Income 1970–99." Paper prepared for the 53rd session of the International Statistical Institute, Seoul, Republic of Korea, 22–29 August.

Djankov Simeon, McLiesh Caralee, Nenova Tatiana and Andrei Shleifer.2001. "Who Owns the Media?" Background paper prepared for *World Development Report 2001/2002.* World Bank, Washington, D.C. [http://econ.worldbank.org/files/2225_wps2620.pdf]. May 2002.

Dollar, David, and Art Kraay. 2001. "Growth Is Good for the Poor." Policy Research Working Paper 2587. World Bank, Washington, D.C. [http://www-wds.worldbank.org/servlet/WDSContentServer/WDSP/IB/2001/05/11//000094946_01042806383524/Rendered/PDF/multi0page.pdf]. April 2002.

The Economist. 2002. "Accountability on Trial." p. 41, 23 March.

Economist Intelligence Unit. 2002. "Country Briefings." [http://www.economist.com/countries/]. April 2002.

Edwards, Michael. 1999. *Future Positive: International Cooperation in the 21st Century.* London: Earthscan.

———. 2000. *NGO Rights and Responsibilities: A New Deal for Global Governance.* London: Foreign Policy Centre.

Edwards, Michael, and John Gaventa, eds. 2001. *Global Citizen Action.* London: Earthscan.

Edwards, Michael, and David Hulme, eds. 1995. *Non-governmental Organisations: Performance and Accountability—Beyond the Magic Bullet.* London: Earthscan.

Edmunds, Timothy. 2002 Email correspondence on civil-military relations in Eastern Europe. King's College, Joint Services Command and Staff College. 14 February. New York.

Edmunds, Timothy, Andrew Cottey and Anthony Forster. Forthcoming. "The Second Generation Problematic: Rethinking Democracy and Civil-Military Relations in Central and Eastern Europe." *Armed Force and Society* (fall 2002).

Eldis. 2002. "Country Profiles." [http://www.eldis.org/country/index.htm]. April 2002.

Esim, Simel. 2000. "Gender-Sensitive Budget Initiatives for Latin America and the Caribbean: A Tool for Improving Accountability and Achieving Effective Policy Implementation." Paper prepared for the Eighth Regional Conference on Women of Latin America and the Caribbean, Lima, Peru, 8–10 February.

EU (European Union). 2002. "EU Commitments: Going Beyond the Monterrey Consensus." Announcement distributed to delegates, nongovernmental organizations and the media at the UN Conference on Financing for Development, Monterrey, Mexico, 20 March.

FAO (Food and Agriculture Organization). 2001. *The State of Food Insecurity in the World.* Rome. [http://www.fao.org/DOCREP/003/Y1500E/Y1500E00.HTM]. April 2002.

Feldstein, Martin. 1998. "Refocusing the IMF." *Foreign Affairs* 77 (2): 20–33.

Filmer, Deon. 1999. "The Structure of Social Disparities in Education: Gender and Wealth." Working paper 5. World Bank, Development Research Group and Poverty Reduction and Economic Management Network. [http://www.worldbank.org/gender/prr/wp5.pdf]. April 2002.

Fomunyoh, Christopher. 2001. "Democratization in Fits and Starts." *Journal of Democracy* 12 (3): 37–50.

Ford, Peter. 2001. "Injustice Seen as Fertile Soil for Terrorists." *The Christian Science Monitor,* 28 November. [http://www.csmonitor.com/2001/1128/p7s1-woeu.html]. April 2002.

Franco, Rolando. 2000. "Democracy, Social Inclusion and Poverty Eradication: Squaring the Circle." Paper presented at the International Institute for Democracy and Electoral Assistance's Democracy Forum 2000, 8–9 June, Stockholm. [http://www.idea.int/2000df/papers_presented_3.html]. March 2002.

Freedom House. 1999. *Democracy's Century. A Survey of Global Political Change in the 20th Century.* [http://freedomhouse.org/century.pdf]. April 2002.

———. 2000. *Press Freedom Survey 2000.* [http://www.freedomhouse.org/pfs2000]. April 2002.

———. 2001. *Freedom in the World 2000/2001: The Annual Survey of Political Rights and Civil Liberties.* New York.

———. 2002. *Freedom in the World 2001/2002. The Democracy Gap.* New York. [http://www.freedomhouse.org/research/survey2002.htm]. April 2002.

Fukuda-Parr, Sakiko. 2002. "Rescuing the Human Development Concept from the HDI—Reflections on a New Agenda." In Sakiko Fukuda-Parr and A K Shiva Kumar, eds., *Human Development: Concepts and Measures—Essential Readings.* New York: Oxford University Press.

Gallup International. 1999. "Millennium Survey." [gallup-international.com/surveys1.htm]. March 2002.

GENIE (Gender Information Exchange). 2001. "Violence against Women. Case studies." [http://www.genie.ids.ac.uk/gem/index_people/vaw_case5.htm]. April 2002.

Global Climate Coalition. 2002. "The GCC's Climate Action Agenda for the 21st Century." [http://www.globalclimate.org/]. April 2002.

Global Compact. 2001. "What It Is." [http://www.unglobalcompact.org/un/gc/unweb.nsf/content/whatitis.htm]. April 2002.

Global Policy Forum. 1997. "Razali Reform Paper." [http://www.globalpolicy.org/security/reform/raz-497.htm]. March 2002.

———. 2002a. "Changing Patterns in the Use of the Veto in the Security Council." [http://www.globalpolicy.org/security/data/vetotab.htm]. March 2002.

———. 2002b. "Reports of the GA Working Group on Security Council Reform." [http://www.globalpolicy.org/security/reform/reports.htm]. March 2002.

———. 2002c. "Security Council Reform." [http://www.globalpolicy.org/security/reform/]. March 2002.

———. 2002d. "Subjects of the UN Security Council Vetoes." [http://www.globalpolicy.org/security/membship/veto/vetosubj.htm]. March 2002.

Grayson, George. 2000. "A Guide to the 2000 Mexican Presidential Election." Washington, D.C.: Center for Strategic and International Studies.

Grunwald, Michael. 2002. "How Enron Sought to Tap the Everglades." *The Washington Post,* 8 February.

Gurr, Ted Robert, Monty G. Marshall and Deepa Khosla. 2001. "Peace and Conflict 2001: A Global Survey of Armed Conflicts, Self-Determination Movements, and Democracy." University of Maryland, Center for International Development and Conflict Management, College Park.

Haggard, Stephan. 1997. "Democratic Institutions and Economic Policy." In Christopher Clague, ed., *Institutions and Economic Development.* Baltimore, Md.: The Johns Hopkins University Press.

Hammond, Allen, and Jonathan Lash. 2000. "Cyber-Activism: The Rise of Civil Accountability and Its Consequences for Governance." [http://www.cisp.org/imp/may_2000/05_00hammond.htm]. April 2002.

Hanmer, Lucia, and Felix Naschold. 2000. "Attaining the International Development Targets: Will Growth Be Enough?" *Development Policy Review* 18 (1): 11–36.

Hayner, Priscilla B. 2001. *Unspeakable Truths: Confronting State Terror and Atrocity.* London. Routledge.

HCCI (Haut Conseil de la Coopération Internationale). 2001. *Les non-dits de la bonne governance.* Paris: Éditions Karthala.

Hegre, Håvard, Tanja Ellingsen, Scott Gates and Nils Petter Gleditsch. 2001. "Toward a Democratic Civil Peace? Democracy, Political Change, and Civil War, 1816–1992." *American Political Science Review* 95 (1): 33–48.

Held, David. 1995. *Democracy and Global Order.* Cambridge: Polity Press.

———. 2001. "Law of States, Law of Peoples: Three Models of Sovereignty." *Legal Theory* 8: 1–44.

Hendrickson, Dylan, and Nicole Ball. 2002. "Off-Budget Military Expenditure and Revenue: Issues and Policy Perspectives for Donors." Occasional Paper 1. King's College, Conflict, Security and Development Group, London. [http://csdg.kcl.ac.uk/Publications/assets/PDF%20files/OP1_Off-Budget%20Military%20Expenditure.pdf]. April 2002.

Hewitt, Guy and Tanni Mukhopadhyay .2001. "Gender Responsive Budget Initiatives: A Report on Commonwealth Experiences." Commonwealth Secretariat, London.

Hills, Alice. 2000. *Policing Africa: Internal Security and the Limits of Liberalization.* Boulder, Colo.: Lynne Rienner.

Himmelweit, Sue. 2000. "The Experience of the UK Women's Budget Group." Paper prepared for the International Workshop on Gender Auditing of Government Budgets, 15–16September, Rome.

Hooper, John. 2000. "Kohl's Colleagues Cannot Escape His Influence." *The Guardian,* 29 August.

Human Rights Watch. 2001. "Chile: New Press Law Welcomed." [http://www.hrw.org/press/2001/04/chilepress0418.htm]. April 2002.

———. 2002. "The Enron Corporation: Corporate Complicity in Human Rights Violations." [http://www.hrw.org/reports/1999/enron/]. May 2002.

Hunger Project. 2002. "The Condition of Women in South Asia." [http://www.thp.org/sac/unit4/index.html]. April 2002.

Huntington, Samuel P. 1991. *The Third Wave: Democratization in the Late Twentieth Century.* Norman: University of Oklahoma Press.

Hyden, Goran, and Julius Court. 2001. "Governance and Development: Sorting Out the Basics." World Governance Survey Working Paper 1. United Nations University, Tokyo.

Imhof, Aviva. Susanne Wong and Peter Bosshard. 2002. *Citizens' Guide to the World Commission on Dams.* Berkeley, Calif.: International Rivers Network. [www.irn.org/wcd/wcdguide.pdf]. March 2002.

ICBL (International Campaign to Ban Landmines). 2001. *Landmine Monitor Report 2001: Toward a Mine-Free World.* [http://www.icbl.org/]. March 2002.

———. 2002. "More about the Campaign." [http://www.icbl.org/]. April 2002.

ILO (International Labour Organization). 1997. *World Labour Report 1997–98: Industrial Relations, Democracy and Social Stability.* Geneva.

IMF (International Monetary Fund). 2002a. "The International Monetary Fund Executive Directors and Voting Power." [www.imf.org/external/np/sec/memdir/eds.htm]. April 2002.

———. 2002b. *Report to the IMF Executive Board of the Quota Formula Review Group.* Washington, D.C.

Instituto Federal Electoral. 2002. "¿Qué es el Instituto Federal Electoral?" [http://www.ife.org.mx/]. April 2002.

International Federation of Journalists. 1999. "Money, Power and Standards: Regulation and Self Regulation in South-east European Journalism—Practices and Procedures in Albania, Bulgaria, Croatia and Romania." Brussels. [http://www.ifj.org/regions/europe/royaumont/monstan.pdf]. April 2002.

International IDEA (Institute for Democracy and Electoral Assistance). 1997. *Voter Turnout from 1945 to 1997: A Global Report.* Stockholm.

———. 2000a. "Chapter 4: Sub-Saharan Africa." Report from the regional workshops of Democracy Forum 2000, 8–9 June, Stockholm. [http://www.idea.int/2000df/regional_reports_chapter_4.html]. March 2002.

———. 2000b. "Former Soviet Union." Report from the regional workshops of Democracy Forum 2000, 8–9 June, Stockholm. [http://www.idea.int/2000df/regional_reports_chapter_1.html]. March 2002.

———. 2000c. "Making Democracy Work for the Poor: Key Messages from the Regional Workshops." Report from the regional workshops of Democracy Forum 2000, 8–9 June, Stockholm. [http://www.idea.int/2000df/regional_reports_democracy_and_the_poor.htm]. March 2002.

———. 2001. "Hague Conference to Discuss External Assistance to Political Parties." Press release. [http://www.idea.int/press/pr20010327.htm]. March 2002.

———. 2002a. *Voter Turnout since 1945: A Global Report.* Stockholm.

———. 2002b. *Women in Parliament: Beyond Numbers* [http://www.idea.int/women/parl/toc.htm]. April 2002.

———. Forthcoming. *Handbook on Funding of Parties and Election Campaigns.* Stockholm.

IPU (Inter-Parliamentary Union). 1995. *Women in Parliaments 1945–1995: A World Statistical Survey.* Geneva.

———. 1998. *Parliamentary Human Rights Bodies: World Directory.* Geneva.

———. 2000a. *Politics: Women's Insight.* Geneva.

———. 2000b. *Women in Politics 1945–2000.* Geneva.

———. 2001. "Women in National Parliaments—Statistical Archive." [http://www.ipu.org/wmn-e/arc/classif121001.htm]. March 2002.

———. 2002a. Correspondence on date of latest elections, political parties represented and voter turnout. March. Geneva.

———. 2002b. *Parline Database.* [http://www.ipu.org/wmn-e/classif.htm]. March 2002.

———. 2002c. "Women in National Parliaments." [http://www.ipu.org/wmn-e/world.htm]. April 2002.

Jenkins, Rhys. 2001. "Corporate Codes of Conduct: Self-Regulation in a Global Economy." UNRISD Programme Paper 2. UN Research Institute for Social Development, New York.

Jubb, Nadine. 2001."Women and Policing in Latin America: A Draft Background Paper." Paper prepared for the meeting of the Latin America Studies Association, 6–8 September, Washington, D.C.

Jubilee Australia. 1999. "Some Background on the Global Jubilee 2000 Debt Coalition Jubilee 2000 Debt Campaign." [http://www.jubilee2000.org.au/who/who.html]. May 2002.

Kaldor, Mary. 2001. *New & Old Wars: Organized Violence in a Global Era.* Stanford, Calif: Stanford University Press.

Kamal, Ahmed. 2000. "Accountable Governance and Poverty Alleviation." Paper commissioned for the regional workshops of the International Institute for Democracy and Electoral Assistance's Democracy Forum 2000, 8–9 June, Stockholm. [http://www.idea.int/2000df/commissioned_papers_2.htm]. March 2002.

Kamal, Simi. 2000. "Democratization and Poverty Alleviation in South Asia." Paper commissioned for the regional workshops of the International Institute for Democracy and Electoral Assistance's Democracy Forum 2000, 8–9 June, Stockholm. [http://www.idea.int/2000df/commissioned_papers_3.htm]. March 2002.

Kapur, Devesh. 2001. "Expansive Agendas and Weak Instruments: Governance Related Conditionalities of International Financial Institutions." *Policy Reform* 4 (3): 207–41.

Kapur, Devesh, John P. Lewis and Richard Webb. 1997. *The World Bank: Its First Half Century.* Washington, D.C.: Brookings Institution Press.

Karam, Azza, ed. 1998. *Women in Parliament: Beyond Numbers.* Stockholm: International Institute for Democracy and Electoral Assistance. [http://www.idea.int/women/parl/toc.htm]. March 2002.

Karl, Terry Lynn. Forthcoming. "The Vicious Cycle of Inequality in Latin America." In Susan Eva Eckstein and Timothy Wickham-Crowley, eds., *The Politics of Injustice in Latin America.* Berkeley: University of California Press. [http://www.cfr.org/public/democracy/Terry_Karl.doc]. April 2002.

Kaufmann, Danny, Aart Kraay and Pablo Zoido-Lobatón. 1999. "Governance Matters." Policy Research Working Paper 2196. World Bank, Washington, D.C. [http://www.worldbank.org/wbi/governance/pdf/govmatrs.pdf]. April 2002.

———. 2002. "Governance Matters II: Updated Indicators for 2000/01." Policy Research Working Paper 2772. World Bank, Washington, D.C. [http://www.worldbank.org/wbi/governance/pdf/govmatters2.pdf]. April 2002.

Kendig, K. 1999. *Civil Society, Global Governance, and the United Nations.* Tokyo: United Nations University.

Kennedy, Paul, Dirk Messner and Franz Nuscheler. 2002. *Global Trends and Global Governance.* London: Pluto Press.

Ketterer, James P. 2001. "From One Chamber to Two: The Case of Morocco." *Journal of Legislative Studies* 7 (1).

King, Jeremy, Walter Dorn and Matthew Hodes. Forthcoming. "An Unprecedented Experiment: Security Sector Reform in Bosnia and Herzegovina." Bonn International Center for Conversion, Bonn, Germany.

Kingma, Kees, ed. 2000. *Demobilization in Sub-Saharan Africa: The Development and Security Impacts.* Basingstoke, U.K.: Macmillan.

Kingma, Kees. 2000. "Post-war Societies." In Natalie Pauwels, ed., *War Force to Work Force: Global Perspectives on Demobilization and Reintegration.* Baden-Baden, Germany: Nomos.

———. 2001. "Demobilizing and Reintegrating Former Combatants." In Luc Reychler and Thania Paffenholz, eds., *Peacebuilding: A Field Guide.* Boulder, Colo.: Lynne Rienner.

Kohli, Atul, ed. 2001. *The Success of India's Democracy.* Cambridge: Cambridge University Press.

Korpela, Sirkka. 2002. Email correspondence on the Global Compact. United Nations Development Programme, Division for Business Partnerships. March. New York.

Korten, David C. 1995. *When Corporations Rule the World.* Bloomfield, Conn.: Kumarian Press. [http://www.thirdworldtraveler.com/Korten/WhenCorpsRuleWorld_Korten.html]

Krause, Keith. 1997. *Military Spending and Social, Economic and Political Development.* Ottawa, Canada: Department of Foreign Affairs and International Trade.

Krueger, Anne O. 1997. "Whither the World Bank and the IMF?" NBER Working Paper 6327. National Bureau of Economic Research, Cambridge, Mass. [http://papers.nber.org/papers/w6327.pdf]. March 2002.

Krugman, Paul. 2002. "America the Polarized." *The New York Times,* 4 January.

Lagos, Marta. 2001. "Between Stability and Crisis in Latin America: How People View Democracy." *Journal of Democracy* 12 (1).

Landman, Todd. 1999. "Economic Development and Democracy: The View from Latin America." *Political Studies* 47: 607–26.

Larson, Alan P. 2002. Press conference transcript, UN Conference on Financing for Development, 19 March, Monterrey, Mexico.

Latinobarómetro. 2002. "Public Policies Time Series." Sent by Marta Lagos, February 2002. Data are private and accesible through purchase or suscription. [www.latinobarometro.org]

Laurenti, Jeffrey, ed. 2002. "Combating Terrorism: Does the UN Matter... And How?" United Nations Association of the USA, New York.

Leaf, Clifton. 2002. "White-Collar Criminals: Enough Is Enough—They Lie They Cheat They Steal and They've Been Getting Away With It for Too Long." *Fortune,* 18 March. [http://www.fortune.com/indexw.jhtml?channel=artcol.jhtml&doc_id=206659]. April 2002.

Lecoq, Herve. 2002. Email correspondence. UN Mission in Sierra Leone. 6 April.

Legault, Albert. 2001. "Démocratie et transfert de normes : les relations civilo-militaires." *Ètudes internationales* 32 (2).

Leitenberg, Milton. 2001. "Death in Wars and Conflicts between 1945 and 2000." University of Maryland, Center for International and Security Studies, College Park.

Lijphart, Arend. 1999. *Patterns of Democracy: Government Forms and Performance in Thirty-six Countries.* London: Yale University Press.

Lindenberg, Marc, and Coralie Bryant. 2001. *Going Global: Transforming Relief and Development NGOs.* Bloomfield, Conn.: Kumarian Press.

Ling, Chee Yoke. 2000. "The Cartagena/Vienna Setting: Towards More Transparent and Democratic Global Negotiations." Third World Network, Penang, Malaysia. [http://www.twnside.org.sg/title/vienna.htm]. March 2002.

Linz, Juan, and Alfred Stepan, eds. 1978. *The Breakdown of Democratic Regimes.* Baltimore, Md.: The Johns Hopkins University Press.

Linz, Juan, and Alfred Stepan. 1996. *Problems of Democratic Transition and Consolidation: Southern Europe, South America, and Post-communist Europe.* London: The Johns Hopkins University Press.

Linz, Juan, and Arturo Valenzuela, eds. 1994. *The Failure of Presidential Democracy.* London: The Johns Hopkins University Press.

Loada, Augustin. 2001 "Review of Critical Issues in Democratic Consolidation: The Case of West Africa." United Nations Development Programme, Bureau of Development Policy, New York.

Londono, Juan L., and Rodrigo Guerrero. 1999. *Violencia en America Latina: epidemiologia y costos.* Washington, D.C.: Inter-American Development Bank.

Londregan, John B., and Keith T. Poole. 1996. "Does High Income Promote Democracy?" *World Politics* 49 (October): 1–30.

Lonsdale, J. 1986. "Political Accountability in African History." In Patrick Chabal, ed., *Political Domination in Africa: Reflections on the Limits of Power.* Cambridge: Cambridge University Press.

Lopez-Pintor, Rafael. 2000. "Electoral Management Bodies as Institutions of Governance." United Nations Development Programme, Bureau of Development Policy, Management Development and Governance Division, New York.

Love, James. 2001. "Overview of the Benefits of the Doha Agreement on TRIPS and Public Health." [http://www.cptech.org/ip/wto/doha/overview.html]. March 2002.

———. 2002. Email correspondence on the Access to Medicine Campaign. CPTech. 25 March. Washington, D.C.

Luckham, Robin, Anne Marie Goetz, Mary Kaldor, Alison Ayers, Sunil Bastian, Emmanuel Gyimah-Boadi, Shireen Hassim and Zarko Puhovski. 2000. "Democratic Institutions and Politics in Contexts of Inequality, Poverty, and Conflict." Working Paper 104. University of Sussex, Institute of Development Studies, Brighton, U.K.

Machel, Graca. 1996. *Impact of Armed Conflict on Children.* New York: United Nations Children's Fund. [http://www.unicef.org/graca/]. April 2002.

Madeley, John. 1999. *Big Business, Poor Peoples: The Impact of Transnational Corporations on the World's Poor.* London: Zed Books.

Maguire Linda. 2002. Correspondence on Mexico's Electoral Commission. United Nations Development Programme, Evaluation Office. 25 March. New York.

Mahbub ul Haq Human Development Centre. 1999. *Human Development in South Asia 1999: The Crisis of Governance.* Karachi, Pakistan: Oxford University Press.

———. 2000. *Human Development in South Asia.* The Gender Question. Karachi, Pakistan: Oxford University Press.

———. 2001. *Human Development in South Asia: Globalisation and Human Development.* Karachi, Pakistan: Oxford

University Press.

Mair, Peter, and Ingrid van Biezen. 2001. "Party Membership in Twenty European Democracies, 1980–2000." *Party Politics* 7: 1.

Marshall, Monty G. 2000. "Major Episodes of Political Violence, 1946–1999." University of Maryland, Center for Systematic Peace, College Park. [http://members.aol.com/CSP-mgm/warlist.htm]. April 2002.

Marshall, Monty G., and Keith Jaggers. 2000. "Polity IV Project: Dataset Users Manual." [http://www.bsos.umd.edu/cidcm/inscr/polity/]. April 2002.

McChesney, Robert. 1999. *Rich Media, Poor Democracy—Communication Politics in Dubious Times.* New York: The New Press.

McCulloch, Lesley. 2000. "Business as Usual." *Inside Indonesia* 63 (July). [http://www.insideindonesia.org/edit63/mcculloch1.htm]. May 2002.

———. Forthcoming. "Trifungsi: The Role of the Indonesian Military in Business." In Jörn Brömmelhörster and Wolf Paes, eds., *Soldiers in Business: The Military as an Economic Player.* London: Ashgate.

McKenzie, Glenn. 2000. "New Breed of Journalists on the Front Lines of African Politics." Associated Press Worldstream, March 23. [http://www.cpj.org/dangerous/2000/Bekoutou/bekoutou.html]. April 2002.

Mehrotra, Santosh. 2001. "The Rhetoric of International Development Targets and the Reality of Official Development Assistance." Working Paper 85. United Nations Children's Fund, Innocenti Research Centre, Florence, Italy.

Mehrotra, Santosh, and Enrique Delamonica. 2002. *Public Spending for the Poor. Basic Services to Enhance Capabilities and Promote Growth.* New York: United Nations Children's Fund.

Méndez, Juan, and Paulo Sérgio Pinheiro, eds. 1999. *The (Un)Rule of Law and the Underprivileged in Latin America.* Notre Dame, Ind.: University of Notre Dame Press.

Mikesell, Raymond F. 1994. "The Bretton Woods Debates: A Memoir." Essays in International Finance 192. Princeton University, International Finance Section, Princeton, N. J.

Milanovic, Branko. 1998. *Income Inequality and Poverty during the Transition from Planned to Market Economy.* Washington, D.C.: World Bank.

———. 2001. "True World Income Distribution, 1988 and 1993: First Calculation Based on Household Surveys Alone." Policy Research Working Paper 2244. World Bank, Washington, D.C. [http://www-wds.worldbank.org/servlet/WDSContentServer/WDSP/IB/1999/12/30/000094946_991211053929 84/Rendered/PDF/multi_page.pdf]. April 2002.

Mitra, Subrata K. 2001. "Making Local Governments Work: Local Elites, Panchayati Raj and Governance in India." In Atul Kohli, ed., *The Success of India's Democracy.* Cambridge: Cambridge University Press.

Morrisey, Oliver. 2002. "ODI Opinions on Effective Expansion of Aid." Opinion 1. Overseas Development Institute, London. [http://www.odi.org.uk/opinions/1_intro_opinions.html]. April 2002.

Muggah, Robert, and Eric Berman. 2001. "Humanitarianism under Threat: The Humanitarian Impacts of Small Arms and Light Weapons." Special Report. Graduate Institute of International Studies, Geneva.

Mulvenon, James C. 2001. *Soldiers of Fortune: The Rise and Fall of the Chinese Military-Business Complex, 1978–1998.* New York: M. E. Sharpe.

Naschold, Felix. 2002. "Aid and the Millennium Development Goals." Opinion 4. Overseas Development Institute, London. [http://www.odi.org.uk/opinions/4_MDGs.html]. April 2002.

Narayan, Deepa, Robert Chambers, Meera Kaul Shaha and Patti

Petesh. 2000. *Voices of the Poor: Crying Out for Change.* New York: Oxford University Press. [http://www.worldbank.org/poverty/voices/reports.htm#crying.]. March 2002.

Narayan, Deepa, Raj Patel, Kai Schafft, Anne Rademacher and Sarah Koch-Schulte. 2000. *Voices of the Poor: Can Anyone Hear Us?* New York: Oxford University Press.

Nathan, Laurie, 1994. *The Changing of the Guard: Armed Forces and Defence Policy in a Democratic South Africa.* Pretoria: Human Sciences Research Council.

———. 2000. "Reform in New Democracies." In *Security Sector Reform.* Brief 15. Bonn: Bonn International Center for Conversion and Johannesburg: Group for Environmental Monitoring.

Nayyar, Deepak, ed. 2001. "The New Role and Functions for the UN and the Bretton Woods Institutions." United Nations University and World Institute for Development Economics Research, Helsinki, Finland. [http://www.wider.unu.edu/search/search.htm]. May 2002.

NDI (National Democratic Institute). 2001. "Political Party Strategies to Combat Corruption." [http://www.ndi.org/worldwide/asia/combatcorruption/executivesummary.asp]. May 2002.

Neild, Rachel. 1998. *Themes and Debates in Public Security Reform: A Manual for Civil Society. Community Policing.* Washington, D.C.: Washington Office on Latin America.

———. 2001a. "Democratic Police Reforms in War-torn States." *Journal of Conflict, Security and Development* 1 (1): 21–43. King's College, Centre for Defence Studies, London. [http://csdg.kcl.ac.uk/Publications/assets/PDF%20files/CSD %201-1.pdf]. March 2002.

———. 2001b. "Democratic Policing." In Luc Reychler and Thania Paffenholz, eds., *Peacebuilding: A Field Guide.* Boulder, Colo.: Lynne Rienner.

Neuffer, Elizabeth. 2001. *The Key to My Neighbor's House: Seeking Justice in Bosnia and Rwanda.* Picador: New York.

Norris, Pippa. 2000. *A Virtuos Circle: Political Communication in Postindustrustrial Societies.* New York: Cambridge University Press.

———. 2002. *Democratic Phoenix: Political Activism Worldwide.* New York: Cambridge University.

Nua Publish. 2002. "Nua Internet Surveys: How Many Online, Worldwide." [http://www.nua.ie/surveys/how_many_online/world.html]. 9 May 2002.

Nübler, Irmgard. 2000. "Human Resources Development and Utilization in Demobilization and Reintegration Programmes." In Kees Kingma, ed., *Demobilization in Sub-Saharan Africa; The Development and Security Impacts.* Basingstoke, U.K.: Macmillan.

Nussbaum, Martha, and Amartya Sen. 1993. *Quality of Life.* Oxford: Clarendon Press.

O'Donnell, Guillermo. 1999. "Horizontal Accountability and New Polyarchies." In Andreas Schedler, Larry Diamond and Mark Plattner, eds., T*he Self-Restraining State: Power and Accountability in New Democracies* Boulder, Colo.: Lynne Rienner.

———. 2000. "Democracy, Law, and Comparative Politics." IDS Working Paper 118. University of Sussex, Institute of Development Studies, Brighton, U.K.

———. 2002. "Human Development/Human Rights/Democracy." Paper prepared for a workshop on the Quality of Democracy sponsored by the United Nations Development Programme, Regional Division for Latin America and the Caribbean, and Proyecto Estado de la Nación, February, Costa Rica.

OECD (Organisation for Economic Co-operation and Development) DAC (Development Assistance Committee). 1997. *Final Report and Follow-up to the 1997 Ottawa Symposium.* Paris. [www.oecd.org/dac.]. March 2002.

OECD (Organisation for Economic Co-operation and Development) and UNESCO (United Nations Educational, Scientific and Cultural Organization) Institute for Statistics. 2001. *Teachers for Tomorrow's Schools: Analysis of World Education Indicators 2001 Edition*. Paris. [http://www.uis.unesco.org/en/pub/doc/WEI/wei_execsum_EN.pdf]. April 2002.

Oeppen, Jim, and James W. Vaupel. 2002. "Enhanced: Broken Limits to Life Expectancy." *Science* 296. 1029-31.

Omitoogun, Olawuyi. 2002. Email correspondence on long-term legacy of military rule in Nigeria. Stockholm International Peace Research Institute. 15 March.

Onishi, Norimitsu. 2002. "Nigeria's President Fears for His Fledgling Democracy." *The New York Times,* 7 February.

Open Society Institute. 2001. *Building Open Societies: Soros Foundation Network Annual Report 2000.* New York. [http://www.soros.org/annual/2000/]. May 2002.

Ottaway, Marina, and Anatol Lieven. 2002. "Rebuilding Afghanistan: Fantasy versus Reality." Policy brief. Carnegie Endowment for International Peace, Washington, D.C.

Parry, Sam. 2001. "Enron's India Disaster." Consortium News.com, 30 December. [http://www.consortiumnews.com/Print/123001a.html]. April 2002.

Paul, James A. 1995. "Security Council Reform: Arguments about the Future of the United Nations." Global Policy Forum, New York. [http://www.globalpolicy.org/security/pubs/secref.htm]. March 2002.

———. 2001. "A Short History of the NGO Working Group on the Security Council." Global Policy Forum, New York. [http://www.globalpolicy.org/security/ngowkgrp/history.htm]. March 2002.

Pauwels, Natalie, ed. 2000. *War Force to Work Force: Global Perspectives on Demobilization and Reintegration.* Baden-Baden, Germany: Nomos.

Pinheiro, Paulo Sergio. 1999. "The Rule of Law and the Underprivileged in Latin America: Introduction." In Juan Mendez, Guillermo O'Donnell and Paulo Sergio Pinheiro, eds., *The Un-Rule of Law and the Underprivileged in Latin America.* Notre Dame, Ind.: University of Notre Dame.

Pityana, Barney. 2000. "Faultlines: Inquiry into Racism in the Media. Executive Summary." South African Human Rights Commission, Johannesburg. [http://www.sahrc.org.za/main_frameset.htm]. March 2002.

Polity IV. 2002. "Political Regime Characteristics and Transitions, 1800–2000." [http://www.bsos.umd.edu/cidcm/inscr/polity/index.htm]. April 2002.

Proyecto Estado de la Nación. 2001. *Auditoría ciudadana sobre la calidad de la democracia.* Volumenes 1 y 2. San Jose, Costa Rica: Editorama.

PRS Group. 2001. Correspondence on International Country Risk Guide Dataset. December. East Syracuse, NY.

Przeworski, Adam. 1998. "The State and the Citizen." Paper prepared for the international seminar on Society and the Reform of the State, 26–28 March, São Paulo, Brazil.

———. 2000. "Democracy and Economic Growth." Paper prepared for the United Nations Development Programme, New York.

Przeworski, Adam, Michael E Alvarez, José Antonio Cheibub and Fernando Limongi. 2000. *Democracy and Development: Political Institutions and Well-being in the World, 1950–1990.* New York: Cambridge University Press.

Quibria, M. G. 2002. "Growth and Poverty: Lessons from the East Asian Miracle Revisited." Research Paper 33. Asian Development Bank, Manila.

Rana, Madhukar S. J. B. 2000. "Democracy and Poverty: Participation." Paper commissioned for the regional workshops on the International Institute for Democracy and Electoral Assistance's Democracy Forum 2000, 8–9 June, Stockholm. [http://www.idea.int/2000df/commissioned_papers_4.htm]. March 2002.

Reid, Angus. 2000. "Face of the Web Study Pegs Global Internet Population at More than 300 Million." [http://www.angus-reid.com/media/content/displaypr.cfm?id_to_view=1001]. 20 February 2001.

Reif, Linda. 2000. "Building Democratic Institutions: The Role of National Human Rights Institutions in Good Governance and Human Rights Protection." *Harvard Human Rights Journal* 13: 45, 56–57.

Reyes, Socorro. 2000. "Seeking Gender Balance, Women Strategize for Change." News and Views 13 (1). Women's Environment and Development Organization. [http://www.wedo.org/news/Mar2000/decision.htm]. March 2002.

Rose, Richard, and Christian Haerpfer. 1999. "New Democracies Barometer V: A 12-Nation Survey." Studies in Public Policy 306. University of Strathclyde, Centre for the Study of Public Policy, Glasgow, U.K.

Rudolph, Lloyd I., and Susanne Hoeber Rudolph. 2001. "Redoing the Constitutional Design: From an Interventionist to a Regulatory State." In Atul Kohli, ed., *The Success of India's Democracy.* Cambridge: Cambridge University Press.

Rummel, Robert J. 1997. *Power Kills: Genocide and Mass Murder.* New Brunswick, N.J.: Transaction Publishers. [http://www.hawaii.edu/powerkills/POWER.TAB4.GIF]. March 2002.

Sachs, Jeffrey D. 2001. *Macroeconomics and Health: Investing in Health for Economic Development.* Geneva: World Health Organization.

Sandbrook, Richard. 2000. "Citizenship, Rights and Poverty: Narrowing the Gap between Theory and Practice." Paper presented at the International Institute for Democracy and Electoral Assistance's Democracy Forum 2000, 8–9 June, Stockholm. [http://www.idea.int/2000df/papers_presented_2.html]. March 2002.

Schmitter, Philippe C., and Terry Lynn Karl. 1991. "What Democracy Is…and Is Not." *Journal of Democracy* 2 (3): 75–88.

Schultz, T Paul. 1998. "Inequality in the Distribution of Personal Income in the World: How It Is Changing and Why." *Journal of Population Economics* 11 (3): 307–44.

Security Industry Association. 2000. *Research Update* 2 (4). Alexandria, Va.

Sen, Amartya. 1989. "Development as Capability Expansion." *Journal of Development Planning* 19: 41–58.

———. 2000. *Development as Freedom.* New York: Random House.

Sen, Amartya, and Jean Drèze. 2002. *India: Development and Participation.* New Delhi: Oxford University Press.

Sharp, Rhonda. 2000. "Gender Budgets: The Australian Experience." Paper prepared for the International Workshop on Gender Auditing of Government Budgets, 15–16 September, Rome.

Shell. 2002. "How We Work." [http://www2.shell.com/home/Framework?siteId=royal-en&FC1=&FC2=%2FLeftHandNav%3FLeftNavState%3D0%2C2&FC3=%2Froyal-en%2Fhtml%2Fiwgen%2FAbout%2Fhow_we_work%2Fprinciple5.html&FC4=%2Froyal-en%2Fhtml%2Fiwgen%2Fimpulse1.html&FC5=]. April 2002.

SIPRI (Stockholm International Peace Research Institute). 2001. *SIPRI Yearbook 2001: Armaments, Disarmament and International Security.* New York: Oxford University Press.

———. 2002. Correspondence on weapons transfer data. Stockholm. March.

Sköns, Elisabeth, Evamaria Loose-Weintraub, Wuyi Omitoogn, Petter Stalenheim and Reinhilde Weidacher. 2001. "Military Expenditure and Arms Production." In Stockholm International Peace Research Institute, *SIPRI Yearbook 2001: Armaments, Disarmament and International Security.* New York: Oxford University Press.

Smeeding, Timothy, with assistance from Andrzej Grodner. 2000.

"Changing Income Inequality in OECD Countries: Updated Results from the Luxembourg Income Study (LIS)." Working Paper 252. Luxembourg Income Study, Luxembourg.

Sridharan, E. 2001 "Reforming Political Finance." [http://www.india-seminar.com/2001/506/506%20e.%20sridharan.htm]. April 2002.

Stewart, Frances. 1998. "The Root Causes of Conflict: Some Conclusions." Working paper 16. Queen Elizabeth House. Oxford. [http://www2.qeh.ox.ac.uk/pdf/qehwp/qehwps16.pdf]. March 2002.

———. 2000. "Crisis Prevention: Tackling Horizontal Inequalities." Working paper 33. Queen Elizabeth House, Oxford. [http://www2.qeh.ox.ac.uk/pdf/qehwp/qehwps33.pdf], March 2002.

Stewart, Frances, and Sam Daws. 2000. *An Economic and Social Security Council at the United Nations.* London: Christian Aid.

Stewart, Frances, and Valpy Fitzgerald. 2000. *The Economic and Social Consequences of Conflict.* Oxford: Oxford University Press.

———. 2001. *War and Underdevelopment.* Oxford. Oxford University Press.

Summers, Lawrence H. 2000. Statement by Treasury Secretary Summers before U.S. Senate Committee on Foreign Relations on progress on International Monetary Fund reform, 29 February. [http://www.useu.be/ISSUES/summ0229.html]. March 2002.

SustainAbility. 2001. "Politics and Persuasion: Corporate Influence on Sustainable Development." Janus Programme, London. [http://www.sustainability.com/programs/janus/Janus-Final.pdf]. April 2002.

Tanzi, Vito, Ke-young Chu and Sanjeev Gupta, eds. 1999. *Economic Policy and Equity.* Washington, D.C.: International Monetary Fund.

Tavares, Jose, and Romain Waczairg. 2001. "How Democracy Affects Growth." *European Economic Review* 45 (August): 1341–78.

Thakur, Ramesh, and Edward Newman, eds. 2000. *New Millennium, New Perspectives: The United Nations, Security, and Governance.* UNU Millennium Series. Tokyo, New York and Paris: United Nations University Press.

Tepperman, Jonathan. 2002. "Truth and Consequences." *Foreign Affairs* 8 (2): 129–30.

Tokman, Víctor E., and Guillermo O'Donnell, eds. 1998. *Poverty and Inequality in Latin America: Issues and New Challenges.* Notre Dame, Ind.: University of Notre Dame Press.

Transparency International. 2001. "Corruption Perceptions Index 2001." [http://www.transparency.org/cpi/index.html] May 2002.

UIA (Union of International Associations). 2000. *Yearbook of International Organizations 2000–2001.* Belgium.

U.K. Department for International Development. 2000. *Security Sector Reform and the Management of Defence Expenditure: High Risks for Donors, High Returns for Development.* Report on an international symposium sponsored by the U.K. Department for International Development. London.

UN (United Nations). 1998. "Cooperating for Development." In *Annual Report of the Secretary-General on the Work of the Organization.* Document A/53/1. New York. [http://www.un.org/Docs/SG/Report98/ch2.htm]. May 2002.

———. 1999. "Disarmament, Demobilization and Reintegration of Ex-Combatants in a Peacekeeping Environment." Department of Peacekeeping Operations, Lessons Learned Unit, New York.

———. 2000a. *Millennium Declaration.* New York. [http://www.un.org/millennium/declaration/ares552e.htm]. April 2002.

———. 2000b. "Report of the Open-ended Working Group on the Question of Equitable Representation on and Increase in the Membership of the Security Council and Other Matters Related to the Security Council." Document A/54/57. General Assembly Official Records, Fifty-fourth Session, New York.

———. 2001a. *Assistance in Mine Action.* Report of the Secretary-General to the General Assembly. New York.

———. 2001b. *DDA 2001 Update* (June). Department of Disarmament Affairs, New York.

———. 2001c. *Road Map towards the Implementation of the United Nations Millennium Declaration: Report of the Secretary-General.* New York. [http://www.un.org/documents/ga/docs/56/a56326.pdf]. April 2002.

———. 2001d. *World Population Prospects 1950–2050: The 2000 Revision.* Database. Department of Economic and Social Affairs, Population Division, New York.

———. 2002a. "Multilateral Treaties Deposited with the Secretary-General." [http://untreaty.un.org]. April 2002.

———. 2002b. "Operations." Department of Peacekeeping Operations, New York. [http://www.un.org/Depts/dpkol/ops.htm]. May 2002.

UN Information Centre Bonn. 2001. "UN Talks on Afghanistan." [http://www.uno.de/frieden/afghanistan/talks.htm]. April 2002.

UNAC (United Nations Associations in Canada). 1995. "Roundtable on Security Council Reform." Ottawa. [http://www.ncrb.unac.org/unreform/roundtables/SCreform.html]. March 2002.

UNAIDS (Joint United Nations Programme on HIV/AIDS). 2000a. "Country Successes." Factsheet. Geneva. [http://www.unaids.org/fact_sheets/files/Successes_Eng.html]. April 2002.

———. 2000b. "Report on the Global HIV/AIDS Epidemic." Geneva. [http://www.unaids.org/epidemic_update/report/index.html]. April 2002.

———. 2001. "AIDS Epidemic Update—December 2001." [http://www.unaids.org/epidemic_update/report_dec01/index.html]. April 2002.

UNCCD (United Nations Convention to Combat Desertification). 2002. "The United Nations Convention to Combat Desertification: An Explanatory Leaflet." [http://www.unccd.int/convention/text/leaflet.php]. April 2002.

UNDESA (United Nations Department of Economic and Social Affairs). 2001. "HIV/AIDS: Population Impact and Policies 2001." [http://www.un.org/esa/population/publications/aidswallchart/MainPage.htm]. May 2002.

UNDP (United Nations Development Programme). 1990. *Human Development Report 1990.* New York: Oxford University Press.

———. 1993 *Human Development Report 1993.* New York: Oxford University Press.

———. 1994. *Human Development Report 1994.* New York: Oxford University Press.

———. 1997a. "Corruption and Good Governance." Discussion Paper 3. Management Development and Governance Division, Bureau for Policy and Programme Support, New York.

———. 1997b. "Governance for Sustainable Human Development: A UNDP Policy Document." Management Development and Governance Division, Bureau for Development Policy and Programme Support, New York. [http://magnet.undp.org/policy/default.htm]. April 2002.

———. 1997c. *Reconceptualising Governance.* Discussion Paper 2. Management Development and Governance Division, Bureau for Policy and Programme Support, New York.

———. 1998. *Nepal Human Development Report 1998.* Kathmundu.

———. 1999a. *China Human Development Report 1999: Transition and the State.* Beijing: China Financial and Economic

Publishing House.

———. 1999b. *Guatemala: el rostro rural del desarrollo humano.* Guatemala City.

———. 1999c. *Human Development Report 1999.* New York: Oxford University Press.

———. 1999d. *Thailand Human Development Report 1999.* Bangkok. [http://www.undp.org/rbap/NHDR/HDRThailand99.PDF]. March 2002.

———. 2000a. *Human Development Report 2000.* New York: Oxford University Press.

———. 2000b. *The South African Human Development Report: Transformation for Human Development.* Pretoria.

———. 2001a. "Fact Sheet on Small Arms and Light Weapons 2001." Bureau for Crisis Prevention and Recovery, New York.

———. 2001b. *Indonesia Human Development Report: Towards a New Consensus.* Jakarta.

———. 2001c. *Latvia Human Development Report 2000/2001: The Public Policy Process in Latvia.* Riga.

———. 2001d. "Learning Lessons: Learning from Experience for Afghanistan." Afghanistan Programming Workshop Report. Evaluation Office and Regional Bureau of Asia and Pacific, New York.

———. 2001e. *Nepal Human Development Report: Poverty Reduction and Governance.* Kathmandu.

———. 2002a. "Albania Moves to Tighten Control on Small Arms." Newsfront, 6 February.

———. 2002b. "Learning Lessons: Learning from Experience for Afghanistan." Second Afghanistan Programming Workshop Report. Evaluation Office and Regional Bureau of Asia and Pacific, New York

———. 2002c. *Bolivia 2002 National Human Development Report: Informe de desarrollo humano en Bolivia 2002].* La Paz.

———. 2002d. "National Human Development Reports." [http://www.undp.org/hdro]. April 2002.

———. 2002e. *Financing the Development Goals: An Analysis of Tanzania, Cameroon, Malawi, Uganda and Philippines.* Summary Report. [http://www.undp.org/ffd/MDG-final.pdf]. April 2002.

UNESCO (United Nations Educational, Scientific and Cultural Organization). 1999a. Correspondence on gross enrolment ratios. April. Paris.

———. 1999b. *Statistical Yearbook 1999.* Paris. [http://www.uis.unesco.org/en/stats/stats0.htm]. April 2002.

———. 2000. "Education For All: 2000 Assessment, Statistical Document." [http://unesdoc.unesco.org/images/0012/001204/120472e.pdf]. April 2002.

———. 2001. Correspondence on net enrolment ratios. March. Paris.

———. 2002. Correspondence on adult and youth literacy rates. UNESCO Institute of Statistics. January. Montreal.

UNHCR (United Nations High Commissioner for Refugees). 2000. *The State of the World's Refugees: Fifty Years of Humanitarian Action.* Oxford: Oxford University Press. [http://www.unhcr.ch/pubs/sowr2000/sowr2000toc.htm]. April 2002.

———. 2001a. "Children." [http://www.unhcr.ch/children/index.html]. April 2002.

———. 2001b. "Refugees by Numbers 2001 Edition." [http://www.unhcr.ch/cgi-bin/texis/vtx/home?page=basics]. April 2002.

———. 2002. Correspondence on refugees and internally displaced persons. February. Geneva.

UNICEF (United Nations Children's Fund). 1996. "Wars against Children." [http://www.unicef.org/graca/]. April 2002.

———. 2002. *The State of the World's Children 2002.* New York: Oxford University Press. [http://www.unicef.org/pubs-gen/sowc02/sowc2002-eng-full.pdf]. April 2002.

UNOHCHR (United Nations Office of the High Commissioner for Human Rights). 2001. "Human Rights Day: Independent Experts Remind States of Obligation to Uphold Fundamental Freedoms." [http://www.unhchr.ch/huricane/huricane.nsf/view01/B6A4C75366A3B305C1256B1E0037F9B1?opendocument]. April 2002.

———. 2002. "Status of Ratifications of the Principal International Human Rights Treaties." [http://www.unhchr.ch/pdf/report.pdf]. April 2002.

UNPAN (United Nations Online Network in Public Administration and Finance). 2002. "Global Survey on E-Government." [www.unpan.org/egovernment2.asp]. April 2002.

U.S. Bureau of Census. 1999. *Statistical Abstract of the United States 1999.* Washington, D.C. [http://www.census.gov/prod/www/statistical-abstract-us.html]. April 2002.

U.S. Bureau of Justice Statistics. 1999. *National Criminal Victimization Survey 1999.* [http://www.ojp.usdoj.gov/bjs/abstract/cvusst.htm]. April 2002.

U.S. Department of State. Bureau of Arms Control. 2000. *World Military Expenditures and Arms Transfers 1998.* Washington, D.C. [http://www.state.gov/www/global/arms/bureau_ac/wmeat98/wmeat98.html]. March 2002.

U.S. Government. 2000. "International Crime Threat Assessment. United States Government Interagency Working Group in Support of and Pursuant to the President's International Crime Control Strategy, December 15, 2000." [http://fas.org/irp/threat/pub45270index.html]. March 2002.

U.S. Institute of Peace. 2002. "Truth Commissions: Selected Commissions of Inquiry and Related Bodies." [http://www.usip.org/library/tc/tc_coi.html]. March 2002.

von Alemann, Ulrich. 2000. "The German Case." Paper prepared for a Transparency International workshop on Corruption and Political Party Funding, October, La Pietra, Italy. [http://www.transparency.org/working_papers/thematic/german_paper.html]. May 2002.

Waczairg, Romain. 2000. "Human Capital and Democracy." Stanford University, Stanford, Calif.

Wallensteen, Peter, and Margareta Sollenberg. 2000. "Armed Conflict, 1989–99." *Journal of Peace Research* 37 (5).

Washington Office on Latin America. 2000. "Mexico Election Monitor 2000." Washington, D.C.

Whaley, John. 2000. "Strengthening Legislative Capacity in Legislative-Executive Relations." Paper 6. National Democratic Institute for International Affairs' Legislative Research Series 25. Washington, D.C.

WHO (World Health Organization). 1997. *Health and Environment in Sustainable Development: Five Years after the Earth Summit.* Geneva.

———. 1998. "Malaria." Factsheet 94. Geneva. [http://www.who.int/inf-fs/en/fact094.html]. April 2002.

———. 2000a. "Tuberculosis." Factsheet 104. Geneva. [http://www.who.int/inf-fs/en/fact104.html]. April 2000.

———. 2000b. "WHO Report on Global Surveillance of Epidemic-prone Infectious Diseases." Department of Communicable Disease Surveillance and Response, Geneva. [http://www.who.int/emc-documents/surveillance/docs/whocdscsrisr2001.pdf/WHO_Report_Infectious_Diseases.pdf]. April 2002.

———. 2001. "WHO and Norvartis Join Forces to Combat Drug Resistant Malaria." Press release. [http://www.who.int/inf-pr-2001/en/pr2001-26.html]. April 2002.

WHO (World Health Organization), UNICEF (United Nations Children's Fund) and WSSCC (Water Supply and Saitation Collaborative Council). 2000. "Global Water Supply and Sanitation Assessment 2000 Report." [http://www.who.int/water_sanitation_health/Globassessment/GlobalTOC.htm]. April 2002.

Willms, Douglas J. 1999. *Inequalities in Literacy Skills among Youth in Canada and the United States.* Statistics Canada

International Adult Literacy Survey Monograph 89-552-MIE99006. National Literacy Secretariat/Human Resources Development, Canada.

Women's Environment and Development Organization. 2002. "Gender Breakdown of Boards of Directors at World Financial Institutions." *News and Views* 15 (1).

Working Group on E-Government in the Developing World. 2002. "Roadmap for E-Government in the Developing World." Pacific Council on International Policy and Council on Foreign Relations, Los Angeles, Calif. [http://www.pacificcouncil.org/pdfs/e-gov.paper.f.pdf]. April 2002.

World Bank. 1998. "Participatory Mechanisms." [http://www.worldbank.org/afr/particip/keycon.htm]. March 2002.

———. 2001a. *Global Economic Prospects and the Developing Countries 2001.* Washington, D.C.

———. 2001b. "IBRD Executive Directors Voting Status." [http://www.worldbank.org/about/organization/voting/librd.htm]. April 2002.

———. 2001c. "World Bank Governance Indicators Dataset." [http://www.worldbank.org/wbi/governance/govdata2001.htm]. May 2002

———. 2001d. *World Development Indicators 2001.* CD-ROM. Washington, D.C.

———. 2001e. *World Development Report 2000/2001.* New York: Oxford University Press.

———. 2002a. "Countries and Regions." [http://www.worldbank.org/html/extdr/regions.htm]. April 2002.

———. 2002b. "GDP per capita." In *World Development Indicators 2002.* CD-ROM. Washington, D.C.

———. 2002c. *Global Economic Prospects and the Developing Countries 2002: Making Trade Work for the World's Poor.* Washington, D.C.

———. 2002d. "The HIPC Initiative: Background and Progress through December 2001." [http://www.worldbank.org/hipc/progress-to-date/may99v3/may99v3.htm]. April 2002.

———. 2002e. *World Development Indicators 2002.* CD-ROM. Washington, D.C.

World Bank and IMF (International Monetary Fund). 2001. "Financing for Development." [http://www.imf.org/external/np/pdr/2001/ffd.pdf]. February 2001.

Wulf, Herbert. 2000. *Security Sector Reform in Developing Countries: An Analysis of the International Debate and Potential for Implementing Reforms with Recommendations for Technical Cooperation.* Eschborn, Germany: Deutsche Gesellschaft für Technische Zusammenarbeit.

Zadek, Simon. 2001. *Third Generation Corporate Citizenship: Public Policy and Business in Society.* London: Foreign Policy Centre.

Zakaria, Fareed. 1997. "The Rise of Illiberal Democracy." *Foreign Affairs* (November/December). [http://www.foreignaffairs.org/19971101faessay3809/fareed-zakaria/the-rise-of-illiberal-democracy.html]. April 2002.

HUMAN DEVELOPMENT INDICATORS

Note on statistics in the Human Development Report   141

I. MONITORING HUMAN DEVELOPMENT: ENLARGING PEOPLE'S CHOICES . . .

1 Human development index   149
2 Human development index trends   153
3 Human and income poverty: developing countries   157
4 Human and income poverty: OECD, Central & Eastern Europe & CIS   160

II. . . . TO LEAD A LONG AND HEALTHY LIFE . . .

5 Demographic trends   162
6 Commitment to health: access, services and resources   166
7 Leading global health crises and challenges   170
8 Survival: progress and setbacks   174

III. . . . TO ACQUIRE KNOWLEDGE . . .

9 Commitment to education: public spending   178
10 Literacy and enrolment   182
11 Technology: diffusion and creation   186

IV. . . . TO HAVE ACCESS TO THE RESOURCES NEEDED FOR A DECENT STANDARD OF LIVING . . .

12 Economic performance   190
13 Inequality in income or consumption   194
14 The structure of trade   198
15 Flows of aid from DAC member countries   202
16 Flows of aid, private capital and debt   203
17 Priorities in public spending   207
18 Unemployment in OECD countries   211

V. . . . WHILE PRESERVING IT FOR FUTURE GENERATIONS . . .

19 Energy and the environment   212

VI. . . . PROTECTING PERSONAL SECURITY . . .

20 Refugees and armaments   216
21 Victims of crime   220

VII. . . . AND ACHIEVING EQUALITY FOR ALL WOMEN AND MEN

22 Gender-related development index   222
23 Gender empowerment measure   226
24 Gender inequality in education   230
25 Gender inequality in economic activity   234
26 Gender, work burden and time allocation   238
27 Women's political participation   239

VIII. HUMAN AND LABOUR RIGHTS INSTRUMENTS

28 Status of major international human rights instruments   243
29 Status of fundamental labour rights conventions   247

30   BASIC INDICATORS FOR OTHER UN MEMBER COUNTRIES   251

Technical note 1: calculating the human development indices   252
Technical note 2: assessing progress towards the Millennium Development Goals   259
Statistical references   260
Definitions of statistical terms   262
Classification of countries   269
Index to indicators   273
Countries and regions that have produced human development reports   276

Note on statistics in the Human Development Report

This Report's primary purpose is to assess the state of human development across the globe and provide a critical analysis of a specific theme each year. It combines thematic policy analysis with detailed country data that focus on human well-being, not just economic trends.

The indicators in the Report reflect the rich body of information available internationally. As a user of data, the Report presents statistical information that has been built up through the collective effort of many people and organizations. The Human Development Report Office gratefully acknowledges the collaboration of the many agencies that made publication of the latest data on human development possible (box 1).

To allow comparisons across countries and over time, where possible the indicator tables in the Report are based on internationally standardized data, collected and processed by sister agencies in the international system or, in a few cases, by other bodies. These organizations, whether collecting data from national sources or through their own surveys, harmonize definitions and collection methods to make their data as internationally comparable as possible. The data produced by these agencies may sometimes differ from data produced by national sources, often because of adjustments to harmonize data. In a few cases where data are not available from international organizations—particularly for the human development indices—other sources have been used. These sources are clearly referenced in the tables.

The text of the Report draws on a much wider variety of sources—commissioned papers, government documents, national human development reports, reports of international organizations, reports of nongovernmental organizations and journal articles and other scholarly publications. Where infor-mation from such sources is used in boxes or tables in the text, the source is shown and the full citation is given in the references. In addition, for each chapter a bibliographic note outlines the major sources for the chapter, and endnotes specify the sources of statistical information not drawn from the Report's indicator tables.

THE INDICATOR TABLES

The indicator tables in this year's Report reflect the continual efforts over the years to publish the best available data and to improve their presentation and transparency. As part of this effort the indicator tables have been streamlined in recent years to focus on indicators that are most reliable, meaningful and comparable across countries.

While many of the indicator tables present conventional indicators, where possible recent innovations in measuring human development are reflected. One example is in the measurement of crime. In previous years the Report relied on data based on crimes reported to the police, information that depended heavily on a country's law enforcement and reporting system. Increasingly, however, data based directly on individuals' experience with crime are available. The Report also recognizes recent efforts in time use and functional literacy statistics. While the Report has featured time use surveys in previous years, recent improvements in survey methods and country coverage have provided a wealth of new information, stepping beyond traditional economic measurement and into the lives and livelihoods of the world's people. This year's Report presents the initial round of results from these new time use surveys. It also presents results from surveys of functional literacy, which allow a

BOX 1

Major sources of data used in the *Human Development Report*

By generously sharing data, the following organizations made it possible for the *Human Development Report* to publish the important human development statistics appearing in the indicator tables.

Carbon Dioxide Information Analysis Center (CDIAC) The CDIAC, a data and analysis centre of the US Department of Energy, focuses on the greenhouse effect and global climate change. It is the source of data on carbon dioxide emissions.

Food and Agriculture Organization (FAO) The FAO collects, analyses and disseminates information and data on food and agriculture. It is the source of data on food insecurity indicators.

International Institute for Strategic Studies (IISS) An independent centre for research, information and debate on the problems of conflict, the IISS maintains an extensive military database. The data on armed forces are from its publication *The Military Balance*.

International Labour Organization (ILO) The ILO maintains an extensive statistical publication programme, with the *Yearbook of Labour Statistics* its most comprehensive collection of labour force data. The ILO is the source of data on wages, employment and occupations and information on the ratification status of labour rights conventions.

International Monetary Fund (IMF) The IMF has an extensive programme for developing and compiling statistics on international financial transactions and balance of payments. Much of the financial data provided to the Human Development Report Office through other agencies originates from the IMF.

International Telecommunication Union (ITU) This specialized UN agency maintains an extensive collection of statistics on information and communications. The data on trends in telecommunications come from its database *World Telecommunication Indicators*.

Inter-Parliamentary Union (IPU) This organization provides data on trends in political participation and structures of democracy. The Human Development Report Office relies on the IPU for election-related data and information on women's political representation.

Joint United Nations Programme on HIV/AIDS (UNAIDS) This joint UN programme monitors the spread of HIV/AIDS and provides regular updates. Its *Report on the Global HIV/AIDS Epidemic* is the primary source of data on HIV/AIDS.

Luxembourg Income Study (LIS) A cooperative research project with 25 member countries, the LIS focuses on poverty and policy issues. It is the source of income poverty estimates for many OECD countries.

Organisation for Economic Co-operation and Development (OECD) The OECD publishes data on a variety of social and economic trends in its member countries as well as on flows of aid. This year's Report presents data from the OECD on aid, employment and education.

Stockholm International Peace Research Institute (SIPRI) SIPRI conducts research on international peace and security. The *SIPRI Year-book: Armaments, Disarmament and International Security* is the source of data on military expenditure and arms transfers.

United Nations Children's Fund (UNICEF) UNICEF monitors the well-being of children and provides a wide array of data. Its *State of the World's Children* is an important source of data for the Report.

United Nations Conference on Trade and Development (UNCTAD) UNCTAD provides trade and economic statistics through a number of publications, including the *World Investment Report*. It is the original source of data on investment flows that the Human Development Report Office receives from other agencies.

United Nations Educational, Scientific and Cultural Organization (UNESCO) This specialized UN agency is the source of data on education-related matters. The Human Development Report Office relies on data published in UNESCO's *Statistical Yearbook* as well as data received directly from its Institute for Statistics.

United Nations High Commissioner for Refugees (UNHCR) This UN organization provides data on refugees through its publication *Refugees and Others of Concern to UNHCR: Statistical Overview*.

United Nations Interregional Crime and Justice Research Institute (UNICRI) This UN institute carries out international comparative research in support of the United Nations Crime Prevention and Criminal Justice Programme. It is the source of data on crime victims.

United Nations Multilateral Treaties Deposited with the Secretary General (UN Treaty Section) The Human Development Report Office compiles information on the status of major international human rights instruments and environmental treaties based on the database maintained by this UN office.

United Nations Population Division (UNPOP) This specialized UN office produces international data on population trends. The Human Development Report Office relies on *World Population Prospects* and *World Urbanization Prospects*, two of the main data products of UNPOP, for demographic estimates and projections.

United Nations Statistics Division (UNSD) The UNSD provides a wide range of statistical outputs and services. Much of the national accounts data provided to the Human Development Report Office by other agencies originates from the UNSD.

World Bank The World Bank produces and compiles data on economic trends as well as a broad array of other indicators. Its *World Development Indicators* is the primary source for a number of indicators in the Report.

World Health Organization (WHO) This specialized agency maintains a large array of data series on health issues, the source for the health-related indicators in the Report.

World Intellectual Property Organization (WIPO) As a specialized UN agency, WIPO promotes the protection of intellectual property rights throughout the world through different kinds of cooperative efforts. The Human Development Report Office relies on WIPO for patent-related data.

more in-depth look at a vital area of human development than conventional literacy surveys have offered (box 2).

While the Report incorporates innovations in many vital areas of human development, in many other areas the challenges of measurement are just beginning to be tackled. In employment, for example, only limited information is provided for developing countries because of the difficulties of measuring the true employment situation (box 3). The environment also poses measurement difficulties, though much new work is being done in this area. One important initiative is the System of Integrated Environmental and Economic Accounting, designed to aid the design and implementation of strategies for sustainable development (box 4).

GAPS IN THE DATA

Despite these strides in measuring human development, many gaps and problems remain. Sufficient and reliable data are still lacking in many areas of human development. Gaps throughout the tables demonstrate the pressing need for improvements in both the quantity and the quality of human development statistics.

Perhaps the starkest demonstration of these data problems is the large number of countries excluded from the human development index (HDI). The intent is to include all UN member countries, along with Hong Kong, China (SAR) and Switzerland, in the HDI exercise. But because of a lack of reliable data, this year 18 countries are excluded from the HDI and

---

BOX 2

Assessing adult literacy on a continuum

The traditional definition of literacy has long been used to classify people into two categories—the literate and the illiterate—based on a simple question asked during a census or survey or on the percentage of adults with a minimum of four years of schooling. By contrast, the International Adult Literacy Survey (IALS) defines literacy on a continuum, according to the ability to understand and use printed information in daily activities at home, at work and in the community.

In the first international comparative assessment of adult literacy skills, the IALS study has combined household survey methods and educational assessment to provide comparable estimates of literacy skills for 24 countries. The survey tests representative samples of adults (aged 16–65) in their homes, asking them to undertake a range of common tasks using authentic materials from a wide range of social and cultural contexts. The cross-country data are compiled so as to ensure that the results are comparable across countries with different languages and cultures and that any known sources of bias are corrected. The IALS study is jointly sponsored by Statistics Canada, the US Center for Education Statistics and the Organisation for Economic Co-operation and Development.

The IALS reports on three areas of literacy:
• *Prose literacy*—the knowledge and skills needed to understand and use information from texts, including editorials, news stories, poems and fiction.
• *Document literacy*—the knowledge and skills required to locate and use information in different formats, including maps, graphs, tables, payroll forms, job applications and transportation schedules.

• *Quantitative literacy*—the knowledge and skills required to apply arithmetic operations to numbers in printed materials, such as balancing a cheque book, figuring out a tip, completing an order form or determining the amount of interest on a loan from an advertisement.

Analysis of IALS data reveals several important facts. First, countries differ greatly in the level and social distribution of literacy skills. Second, these differences can be attributed to a handful of underlying factors, including differences among countries in the quantity and quality of initial education. The evidence also suggests, however, that several aspects of adult life, including the use of literacy skills at home and at work, transform skills after formal education. Finally, in many countries literacy skills play an important part in allocating economic opportunity, rewarding the skilled and penalizing the relatively unskilled. A full analysis of the currently available data can be found in OECD and Statistics Canada (2000).

The IALS has begun a new cycle of data collection in 2002 to better understand the role of literacy skills in determining economic outcomes for individuals. Participating countries are Argentina, Belgium (French and Flemish communities), Bermuda, Bolivia, Canada, Costa Rica, Italy, the Republic of Korea, Luxembourg, the Netherlands, Norway, Switzerland and the United States (for more detailed information see http://nces.ed.gov/surveys/all/index.asp).

This Report uses the percentage of adults lacking prose literacy skills in the human poverty index for selected OECD countries, presented in table 4.

Source: Based on Murray 2001.

Measuring unemployment in developing countries— the limitations of labour statistics

The performance of labour markets has conventionally been assessed on the basis of the unemployment rate. But the relevance and usefulness of the unemployment rate for this purpose differ across countries and over time. As currently defined and measured, the unemployment rate in many developing countries is lower than rates in OECD countries. That does not mean that labour markets are more effective in those developing countries. Unemployment, defined as a complete lack of work, is only one manifestation of the employment problems these countries face.

The concept of unemployment is not always meaningful in developing countries, for several reasons. First, most developing countries lack unemployment relief programmes, leaving those who find themselves without formal employment to engage in informal sector activities to survive. Often this work will not employ them full time or generate sufficient income for a decent living. Second, a large share of people are self-employed. When these workers face periods of no work, they tend not to seek formal employment but to engage in alternative self-employment activities instead, even though these may generate a lower income than their usual activ-

ities. Third, work in rural communities is often organized according to traditional arrangements, with the available labour distributed among all workers at the cost of lowering their average hours. Thus the problem in developing countries is often summarized as underemployment—a partial lack of work, low employment income and underutilization of skills or low productivity—rather than unemployment as normally measured.

Underemployment has recently come to be recognized as an important phenomenon in OECD countries and Central and Eastern Europe and the CIS as well, as workers experience downsizings and reorganizations. Many workers in these economies lack opportunities to perform the type of work that they could and would like to do. As a result, they may work less productively or fewer hours than they could and would like to work, experience unemployment or drop out of the labour force permanently.

Although measuring these aspects of employment is difficult, statistics on underemployment are being gathered in more than 50 countries around the world. The next step is to compile these data and work towards an international database of underemployment statistics.

Source: ILO 2002a.

---

therefore from the main indicator tables. What key indicators are available for these countries are presented in table 30.

There are many links in the chain from measuring a concept to verifying statistics at the international level—and no easy ways to reinforce those links where they are weak. But improving the statistical capacity of countries is widely recognized as vital, and so is the need for both financial and political commitment at the national and international levels. Also vital is a stronger relationship between national and international statistics—often data are available nationally but not internationally. Steps are being taken to strengthen this link. In education, for example, the United Nations Educational, Scientific and Cultural Organization (UNESCO) is conducting workshops to help train national statisticians from around the world in the rigours of international data collection. Clearly, however, further efforts are needed at both the national and the international level.

DATA USED IN THE HUMAN DEVELOPMENT INDEX

The human development index is calculated using international data available at the time the Report is prepared. For a country to be included in the index, data ideally should be available from the relevant international statistical agency for all four components of the index. However, a country will still be included if reasonable estimates can be found from another source.

As a result of revisions in data and in the methodology of the HDI over time, HDI values and ranks are not comparable across editions of the Report. Table 2, however, presents comparable HDI trends based on a consistent methodology and consistent data.

LIFE EXPECTANCY AT BIRTH

The life expectancy estimates used in the Report are from the 2000 revision of the United Nations

BOX 4

Accounting for the environment

Strategies for sustainable development rely on information about the interaction between the economy and the environment. This information is needed to monitor progress towards meeting environmental goals, to assess alternative development strategies and to design environmental policy instruments.

In response to these needs, the System of Integrated Environmental and Economic Accounting (commonly referred to as the SEEA) was developed. Based on the revised UN System of National Accounts (UN 1993), the SEEA brings together economic and environmental information in a common framework to measure the contribution of the environment to the economy and the impact of the economy on the environment. In the early 1990s several developing and developed countries began experimenting with the compilation of the SEEA, and in 1994 the London Group on Environmental Accounting was created to provide practitioners a forum for sharing their experience in developing and implementing environmental accounts.

The SEEA provides policy-makers with indicators and descriptive statistics to monitor the interactions between the environment and the economy as well as a database for strategic planning and policy analysis to identify more sustainable paths of development. The SEEA thus enables governments to formulate and monitor economic policies more effectively, enact more effective environmental regulations and resource management strategies and use taxes and subsidies more efficiently. It also offers a way to improve policy dialogue among different stakeholders by providing a transparent system of information about the relationship between human activities and the environment.

The SEEA, which aims to systematically measure the interaction between the economy and the environment, represents a major step towards standardizing and harmonizing concepts, definitions and methods. The system has four components:

• *Natural resource asset accounts.* These accounts record stocks and changes in stocks of natural resources such as land, fish, forest, water and minerals, allowing more effective monitoring of a nation's wealth. They also allow the calculation of such indi-

cators as the total value of natural capital and the economic costs of natural resource depletion.

• *Flow accounts for pollution, energy and materials.* These accounts provide information at the industry level about the use of energy and materials as inputs to production and the generation of pollutants and solid waste. They produce eco-efficiency and pollution and material intensity indicators that can be used to assess the pressure on the environment and to evaluate alternative options for reducing this pressure.

• *Environmental protection and resource management expenditure accounts.* These accounts identify expenditures incurred by industry, government and households to protect the environment or to manage natural resources. They can be used to assess the economic impact of environmental regulation and taxes and their effect in reducing pollution.

• *Valuation of non-market flow and environmentally adjusted aggregates.* This component presents non-market valuation techniques and their applicability in answering specific policy questions. It discusses the calculation of several macroeconomic aggregates adjusted for depletion and degradation costs and their advantages and disadvantages.

An increasing number of OECD and developing countries have introduced environmental accounts, compiling different components according to their environmental concerns and priorities. Resource-rich countries have usually developed asset accounts in order to design policies for better natural resource management. Countries in which pollution is a main concern have implemented physical flow accounts, often linked to environmental protection accounts so as to analyse the impact of consumption and production patterns on the environment and the impact of environmental expenditure in reducing emissions.

Pilot projects have shown that some of the components of the SEEA can be compiled using existing information from various data sources. These exercises have identified data gaps and inconsistencies, helping to improve both environmental and economic data. The results have already been used by government planning agencies in designing policies and by non-governmental organizations and academia in advocacy efforts.

Source: Prepared by the United Nations Statistics Division based on London Group on Environmental Accounting (2002) and UNSD and UNEP (2000).

Population Division's database *World Population Prospects* (UN 2001). The United Nations Population Division derives global demographic estimates and projections biannually. In the 2000 revision it made significant adjustments to further incorporate the demographic impact of HIV/AIDS, which has led to substantial changes in life expectancy estimates and projections for a number of countries, particularly in Sub-Saharan Africa.

The life expectancy estimates published by the United Nations Population Division are five-year averages. The life expectancy estimates for 2000 shown in table 1 (on the HDI) were obtained through linear interpolation based on these five-year averages. While the human development index requires yearly estimates, other tables showing data of this type, such as table 8 (on survival), present the unaltered five-year averages. Estimates for years after 2000 refer to medium-variant projections.

ADULT LITERACY

The adult literacy rates presented in the Report are estimates and projections from UNESCO's January 2002 literacy assessment. These estimates and projections are based on population data from the 1998 revision of the *World Population Prospects* database (UN 1998) and literacy statistics collected through national population censuses, as well as refined estimation procedures.

COMBINED PRIMARY, SECONDARY AND TERTIARY GROSS ENROLMENT

The 1999 gross enrolment ratios presented in the Report are preliminary estimates from UNESCO based on the 1998 revision of population estimates and projections. Gross enrolment ratios are calculated by dividing the number of children enrolled in each level of schooling by the number of children in the age group corresponding to that level. Thus the ratios are affected by the age- and sex-specific population estimates published by the United Nations Population Division and by the timing and methods of surveys by administrative registries, of population censuses and of national education surveys. Moreover, UNESCO periodically revises its methodology for estimating and projecting enrolment.

Gross enrolment ratios can hide important differences among countries because of differences in the age range corresponding to a level of education and in the duration of education programmes. Such factors as grade repetition can also lead to distortions in the data. For the HDI a preferred indicator of access to education as a proxy of knowledge would be net enrolment,

for which data are collected for single years of age. Because this indicator measures enrolments only of a particular age group, the data could be more easily and reliably aggregated and used for international comparisons. But net enrolment data are available for too few countries to be used in the HDI.

GDP PER CAPITA (PPP US$)

The GDP per capita (PPP US$) data used in calculating the HDI are based on purchasing power parity (PPP) rates of exchange. The data are provided by the World Bank based on the latest International Comparison Programme (ICP) surveys. This most recent round of ICP surveys covers 118 countries, the largest number ever. The World Bank has also provided estimates based on these surveys for another 44 countries and areas.

The surveys were carried out separately in different world regions. Because regional data are expressed in different currencies and may be based on different classification schemes or aggregation formulas, the data are not strictly comparable across regions. Price and expenditure data from the regional surveys were linked using a standard classification scheme to compile internationally comparable PPP data (box 5). The base year for the PPP data is 1996; data for the reference year, 2000, were extrapolated using relative price movements over time between each country and the United States, the base country. For countries not covered by the World Bank, PPP estimates are from the Penn World Tables 6.0 (Aten, Heston and Summers 2001).

DATA, METHODOLOGY AND PRESENTATION OF THE HUMAN DEVELOPMENT INDICATORS

This year's Report presents data for most key indicators with only a two-year lag between the reference date for the indicators and the date of the Report's release. All sources of data used in the indicator tables have been clearly referenced. When an agency provides data it has collected from another source, both sources are credited in the table notes. But when an international statistical organization has built on the work of many other contributors, only the ultimate source is given. The source notes also

The why's and wherefore's of purchasing power parities

To compare economic statistics across countries, the data must first be converted into a common currency. Unlike conventional exchange rates, purchasing power parity (PPP) rates of exchange allow this conversion to take account of price differences between countries. By eliminating differences in national price levels, the method aids comparisons of real values for income, poverty, inequality and expenditure patterns.

While the conceptual case for using PPP rates of exchange is clear, practical issues remain. The World Bank has compiled PPPs directly for 118 of the world's approximately 220 distinct national political entities. For countries for which it does not directly compile PPPs, it produces estimates using econometric regression. This approach assumes that the economic characteristics and relationships commonly observed in surveyed countries also apply to the non-surveyed countries. While this assumption may not necessarily hold, fundamental economic relationships are thought to have general relevance and can be associated with independently observed variables in the non-surveyed countries.

The intricacies of the survey procedure and the need to link countries globally and regionally have raised a number of issues relating to data reporting. In the past they have also led to significant delays in generating PPP results. As a result of these concerns, some governments and international institutions still refrain from using PPPs in regular operational policy decisions, but use the method extensively in analyses.

The importance of PPPs in economic analysis underlines the need to improve PPP data. That effort requires both institutional and financial support. In collaboration with Eurostat and the Organisation for Economic Co-operation and Development, the World Bank has set up an initiative to further improve the quality and availability of PPPs.

Source: Ward 2001.

---

show the original data components used in any calculations by the Human Development Report Office to ensure that all calculations can be easily replicated. Indicators for which short, meaningful definitions can be given are included in the definitions of statistical terms.

COUNTRY CLASSIFICATIONS

The indicator tables cover UN member countries, along with Hong Kong, China (SAR) and Switzerland. Countries are classified in four ways: in major world aggregates, by region, by human development level and by income (see the classification of countries). These designations do not necessarily express a judgement about the development stage of a particular country or area. Instead, they are classifications used by different organizations for operational purposes. The term *country* as used in the text and tables refers, as appropriate, to territories or areas.

Major world classifications. The three global groups are *developing countries, Central and Eastern Europe and the CIS* and *OECD.* These groups are not mutually exclusive. (Replacing the OECD group with the high-income OECD group would produce mutually exclusive groups; see country classifications.) Unless otherwise specified, the classification

world represents the universe of 173 countries covered in the main indicator tables.

Regional classifications. Developing countries are further classified into the following regions: Arab States, East Asia and the Pacific, Latin America and the Caribbean (including Mexico), South Asia, Southern Europe and Sub-Saharan Africa. These regional classifications are consistent with the Regional Bureaux of UNDP. An additional classification is *least developed countries,* as defined by the United Nations (UNCTAD 2001).

Human development classifications. All countries are classified into three clusters by achievement in human development: high human development (with an HDI of 0.800 or above), medium human development (0.500–0.799) and low human development (less than 0.500).

Income classifications. All countries are grouped by income using World Bank classifications: high income (GNP per capita of $9,266 or more in 2000), middle income ($756–9,265) and low income ($755 or less).

AGGREGATES AND GROWTH RATES

Aggregates. Aggregates for the classifications described above are presented at the end of most tables. Aggregates that are the total for the classification (such as for population) are indicated by a T. As a result of rounding, world totals may not always equal the sum of the totals for subgroups. All other aggregates are weighted averages.

In general, an aggregate is shown for a classification only when data are available for half the countries and represent two-thirds of the available weight in that classification. The Human Development Report Office does not fill in missing data for the purpose of aggregation. Therefore, unless otherwise specified, aggregates for each classification represent only the countries for which data are shown in the tables, refer to the year or period specified and refer only to data from the primary sources listed. Aggregates are not shown where appropriate weighting procedures were unavailable.

Aggregates for indices, for growth rates and for indicators covering more than one point in time are based only on countries for which data exist for all necessary points in time. For the world classification, which refers only to the universe of 173 countries (unless otherwise specified), aggregates are not always shown where no aggregate is shown for one or more regions.

Aggregates in the *Human Development Report* will not always conform to those in other publications because of differences in country classifications and methodology. Where indicated, aggregates are calculated by the statistical agency that provides the indicator itself.

Growth rates. Multiyear growth rates are expressed as average annual rates of change. In calculations of rates by the Human Development Report Office, only the beginning and end points are used. Year-to-year growth rates are expressed as annual percentage changes.

PRESENTATION

In the indicator tables countries and areas are ranked in descending order by their HDI value. To locate a country in the tables, refer to the key to countries on the back cover flap, which lists countries alphabetically with their HDI rank.

Short citations of sources are given at the end of each table. These correspond to full references in the statistical references, which follow the indicator tables and technical notes. Where appropriate, definitions of indicators appear in the definitions of statistical terms. All other relevant information appears in the notes at the end of each table.

Owing to a lack of comparable data, not all countries have been included in the indicator tables. For UN member countries not included in the main indicator tables, basic human development indicators are presented in a separate table (table 30).

In the absence of the words *annual, annual rate* or *growth rate*, a hyphen between two years indicates that the data were collected during one of the years shown, such as 1995-2000. A slash between two years indicates an average for the years shown, such as 1997/99. The following signs have been used:

.. Data not available.
(.) Less than half the unit shown.
<   Less than.
–   Not applicable.
T   Total.

1 Human development index

HDI rank [a]		Life expectancy at birth (years) 2000	Adult literacy rate (% age 15 and above) 2000	Combined primary, secondary and tertiary gross enrolment ratio (%) [b] 1999	GDP per capita (PPP US$) 2000	Life expectancy index	Education index	GDP index	Human development index (HDI) value 2000	GDP per capita (PPP US$) rank minus HDI rank [c]
High human development										
1	Norway	78.5	.. [d]	97	29,918	0.89	0.98	0.95	0.942	2
2	Sweden	79.7	.. [d]	101 [e]	24,277	0.91	0.99	0.92	0.941	15
3	Canada	78.8	.. [d]	97	27,840	0.90	0.98	0.94	0.940	4
4	Belgium	78.4	.. [d]	109 [e]	27,178	0.89	0.99	0.94	0.939	5
5	Australia	78.9	.. [d]	116 [e]	25,693	0.90	0.99	0.93	0.939	7
6	United States	77.0	.. [d]	95	34,142	0.87	0.98	0.97	0.939	-4
7	Iceland	79.2	.. [d]	89	29,581	0.90	0.96	0.95	0.936	-2
8	Netherlands	78.1	.. [d]	102 [e]	25,657	0.89	0.99	0.93	0.935	5
9	Japan	81.0	.. [d]	82	26,755	0.93	0.93	0.93	0.933	2
10	Finland	77.6	.. [d]	103 [e]	24,996	0.88	0.99	0.92	0.930	6
11	Switzerland	78.9	.. [d]	84	28,769	0.90	0.94	0.94	0.928	-5
12	France	78.6	.. [d]	94	24,223	0.89	0.97	0.92	0.928	6
13	United Kingdom	77.7	.. [d]	106 [e]	23,509	0.88	0.99	0.91	0.928	7
14	Denmark	76.2	.. [d]	97	27,627	0.85	0.98	0.94	0.926	-6
15	Austria	78.1	.. [d]	90	26,765	0.89	0.96	0.93	0.926	-5
16	Luxembourg	77.4	.. [d]	72 [f]	50,061 [g]	0.87	0.90	1.00	0.925	-15
17	Germany	77.7	.. [d]	94	25,103	0.88	0.97	0.92	0.925	-2
18	Ireland	76.6	.. [d]	91	29,866	0.86	0.96	0.95	0.925	-14
19	New Zealand	77.6	.. [d]	99	20,070	0.88	0.99	0.88	0.917	5
20	Italy	78.5	98.4	84	23,626	0.89	0.94	0.91	0.913	-1
21	Spain	78.5	97.6	95	19,472	0.89	0.97	0.88	0.913	4
22	Israel	78.7	94.6	83	20,131	0.90	0.91	0.89	0.896	1
23	Hong Kong, China (SAR)	79.5	93.5	63	25,153	0.91	0.83	0.92	0.888	-9
24	Greece	78.2	97.2	81	16,501	0.89	0.92	0.85	0.885	10
25	Singapore	77.6	92.3	75	23,356	0.88	0.87	0.91	0.885	-4
26	Cyprus	78.0	97.1	68 [h]	20,824	0.88	0.88	0.89	0.883	-4
27	Korea, Rep. of	74.9	97.8	90	17,380	0.83	0.95	0.86	0.882	1
28	Portugal	75.7	92.2	96	17,290	0.84	0.94	0.86	0.880	2
29	Slovenia	75.5	99.6 [d]	83	17,367	0.84	0.94	0.86	0.879	0
30	Malta	78.0	92.0	80	17,273	0.88	0.88	0.86	0.875	1
31	Barbados	76.8	98.0 [i, j]	77	15,494	0.86	0.91	0.84	0.871	5
32	Brunei Darussalam	75.9	91.5	76	16,779 [k]	0.85	0.86	0.86	0.856	1
33	Czech Republic	74.9	.. [d]	70	13,991	0.83	0.89	0.82	0.849	6
34	Argentina	73.4	96.8	83	12,377	0.81	0.92	0.80	0.844	10
35	Hungary	71.3	99.3 [d]	81	12,416	0.77	0.93	0.80	0.835	8
36	Slovakia	73.3	100.0 [d, i, j]	76	11,243	0.80	0.91	0.79	0.835	10
37	Poland	73.3	99.7 [d]	84	9,051	0.81	0.94	0.75	0.833	16
38	Chile	75.3	95.8	78	9,417	0.84	0.90	0.76	0.831	12
39	Bahrain	73.3	87.6	80	15,084 [l]	0.81	0.85	0.84	0.831	-2
40	Uruguay	74.4	97.7	79	9,035	0.82	0.92	0.75	0.831	14
41	Bahamas	69.2	95.4	74	17,012	0.74	0.88	0.86	0.826	-9
42	Estonia	70.6	99.8 [d, m]	86	10,066	0.76	0.95	0.77	0.826	6
43	Costa Rica	76.4	95.6	67	8,650	0.86	0.86	0.74	0.820	14
44	Saint Kitts and Nevis	70.0 [n]	97.8 [n]	70 [n]	12,510	0.75	0.89	0.81	0.814	-3
45	Kuwait	76.2	82.0	59	15,799	0.85	0.74	0.84	0.813	-10
46	United Arab Emirates	75.0	76.3	68	17,935 [k]	0.83	0.74	0.87	0.812	-19
47	Seychelles	72.7 [o]	88.0 [i, j]	.. [p]	12,508 [k, q]	0.80	0.83	0.81	0.811	-5
48	Croatia	73.8	98.3	68	8,091	0.81	0.88	0.73	0.809	11
49	Lithuania	72.1	99.6 [d]	80	7,106	0.78	0.93	0.71	0.808	16
50	Trinidad and Tobago	74.3	93.8	65	8,964	0.82	0.84	0.75	0.805	6

HDI rank [a]		Life expectancy at birth (years) 2000	Adult literacy rate (% age 15 and above) 2000	Combined primary, secondary and tertiary gross enrolment ratio (%) [b] 1999	GDP per capita (PPP US$) 2000	Life expectancy index	Education index	GDP index	Human development index (HDI) value 2000	GDP per capita (PPP US$) rank minus HDI rank [c]
51	Qatar	69.6	81.2	75	18,789 [q,r]	0.74	0.79	0.87	0.803	-25
52	Antigua and Barbuda	73.9 [n]	86.6 [n]	69 [n]	10,541	0.82	0.81	0.78	0.800	-5
53	Latvia	70.4	99.8 [d]	82	7,045	0.76	0.93	0.71	0.800	13

Medium human development

54	Mexico	72.6	91.4	71	9,023	0.79	0.84	0.75	0.796	1
55	Cuba	76.0	96.7	76	.. [s]	0.85	0.90	0.64	0.795	35
56	Belarus	68.5	99.6 [d]	77	7,544	0.73	0.92	0.72	0.788	7
57	Panama	74.0	91.9	74	6,000	0.82	0.86	0.68	0.787	18
58	Belize	74.0	93.2	73	5,606	0.82	0.86	0.67	0.784	24
59	Malaysia	72.5	87.5	66	9,068	0.79	0.80	0.75	0.782	-7
60	Russian Federation	66.1	99.6 [d]	78	8,377	0.68	0.92	0.74	0.781	-2
61	Dominica	72.9 [n]	96.4 [n]	65 [n]	5,880	0.80	0.86	0.68	0.779	16
62	Bulgaria	70.8	98.4	72	5,710	0.76	0.90	0.68	0.779	18
63	Romania	69.8	98.1	69	6,423	0.75	0.88	0.69	0.775	6
64	Libyan Arab Jamahiriya	70.5	80.0	92	7,570 [q,r]	0.76	0.84	0.72	0.773	-2
65	Macedonia, TFYR	73.1	94.0 [j,t]	70	5,086	0.80	0.86	0.66	0.772	20
66	Saint Lucia	73.4	90.2 [n]	70 [n]	5,703	0.81	0.83	0.67	0.772	15
67	Mauritius	71.3	84.5	63	10,017	0.77	0.77	0.77	0.772	-18
68	Colombia	71.2	91.7	73	6,248	0.77	0.85	0.69	0.772	4
69	Venezuela	72.9	92.6	65	5,794	0.80	0.83	0.68	0.770	10
70	Thailand	70.2	95.5	60	6,402	0.75	0.84	0.69	0.762	0
71	Saudi Arabia	71.6	76.3	61	11,367	0.78	0.71	0.79	0.759	-26
72	Fiji	69.1	92.9	83	4,668	0.73	0.90	0.64	0.758	17
73	Brazil	67.7	85.2	80	7,625	0.71	0.83	0.72	0.757	-13
74	Suriname	70.6	94.0 [i,j]	82	3,799	0.76	0.90	0.61	0.756	29
75	Lebanon	73.1	86.0	78	4,308	0.80	0.83	0.63	0.755	20
76	Armenia	72.9	98.4	80	2,559	0.80	0.92	0.54	0.754	41
77	Philippines	69.3	95.3	82	3,971	0.74	0.91	0.61	0.754	20
78	Oman	71.0	71.7	58	13,356 [q,r]	0.77	0.67	0.82	0.751	-38
79	Kazakhstan	64.6	98.0 [i,j]	77	5,871	0.66	0.91	0.68	0.750	-1
80	Ukraine	68.1	99.6 [d]	77	3,816	0.72	0.92	0.61	0.748	22
81	Georgia	73.2	100.0 [d,i,j]	70	2,664	0.80	0.89	0.55	0.748	34
82	Peru	68.8	89.9	80	4,799	0.73	0.87	0.65	0.747	6
83	Grenada	65.3 [n]	94.4 [n]	65 [n]	7,580	0.67	0.85	0.72	0.747	-22
84	Maldives	66.5	96.7	77	4,485	0.69	0.90	0.63	0.743	9
85	Turkey	69.8	85.1	62	6,974	0.75	0.77	0.71	0.742	-18
86	Jamaica	75.3	86.9	62	3,639	0.84	0.79	0.60	0.742	18
87	Turkmenistan	66.2	98.0 [j,t]	81	3,956	0.69	0.92	0.61	0.741	13
88	Azerbaijan	71.6	97.0 [i,j]	71	2,936	0.78	0.88	0.56	0.741	24
89	Sri Lanka	72.1	91.6	70	3,530	0.79	0.84	0.59	0.741	19
90	Paraguay	70.1	93.3	64	4,426	0.75	0.83	0.63	0.740	4
91	St. Vincent & the Grenadines	69.6 [n]	88.9 [n]	58 [n]	5,555	0.74	0.79	0.67	0.733	-8
92	Albania	73.2	84.7	71	3,506	0.80	0.80	0.59	0.733	17
93	Ecuador	70.0	91.6	77	3,203	0.75	0.87	0.58	0.732	17
94	Dominican Republic	67.1	83.6	72	6,033	0.70	0.80	0.68	0.727	-20
95	Uzbekistan	69.0	99.2 [d]	76	2,441	0.73	0.91	0.53	0.727	24
96	China	70.5	84.1	73	3,976	0.76	0.80	0.61	0.726	0
97	Tunisia	70.2	71.0	74	6,363	0.75	0.72	0.69	0.722	-26
98	Iran, Islamic Rep. of	68.9	76.3	73	5,884	0.73	0.75	0.68	0.721	-22
99	Jordan	70.3	89.7	55	3,966	0.76	0.78	0.61	0.717	-1
100	Cape Verde	69.7	73.8	77	4,863	0.75	0.75	0.65	0.715	-13

HDI rank [a]		Life expectancy at birth (years) 2000	Adult literacy rate (% age 15 and above) 2000	Combined primary, secondary and tertiary gross enrolment ratio (%) [b] 1999	GDP per capita (PPP US$) 2000	Life expectancy index	Education index	GDP index	Human development index (HDI) value 2000	GDP per capita (PPP US$) rank minus HDI rank [c]
101	Samoa (Western)	69.2	80.2	65	5,041	0.74	0.75	0.65	0.715	-15
102	Kyrgyzstan	67.8	97.0 [i,j]	68	2,711	0.71	0.87	0.55	0.712	12
103	Guyana	63.0	98.5	66	3,963	0.63	0.88	0.61	0.708	-4
104	El Salvador	69.7	78.7	63	4,497	0.75	0.74	0.64	0.706	-13
105	Moldova, Rep. of	66.6	98.9	72	2,109	0.69	0.90	0.51	0.701	21
106	Algeria	69.6	66.7	72	5,308	0.74	0.69	0.66	0.697	-22
107	South Africa	52.1	85.3	93	9,401	0.45	0.88	0.76	0.695	-56
108	Syrian Arab Republic	71.2	74.4	63	3,556	0.77	0.71	0.60	0.691	-2
109	Viet Nam	68.2	93.4	67	1,996	0.72	0.84	0.50	0.688	19
110	Indonesia	66.2	86.9	65	3,043	0.69	0.79	0.57	0.684	1
111	Equatorial Guinea	51.0	83.2	64	15,073	0.43	0.77	0.84	0.679	-73
112	Tajikistan	67.6	99.2 [d]	67	1,152	0.71	0.88	0.41	0.667	39
113	Mongolia	62.9	98.9	58	1,783	0.63	0.85	0.48	0.655	21
114	Bolivia	62.4	85.5	70	2,424	0.62	0.80	0.53	0.653	6
115	Egypt	67.3	55.3	76	3,635	0.70	0.62	0.60	0.642	-10
116	Honduras	65.7	74.6	61	2,453	0.68	0.70	0.53	0.638	2
117	Gabon	52.7	71.0 [i,j]	86	6,237	0.46	0.76	0.69	0.637	-44
118	Nicaragua	68.4	66.5	63	2,366	0.72	0.65	0.53	0.635	4
119	São Tomé and Principe	65.1 [u]	83.1 [o]	58 [o]	1,792 [q,v]	0.67	0.75	0.48	0.632	14
120	Guatemala	64.8	68.6	49	3,821	0.66	0.62	0.61	0.631	-19
121	Solomon Islands	68.3	76.6 [o]	50 [o]	1,648	0.72	0.68	0.47	0.622	17
122	Namibia	44.7	82.0	78	6,431	0.33	0.81	0.69	0.610	-54
123	Morocco	67.6	48.9	52	3,546	0.71	0.50	0.60	0.602	-16
124	India	63.3	57.2	55	2,358	0.64	0.57	0.53	0.577	-1
125	Swaziland	44.4	79.6	72	4,492	0.32	0.77	0.64	0.577	-33
126	Botswana	40.3	77.2	70	7,184	0.25	0.75	0.71	0.572	-62
127	Myanmar	56.0	84.7	55	1,027 [q,r]	0.52	0.75	0.39	0.552	25
128	Zimbabwe	42.9	88.7	65	2,635	0.30	0.81	0.55	0.551	-12
129	Ghana	56.8	71.5	42	1,964	0.53	0.62	0.50	0.548	1
130	Cambodia	56.4	67.8	62	1,446	0.52	0.66	0.45	0.543	15
131	Vanuatu	68.0	34.0 [o]	.. [p]	2,802	0.72	0.35	0.56	0.542	-18
132	Lesotho	45.7	83.4	61	2,031	0.34	0.76	0.50	0.535	-5
133	Papua New Guinea	56.7	63.9	38	2,280	0.53	0.55	0.52	0.535	-9
134	Kenya	50.8	82.4	51	1,022	0.43	0.72	0.39	0.513	19
135	Cameroon	50.0	75.8	43	1,703	0.42	0.65	0.47	0.512	0
136	Congo	51.3	80.7	63	825	0.44	0.75	0.35	0.512	27
137	Comoros	59.8	55.9	35	1,588	0.58	0.49	0.46	0.511	4
Low human development										
138	Pakistan	60.0	43.2	40	1,928	0.58	0.42	0.49	0.499	-7
139	Sudan	56.0	57.8	34	1,797	0.52	0.50	0.48	0.499	-7
140	Bhutan	62.0	47.0 [i,j]	33 [w]	1,412	0.62	0.42	0.44	0.494	7
141	Togo	51.8	57.1	62	1,442	0.45	0.59	0.45	0.493	5
142	Nepal	58.6	41.8	60	1,327	0.56	0.48	0.43	0.490	6
143	Lao People's Dem. Rep.	53.5	48.7	58	1,575	0.47	0.52	0.46	0.485	-1
144	Yemen	60.6	46.3	51	893	0.59	0.48	0.37	0.479	14
145	Bangladesh	59.4	41.3	37	1,602	0.57	0.40	0.46	0.478	-5
146	Haiti	52.6	49.8	52	1,467	0.46	0.50	0.45	0.471	-2
147	Madagascar	52.6	66.5	44	840	0.46	0.59	0.36	0.469	14
148	Nigeria	51.7	63.9	45	896	0.44	0.58	0.37	0.462	9
149	Djibouti	43.1	64.6	22	2,377 [q,r]	0.30	0.50	0.53	0.445	-28
150	Uganda	44.0	67.1	45	1,208	0.32	0.60	0.42	0.444	-1

HDI rank [a]		Life expectancy at birth (years) 2000	Adult literacy rate (% age 15 and above) 2000	Combined primary, secondary and tertiary gross enrolment ratio (%) [b] 1999	GDP per capita (PPP US$) 2000	Life expectancy index	Education index	GDP index	Human development index (HDI) value 2000	GDP per capita (PPP US$) rank minus HDI rank [c]
151	Tanzania, U. Rep. of	51.1	75.1	32	523	0.43	0.61	0.28	0.440	21
152	Mauritania	51.5	40.2	40	1,677	0.44	0.40	0.47	0.438	-16
153	Zambia	41.4	78.1	49	780	0.27	0.68	0.34	0.433	12
154	Senegal	53.3	37.3	36	1,510	0.47	0.37	0.45	0.431	-11
155	Congo, Dem. Rep. of the	51.3	61.4	31	765 [k]	0.44	0.51	0.34	0.431	11
156	Côte d'Ivoire	47.8	46.8	38	1,630	0.38	0.44	0.47	0.428	-17
157	Eritrea	52.0	55.7	26	837	0.45	0.46	0.35	0.421	5
158	Benin	53.8	37.4	45	990	0.48	0.40	0.38	0.420	-4
159	Guinea	47.5	41.0 [i, j]	28	1,982	0.38	0.37	0.50	0.414	-30
160	Gambia	46.2	36.6	45	1,649	0.35	0.39	0.47	0.405	-23
161	Angola	45.2	42.0 [j, t]	23	2,187	0.34	0.36	0.51	0.403	-36
162	Rwanda	40.2	66.8	40	943	0.25	0.58	0.37	0.403	-6
163	Malawi	40.0	60.1	73	615	0.25	0.65	0.30	0.400	7
164	Mali	51.5	41.5	28	797	0.44	0.37	0.35	0.386	0
165	Central African Republic	44.3	46.7	24	1,172	0.32	0.39	0.41	0.375	-15
166	Chad	45.7	42.6	31	871	0.35	0.39	0.36	0.365	-7
167	Guinea-Bissau	44.8	38.5	37	755	0.33	0.38	0.34	0.349	0
168	Ethiopia	43.9	39.1	27	668	0.31	0.35	0.32	0.327	1
169	Burkina Faso	46.7	23.9	23	976	0.36	0.23	0.38	0.325	-14
170	Mozambique	39.3	44.0	23	854	0.24	0.37	0.36	0.322	-10
171	Burundi	40.6	48.0	18	591	0.26	0.38	0.30	0.313	0
172	Niger	45.2	15.9	16	746	0.34	0.16	0.34	0.277	-4
173	Sierra Leone	38.9	36.0 [i, j]	27	490	0.23	0.33	0.27	0.275	0
	Developing countries	64.7	73.7	61	3,783	0.66	0.69	0.61	0.654	–
	Least developed countries	51.9	52.8	38	1,216	0.45	0.48	0.41	0.445	–
	Arab States	66.8	62.0	62	4,793	0.70	0.62	0.64	0.653	–
	East Asia and the Pacific	69.5	85.9	71	4,290	0.74	0.81	0.63	0.726	–
	Latin America and the Caribbean	70.0	88.3	74	7,234	0.75	0.84	0.72	0.767	–
	South Asia	62.9	55.6	53	2,404	0.63	0.55	0.53	0.570	–
	Sub-Saharan Africa	48.7	61.5	42	1,690	0.40	0.55	0.47	0.471	–
	Central and Eastern Europe and the CIS	68.6	99.3	77	6,930	0.73	0.91	0.71	0.783	–
	OECD	76.8	..	87	23,569	0.86	0.94	0.91	0.905	–
	High-income OECD	78.2	..	94	27,848	0.89	0.97	0.94	0.932	–
	High human development	77.4	..	91	24,973	0.87	0.96	0.92	0.918	–
	Medium human development	67.1	78.9	67	4,141	0.70	0.75	0.62	0.691	–
	Low human development	52.9	49.7	38	1,251	0.46	0.46	0.42	0.448	–
	High income	78.2	..	93	27,639	0.89	0.97	0.94	0.930	–
	Middle income	69.7	86.0	73	5,734	0.75	0.82	0.68	0.747	–
	Low income	59.7	62.4	51	2,002	0.58	0.59	0.50	0.554	–
	World	66.9	..	65	7,446	0.70	0.75	0.72	0.722	–

Note: As a result of revisions to data and methodology, human development index values are not strictly comparable with those in earlier *Human Development Reports*. The index has been calculated for UN member countries with reliable data in each of its components as well as for Hong Kong, China (SAR) and Switzerland. For data on the remaining 18 UN member countries see table 30. Aggregates for columns 5-8 are based on all data in the table.

a. The HDI rank is determined using HDI values to the sixth decimal point. b. Preliminary UNESCO estimates subject to further revision. c. A positive figure indicates that the HDI rank is higher than the GDP per capita (PPP US$) rank, a negative the opposite. d. For purposes of calculating the HDI a value of 99.0% was applied. e. For purposes of calculating the HDI a value of 100% was applied. f. The ratio is an underestimate, as many secondary and tertiary students pursue their studies in nearby countries. g. For purposes of calculating the HDI a value of $40,000 (PPP US$) was applied. h. Excludes Turkish students and population. i. UNICEF 2002b. j. Data refer to a year or period other than that specified, differ from the standard definition or refer to only part of a country. k. Data refer to 1998. l. Data refer to 1999. m. UNESCO 1997b. Data refer to 1995. n. Data are from the Secretariat of the Organization of Eastern Caribbean States, based on national sources. o. Data are from national sources. p. Because the combined gross enrolment ratio was unavailable, Human Development Report Office estimates were used for Seychelles (73%) and Vanuatu (38%). q. Aten, Heston and Summers 2001. Data differ from the standard definition. r. Data refer to 1996. s. Pending the outcome of ongoing efforts to calculate GDP per capita (PPP US$) for Cuba, the Human Development Report Office estimate of the subregional weighted average for the Caribbean of $4,519 (PPP US$) was used. t. UNICEF 2000. u. World Bank 2002b. v. Data refer to 1997. w. Human Development Report Office estimate based on national sources.

Source: Column 1: calculated on the basis of data on life expectancy from UN (2001); *column 2:* unless otherwise noted, UNESCO (2002a); *column 3:* unless otherwise noted, UNESCO (2001a); *column 4:* unless otherwise noted, World Bank (2002b); aggregates calculated for the Human Development Report Office by the World Bank; *column 5:* calculated on the basis of data in column 1; *column 6:* calculated on the basis of data in columns 2 and 3; *column 7:* calculated on the basis of data in column 4; *column 8:* calculated on the basis of data in columns 5-7; see technical note 1 for details; *column 9:* calculated on the basis of data in columns 4 and 8.

2 Human development index trends

HDI rank	1975	1980	1985	1990	1995	2000
High human development						
1 Norway	0.859	0.877	0.888	0.901	0.925	0.942
2 Sweden	0.863	0.872	0.883	0.894	0.925	0.941
3 Canada	0.868	0.883	0.906	0.926	0.932	0.940
4 Belgium	0.844	0.861	0.875	0.896	0.927	0.939
5 Australia	0.844	0.861	0.873	0.888	0.927	0.939
6 United States	0.863	0.884	0.898	0.914	0.925	0.939
7 Iceland	0.863	0.885	0.894	0.913	0.918	0.936
8 Netherlands	0.861	0.873	0.888	0.902	0.922	0.935
9 Japan	0.854	0.878	0.893	0.909	0.923	0.933
10 Finland	0.836	0.856	0.873	0.896	0.908	0.930
11 Switzerland	0.874	0.886	0.892	0.905	0.914	0.928
12 France	0.848	0.863	0.875	0.897	0.914	0.928
13 United Kingdom	0.841	0.848	0.858	0.878	0.916	0.928
14 Denmark	0.868	0.876	0.883	0.891	0.907	0.926
15 Austria	0.840	0.854	0.867	0.890	0.909	0.926
16 Luxembourg	0.831	0.846	0.860	0.884	0.912	0.925
17 Germany	..	0.859	0.868	0.885	0.907	0.925
18 Ireland	0.818	0.831	0.846	0.870	0.894	0.925
19 New Zealand	0.849	0.855	0.866	0.875	0.902	0.917
20 Italy	0.828	0.846	0.856	0.879	0.897	0.913
21 Spain	0.819	0.838	0.855	0.876	0.895	0.913
22 Israel	0.790	0.814	0.836	0.855	0.877	0.896
23 Hong Kong, China (SAR)	0.756	0.795	0.823	0.859	0.877	0.888
24 Greece	0.808	0.829	0.845	0.859	0.868	0.885
25 Singapore	0.722	0.755	0.782	0.818	0.857	0.885
26 Cyprus	..	0.801	0.821	0.845	0.866	0.883
27 Korea, Rep. of	0.691	0.732	0.774	0.815	0.852	0.882
28 Portugal	0.737	0.760	0.787	0.819	0.855	0.880
29 Slovenia	..	..	..	0.845	0.852	0.879
30 Malta	0.731	0.766	0.793	0.826	0.850	0.875
31 Barbados	..	..	..	..	..	0.871
32 Brunei Darussalam	..	..	..	..	..	0.856
33 Czech Republic	..	..	..	0.835	0.843	0.849
34 Argentina	0.785	0.799	0.805	0.808	0.830	0.844
35 Hungary	0.777	0.793	0.805	0.804	0.809	0.835
36 Slovakia	..	..	0.813	0.820	0.817	0.835
37 Poland	..	..	..	0.792	0.808	0.833
38 Chile	0.702	0.737	0.754	0.782	0.811	0.831
39 Bahrain	..	..	..	..	..	0.831
40 Uruguay	0.757	0.777	0.781	0.801	0.815	0.831
41 Bahamas	..	0.805	0.817	0.822	0.816	0.826
42 Estonia	..	..	..	..	..	0.826
43 Costa Rica	0.745	0.769	0.770	0.787	0.805	0.820
44 Saint Kitts and Nevis	..	..	..	..	..	0.814
45 Kuwait	0.753	0.773	0.777	..	0.812	0.813
46 United Arab Emirates	..	..	..	..	..	0.812
47 Seychelles	..	..	..	..	..	0.811
48 Croatia	..	..	..	0.797	0.789	0.809
49 Lithuania	..	..	..	0.816	0.781	0.808
50 Trinidad and Tobago	0.722	0.755	0.774	0.781	0.787	0.805

HUMAN DEVELOPMENT INDICATORS

HDI rank	1975	1980	1985	1990	1995	2000
51 Qatar	..	..	..	..	..	0.803
52 Antigua and Barbuda	..	..	..	..	..	0.800
53 Latvia	..	0.790	0.802	0.804	0.763	0.800
Medium human development						
54 Mexico	0.689	0.734	0.752	0.761	0.774	0.796
55 Cuba	..	..	..	..	..	0.795
56 Belarus	..	..	..	0.809	0.776	0.788
57 Panama	0.712	0.731	0.745	0.747	0.770	0.787
58 Belize	..	0.710	0.718	0.750	0.772	0.784
59 Malaysia	0.616	0.659	0.693	0.722	0.760	0.782
60 Russian Federation	..	0.809	0.827	0.824	0.779	0.781
61 Dominica	..	..	..	..	..	0.779
62 Bulgaria	..	0.763	0.784	0.786	0.778	0.779
63 Romania	0.755	0.788	0.794	0.777	0.772	0.775
64 Libyan Arab Jamahiriya	..	..	..	..	..	0.773
65 Macedonia, TFYR	..	..	..	..	..	0.772
66 Saint Lucia	..	..	..	..	..	0.772
67 Mauritius	0.630	0.656	0.686	0.723	0.746	0.772
68 Colombia	0.660	0.690	0.704	0.724	0.750	0.772
69 Venezuela	0.716	0.731	0.738	0.757	0.766	0.770
70 Thailand	0.604	0.645	0.676	0.713	0.749	0.762
71 Saudi Arabia	0.587	0.646	0.670	0.706	0.737	0.759
72 Fiji	0.660	0.683	0.697	0.723	0.743	0.758
73 Brazil	0.644	0.679	0.692	0.713	0.737	0.757
74 Suriname	..	..	..	..	..	0.756
75 Lebanon	..	..	..	0.680	0.730	0.755
76 Armenia	..	..	..	0.759	0.715	0.754
77 Philippines	0.652	0.684	0.688	0.716	0.733	0.754
78 Oman	..	..	..	..	..	0.751
79 Kazakhstan	..	..	..	..	..	0.750
80 Ukraine	..	..	..	0.795	0.745	0.748
81 Georgia	..	..	..	..	..	0.748
82 Peru	0.641	0.669	0.692	0.704	0.730	0.747
83 Grenada	..	..	..	..	..	0.747
84 Maldives	..	..	0.629	0.676	0.707	0.743
85 Turkey	0.593	0.617	0.654	0.686	0.717	0.742
86 Jamaica	0.687	0.690	0.692	0.720	0.736	0.742
87 Turkmenistan	..	..	..	..	..	0.741
88 Azerbaijan	..	..	..	..	..	0.741
89 Sri Lanka	0.616	0.650	0.676	0.697	0.719	0.741
90 Paraguay	0.665	0.699	0.705	0.717	0.735	0.740
91 St. Vincent & the Grenadines	..	..	..	..	..	0.733
92 Albania	..	0.673	0.691	0.702	0.702	0.733
93 Ecuador	0.627	0.673	0.694	0.705	0.719	0.732
94 Dominican Republic	0.617	0.646	0.667	0.677	0.698	0.727
95 Uzbekistan	..	..	..	0.731	0.714	0.727
96 China	0.523	0.554	0.591	0.625	0.681	0.726
97 Tunisia	0.514	0.566	0.613	0.646	0.682	0.722
98 Iran, Islamic Rep. of	0.556	0.563	0.607	0.645	0.688	0.721
99 Jordan	..	0.636	0.658	0.677	0.703	0.717
100 Cape Verde	..	..	0.587	0.626	0.678	0.715

HDI rank		1975	1980	1985	1990	1995	2000
101	Samoa (Western)	..	..	0.650	0.666	0.689	0.715
102	Kyrgyzstan	..	..	..	..	..	0.712
103	Guyana	0.676	0.679	0.671	0.680	0.703	0.708
104	El Salvador	0.586	0.586	0.606	0.644	0.682	0.706
105	Moldova, Rep. of	..	0.720	0.741	0.759	0.704	0.701
106	Algeria	0.501	0.550	0.600	0.639	0.663	0.697
107	South Africa	0.649	0.663	0.683	0.714	0.724	0.695
108	Syrian Arab Republic	0.538	0.580	0.614	0.634	0.665	0.691
109	Viet Nam	..	..	0.583	0.605	0.649	0.688
110	Indonesia	0.469	0.530	0.582	0.623	0.664	0.684
111	Equatorial Guinea	..	..	0.533	0.553	0.582	0.679
112	Tajikistan	..	..	0.740	0.740	0.669	0.667
113	Mongolia	..	..	0.650	0.657	0.636	0.655
114	Bolivia	0.514	0.548	0.573	0.597	0.630	0.653
115	Egypt	0.435	0.482	0.532	0.574	0.605	0.642
116	Honduras	0.518	0.566	0.597	0.615	0.628	0.638
117	Gabon	..	..	..	..	..	0.637
118	Nicaragua	0.565	0.576	0.584	0.592	0.615	0.635
119	São Tomé and Principe	..	..	..	..	..	0.632
120	Guatemala	0.506	0.543	0.555	0.579	0.609	0.631
121	Solomon Islands	..	..	..	..	..	0.622
122	Namibia	..	..	..	..	0.629	0.610
123	Morocco	0.429	0.474	0.508	0.540	0.569	0.602
124	India	0.407	0.434	0.473	0.511	0.545	0.577
125	Swaziland	0.512	0.543	0.569	0.615	0.620	0.577
126	Botswana	0.494	0.556	0.613	0.653	0.620	0.572
127	Myanmar	..	..	..	..	..	0.552
128	Zimbabwe	0.547	0.572	0.621	0.597	0.563	0.551
129	Ghana	0.438	0.468	0.481	0.506	0.525	0.548
130	Cambodia	..	..	..	0.501	0.531	0.543
131	Vanuatu	..	..	..	..	..	0.542
132	Lesotho	0.478	0.518	0.547	0.574	0.572	0.535
133	Papua New Guinea	0.420	0.441	0.462	0.479	0.519	0.535
134	Kenya	0.443	0.489	0.512	0.533	0.523	0.513
135	Cameroon	0.410	0.455	0.505	0.513	0.499	0.512
136	Congo	0.417	0.467	0.517	0.510	0.511	0.512
137	Comoros	..	0.480	0.498	0.502	0.506	0.511
Low human development							
138	Pakistan	0.345	0.372	0.404	0.442	0.473	0.499
139	Sudan	0.346	0.374	0.395	0.419	0.462	0.499
140	Bhutan	..	..	..	..	..	0.494
141	Togo	0.394	0.443	0.440	0.465	0.476	0.493
142	Nepal	0.289	0.328	0.370	0.416	0.453	0.490
143	Lao People's Dem. Rep.	..	..	0.374	0.404	0.445	0.485
144	Yemen	..	..	..	0.399	0.439	0.479
145	Bangladesh	0.335	0.353	0.386	0.416	0.445	0.478
146	Haiti	..	0.430	0.445	0.447	0.457	0.471
147	Madagascar	0.399	0.433	0.427	0.434	0.441	0.469
148	Nigeria	0.328	0.388	0.403	0.425	0.448	0.462
149	Djibouti	..	..	..	..	..	0.445
150	Uganda	..	..	0.386	0.388	0.404	0.444

HDI rank		1975	1980	1985	1990	1995	2000
151	Tanzania, U. Rep. of	..	..	..	0.422	0.427	0.440
152	Mauritania	0.337	0.360	0.379	0.390	0.418	0.438
153	Zambia	0.449	0.463	0.480	0.468	0.432	0.433
154	Senegal	0.313	0.330	0.356	0.380	0.400	0.431
155	Congo, Dem. Rep. of the	..	..	..	..	..	0.431
156	Côte d'Ivoire	0.369	0.403	0.412	0.415	0.416	0.428
157	Eritrea	..	..	..	..	0.408	0.421
158	Benin	0.288	0.324	0.350	0.358	0.388	0.420
159	Guinea	..	..	..	..	..	0.414
160	Gambia	0.272	..	..	..	0.375	0.405
161	Angola	..	..	..	..	..	0.403
162	Rwanda	0.336	0.380	0.396	0.346	0.335	0.403
163	Malawi	0.316	0.341	0.354	0.362	0.403	0.400
164	Mali	0.252	0.279	0.292	0.312	0.346	0.386
165	Central African Republic	0.333	0.351	0.371	0.372	0.369	0.375
166	Chad	0.256	0.257	0.298	0.322	0.335	0.365
167	Guinea-Bissau	0.248	0.253	0.283	0.304	0.331	0.349
168	Ethiopia	..	..	0.275	0.297	0.308	0.327
169	Burkina Faso	0.232	0.259	0.282	0.290	0.300	0.325
170	Mozambique	..	0.302	0.290	0.310	0.313	0.322
171	Burundi	0.280	0.307	0.338	0.344	0.316	0.313
172	Niger	0.234	0.254	0.246	0.256	0.262	0.277
173	Sierra Leone	..	..	..	..	..	0.275

Note: The human development index values in this table were calculated using a consistent methodology and consistent data series. They are not strictly comparable with those in earlier *Human Development Reports*.
Source: Columns 1-5: calculated on the basis of data on life expectancy from UN (2001), data on adult literacy rates from UNESCO (2002a), data on combined primary, secondary and tertiary gross enrolment ratios from UNESCO (2001a) and data on GDP at market prices (constant 1995 US$), population and GDP per capita (PPP US$) from World Bank (2002b); *column 6:* column 8 of table 1.

3 Human and income poverty
Developing countries

HDI rank		Human poverty index (HPI-1) Rank	Value (%)	Probability at birth of not surviving to age 40 [l] (% of cohort) 1995-2000 [a]	Adult illiteracy rate [†] (% age 15 and above) 2000	Population not using improved water sources [l] (%) 2000	Underweight children under age five [l] (%) 1995-2000 [b]	Population below income poverty line (%) $1 a day (1993 PPP US$) 1983-2000 [b]	$2 a day (1993 PPP US$) 1983-2000 [b]	National poverty line 1987-2000 [b]	HPI-1 rank minus Income poverty rank [c]
High human development											
23	Hong Kong, China (SAR)	..	..	2.0	6.5	..	..	..	..	..	..
25	Singapore	5	6.5	2.3	7.7	0	14 [d]	..	..	..	..
26	Cyprus	..	..	3.1	2.9	0	..	..	..	..	..
27	Korea, Rep. of	..	..	4.0	2.2	8	..	<2	<2	..	..
31	Barbados	..	..	3.0	..	0	5 [d]	..	..	..	..
32	Brunei Darussalam	..	..	3.2	8.5	..	..	..	..	..	..
34	Argentina	..	..	5.6	3.2	21	..	..	..	17.6	..
38	Chile	3	4.1	4.5	4.2	6	1	<2	8.7	21.2	2
39	Bahrain	..	..	4.7	12.4	..	9	..	..	..	..
40	Uruguay	1	3.9	5.1	2.3	2	5	<2	6.6	..	0
41	Bahamas	..	..	11.8	4.6	4	..	..	..	..	..
43	Costa Rica	2	4.0	4.0	4.4	2	5	12.6	26.0	22.0	-15
44	Saint Kitts and Nevis	..	..	..	..	2	..	..	..	..	..
45	Kuwait	..	..	3.0	18.0	..	10	..	..	..	..
46	United Arab Emirates	..	..	5.4	23.7	..	14	..	..	..	..
47	Seychelles	..	..	..	..	..	6 [d]	..	..	..	..
50	Trinidad and Tobago	6	7.9	4.1	6.2	14	7 [d]	12.4	39.0	21.0	-12
51	Qatar	..	..	4.8	18.8	..	6	..	..	..	..
52	Antigua and Barbuda	..	..	..	..	9	10 [d]	..	..	..	..
Medium human development											
54	Mexico	11	9.4	8.3	8.6	14	8	15.9	37.7	10.1	-14
55	Cuba	4	4.1	4.4	3.3	5	4	..	..	..	..
57	Panama	8	8.4	6.4	8.1	13	7	14.0	29.0	37.3	-13
58	Belize	14	11.0	6.8	6.8	24	6 [d]	..	..	..	..
59	Malaysia	..	..	5.0	12.5	..	18	..	..	15.5	..
61	Dominica	..	..	..	..	3	5 [d]	..	..	..	..
64	Libyan Arab Jamahiriya	27	16.2	6.4	20.0	28	5	..	..	..	..
66	Saint Lucia	..	..	5.3	..	2	14 [d]	..	..	..	..
67	Mauritius	15	11.3	5.4	15.5	0	16	..	..	10.6	..
68	Colombia	10	8.9	10.1	8.3	9	7	19.7	36.0	17.7	-18
69	Venezuela	9	8.5	6.5	7.4	16	5	23.0	47.0	31.3	-23
70	Thailand	21	14.0	9.0	4.5	20	19 [d]	<2	28.2	13.1	14
71	Saudi Arabia	29	16.9	6.4	23.7	5	14	..	..	..	..
72	Fiji	38	21.3	6.3	7.1	53	8 [d]	..	..	..	..
73	Brazil	17	12.2	11.3	14.8	13	6	11.6	26.5	17.4	-3
74	Suriname	..	..	7.4	..	5	..	..	..	..	..
75	Lebanon	12	9.9	5.0	14.0	0	3	..	..	..	..
77	Philippines	23	14.6	8.9	4.7	13	28	..	..	36.8	..
78	Oman	52	32.1	6.8	28.3	61	24	..	..	..	..
82	Peru	19	12.8	11.6	10.1	23	8	15.5	41.4	49.0	-8
83	Grenada	..	..	..	..	6	..	..	..	..	..
84	Maldives	25	15.8	12.5	3.3	0	43	..	..	..	..
85	Turkey	18	12.7	9.6	14.9	17	8	2.4	18.0	..	5
86	Jamaica	20	13.2	5.4	13.1	29	4	3.2	25.2	18.7	5
89	Sri Lanka	31	17.6	5.8	8.4	17	33	6.6	45.4	25.0	9
90	Paraguay	13	10.2	8.7	6.7	21	5	19.5	49.3	21.8	-15
91	St. Vincent & the Grenadines	..	..	..	..	7	..	..	..	..	..
93	Ecuador	26	16.1	11.1	8.4	29	15	20.2	52.3	35.0	-10
94	Dominican Republic	22	14.0	11.9	16.4	21	5	3.2	16.0	20.6	6
96	China	24	14.9	7.9	15.9	25	10	18.8	52.6	4.6	-7

HDI rank		Human poverty index (HPI-1)		Probability at birth of not surviving to age 40 [†] (% of cohort) 1995-2000 [a]	Adult illiteracy rate [†] (% age 15 and above) 2000	Population not using improved water sources [†] (%) 2000	Underweight children under age five [†] (%) 1995-2000 [b]	Population below income poverty line (%)			HPI-1 rank minus income poverty rank [c]
		Rank	Value (%)					$1 a day (1993 PPP US$) 1983-2000 [b]	$2 a day (1993 PPP US$) 1983-2000 [b]	National poverty line 1987-2000 [b]	
97	Tunisia	..	..	7.8	29.0	..	4	<2	10.0	14.1	..
98	Iran, Islamic Rep. of	30	17.0	9.3	23.7	5	11	..	..	..	..
99	Jordan	7	8.2	7.9	10.3	4	5	<2	7.4	11.7	4
100	Cape Verde	37	20.8	10.4	26.2	26	14 [d]	..	..	..	..
101	Samoa (Western)	..	..	7.8	19.8	1	..	..	..	..	..
103	Guyana	16	11.4	15.4	1.5	6	12	..	..	43.2	..
104	El Salvador	32	18.1	10.9	21.3	26	12	21.0	44.5	48.3	-8
106	Algeria	39	23.4	10.5	33.3	6	6	<2	15.1	22.6	24
107	South Africa	..	..	24.4	14.7	14	..	11.5	35.8	..	..
108	Syrian Arab Republic	34	19.3	6.9	25.6	20	13	..	..	..	..
109	Viet Nam	43	27.1	12.8	6.6	44	33	..	..	50.9	..
110	Indonesia	33	18.8	12.8	13.1	24	26	7.7	55.3	27.1	10
111	Equatorial Guinea	..	..	33.7	16.8	57	..	..	..	..	..
113	Mongolia	35	19.4	15.0	1.1	40	13	13.9	50.0	36.3	5
114	Bolivia	28	16.3	18.4	14.5	21	10	14.4	34.3	..	-1
115	Egypt	48	31.2	10.3	44.7	5	12	3.1	52.7	22.9	22
116	Honduras	36	20.5	16.0	25.4	10	25	24.3	45.1	53.0	-7
117	Gabon	..	..	32.0	..	30	..	..	..	..	..
118	Nicaragua	41	24.4	11.5	33.5	21	12	..	..	50.3	..
119	São Tomé and Principe	..	..	..	..	..	16	..	..	..	..
120	Guatemala	40	23.5	15.6	31.4	8	24	10.0	33.8	57.9	13
121	Solomon Islands	..	..	8.2	..	29	21 [d]	..	..	..	..
122	Namibia	57	34.5	46.7	18.0	23	26 [d]	34.9	55.8	..	-6
123	Morocco	59	35.8	11.8	51.1	18	9 [d]	<2	7.5	19.0	35
124	India	55	33.1	16.7	42.8	12	47	44.2	86.2	35.0	-13
125	Swaziland	..	..	36.3	20.4	..	10 [d]	..	..	40.0	..
126	Botswana	..	..	49.5	22.8	..	13	33.3	61.4	..	..
127	Myanmar	44	27.2	26.0	15.3	32	36	..	..	..	..
128	Zimbabwe	60	36.1	51.6	11.3	15	13	36.0	64.2	25.5	-5
129	Ghana	45	28.7	27.0	28.5	36	25	44.8	78.5	31.4	-19
130	Cambodia	75	43.3	24.4	32.2	70	46	..	..	36.1	..
131	Vanuatu	..	..	8.6	..	12	20 [d]	..	..	..	..
132	Lesotho	42	25.7	35.4	16.6	9	16	43.1	65.7	49.2	-18
133	Papua New Guinea	62	37.5	21.6	36.1	58	35 [d]	..	..	..	..
134	Kenya	49	31.9	34.6	17.6	51	23	26.5	62.3	42.0	-3
135	Cameroon	47	30.7	36.2	24.2	38	21	33.4	64.4	40.0	-10
136	Congo	46	30.0	34.8	19.3	49	14	..	..	..	..
137	Comoros	51	31.9	20.6	44.1	4	25	..	..	..	..

Low human development

HDI rank		Human poverty index (HPI-1)		Probability at birth of not surviving to age 40	Adult illiteracy rate	Population not using improved water sources	Underweight children under age five	$1 a day	$2 a day	National poverty line	HPI-1 rank minus income poverty rank
138	Pakistan	68	41.0	20.1	56.8	12	38	31.0	84.6	34.0	4
139	Sudan	53	32.7	27.3	42.2	25	17	..	..	..	..
140	Bhutan	..	..	20.2	..	38	19	..	..	..	..
141	Togo	63	37.9	34.1	42.9	46	25	..	..	32.3	..
142	Nepal	76	43.4	22.5	58.2	19	47	37.7	82.5	42.0	2
143	Lao People's Dem. Rep.	64	39.1	30.5	51.3	10	40	26.3	73.2	46.1	6
144	Yemen	69	41.8	20.0	53.7	31	46	15.7	45.2	19.1	20
145	Bangladesh	72	42.4	21.4	58.7	3	48	29.1	77.8	35.6	8
146	Haiti	71	42.3	31.6	50.2	54	28	..	..	65.0	..
147	Madagascar	61	36.7	31.6	33.5	53	33	49.1	83.3	70.0	-10

HDI rank		Human poverty index (HPI-1)		Probability at birth of not surviving to age 40 † (% of cohort) 1995-2000 ᵃ	Adult illiteracy rate † (% age 15 and above) 2000	Population not using improved water sources † (%) 2000	Underweight children under age five † (%) 1995-2000 ᵇ	Population below income poverty line (%)			HPI-1 rank minus income poverty rank ᶜ
		Rank	Value (%)					$1 a day (1993 PPP US$) 1983-2000 ᵇ	$2 a day (1993 PPP US$) 1983-2000 ᵇ	National poverty line 1987-2000 ᵇ	
148	Nigeria	58	34.9	33.7	36.1	43	27	70.2	90.8	34.1	-18
149	Djibouti	56	34.3	42.3	35.4	0	18	..	..	45.1	..
150	Uganda	67	40.8	48.4	32.9	50	26	..	..	55.0	..
151	Tanzania, U. Rep. of	54	32.7	33.3	24.9	46	29	19.9	59.6	41.6	5
152	Mauritania	82	47.9	33.1	59.8	63	23	28.6	68.7	57.0	15
153	Zambia	66	40.0	53.6	21.9	36	25	63.6	87.4	86.0	-11
154	Senegal	79	45.2	28.5	62.7	22	18	26.3	67.8	33.4	16
155	Congo, Dem. Rep. of the	65	39.7	34.7	38.6	55	34	..	..	..	..
156	Côte d'Ivoire	70	42.3	40.2	53.2	23	21	12.3	49.4	36.8	28
157	Eritrea	74	42.9	31.7	44.3	54	44	..	..	53.0	..
158	Benin	80	46.8	29.7	62.6	37	29	..	..	33.0	..
159	Guinea	..	..	38.3	..	52	23	..	..	40.0	..
160	Gambia	84	48.5	40.5	63.4	38	17	59.3	82.9	64.0	3
161	Angola	..	..	41.6	..	62	..	..	..	..	..
162	Rwanda	77	44.3	51.9	33.2	59	29	35.7	84.6	51.2	5
163	Malawi	73	42.5	50.4	39.9	43	25	..	..	54.0	..
164	Mali	81	47.3	38.5	58.5	35	43	72.8	90.6	..	-5
165	Central African Republic	78	45.2	45.3	53.3	40	24	66.6	84.0	..	-5
166	Chad	86	50.5	41.0	57.4	73	28	..	..	64.0	..
167	Guinea-Bissau	85	49.3	42.2	61.5	51	23	..	..	48.7	..
168	Ethiopia	87	56.5	43.6	60.9	76	47	31.2	76.4	..	15
169	Burkina Faso	..	..	43.0	76.1	..	34	61.2	85.8	..	..
170	Mozambique	83	47.9	49.2	56.0	40	26	37.8	78.4	..	7
171	Burundi	..	..	50.1	52.0	..	45	..	..	36.2	..
172	Niger	88	62.5	41.4	84.1	41	40	61.4	85.3	63.0	4
173	Sierra Leone	..	..	51.6	..	72	27	57.0	74.5	68.0	..

† Denotes indicators used to calculate the human poverty index (HPI-1). For further details see technical note 1.

a. Data refer to the probability at birth of not surviving to age 40, times 100. They are estimates for the period specified. b. Data refer to the most recent year available during the period specified. c. Income poverty refers to the percentage of the population living on less than $1 (PPP US$) a day. The rankings are based on countries with data available for both indicators. A positive figure indicates that the country performs better in income poverty than in human poverty, a negative the opposite. d. Data refer to a year or period other than that specified, differ from the standard definition or refer to only part of a country. *Source: Column 1:* determined on the basis of the HPI-1 values in column 2; *column 2:* calculated on the basis of data in columns 3-6; see technical note 1 for details; *column 3:* UN 2001; *column 4:* UNESCO 2002a; *column 5:* calculated on the basis of data on population using improved water sources from WHO, UNICEF and WSSCC (2000); *column 6:* UNICEF 2002b; *columns 7-9:* World Bank 2002b; *column 10:* calculated on the basis of data in columns 1 and 7.

HPI-1 ranks for 88 developing countries					
1 Uruguay	17 Brazil	36 Honduras	55 India	74 Eritrea	
2 Costa Rica	18 Turkey	37 Cape Verde	56 Djibouti	75 Cambodia	
3 Chile	19 Peru	38 Fiji	57 Namibia	76 Nepal	
4 Cuba	20 Jamaica	39 Algeria	58 Nigeria	77 Rwanda	
5 Singapore	21 Thailand	40 Guatemala	59 Morocco	78 Central African Republic	
6 Trinidad and Tobago	22 Dominican Republic	41 Nicaragua	60 Zimbabwe	79 Senegal	
7 Jordan	23 Philippines	42 Lesotho	61 Madagascar	80 Benin	
8 Panama	24 China	43 Viet Nam	62 Papua New Guinea	81 Mali	
9 Venezuela	25 Maldives	44 Myanmar	63 Togo	82 Mauritania	
10 Colombia	26 Ecuador	45 Ghana	64 Lao People's Dem. Rep.	83 Mozambique	
11 Mexico	27 Libyan Arab Jamahiriya	46 Congo	65 Congo, Dem. Rep. of the	84 Gambia	
12 Lebanon	28 Bolivia	47 Cameroon	66 Zambia	85 Guinea-Bissau	
13 Paraguay	29 Saudi Arabia	48 Egypt	67 Uganda	86 Chad	
14 Belize	30 Iran, Islamic Rep. of	49 Kenya	68 Pakistan	87 Ethiopia	
15 Mauritius	31 Sri Lanka	50 Iraq	69 Yemen	88 Niger	
16 Guyana	32 El Salvador	51 Comoros	70 Côte d'Ivoire		
	33 Indonesia	52 Oman	71 Haiti		
	34 Syrian Arab Republic	53 Sudan	72 Bangladesh		
	35 Mongolia	54 Tanzania, U. Rep. of	73 Malawi		

4 Human and income poverty
OECD, Central & Eastern Europe & CIS

HDI rank		Human poverty index (HPI-2) Rank	Value (%)	Probability at birth of not surviving to age 60 [†] (% of cohort) 1995-2000 [a]	People lacking functional literacy skills [†] (% age 16-65) 1994-98 [b]	Long-term unemployment [†] (as % of labour force) [c] 2000	Population below income poverty line (%) 50% of median income [d, †] 1987-98 [e]	$11 a day (1994 PPP US$) [f] 1994-95 [e]	$4 a day (1990 PPP US$) 1996-99 [e]	HPI-2 rank minus income poverty rank [g]
High human development										
1	Norway	2	7.5	9.1	8.5	0.2	6.9	4.3	..	-2
2	Sweden	1	6.7	8.0	7.5	1.4	6.6	6.3	..	-2
3	Canada	12	12.3	9.5	16.6	0.8	12.8	7.4	..	0
4	Belgium	13	12.6	10.5	18.4 [h]	4.0	8.2	..	..	5
5	Australia	14	12.9	9.1	17.0	1.8	14.3	17.6	..	-1
6	United States	17	15.8	12.8	20.7	0.2	16.9	13.6	..	1
7	Iceland	..	..	8.7	..	0.2	..	..	..	..
8	Netherlands	3	8.5	9.2	10.5	0.9	8.1	7.1	..	-4
9	Japan	9	11.2	8.2	.. [i]	1.2	11.8 [j]	..	..	-8
10	Finland	4	8.8	11.3	10.4	2.4	5.1	4.8	..	2
11	Switzerland	..	..	9.6	..	0.6	9.3	..	..	..
12	France	8	11.1	11.4	.. [i]	3.8	8.0	9.9	..	2
13	United Kingdom	15	15.1	9.9	21.8	1.5	13.4	15.7	..	2
14	Denmark	5	9.5	12.0	9.6	0.9	9.2	..	..	-4
15	Austria	..	..	10.6	..	1.3	10.6	..	..	..
16	Luxembourg	7	10.8	11.4	.. [i]	0.6	3.9	0.3	..	6
17	Germany	6	10.5	10.6	14.4	3.9	7.5	7.3	..	1
18	Ireland	16	15.3	10.4	22.6	5.6 [k]	11.1	..	..	5
19	New Zealand	..	..	10.7	18.4	1.2	..	..	..	..
20	Italy	11	12.2	9.1	.. [i]	6.5	14.2	..	..	-3
21	Spain	10	11.3	10.3	.. [i]	6.0	10.1	..	..	0
22	Israel	..	..	8.0	..	..	13.5	..	..	..
24	Greece	..	..	9.4	..	6.4	..	..	..	..
28	Portugal	..	..	13.1	48.0	1.7	..	..	..	..
29	Slovenia	..	..	13.8	42.2	..	..	..	<1	..
30	Malta	..	..	8.4	..	..	..	..	..	..
33	Czech Republic	..	..	13.7	15.7	4.4	4.9	..	<1	..
35	Hungary	..	..	21.9	33.8	3.1	10.1	..	<1	..
36	Slovakia	..	..	16.6	..	10.2	2.1	..	8	..
37	Poland	..	..	17.5	42.6	6.1	11.6	..	10	..
42	Estonia	..	..	23.8	..	..	..	..	18	..
48	Croatia	..	..	15.8	..	..	..	..	..	..
49	Lithuania	..	..	21.6	..	..	..	..	17	..
53	Latvia	..	..	23.7	..	..	..	..	28	..
Medium human development										
56	Belarus	..	..	26.0	..	..	..	..	..	..
60	Russian Federation	..	..	30.1	..	..	20.1	..	53	..
62	Bulgaria	..	..	18.8	..	..	..	..	22	..
63	Romania	..	..	21.6	..	..	..	..	23	..
65	Macedonia, TFYR	..	..	14.5	..	..	..	..	..	..
76	Armenia	..	..	14.7	..	..	..	..	..	..
79	Kazakhstan	..	..	31.6	..	..	..	..	62	..
80	Ukraine	..	..	26.3	..	..	..	..	25	..
81	Georgia	..	..	17.5	..	..	..	..	..	..
87	Turkmenistan	..	..	27.6	..	..	..	..	..	..

4 Human and income poverty
OECD, Central & Eastern Europe & CIS

HDI rank	Human poverty index (HPI-2) Rank	Human poverty index (HPI-2) Value (%)	Probability at birth of not surviving to age 60 [t] (% of cohort) 1995-2000 [a]	People lacking functional literacy skills [t] (% age 16-65) 1994-98 [b]	Long-term unemployment [t] (as % of labour force) [c] 2000	Population below income poverty line (%) 50% of median income [d, t] 1987-98 [e]	Population below income poverty line (%) $11 a day (1994 PPP US$) [f] 1994-95 [e]	Population below income poverty line (%) $4 a day (1990 PPP US$) 1996-99 [e]	HPI-2 rank minus income poverty rank [g]
88 Azerbaijan	..	..	20.4	..	..	..	..	..	..
92 Albania	..	..	12.4	..	..	..	..	..	..
95 Uzbekistan	..	..	23.9	..	..	..	..	..	..
102 Kyrgyzstan	..	..	26.4	..	..	..	..	88	..
105 Moldova, Rep. of	..	..	27.4	..	..	..	..	82	..
112 Tajikistan	..	..	25.3	..	..	..	..	..	..

† Denotes indicators used to calculate the human poverty index (HPI-2). For further details see technical note 1.

Note: This table includes Israel and Malta, which are not OECD member countries, but excludes the Republic of Korea, Mexico and Turkey, which are. For the human poverty index and related indicators for these countries see table 3.

a. Data refer to the probability at birth of not surviving to age 60, times 100. They are estimates for the period specified. b. Based on scoring at level 1 on the prose literacy scale of the International Adult Literacy Survey. Data refer to the most recent year available during the period specified. c. Data refer to unemployment lasting 12 months or longer. d. Poverty line is measured at 50% of equivalent median disposable household income. e. Data refer to the most recent year available during the period specified. f. Based on the US poverty line, $11 (1994 PPP US$) a day per person for a family of three. g. Income poverty refers to the percentage of the population living on less than 50% of the median disposable household income. A positive figure indicates that the country performs better in income poverty than in human poverty, a negative the opposite. h. Data refer to Flanders. i. For purposes of calculating the HPI-2 an estimate of 15.1%, the unweighted average for countries with available data, was applied. j. Data refer to an estimate for 2001 (LIS 2001). k. Data refer to 1999.

Source: Column 1: determined on the basis of the HPI-2 values in column 2; *column 2:* calculated on the basis of data in columns 3-6; see technical note 1 for details; *column 3:* calculated on the basis of survival data from UN (2001); *column 4:* unless otherwise noted, OECD and Statistics Canada (2000); *column 5:* OECD 2001b; *column 6:* LIS 2002; *column 7:* Smeeding, Rainwater and Burtless 2000; *column 8:* Milanovic 2002; *column 9:* calculated on the basis of data in columns 1 and 6.

HPI-2 ranks for 17 selected OECD countries

1 Sweden	6 Germany	13 Belgium
2 Norway	7 Luxembourg	14 Australia
3 Netherlands	8 France	15 United Kingdom
4 Finland	9 Japan	16 Ireland
5 Denmark	10 Spain	17 United States
	11 Italy	
	12 Canada	

HDI rank	Total population (millions)			Annual population growth rate (%)		Urban population (as % of total) [a]			Population under age 15 (as % of total)		Population aged 65 and above (as % of total)		Total fertility rate (per woman)	
	1975	2000	2015 [b]	1975-2000	2000-15	1975	2000	2015 [b]	2000	2015 [b]	2000	2015 [b]	1970-75 [c]	1995-2000 [c]
High human development														
1 Norway	4.0	4.5	4.7	0.4	0.3	68.2	74.7	78.9	19.8	15.8	15.4	18.2	2.2	1.8
2 Sweden	8.2	8.8	8.6	0.3	-0.2	82.7	83.3	84.2	18.2	12.4	17.4	22.3	1.9	1.5
3 Canada	23.1	30.8	34.4	1.1	0.8	75.6	78.7	81.9	19.1	15.9	12.6	16.1	2.0	1.6
4 Belgium	9.8	10.2	10.3	0.2	(.)	94.9	97.3	98.0	17.3	13.9	17.0	19.9	1.9	1.5
5 Australia	13.9	19.1	21.9	1.3	0.9	85.9	90.7	94.8	20.5	18.0	12.3	15.2	2.5	1.8
6 United States	220.2	283.2	321.2	1.0	0.8	73.7	77.2	81.0	21.7	18.7	12.3	14.4	2.0	2.0
7 Iceland	0.2	0.3	0.3	1.0	0.6	86.6	92.5	94.3	23.3	18.7	11.7	14.0	2.8	2.0
8 Netherlands	13.7	15.9	16.4	0.6	0.2	88.4	89.5	91.0	18.3	14.7	13.6	17.8	2.1	1.5
9 Japan	111.5	127.1	127.5	0.5	(.)	75.7	78.8	81.5	14.7	13.3	17.2	25.8	2.1	1.4
10 Finland	4.7	5.2	5.2	0.4	(.)	58.3	59.0	59.0	18.0	14.2	14.9	20.7	1.6	1.7
11 Switzerland	6.3	7.2	7.0	0.5	-0.2	55.7	67.4	69.5	16.7	12.1	16.0	22.1	1.8	1.5
12 France	52.7	59.2	61.9	0.5	0.3	73.0	75.4	78.4	18.7	17.4	16.0	18.6	2.3	1.7
13 United Kingdom	56.2	59.4	60.6	0.2	0.1	88.7	89.5	90.8	19.0	15.1	15.8	18.9	2.0	1.7
14 Denmark	5.1	5.3	5.4	0.2	0.1	81.8	85.1	85.7	18.3	15.1	15.0	19.5	2.0	1.7
15 Austria	7.6	8.1	7.8	0.3	-0.2	67.4	67.3	71.0	16.6	11.8	15.6	20.0	2.0	1.4
16 Luxembourg	0.4	0.4	0.5	0.8	1.1	73.7	91.5	95.0	18.7	17.3	14.4	16.0	2.0	1.7
17 Germany	78.7	82.0	80.7	0.2	-0.1	81.2	87.5	89.9	15.5	12.1	16.4	21.0	1.6	1.3
18 Ireland	3.2	3.8	4.4	0.7	1.0	53.6	59.0	64.0	21.6	21.8	11.3	13.1	3.8	1.9
19 New Zealand	3.1	3.8	4.1	0.8	0.6	82.8	85.8	87.5	23.0	18.8	11.7	14.5	2.8	2.0
20 Italy	55.4	57.5	55.2	0.1	-0.3	65.6	66.9	70.6	14.3	12.0	18.1	22.4	2.3	1.2
21 Spain	35.6	39.9	39.0	0.5	-0.2	69.6	77.6	81.1	14.7	12.5	17.0	19.8	2.9	1.2
22 Israel	3.4	6.0	7.7	2.3	1.6	86.6	91.6	93.5	28.3	24.3	9.9	11.5	3.8	2.9
23 Hong Kong, China (SAR)	4.4	6.9	8.0	1.8	1.0	89.7	100.0	100.0	16.3	13.9	10.6	13.4	2.9	1.2
24 Greece	9.0	10.6	10.5	0.6	-0.1	55.3	60.1	65.1	15.1	12.7	17.6	21.2	2.3	1.3
25 Singapore	2.3	4.0	4.8	2.3	1.1	100.0	100.0	100.0	21.9	14.0	7.2	12.9	2.6	1.6
26 Cyprus	0.6	0.8	0.9	1.0	0.7	45.2	69.9	74.6	23.1	19.2	11.5	14.8	2.5	2.0
27 Korea, Rep. of	35.3	46.7	50.6	1.1	0.5	48.0	81.9	88.2	20.8	17.2	7.1	11.6	4.3	1.5
28 Portugal	9.1	10.0	10.0	0.4	(.)	27.7	64.4	77.5	16.7	15.3	15.6	18.0	2.7	1.5
29 Slovenia	1.7	2.0	1.9	0.5	-0.2	42.4	49.2	51.6	15.9	12.0	13.9	18.5	2.2	1.2
30 Malta	0.3	0.4	0.4	1.0	0.4	80.4	90.9	93.7	20.2	16.9	12.4	18.1	2.1	1.9
31 Barbados	0.2	0.3	0.3	0.3	0.3	38.6	50.0	58.4	20.7	16.7	10.4	11.4	2.7	1.5
32 Brunei Darussalam	0.2	0.3	0.4	2.9	1.6	62.0	72.2	78.7	31.9	23.0	3.2	6.4	5.4	2.8
33 Czech Republic	10.0	10.3	10.0	0.1	-0.2	63.7	74.5	76.4	16.4	12.8	13.8	18.7	2.2	1.2
34 Argentina	26.0	37.0	43.5	1.4	1.1	80.7	88.2	90.2	27.7	24.5	9.7	10.7	3.1	2.6
35 Hungary	10.5	10.0	9.3	-0.2	-0.5	52.8	64.5	69.4	16.9	13.3	14.6	17.4	2.1	1.4
36 Slovakia	4.7	5.4	5.4	0.5	(.)	46.3	57.4	62.0	19.5	14.9	11.4	13.7	2.5	1.4
37 Poland	34.0	38.6	38.0	0.5	-0.1	55.4	62.3	66.5	19.2	14.6	12.1	14.8	2.2	1.5
38 Chile	10.3	15.2	17.9	1.5	1.1	78.4	85.8	89.1	28.5	23.7	7.2	9.7	3.6	2.4
39 Bahrain	0.3	0.6	0.8	3.4	1.4	79.2	92.2	95.0	28.2	20.2	2.9	6.1	5.9	2.6
40 Uruguay	2.8	3.3	3.7	0.7	0.6	83.1	91.9	94.4	24.8	22.6	12.9	13.4	3.0	2.4
41 Bahamas	0.2	0.3	0.4	1.9	1.1	73.4	88.5	91.5	29.6	24.5	5.4	7.7	3.4	2.4
42 Estonia	1.4	1.4	1.2	-0.1	-1.1	67.6	69.4	71.3	17.7	13.7	14.4	16.9	2.1	1.2
43 Costa Rica	2.0	4.0	5.2	2.9	1.8	42.5	59.0	66.5	32.4	27.1	5.1	7.1	4.3	2.8
44 Saint Kitts and Nevis	(.)	(.)	(.)	-0.7	-0.6	35.0	34.1	39.3	..	..	..	..	..	..
45 Kuwait	1.0	1.9	2.8	2.6	2.5	83.8	96.0	96.9	31.3	25.9	2.2	6.6	6.9	2.9
46 United Arab Emirates	0.5	2.6	3.2	6.6	1.4	65.4	86.7	91.6	26.0	21.1	2.7	9.2	6.4	3.2
47 Seychelles	0.1	0.1	0.1	1.2	1.3	33.3	63.8	72.3	..	..	..	..	..	..
48 Croatia	4.3	4.7	4.6	0.4	(.)	45.1	57.7	64.4	18.0	16.8	14.1	16.9	2.0	1.7
49 Lithuania	3.3	3.7	3.5	0.5	-0.3	55.7	68.5	71.6	19.5	13.0	13.4	16.6	2.3	1.4
50 Trinidad and Tobago	1.0	1.3	1.4	1.0	0.5	63.0	74.1	79.3	25.0	19.4	6.7	9.6	3.4	1.6

HDI rank		Total population (millions)			Annual population growth rate (%)		Urban population (as % of total) [a]			Population under age 15 (as % of total)		Population aged 65 and above (as % of total)		Total fertility rate (per woman)	
		1975	2000	2015[b]	1975-2000	2000-15	1975	2000	2015[b]	2000	2015[b]	2000	2015[b]	1970-75[c]	1995-2000[c]
51	Qatar	0.2	0.6	0.7	4.8	1.4	82.9	92.7	95.0	26.7	22.7	1.5	5.7	6.8	3.7
52	Antigua and Barbuda	0.1	0.1	0.1	0.4	0.3	34.2	36.8	43.3	..	..	..	..	..	..
53	Latvia	2.5	2.4	2.2	-0.1	-0.6	65.4	60.4	60.4	17.4	12.6	14.8	17.8	2.0	1.1
Medium human development															
54	Mexico	59.1	98.9	119.2	2.1	1.2	62.8	74.4	77.9	33.1	26.3	4.7	6.8	6.5	2.8
55	Cuba	9.3	11.2	11.6	0.7	0.3	64.2	75.3	78.5	21.2	16.4	9.6	14.1	3.6	1.6
56	Belarus	9.4	10.2	9.7	0.3	-0.4	50.3	69.4	72.6	18.7	14.3	13.3	14.0	2.2	1.3
57	Panama	1.7	2.9	3.5	2.0	1.3	49.0	56.3	61.7	31.3	24.9	5.5	7.8	4.9	2.6
58	Belize	0.1	0.2	0.3	2.1	1.6	50.2	48.0	51.7	38.4	27.9	4.2	4.9	6.2	3.4
59	Malaysia	12.3	22.2	27.9	2.4	1.5	37.7	57.4	66.4	34.1	26.7	4.1	6.2	5.2	3.3
60	Russian Federation	134.2	145.5	133.3	0.3	-0.6	66.4	72.9	74.0	18.0	13.6	12.5	13.8	2.0	1.2
61	Dominica	0.1	0.1	0.1	-0.1	(.)	55.3	71.0	76.0	..	..	..	..	..	..
62	Bulgaria	8.7	7.9	6.8	-0.4	-1.0	57.5	67.5	69.3	15.7	12.2	16.1	17.9	2.2	1.1
63	Romania	21.2	22.4	21.4	0.2	-0.3	46.2	55.1	59.3	18.3	15.2	13.3	14.6	2.6	1.3
64	Libyan Arab Jamahiriya	2.4	5.3	7.1	3.1	1.9	60.9	87.6	90.3	33.9	30.4	3.4	5.1	7.6	3.8
65	Macedonia, TFYR	1.7	2.0	2.1	0.8	0.1	50.6	59.4	62.0	22.6	15.1	10.0	13.0	3.0	1.9
66	Saint Lucia	0.1	0.1	0.2	1.4	0.9	38.6	37.8	43.6	32.1	27.2	5.7	6.0	5.7	2.7
67	Mauritius	0.9	1.2	1.3	1.1	0.8	43.4	41.3	48.6	25.6	21.1	6.2	8.3	3.2	2.0
68	Colombia	25.4	42.1	52.6	2.0	1.5	60.0	75.0	81.3	32.8	27.0	4.7	6.4	5.0	2.8
69	Venezuela	12.7	24.2	30.9	2.6	1.6	75.8	86.9	90.0	34.0	27.6	4.4	6.5	4.9	3.0
70	Thailand	41.1	62.8	72.5	1.7	1.0	15.1	19.8	24.2	26.7	22.0	5.2	7.8	5.0	2.1
71	Saudi Arabia	7.3	20.3	31.7	4.1	3.0	58.4	86.2	91.0	42.9	38.6	3.0	4.4	7.3	6.2
72	Fiji	0.6	0.8	0.9	1.4	0.9	36.7	49.4	59.9	33.3	28.2	3.4	5.7	4.2	3.2
73	Brazil	108.1	170.4	201.4	1.8	1.1	61.8	81.2	87.7	28.8	24.3	5.1	7.3	4.7	2.3
74	Suriname	0.4	0.4	0.4	0.5	0.3	49.5	74.1	81.3	30.5	23.1	5.6	6.3	5.3	2.2
75	Lebanon	2.8	3.5	4.2	0.9	1.3	67.0	89.7	92.6	31.1	23.8	6.1	6.5	4.9	2.3
76	Armenia	2.8	3.8	3.8	1.2	(.)	63.0	67.2	69.8	23.7	14.0	8.6	10.3	3.0	1.4
77	Philippines	42.0	75.7	95.9	2.4	1.6	35.6	58.6	69.0	37.5	29.6	3.5	4.9	6.0	3.6
78	Oman	0.9	2.5	4.1	4.2	3.2	19.6	76.0	82.6	44.1	41.5	2.5	3.7	7.2	5.8
79	Kazakhstan	14.1	16.2	16.0	0.5	-0.1	52.2	55.8	58.2	27.0	22.2	6.9	8.1	3.5	2.1
80	Ukraine	49.0	49.6	43.3	(.)	-0.9	58.3	67.9	70.4	17.8	12.8	13.8	15.7	2.2	1.3
81	Georgia	4.9	5.3	4.8	0.3	-0.6	49.5	56.3	61.4	20.5	14.8	12.9	15.0	2.6	1.6
82	Peru	15.2	25.7	31.9	2.1	1.4	61.5	72.8	77.9	33.4	26.7	4.8	6.5	6.0	3.0
83	Grenada	0.1	0.1	0.1	0.1	0.3	32.6	37.9	47.2	..	..	..	..	..	..
84	Maldives	0.1	0.3	0.5	3.0	2.9	18.1	27.6	35.2	43.7	40.5	3.5	3.2	7.0	5.8
85	Turkey	40.0	66.7	79.0	2.0	1.1	41.6	65.8	71.8	30.0	24.1	5.8	7.2	5.2	2.7
86	Jamaica	2.0	2.6	3.0	1.0	0.9	44.1	56.1	63.5	31.5	25.4	7.2	7.8	5.0	2.5
87	Turkmenistan	2.5	4.7	6.1	2.5	1.6	47.6	44.8	49.9	37.6	28.4	4.3	4.5	6.2	3.6
88	Azerbaijan	5.7	8.0	8.7	1.4	0.5	51.5	51.9	53.9	29.0	17.5	6.8	8.1	4.3	1.9
89	Sri Lanka	13.5	18.9	21.5	1.3	0.8	22.0	22.8	29.9	26.3	22.5	6.3	8.8	4.1	2.1
90	Paraguay	2.7	5.5	7.8	2.9	2.3	39.0	56.0	65.0	39.5	34.1	3.5	4.3	5.7	4.2
91	St. Vincent & the Grenadines	0.1	0.1	0.1	0.8	0.6	27.0	54.8	68.0	..	..	..	..	..	..
92	Albania	2.4	3.1	3.4	1.1	0.6	32.7	42.3	51.9	30.0	22.7	5.9	8.0	4.7	2.6
93	Ecuador	6.9	12.6	15.9	2.4	1.5	42.4	63.0	69.4	33.8	27.1	4.7	6.2	6.0	3.1
94	Dominican Republic	5.0	8.4	10.1	2.0	1.3	45.3	65.4	73.0	33.5	28.4	4.3	6.2	5.6	2.9
95	Uzbekistan	14.0	24.9	30.6	2.3	1.4	39.1	36.7	38.4	36.3	25.9	4.7	5.0	6.3	2.8
96	China	927.8[d]	1,275.1[d]	1,410.2[d]	1.3[d]	0.7[d]	17.4	35.8	49.5	24.8	19.4	6.9	9.3	4.9	1.8
97	Tunisia	5.7	9.5	11.3	2.0	1.2	49.8	65.5	73.5	29.7	24.8	5.9	6.2	6.2	2.3
98	Iran, Islamic Rep. of	33.5	70.3	87.1	3.0	1.4	45.8	64.0	73.2	37.4	27.2	3.4	5.0	6.4	3.2
99	Jordan	1.9	4.9	7.2	3.7	2.5	57.8	78.7	81.1	40.0	36.4	2.8	3.7	7.8	4.7
100	Cape Verde	0.3	0.4	0.6	1.7	1.9	21.4	62.2	73.5	39.3	31.9	4.6	3.3	7.0	3.6

HDI rank		Total population (millions)			Annual population growth rate (%)		Urban population (as % of total) [a]			Population under age 15 (as % of total)		Population aged 65 and above (as % of total)		Total fertility rate (per woman)	
		1975	2000	2015 [b]	1975-2000	2000-15	1975	2000	2015 [b]	2000	2015 [b]	2000	2015 [b]	1970-75 [c]	1995-2000 [c]
101	Samoa (Western)	0.2	0.2	0.2	0.2	0.8	21.1	22.1	27.6	41.2	36.6	4.6	4.7	5.7	4.5
102	Kyrgyzstan	3.3	4.9	5.8	1.6	1.1	37.9	34.4	36.0	33.9	25.0	6.0	6.0	4.7	2.9
103	Guyana	0.7	0.8	0.7	0.1	-0.1	30.0	36.3	44.0	30.6	25.7	5.0	6.5	4.9	2.4
104	El Salvador	4.1	6.3	8.0	1.7	1.6	41.5	60.3	73.2	35.6	29.5	5.0	6.1	6.1	3.2
105	Moldova, Rep. of	3.8	4.3	4.2	0.4	-0.2	35.8	41.6	45.2	23.1	16.7	9.3	10.2	2.6	1.6
106	Algeria	16.0	30.3	38.0	2.5	1.5	40.3	57.1	65.2	34.8	26.8	4.1	4.9	7.4	3.2
107	South Africa	25.8	43.3	44.6	2.1	0.2	48.0	56.9	67.2	34.0	30.5	3.6	5.4	5.4	3.1
108	Syrian Arab Republic	7.4	16.2	23.2	3.1	2.4	45.1	51.4	57.9	40.8	34.3	3.1	3.4	7.7	4.0
109	Viet Nam	48.0	78.1	94.4	2.0	1.3	18.8	24.1	31.6	33.4	25.1	5.3	5.5	6.7	2.5
110	Indonesia	134.6	212.1	250.1	1.8	1.1	19.4	41.0	55.0	30.8	24.7	4.8	6.4	5.2	2.6
111	Equatorial Guinea	0.2	0.5	0.7	2.8	2.8	27.1	48.2	61.4	43.7	43.4	3.9	3.5	5.7	5.9
112	Tajikistan	3.4	6.1	7.1	2.3	1.0	35.5	27.6	29.6	39.4	27.1	4.6	4.6	6.8	3.7
113	Mongolia	1.4	2.5	3.1	2.2	1.3	48.7	56.6	59.5	35.2	25.9	3.8	4.2	7.3	2.7
114	Bolivia	4.8	8.3	11.2	2.2	2.0	41.3	62.4	69.9	39.6	33.7	4.0	4.9	6.5	4.4
115	Egypt	38.8	67.9	84.4	2.2	1.5	43.5	42.7	45.8	35.4	26.9	4.1	5.2	5.5	3.4
116	Honduras	3.0	6.4	8.7	3.0	2.0	32.1	52.7	64.3	41.8	33.7	3.4	4.1	7.0	4.3
117	Gabon	0.6	1.2	1.8	2.9	2.4	40.0	81.4	88.9	40.2	40.8	5.8	5.5	4.3	5.4
118	Nicaragua	2.5	5.1	7.2	2.8	2.4	48.9	56.1	62.6	42.6	35.2	3.0	3.7	6.8	4.3
119	São Tomé and Principe	0.1	0.1	0.2	2.1	1.7	27.0	47.0	56.4	..	..	..	..	..	..
120	Guatemala	6.0	11.4	16.3	2.6	2.4	36.7	39.7	46.2	43.6	37.3	3.5	3.8	6.4	4.9
121	Solomon Islands	0.2	0.4	0.7	3.4	3.2	9.1	19.7	28.6	44.8	41.6	2.6	2.9	7.2	5.6
122	Namibia	0.9	1.8	2.3	2.7	1.8	20.6	30.9	39.4	43.7	39.0	3.8	3.9	6.5	5.3
123	Morocco	17.3	29.9	37.7	2.2	1.5	37.8	55.5	64.4	34.7	28.1	4.1	4.9	6.9	3.4
124	India	620.7	1,008.9	1,230.5	1.9	1.3	21.3	27.7	32.2	33.5	26.9	5.0	6.4	5.4	3.3
125	Swaziland	0.5	0.9	1.0	2.6	0.7	14.0	26.4	32.7	41.6	38.7	3.5	4.3	6.5	4.8
126	Botswana	0.8	1.5	1.7	2.8	0.6	12.8	49.0	56.0	42.1	36.8	2.8	3.9	6.6	4.4
127	Myanmar	30.2	47.7	55.3	1.8	1.0	23.9	27.7	36.7	33.1	25.3	4.6	6.0	5.8	3.3
128	Zimbabwe	6.1	12.6	16.4	2.9	1.7	19.6	35.3	45.9	45.2	39.9	3.2	3.1	7.4	5.0
129	Ghana	9.9	19.3	26.4	2.7	2.1	30.1	36.1	42.4	40.9	36.0	3.2	4.0	6.9	4.6
130	Cambodia	7.1	13.1	18.6	2.5	2.3	10.3	16.9	26.1	43.9	38.6	2.8	3.4	5.5	5.2
131	Vanuatu	0.1	0.2	0.3	2.7	2.4	15.7	21.7	28.6	42.0	36.2	3.2	3.7	6.1	4.6
132	Lesotho	1.2	2.0	2.1	2.0	0.3	10.8	28.0	38.9	39.3	36.6	4.2	5.6	5.7	4.8
133	Papua New Guinea	2.6	4.8	6.6	2.5	2.2	11.9	17.4	22.3	40.1	36.0	2.4	2.9	6.1	4.6
134	Kenya	13.6	30.7	40.0	3.3	1.8	12.9	33.4	47.2	43.5	38.3	2.8	3.0	8.1	4.6
135	Cameroon	7.5	14.9	20.2	2.7	2.0	26.9	48.9	58.9	43.1	39.5	3.7	3.8	6.3	5.1
136	Congo	1.4	3.0	4.7	2.9	3.0	35.0	65.4	72.6	46.3	46.0	3.3	3.1	6.3	6.3
137	Comoros	0.3	0.7	1.1	3.2	2.8	21.2	33.2	42.6	43.0	39.8	2.6	3.0	7.0	5.4
Low human development															
138	Pakistan	70.3	141.3	204.3	2.8	2.5	26.4	33.1	39.5	41.8	38.4	3.7	4.0	6.3	5.5
139	Sudan	16.7	31.1	42.4	2.5	2.1	18.9	36.1	48.7	40.1	35.4	3.4	4.3	6.7	4.9
140	Bhutan	1.2	2.1	3.1	2.3	2.6	3.4	7.1	11.6	42.7	38.8	4.2	4.5	5.9	5.5
141	Togo	2.3	4.5	6.6	2.8	2.5	16.3	33.4	42.7	44.3	41.2	3.1	3.3	7.1	5.8
142	Nepal	13.1	23.0	32.1	2.2	2.2	5.0	11.8	17.9	41.0	37.2	3.7	4.2	5.8	4.8
143	Lao People's Dem. Rep.	3.0	5.3	7.3	2.2	2.2	11.1	19.3	27.1	42.7	37.3	3.5	3.7	6.2	5.3
144	Yemen	7.0	18.3	33.1	3.9	3.9	16.6	24.7	31.2	50.1	48.9	2.3	2.0	7.6	7.6
145	Bangladesh	75.6	137.4	183.2	2.4	1.9	9.9	25.0	34.4	38.7	32.9	3.1	3.7	6.4	3.8
146	Haiti	4.9	8.1	10.2	2.0	1.5	21.7	35.7	45.6	40.6	35.1	3.7	4.1	5.8	4.4
147	Madagascar	7.9	16.0	24.1	2.8	2.7	16.3	29.5	39.4	44.7	41.9	3.0	3.1	6.6	6.1
148	Nigeria	54.9	113.9	165.3	2.9	2.5	23.4	44.1	55.5	45.1	41.4	3.0	3.3	6.9	5.9
149	Djibouti	0.2	0.6	0.7	4.4	0.7	68.9	84.0	86.9	43.2	41.5	3.2	5.2	6.7	6.1
150	Uganda	10.8	23.3	38.7	3.1	3.4	8.3	14.2	20.7	49.2	49.3	2.5	2.2	7.1	7.1

HDI rank		Total population (millions)			Annual population growth rate (%)		Urban population (as % of total) [a]			Population under age 15 (as % of total)		Population aged 65 and above (as % of total)		Total fertility rate (per woman)	
		1975	2000	2015 [b]	1975-2000	2000-15	1975	2000	2015 [b]	2000	2015 [b]	2000	2015 [b]	1970-75 [c]	1995-2000 [c]
151	Tanzania, U. Rep. of	16.2	35.1	49.3	3.1	2.3	10.1	32.3	46.2	45.0	40.4	2.4	3.0	6.8	5.5
152	Mauritania	1.4	2.7	4.1	2.7	2.9	20.3	57.7	73.8	44.1	43.5	3.2	3.0	6.5	6.0
153	Zambia	5.0	10.4	14.8	2.9	2.3	34.8	39.6	45.2	46.5	44.2	2.9	2.9	7.8	6.0
154	Senegal	4.8	9.4	13.5	2.7	2.4	34.2	47.4	57.4	44.3	40.1	2.5	2.7	7.0	5.6
155	Congo, Dem. Rep. of the	23.1	50.9	84.0	3.2	3.3	29.5	30.3	39.3	48.8	48.0	2.9	2.8	6.3	6.7
156	Côte d'Ivoire	6.8	16.0	21.5	3.5	2.0	32.1	43.6	50.9	42.1	38.4	3.1	3.8	7.4	5.1
157	Eritrea	2.1	3.7	5.7	2.2	3.0	12.7	18.7	26.2	43.9	40.4	2.9	3.5	6.5	5.7
158	Benin	3.0	6.3	9.4	2.9	2.7	21.9	42.3	53.0	46.4	42.8	2.7	2.8	7.1	6.1
159	Guinea	4.1	8.2	11.3	2.8	2.2	16.3	27.5	35.5	44.1	41.6	2.8	3.0	7.0	6.3
160	Gambia	0.5	1.3	1.8	3.5	2.1	17.0	30.7	40.5	40.3	36.7	3.1	4.0	6.5	5.2
161	Angola	6.2	13.1	20.8	3.0	3.1	17.8	34.2	44.1	48.2	48.5	2.8	2.6	6.6	7.2
162	Rwanda	4.4	7.6	10.5	2.2	2.1	4.0	6.2	8.9	44.3	42.8	2.6	2.8	8.3	6.2
163	Malawi	5.2	11.3	15.7	3.1	2.2	7.7	14.7	21.3	46.3	44.2	2.9	3.2	7.4	6.8
164	Mali	6.2	11.4	17.7	2.4	2.9	16.2	30.2	40.7	46.1	46.3	4.0	3.8	7.1	7.0
165	Central African Republic	2.1	3.7	4.9	2.4	1.8	33.7	41.2	49.7	43.0	40.5	4.0	4.0	5.7	5.3
166	Chad	4.1	7.9	12.4	2.6	3.0	15.6	23.8	30.9	46.5	46.4	3.1	2.8	6.7	6.6
167	Guinea-Bissau	0.6	1.2	1.7	2.5	2.4	16.0	31.5	43.0	43.5	43.6	3.6	3.3	6.0	6.0
168	Ethiopia	32.8	62.9	89.8	2.6	2.4	9.5	15.5	22.0	45.2	44.4	3.0	3.2	6.8	6.8
169	Burkina Faso	6.2	11.5	18.5	2.5	3.2	6.3	16.5	23.1	48.7	47.7	3.2	2.6	7.8	6.9
170	Mozambique	10.3	18.3	23.5	2.3	1.7	8.7	32.1	48.2	43.9	41.8	3.2	3.4	6.6	6.3
171	Burundi	3.7	6.4	9.8	2.2	2.9	3.2	9.0	14.5	47.6	45.0	2.9	2.4	6.8	6.8
172	Niger	4.8	10.8	18.5	3.2	3.6	10.6	20.6	29.1	49.9	49.7	2.0	1.9	8.1	8.0
173	Sierra Leone	2.9	4.4	7.1	1.6	3.2	21.4	36.6	46.7	44.2	45.0	2.9	2.9	6.5	6.5
	Developing countries	2,908 T	4,695 T	5,773 T	1.9	1.4	26.1	40.0	48.5	32.7	28.1	5.1	6.4	5.4	3.1
	Least developed countries	332 T	634 T	907 T	2.6	2.4	14.6	25.7	34.5	43.1	40.4	3.1	3.4	6.6	5.4
	Arab States	126 T	246 T	333 T	2.7	2.0	40.3	52.8	59.0	37.6	32.2	3.7	4.6	6.5	4.1
	East Asia and the Pacific	1,293 T	1,859 T	2,108 T	1.5	0.8	19.7	37.7	50.1	26.9	21.3	6.2	8.4	5.0	2.1
	Latin America and the Caribbean	318 T	513 T	624 T	1.9	1.3	61.4	75.4	80.5	31.6	26.3	5.4	7.2	5.1	2.7
	South Asia	828 T	1,402 T	1,762 T	2.1	1.5	21.4	29.4	35.0	35.1	29.0	4.6	5.7	5.6	3.6
	Sub-Saharan Africa	303 T	606 T	866 T	2.8	2.4	20.9	33.9	42.7	44.6	42.4	3.0	3.2	6.8	5.8
	Central and Eastern Europe and the CIS	354 T	397 T	383 T	0.5	-0.2	57.7	63.4	64.8	20.8	15.9	11.6	12.9	2.5	1.5
	OECD	925 T	1,129 T	1,209 T	0.8	0.5	70.4	76.9	80.4	20.4	17.3	13.0	16.2	2.5	1.8
	High-income OECD	732 T	852 T	898 T	0.6	0.3	74.9	78.7	81.9	18.3	15.7	14.9	18.5	2.1	1.7
	High human development	895 T	1,063 T	1,127 T	0.7	0.4	72.6	78.5	82.0	19.1	16.3	13.9	17.3	2.3	1.7
	Medium human development	2,678 T	4,048 T	4,717 T	1.7	1.0	29.5	42.6	50.9	29.8	24.2	5.9	7.5	4.9	2.6
	Low human development	424 T	839 T	1,218 T	2.7	2.5	17.4	29.7	38.5	43.7	40.9	3.1	3.4	6.7	5.6
	High income	747 T	878 T	929 T	0.7	0.4	75.0	79.1	82.3	18.4	15.8	14.7	18.3	2.1	1.7
	Middle income	1,855 T	2,675 T	3,037 T	1.5	0.8	35.0	51.2	60.9	27.4	22.2	6.6	8.5	4.6	2.2
	Low income	1,396 T	2,397 T	3,096 T	2.2	1.7	21.8	31.0	38.0	36.9	32.4	4.5	5.2	5.7	4.0
	World	4,066 T [e]	6,057 T [e]	7,207 T [e]	1.6	1.2	37.9	47.2	53.7	29.9	25.8	6.9	8.3	4.5	2.8

a. Because data are based on national definitions of what constitutes a city or metropolitan area, cross-country comparisons should be made with caution. b. Data refer to medium-variant projections. c. Data refer to estimates for the period specified. d. Population estimates include Taiwan, province of China. e. Data refer to the total world population according to UN (2001). The total population of the 173 countries included in the main indicator tables was estimated to be 3,998 million in 1975 and 5,951 million in 2000 and is projected to be 7,061 million in 2015.

Source: Columns 1-3, 13 and 14: UN 2001; *column 4:* calculated on the basis of data in columns 1 and 2; *column 5:* calculated on the basis of data in columns 2 and 3; *columns 6-8:* UN 2002d; *columns 9 and 10:* calculated on the basis of data on population under age 15 and total population from UN (2001); *columns 11 and 12:* calculated on the basis of data on population aged 65 and above and total population from UN (2001).

6 Commitment to health: access, services and resources

HDI rank		Population using adequate sanitation facilities (%) 2000	Population using improved water sources (%) 2000	Population with access to essential drugs (%)a 1999	One-year-olds fully immunized		Oral rehydration therapy use rate (%) 1994-2000b	Contraceptive prevalence (%)c 1995-2000b	Births attended by skilled health staff (%) 1995-2000d	Physicians (per 100,000 people) 1990-99b	Health expenditure		
					Against tuberculosis (%) 1999	Against measles (%) 1999					Public (as % of GDP) 1998	Private (as % of GDP) 1998	Per capita (PPP US$) 1998
High human development													
1	Norway	..	100	95-100	98	93	..	..	..	413	7.0 e	2.2 e	3,182 e
2	Sweden	100	100	95-100	13	96	..	..	..	311	6.6	1.3	2,145
3	Canada	100	100	95-100	..	96	..	75	98	229	6.6 e	2.7 e	1,939 e
4	Belgium	..	..	95-100	..	83	..	..	..	395	6.3 e	2.5 e	2,137 e
5	Australia	100	100	95-100	..	89	..	..	100	240	6.0	2.6	1,714
6	United States	100	100	95-100	..	92	..	76	99	279	5.7 e	7.1 e	4,271 e
7	Iceland	..	..	95-100	..	99	..	..	..	326	7.4 e	1.3 e	2,701 e
8	Netherlands	100	100	95-100	..	96	..	..	100	251	6.0 e	2.8 e	2,173 e
9	Japan	..	..	95-100	..	94	..	..	100	193	5.7	1.6	2,243
10	Finland	100	100	95-100	99	96	..	..	..	299	5.2 e	1.7 e	1,704 e
11	Switzerland	100	100	95-100	..	81	..	82 f	..	323	7.6	2.8	3,857
12	France	..	..	95-100	84	84	..	..	..	303	7.3 e	2.0 e	2,288 e
13	United Kingdom	100	100	95-100	..	91	..	..	99	164	5.8 e	1.2 e	1,675 e
14	Denmark	..	100	95-100	..	92	..	..	..	290	6.9 e	1.5 e	2,785 e
15	Austria	100	100	95-100	..	90	..	51	..	302	5.9 e	2.3 e	2,121 e
16	Luxembourg	..	..	95-100	59	91	..	..	..	272	5.7 e	0.4 e	2,731 e
17	Germany	..	..	95-100	..	75	..	..	..	350	7.9 e	2.6 e	2,697 e
18	Ireland	..	..	95-100	90	77	..	..	..	219	5.2	1.6 e	1,569
19	New Zealand	..	..	95-100	..	83	..	75	100 g	218	6.3 e	1.8 e	1,163 e
20	Italy	..	..	95-100	81	70	..	60	..	554	5.6 e	2.6 e	1,676 e
21	Spain	..	..	95-100	..	93	..	81	..	424	5.4	1.6	1,043
22	Israel	..	..	95-100	..	94	..	..	..	385	6.0	3.6	1,607
23	Hong Kong, China (SAR)	..	..	..	..	..	..	..	100	..	..	..	..
24	Greece	..	..	95-100	88	88	..	..	..	392	4.7	3.6	965
25	Singapore	100	100	95-100	98	93	..	..	100 g	163	1.1	2.1	678
26	Cyprus	100	100	95-100	..	..	..	..	..	255	..	..	..
27	Korea, Rep. of	63	92	95-100	75	85	..	80	100 g	136	2.4 e	3.0 e	470 e
28	Portugal	..	..	95-100	88	96	..	..	100	312	5.1	2.5	859
29	Slovenia	..	100	95-100	96	98	..	..	..	228	6.7	0.9	746
30	Malta	100	100	95-100	91	60	..	..	..	261	..	..	..
31	Barbados	100	100	95-100	..	86	..	..	91	125	4.5	2.2	601
32	Brunei Darussalam	..	..	95-100	98	94	..	..	99 g	85	..	..	..
33	Czech Republic	..	..	80-94	98	95	..	..	..	303	6.6 e	0.6 e	380 e
34	Argentina	85	79	50-79	99	99	..	..	98	268	2.4 e	6.1 e	654 e
35	Hungary	99	99	95-100	99	99	..	..	..	357	5.2	1.6	318
36	Slovakia	100	100	95-100	96	99	..	..	..	353	5.7	1.5	285
37	Poland	..	..	80-94	96	97	..	..	..	236	4.7 e	1.5 e	248 e
38	Chile	97	94	80-94	94	96	..	..	100	110	2.7	3.1	289
39	Bahrain	..	..	95-100	..	94	..	62	98	100	2.6	1.6	358
40	Uruguay	95	98	50-79	99	93	..	..	99	370	1.9	7.3	621
41	Bahamas	93	96	80-94	..	86	..	..	..	152	2.5	1.8	612
42	Estonia	..	..	95-100	99	92	..	..	..	297	5.1 e	1.3 e	243 e
43	Costa Rica	96	98	95-100	89	88	..	..	98	141	5.2	1.5	257
44	Saint Kitts and Nevis	96	98	50-79	99	99	..	..	100	117	3.1	2.7	408
45	Kuwait	..	..	95-100	..	96	..	50	98	189	..	..	..
46	United Arab Emirates	..	..	95-100	98	95	..	28	99	181	0.8	7.6	1,428
47	Seychelles	..	..	80-94	99	99	..	..	..	132	4.8	..	..
48	Croatia	..	..	95-100	96	92	..	..	..	229	9.5 e	2.0 e	..
49	Lithuania	..	..	80-94	99	97	..	58 f	..	395	4.7 e	1.5	183
50	Trinidad and Tobago	88	86	50-79	..	91	..	..	99	79	2.5	1.8	204

HDI rank		Population using adequate sanitation facilities (%) 2000	Population using improved water sources (%) 2000	Population with access to essential drugs (%) [a] 1999	One-year-olds fully immunized		Oral rehydration therapy use rate (%) 1994-2000 [b]	Contraceptive prevalence (%) [c] 1995-2000 [b]	Births attended by skilled health staff (%) 1995-2000 [d]	Physicians (per 100,000 people) 1990-99 [b]	Health expenditure		
					Against tuberculosis (%) 1999	Against measles (%) 1999					Public (as % of GDP) 1998	Private (as % of GDP) 1998	Per capita (PPP US$) 1998
51	Qatar	..	..	95-100	99	87	..	43	..	126	..	..	..
52	Antigua and Barbuda	96	91	50-79	..	99	..	..	..	114	0.4	1.6	179
53	Latvia	..	..	80-94	99	97	..	48	100	282	4.0 e	2.6	166
Medium human development													
54	Mexico	73	86	80-94	99	95	..	66	86	186	2.6	2.8	236
55	Cuba	95	95	95-100	99	96	..	..	100	530	..	..	..
56	Belarus	..	100	50-79	99	98	..	50	..	443	4.6	1.0	85
57	Panama	94	87	80-94	99	90	7	..	90	167	4.9	2.3	246
58	Belize	42	76	80-94	96	82	..	..	..	55	2.3	0.5	82
59	Malaysia	..	..	50-79	99	88	..	..	96	66	1.4	1.0	81
60	Russian Federation	..	99	50-79	96	97	..	..	..	421	..	1.2	..
61	Dominica	..	97	80-94	99	99	..	..	100	49	3.8	2.2	208
62	Bulgaria	100	100	80-94	98	96	..	86	..	345	3.9 c	0.2 c	62 c
63	Romania	53	58	80-94	99	98	..	64	98	184	3.8 e	1.5	86
64	Libyan Arab Jamahiriya	97	72	95-100	97	92	..	40	94	128	..	..	..
65	Macedonia, TFYR	..	..	50-79	97	98	..	..	..	204	5.3	1.0	90 e
66	Saint Lucia	..	98	50-79	99	95	..	..	100	47	2.4	1.2	151
67	Mauritius	99	100	95-100	86	79	..	..	..	85	1.8	1.6	120
68	Colombia	85	91	80-94	93	75	..	77	86	116	5.2	4.2	227
69	Venezuela	74	84	80-94	97	82	..	..	95	236	2.6	1.6	171
70	Thailand	96	80	95-100	98	96	..	72	85	24	1.9	4.1	112
71	Saudi Arabia	100	95	95-100	99	94	..	32	91	166	..	..	..
72	Fiji	43	47	95-100	95	75	..	..	100 g	48	2.9	1.4	86
73	Brazil	77	87	0-49	93	99	18	77	88	127	2.9 e	3.6	308
74	Suriname	83	95	95-100	..	85	24	..	84	25	..	..	..
75	Lebanon	99	100	80-94	..	88	30	61	88	210	2.2	9.7	469
76	Armenia	..	..	0-49	93	91	30	60	97	316	4.0 e	4.2	..
77	Philippines	83	87	50-79	87	79	28	46	56	123	1.6 e	2.1 e	37 e
78	Oman	92	39	80-94	98	99	88	24	91	133	2.9	0.6	..
79	Kazakhstan	99	91	50-79	99	99	20	66	99	353	2.7 e	2.9 e	62 e
80	Ukraine	..	..	50-79	99	99	..	68	99	299	2.9 e	1.5 e	28 e
81	Georgia	..	..	0-49	94	80	33	40	96	436	0.8 e	2.0 e	16 e
82	Peru	76	77	50-79	97	93	29	64	56	93	2.4	3.8	141
83	Grenada	97	94	95-100	..	94	..	..	..	50	2.9	2.5	193
84	Maldives	56	100	50-79	98	86	..	..	..	40	3.7	4.0	150
85	Turkey	91	83	95-100	89	80	15	64	81	121	3.3 e	1.4	153
86	Jamaica	84	71	95-100	88	96	..	66	95	140	3.0	2.5	157
87	Turkmenistan	..	..	50-79	99	97	31	62	97	300	4.1	1.1	30
88	Azerbaijan	..	..	50-79	99	99	27	..	88	360	1.0 e	0.6	..
89	Sri Lanka	83	83	95-100	97	95	..	..	..	36	1.7 e	1.8 e	29 e
90	Paraguay	95	79	0-49	72	92	..	57	58	110	1.7	3.6	86
91	St. Vincent & the Grenadines	96	93	80-94	99	87	..	..	..	88	4.2	2.1	175
92	Albania	..	..	50-79	93	85	48	..	99	129	2.0 e	0.9 e	36 e
93	Ecuador	59	71	0-49	99	99	..	66	69	170	1.7	2.0	59
94	Dominican Republic	71	79	50-79	90	96	22	64	96	216	1.9	3.0	95
95	Uzbekistan	100	85	50-79	98	96	19	56	96	309	3.4	0.6	25
96	China	38	75	80-94	92	90	29	84	89 g	162	2.1 e	3.0 e	40 e
97	Tunisia	..	..	50-79	97	84	..	..	90	70	2.2	2.9	108
98	Iran, Islamic Rep. of	81	95	80-94	99	99	..	73	..	85	1.7	2.5	128
99	Jordan	99	96	95-100	..	94	..	53	97	166	3.6	3.8	139
100	Cape Verde	71	74	80-94	..	..	..	53	53	17	1.8	1.0	37

HDI rank		Population using adequate sanitation facilities (%) 2000	Population using improved water sources (%) 2000	Population with access to essential drugs (%)[a] 1999	One-year-olds fully immunized Against tuberculosis (%) 1999	One-year-olds fully immunized Against measles (%) 1999	Oral rehydration therapy use rate (%) 1994-2000[b]	Contraceptive prevalence (%)[c] 1995-2000[b]	Births attended by skilled health staff (%) 1995-2000[d]	Physicians (per 100,000 people) 1990-99[b]	Health expenditure Public (as % of GDP) 1998	Health expenditure Private (as % of GDP) 1998	Health expenditure Per capita (PPP US$) 1998
101	Samoa (Western)	99	99	95-100	..	..	..	..	100 [g]	34	4.8 [e]	1.3 [e]	85 [e]
102	Kyrgyzstan	100	77	50-79	98	97	13	60	98	301	2.2 [e]	2.2 [e]	11 [e]
103	Guyana	87	94	0-49	91	87	..	..	95	18	4.5	0.8	51
104	El Salvador	83	74	80-94	99	99	..	60	51	107	2.6	4.6	143
105	Moldova, Rep. of	..	100	50-79	99	99	19	74	99	350	2.9 [e]	2.1	25
106	Algeria	73	94	95-100	97	83	24	57	92	85	2.6	1.0	..
107	South Africa	86	86	80-94	97	82	..	56	84	56	3.3	3.8	230
108	Syrian Arab Republic	90	80	80-94	95	97	..	..	..	144	0.9	1.6	116
109	Viet Nam	73	56	80-94	95	93	20	75	70	48	0.8	4.0	17
110	Indonesia	66	76	80-94	85	71	28	57	56	16	0.8 [e]	0.9	8
111	Equatorial Guinea	53	43	0-49	48	24	..	..	..	25	..	..	..
112	Tajikistan	..	..	0-49	98	79	20	..	77	201	5.2	0.9	13
113	Mongolia	30	60	50-79	97	93	32	60	97	243	..	..	..
114	Bolivia	66	79	50-79	96	79	40	48	59	130	4.1	2.4	69
115	Egypt	94	95	80-94	99	95	..	56	61	202	..	..	..
116	Honduras	77	90	0-49	93	98	..	50	54	83	3.9	4.7	74
117	Gabon	21	70	0-49	89	55	..	33	86	...	2.1	1.0	122
118	Nicaragua	84	79	0-49	99	99	18	60	65	86	8.5	4.0	54
119	São Tomé and Principe	..	..	0-49	..	..	25	..	..	47	..	..	..
120	Guatemala	85	92	50-79	91	83	15	38	41	93	2.1	2.3	78
121	Solomon Islands	34	71	80-94	..	..	..	..	85 [g]	14	..	..	..
122	Namibia	41	77	80-94	80	66	..	..	76	30	3.3 [e]	3.3	142
123	Morocco	75	82	50-79	93	90	..	50	40	46	1.2	3.2	..
124	India	31	88	0-49	68	50	..	48	42	48	..	4.2	..
125	Swaziland	..	..	95-100	97	82	7	..	..	15	2.5	1.0	46
126	Botswana	..	..	80-94	97	86	..	..	98	24	2.5	1.5	127
127	Myanmar	46	68	50-79	88	85	24	33	..	30	0.2	1.6	97
128	Zimbabwe	68	85	50-79	88	79	50	54	72	14	3.0 [e]	4.0 [e]	36 [e]
129	Ghana	63	64	0-49	88	73	22	22	44	6	1.7 [e]	2.9	19
130	Cambodia	18	30	0-49	71	55	..	24	34	30	0.6	6.3	17
131	Vanuatu	100	88	..	..	..	..	..	89 [g]	12	..	..	..
132	Lesotho	92	91	80-94	95	77	..	..	60	5	..	..	..
133	Papua New Guinea	82	42	80-94	70	58	..	26	53	7	2.5	0.7	25
134	Kenya	86	49	0-49	96	79	30	39	44	13	2.4	5.5	31
135	Cameroon	92	62	50-79	77	62	23	19	56	7	1.0	..	..
136	Congo	..	51	50-79	39	23	13	..	..	25	2.0	3.8	40
137	Comoros	98	96	80-94	..	..	22	21	62	7	..	..	..

Low human development

HDI rank		Population using adequate sanitation facilities (%) 2000	Population using improved water sources (%) 2000	Population with access to essential drugs (%)[a] 1999	One-year-olds fully immunized Against tuberculosis (%) 1999	One-year-olds fully immunized Against measles (%) 1999	Oral rehydration therapy use rate (%) 1994-2000[b]	Contraceptive prevalence (%)[c] 1995-2000[b]	Births attended by skilled health staff (%) 1995-2000[d]	Physicians (per 100,000 people) 1990-99[b]	Health expenditure Public (as % of GDP) 1998	Health expenditure Private (as % of GDP) 1998	Health expenditure Per capita (PPP US$) 1998
138	Pakistan	61	88	50-79	78	54	19	24	20	57	0.7 [e]	3.1	18
139	Sudan	62	75	0-49	65	53	..	..	..	9	..	..	..
140	Bhutan	69	62	80-94	90	76	..	..	..	16	3.2	3.6	36
141	Togo	34	54	50-79	76	43	23	24	50	8	1.3	1.3	9
142	Nepal	27	81	0-49	86	73	11	28	12	4	1.3	4.2	11
143	Lao People's Dem. Rep.	46	90	50-79	63	71	20	..	21	24	1.2	1.3	6
144	Yemen	45	69	50-79	78	74	..	21	22	23	..	..	..
145	Bangladesh	53	97	50-79	91	71	..	54	12	20	1.7	1.9	12
146	Haiti	28	46	0-49	71	54	..	28	24	8	1.4	2.8	21
147	Madagascar	42	47	50-79	72	55	16	19	47	11	1.1	1.0	5
148	Nigeria	63	57	0-49	54	41	24	15	42	18	0.8	2.0	30
149	Djibouti	91	100	80-94	26	21	..	..	..	14	5.4	1.6	..
150	Uganda	75	50	50-79	83	53	..	15	38	..	1.9	4.1	18

HDI rank	Population using adequate sanitation facilities (%) 2000	Population using improved water sources (%) 2000	Population with access to essential drugs (%)[a] 1999	One-year-olds fully immunized — Against tuberculosis (%) 1999	One-year-olds fully immunized — Against measles (%) 1999	Oral rehydration therapy use rate (%) 1994-2000[b]	Contraceptive prevalence (%)[c] 1995-2000[b]	Births attended by skilled health staff (%) 1995-2000[d]	Physicians (per 100,000 people) 1990-99[b]	Health expenditure Public (as % of GDP) 1998	Health expenditure Private (as % of GDP) 1998	Health expenditure Per capita (PPP US$) 1998
151 Tanzania, U. Rep. of	90	54	50-79	87	72	21	24	36	4	1.3	1.8	8
152 Mauritania	33	37	50-79	75	62	..	..	..	14	1.4	3.4	19
153 Zambia	78	64	50-79	94	90	36	25	46	7	3.6	3.4	23
154 Senegal	70	78	50-79	90	60	..	13	50	8	2.6	1.9	23
155 Congo, Dem. Rep. of the	20	45	..	30	15	..	..	70	7	..	..	..
156 Côte d'Ivoire	..	77	80-94	84	62	25	15	47	9	1.2	2.5	28
157 Eritrea	13	46	50-79	98	88	..	5	21	3	..	..	..
158 Benin	23	63	50-79	90	79	18	16	60	6	1.6	1.6	12
159 Guinea	58	48	80-94	72	52	21	6	35	13	2.3	1.5	19
160 Gambia	37	62	80-94	96	88	26	..	51	4	2.3 [e]	1.9	13
161 Angola	44	38	0-49	52	46	..	..	22	8	..	..	..
162 Rwanda	8	41	0-49	94	87	..	13	31	..	2.0	2.1	10
163 Malawi	77	57	0-49	84	83	..	31	56	..	2.8	3.5	11
164 Mali	69	65	50-79	84	57	22	7	24	5	2.1	2.2	11
165 Central African Republic	31	60	50-79	62	39	39	15 [f]	44	4	2.0	1.0	9
166 Chad	29	27	0-49	45	30	36	4	16	3	2.3	0.6	7
167 Guinea-Bissau	47	49	0-49	74	70	13	..	35	17	..	..	..
168 Ethiopia	15	24	50-79	46	27	..	8	10	..	1.2 [e]	2.4	4
169 Burkina Faso	29	..	50-79	76	53	37	12	31	3	1.5 [e]	2.8	9
170 Mozambique	43	60	50-79	84	57	27	6	44	..	2.8	0.7	8
171 Burundi	..	..	0-49	84	75	..	..	25	..	0.6	3.0	5
172 Niger	20	59	50-79	47	36	38	8	16	4	1.2	1.4	5
173 Sierra Leone	28	28	0-49	73	62	28	..	42	7	0.9	4.4	8
Developing countries	52	78	..	80	69	..	..	..	..	..	..	..
Least developed countries	45	63	..	72	56	..	..	..	..	..	..	..
Arab States	81	86	..	89	84	..	..	..	..	..	..	..
East Asia and the Pacific	48	75	..	90	86	..	..	..	..	..	..	..
Latin America and the Caribbean	78	85	..	95	92	..	..	..	..	..	..	..
South Asia	39	89	..	74	56	..	..	..	..	..	..	..
Sub-Saharan Africa	55	54	..	67	51	..	..	..	..	..	..	..
Central and Eastern Europe and the CIS	..	..	..	97	96	..	..	..	..	..	..	..
OECD	..	..	..	..	89	..	..	..	..	..	..	..
High-income OECD	..	..	..	..	89	..	..	..	..	..	..	..
High human development	..	..	..	..	90	..	..	..	..	..	..	..
Medium human development	52	81	..	85	76	..	..	..	..	..	..	..
Low human development	50	67	..	70	52	..	..	..	..	..	..	..
High income	..	..	..	..	89	..	..	..	..	..	..	..
Middle income	59	81	..	93	91	..	..	..	..	..	..	..
Low income	46	77	..	72	56	..	..	..	..	..	..	..
World	56	81	..	81	72	..	..	..	..	..	..	..

a. The data on access to essential drugs are based on statistical estimates received from World Health Organization (WHO) country and regional offices and regional advisers and through the World Drug Situation Survey carried out in 1998-99. These estimates represent the best information available to the WHO Department of Essential Drugs and Medicines Policy to date and are currently being validated by WHO member states. The department assigns the estimates to four groupings: very low access (0-49%), low access (50-79%), medium access (80-94%) and good access (95-100%). These groupings, used here in presenting the data, are often employed by the WHO in interpreting the data, as the actual estimates may suggest a higher level of accuracy than the data afford. b. Data refer to the most recent year available during the period specified. c. Data refer to married women aged 15-49, but the actual age range covered may vary across countries. d. Definitions of skilled health staff may vary across countries. Data refer to the most recent year available during the period specified or to a running average for a series of years surrounding that period. e. Data refer to 1999. f. Data refer to the survey period 1994-95. g. Preliminary estimate subject to further revision.
Source: Columns 1 and 2: WHO, UNICEF and WSSCC 2000; *column 3:* WHO 2001a; *columns 4-6:* UNICEF 2002b; *column 7:* UN 2002c; *column 8:* WHO 2002a; *column 9:* WHO 2002d; *columns 10-12:* World Bank 2002b.

7 Leading global health crises and challenges

HDI rank		Under-nourished people (as % of total population) 1997/99	Children under weight for age (% under age 5) 1995-2000 [a]	Children under height for age (% under age 5) 1995-2000 [a]	Infants with low birth-weight (%) 1995-2000 [a]	People living with HIV/AIDS			Malaria cases (per 100,000 people) [c] 2000	Tuberculosis cases (per 100,000 people) [d] 1999	Cigarette consumption per adult (annual average) 1992-2000 [e]
						Adults (% age 15-49) 2001 [b]	Women (age 15-49) 2001 [b]	Children (age 0-14) 2001 [b]			
High human development											
1	Norway	..	..	..	5	0.08	400	<100	..	5	763
2	Sweden	..	..	..	4	0.08	880	<100	..	5	1,060
3	Canada	..	..	..	6	0.31	14,000	<500	..	7 [f]	1,980
4	Belgium	..	..	..	8	0.16	2,900	330	..	11	1,910 [g]
5	Australia	..	..	..	7	0.07	800	140	..	6	1,906
6	United States	..	1 [h]	2 [h]	8	0.61	180,000	10,000	..	6	2,193
7	Iceland	..	..	..	4	0.15	<100	<100	..	4	2,035
8	Netherlands	..	..	..	..	0.21	3,300	160	..	9	2,377
9	Japan	..	..	..	7 [h]	<0.10	6,600	110	..	32	3,076
10	Finland	..	..	..	6	<0.10	330	<100	..	11	1,222
11	Switzerland	..	..	..	6	0.50	6,000	300	..	10	2,871
12	France	..	..	..	6	0.33	27,000	1,000	..	10	1,772
13	United Kingdom	..	..	..	8	0.10	7,400	550	..	11	1,790
14	Denmark	..	..	..	6	0.15	770	<100	..	11	1,963
15	Austria	..	..	..	7	0.24	2,200	<100	..	13	1,709
16	Luxembourg	..	..	..	4	0.16	..	..	..	9	..
17	Germany	..	..	..	7	0.10	8,100	550	..	12	1,803
18	Ireland	..	..	..	4 [h]	0.11	660	190	..	12	2,246
19	New Zealand	..	..	..	6	0.06	180	<100	..	12	1,235
20	Italy	..	..	..	6	0.37	33,000	770	..	8	1,960
21	Spain	..	..	..	6	0.50	26,000	1,300	..	21	2,572
22	Israel	..	..	..	8	0.10	..	..	..	8	2,223
23	Hong Kong, China (SAR)	..	..	..	..	0.08	660	<100	..	113	952
24	Greece	..	..	..	7	0.17	1,800	<100	..	9	3,571
25	Singapore	..	14 [h]	11 [h]	8	0.20	860	<100	..	47	1,156
26	Cyprus	..	..	..	..	0.25	150	..	..	5	..
27	Korea, Rep. of	..	..	..	..	<0.10	960	<100	9	52	2,778
28	Portugal	..	..	..	7	0.52	5,100	350	..	47	2,071
29	Slovenia	..	..	..	6	<0.10	<100	<100	..	21	2,944
30	Malta	..	..	..	7	0.13	..	..	..	6	..
31	Barbados	..	5 [h]	7 [h]	10	1.20 [i]	..	..	..	1	512
32	Brunei Darussalam	..	..	..	..	..	..	..	..	52 [f]	..
33	Czech Republic	..	1 [h]	2 [h]	6	<0.10	<100	<10	..	16	2,498
34	Argentina	..	..	..	7	0.69	30,000	3,000	1	31	1,524
35	Hungary	..	2 [h]	3 [h]	9	0.06	300	<100	..	35	2,742
36	Slovakia	..	..	..	7	<0.10	<100	..	..	20	2,166
37	Poland	..	..	..	6	0.10 [i]	..	..	..	31	2,631
38	Chile	4	1	2	5	0.30	4,300	<500	..	23	1,185
39	Bahrain	..	9	10	10	0.26	150	..	..	33	1,785
40	Uruguay	3	5	8	..	0.30	1,400	100	..	19	1,562
41	Bahamas	..	..	..	..	3.50	2,700	<100	..	25	370
42	Estonia	4	..	..	5	1.00	1,500	..	..	52	2,009
43	Costa Rica	5	5	6	6	0.55	2,800	320	38	22	..
44	Saint Kitts and Nevis	..	..	..	13 [h]	..	..	..	..	8	..
45	Kuwait	4	10	24	7	..	..	..	..	31 [j]	3,080
46	United Arab Emirates	..	14	17	..	..	..	..	..	33 [j]	..
47	Seychelles	..	6 [h]	5 [h]	10 [h]	..	..	..	..	14 [j]	..
48	Croatia	15	1	1	6	<0.10	<100	<10	..	39	2,303
49	Lithuania	3	..	..	4	0.07	260	<100	..	76	..
50	Trinidad and Tobago	13	7 [h]	4 [h]	..	2.50	5,600	300	..	12	2,015

7 Leading global health crises and challenges

HDI rank		Under-nourished people (as % of total population) 1997/99	Children under weight for age (% under age 5) 1995-2000 [a]	Children under height for age (% under age 5) 1995-2000 [a]	Infants with low birth-weight (%) 1995-2000 [a]	People living with HIV/AIDS			Malaria cases (per 100,000 people) [c] 2000	Tuberculosis cases (per 100,000 people) [d] 1999	Cigarette consumption per adult (annual average) 1992-2000 [e]
						Adults (% age 15-49) 2001 [b]	Women (age 15-49) 2001 [b]	Children (age 0-14) 2001 [b]			
51	Qatar	..	6	8	10	..	..	..	..	44	..
52	Antigua and Barbuda	..	10 [h]	7 [h]	8	..	..	..	..	4	..
53	Latvia	4	..	..	5	0.40	1,000	<100	..	79	..
Medium human development											
54	Mexico	5	8	18	9	0.28	32,000	3,600	6 [h]	16	794
55	Cuba	17	4	5	6	<0.10	830	<100	..	10	..
56	Belarus	..	..	..	5	0.27	3,700	..	..	71	2,043
57	Panama	16	7	14	10	1.50	8,700	800	36	51	271
58	Belize	..	6 [h]	..	4	2.00	1,000	180	856 [h]	40 [f]	582
59	Malaysia	..	18	..	9	0.35	11,000	770	57	68	844
60	Russian Federation	6	3	13	7	0.90	180,000	..	1	91	2,081
61	Dominica	..	5 [h]	6 [h]	8 [h]	..	..	..	..	7 [j]	..
62	Bulgaria	11	..	..	9	<0.10 [i]	..	..	..	43	3,458
63	Romania	..	6 [h]	8 [h]	9	<0.10	..	4,000	..	117	1,726
64	Libyan Arab Jamahiriya	..	5	15	7 [h]	0.24	1,100	..	2	30	..
65	Macedonia, TFYR	5	6	7	6	<0.10	<100	<100	..	28	..
66	Saint Lucia	..	14 [h]	11 [h]	8 [h]	..	..	..	..	10	..
67	Mauritius	6	16	10	13	0.10	350	<100	1 [h]	15	1,401
68	Colombia	13	7	14	7	0.40	20,000	4,000	250	26	517
69	Venezuela	21	5	14	6	0.50 [i]	..	..	94	28	1,185
70	Thailand	21	19 [h]	16 [h]	7	1.79	220,000	21,000	130	48	1,014
71	Saudi Arabia	..	14	20	3	..	..	..	33	17	..
72	Fiji	..	8 [h]	3 [h]	12 [h]	0.07	<100	..	..	24	1,107
73	Brazil	10	6	11	9	0.65	220,000	13,000	344	47	813
74	Suriname	11	..	..	11	1.20	1,800	190	3,485 [h]	22	2,081
75	Lebanon	..	3	12	6	..	..	..	1	21	..
76	Armenia	35	3	14	9	0.15	480	<100	4	42	925
77	Philippines	24	28	30	18	<0.10	2,500	<10	15	196	1,587
78	Oman	..	24	23	8	0.11	200	..	28	10	..
79	Kazakhstan	11	4	10	6	0.07	1,200	<100	<1	154	1,880
80	Ukraine	5	3	15	6	0.99	76,000	..	..	65	1,405
81	Georgia	18	3	12	6	<0.10	180	..	5	96	..
82	Peru	13	8	26	10	0.35	13,000	1,500	257	160	189
83	Grenada	..	..	..	11 [h]	..	..	..	..	2 [j]	..
84	Maldives	..	43	27	12	0.06	..	..	..	55	..
85	Turkey	..	8	16	15	<0.10 [i]	..	..	17	34	2,068
86	Jamaica	8	4	3	11	1.22	7,200	800	..	4	766
87	Turkmenistan	9	..	..	5	<0.10	<100	..	1	93	..
88	Azerbaijan	37	17	20	10	<0.10	280	..	19	60	600
89	Sri Lanka	23	33	17	17	<0.10	1,400	<100	1,111	38	392
90	Paraguay	13	5	11	9	..	..	..	124	40	..
91	St. Vincent & the Grenadines	..	..	..	10	..	..	..	..	4 [j]	..
92	Albania	10	14	32	5	..	..	..	..	24	..
93	Ecuador	5	15	27	16	0.30	5,100	660	686	50	272
94	Dominican Republic	25	5	6	13	2.50	61,000	4,700	6	72	800
95	Uzbekistan	4	19	31	6	<0.10	150	<100	1	63	1,234
96	China	9	10	17	6	0.11	220,000	2,000	1	36	1,790
97	Tunisia	..	4	12	5	..	..	..	..	23	1,436
98	Iran, Islamic Rep. of	5	11	15	7	<0.10	5,000	<200	27	18	789
99	Jordan	5	5	8	10	<0.10	150	..	..	6	1,725
100	Cape Verde	..	14 [h]	16 [h]	13	..	..	..	..	50 [j]	..

7 Leading global health crises and challenges

HDI rank	Under-nourished people (as % of total population) 1997/99	Children under weight for age (% under age 5) 1995-2000 [a]	Children under height for age (% under age 5) 1995-2000 [a]	Infants with low birth-weight (%) 1995-2000 [a]	People living with HIV/AIDS — Adults (% age 15-49) 2001 [b]	People living with HIV/AIDS — Women (age 15-49) 2001 [b]	People living with HIV/AIDS — Children (age 0-14) 2001 [b]	Malaria cases (per 100,000 people) [c] 2000	Tuberculosis cases (per 100,000 people) [d] 1999	Cigarette consumption per adult (annual average) 1992-2000 [e]
101 Samoa (Western)	..	..	..	..	..	..	..	..	18	..
102 Kyrgyzstan	10	11	25	6	<0.10	<100	..	<1	137	..
103 Guyana	14	12	10	14	2.70	8,500	800	3,340	37 [j]	1,565
104 El Salvador	12	12	23	13	0.60	6,300	830	..	26	524
105 Moldova, Rep. of	10	3	10	7	0.24	1,200	..	..	62	..
106 Algeria	6	6	18	7	0.10 [i]	..	..	..	48	930
107 South Africa	..	..	25 [h]	..	20.10	2,700,000	250,000	143	323	1,088
108 Syrian Arab Republic	..	13	21	6	..	..	..	<1	35	1,255
109 Viet Nam	19	33	36	9	0.30	35,000	2,500	95	113	1,085
110 Indonesia	6	26	..	9	0.10	27,000	1,300	48	33	1,504
111 Equatorial Guinea	..	..	..	..	3.38	3,000	420	2,506 [h]	97 [j]	..
112 Tajikistan	47	..	..	13	<0.10	<100	..	302	42	..
113 Mongolia	42	13	25	6	<0.10	..	..	..	128	..
114 Bolivia	22	10	26	8	0.10	1,200	160	379	121	279
115 Egypt	4	12	25	10	<0.10	780	..	..	18	1,221
116 Honduras	21	25	39	6	1.60	27,000	3,000	543	72	912
117 Gabon	9	..	..	..	..	..	..	2,202 [h]	134	532
118 Nicaragua	29	12	25	13	0.20	1,500	210	400	52	..
119 São Tomé and Principe	..	16	26	7 [h]	..	..	..	31,614 [h]	67	..
120 Guatemala	22	24	46	12	1.00	27,000	4,800	350	28	442
121 Solomon Islands	..	21 [h]	27 [h]	..	..	..	..	16,971	67	638
122 Namibia	33	26 [h]	28 [h]	15 [h]	22.50	110,000	30,000	1,466	469	..
123 Morocco	6	9 [h]	23 [h]	9 [h]	0.08	2,000	..	<1	107	817
124 India	23	47	46	26	0.79	1,500,000	170,000	193	123	119
125 Swaziland	12	10 [h]	30 [h]	..	33.44	89,000	14,000	2,913	..	..
126 Botswana	23	13	23	11	38.80	170,000	28,000	4,760	513	..
127 Myanmar	7	36	37	16	..	..	..	225	44	..
128 Zimbabwe	39	13	27	10	33.73	1,200,000	240,000	5,422	435	309
129 Ghana	15	25	26	9	3.00	170,000	34,000	15,348	53	174
130 Cambodia	37	46	46	9	2.70	74,000	12,000	477	176	..
131 Vanuatu	..	20 [h]	19 [h]	7 [h]	..	..	..	3,208	63	..
132 Lesotho	25	16	44	..	31.00	180,000	27,000	..	291 [j]	..
133 Papua New Guinea	26	35 [h]	..	..	0.65	4,100	500	1,692	278	..
134 Kenya	46	23	37	9	15.01	1,400,000	220,000	545	194	329
135 Cameroon	25	21	35	10	11.83	500,000	69,000	3,423 [h]	52	..
136 Congo	32	14	19	..	7.15	59,000	15,000	5,916	175	422
137 Comoros	..	25	42	18	..	..	..	1,946	20 [j]	..
Low human development										
138 Pakistan	18	38	..	21 [h]	0.11	16,000	2,200	58	14	620
139 Sudan	21	17	..	..	2.60	230,000	30,000	13,932	80	..
140 Bhutan	..	19	40	15	<0.10	..	..	283	57	..
141 Togo	17	25	22	13	6.00	76,000	15,000	8,939 [h]	28 [j]	390
142 Nepal	23	47	54	21	0.49	14,000	1,500	33	117	604
143 Lao People's Dem. Rep.	28	40	41	..	<0.10	350	<100	755	42 [j]	..
144 Yemen	34	46	52	26	0.12	1,500	..	15,200 [h]	73 [j]	797
145 Bangladesh	33	48	45	30	<0.10	3,100	310	40	62	232
146 Haiti	56	28	32	28 [h]	6.10	120,000	12,000	15 [h]	113	231
147 Madagascar	40	33	49	15	0.29	12,000	1,000	2,363 [h]	97 [j]	308
148 Nigeria	7	27	46	9	5.80	1,700,000	270,000	30	22	188
149 Djibouti	..	18	26	..	..	..	..	753 [h]	694	..
150 Uganda	28	26	38	13	5.00	280,000	110,000	46	166	155

HDI rank		Under-nourished people (as % of total population) 1997/99	Children under weight for age (% under age 5) 1995-2000 [a]	Children under height for age (% under age 5) 1995-2000 [a]	Infants with low birth-weight (%) 1995-2000 [a]	People living with HIV/AIDS			Malaria cases (per 100,000 people) [c] 2000	Tuberculosis cases (per 100,000 people) [d] 1999	Cigarette consumption per adult (annual average) 1992-2000 [e]
						Adults (% age 15-49) 2001 [b]	Women (age 15-49) 2001 [b]	Children (age 0-14) 2001 [b]			
151	Tanzania, U. Rep. of	46	29	44	11	7.83	750,000	170,000	1,208 [h]	160	188
152	Mauritania	11	23	44	..	..	..	..	..	140	..
153	Zambia	47	25	59	11	21.52	590,000	150,000	34,274	..	..
154	Senegal	24	18	19	12	0.50	14,000	2,900	553	79	374
155	Congo, Dem. Rep. of the	64	34	45	15	4.90	670,000	170,000	2,963 [h]	118	139
156	Côte d'Ivoire	16	21	22	17	9.65	400,000	84,000	12,162	104	313
157	Eritrea	57	44	38	14	2.80	30,000	4,000	3,440	162	..
158	Benin	15	29	25	15	3.61	67,000	12,000	11,915	46	..
159	Guinea	34	23	26	10	..	..	..	11,161	69	..
160	Gambia	15	17	19	14	1.60	4,400	460	17,376 [h]	127 [j]	..
161	Angola	51	..	..	..	5.50	190,000	37,000	8,796	129	..
162	Rwanda	40	29	43	12 [h]	8.88	250,000	65,000	6,518	90	..
163	Malawi	35	25	49	13 [h]	15.00	440,000	65,000	27,682	229	194
164	Mali	28	43	..	16	1.65	54,000	13,000	4,505 [h]	41	..
165	Central African Republic	43	24	39	13 [h]	12.90	130,000	25,000	2,487 [h]	141	..
166	Chad	34	28	28	24	3.61	76,000	18,000	196 [h]	63	157
167	Guinea-Bissau	..	23	28	20	2.81	9,300	1,500	16,454 [h]	..	107
168	Ethiopia	49	47	51	12	6.41	1,100,000	230,000	635 [h]	118	62
169	Burkina Faso	24	34	37	18	6.50	220,000	61,000	6,061 [h]	18	194
170	Mozambique	54	26	36	13	13.00	630,000	80,000	18,108	104 [j]	..
171	Burundi	66	45	57	16 [h]	8.30	190,000	55,000	48,528	97	113
172	Niger	41	40	40	12	..	..	..	2,132 [h]	34 [j]	..
173	Sierra Leone	41	27	34	22	7.00	90,000	16,000	9,311 [h]	72 [j]	..
	Developing countries	17	..	..	..	1.32	18,000,000 T	2,900,000 T	..	72	..
	Least developed countries	36	..	..	..	3.55	6,500,000 T	1,400,000 T	..	95	..
	Arab States	..	..	..	..	0.35	250,000 T	35,000 T	..	48	..
	East Asia and the Pacific	10	..	..	..	0.20	600,000 T	40,000 T	..	49	..
	Latin America and the Caribbean	12	..	..	..	0.61	640,000 T	60,000 T	..	43	..
	South Asia	23	..	..	..	0.55	1,500,000 T	170,000 T	..	99	..
	Sub-Saharan Africa	34	..	..	..	9.00	15,000,000 T	2,600,000 T	..	121	..
	Central and Eastern Europe and the CIS	9	..	..	..	0.48	270,000 T	15,000 T	..	75	..
	OECD	..	..	..	..	0.28	360,000 T	19,000 T	..	17	..
	High-income OECD	..	..	..	..	0.36	330,000 T	16,000 T	..	13	..
	High human development	..	..	..	..	0.31	380,000 T	19,000 T	..	18	..
	Medium human development	14	..	..	..	0.86	9,400,000 T	1,200,000 T	..	74	..
	Low human development	31	..	..	..	3.75	8,400,000 T	1,700,000 T	..	73	..
	High income	..	..	..	..	0.34	330,000 T	16,000 T	..	14	..
	Middle income	10	..	..	..	0.61	4,200,000 T	390,000 T	..	53	..
	Low income	24	..	..	..	2.08	14,000,000 T	2,500,000 T	..	95	..
	World	..	..	..	..	1.20	18,500,000 T	3,000,000 T	..	64	..

a. Data refer to the most recent year available during the period specified. b. Data refer to the end of 2001. Aggregates are rounded estimates; regional totals may not sum to the world total. c. Data refer to malaria cases reported to the World Health Organization and may represent only a fraction of the true number in a country because of incomplete reporting systems or incomplete coverage by health services, or both. Because of the diversity of case detection and reporting systems, country comparisons should be made with caution. d. Data refer to tuberculosis cases reported to the World Health Organization and may represent only a fraction of the true number in a country because of incomplete coverage by health services, inaccurate diagnosis or deficient recording and reporting. e. Data refer to estimates of apparent consumption based on data on cigarette production, imports and exports. Such estimates may under- or overstate true consumption in countries where tobacco products are illegally imported or exported, where there is significant stock-piling of cigarettes or where there are large transient populations. Estimates of apparent consumption cannot provide insights into smoking patterns in a population. Data refer to the most recent three-year moving average available during the period specified. f. Data refer to 1997. g. Includes Luxembourg. h. Data refer to a year or period other than that specified, differ from the standard definition or refer to only part of a country. i. Data refer to the end of 1999. j. Data refer to 1998.

Source: Column 1: FAO 2001; columns 2-4: UNICEF 2002b; columns 5-7: UNAIDS and WHO 2002; aggregates calculated for the Human Development Report Office by UNAIDS; column 8: WHO 2002c; column 9: WHO 2001b; column 10: WHO 2002b.

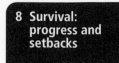

8 Survival: progress and setbacks

	Life expectancy at birth (years)		Infant mortality rate (per 1,000 live births)		Under-five mortality rate (per 1,000 live births)		Probability at birth of surviving to age 65 [a]		Maternal mortality ratio reported (per 100,000 live births)
							Female (% of cohort)	Male (% of cohort)	
HDI rank	1970-75 [b]	1995-2000 [b]	1970	2000	1970	2000	1995-2000 [b]	1995-2000 [b]	1985-99 [c]
High human development									
1 Norway	74.4	78.1	13	4	15	4	90.0	82.2	6
2 Sweden	74.7	79.3	11	3	14	4	90.8	84.8	5
3 Canada	73.2	78.5	19	6	23	6	89.3	82.3	..
4 Belgium	71.4	77.9	21	6	29	6	89.5	80.7	..
5 Australia	71.7	78.7	17	6	20	6	90.2	83.1	..
6 United States	71.5	76.5	20	7	26	8	85.7	77.4	8
7 Iceland	74.3	78.9	12	4	14	4	90.0	84.4	..
8 Netherlands	74.0	77.9	13	5	15	5	89.1	82.7	7
9 Japan	73.3	80.5	14	4	21	4	92.1	84.0	8
10 Finland	70.7	77.2	13	4	16	4	90.3	77.9	6
11 Switzerland	73.8	78.6	15	3	18	4	90.5	82.2	5
12 France	72.4	78.1	18	4	24	5	90.1	78.0	10
13 United Kingdom	72.0	77.2	18	6	23	6	88.3	81.5	7
14 Denmark	73.6	75.9	14	4	19	4	85.5	78.3	10
15 Austria	70.6	77.7	26	5	33	5	89.9	79.7	..
16 Luxembourg	70.7	77.0	19	5	26	5	88.4	80.1	(.)
17 Germany	71.0	77.3	22	4	26	5	89.3	79.2	8
18 Ireland	71.3	76.1	20	6	26	6	87.7	80.0	6
19 New Zealand	71.7	77.2	17	6	20	6	87.6	80.9	15
20 Italy	72.1	78.2	30	6	33	6	90.9	81.6	7
21 Spain	72.8	78.1	27	5	34	5	91.4	79.8	6
22 Israel	71.6	78.3	24	6	27	6	89.7	85.1	5
23 Hong Kong, China (SAR)	72.0	79.1	..	..	..	..	91.6	83.1	..
24 Greece	72.3	78.0	38	5	54	6	91.4	81.6	1
25 Singapore	69.5	77.1	22	4	26	4	86.6	79.6	6
26 Cyprus	71.4	77.8	29	6	33	7	90.3	83.2	(.)
27 Korea, Rep. of	62.6	74.3	43	5	54	5	87.5	72.1	20
28 Portugal	68.0	75.2	53	6	62	6	88.4	75.3	8
29 Slovenia	69.8	75.0	25	4	29	5	87.3	72.8	11
30 Malta	70.6	77.6	25	5	32	6	89.7	84.2	..
31 Barbados	69.4	76.4	40	12	54	14	88.1	80.6	(.)
32 Brunei Darussalam	68.3	75.5	58	6	78	6	87.8	79.4	(.)
33 Czech Republic	70.1	74.3	21	5	24	5	87.0	72.0	9
34 Argentina	67.1	72.9	59	18	71	21	84.1	70.6	41
35 Hungary	69.3	70.7	36	8	39	9	81.1	59.0	15
36 Slovakia	70.0	72.8	25	8	29	9	85.4	66.4	9
37 Poland	70.4	72.8	32	9	36	10	85.1	65.8	8
38 Chile	63.4	74.9	76	10	96	12	85.4	75.6	23
39 Bahrain	63.5	72.9	55	13	75	16	84.0	75.5	46
40 Uruguay	68.7	73.9	48	14	57	16	84.7	71.4	26
41 Bahamas	66.5	69.0	38	15	49	18	76.0	57.4	..
42 Estonia	70.5	70.0	21	17	26	21	81.9	54.8	50
43 Costa Rica	67.9	76.0	58	10	76	12	87.2	80.1	29
44 Saint Kitts and Nevis	..	..	..	21	..	25	..	..	130
45 Kuwait	67.2	75.9	49	9	59	10	86.2	80.7	5
46 United Arab Emirates	62.5	74.6	61	8	83	9	83.6	75.8	3
47 Seychelles	..	..	..	13	..	17	..	..	..
48 Croatia	69.6	73.3	34	8	42	8	85.3	69.5	6
49 Lithuania	71.3	71.4	23	17	28	21	83.6	59.7	18
50 Trinidad and Tobago	65.9	73.8	48	17	57	20	82.4	73.9	70

HDI rank	Life expectancy at birth (years)		Infant mortality rate (per 1,000 live births)		Under-five mortality rate (per 1,000 live births)		Probability at birth of surviving to age 65 [a]		Maternal mortality ratio reported (per 100,000 live births)
							Female (% of cohort)	Male (% of cohort)	
	1970-75 [b]	1995-2000 [b]	1970	2000	1970	2000	1995-2000 [b]	1995-2000 [b]	1985-99 [c]
51 Qatar	62.6	68.9	45	12	65	16	75.7	69.4	10
52 Antigua and Barbuda	..	..	..	13	..	15	..	..	150
53 Latvia	70.1	69.6	21	17	26	21	79.8	56.9	45
Medium human development									
54 Mexico	62.4	72.2	79	25	110	30	80.8	69.9	55
55 Cuba	70.6	75.7	34	7	43	9	84.1	78.1	33
56 Belarus	71.5	68.5	22	17	27	20	80.0	51.3	20
57 Panama	66.2	73.6	46	20	68	26	83.5	76.0	70
58 Belize	67.6	73.6	56	34	77	41	82.1	77.4	140
59 Malaysia	63.0	71.9	46	8	63	9	82.0	70.8	41
60 Russian Federation	69.7	66.1	29	18	36	22	77.0	46.4	44
61 Dominica	..	..	..	14	..	16	..	..	65
62 Bulgaria	71.0	70.8	28	14	32	16	83.5	64.2	15
63 Romania	69.2	69.8	46	19	56	22	79.9	62.5	42
64 Libyan Arab Jamahiriya	52.9	70.0	105	17	160	20	76.0	68.3	75
65 Macedonia, TFYR	67.5	72.7	85	22	120	26	82.5	74.2	7
66 Saint Lucia	65.3	73.0	..	17	..	19	80.4	70.1	30
67 Mauritius	62.9	70.7	64	17	86	20	80.6	63.0	21
68 Colombia	61.6	70.4	70	25	113	30	79.1	67.6	80
69 Venezuela	65.7	72.4	47	20	61	23	82.3	71.6	60
70 Thailand	59.5	69.6	74	25	102	29	78.8	66.5	44
71 Saudi Arabia	53.9	70.9	118	24	185	29	78.4	73.4	..
72 Fiji	60.6	68.4	50	18	61	22	72.8	63.7	38
73 Brazil	59.5	67.2	95	32	135	38	75.4	59.3	160
74 Suriname	64.0	70.1	51	27	68	33	77.7	66.4	110
75 Lebanon	65.0	72.6	45	28	54	32	81.8	75.7	100
76 Armenia	72.5	72.4	24	25	30	30	85.1	70.8	35
77 Philippines	58.1	68.6	60	30	90	40	75.7	67.2	170
78 Oman	49.0	70.5	126	12	200	14	78.1	72.1	14
79 Kazakhstan	64.4	64.1	..	60	..	75	72.7	47.6	65
80 Ukraine	70.1	68.1	22	17	27	21	79.0	51.8	25
81 Georgia	69.2	72.7	36	24	46	29	84.5	67.1	50
82 Peru	55.4	68.0	115	40	178	50	75.2	66.2	270
83 Grenada	..	..	..	21	..	26	..	..	1
84 Maldives	51.4	65.4	157	59	255	80	65.4	66.8	350
85 Turkey	57.9	69.0	150	38	201	45	78.6	68.7	130 [d]
86 Jamaica	69.0	74.8	49	17	64	20	84.1	77.5	95
87 Turkmenistan	60.6	65.4	82	52	120	70	71.7	56.9	65
88 Azerbaijan	69.0	71.0	..	74	..	105	79.8	65.0	80
89 Sri Lanka	65.1	71.6	65	17	100	19	82.8	71.8	60
90 Paraguay	65.9	69.6	56	26	76	31	78.2	69.4	190
91 St. Vincent & the Grenadines	..	..	..	21	..	24	..	..	43
92 Albania	67.7	72.8	68	27	82	31	87.0	78.6	..
93 Ecuador	58.8	69.5	87	25	140	32	77.3	69.0	160
94 Dominican Republic	59.7	67.3	91	42	128	48	74.5	64.9	230 [d]
95 Uzbekistan	64.2	68.3	..	51	..	67	75.0	62.9	21
96 China	63.2	69.8	85	32	120	40	79.4	70.9	55
97 Tunisia	55.6	69.5	135	22	201	28	75.8	70.6	70
98 Iran, Islamic Rep. of	53.9	68.0	122	36	191	44	74.3	68.9	37
99 Jordan	56.6	69.7	77	28	107	34	74.4	68.9	41
100 Cape Verde	57.5	68.9	..	30	..	40	76.2	64.6	35

8 Survival: progress and setbacks

HDI rank	Life expectancy at birth (years)		Infant mortality rate (per 1,000 live births)		Under-five mortality rate (per 1,000 live births)		Probability at birth of surviving to age 65 [a]		Maternal mortality ratio reported (per 100,000 live births)
	1970-75 [b]	1995-2000 [b]	1970	2000	1970	2000	Female (% of cohort) 1995-2000 [b]	Male (% of cohort) 1995-2000 [b]	1985-99 [c]
101 Samoa (Western)	56.1	68.5	106	21	160	26	75.8	62.0	..
102 Kyrgyzstan	63.1	66.9	111	53	146	63	75.3	57.8	65
103 Guyana	60.0	63.7	80	55	101	74	70.2	54.1	110
104 El Salvador	58.2	69.1	111	34	162	40	75.9	65.6	120
105 Moldova, Rep. of	64.8	66.6	46	27	61	33	72.5	53.6	28
106 Algeria	54.5	68.9	143	50	234	65	75.4	72.2	220 [d]
107 South Africa	53.7	56.7	80	55	115	70	53.7	40.2	..
108 Syrian Arab Republic	57.0	70.5	90	24	128	29	77.4	72.5	110 [d]
109 Viet Nam	50.3	67.2	112	30	157	39	74.1	65.6	95
110 Indonesia	49.2	65.1	104	35	172	48	69.5	61.7	380
111 Equatorial Guinea	40.5	50.0	165	103	281	156	47.0	41.0	..
112 Tajikistan	63.4	67.2	78	54	111	73	73.6	62.7	65
113 Mongolia	53.8	61.9	..	62	..	78	64.0	53.9	150
114 Bolivia	46.7	61.4	144	62	243	80	63.9	57.0	390
115 Egypt	52.1	66.3	157	37	235	43	72.8	63.9	170
116 Honduras	53.8	65.6	116	32	170	40	70.5	59.3	110
117 Gabon	45.0	52.4	..	60	..	90	48.7	43.5	520
118 Nicaragua	55.1	67.7	113	37	165	45	72.7	63.9	150
119 São Tomé and Principe	..	..	..	58	..	75	..	..	..
120 Guatemala	53.7	64.0	115	44	168	59	67.9	56.2	190
121 Solomon Islands	55.6	67.4	70	21	99	25	72.5	67.4	550 [d]
122 Namibia	49.4	45.1	104	56	155	69	31.3	28.0	230
123 Morocco	52.9	66.6	119	41	184	46	74.1	66.3	230
124 India	50.3	62.3	127	69	202	96	64.7	59.9	540
125 Swaziland	47.3	50.8	132	101	196	142	45.1	39.2	230
126 Botswana	53.2	44.4	99	74	142	101	29.6	24.5	330
127 Myanmar	49.3	55.8	122	78	179	110	55.9	46.6	230
128 Zimbabwe	56.0	42.9	86	73	138	117	23.7	22.1	700
129 Ghana	49.9	56.3	112	58	190	102	53.8	48.3	210 [d]
130 Cambodia	40.3	56.5	..	95	..	135	55.8	46.3	440
131 Vanuatu	54.0	67.2	107	35	160	44	70.4	63.1	..
132 Lesotho	49.5	51.2	125	92	190	133	46.9	42.5	..
133 Papua New Guinea	44.7	55.6	90	79	130	112	48.0	41.4	370
134 Kenya	51.0	52.2	96	77	156	120	43.6	38.5	590
135 Cameroon	45.7	50.0	127	95	215	154	42.6	38.4	430
136 Congo	46.7	50.9	100	81	160	108	45.4	37.9	..
137 Comoros	48.9	58.8	159	61	215	82	58.6	52.1	..
Low human development									
138 Pakistan	49.0	59.0	117	85	181	110	58.8	56.9	..
139 Sudan	43.7	55.0	104	66	172	108	53.9	48.3	550
140 Bhutan	43.2	60.7	156	77	267	100	62.3	57.2	380
141 Togo	45.5	51.3	128	80	216	142	45.3	40.1	480
142 Nepal	43.3	57.3	165	72	250	100	53.7	52.4	540
143 Lao People's Dem. Rep.	40.4	52.5	145	90	218	105	50.0	44.9	650
144 Yemen	42.1	59.4	194	85	303	117	58.9	53.4	350
145 Bangladesh	44.9	58.1	145	54	239	82	55.4	53.2	350
146 Haiti	48.5	52.0	148	81	221	125	46.3	34.2	520
147 Madagascar	44.9	51.6	109	86	180	139	48.7	43.8	490
148 Nigeria	44.0	51.3	120	110	201	184	44.6	42.1	..
149 Djibouti	41.0	45.5	160	102	241	146	39.1	32.9	..
150 Uganda	46.4	41.9	110	81	185	127	28.1	24.9	510

HDI rank	Life expectancy at birth (years)		Infant mortality rate (per 1,000 live births)		Under-five mortality rate (per 1,000 live births)		Probability at birth of surviving to age 65 [a]		Maternal mortality ratio reported (per 100,000 live births)
	1970-75 [b]	1995-2000 [b]	1970	2000	1970	2000	Female (% of cohort) 1995-2000 [b]	Male (% of cohort) 1995-2000 [b]	1985-99 [c]
151 Tanzania, U. Rep. of	46.5	51.1	129	104	218	165	43.2	37.9	530
152 Mauritania	43.5	50.5	150	120	250	183	47.7	41.6	550 [d]
153 Zambia	47.2	40.5	109	112	181	202	22.8	21.7	650
154 Senegal	41.8	52.3	164	80	279	139	51.0	39.4	560
155 Congo, Dem. Rep. of the	46.0	50.5	147	128	245	207	44.9	39.4	..
156 Côte d'Ivoire	45.4	47.7	158	102	239	173	37.3	35.4	600
157 Eritrea	44.3	51.5	..	73	..	114	47.1	40.7	1,000
158 Benin	44.0	53.5	149	98	252	154	51.4	44.8	500
159 Guinea	37.3	46.5	197	112	345	175	40.6	37.7	530
160 Gambia	37.0	45.4	183	92	319	128	39.6	34.2	..
161 Angola	38.0	44.6	180	172	300	295	38.1	32.9	..
162 Rwanda	44.6	39.4	124	100	209	187	26.3	22.9	..
163 Malawi	41.0	40.7	189	117	330	188	30.4	28.2	1,100
164 Mali	42.9	50.9	221	142	391	233	48.5	45.5	580
165 Central African Republic	43.0	44.3	149	115	248	180	34.4	28.5	1,100
166 Chad	39.0	45.2	149	118	252	198	38.6	33.6	830
167 Guinea-Bissau	36.5	44.1	..	132	..	215	37.8	32.5	910
168 Ethiopia	41.8	44.5	160	117	239	174	35.6	31.4	..
169 Burkina Faso	41.5	45.3	163	105	290	198	34.8	29.7	480
170 Mozambique	42.5	40.6	163	126	278	200	31.0	26.3	1,100
171 Burundi	44.0	40.6	138	114	233	190	28.5	23.5	..
172 Niger	38.2	44.2	197	159	330	270	37.1	34.9	590
173 Sierra Leone	35.0	37.3	206	180	363	316	28.2	23.4	..
Developing countries	55.6	64.1	108	61	166	89	68.4	61.3	..
Least developed countries	44.2	51.3	148	98	240	155	46.1	41.7	..
Arab States	51.9	65.9	132	46	204	61	71.1	64.9	..
East Asia and the Pacific	60.4	68.8	87	33	126	43	77.2	68.5	..
Latin America and the Caribbean	61.1	69.4	86	30	123	37	77.6	65.2	..
South Asia	49.9	61.9	128	68	203	94	63.8	59.4	..
Sub-Saharan Africa	45.3	48.8	135	107	223	174	41.4	36.6	..
Central and Eastern Europe and the CIS	69.2	68.4	34	20	42	25	79.0	55.3	..
OECD	70.4	76.4	40	12	53	14	87.2	77.3	..
High-income OECD	72.1	77.8	20	6	26	6	88.8	80.0	..
High human development	71.3	77.0	25	7	32	7	88.2	78.1	..
Medium human development	58.4	66.5	100	46	150	62	72.9	63.8	..
Low human development	44.6	52.2	141	99	230	154	47.0	43.8	..
High income	72.0	77.8	21	6	26	6	88.8	80.0	..
Middle income	62.6	69.2	85	31	121	38	78.2	67.1	..
Low income	49.5	59.0	126	80	202	120	59.0	53.6	..
World	59.9	66.4	96	56	146	81	72.2	63.6	..

a. Data refer to the probability at birth of surviving to age 65, times 100. b. Data refer to estimates for the period specified. c. The maternal mortality data are those reported by national authorities. UNICEF and the World Health Organization periodically evaluate these data and make adjustments to account for the well-documented problems of underreporting and misclassification of maternal deaths and to develop estimates for countries with no data (for details on the most recent estimates see Hill, AbouZahr and Wardlaw 2001). Data refer to the most recent year available during the period specified. d. Data refer to a year or period other than that specified, differ from the standard definition or refer to only part of a country.

Source: Columns 1, 2, 7 and 8: UN 2001; columns 3 and 5: UNICEF 2002a; columns 4, 6 and 9: UNICEF 2002b.

9 Commitment to education: public spending

HDI rank		Public education expenditure [a]				Public education expenditure by level (as % of all levels) [b]					
		As % of GNP		As % of total government expenditure		Pre-primary and primary		Secondary		Tertiary	
		1985-87 [c]	1995-97 [c]	1985-87 [c]	1995-97 [c]	1985-86 [c]	1995-97 [c]	1985-86 [c]	1995-97 [c]	1985-86 [c]	1995-97 [c]
High human development											
1	Norway	6.5	7.7 [d]	14.7	16.8 [d]	45.2	38.7 [e]	28.3	23.0 [e]	13.5	27.9 [e]
2	Sweden	7.3	8.3 [d]	12.8	12.2 [d]	48.0	34.1 [e, f]	20.1	38.7 [e, f]	13.1	27.2 [e, f]
3	Canada	6.7	6.9 [d, g]	14.1	12.9 [d, g]	..	..	63.6 [h]	64.7 [e, f, g, h]	28.7	35.3 [e, f, g]
4	Belgium	5.1 [i]	3.1 [d, j]	14.3 [i]	6.0 [d, j]	24.7 [i]	29.9 [e, j]	46.4 [i]	45.5 [e, j]	16.7 [i]	21.5 [e, j]
5	Australia	5.1	5.5 [d]	12.5	13.5 [d]	..	30.6 [e]	61.9 [h]	38.9 [e]	30.5	30.5 [e]
6	United States	5.0	5.4 [d, g]	11.9	14.4 [d, g]	44.7	38.7 [e, f, g]	30.3	36.1 [e, f, g]	25.1	25.2 [e, f, g]
7	Iceland	4.8	5.4 [d]	14.0	13.6 [d]	..	35.9 [e]	..	41.9 [e]	..	17.7 [e]
8	Netherlands	6.9	5.1 [d]	..	9.8 [d]	22.6	30.9 [e]	35.9	39.8 [e]	26.4	29.3 [e]
9	Japan [g]	..	3.6	..	9.9 [d]	..	39.3 [e, f]	..	41.8 [e, f]	..	12.1 [e, f]
10	Finland	5.5	7.5 [d]	11.6	12.2 [d]	30.8	33.0 [e]	41.6	36.2 [e]	18.7	28.9 [e]
11	Switzerland	4.7	5.4 [d]	18.8	15.4 [d]	..	30.6 [e]	73.6	48.1 [e]	18.1	19.3 [e]
12	France	5.5	6.0 [d]	18.0 [g]	10.9 [d]	29.4	31.4 [e]	40.8	49.5 [e]	12.9	17.9 [e]
13	United Kingdom	4.8	5.3 [d]	11.3 [g]	11.6 [d]	26.7	32.3 [e, f]	45.9	44.0 [e, f]	19.8	23.7 [e, f]
14	Denmark	7.2	8.1 [d]	13.7	13.1 [d]	..	33.6 [e]	..	39.3 [e]	..	22.0 [e]
15	Austria	5.9	5.4 [d]	7.8	10.4 [d]	23.1	28.1 [e]	46.9	49.0 [e]	16.6	21.2 [e]
16	Luxembourg	4.1	4.0 [d]	9.5 [i]	11.5 [g, i]	43.5	51.9 [e]	42.7	43.4 [e]	3.3	4.7 [e]
17	Germany	..	4.8 [d]	..	9.6 [d]	..	..	..	72.2 [e, h]	..	22.5 [e]
18	Ireland	6.7	6.0 [d]	9.5	13.5 [d]	39.4	32.2 [e]	39.7	41.5 [e]	17.7	23.8 [e]
19	New Zealand	5.4	7.3 [d]	20.9	17.1 [d, g]	38.3	28.7 [e]	28.5	40.3 [e]	28.3	29.1 [e]
20	Italy	5.0	4.9 [d]	8.3	9.1 [d]	30.1	32.0 [e]	35.5	49.2 [e]	10.2	15.1 [e]
21	Spain	3.7	5.0 [d]	8.8	11.0 [d]	..	33.3 [e]	..	47.9 [e]	..	16.6 [e]
22	Israel	6.7	7.6 [d, g]	10.0	12.3 [d, g]	42.8	42.3 [e, g]	30.8	31.2 [e, g]	18.9	18.2 [e, g]
23	Hong Kong, China (SAR)	2.5	2.9	19.8	17.0 [g]	31.5 [g]	21.9	37.9 [g]	35.0	25.1 [g]	37.1
24	Greece	2.2	3.1 [d]	6.1	8.2 [d]	37.6	35.3 [e, f]	41.3	38.0 [e, f]	20.1	25.0 [e, f]
25	Singapore	3.9	3.0	11.5	23.3	30.5	25.7	36.9	34.6	27.9	34.8
26	Cyprus [k]	3.6	4.5	11.9	13.2	37.6	36.7	50.7	50.8	4.2	6.5
27	Korea, Rep. of	3.8	3.7 [d]	..	17.5 [d]	47.0	45.3 [e, f]	36.7	36.6 [e, f]	10.9	8.0 [e, f]
28	Portugal	3.8 [i]	5.8 [d]	..	11.7 [d]	51.0	34.2 [e]	30.6	41.6 [e]	12.7	16.4 [e]
29	Slovenia	..	5.7	..	12.6	..	29.9	..	48.4	..	16.9
30	Malta	3.4	5.1	7.4	10.8	31.0	22.6 [g]	43.3	32.0 [g]	8.2	10.9 [g]
31	Barbados [g]	6.2	7.2	17.2	19.0	31.0	..	32.5	..	22.3	..
32	Brunei Darussalam	..	..	..	..	..	..	..	..	..	..
33	Czech Republic	..	5.1 [d]	..	13.6 [d]	..	31.3 [e]	..	50.2 [e]	..	15.8 [e]
34	Argentina	1.4 [i]	3.5	8.9 [i]	12.6	37.7 [g]	45.7	27.4 [g]	34.8	19.2 [g]	19.5
35	Hungary	5.6	4.6 [d]	6.3	6.9 [g]	51.1	36.8 [e]	19.9	46.3 [e]	16.9	15.5 [e]
36	Slovakia	..	4.7	..	14.6	..	40.5	..	28.0	..	12.7
37	Poland	4.6	7.5 [d]	12.5	24.8 [d]	44.2	37.6 [e, f]	17.9	15.1 [e, f]	18.2	11.1 [e, f]
38	Chile	3.3	3.6	15.3	15.5	57.0	58.3	19.5	18.8	20.3	16.1
39	Bahrain	5.2	4.4	12.3	12.0	..	30.1 [f]	..	34.5 [f]	..	..
40	Uruguay	3.2	3.3	15.0	15.5	37.7	32.6	28.4	29.0	22.4	19.6
41	Bahamas	4.0	..	18.9	13.2	..	..	..	..	..	..
42	Estonia	..	7.2	..	25.5	..	18.5	..	50.7	..	17.9
43	Costa Rica	4.5	5.4	21.6	22.8	35.1	40.2	22.3	24.3	41.4	28.3
44	Saint Kitts and Nevis	3.7 [l]	3.8	14.6 [l]	8.8	50.3	38.1	40.1	42.5	2.1	11.4
45	Kuwait	4.8	5.0	13.4	14.0	..	..	..	69.8 [f, h]	..	30.2 [f]
46	United Arab Emirates	2.1	1.7	13.2	20.3	..	..	..	..	..	..
47	Seychelles	10.2	7.9	16.0	16.3	29.5	27.0	54.3	38.7	..	16.2
48	Croatia	..	5.3	..	..	..	..	..	..	..	..
49	Lithuania	5.3 [g]	5.9	12.9	22.8	..	15.1	..	50.9	..	18.3
50	Trinidad and Tobago	6.3	4.4 [g]	14.0	..	47.5	40.5 [g]	36.8	33.1 [g]	8.9	13.3 [g]

		Public education expenditure [a]				Public education expenditure by level (as % of all levels) [b]					
		As % of GNP		As % of total government expenditure		Pre-primary and primary		Secondary		Tertiary	
HDI rank		1985-87 [c]	1995-97 [c]	1985-87 [c]	1995-97 [c]	1985-86 [c]	1995-97 [c]	1985-86 [c]	1995-97 [c]	1985-86 [c]	1995-97 [c]
51	Qatar	4.7	3.4 [g]	..	..	..	..	..	..	..	..
52	Antigua and Barbuda [g]	2.7	..	7.6	..	36.6	..	30.6	..	12.7	..
53	Latvia	3.4	6.5	12.4	16.5	15.8	12.1	56.2	58.9	10.3	12.2
Medium human development											
54	Mexico	3.5	4.9 [d]	..	23.0 [d]	31.5 [i]	50.3 [e]	26.8 [i]	32.5 [e]	17.6 [i]	17.2 [e]
55	Cuba	6.8	6.7	18.4	12.6	26.3	31.9	42.0	33.0	12.9	14.9
56	Belarus	5.0	5.9	..	17.8	..	..	74.8 [h]	72.5 [h]	14.0	11.1
57	Panama	4.8	5.1	14.3	16.3	38.3	31.1	25.2	19.8	20.4	26.1
58	Belize	4.7	5.0	15.4	19.5	55.7	62.8	27.7	25.8	2.3	6.9
59	Malaysia	6.9	4.9	18.8	15.4	37.8	32.7	37.1	30.6	14.6	25.5
60	Russian Federation	3.4	3.5 [d]	..	9.6 [g]	..	23.2 [e, f]	..	57.4 [e, f]	..	19.3 [e, f]
61	Dominica	5.6	..	14.1	..	62.4	..	26.2	..	2.6	..
62	Bulgaria	5.4	3.2	..	7.0	..	..	65.3 [h]	73.8 [h]	12.4	18.0
63	Romania	2.2	3.6	7.5 [g]	10.5	..	42.7 [f]	..	23.8 [f]	..	16.0 [f]
64	Libyan Arab Jamahiriya	9.6	..	20.8	..	..	..	..	..	..	..
65	Macedonia, TFYR	..	5.1	..	20.0	..	54.4	..	23.6	..	22.0
66	Saint Lucia	5.5	9.8 [g]	..	22.2 [g]	..	..	..	..	..	..
67	Mauritius	3.3	4.6	10.0	17.4	45.2	31.0	37.6	36.3	5.6	24.7
68	Colombia [i]	2.6	4.1	22.4	16.6	42.0	40.5	32.5	31.5	21.2	19.2
69	Venezuela	5.0	5.2 [g]	19.6	22.4 [g]	..	..	..	29.5 [g, h]	..	34.7 [g]
70	Thailand	3.4	4.8	17.9	20.1	58.4	50.4	21.1	20.0	13.2	16.4
71	Saudi Arabia	7.4	7.5	13.6	22.8	..	..	72.9 [h]	84.4 [h]	27.1	15.6
72	Fiji	6.0	..	..	..	..	..	..	..	..	..
73	Brazil	4.7	5.1	17.7	..	45.9 [f]	53.5	7.7 [f]	20.3	19.6 [f]	26.2
74	Suriname	10.2	3.5 [g]	22.8	..	63.7	..	13.5	..	7.7	..
75	Lebanon [i]	..	2.5	11.7	8.2	..	..	..	68.9 [f, h]	..	16.2 [f]
76	Armenia	..	2.0	..	10.3	..	15.8	..	63.0	..	13.2
77	Philippines	2.1	3.4	11.2	15.7	63.9	56.1	10.1	23.3	22.5	18.0
78	Oman	4.1	4.5	15.0	16.4	..	40.9	..	51.3	..	7.0
79	Kazakhstan	3.4	4.4	19.8	17.6	..	7.2 [f]	..	63.0 [f]	..	13.9 [f]
80	Ukraine	5.3	5.6	21.2	14.8	..	..	74.2 [h]	73.5 [h]	13.5	10.7
81	Georgia [g]	..	5.2	..	6.9	..	22.0	..	45.1	..	18.5
82	Peru	3.6	2.9	15.7	19.2	39.5	35.2	20.5	21.2	2.7	16.0
83	Grenada	4.5	4.7	8.6	10.6	..	..	..	..	..	..
84	Maldives	5.2	6.4	8.5	10.5	..	..	..	..	..	..
85	Turkey	1.2 [l]	2.2 [d]	..	14.7 [d, g]	45.9	43.3 [e, f]	22.4	22.0 [e, f]	23.9	34.7 [e, f]
86	Jamaica	4.9	7.5	11.0	12.9	31.9	31.3	34.0	37.4	19.4	22.4
87	Turkmenistan	4.1	..	29.3	..	..	..	..	..	..	..
88	Azerbaijan	5.8	3.0	29.3	18.8	..	14.6	..	63.9	..	7.5
89	Sri Lanka	2.7	3.4	7.8	8.9	..	..	90.2 [h]	74.8 [h]	9.8	9.3
90	Paraguay	1.1 [i]	4.0 [i]	14.3 [i]	19.8 [i]	36.6	50.0 [f, i]	29.7	18.1 [f, i]	23.8	19.7 [f, i]
91	St. Vincent & the Grenadines	6.0	6.3 [g]	11.6	13.8 [g]	73.3	..	26.6	..	..	..
92	Albania	..	..	11.2	..	..	63.9 [g]	..	20.6 [g]	..	10.3 [g]
93	Ecuador	3.5	3.5	21.3	13.0	45.5	38.4	35.8	36.0	17.8	21.3
94	Dominican Republic	1.3	2.3	10.0	13.8	47.3	49.5	19.7	12.5	20.8	13.0
95	Uzbekistan	9.2 [g]	7.7	25.1	21.1	..	..	..	..	..	..
96	China	2.3	2.3	11.1	12.2 [g]	29.5 [m]	37.4	33.2 [m]	32.2	21.8 [m]	15.6
97	Tunisia	6.2	7.7	14.8	19.9	44.0 [i]	42.5	37.0 [i]	37.2	18.2 [i]	18.5
98	Iran, Islamic Rep. of	3.7	4.0	18.1	17.8	42.0	29.0	37.9	33.9	10.7	22.9
99	Jordan	6.8	7.9	15.8	19.8	..	..	62.9 [h]	64.5 [h]	34.1	33.0
100	Cape Verde	2.9	..	14.8	..	61.5	..	15.9	..	..	..

		Public education expenditure [a]				Public education expenditure by level (as % of all levels) [b]					
		As % of GNP		As % of total government expenditure		Pre-primary and primary		Secondary		Tertiary	
HDI rank		1985-87 [c]	1995-97 [c]	1985-87 [c]	1995-97 [c]	1985-86 [c]	1995-97 [c]	1985-86 [c]	1995-97 [c]	1985-86 [c]	1995-97 [c]
101	Samoa (Western)	..	..	..	..	..	..	..	..	..	..
102	Kyrgyzstan	9.7	5.3	22.4	23.5	10.9	6.6	60.4	68.0	8.8	14.1
103	Guyana	8.5	5.0	7.3	10.0	38.8	..	23.8	71.3 [h]	17.8	7.7
104	El Salvador	3.1 [g]	2.5	12.5 [g]	16.0	..	63.5	..	6.5	..	7.2
105	Moldova, Rep. of	3.6	10.6	..	28.1	..	24.5	..	52.9	..	13.3
106	Algeria	9.8	5.1 [l]	27.8	16.4 [l]	..	..	..	95.3 [h, l]	..	..
107	South Africa	6.1	7.6	..	22.0	..	43.5	73.1 [h]	29.5	24.8	14.3
108	Syrian Arab Republic	4.8	4.2	14.0	13.6	38.4	41.9	25.3	29.8	33.6 [f]	25.9 [f]
109	Viet Nam	..	3.0	..	7.4 [g]	..	43.0	..	26.0	..	22.0
110	Indonesia	0.9 [g, i]	1.4 [n]	4.3 [g, i]	7.9 [n]	..	..	..	73.5 [h, i]	..	24.4 [i]
111	Equatorial Guinea [g]	1.7	1.7	3.9	5.6	..	..	..	..	..	..
112	Tajikistan	..	2.2	29.5	11.5	9.2	14.9	55.7	71.2	7.7	7.1
113	Mongolia	11.7	5.7	17.1	15.1	10.7 [f]	19.9 [f]	51.2 [f]	56.0 [f]	17.3 [f]	14.3 [f]
114	Bolivia	2.1	4.9	20.1 [g]	11.1	..	50.7	..	9.8	..	27.7
115	Egypt	4.5	4.8	..	14.9	..	..	..	66.7 [h]	..	33.3
116	Honduras	4.8	3.6	19.5	16.5	49.1	52.5	16.7	21.5	21.3	16.6
117	Gabon	5.8	2.9 [l]	9.4	..	..	..	..	..	..	..
118	Nicaragua	5.4	3.9 [l]	12.0	8.8 [l]	45.6	68.6 [l]	16.7	13.9 [l]	23.2	..
119	São Tomé and Principe	3.8	..	18.8	..	55.7	..	27.0	..	..	..
120	Guatemala [i]	1.9	1.7	13.8	15.8	..	63.0	..	12.1	..	15.2
121	Solomon Islands	4.7 [g]	3.8 [g]	12.4 [g]	7.9 [g]	..	..	..	..	..	..
122	Namibia	..	9.1	..	25.6	..	58.0	..	28.9	..	13.1
123	Morocco [i]	6.2	5.3	21.5	24.9	35.3	34.6	47.6	48.8	17.1	16.5
124	India	3.2	3.2	8.5	11.6	38.0	39.5	25.3	26.5	15.3	13.7
125	Swaziland	5.6	5.7	20.6	18.1	39.4	35.8	29.6	27.1	19.5	26.6
126	Botswana	7.3	8.6	15.9	20.6	36.3	..	40.7	..	17.2	..
127	Myanmar [i]	1.9	1.2 [g]	..	14.4 [g]	..	47.7 [g]	..	40.3 [g]	..	11.7 [g]
128	Zimbabwe	7.7	7.1 [g]	15.0	..	..	51.7 [g]	..	26.4 [g]	..	17.3 [g]
129	Ghana	3.4	4.2	24.3	19.9	24.5 [g]	..	29.5 [g]	..	12.5 [g]	..
130	Cambodia	..	2.9	..	..	..	..	..	..	..	..
131	Vanuatu	7.4	4.8	24.6	18.8 [g]	..	..	..	..	..	..
132	Lesotho	4.1	8.4	13.4	..	39.1 [g]	41.2	32.7 [g]	29.2	22.3 [g]	28.7
133	Papua New Guinea	..	..	..	..	..	..	..	..	..	..
134	Kenya	7.1	6.5	14.8 [g]	16.7	59.9	..	17.7	..	12.4	..
135	Cameroon	2.8	..	16.4	16.9 [g]	..	..	72.6 [h]	86.8 [h]	27.4	13.2
136	Congo	4.9 [g]	6.1	9.8 [g]	14.7	30.0 [g]	50.4	35.6 [g]	11.6	34.4 [g]	28.0
137	Comoros	..	..	..	..	..	36.6 [i]	..	35.1 [i]	..	17.2 [i]
Low human development											
138	Pakistan	3.1	2.7	8.8	7.1	36.0	51.8	33.3	27.9	18.2	13.0
139	Sudan	..	1.4	..	..	..	..	..	..	..	..
140	Bhutan	3.7	4.1	..	7.0	..	44.0	..	35.6	..	20.4
141	Togo	4.9	4.5	19.7	24.6	34.0	45.9	29.1	26.9	22.8	24.7
142	Nepal	2.2	3.2	10.4	13.5	35.7	45.1	19.9	19.0	33.4	19.0
143	Lao People's Dem. Rep.	0.5	2.1	6.6	8.7	..	48.3	..	30.7	..	7.4
144	Yemen	..	7.0	..	21.6 [g]	..	..	..	..	..	..
145	Bangladesh [i]	1.4	2.2	9.9	13.8	46.1	44.8	34.7	43.8	10.4	7.9
146	Haiti	1.9	..	20.6	..	51.0	..	18.1	..	10.8	..
147	Madagascar	1.9 [l]	1.9	..	16.1 [g]	42.3	30.0	26.5	33.4	27.2	21.1
148	Nigeria [n]	1.7	0.7	12.0	11.5	..	..	..	..	..	..
149	Djibouti	..	..	..	..	..	..	..	..	..	..
150	Uganda	3.5 [g, i]	2.6	..	..	44.5 [g, i]	..	32.4 [g, i]	..	13.2 [g, i]	..

HDI rank	Public education expenditure [a]				Public education expenditure by level (as % of all levels) [b]					
	As % of GNP		As % of total government expenditure		Pre primary and primary		Secondary		Tertiary	
	1985-87 [c]	1995-97 [c]	1985-87 [c]	1995-97 [c]	1985-86 [c]	1995-97 [c]	1985-86 [c]	1995-97 [c]	1985-86 [c]	1995-97 [c]
151 Tanzania, U. Rep. of	..	..	9.9	..	57.5	..	20.5	..	12.7	..
152 Mauritania [i]	..	5.1	..	16.2	32.6	39.4	36.2	35.3	27.4	21.2
153 Zambia	3.1	2.2	9.8	7.1	43.9	41.5	26.9	18.4	18.3	23.2
154 Senegal	..	3.7	..	33.1	50.1	34.2	25.1	42.5	19.0	23.2
155 Congo, Dem. Rep. of the	1.0	..	8.2	..	..	..	71.3 [h]	..	28.7	..
156 Côte d'Ivoire	..	5.0	..	24.9	40.2	45.2	42.7	36.2	17.1	18.6
157 Eritrea [l]	..	1.8	..	..	..	44.5	..	17.6	..	..
158 Benin	..	3.2	..	15.2	..	59.1	..	21.7	..	18.8
159 Guinea	1.8	1.9	13.0	26.8	30.8 [g]	35.1 [f]	36.9 [g]	29.6 [f]	23.5 [g]	26.1 [f]
160 Gambia	3.7	4.9	8.8 [g]	21.2	49.0	48.9	21.3	31.6	13.8	12.9
161 Angola	6.2	..	13.8	..	..	..	86.8 [h, i]	..	5.0 [i]	..
162 Rwanda	3.5	..	22.9	..	67.6	..	15.3	..	11.5	..
163 Malawi	3.5	5.4	9.0	18.3 [g]	41.3	58.8	15.2	8.9	23.3	20.5
164 Mali	3.2	2.2	17.3	..	48.4	45.9	22.6	21.6	13.4	17.7
165 Central African Republic	2.6	..	16.8	..	55.2 [i]	53.2 [i]	17.6 [i]	16.5 [i]	18.8 [i]	24.0 [i]
166 Chad	..	2.2	..	..	..	43.5	..	24.2	..	9.0
167 Guinea-Bissau	1.8	..	..	..	..	..	..	..	..	..
168 Ethiopia	3.1	4.0	9.3	13.7	51.5	46.2 [f]	28.3	23.7 [f]	14.4	15.9 [f]
169 Burkina Faso	2.3	3.6 [g]	14.9	11.1 [g]	38.1	56.6	20.3	25.1	30.7	18.3
170 Mozambique	2.1	..	5.6	..	..	..	..	..	..	..
171 Burundi	3.1	4.0	18.1	18.3	45.0	42.7	32.2	36.7	19.8	17.1
172 Niger [l]	..	2.3	..	12.8	..	59.7 [f]	..	32.3 [f]	..	..
173 Sierra Leone	1.7	..	12.4	..	33.2	..	29.3	..	24.2	..

Note: As a result of a number of limitations in the data, comparisons of education expenditure data over time and across countries should be made with caution. For detailed notes on the data see UNESCO (1999b).
a. Data refer to total public expenditure on education, including current and capital expenditure. See the definitions of statistical terms. b. Data refer to current public expenditure on education. Expenditures by level may not sum to 100 as a result of rounding or the omission of the categories "other types" and "not distributed". c. Data refer to the most recent year available during the period specified. d. Data may not be strictly comparable with those for earlier years as a result of methodological changes. e. Expenditures previously classified as "other types" have been distributed across the different education levels. f. Data include capital expenditure. g. Data refer to a year or period other than that specified. h. Data refer to combined expenditures for pre-primary, primary and secondary levels. i. Data refer to the ministry of education only. j. Data refer to the Flemish community only. k. Data refer to the Office of Greek Education only. l. Data do not include expenditure on tertiary education. m. Data do not include expenditure on mid-level specialized colleges and technical schools. n. Data refer to the central government only.
Source: Columns 1-4: UNESCO 2000; *columns 5-10:* UNESCO 1999b.

. . . TO ACQUIRE KNOWLEDGE . . .

HDI rank		Adult literacy rate (% age 15 and above)		Youth literacy rate (% age 15-24)		Net primary enrolment ratio (%)		Net secondary enrolment ratio (%)		Children reaching grade 5 (%)	Tertiary students in science, math and engineering (as % of all tertiary students)
		1985	2000	1985	2000	1985-87 [a]	1998 [b]	1985-87 [a]	1998 [b]	1995-97 [a]	1994-97 [a]
High human development											
1	Norway	..	..	..	..	97	100	85	96	..	18
2	Sweden	..	..	..	..	98	100	..	100	97	31
3	Canada	..	..	..	..	94	96	89	94	..	..
4	Belgium	..	..	..	..	96	100	89	95	..	..
5	Australia	..	..	..	..	97	..	79	..	..	32
6	United States	..	..	..	..	94	95	91	90	..	..
7	Iceland	..	..	..	..	..	99	..	85	..	20
8	Netherlands	..	..	..	..	95	100	86	93	..	20
9	Japan	..	..	..	..	99	100	97	..	..	23
10	Finland	..	..	..	..	..	99	..	95	100	37
11	Switzerland	..	..	..	..	..	94	..	83	..	31
12	France	..	..	..	..	100	100	82	94	..	25
13	United Kingdom	..	..	..	..	98	100	79	94	..	29
14	Denmark	..	..	..	..	99	100	85	89	..	21
15	Austria	..	..	..	..	..	88	..	..	..	28
16	Luxembourg	..	..	..	..	85	100	60	..	..	..
17	Germany	..	..	..	..	..	87	..	88	..	31
18	Ireland	..	..	..	..	90	100	81	77	..	30
19	New Zealand	..	..	..	..	100	100	84	..	..	21
20	Italy	97.1	98.4	99.8	99.8	96 [c]	100	68 [c]	88	99	28
21	Spain	95.3	97.6	99.4	99.8	100	100	..	92	..	30
22	Israel	88.0	94.6	98.2	99.4	..	95	..	85	..	..
23	Hong Kong, China (SAR)	87.8	93.5	97.7	99.2	96 [c]	..	65 [c]	..	..	..
24	Greece	93.2	97.2	99.4	99.8	98	95	82	86	..	..
25	Singapore	85.6	92.3	98.2	99.7	99 [c]	..	..	..	..	..
26	Cyprus	92.5	97.1	99.6	99.8	96	81	76	73	100	17
27	Korea, Rep. of	94.5	97.8	99.8	99.8	96	97	85	..	98	34
28	Portugal	84.4	92.2	98.8	99.8	100	100	..	88	..	31
29	Slovenia	99.5	99.6	99.7	99.8	..	94	..	89	..	29
30	Malta	86.1	92.0	96.7	98.6	95	100	74	81	100	13
31	Barbados	..	..	..	..	..	..	77 [c]	100	..	21
32	Brunei Darussalam	80.9	91.5	96.4	99.4	80	..	51 [c]	..	..	6
33	Czech Republic	..	..	..	..	..	90	..	79	..	34
34	Argentina	95.1	96.8	97.8	98.6	96	100	..	74	..	30
35	Hungary	98.8	99.3	99.7	99.8	97	82	66	85	..	32
36	Slovakia	..	..	..	..	..	..	..	..	..	43
37	Poland	99.4	99.7	99.8	99.8	99	96	75	57	..	..
38	Chile	93.0	95.8	97.5	98.8	89 [c]	88	..	70	100	43
39	Bahrain	76.8	87.6	93.2	98.4	97	97	82	80	95	..
40	Uruguay	95.8	97.7	98.7	99.3	89	92	56 [c]	66	98	24
41	Bahamas	93.8	95.4	96.0	97.2	100	87	83	100	..	..
42	Estonia	..	..	..	..	..	96	..	77	..	32
43	Costa Rica	92.9	95.6	97.1	98.3	86	..	35	..	90	18
44	Saint Kitts and Nevis	..	..	..	..	..	..	..	..	..	..
45	Kuwait	72.2	82.0	84.2	92.4	82	67	..	57	..	23
46	United Arab Emirates	69.0	76.3	79.7	90.7	89	83	..	70	..	27
47	Seychelles	..	..	..	..	..	..	..	..	99	..
48	Croatia	95.8	98.3	99.5	99.8	..	77	..	81	..	38
49	Lithuania	99.1	99.6	99.8	99.8	..	94	..	85	..	38
50	Trinidad and Tobago	90.2	93.8	95.5	97.5	93	93	73	72	97	41

HDI rank	Adult literacy rate (% age 15 and above)		Youth literacy rate (% age 15-24)		Net primary enrolment ratio (%)		Net secondary enrolment ratio (%)		Children reaching grade 5 (%)	Tertiary students in science, math and engineering (as % of all tertiary students)
	1985	2000	1985	2000	1985-87 [a]	1998 [b]	1985-87 [a]	1998 [b]	1995-97 [a]	1994-97 [a]
51 Qatar	74.4	81.2	86.8	94.8	92	86	66	67	..	..
52 Antigua and Barbuda	..	..	..	..	..	..	..	..	..	..
53 Latvia	99.8	99.8	99.8	99.8	..	94	..	83	..	29
Medium human development										
54 Mexico	85.3	91.4	93.9	97.0	99	100	46	56	86	31
55 Cuba	94.0	96.7	98.8	99.8	88	97	69	75	..	21
56 Belarus	99.0	99.6	99.8	99.8	..	..	..	..	..	33
57 Panama	87.1	91.9	94.4	96.8	91	..	49	..	..	26
58 Belize	86.4	93.2	94.9	98.0	..	99	..	39	..	..
59 Malaysia	76.4	87.5	92.7	97.6	..	98	..	93	..	..
60 Russian Federation	99.0	99.6	99.8	99.8	..	73	..	..	..	48
61 Dominica	..	..	..	..	..	..	..	..	..	..
62 Bulgaria	96.3	98.4	99.4	99.7	97 [c]	93	79 [c]	81	..	25
63 Romania	96.3	98.1	99.2	99.6	..	94	..	76	..	32
64 Libyan Arab Jamahiriya	60.8	80.0	86.7	96.5	..	..	..	71	..	..
65 Macedonia, TFYR	..	..	..	..	..	96	..	79	95	38
66 Saint Lucia	..	..	..	..	..	..	..	..	..	..
67 Mauritius	77.2	84.5	89.3	93.9	100	93	..	63	99	17
68 Colombia	86.6	91.7	94.0	96.9	65	87	32	..	73	31
69 Venezuela	86.7	92.6	94.9	98.0	86	..	18	..	89	..
70 Thailand	90.3	95.5	97.4	98.9	..	77	..	55	..	21
71 Saudi Arabia	59.4	76.3	80.0	92.7	53	59	29	..	89	18
72 Fiji	86.1	92.9	96.8	99.1	98	100	..	76	..	..
73 Brazil	78.4	85.2	88.8	92.5	82	98	15	..	..	22
74 Suriname	..	..	..	..	84	..	43	..	..	..
75 Lebanon	76.3	86.0	90.0	95.2	..	78	..	76	..	17
76 Armenia	96.8	98.4	99.4	99.7	..	..	..	..	..	33
77 Philippines	90.9	95.3	96.4	98.7	98	..	51	..	..	..
78 Oman	45.5	71.7	74.0	97.9	69	66	..	58	96	30
79 Kazakhstan	..	..	..	..	..	..	..	74	..	42
80 Ukraine	99.3	99.6	99.8	99.9	..	..	..	..	..	..
81 Georgia	..	..	..	..	..	..	..	..	..	48
82 Peru	82.7	89.9	93.0	96.8	96	100	49	61	..	..
83 Grenada	..	..	..	..	..	..	..	..	..	..
84 Maldives	93.2	96.7	97.3	99.1	..	..	..	..	..	..
85 Turkey	73.9	85.1	90.7	96.5	95	100	38	..	..	22
86 Jamaica	79.5	86.9	89.6	94.0	91	92	62	79	..	20
87 Turkmenistan	..	..	..	..	..	..	..	..	..	..
88 Azerbaijan	..	..	..	..	..	96	..	82	..	..
89 Sri Lanka	87.1	91.6	93.9	96.8	..	100	60	..	..	28
90 Paraguay	88.4	93.3	94.7	97.1	89	92	25	42	78	22
91 St. Vincent & the Grenadines	..	..	..	..	..	..	..	..	..	..
92 Albania	71.7	84.7	93.1	97.8	..	..	..	..	..	22
93 Ecuador	85.1	91.6	94.3	97.3	..	97	..	46	85	..
94 Dominican Republic	76.9	83.6	85.2	91.1	..	87	..	53	..	25
95 Uzbekistan	98.3	99.2	99.6	99.7	..	..	..	..	..	..
96 China	71.9	84.1	93.1	97.8	94	91	..	50	94	53
97 Tunisia	52.6	71.0	78.3	93.4	94	98	32 [c]	55	91	27
98 Iran, Islamic Rep. of	56.2	76.3	80.7	94.0	85	..	..	..	..	36
99 Jordan	74.8	89.7	94.6	99.3	..	64	..	60	..	27
100 Cape Verde	57.3	73.8	77.0	88.1	100	99	12	..	..	..

HDI rank	Adult literacy rate (% age 15 and above)		Youth literacy rate (% age 15-24)		Net primary enrolment ratio (%)		Net secondary enrolment ratio (%)		Children reaching grade 5 (%)	Tertiary students in science, math and engineering (as % of all tertiary students)
	1985	2000	1985	2000	1985-87 [a]	1998 [b]	1985-87 [a]	1998 [b]	1995-97 [a]	1994-97 [a]
101 Samoa (Western)	73.5	80.2	81.2	87.1	..	96	..	65	85	..
102 Kyrgyzstan	..	..	..	..	..	85	..	..	..	..
103 Guyana	96.1	98.5	99.7	99.8	..	85	..	..	91	25
104 El Salvador	69.1	78.7	81.4	88.2	74	81	15 [c]	37	77	20
105 Moldova, Rep. of	96.3	98.9	99.8	99.8	..	..	..	..	..	44
106 Algeria	44.5	66.7	69.5	89.0	89	94	50	58	94	50
107 South Africa	78.9	85.3	86.8	91.3	..	100	..	..	..	18
108 Syrian Arab Republic	59.4	74.4	75.5	87.2	100	93	52	38	94	31
109 Viet Nam	88.9	93.4	94.5	97.0	..	97	..	49	..	..
110 Indonesia	74.7	86.9	92.6	97.7	98	..	42	..	88	28
111 Equatorial Guinea	66.7	83.2	89.1	96.9	..	83	..	26	..	..
112 Tajikistan	97.2	99.2	99.7	99.8	..	..	..	..	..	23
113 Mongolia	97.8	98.9	99.1	99.6	94	85	..	53	..	25
114 Bolivia	73.6	85.5	89.9	95.9	92	97	28	..	..	..
115 Egypt	43.2	55.3	57.0	69.8	..	92	..	..	..	15
116 Honduras	65.1	74.6	75.8	83.4	92	..	23	..	..	26
117 Gabon	..	..	..	..	..	..	..	..	..	..
118 Nicaragua	60.8	66.5	66.5	71.7	72	..	22	..	51	31
119 São Tomé and Principe	..	..	..	..	..	..	..	..	..	..
120 Guatemala	57.1	68.6	69.6	79.3	..	83	..	..	50	..
121 Solomon Islands	..	..	..	..	..	..	..	..	..	..
122 Namibia	70.8	82.0	84.7	91.6	..	86	..	31	86	4
123 Morocco	33.5	48.9	48.3	67.4	58	79	..	..	75	29
124 India	45.2	57.2	60.0	72.6	..	..	..	39	..	25
125 Swaziland	66.1	79.6	81.5	90.4	81	77	..	35	76	22
126 Botswana	63.3	77.2	78.2	88.3	92	81	24	57	90	27
127 Myanmar	78.2	84.7	86.5	90.9	..	..	..	..	..	37
128 Zimbabwe	75.8	88.7	90.2	97.2	..	..	..	..	79	23
129 Ghana	51.1	71.5	74.8	91.0	..	..	..	..	..	..
130 Cambodia	57.9	67.8	69.9	78.9	..	100	..	20	49	23
131 Vanuatu	..	..	..	..	..	100	..	..	..	..
132 Lesotho	74.8	83.4	85.1	90.5	73	60	14	14	..	13
133 Papua New Guinea	52.7	63.9	65.1	75.7	..	85	..	22	..	..
134 Kenya	63.8	82.4	85.0	95.1	..	..	..	..	..	..
135 Cameroon	54.8	75.8	81.7	93.7	76	..	..	..	..	..
136 Congo	58.9	80.7	87.6	97.4	..	..	..	..	..	..
137 Comoros	52.7	55.9	55.8	58.7	55	50	..	..	..	..
Low human development										
138 Pakistan	31.4	43.2	41.4	57.0	..	..	..	..	..	..
139 Sudan	40.0	57.8	57.7	77.2	..	46	..	..	..	..
140 Bhutan	..	..	..	..	..	16	..	5	..	..
141 Togo	38.3	57.1	56.9	75.4	72	88	..	23	..	11
142 Nepal	26.5	41.8	39.5	60.5	58 [c]	..	19 [c]	..	..	14
143 Lao People's Dem. Rep.	30.7	48.7	47.5	70.5	71	76	..	27	55	..
144 Yemen	25.9	46.3	40.7	64.9	..	61	..	35	..	6
145 Bangladesh	32.0	41.3	40.2	50.7	54	100	19 [c]	..	..	..
146 Haiti	35.1	49.8	50.2	64.4	25	80	..	..	..	..
147 Madagascar	52.8	66.5	67.7	80.1	..	63	..	13	..	20
148 Nigeria	40.7	63.9	64.7	86.8	..	..	..	..	..	41
149 Djibouti	46.7	64.6	66.6	84.0	32	32	11	..	79	..
150 Uganda	50.8	67.1	65.3	78.8	57	100	..	9	..	15

HDI rank		Adult literacy rate (% age 15 and above)		Youth literacy rate (% age 15-24)		Net primary enrolment ratio (%)		Net secondary enrolment ratio (%)		Children reaching grade 5 (%)	Tertiary students in science, math and engineering (as % of all tertiary students)
		1985	2000	1985	2000	1985-87 [a]	1998 [b]	1985-87 [a]	1998 [b]	1995-97 [a]	1994-97 [a]
151	Tanzania, U. Rep. of	56.2	75.1	77.4	90.6	54	48	..	4	81	39
152	Mauritania	31.9	40.2	37.9	48.9	33 [c]	60	..	..	64	..
153	Zambia	63.3	78.1	77.2	88.2	88	73	..	22	..	..
154	Senegal	24.5	37.3	34.9	50.7	49	59	12	..	85	..
155	Congo, Dem. Rep. of the	40.6	61.4	61.4	81.7	58	32	17	12	..	..
156	Côte d'Ivoire	27.7	46.8	42.9	65.0	..	59	..	..	75	..
157	Eritrea	41.9	55.7	55.9	70.2	..	34	..	19	70	..
158	Benin	22.0	37.4	33.9	53.1	51	..	13	16	..	18
159	Guinea	..	..	..	..	27	46	9	13	..	42
160	Gambia	20.5	36.6	35.2	57.1	62	61	14	23	..	..
161	Angola	..	..	..	..	..	57	..	..	..	..
162	Rwanda	46.5	66.8	65.9	83.3	62	91	..	..	..	..
163	Malawi	48.2	60.1	59.3	71.1	45	..	..	7	..	..
164	Mali	19.2	41.5	34.9	66.3	18	42	..	..	84	..
165	Central African Republic	27.8	46.7	45.1	67.2	48	53	..	..	..	..
166	Chad	21.8	42.6	39.0	66.6	37	55	..	7	59	14
167	Guinea-Bissau	22.7	38.5	38.0	58.2	45	..	..	..	..	..
168	Ethiopia	24.2	39.1	37.5	54.8	31	35	..	16	51	36
169	Burkina Faso	13.4	23.9	20.9	34.6	25	34	3	9	..	18
170	Mozambique	28.9	44.0	43.2	60.6	48	41	..	7	..	46
171	Burundi	32.3	48.0	45.5	63.9	50	38	3	..	..	..
172	Niger	9.6	15.9	14.2	23.0	25	26	..	6	73	..
173	Sierra Leone	..	..	..	..	..	..	..	..	..	..
Developing countries		62.7	73.7	78.4	84.6	..	..	..	..	..	..
Least developed countries		39.4	52.8	52.3	66.0	..	..	..	..	..	..
Arab States		45.8	62.0	63.1	79.1	..	..	..	..	..	..
East Asia and the Pacific		74.7	85.9	93.1	97.4	..	..	..	..	..	..
Latin America and the Caribbean		82.4	88.3	90.8	94.0	..	..	..	..	..	..
South Asia		43.7	55.6	57.4	69.8	..	..	..	..	..	..
Sub-Saharan Africa		44.4	61.5	61.7	77.7	..	..	..	..	..	..
Central and Eastern Europe and the CIS		98.5	99.3	99.6	99.8	..	..	..	..	..	..
OECD		..	..	..	..	..	..	..	..	..	..
High-income OECD		..	..	..	..	..	..	..	..	..	..
High human development		..	..	..	..	..	..	..	..	..	..
Medium human development		69.2	78.9	83.9	89.4	..	..	..	..	..	..
Low human development		34.5	49.7	48.8	65.5	..	..	..	..	..	..
High income		..	..	..	..	..	..	..	..	..	..
Middle income		77.1	86.0	91.5	95.6	..	..	..	..	..	..
Low income		50.8	62.4	64.0	75.4	..	..	..	..	..	..
World		..	..	..	..	..	..	..	..	..	..

a. Data refer to the most recent year available during the period specified. b. Enrolment ratios are based on the new International Standard Classification of Education, adopted in 1997 (UNESCO 1997a), and so may not be strictly comparable with those for earlier years. c. Data refer to 1984.
Source: Columns 1-4: UNESCO 2002a; columns 5-8: UNESCO 2002c; column 9: UNESCO 1999b; column 10: calculated on the basis of data on tertiary students from UNESCO (1999b).

. . . TO ACQUIRE KNOWLEDGE . . .

HDI rank		Telephone mainlines (per 1,000 people)		Cellular mobile subscribers (per 1,000 people)		Internet hosts (per 1,000 people)		Patents granted to residents (per million people)	Receipts of royalties and licence fees (US$ per person)	Research and development (R&D) expenditures (as % of GNP)	Scientists and engineers in R&D (per million people)
		1990	2000	1990	2000	1990	2000	1998	2000	1990-2000[a]	1990-2000[a]
High human development											
1	Norway	502	532	46	751	19.3	101.1	103	29.3	1.7	4,095
2	Sweden	681	682	54	717	16.4	67.3	271	144.2	3.8	4,507
3	Canada	565	677	22	285	12.7	77.4	31	44.7	1.7	3,009
4	Belgium	393	498	4	525	3.0	29.4	72	76.4	1.6	2,307
5	Australia	456	525	11	447	17.1	85.7	75	17.9	1.7	3,320
6	United States	545	700	21	398	23.0	295.2	289	134.3	2.5	4,103
7	Iceland	510	701	39	783	31.0	143.0	15	0.0	2.1	5,686
8	Netherlands	464	618	5	670	11.1	101.9	189	137.1	2.0	2,490
9	Japan	441	586	7	526	2.1	36.5	994	80.5	2.8	4,960
10	Finland	534	550	52	720	41.7	102.3	187	219.9	..	..
11	Switzerland	574	727	18	644	11.3	36.7	183	..	2.6	3,058
12	France	495	579	5	493	2.6	19.1	205	39.0	2.2	2,686
13	United Kingdom	441	589	19	727	7.5	28.2	82	123.9	1.8	2,678
14	Denmark	567	720	29	631	9.7	62.9	52	..	1.9	3,240
15	Austria	418	467	10	762	6.6	59.0	165	20.0	1.6	1,605
16	Luxembourg	478	750	2	861	4.6	27.1	202	307.0	..	..
17	Germany	441	611	4	586	5.8	24.8	235	34.4	2.3	2,873
18	Ireland	281	420	7	658	3.7	29.7	106	132.5	1.5	2,132
19	New Zealand	434	500	16	563	14.8	90.6	103	12.9	1.2	2,197
20	Italy	388	474	5	737	1.3	17.8	13	9.8	1.0	1,322
21	Spain	316	421	1	609	1.3	11.3	42	10.1	0.8	1,562
22	Israel	343	482	3	702	4.9	29.5	74	82.8	3.7	1,570
23	Hong Kong, China (SAR)	450	583	24	809	2.9	34.3	6	..	..	93
24	Greece	389	532	0	557	0.7	10.5	(.)	0.5	0.5	1,045
25	Singapore	349	484	17	684	6.6	45.2	8	..	1.1	2,182
26	Cyprus	419	647	5	321	0.6	11.9	..	..	0.2	369
27	Korea, Rep. of	310	464	2	567	0.6	8.5	779	14.7	2.7	2,139
28	Portugal	243	430	1	665	1.2	6.2	6	2.1	0.6	1,583
29	Slovenia	211	386	0	612	2.8	11.0	105	5.9	1.5	2,161
30	Malta	360	522	0	292	0.2	17.1	18	0.0 [b]	(.) [c]	96 [c]
31	Barbados	281	437	0	111 [b]	(.)	0.4	..	0.9	..	..
32	Brunei Darussalam	136	245	7	289	0.5	14.4	..	..	..	..
33	Czech Republic	158	378	0	424	2.1	15.4	28	4.3	1.3	1,317
34	Argentina	93	213	(.)	163	0.2	7.4	8	0.4	0.5	711
35	Hungary	96	372	(.)	302	1.5	10.4	26	11.2	0.7	1,249
36	Slovakia	135	314	0	205	0.5	7.0	24	3.0	1.0	1,706
37	Poland	86	282	0	174	0.6	8.8	30	0.9	0.7	1,460
38	Chile	66	221	1	222	0.6	4.9	..	6.7	0.6	370
39	Bahrain	192	250	10	300	0.2	1.7	..	..	..	..
40	Uruguay	134	278	0	132	0.2	16.3	2	0.0	..	..
41	Bahamas	274	376	8	104	1.0	0.1	..	..	..	..
42	Estonia	204	363	0	387	2.4	28.4	1	1.1	0.8	2,164
43	Costa Rica	101	249	0	52	0.5	1.9	..	0.3 [b]	0.1	533
44	Saint Kitts and Nevis	237	569	..	31	0.0	0.1	..	0.0	..	..
45	Kuwait	247	244	15	249	0.7	1.8	..	0.0	..	214
46	United Arab Emirates	206	391	17	548	0.2	14.3	..	..	..	..
47	Seychelles	124	235	0	320	0.0	0.1	..	..	..	..
48	Croatia	172	365 [b]	(.)	231	0.5	3.7	9	..	1.2	1,494
49	Lithuania	212	321	0	142	0.1	4.8	27	(.)	..	2,031
50	Trinidad and Tobago	141	231	0	103	(.)	5.1	..	..	0.1	145

HDI rank		Telephone mainlines (per 1,000 people)		Cellular mobile subscribers (per 1,000 people)		Internet hosts (per 1,000 people)		Patents granted to residents (per million people)	Receipts of royalties and licence fees (US$ per person)	Research and development (R&D) expenditures (as % of GNP)	Scientists and engineers in R&D (per million people)
		1990	2000	1990	2000	1990	2000	1998	2000	1990-2000 [a]	1990-2000 [a]
51	Qatar	190	268	8	202	0.0	0.1	..	..	..	..
52	Antigua and Barbuda	253	499	..	287	2.4	4.2	..	0.0	..	..
53	Latvia	234	303	0	166	0.5	10.7	71	1.0	0.4	1,090
Medium human development											
54	Mexico	65	125	1	142	0.1	5.7	1	0.4	0.4	213
55	Cuba	31	44	0	0	(.)	0.1	..	..	..	1,611
56	Belarus	153	269	0	5	(.)	0.2	50	0.1	0.6	2,296
57	Panama	93	151	0	145	0.1	5.4	..	0.0 [b]	..	..
58	Belize	92	149	0	70	(.)	1.2	..	..	..	..
59	Malaysia	89	199	5	213	0.2	3.1	..	0.0 [b]	0.4	154
60	Russian Federation	140	218	0	22	0.1	2.2	131	0.6	1.1	3,397
61	Dominica	164	294	0	16	0.0	2.4	..	0.4	..	..
62	Bulgaria	242	350	0	90	0.1	2.2	23	0.4	(.)	1,289
63	Romania	102	175	0	112	0.1	1.9	71	0.1	0.8	1,393
64	Libyan Arab Jamahiriya	48	108	0	7	0.0	(.)	..	..	..	361
65	Macedonia, TFYR	148	255	0	57	(.)	0.8	19	1.4	0.3	387
66	Saint Lucia	127	313	..	16	0.0	0.2	..	0.0	..	..
67	Mauritius	52	235	2	151	0.0	2.8	..	(.)	0.2 [c]	360
68	Colombia	69	169	0	53	0.1	1.1	1	0.1	..	..
69	Venezuela	76	108	(.)	217	0.1	0.7	..	0.0	0.3	194
70	Thailand	24	92	1	50	0.1	1.1	1	0.1	0.1	102
71	Saudi Arabia	77	137	1	64	(.)	0.2	(.)	0.0	..	..
72	Fiji	57	106	0	68	0.1	0.7	..	..	..	..
73	Brazil	65	182	(.)	136	0.1	5.2	2	0.7	0.8	168
74	Suriname	92	174	0	94	(.)	(.)	..	0.0 [b]	..	..
75	Lebanon	118	195	0	212	(.)	1.7	..	..	..	..
76	Armenia	157	152	0	5	(.)	0.8	8	..	0.2	1,308
77	Philippines	10	40	0	84	(.)	0.3	(.)	0.1	0.2	156
78	Oman	60	89	2	65	0.0	0.3	..	..	..	..
79	Kazakhstan	80	113	0	12	(.)	0.5	55	0.0	0.3	..
80	Ukraine	136	206	0	16	(.)	0.7	84	(.)	1.0	2,121
81	Georgia	99	139	0	34	(.)	0.3	67	..	..	..
82	Peru	26	67	(.)	50	(.)	0.4	..	0.0	(.) [c]	229
83	Grenada	177	332	2	46	0.0	(.)	..	0.0	..	..
84	Maldives	29	91	0	28	0.0	1.0	..	12.7	..	..
85	Turkey	121	280	0	246	0.1	1.1	(.)	..	0.5	303
86	Jamaica	45	199	0	142	0.1	0.6	..	2.5	..	..
87	Turkmenistan	60	82	0	2	0.0	0.3	10	..	..	..
88	Azerbaijan	86	104	0	56	(.)	0.2	..	..	..	2,735
89	Sri Lanka	7	40	(.)	23	(.)	0.1	..	..	..	188
90	Paraguay	27	50 [b]	0	149	0.0	0.2	..	36.9	..	..
91	St. Vincent & the Grenadines	124	220	0	21	0.0	(.)	..	0.0	..	..
92	Albania	12	39	0	8	(.)	0.1	..	..	..	..
93	Ecuador	48	100	0	38	(.)	(.)	..	..	..	140
94	Dominican Republic	48	105	(.)	82	(.)	0.9	..	..	..	..
95	Uzbekistan	69	67	0	2	(.)	(.)	25	..	..	1,754
96	China	6	112	(.)	66	(.)	0.1	1	0.1	0.1	459
97	Tunisia	38	90 [b]	(.)	6 [b]	(.)	(.)	..	0.9	0.3	124
98	Iran, Islamic Rep. of	40	149	0	15	(.)	(.)	1	0.0	0.5	590
99	Jordan	58	92	(.)	58	(.)	0.1	..	..	..	..
100	Cape Verde	24	126	0	45	0.0	0.1	..	..	..	..

11 Technology: diffusion and creation

		Telephone mainlines (per 1,000 people)		Cellular mobile subscribers (per 1,000 people)		Internet hosts (per 1,000 people)		Patents granted to residents (per million people)	Receipts of royalties and licence fees (US$ per person)	Research and development (R&D) expenditures (as % of GNP)	Scientists and engineers in R&D (per million people)
HDI rank		1990	2000	1990	2000	1990	2000	1998	2000	1990-2000 [a]	1990-2000 [a]
101	Samoa (Western)	26	47	0	17 [b]	0.0	14.2	..	..	..	..
102	Kyrgyzstan	72	77	0	2	0.0	0.4	14	0.1	0.2	574
103	Guyana	20	79	0	46	0.0	0.1	..	..	..	..
104	El Salvador	24	100	0	118	(.)	0.1	..	0.4	2.2	19
105	Moldova, Rep. of	106	133	0	32	(.)	0.4	42	0.2	0.8	334
106	Algeria	32	57	(.)	3	(.)	(.)	..	..	..	..
107	South Africa	93	114	(.)	190	1.2	4.4	..	1.4	0.6	992
108	Syrian Arab Republic	41	103	0	2	0.0	(.)	..	..	..	29
109	Viet Nam	1	32	0	10	0.0	(.)	..	..	..	274
110	Indonesia	6	31	(.)	17	(.)	0.1	..	..	0.1	..
111	Equatorial Guinea	4	13	0	..	0.0	0.0	..	..	..	..
112	Tajikistan	45	36	0	(.)	0.0	(.)	2	..	..	660
113	Mongolia	32	56	0	45	0.0	0.1	56	0.4 [b]	0.1	468
114	Bolivia	28	60	0	70	(.)	0.2	..	0.2	..	171
115	Egypt	30	86	(.)	21	(.)	(.)	(.)	0.9	1.9	493
116	Honduras	17	46	0	24	0.0	(.)	..	0.0	..	..
117	Gabon	22	32	0	98	0.0	(.)	..	..	..	..
118	Nicaragua	13	31	0	18	(.)	0.3	..	..	..	203 [c]
119	São Tomé and Principe	19	31	0	0	0.0	5.4	..	..	..	..
120	Guatemala	21	57	(.)	61	(.)	0.5	(.)	..	0.2 [c]	103 [c]
121	Solomon Islands	15	18	0	3	(.)	0.8	..	0.1 [b]	..	..
122	Namibia	39	63	0	47	(.)	1.9	..	..	..	..
123	Morocco	16	50	(.)	83	(.)	0.1	3	1.3	..	..
124	India	6	32	0	4	(.)	(.)	1	0.1	0.6	158
125	Swaziland	17	32	0	33	(.)	1.0	..	0.2	..	..
126	Botswana	21	93	0	123	(.)	1.5	1	(.) [b]	..	..
127	Myanmar	2	6	0	(.)	0.0	(.)	..	(.)	..	..
128	Zimbabwe	12	18	0	23	(.)	0.3	(.)	..	..	..
129	Ghana	3	12	0	6	(.)	(.)	(.)	..	..	..
130	Cambodia	(.)	2	0	10	0.0	(.)	..	..	..	..
131	Vanuatu	18	34	0	2	0.0	1.1	..	..	..	..
132	Lesotho	7	10	0	10	0.0	(.)	..	5.7	..	..
133	Papua New Guinea	8	13	0	2 [b]	0.0	0.1	..	..	..	..
134	Kenya	8	10	0	4	(.)	0.1	(.)	0.2	..	..
135	Cameroon	3	6 [b]	0	10	0.0	(.)	..	..	..	..
136	Congo	7	7	0	24	0.0	(.)	..	..	..	34
137	Comoros	8	10	0	0	0.0	0.1	..	..	..	..
Low human development											
138	Pakistan	8	22	(.)	2	(.)	(.)	..	(.) [b]	..	78
139	Sudan	2	12	0	1	0.0	0.0	..	0.0	..	..
140	Bhutan	4	20	0	0	0.0	1.2	..	..	..	..
141	Togo	3	9	0	11	0.0	(.)	..	0.0 [b]	8.4	102
142	Nepal	3	12	0	(.)	(.)	(.)	..	..	..	..
143	Lao People's Dem. Rep.	2	8	0	2	0.0	(.)	..	..	..	..
144	Yemen	11	19	0	2	0.0	(.)	..	..	..	..
145	Bangladesh	2	4	0	1	0.0	(.)	(.)	(.)	..	51
146	Haiti	7	9	0	3 [b]	0.0	(.)	..	..	..	..
147	Madagascar	2	3	0	4	0.0	(.)	..	(.)	0.2	12
148	Nigeria	3	4	0	(.)	0.0	(.)	..	..	0.1 [c]	15 [c]
149	Djibouti	11	15	0	(.)	0.0	(.)	..	..	..	..
150	Uganda	2	3	0	8	(.)	(.)	..	..	0.8	25

HDI rank	Telephone mainlines (per 1,000 people)		Cellular mobile subscribers (per 1,000 people)		Internet hosts (per 1,000 people)		Patents granted to residents (per million people)	Receipts of royalties and licence fees (US$ per person)	Research and development (R&D) expenditures (as % of GNP)	Scientists and engineers in R&D (per million people)
	1990	2000	1990	2000	1990	2000	1998	2000	1990-2000 [a]	1990-2000 [a]
151 Tanzania, U. Rep. of	3	5	0	5	0.0	(.)	..	(.)	..	..
152 Mauritania	3	7	0	3	0.0	(.)	..	..	..	..
153 Zambia	9	8	0	9	(.)	0.1	(.)	..	..	..
154 Senegal	6	22	0	26	(.)	0.2	..	0.2 [b]	..	2
155 Congo, Dem. Rep. of the	1	(.)	0	(.)	0.0	(.)	..	..	..	..
156 Côte d'Ivoire	6	18	0	30	(.)	(.)	..	(.)	..	..
157 Eritrea	..	8	..	0	0.0	(.)	..	..	..	..
158 Benin	3	8	0	9	0.0	0.0	..	..	..	174 [c]
159 Guinea	2	8	0	5	(.)	(.)	..	..	..	..
160 Gambia	7	26	0	4	0.0	(.)	1	..	..	..
161 Angola	8	5	0	2	0.0	(.)	..	0.2 [b]	..	..
162 Rwanda	2	2	0	5	0.0	0.1	..	0.0	..	..
163 Malawi	3	4	0	5	0.0	(.)	..	..	..	..
164 Mali	1	3	0	1	0.0	(.)	..	..	..	..
165 Central African Republic	2	3	0	1	0.0	(.)	..	..	(.)	47
166 Chad	1	1 [b]	0	1	0.0	(.)	..	..	..	..
167 Guinea-Bissau	6	9	0	0	0.0	(.)	..	..	..	..
168 Ethiopia	3	4	0	(.)	(.)	(.)	..	..	..	..
169 Burkina Faso	2	4	0	2	0.0	(.)	..	..	..	17
170 Mozambique	3	4	0	2	0.0	(.)	..	..	..	..
171 Burundi	2	3	0	2	0.0	0.0	..	0.0 [b]	0.3 [c]	21 [c]
172 Niger	1	2	0	(.)	0.0	(.)	..	..	..	..
173 Sierra Leone	3	4	0	2	0.0	(.)	..	..	..	..
Developing countries	21	78	(.)	52	(.)	0.7	..	1.0	..	..
Least developed countries	3	6	0	3	(.)	(.)	..	16.0	..	..
Arab States	35	77	(.)	38	(.)	0.2	..	106.0	..	..
East Asia and the Pacific	17	104	(.)	74	(.)	0.6	..	784.0	0.9	496
Latin America and the Caribbean	62	147	(.)	121	0.1	3.9	..	501.0	0.6	287
South Asia	7	33	(.)	4	(.)	(.)	..	86.0	..	158
Sub-Saharan Africa	11	15	(.)	19	0.1	0.4	..	81.0	..	..
Central and Eastern Europe and the CIS	124	210	(.)	69	0.3	3.0	78	325.0	0.9	2,544
OECD	392	524	10	459	8.5	92.0	266	70.0	2.2	2,973
High-income OECD	473	609	13	524	11.1	120.0	306	69.0	2.3	3,369
High human development	416	556	11	487	9.1	98.1	290	71.0	2.3	2,989
Medium human development	28	92	(.)	50	(.)	0.6	..	859.0	..	584
Low human development	4	8	(.)	3	(.)	(.)	..	1.0	..	..
High income	470	605	13	527	10.9	117.2	300	70.0	2.3	3,344
Middle income	45	139	(.)	92	0.1	1.5	..	1.0	..	818
Low income	10	27	(.)	5	(.)	0.1	..	105.0	..	..
World	99	163	2	121	1.7	17.8	..	72.0	..	..

a. Data refer to the most recent year available during the period specified. b. Data refer to 1999. c. Data refer to a year before 1990.

Source: Columns 1-6: ITU 2002; *column 7:* WIPO 2001; *columns 8-10:* World Bank 2002b; aggregates calculated for the Human Development Report Office by the World Bank.

... TO HAVE ACCESS TO THE RESOURCES NEEDED FOR A DECENT STANDARD OF LIVING ...

HDI rank	GDP US$ billions 2000	GDP PPP US$ billions 2000	GDP per capita (PPP US$) 2000	GDP per capita annual growth rate (%) 1975-2000	GDP per capita annual growth rate (%) 1990-2000	GDP per capita Highest value during 1975-2000 (PPP US$)	Year of highest value	Average annual change in consumer price index (%) 1990-2000	Average annual change in consumer price index (%) 1999-2000
High human development									
1 Norway	161.8	134.4	29,918	2.6	3.1	29,918	2000	2.2	3.1
2 Sweden	227.3	215.3	24,277	1.4	1.6	24,277	2000	1.9	1.0
3 Canada	687.9	856.1	27,840	1.5	1.9	27,840	2000	1.7	2.7
4 Belgium	226.6	278.6	27,178	1.9	1.8	27,178	2000	1.6	1.6
5 Australia	390.1	492.8	25,693	1.9	2.9	25,693	2000	2.1	4.5
6 United States	9,837.4	9,612.7 [a]	34,142	2.0	2.2	34,142	2000	2.7	3.4
7 Iceland	8.5	8.3	29,581	1.7	1.8	29,581	2000	2.7	5.2
8 Netherlands	364.8	408.4	25,657	1.8	2.2	25,657	2000	2.4	2.5
9 Japan	4,841.6	3,394.4	26,755	2.7	1.1	26,755	2000	0.7	-0.7
10 Finland	121.5	129.4	24,996	2.0	2.4	24,996	2000	1.5	3.4
11 Switzerland	239.8	206.6	28,769	1.0	0.2	28,769	2000	1.6	1.6
12 France	1,294.2	1,426.6	24,223	1.7	1.3	24,223	2000	1.6	1.7
13 United Kingdom	1,414.6	1,404.4	23,509	2.0	2.2	23,509	2000	2.9	2.9
14 Denmark	162.3	147.4	27,627	1.6	2.1	27,627	2000	2.1	2.9
15 Austria	189.0	217.1	26,765	2.0	1.7	26,765	2000	2.2	2.4
16 Luxembourg	18.9	21.9	50,061	3.9	4.1	50,061	2000	2.0	3.1
17 Germany	1,873.0	2,062.2	25,103	1.9	1.2	25,103	2000	2.2	1.9
18 Ireland	93.9	113.3	29,866	4.0	6.5	29,866	2000	2.3	5.6
19 New Zealand	49.9	76.9	20,070	0.8	1.8	20,070	2000	1.8	2.6
20 Italy	1,074.0	1,363.0	23,626	2.1	1.4	23,626	2000	3.7	2.5
21 Spain	558.6	768.5	19,472	2.2	2.3	19,472	2000	3.8	3.4
22 Israel	110.4	125.5	20,131	2.0	2.2	20,131	2000	9.7	1.1
23 Hong Kong, China (SAR)	162.6	171.0	25,153	4.6	1.9	25,153	2000	5.8	-3.7
24 Greece	112.6	174.3	16,501	0.9	1.8	16,501	2000	9.0	3.2
25 Singapore	92.3	93.8	23,356	5.2	4.7	23,356	2000	1.7	1.4
26 Cyprus	8.7	15.8	20,824	4.8	3.1	20,824	2000	3.7	4.1
27 Korea, Rep. of	457.2	821.7	17,380	6.2	4.7	17,380	2000	5.1	2.3
28 Portugal	105.1	173.0	17,290	2.9	2.5	17,290	2000	4.5	2.9
29 Slovenia	18.1	34.5	17,367	..	2.8	17,367 [b]	2000	24.6 [b]	10.8
30 Malta	3.6	6.7	17,273	4.6	4.0	17,273	2000	3.0	2.4
31 Barbados	2.6	4.1	15,494	1.3	1.7	15,494	2000	2.5	2.4
32 Brunei Darussalam	4.8 [c]	5.4 [c]	16,779 [c]	-2.2 [b]	-0.7 [b]	..	..	..	..
33 Czech Republic	50.8	143.7	13,991	..	1.0	13,991 [b]	2000	7.8 [b]	3.9
34 Argentina	285.0	458.3	12,377	0.4	3.0	13,204	1998	8.9	-0.9
35 Hungary	45.6	124.4	12,416	0.9	1.9	12,416	2000	20.3	9.8
36 Slovakia	19.1	60.7	11,243	-0.1 [b]	1.9	11,243 [b]	2000	8.4 [b]	12.0
37 Poland	157.7	349.8	9,051	..	4.5	9,051 [b]	2000	25.3	10.1
38 Chile	70.5	143.2	9,417	4.1	5.2	9,417	2000	8.9	3.8
39 Bahrain	8.0	10.1 [d]	15,084 [d]	0.9 [b]	1.7 [b]	..	..	1.2 [b]	..
40 Uruguay	19.7	30.1	9,035	1.4	2.6	9,557	1998	33.9	4.8
41 Bahamas	4.8	5.2	17,012	1.5	0.1	17,103	1989	2.1	1.6
42 Estonia	5.0	13.8	10,066	-0.9 [b]	1.0	10,982 [b]	1989	21.6 [b]	4.0
43 Costa Rica	15.9	33.0	8,650	1.1	3.0	8,691	1999	15.6	11.0
44 Saint Kitts and Nevis	0.3	0.5	12,510	5.7 [b]	4.7	12,510 [b]	2000	3.4 [b]	..
45 Kuwait	37.8	31.4	15,799	-0.9 [b]	-1.4 [b]	25,382 [b]	1979	2.0	1.8
46 United Arab Emirates	46.5 [c]	48.9 [c]	17,935 [c]	-3.7 [b]	-1.6 [b]	..	..	..	..
47 Seychelles	0.6	..	..	2.8	1.1	..	..	1.7	6.3
48 Croatia	19.0	35.4	8,091	..	1.8	8,551 [b]	1990	86.3	5.4
49 Lithuania	11.3	26.3	7,106	-3.1 [b]	-2.9	10,320 [b]	1990	32.6 [b]	1.0
50 Trinidad and Tobago	7.3	11.7	8,964	0.5	2.3	9,005	1982	5.7	3.6

		GDP		GDP per capita (PPP US$)	GDP per capita annual growth rate (%)		GDP per capita Highest value during 1975-2000 (PPP US$)	Year of highest value	Average annual change in consumer price index (%)	
HDI rank		US$ billions 2000	PPP US$ billions 2000	2000	1975-2000	1990-2000	2000		1990-2000	1999-2000
51	Qatar	14.5	..	..	..	..	..	..	2.7	-1.0
52	Antigua and Barbuda	0.7	0.7	10,541	4.6 [b]	2.8	10,541 [b]	2000	..	..
53	Latvia	7.2	16.7	7,045	-0.9	-2.3	10,121	1989	29.2 [b]	2.7
Medium human development										
54	Mexico	574.5	884.0	9,023	0.9	1.4	9,023	2000	19.4	9.5
55	Cuba	..	..	..	..	3.7 [b]	..	..	..	..
56	Belarus	29.9	75.5	7,544	-1.8 [b]	-1.4	8,486 [b]	1989	336.7 [b]	168.6
57	Panama	9.9	17.1	6,000	0.8	2.3	6,000	2000	1.1	1.4
58	Belize	0.8	1.3	5,606	2.9	1.6	5,606	2000	2.0	0.6
59	Malaysia	89.7	211.0	9,068	4.1	4.4	9,151	1997	3.6	1.5
60	Russian Federation	251.1	1,219.4	8,377	-1.2	-4.6	12,947	1989	99.1 [b]	20.8
61	Dominica	0.3	0.4	5,880	..	..	..	..	1.8	0.8
62	Bulgaria	12.0	46.6	5,710	0.2 [b]	-1.5	7,200 [b]	1988	117.5	10.3
63	Romania	36.7	144.1	6,423	-0.5	-0.4	9,073	1986	100.5	45.7
64	Libyan Arab Jamahiriya	..	..	..	-6.7 [b]	..	..	..	..	..
65	Macedonia, TFYR	3.6	10.3	5,086	..	-1.5	5,965 [b]	1990	13.0 [b]	..
66	Saint Lucia	0.7	0.9	5,703	4.4 [b]	0.9	5,703 [b]	2000	2.9 [b]	..
67	Mauritius	4.4	11.9	10,017	4.1	4.0	10,017	2000	6.9	4.2
68	Colombia	81.3	264.3	6,248	1.6	1.1	6,653	1997	20.6	9.5
69	Venezuela	120.5	140.0	5,794	-0.9	-0.6	7,845	1977	20.9	-98.8
70	Thailand	122.2	388.8	6,402	5.5	3.3	6,896	1996	4.9	1.5
71	Saudi Arabia	173.3	235.6	11,367	-2.2	-1.2	19,525	1980	1.0	-0.9
72	Fiji	1.5	3.8	4,668	0.7	0.7	5,143	1999	3.3	1.1
73	Brazil	595.5	1,299.4	7,625	0.8	1.5	7,625	2000	199.5	7.0
74	Suriname	0.8	1.6	3,799	-0.1	3.0	4,298	1998	88.0 [b]	..
75	Lebanon	16.5	18.6	4,308	..	4.2	4,385 [b]	1998	..	..
76	Armenia	1.9	9.7	2,559	..	-2.5	4,044 [b]	1990	72.0 [b]	-0.8
77	Philippines	74.7	300.1	3,971	0.1	1.1	4,072	1982	8.2	4.4
78	Oman	15.0 [c]	..	..	2.8 [b]	0.3 [b]	..	..	0.1	-1.1
79	Kazakhstan	18.2	87.3	5,871	..	-3.1	8,127 [b]	1989	67.8 [b]	13.2
80	Ukraine	31.8	188.9	3,816	-8.4 [b]	-8.8	8,977 [b]	1989	200.4 [b]	..
81	Georgia	3.0	13.4	2,664	-7.6	-12.4	14,328	1985	24.7 [b]	4.1
82	Peru	53.5	123.2	4,799	-0.7	2.9	5,442	1981	27.3	3.8
83	Grenada	0.4	0.7	7,580	3.9 [b]	2.9	7,580 [b]	2000	2.3 [b]	..
84	Maldives	0.6	1.2	4,485	5.8 [b]	5.4	4,485 [b]	2000	7.1	-1.1
85	Turkey	199.9	455.3	6,974	2.1	2.1	7,063	1998	79.9	54.9
86	Jamaica	7.4	9.6	3,639	0.5	-0.4	3,981	1975	23.5	8.2
87	Turkmenistan	4.4	20.6	3,956	-7.9 [b]	-8.0	8,049 [b]	1988	..	..
88	Azerbaijan	5.3	23.6	2,936	-9.6 [b]	-7.3	8,435 [b]	1986	170.8 [b]	1.8
89	Sri Lanka	16.3	68.3	3,530	3.2	3.9	3,530	2000	9.9	6.2
90	Paraguay	7.5	24.3	4,426	0.7	-0.4	5,149	1981	13.1	9.0
91	St. Vincent & the Grenadines	0.3	0.6	5,555	3.9 [b]	2.6	5,555 [b]	2000	2.3	0.2
92	Albania	3.8	12.0	3,506	-1.3 [b]	2.7	3,710 [b]	1982	27.8 [b]	(.)
93	Ecuador	13.6	40.5	3,203	0.2	-0.3	3,561	1997	37.1	96.1
94	Dominican Republic	19.7	50.5	6,033	1.7	4.2	6,033	2000	8.7	7.7
95	Uzbekistan	7.7	60.4	2,441	-2.6 [b]	-2.4	3,091 [b]	1989	..	..
96	China	1,080.0	5,019.4	3,976	8.1	9.2	3,976	2000	8.6	0.3
97	Tunisia	19.5	60.8	6,363	2.0	3.0	6,363	2000	4.4	2.9
98	Iran, Islamic Rep. of	104.9	374.6	5,884	-0.7	1.9	7,959	1976	26.0	14.5
99	Jordan	8.3	19.4	3,966	0.4	1.0	4,881	1986	3.5	0.7
100	Cape Verde	0.6	2.1	4,863	3.0 [b]	3.3	4,863 [b]	2000	6.0 [b]	..

		GDP		GDP per capita (PPP US$)	GDP per capita annual growth rate (%)		GDP per capita Highest value during 1975-2000 (PPP US$)	Year of highest value	Average annual change in consumer price index (%)	
HDI rank		US$ billions 2000	PPP US$ billions 2000	2000	1975-2000	1990-2000			1990-2000	1999-2000
101	Samoa (Western)	0.2	0.9	5,041	0.4 b	1.9	5,041 b	2000	3.8	1.0
102	Kyrgyzstan	1.3	13.3	2,711	-4.7 b	-5.1	4,570 b	1990	23.1 b	18.7
103	Guyana	0.7	3.0	3,963	0.3	5.0	4,016	1999	6.3 b	6.1
104	El Salvador	13.2	28.2	4,497	-0.1	2.6	5,018	1978	8.5	2.3
105	Moldova, Rep. of	1.3	9.0	2,109	-5.7 b	-9.5	6,030 b	1989	18.9 b	31.3
106	Algeria	53.3	161.3	5,308	-0.3	-0.1	5,997	1985	19.5 b	..
107	South Africa	125.9	402.4	9,401	-0.7	(.)	11,484	1981	8.7	5.3
108	Syrian Arab Republic	17.0	57.6	3,556	1.0	2.8	3,714	1998	6.7	-0.5
109	Viet Nam	31.3	156.8	1,996	4.8 b	6.0	1,996 b	2000	4.1 b	-1.7
110	Indonesia	153.3	640.3	3,043	4.4	2.5	3,481	1997	13.7	3.7
111	Equatorial Guinea	1.3	6.9	15,073	10.4 b	18.9	15,073 b	2000	..	..
112	Tajikistan	1.0	7.1	1,152	-10.8 b	-11.8	3,999 b	1988	..	..
113	Mongolia	1.0	4.3	1,783	-0.4 b	-0.3	2,127 b	1989	53.7 b	..
114	Bolivia	8.3	20.2	2,424	-0.5	1.6	2,721	1978	8.7	4.6
115	Egypt	98.7	232.5	3,635	2.9	2.5	3,635	2000	8.8	2.7
116	Honduras	5.9	15.7	2,453	0.1	0.4	2,601	1979	17.3	-15.1
117	Gabon	4.9	7.7	6,237	-1.5	0.1	12,112	1976	5.7 b	..
118	Nicaragua	2.4	12.0	2,366	-3.5	0.6	5,284	1977	35.1 b	..
119	São Tomé and Principe	(.)	..	..	-0.9 b	-0.8	..	..	..	..
120	Guatemala	19.0	43.5	3,821	(.)	1.4	3,917	1980	10.1	6.0
121	Solomon Islands	0.3	0.7	1,648	2.2	-1.0	2,226	1996	10.8 b	..
122	Namibia	3.5	11.3	6,431	-0.1 b	1.8	6,596 b	1980	9.9 b	..
123	Morocco	33.3	101.8	3,546	1.3	0.6	3,632	1998	3.8	1.9
124	India	457.0	2,395.4	2,358	3.2	4.1	2,358	2000	9.1	4.0
125	Swaziland	1.5	4.7	4,492	1.9	0.2	4,492	2000	9.4	12.2
126	Botswana	5.3	11.5	7,184	5.1	2.3	7,184	2000	10.4	8.6
127	Myanmar	..	..	..	1.3 b	4.8 b	..	..	25.9	-0.1
128	Zimbabwe	7.4	33.3	2,635	0.3	0.4	2,898	1998	27.0 b	..
129	Ghana	5.2	37.9	1,964	0.1	1.8	1,989	1978	28.4	25.2
130	Cambodia	3.2	17.4	1,446	1.9 b	2.0	1,446 b	2000	6.3 b	-0.8
131	Vanuatu	0.2	0.6	2,802	0.1 b	-0.9	3,189 b	1991	2.8 b	..
132	Lesotho	0.9	4.1	2,031	2.6	2.1	2,101	1997	9.8 b	6.1
133	Papua New Guinea	3.8	11.7	2,280	0.5	1.4	2,666	1994	9.3	15.6
134	Kenya	10.4	30.8	1,022	0.4	-0.5	1,115	1990	15.1	5.9
135	Cameroon	8.9	25.3	1,703	-0.6	-0.8	2,574	1986	6.5	1.2
136	Congo	3.2	2.5	825	(.)	-3.4	1,326	1984	9.2 b	-0.9
137	Comoros	0.2	0.9	1,588	-1.4 b	-2.4	2,147 b	1984	..	..
Low human development										
138	Pakistan	61.6	266.2	1,928	2.8	1.2	1,928	2000	9.7	4.4
139	Sudan	11.5	55.9	1,797	0.6	5.6	1,797	2000	81.1 b	..
140	Bhutan	0.5	1.1	1,412	4.0 b	3.4	1,412 b	2000	9.6 b	..
141	Togo	1.2	6.5	1,442	-1.2	-0.4	2,059	1980	8.5	1.9
142	Nepal	5.5	30.6	1,327	2.1	2.4	1,327	2000	8.6	1.5
143	Lao People's Dem. Rep.	1.7	8.3	1,575	3.2 b	3.9	1,575 b	2000	28.2	25.1
144	Yemen	8.5	15.6	893	..	2.3	893 b	2000	32.6 b	..
145	Bangladesh	47.1	209.9	1,602	2.2	3.0	1,602	2000	5.5	2.4
146	Haiti	4.0	11.7	1,467	-2.0	-2.7	2,423	1980	21.9	13.7
147	Madagascar	3.9	13.0	840	-1.7	-0.9	1,246	1975	18.7	12.0
148	Nigeria	41.1	113.7	896	-0.7	-0.4	1,160	1977	32.5	6.9
149	Djibouti	0.6	..	..	-5.0 b	-3.9	..	..	..	..
150	Uganda	6.2	26.8	1,208	2.5 b	3.8	1,208 b	2000	10.5	2.8

HDI rank	GDP US$ billions 2000	GDP PPP US$ billions 2000	GDP per capita (PPP US$) 2000	GDP per capita annual growth rate (%) 1975-2000	GDP per capita annual growth rate (%) 1990-2000	GDP per capita Highest value during 1975-2000 (PPP US$)	Year of highest value	Average annual change in consumer price index (%) 1990-2000	Average annual change in consumer price index (%) 1999-2000
151 Tanzania, U. Rep. of	9.0	17.6	523	..	0.1	523 [b]	2000	20.9	5.9
152 Mauritania	0.9	4.5	1,677	-0.1	1.2	1,715	1976	6.1	3.3
153 Zambia	2.9	7.9	780	-2.3	-2.1	1,389	1976	80.8 [b]	..
154 Senegal	4.4	14.4	1,510	-0.2	0.9	1,584	1976	5.4	0.7
155 Congo, Dem. Rep. of the	5.6 [c]	36.9 [c]	765 [c]	-4.7 [b]	-8.2 [b]	..	..	2,089.0 [b]	..
156 Côte d'Ivoire	9.4	26.1	1,630	-2.1	0.4	2,717	1978	7.2	2.5
157 Eritrea	0.6	3.4	837	..	1.1 [b]	..	..	..	..
158 Benin	2.2	6.2	990	0.5	1.8	990	2000	8.7 [b]	4.2
159 Guinea	3.0	14.7	1,982	1.4 [b]	1.7	1,987 [b]	1999	..	..
160 Gambia	0.4	2.1	1,649	-0.3	-0.3	1,744	1984	4.0	0.8
161 Angola	8.8	28.7	2,187	-1.9 [b]	-1.8	3,016 [b]	1980	708.7	325.0
162 Rwanda	1.8	8.0	943	-1.3	-2.1	1,298	1983	16.2 [b]	3.9
163 Malawi	1.7	6.3	615	0.2	1.8	618	1999	33.8	29.5
164 Mali	2.3	8.6	797	-0.5	1.3	904	1979	5.2	-0.7
165 Central African Republic	1.0	4.4	1,172	-1.6	-0.5	1,646	1977	5.9 [b]	..
166 Chad	1.4	6.7	871	(.)	-0.8	1,025	1977	8.1	3.8
167 Guinea-Bissau	0.2	0.9	755	0.4	-1.1	965	1997	34.0	8.6
168 Ethiopia	6.4	43.0	668	-0.1 [b]	2.4	696 [b]	1983	5.3	(.)
169 Burkina Faso	2.2	11.0	976	1.4	2.4	980	1999	5.5	-0.3
170 Mozambique	3.8	15.1	854	1.5 [b]	3.9	860 [b]	1999	34.9 [b]	..
171 Burundi	0.7	4.0	591	-0.7	-4.7	886	1991	16.1	24.3
172 Niger	1.8	8.1	746	-2.1	-1.0	1,267	1979	6.1	2.9
173 Sierra Leone	0.6	2.5	490	-2.6	-6.5	1,002	1982	29.3	-0.8
Developing countries	6,059.4 T	17,438.0 T	3,783	2.3	3.1	..	..	..	..
Least developed countries	178.5 T	669.4 T	1,216	0.3	1.3	..	..	..	..
Arab States	603.5 T	1,049.5 T	4,793	0.3	0.7	..	..	..	..
East Asia and the Pacific	2,296.3 T	7,855.9 T	4,290	5.9	5.7	..	..	..	..
Latin America and the Caribbean	1,961.2 T	3,679.7 T	7,234	0.7	1.7	..	..	..	..
South Asia	693.5 T	3,347.3 T	2,404	2.4	3.3	..	..	..	..
Sub-Saharan Africa	307.6 T	1,034.4 T	1,690	-0.9	-0.3	..	..	..	..
Central and Eastern Europe and the CIS	746.8 T	2,746.7 T	6,930	..	-2.4	..	..	..	..
OECD	25,558.2 T	26,525.3 T	23,569	2.0	1.7	..	..	..	..
High-income OECD	24,053.3 T	23,685.6 T	27,848	2.1	1.7	..	..	..	..
High human development	25,744.2 T	26,508.0 T	24,973	2.1	1.8	..	..	..	..
Medium human development	4,960.5 T	16,453.9 T	4,141	1.6	1.9	..	..	..	..
Low human development	264.8 T	1,040.5 T	1,251	0.5	1.0	..	..	..	..
High income	24,563.2 T	24,227.8 T	27,639	2.1	1.7	..	..	..	..
Middle income	5,390.3 T	15,047.0 T	5,734	1.8	2.4	..	..	..	..
Low income	1,017.2 T	4,727.7 T	2,002	1.5	1.2	..	..	..	..
World	30,971.1 T	44,002.4 T	7,446	1.2	1.2	..	..	..	..

a. In theory, for the United States the value of GDP in PPP US dollars should be the same as that in US dollars, but practical issues arising in the calculation of the PPP US dollar GDP prevent this. b. Data refer to a period shorter than that specified. c. Data refer to 1998. d. Data refer to 1999.

Source: Columns 1-3: World Bank 2002b; aggregates calculated for the Human Development Report Office by the World Bank; *columns 4 and 5:* World Bank 2002a; aggregates calculated for the Human Development Report Office by the World Bank; *columns 6 and 7:* calculated on the basis of data on GDP at market prices (constant 1995 US$), population and GDP per capita (PPP US$) from World Bank (2002b); *column 8:* calculated for the Human Development Report Office by the World Bank on the basis of data on the consumer price index from World Bank (2002b); *column 9:* calculated on the basis of data on the consumer price index from World Bank (2002b).

13 Inequality in income or consumption

			Share of income or consumption (%) [a]				Inequality measures		
HDI rank		Survey year	Poorest 10%	Poorest 20%	Richest 20%	Richest 10%	Richest 10% to poorest 10% [b]	Richest 20% to poorest 20% [b]	Gini index [c]
High human development									
1	Norway	1995 [d]	4.1	9.7	35.8	21.8	5.3	3.7	25.8
2	Sweden	1992 [d]	3.7	9.6	34.5	20.1	5.4	3.6	25.0
3	Canada	1994 [d]	2.8	7.5	39.3	23.8	8.5	5.2	31.5
4	Belgium	1996 [d]	3.2	8.3	37.3	23.0	7.3	4.5	28.7
5	Australia	1994 [d]	2.0	5.9	41.3	25.4	12.5	7.0	35.2
6	United States	1997 [d]	1.8	5.2	46.4	30.5	16.6	9.0	40.8
7	Iceland	..	..	..	..	..	..	..	..
8	Netherlands	1994 [d]	2.8	7.2	40.1	25.1	9.0	5.5	32.6
9	Japan	1993 [d]	4.8	10.6	35.6	21.7	4.5	3.4	24.8
10	Finland	1991 [d]	4.2	10.0	35.8	21.6	5.1	3.6	25.6
11	Switzerland	1992 [d]	2.6	6.9	40.3	25.2	9.9	5.8	33.1
12	France	1995 [d]	2.8	7.2	40.2	25.1	9.1	5.6	32.7
13	United Kingdom	1995 [d]	2.2	6.1	43.2	27.7	12.3	7.1	36.8
14	Denmark	1992 [d]	3.6	9.6	34.5	20.5	5.7	3.6	24.7
15	Austria	1995 [d]	2.5	6.9	38.0	22.5	9.1	5.5	31.0
16	Luxembourg	1994 [d]	4.0	9.4	36.5	22.0	5.4	3.9	26.9
17	Germany	1994 [d]	3.3	8.2	38.5	23.7	7.1	4.7	30.0
18	Ireland	1987 [d]	2.5	6.7	42.9	27.4	11.0	6.4	35.9
19	New Zealand	..	..	..	..	..	..	..	..
20	Italy	1995 [d]	3.5	8.7	36.3	21.8	6.2	4.2	27.3
21	Spain	1990 [d]	2.8	7.5	40.3	25.2	9.0	5.4	32.5
22	Israel	1997 [d]	2.4	6.1	44.2	28.3	11.6	7.3	38.1
23	Hong Kong, China (SAR)	..	..	..	..	..	..	..	..
24	Greece	1993 [d]	3.0	7.5	40.3	25.3	8.5	5.3	32.7
25	Singapore	..	..	..	..	..	..	..	..
26	Cyprus	..	..	..	..	..	..	..	..
27	Korea, Rep. of	1993 [e]	2.9	7.5	39.3	24.3	8.4	5.3	31.6
28	Portugal	1994-95 [d]	3.1	7.3	43.4	28.4	9.3	5.9	35.6
29	Slovenia	1998 [d]	3.9	9.1	37.7	23.0	5.8	4.1	28.4
30	Malta	..	..	..	..	..	..	..	..
31	Barbados	..	..	..	..	..	..	..	..
32	Brunei Darussalam	..	..	..	..	..	..	..	..
33	Czech Republic	1996 [d]	4.3	10.3	35.9	22.4	5.2	3.5	25.4
34	Argentina	..	..	..	..	..	..	..	..
35	Hungary	1998 [e]	4.1	10.0	34.4	20.5	5.0	3.5	24.4
36	Slovakia	1992 [d]	5.1	11.9	31.4	18.2	3.6	2.6	19.5
37	Poland	1998 [e]	3.2	7.8	39.7	24.7	7.8	5.1	31.6
38	Chile	1998 [d]	1.3	3.3	61.0	45.6	35.6	18.6	56.6
39	Bahrain	..	..	..	..	..	..	..	..
40	Uruguay	1989 [d]	2.1	5.4	48.3	32.7	15.4	8.9	42.3
41	Bahamas	..	..	..	..	..	..	..	..
42	Estonia	1998 [d]	3.0	7.0	45.1	29.8	10.0	6.5	37.6
43	Costa Rica	1997 [d]	1.7	4.4	51.0	34.6	20.7	11.5	45.9
44	Saint Kitts and Nevis	..	..	..	..	..	..	..	..
45	Kuwait	..	..	..	..	..	..	..	..
46	United Arab Emirates	..	..	..	..	..	..	..	..
47	Seychelles	..	..	..	..	..	..	..	..
48	Croatia	1998 [d]	3.7	8.8	38.0	23.3	6.3	4.3	29.0
49	Lithuania	1996 [e]	3.1	7.8	40.3	25.6	8.3	5.2	32.4
50	Trinidad and Tobago	1992 [d]	2.1	5.5	45.9	29.9	14.4	8.3	40.3

| HDI rank | Survey year | Share of income or consumption (%) [a] | | | | Inequality measures | | |
		Poorest 10%	Poorest 20%	Richest 20%	Richest 10%	Richest 10% to poorest 10% [b]	Richest 20% to poorest 20% [b]	Gini index [c]
51 Qatar	..	..	..	..	..	..	..	..
52 Antigua and Barbuda	..	..	..	..	..	..	..	..
53 Latvia	1998 [d]	2.9	7.6	40.3	25.9	8.9	5.3	32.4
Medium human development								
54 Mexico	1998 [d]	1.3	3.5	57.4	41.7	32.6	16.5	53.1
55 Cuba	..	..	..	..	..	..	..	..
56 Belarus	1998 [e]	5.1	11.4	33.3	20.0	3.9	2.9	21.7
57 Panama	1997 [e]	1.2	3.6	52.8	35.6	29.0	14.8	48.5
58 Belize	..	..	..	..	..	..	..	..
59 Malaysia	1997 [d]	1.7	4.4	54.3	38.4	22.1	12.4	49.2
60 Russian Federation	1998 [e]	1.7	4.4	53.7	38.7	23.3	12.2	48.7
61 Dominica	..	..	..	..	..	..	..	..
62 Bulgaria	1997 [d]	4.5	10.1	36.8	22.8	5.0	3.6	26.4
63 Romania	1998 [e]	3.2	8.0	39.4	25.0	7.8	4.9	31.1
64 Libyan Arab Jamahiriya	..	..	..	..	..	..	..	..
65 Macedonia, TFYR	..	..	..	..	..	..	..	..
66 Saint Lucia	1995 [d]	2.0	5.2	48.3	32.5	16.2	9.2	42.6
67 Mauritius	..	..	..	..	..	..	..	..
68 Colombia	1996 [d]	1.1	3.0	60.9	46.1	42.7	20.3	57.1
69 Venezuela	1998 [d]	0.8	3.0	53.2	36.5	44.0	17.7	49.5
70 Thailand	1998 [e]	2.8	6.4	48.4	32.4	11.6	7.6	41.4
71 Saudi Arabia	..	..	..	..	..	..	..	..
72 Fiji	..	..	..	..	..	..	..	..
73 Brazil	1998 [d]	0.7	2.2	64.1	48.0	65.8	29.7	60.7
74 Suriname	..	..	..	..	..	..	..	..
75 Lebanon	..	..	..	..	..	..	..	..
76 Armenia	1996 [e]	2.3	5.5	50.6	35.2	15.3	9.2	44.4
77 Philippines	1997 [e]	2.3	5.4	52.3	36.6	16.1	9.8	46.2
78 Oman	..	..	..	..	..	..	..	..
79 Kazakhstan	1996 [e]	2.7	6.7	42.3	26.3	9.8	6.3	35.4
80 Ukraine	1999 [e]	3.6	8.8	37.8	23.2	6.4	4.3	29.0
81 Georgia	1996 [d]	2.3	6.1	43.6	27.9	12.0	7.1	37.1
82 Peru	1996 [d]	1.6	4.4	51.2	35.4	22.3	11.7	46.2
83 Grenada	..	..	..	..	..	..	..	..
84 Maldives	..	..	..	..	..	..	..	..
85 Turkey	1994 [e]	2.3	5.8	47.7	32.3	14.2	8.2	41.5
86 Jamaica	2000 [e]	2.7	6.7	46.0	30.3	11.2	6.9	37.9
87 Turkmenistan	1998 [e]	2.6	6.1	47.5	31.7	12.3	7.7	40.8
88 Azerbaijan	1995 [d]	2.8	6.9	43.3	27.8	9.8	6.3	36.0
89 Sri Lanka	1995 [e]	3.5	8.0	42.8	28.0	7.9	5.3	34.4
90 Paraguay	1998 [d]	0.5	1.9	60.7	43.8	91.1	31.8	57.7
91 St. Vincent & the Grenadines	..	..	..	..	..	..	..	..
92 Albania	..	..	..	..	..	..	..	..
93 Ecuador	1995 [e]	2.2	5.4	49.7	33.8	15.4	9.2	43.7
94 Dominican Republic	1998 [d]	2.1	5.1	53.3	37.8	17.7	10.5	47.4
95 Uzbekistan	1998 [e]	1.2	4.0	49.1	32.8	26.9	12.4	44.6
96 China	1998 [d]	2.4	5.9	46.6	30.4	12.7	8.0	40.3
97 Tunisia	1995 [e]	2.3	5.7	47.9	31.8	13.8	8.5	41.7
98 Iran, Islamic Rep. of	..	..	..	..	..	..	..	..
99 Jordan	1997 [e]	3.3	7.6	44.4	29.8	9.1	5.9	36.4
100 Cape Verde	..	..	..	..	..	..	..	..

		Share of income or consumption (%) [a]				Inequality measures		
HDI rank	Survey year	Poorest 10%	Poorest 20%	Richest 20%	Richest 10%	Richest 10% to poorest 10% [b]	Richest 20% to poorest 20% [b]	Gini index [c]
101 Samoa (Western)	..	..	..	..	..	..	..	..
102 Kyrgyzstan	1999 [e]	3.2	7.6	42.5	27.2	8.4	5.6	34.6
103 Guyana	1993 [e]	2.4	6.3	46.9	32.0	13.3	7.4	40.2
104 El Salvador	1998 [d]	1.2	3.3	56.4	39.5	33.5	17.2	52.2
105 Moldova, Rep. of	1997 [d]	2.2	5.6	46.8	30.7	13.7	8.3	40.6
106 Algeria	1995 [e]	2.8	7.0	42.6	26.8	9.6	6.1	35.3
107 South Africa	1993-94 [e]	1.1	2.9	64.8	45.9	42.5	22.6	59.3
108 Syrian Arab Republic	..	..	..	..	..	..	..	..
109 Viet Nam	1998 [e]	3.6	8.0	44.5	29.9	8.4	5.6	36.1
110 Indonesia	1999 [e]	4.0	9.0	41.1	26.7	6.6	4.6	31.7
111 Equatorial Guinea	..	..	..	..	..	..	..	..
112 Tajikistan	1998 [e]	3.2	8.0	40.0	25.2	7.9	5.0	34.7
113 Mongolia	1995 [e]	2.9	7.3	40.9	24.5	8.4	5.6	33.2
114 Bolivia	1999 [e]	1.3	4.0	49.1	32.0	24.2	12.4	44.7
115 Egypt	1995 [e]	4.4	9.8	39.0	25.0	5.7	4.0	28.9
116 Honduras	1998 [d]	0.6	2.2	59.4	42.7	72.3	27.4	56.3
117 Gabon	..	..	..	..	..	..	..	..
118 Nicaragua	1998 [e]	0.7	2.3	63.6	48.8	70.7	27.9	60.3
119 São Tomé and Principe	..	..	..	..	..	..	..	..
120 Guatemala	1998 [d]	1.6	3.8	60.6	46.0	29.1	15.8	55.8
121 Solomon Islands	..	..	..	..	..	..	..	..
122 Namibia	..	..	..	..	..	..	..	..
123 Morocco	1998-99 [e]	2.6	6.5	46.6	30.9	11.7	7.2	39.5
124 India	1997 [e]	3.5	8.1	46.1	33.5	9.5	5.7	37.8
125 Swaziland	1994 [d]	1.0	2.7	64.4	50.2	49.7	23.8	60.9
126 Botswana	..	..	..	..	..	..	..	..
127 Myanmar	..	..	..	..	..	..	..	..
128 Zimbabwe	1995 [e]	2.0	4.7	55.7	40.4	20.5	11.9	50.1
129 Ghana	1999 [e]	2.2	5.6	46.7	30.1	13.4	8.4	40.7
130 Cambodia	1997 [e]	2.9	6.9	47.6	33.8	11.6	6.9	40.4
131 Vanuatu	..	..	..	..	..	..	..	..
132 Lesotho	1986-87 [e]	0.9	2.8	60.1	43.4	48.2	21.5	56.0
133 Papua New Guinea	1996 [e]	1.7	4.5	56.5	40.5	23.8	12.6	50.9
134 Kenya	1997 [e]	2.4	5.6	51.2	36.1	15.2	9.1	44.9
135 Cameroon	1996 [e]	1.9	4.6	53.1	36.6	19.5	11.6	47.7
136 Congo	..	..	..	..	..	..	..	..
137 Comoros	..	..	..	..	..	..	..	..
Low human development								
138 Pakistan	1996-97 [e]	4.1	9.4	41.1	27.6	6.7	4.3	31.2
139 Sudan	..	..	..	..	..	..	..	..
140 Bhutan	..	..	..	..	..	..	..	..
141 Togo	..	..	..	..	..	..	..	..
142 Nepal	1995-96 [e]	3.2	7.6	44.8	29.8	9.3	5.9	36.7
143 Lao People's Dem. Rep.	1997 [e]	3.2	7.6	45.0	30.6	9.7	6.0	37.0
144 Yemen	1998 [e]	3.0	7.4	41.2	25.9	8.6	5.6	33.4
145 Bangladesh	1995-96 [e]	3.9	8.7	42.8	28.6	7.3	4.9	33.6
146 Haiti	..	..	..	..	..	..	..	..
147 Madagascar	1999 [e]	2.6	6.4	44.8	28.6	10.9	7.1	38.1
148 Nigeria	1996-97 [e]	1.6	4.4	55.7	40.8	24.9	12.8	50.6
149 Djibouti	..	..	..	..	..	..	..	..
150 Uganda	1996 [e]	3.0	7.1	44.9	29.8	9.9	6.4	37.4

HDI rank		Survey year	Share of income or consumption (%) [a]				Inequality measures		
			Poorest 10%	Poorest 20%	Richest 20%	Richest 10%	Richest 10% to poorest 10% [b]	Richest 20% to poorest 20% [b]	Gini index [c]
151	Tanzania, U. Rep. of	1993 [e]	2.8	6.8	45.5	30.0	10.8	6.7	38.2
152	Mauritania	1995 [e]	2.5	6.4	44.1	28.4	11.2	6.9	37.3
153	Zambia	1998 [e]	1.1	3.3	56.6	41.0	36.6	17.3	52.6
154	Senegal	1995 [e]	2.6	6.4	48.2	33.5	12.8	7.5	41.3
155	Congo, Dem. Rep. of the	..	..	..	..	..	..	..	..
156	Côte d'Ivoire	1995 [e]	3.0	7.1	44.2	28.8	9.4	6.2	36.7
157	Eritrea	..	..	..	..	..	..	..	..
158	Benin	..	..	..	..	..	..	..	..
159	Guinea	1994 [e]	2.6	6.4	47.2	32.0	12.3	7.3	40.3
160	Gambia	1998 [e]	1.6	4.0	55.2	38.2	23.6	13.7	50.2
161	Angola	..	..	..	..	..	..	..	..
162	Rwanda	1983-85 [e]	4.2	9.7	39.1	24.2	5.8	4.0	28.9
163	Malawi	..	..	..	..	..	..	..	..
164	Mali	1994 [e]	1.8	4.6	56.2	40.4	23.1	12.2	50.5
165	Central African Republic	1993 [e]	0.7	2.0	65.0	47.7	69.2	32.7	61.3
166	Chad	..	..	..	..	..	..	..	..
167	Guinea-Bissau	1991 [e]	0.5	2.1	58.9	42.4	84.8	28.0	56.2
168	Ethiopia	1995 [e]	3.0	7.1	47.7	33.7	11.4	6.7	40.0
169	Burkina Faso	1998 [e]	2.0	4.6	60.4	46.8	23.5	13.2	55.1
170	Mozambique	1996-97 [e]	2.5	6.5	46.5	31.7	12.5	7.2	39.6
171	Burundi	1998 [e]	1.8	5.1	48.0	32.9	18.3	9.5	42.5
172	Niger	1995 [e]	0.8	2.6	53.3	35.4	46.0	20.7	50.5
173	Sierra Leone	1989 [e]	0.5	1.1	63.4	43.6	87.2	57.6	62.9

Note: Because data come from surveys covering different years and using different methodologies, comparisons between countries must be made with caution.

a. The distribution of income is typically more unequal than the distribution of consumption. b. Data show the ratio of the income or consumption share of the richest group to that of the poorest. Because of rounding, results may differ from ratios calculated using the income or consumption shares in columns 2-5. c. The Gini index measures inequality over the entire distribution of income or consumption. A value of 0 represents perfect equality, and a value of 100 perfect inequality. d. Survey based on income. e. Survey based on consumption.

Source: Columns 1-5 and 8: World Bank 2002b; *columns 6 and 7:* calculated on the basis of income or consumption data from World Bank (2002b).

14 The structure of trade

HDI rank	Imports of goods and services (as % of GDP)		Exports of goods and services (as % of GDP)		Primary exports (as % of merchandise exports)		Manufactured exports (as % of merchandise exports)		High-technology exports (as % of manufactured exports)		Terms of trade (1980 = 100)[a]
	1990	2000	1990	2000	1990	2000	1990	2000	1990	2000	1999
High human development											
1 Norway	34	30	41	47	67	77	33	18	12	17	86
2 Sweden	29	42	30	47	16	9	83	85	13	22	110
3 Canada	26	41 [b]	26	44 [b]	36	30	59	64	14	19	..
4 Belgium	69	85	71	88	..	18	..	78	5	10	..
5 Australia	17	22 [b]	17	20 [b]	64	65	16	29	12	15	79
6 United States	11	13 [b]	10	11 [b]	22	13	74	83	33	34	116
7 Iceland	33	39 [b]	34	34 [b]	91	86	8	13	10	12	..
8 Netherlands	55	56 [b]	59	61 [b]	37	30	59	70	16	35	102
9 Japan	9	8 [b]	10	10 [b]	3	3	96	94	24	28	196
10 Finland	24	32	23	42	17	15	83	85	8	27	116
11 Switzerland	36	37 [b]	36	42 [b]	6	9	94	91	12	19	..
12 France	22	27	21	29	23	17	77	81	16	24	116
13 United Kingdom	27	29	24	27	19	17	79	82	24	32	101
14 Denmark	31	37	36	42	35	30	60	64	15	21	..
15 Austria	38	46 [b]	40	45 [b]	12	12	88	83	8	14	..
16 Luxembourg	105	99	109	120	..	13	..	86	..	17	..
17 Germany	25	33	29	33	10	9	89	85	11	18	112
18 Ireland	52	74 [b]	57	88 [b]	26	9	70	86	41	48	96
19 New Zealand	27	33 [b]	28	32 [b]	75	67	23	28	4	10	109
20 Italy	20	27	20	28	11	10	88	88	8	9	132
21 Spain	20	32	16	30	24	21	75	78	6	8	126
22 Israel	45	47	35	40	13	6	87	94	10	25	129
23 Hong Kong, China (SAR)	126	145	134	150	4	4	95	95	..	23	101
24 Greece	28	29 [b]	18	20 [b]	46	49 [b]	54	50 [b]	2	9 [b]	72
25 Singapore	195	161	202	180	27	14	72	86	40	63	81
26 Cyprus	57	48 [b]	52	45 [b]	45	48	55	52	6	2	79
27 Korea, Rep. of	30	42	29	45	6	9	94	91	18	35	99
28 Portugal	40	43	33	31	19	14	80	85	4	5 [b]	..
29 Slovenia	..	63	..	59	..	10	..	90	..	5	..
30 Malta	99	114	85	103	4	3	96	97	45	72	..
31 Barbados	52	56	49	51	55	46	43	52	..	23	80
32 Brunei Darussalam	..	..	..	..	100	89 [c]	(.)	11 [c]	..	9 [c]	68
33 Czech Republic	43	75	45	71	..	11	..	88	..	8	..
34 Argentina	5	11	10	11	71	66	29	32	..	9	74
35 Hungary	29	67	31	63	35	12	63	86	..	26	102
36 Slovakia	36	76	27	74	..	15 [b]	..	85 [b]	..	4 [b]	..
37 Poland	22	34	29	27	36	20	59	80	..	3	285
38 Chile	31	31	35	32	87	81	11	16	5	3	41
39 Bahrain	95	63	116	82	91	89	9	11	..	(.)	..
40 Uruguay	18	21	24	19	61	58	39	42	0	2	112
41 Bahamas	..	..	..	..	..	..	..	..	..	..	..
42 Estonia	..	88	..	84	..	27	..	73	..	30	..
43 Costa Rica	41	46	35	48	66	34	27	66	..	..	131
44 Saint Kitts and Nevis	83	79	52	52	..	27	..	73	..	1	..
45 Kuwait	58	31	45	57	94	80 [b]	6	20 [b]	3	1 [b]	73
46 United Arab Emirates	40	..	65	..	54	..	46	..	..	..	40
47 Seychelles	67	86	62	78	..	..	(.)	..	0	..	..
48 Croatia	..	51	..	45	..	27	..	73	..	8	..
49 Lithuania	61	52	52	45	..	40	..	60	..	4	..
50 Trinidad and Tobago	29	52	45	65	73	71	27	29	0	1	60

HDI rank	Imports of goods and services (as % of GDP)		Exports of goods and services (as % of GDP)		Primary exports (as % of merchandise exports)		Manufactured exports (as % of merchandise exports)		High-technology exports (as % of manufactured exports)		Terms of trade (1980 = 100) [a]
	1990	2000	1990	2000	1990	2000	1990	2000	1990	2000	1999
51 Qatar	..	..	..	..	84	90 [b]	16	10 [b]	..	..	53
52 Antigua and Barbuda	87	80	89	71	..	..	..	..	..	..	..
53 Latvia	49	54	48	46	..	44	..	56	..	4	..
Medium human development											
54 Mexico	20	33	19	31	56	16	43	83	8	22	31
55 Cuba	..	18	..	16	..	..	..	..	..	..	74
56 Belarus	44	69	46	68	..	31	..	67	..	4	..
57 Panama	34	39	38	33	78	84	21	16	..	(.) [b]	91
58 Belize	62	64	64	47	..	..	15	13 [b]	..	(.) [c]	..
59 Malaysia	72	104	75	125	46	19	54	80	38	59 [b]	47
60 Russian Federation	18	25	18	46	..	65	..	22	..	14	..
61 Dominica	81	64	55	51	..	..	32	56	..	7	..
62 Bulgaria	37	64	33	58	..	37	..	57	..	..	..
63 Romania	26	40	17	34	26	22	73	77	2	6	..
64 Libyan Arab Jamahiriya	..	..	..	..	95	..	5	..	..	..	50
65 Macedonia, TFYR	36	62	26	45	..	31 [b]	..	66 [b]	..	1 [b]	..
66 Saint Lucia	84	66	73	56	..	81	28	19	..	8	..
67 Mauritius	72	67	65	64	34	19	66	81	1	1	97
68 Colombia	15	20	21	22	74	66	25	34	..	7	78
69 Venezuela	20	17	39	29	90	91	10	9	4	3	45
70 Thailand	42	59	34	67	36	22	63	76	21	32 [b]	72
71 Saudi Arabia	36	26	46	50	93	93	7	7	..	(.)	45
72 Fiji	66	63	64	69	63	..	36	52	12	..	80
73 Brazil	7	12	8	11	47	40	52	59	7	19	142
74 Suriname	27	17	28	17	26	22	74	78	0	1 [c]	67
75 Lebanon	100	38	18	13	..	..	..	..	..	..	82
76 Armenia	46	51	35	23	..	52	..	43	..	5	..
77 Philippines	33	50	28	56	31	8	38	92	..	59 [b]	119
78 Oman	31	..	53	..	94	87	5	12	2	4 [b]	79
79 Kazakhstan	..	47	..	59	..	80	..	20	..	10	..
80 Ukraine	29	57	28	61	..	..	..	..	..	..	..
81 Georgia	46	47	40	37	..	..	..	..	..	..	..
82 Peru	14	18	16	16	82	80	18	20	..	3 [b]	42
83 Grenada	63	75	42	61	..	..	20	13 [b]	..	(.) [b]	..
84 Maldives	70	86	27	104	..	..	..	46	..	..	..
85 Turkey	18	31	13	24	32	18	68	81	1	5	..
86 Jamaica	56	55	52	44	31	27	69	73	..	(.)	73
87 Turkmenistan	..	53	..	63	..	92	..	7	..	5	..
88 Azerbaijan	..	38	..	41	..	92	..	8	..	4	..
89 Sri Lanka	38	51	29	40	42	23 [b]	54	75 [b]	1	3 [b]	95
90 Paraguay	39	35	33	20	..	81	10	19	(.)	3	154
91 St. Vincent & the Grenadines	77	70	66	59	..	..	..	13	..	0	..
92 Albania	23	40	15	19	..	18	..	82	..	1	..
93 Ecuador	27	31	33	42	98	90	2	10	(.)	6	40
94 Dominican Republic	44	39	34	30	..	..	..	..	..	..	58
95 Uzbekistan	48	39	29	44	..	..	..	..	..	..	..
96 China	14	23	18	26	27	12	72	88	..	19	105
97 Tunisia	51	48	44	44	31	23	69	77	2	3 [b]	84
98 Iran, Islamic Rep. of	24	21	22	35	..	93	..	7	..	2	35
99 Jordan	93	69	62	42	..	31	51	69	1	8	120
100 Cape Verde	44	62	13	23	..	..	..	..	..	..	100

14 The structure of trade

HDI rank	Imports of goods and services (as % of GDP)		Exports of goods and services (as % of GDP)		Primary exports (as % of merchandise exports)		Manufactured exports (as % of merchandise exports)		High-technology exports (as % of manufactured exports)		Terms of trade (1980 = 100)[a]
	1990	2000	1990	2000	1990	2000	1990	2000	1990	2000	1999
101 Samoa (Western)	..	82	..	33	..	..	4	..	0	..	..
102 Kyrgyzstan	50	55	29	43	..	40 [b]	..	20 [b]	..	5 [b]	..
103 Guyana	80	111	63	97	..	..	..	..	..	..	70
104 El Salvador	31	43	19	28	62	50	38	48	0	6	112
105 Moldova, Rep. of	51	77	49	50	..	66	..	33	..	3	..
106 Algeria	25	22	23	42	97	98	3	2	..	4 [b]	36
107 South Africa	19	26	24	29	30 [d]	33 [d]	22 [d]	54 [d]	0	1	..
108 Syrian Arab Republic	28	35	28	38	64	90	36	8	0	1	57
109 Viet Nam	33	..	26	..	..	..	..	..	..	..	..
110 Indonesia	24	31	25	39	65	43	35	57	1	16	56
111 Equatorial Guinea	70	58	32	95	..	..	..	..	..	..	..
112 Tajikistan	35	85	28	81	..	..	..	..	..	..	..
113 Mongolia	53	82	24	65	..	..	..	..	..	..	..
114 Bolivia	24	25	23	18	95	71	5	29	..	..	52
115 Egypt	33	23	20	16	57	58 [b]	42	37 [b]	..	(.) [b]	49
116 Honduras	40	56	36	42	91	67	9	33	..	2 [b]	95
117 Gabon	31	35	46	37	..	..	..	..	..	..	49
118 Nicaragua	46	81	25	40	92	92	8	8	..	5	64
119 São Tomé and Principe	72	82	14	33	..	..	..	..	..	..	..
120 Guatemala	25	28	21	20	76	68	24	32	..	8	77
121 Solomon Islands	73	..	47	..	..	..	..	..	..	..	..
122 Namibia	56	56 [b]	47	49 [b]	.. [e]	.. [e]	.. [e]	.. [e]	..	..	..
123 Morocco	32	37	26	31	48	36	52	64	..	12 [b]	116
124 India	10	17	7	14	28	19 [b]	71	79 [b]	2	4 [b]	148
125 Swaziland	76	81	76	66	.. [e]	.. [e]	.. [e]	.. [e]	..	..	70
126 Botswana	50	33 [b]	55	28 [b]	.. [e]	.. [e]	.. [e]	.. [e]	..	..	..
127 Myanmar	5	1 [b]	3	(.) [b]	..	..	..	..	..	..	26
128 Zimbabwe	23	31	23	30	68	72	31	28	2	2	115
129 Ghana	26	70	17	49	..	85	..	15	..	14 [b]	47
130 Cambodia	13	47	6	40	..	..	..	..	..	..	..
131 Vanuatu	77	..	46	..	..	..	13	..	20	..	..
132 Lesotho	122	88	17	28	.. [e]	.. [e]	.. [e]	.. [e]	..	..	73
133 Papua New Guinea	49	42 [b]	41	45 [b]	89	98	10	2	..	42 [c]	..
134 Kenya	31	36	26	26	71	79	29	21	4	4	110
135 Cameroon	17	27	20	31	91	92 [b]	9	5 [b]	3	1 [b]	84
136 Congo	46	42	54	79	..	..	..	..	..	..	71
137 Comoros	37	32	14	26	..	..	..	8	..	1	57
Low human development											
138 Pakistan	23	19	16	16	21	15	79	85	(.)	(.)	107
139 Sudan	..	16	..	17	..	..	..	3 [c]	..	(.) [c]	61
140 Bhutan	32	60	28	30	..	60 [b]	..	40 [b]	..	..	..
141 Togo	45	50	33	36	89	69	9	31	0	0	109
142 Nepal	21	32	11	24	..	23 [b]	83	77 [b]	..	(.) [c]	..
143 Lao People's Dem. Rep.	..	48 [c]	..	36 [c]	..	..	..	..	..	..	..
144 Yemen	20	41	14	50	..	99 [c]	..	1 [c]	..	0 [c]	..
145 Bangladesh	14	19	6	14	..	9 [c]	77	91 [c]	(.)	(.) [c]	97
146 Haiti	29	27	16	12	15	..	85	..	14	..	48
147 Madagascar	27	35	17	25	85	48 [b]	14	50 [b]	8	3 [b]	101
148 Nigeria	29	41	43	52	..	100	..	(.)	..	13 [b]	33
149 Djibouti	..	63	..	45	44	..	8	..	..	..	..
150 Uganda	19	26	7	10	..	94	..	6	..	10 [b]	20

HDI rank	Imports of goods and services (as % of GDP)		Exports of goods and services (as % of GDP)		Primary exports (as % of merchandise exports)		Manufactured exports (as % of merchandise exports)		High-technology exports (as % of manufactured exports)		Terms of trade (1980 = 100)[a]
	1990	2000	1990	2000	1990	2000	1990	2000	1990	2000	1999
151 Tanzania, U. Rep. of	37	23	13	15	..	84 [b]	..	15 [b]	..	6 [b]	41
152 Mauritania	61	57	46	41	..	..	..	..	..	..	144
153 Zambia	37	46	36	31	..	..	..	..	..	..	40
154 Senegal	30	40	25	31	77	69	23	30	..	13 [b]	102
155 Congo, Dem. Rep. of the	29	..	30	..	..	..	..	..	..	..	74
156 Côte d'Ivoire	27	39	32	46	..	85	..	14	..	..	82
157 Eritrea	..	86	..	16	..	..	..	..	..	..	..
158 Benin	26	29	14	15	..	97 [c]	..	3 [c]	..	(.) [c]	101
159 Guinea	31	31	31	26	..	70	..	30	..	..	..
160 Gambia	72	61	60	48	..	94 [c]	..	5 [c]	..	17 [c]	..
161 Angola	21	74	39	90	100	..	(.)	..	..	..	71
162 Rwanda	14	24	6	8	..	..	..	..	..	..	160
163 Malawi	33	38	24	26	95	..	5	..	(.)	..	65
164 Mali	34	40	17	25	..	..	2	..	..	..	85
165 Central African Republic	28	16	15	13	..	..	..	..	..	..	41
166 Chad	29	32	13	17	..	..	..	..	..	..	85
167 Guinea-Bissau	37	58	10	32	..	..	..	..	..	..	83
168 Ethiopia	12	31	8	15	..	..	..	10	..	(.)	..
169 Burkina Faso	26	30	13	11	..	..	..	..	..	..	170
170 Mozambique	36	39	8	15	..	90 [b]	..	10 [b]	..	2 [b]	34
171 Burundi	28	24	8	9	..	..	..	(.)	..	..	51
172 Niger	22	23	15	15	..	97 [c]	..	2 [c]	..	5 [c]	41
173 Sierra Leone	25	33	24	17	..	..	..	..	..	..	105
Developing countries	26	32	26	34	38	28	60	71	..	23	..
Least developed countries	23	31	14	22	..	..	..	..	..	..	..
Arab States	39	29	40	40	81	81	20	19	..	2	..
East Asia and the Pacific	40	51	41	56	24	13	75	86	..	31	..
Latin America and the Caribbean	12	18	14	17	66	51	34	48	6	16	..
South Asia	15	19	11	18	..	40	71	58	..	3	..
Sub-Saharan Africa	26	33	27	32	..	57	..	36	..	8	..
Central and Eastern Europe and the CIS	25	41	25	49	..	42	..	52	..	11	..
OECD	18	21 [b]	18	21 [b]	20	15	78	81	17	20	..
High-income OECD	18	20 [b]	18	20 [b]	19	16	78	81	18	19	..
High human development	20	22 [b]	20	22 [b]	20	16	78	82	18	22	..
Medium human development	19	27	20	30	49	40	48	58	..	13	..
Low human development	24	28	20	24	..	69	..	32	..	1	..
High income	19	21 [b]	19	22 [b]	19	15	78	82	18	22	..
Middle income	20	29	21	32	43	35	54	63	..	16	..
Low income	20	28	17	28	..	45	..	53	..	7	..
World	20	22 [b]	20	23 [b]	24	20	73	77	..	20	..

a. The ratio of the export price index to the import price index measured relative to the base year 1980. A value of more than 100 implies that the price of exports has risen relative to the price of imports.
b. Data refer to 1999. c. Data refer to 1998. d. Data refer to the South African Customs Union, which comprises Botswana, Lesotho, Namibia, South Africa and Swaziland. e. Included in the data for South Africa.
Source: Columns 1-4 and 7-10: World Bank 2002b; aggregates calculated for the Human Development Report Office by the World Bank; *columns 5 and 6:* calculated on the basis of data on merchandise trade and exports of food, agricultural raw materials, fuels, ores and metals from World Bank (2002b); *column 11:* calculated on the basis of data on terms of trade from World Bank (2002b).

15 Flows of aid from DAC member countries

HDI rank		Net official development assistance (ODA) disbursed			ODA per capita of donor country (2000 US$)		ODA to least developed countries (as % of total) [b]		Net grants by NGOs (as % of GNP) [c]	
		Total (US$ millions) [a]	As % of GNP							
		2000	1990 [d]	2000	1990	2000	1990	2000	1990	2000
1	Norway	1,264	1.17	0.80	277	276	43	33	0.13	0.11
2	Sweden	1,799	0.91	0.80	207	223	38	29	0.06	0.01
3	Canada	1,744	0.44	0.25	79	55	28	17	0.05	0.02
4	Belgium	820	0.46	0.36	95	91	40	25	0.03	0.03
5	Australia	987	0.34	0.27	52	56	18	21	0.02	0.04
6	United States	9,955	0.21	0.10	55	35	18	20	0.05	0.04
8	Netherlands	3,135	0.92	0.84	178	221	32	25	0.09	0.08
9	Japan	13,508	0.31	0.28	96	102	18	15	(.)	(.)
10	Finland	371	0.65	0.31	137	80	37	29	0.03	(.)
11	Switzerland	890	0.32	0.34	120	137	41	30	0.05	0.06
12	France	4,105	0.60	0.32	129	80	28	24	0.02	..
13	United Kingdom	4,501	0.27	0.32	55	79	31	31	0.03	0.04
14	Denmark	1,664	0.94	1.06	246	348	39	32	0.02	0.02
15	Austria	423	0.25	0.23	55	60	26	23	0.02	0.03
16	Luxembourg	127	0.21	0.71	71	320	31	32	..	0.04
17	Germany	5,030	0.42	0.27	108	71	26	23	0.05	0.05
18	Ireland	235	0.16	0.30	18	68	36	48	0.07	0.11
19	New Zealand	113	0.23	0.25	29	34	19	24	0.03	0.03
20	Italy	1,376	0.31	0.13	56	27	39	27	..	(.)
21	Spain	1,195	0.20	0.22	23	34	19	12	0.01	..
24	Greece	226	..	0.20	..	25	..	8	..	..
28	Portugal	271	0.24	0.26	18	30	70	43	(.)	..
DAC		53,737 T	0.33	0.22	78	67	26	22	0.03	0.03

Note: DAC is the Development Assistance Committee of the Organisation for Economic Co-operation and Development (OECD).

a. Some non-DAC countries and areas also provide ODA. According to OECD, Development Assistance Committee (2002c), net ODA disbursed in 2000 by the Czech Republic, Estonia, Israel, the Republic of Korea, Kuwait, Poland, Saudi Arabia, Slovakia, Turkey and the United Arab Emirates totalled $1,120 million. China also provides aid but does not disclose the amount. b. Includes imputed multilateral flows that make allowance for contributions through multilateral organizations. These are calculated using the geographic distribution of disbursements for the year of reference. c. Does not include disbursements from non-governmental organizations (NGOs) that originate from official sources and are already included in ODA. d. Data for individual countries (but not the DAC average) include forgiveness of non-ODA claims.

Source: Columns 1-7: OECD, Development Assistance Committee 2002b; aggregates calculated for the Human Development Report Office by the OECD; *columns 8 and 9:* OECD, Development Assistance Committee 2002a; aggregates calculated for the Human Development Report Office by the OECD.

16 Flows of aid, private capital and debt

HDI rank	Official development assistance (ODA) received (net disbursements) [a] Total (US$ millions) 2000	Per capita (US$) 2000	As % of GDP 1990	As % of GDP 2000	Net foreign direct investment inflows (as % of GDP) [b] 1990	2000	Other private flows (as % of GDP) [b, c] 1990	2000	Total debt service As % of GDP 1990	As % of GDP 2000	As % of exports of goods and services 1990	2000
High human development												
22 Israel	800.0 [d]	132.4 [d]	2.6	0.7 [d]	0.3	4.0	..	..	..	..	..	..
23 Hong Kong, China (SAR)	4.3 [d]	0.6 [d]	0.1	(.) [d]	..	..	..	..	..	..	..	..
25 Singapore	1.1 [d]	0.3 [d]	(.)	(.) [d]	15.2	6.9	..	..	..	..	..	..
26 Cyprus	54.5 [d]	69.5 [d]	0.7	0.6 [d]	2.3	1.8	..	..	..	..	..	..
27 Korea, Rep. of	-198.0 [d]	-4.2 [d]	(.)	(.) [d]	0.3	2.0	0.1	0.9	3.3	5.1	10.8	10.9
29 Slovenia	60.9	30.6	..	0.3	..	1.0	..	..	..	..	..	..
30 Malta	21.2	54.5	0.2	0.6	2.0	17.7	..	..	..	..	..	..
31 Barbados	0.2	0.9	0.2	(.)	0.7	0.7	..	..	..	..	..	..
32 Brunei Darussalam	0.6 [d]	1.9 [d]	0.1	..	..	..	..	..	..	..	..	..
33 Czech Republic	438.2 [d]	42.7 [d]	(.) [d]	0.9 [d]	0.6	9.0	1.9	-2.5	3.0	9.4	..	12.7
34 Argentina	76.3	2.1	0.1	(.)	1.3	4.1	-1.4	1.7	4.4	9.6	37.0	71.3
35 Hungary	252.2 [d]	25.3 [d]	0.2 [d]	0.6 [d]	0.0	3.7	-0.9	0.1	12.8	17.4	34.3	24.4
36 Slovakia	113.1 [d]	20.9 [d]	(.) [d]	0.6 [d]	0.0	10.7	1.8	0.7	2.1	13.5	..	18.0
37 Poland	1,396.2 [d]	36.2 [d]	2.2 [d]	0.9 [d]	0.2	5.9	(.)	2.4	1.6	6.5	4.9	20.9
38 Chile	49.3	3.2	0.3	0.1	1.9	5.2	5.0	1.6	9.1	8.7	25.9	26.0
39 Bahrain	49.1	76.7	3.2	0.6	..	..	..	..	..	..	..	..
40 Uruguay	17.4	5.2	0.6	0.1	0.0	1.5	-2.1	1.4	10.6	6.7	40.8	29.2
41 Bahamas	5.5 [d]	18.1 [d]	0.1	0.1 [d]	-0.6	5.2	..	..	..	..	..	..
42 Estonia	63.8 [d]	45.8 [d]	..	1.3 [d]	..	7.8	..	2.0	..	8.6	..	8.7
43 Costa Rica	11.8	2.9	4.0	0.1	2.9	2.6	-2.5	1.3	8.8	4.1	23.9	8.2
44 Saint Kitts and Nevis	3.9	101.6	5.1	1.2	30.8	30.6	-0.3	-0.3	1.9	6.2	2.9	12.5
45 Kuwait	2.8 [d]	1.5 [d]	(.)	(.) [d]	..	(.)	..	..	..	..	..	..
46 United Arab Emirates	4.0 [d]	1.5 [d]	(.)	..	..	..	..	..	..	..	..	..
47 Seychelles	18.3	227.3	9.8	3.0	5.4	9.1	-1.7	-0.7	5.9	2.8	9.0	3.4
48 Croatia	65.5	14.1	..	0.3	..	4.9	..	8.0	..	12.8	..	25.5
49 Lithuania	99.0 [d]	26.8 [d]	..	0.9 [d]	..	3.3	..	3.7	..	8.0	..	17.1
50 Trinidad and Tobago	-1.5	-1.2	0.4	(.)	2.2	8.9	-3.5	0.3	8.9	6.8	19.3	10.3
51 Qatar	0.5 [d]	0.9 [d]	(.)	(.) [d]	..	..	..	..	..	..	..	..
52 Antigua and Barbuda	9.8	151.0	1.2	1.4	..	..	..	..	..	..	..	..
53 Latvia	91.1 [d]	37.6 [d]	..	1.3 [d]	..	5.7	..	2.5	..	7.9	..	15.8
Medium human development												
54 Mexico	-54.1	-0.5	0.1	(.)	1.0	2.3	2.1	-0.3	4.3	10.1	20.7	30.2
55 Cuba	44.0	3.9	..	..	..	..	..	..	..	..	..	..
56 Belarus	39.6 [d]	3.9 [d]	..	0.1 [d]	..	0.3	..	0.1	..	0.8	..	2.9
57 Panama	16.5	5.8	1.9	0.2	2.5	6.1	-0.1	3.5	6.5	9.4	6.2	10.0
58 Belize	14.7	64.8	7.6	1.8	4.2	2.2	1.4	17.6	5.0	8.1	7.5	16.1
59 Malaysia	45.4	2.0	1.1	0.1	5.3	1.9	-3.6	1.7	9.8	6.7	12.6	5.3
60 Russian Federation	1,564.6 [d]	10.8 [d]	(.) [d]	0.6 [d]	0.0	1.1	1.0	-0.2	2.0	4.6	..	10.1
61 Dominica	15.5	219.4	11.9	5.7	7.8	3.9	-0.1	0.0	3.5	3.8	5.6	7.1
62 Bulgaria	311.1 [d]	39.1 [d]	0.1 [d]	2.6 [d]	(.)	8.3	-0.2	0.9	6.6	9.9	19.4	16.2
63 Romania	432.0 [d]	19.3 [d]	0.6 [d]	1.2 [d]	0.0	2.8	(.)	2.4	(.)	6.4	0.3	18.8
64 Libyan Arab Jamahiriya	15.4 [d]	2.9 [d]	..	..	..	..	..	..	..	..	..	..
65 Macedonia, TFYR	251.9	123.8	..	7.0	..	4.9	..	0.3	..	4.5	..	9.3
66 Saint Lucia	11.0	74.3	3.1	1.6	11.3	6.9	-0.2	3.5	1.6	5.7	2.1	11.0
67 Mauritius	20.4	17.6	3.4	0.5	1.6	6.1	1.7	-6.2	5.9	12.6	8.8	20.8
68 Colombia	186.9	4.4	0.2	0.2	1.2	2.9	-0.4	0.9	9.7	6.4	40.9	28.6
69 Venezuela	76.6	3.2	0.2	0.1	0.9	3.7	-1.2	0.8	10.3	4.9	23.2	15.7
70 Thailand	640.7	10.2	0.9	0.5	2.9	2.8	2.3	-3.9	6.2	11.5	16.9	16.3
71 Saudi Arabia	31.0	1.5	(.)	(.)	..	..	..	..	..	..	..	..
72 Fiji	29.1	35.8	3.7	1.9	6.7	0.0	-1.1	-0.4	7.7	2.0	12.0	2.5
73 Brazil	322.4	1.9	(.)	0.1	0.2	5.5	-0.1	2.2	1.8	10.5	22.2	90.7

HDI rank		Official development assistance (ODA) received (net disbursements) [a]				Net foreign direct investment inflows (as % of GDP) [b]		Other private flows (as % of GDP) [b, c]		Total debt service			
		Total (US$ millions)	Per capita (US$)	As % of GDP						As % of GDP		As % of exports of goods and services	
		2000	2000	1990	2000	1990	2000	1990	2000	1990	2000	1990	2000
74	Suriname	34.4	82.4	19.4	4.1	..	..	..	..	..	..	..	..
75	Lebanon	196.5	56.2	9.1	1.2	0.2	1.8	0.2	10.5	3.5	11.0	3.3	..
76	Armenia	215.9	57.0	..	11.3	..	7.3	..	1.0	..	2.2	..	7.6
77	Philippines	577.7	7.6	2.9	0.8	1.2	2.7	0.2	0.6	8.1	9.0	27.0	13.6
78	Oman	45.6	18.0	0.6	..	1.3	0.7 [e]	-3.8	-2.1	7.0	7.7 [e]	12.3	7.3 [e]
79	Kazakhstan	189.1	11.7	..	1.0	..	6.9	..	3.6	..	10.1	..	16.8
80	Ukraine	541.0 [d]	10.9 [d]	0.3 [d]	1.7 [d]	..	1.9	..	1.0	..	11.5	..	18.6
81	Georgia	169.5	32.2	..	5.6	..	4.3	..	0.8	..	3.9	..	9.5
82	Peru	401.1	15.6	1.5	0.8	0.2	1.3	0.1	1.6	1.8	8.1	10.8	42.8
83	Grenada	16.5	176.6	6.3	4.0	5.9	9.0	0.1	7.3	1.9	2.9	4.0	5.0
84	Maldives	19.3	66.2	10.7	3.5	3.0	2.3	0.6	0.1	4.4	3.6	4.8	4.3
85	Turkey	324.9	4.9	0.8	0.2	0.5	0.5	0.7	5.2	4.9	10.6	29.4	36.1
86	Jamaica	10.0	3.9	6.4	0.1	3.3	6.2	-1.1	6.0	15.6	8.7	26.9	14.1
87	Turkmenistan	31.5	6.7	..	0.7	..	4.5 [e]	..	12.0	..	10.9 [e]	..	31.8 [e]
88	Azerbaijan	139.4	17.3	..	2.6	..	2.5	..	0.9	..	3.4	..	8.0
89	Sri Lanka	276.3	14.6	9.1	1.7	0.5	1.1	0.1	0.5	4.8	4.5	13.8	9.6
90	Paraguay	81.8	14.9	1.1	1.1	1.4	1.1	-0.2	-1.3	6.2	4.4	12.2	10.4
91	St. Vincent & the Grenadines	6.2	54.8	7.8	1.9	4.0	8.4	0.0	-0.1	2.2	4.6	2.9	8.5
92	Albania	318.5	101.6	0.5	8.5	0.0	3.8	1.5	(.)	0.1	0.7	0.9	2.0
93	Ecuador	146.8	11.6	1.5	1.1	1.2	5.2	0.5	1.4	10.1	9.4	32.5	17.3
94	Dominican Republic	62.4	7.5	1.4	0.3	1.9	4.8	(.)	1.0	3.3	2.6	10.4	4.8
95	Uzbekistan	185.9	7.5	..	2.4	..	1.3	..	-1.1	..	11.7	..	26.4
96	China	1,735.0	1.4	0.6	0.2	1.0	3.6	1.3	1.8	2.0	2.0	11.7	7.4
97	Tunisia	222.8	23.5	3.2	1.1	0.6	3.9	-1.6	1.1	11.6	9.8	24.5	20.2
98	Iran, Islamic Rep. of	130.1	1.9	0.1	0.1	-0.3	(.)	(.)	-0.6	0.5	3.3	3.2	11.4
99	Jordan	552.4	112.4	22.1	6.6	0.9	6.7	5.4	-1.2	15.5	8.0	20.3	11.4
100	Cape Verde	94.1	220.3	31.8	16.9	0.0	1.8	(.)	-0.3	1.7	2.9	4.8	7.5
101	Samoa (Western)	27.4	172.5	23.7	11.6	3.5	0.0	0.0	0.0	2.7	3.6	5.8	10.8
102	Kyrgyzstan	215.0	43.7	..	16.5	..	-0.2	..	-4.8	..	13.3	..	29.3
103	Guyana	108.3	142.4	42.6	15.2	0.0	9.4	-4.1	-0.1	74.5	16.2	..	19.5
104	El Salvador	180.0	28.7	7.2	1.4	(.)	1.4	0.1	1.2	4.3	2.8	15.3	6.7
105	Moldova, Rep. of	122.6	28.5	..	9.5	..	10.0	..	6.3	..	10.5	..	16.7
106	Algeria	162.4	5.4	0.4	0.3	0.0	(.)	-0.7	-2.3	14.2	8.4	63.4	19.6
107	South Africa	487.5	11.3	..	0.4	..	0.8	..	1.4	..	3.1	..	10.0
108	Syrian Arab Republic	158.4	9.8	5.6	0.9	0.6	0.7	-0.1	(.)	9.7	2.0	21.8	4.8
109	Viet Nam	1,699.5	21.8	2.9	5.4	0.2	4.1	0.0	-2.3	2.7	4.2	8.9	7.5
110	Indonesia	1,731.0	8.2	1.5	1.1	1.0	-3.0	1.9	-4.3	8.7	12.2	33.3	25.3
111	Equatorial Guinea	21.3	46.6	46.0	1.6	8.3	8.9	0.0	0.0	3.9	0.4	12.1	0.2
112	Tajikistan	142.3	23.4	..	14.4	..	2.4	..	4.0	..	8.8	..	10.9
113	Mongolia	217.5	85.8	..	22.4	..	3.1	..	-0.4	..	3.0	..	4.7
114	Bolivia	476.6	57.2	11.2	5.8	0.6	8.9	-0.5	2.3	7.9	8.0	38.6	39.1
115	Egypt	1,328.4	19.6	12.6	1.3	1.7	1.3	-0.2	0.7	7.1	1.8	22.5	8.4
116	Honduras	449.1	70.0	14.7	7.6	1.4	4.8	1.0	0.3	12.8	9.7	35.3	19.3
117	Gabon	11.8	9.6	2.2	0.2	1.2	3.0	0.5	-0.2	3.0	9.5	6.4	15.0
118	Nicaragua	561.7	110.8	32.9	23.4	0.0	10.6	2.0	5.9	1.6	12.5	3.9	23.0
119	São Tomé and Principe	35.0	253.9	95.0	75.2	0.0	21.5	-0.2	0.0	4.9	9.5	34.0	31.7
120	Guatemala	263.6	23.2	2.6	1.4	0.6	1.2	-0.1	-0.3	2.8	2.3	12.6	9.4
121	Solomon Islands	68.4	152.9	21.7	24.9	4.7	3.6	-1.5	-1.3	5.5	3.3	11.9	6.7
122	Namibia	151.7	86.3	4.8	4.4	..	..	..	..	..	..	..	..
123	Morocco	419.3	14.0	4.1	1.3	0.6	(.)	0.7	-0.9	6.9	10.0	21.5	25.9

HDI rank		Official development assistance (ODA) received (net disbursements) [a]				Net foreign direct investment inflows (as % of GDP) [b]		Other private flows (as % of GDP) [b, c]		Total debt service			
		Total (US$ millions)	Per capita (US$)	As % of GDP						As % of GDP		As % of exports of goods and services	
		2000	2000	1990	2000	1990	2000	1990	2000	1990	2000	1990	2000
124	India	1,487.2	1.5	0.4	0.3	0.1	0.5	0.5	1.4	2.6	2.2	32.4	12.8
125	Swaziland	13.2	14.3	6.4	0.9	3.6	-3.0	-0.2	0.0	5.6	1.6	5.7	2.3
126	Botswana	30.7	19.9	3.9	0.6	2.5	0.6	-0.5	-0.1	2.8	1.3	4.4	1.8
127	Myanmar	106.8	2.2	..	..	..	..	..	..	..	..	9.0	4.7
128	Zimbabwe	178.1	14.1	3.9	2.4	-0.1	1.1	1.1	-0.7	5.4	6.4	23.1	22.1
129	Ghana	609.4	31.6	9.6	11.7	0.3	2.1	-0.3	-0.8	6.3	9.1	36.9	19.3
130	Cambodia	398.5	30.4	3.7	12.5	0.0	3.9	0.0	0.0	2.7	1.0	..	2.0
131	Vanuatu	45.8	232.7	32.6	21.6	8.5	9.4	-0.1	0.0	1.6	1.0	2.1	1.4
132	Lesotho	41.5	20.4	23.0	4.6	2.8	13.1	(.)	-0.7	3.8	7.3	4.2	12.1
133	Papua New Guinea	275.4	57.3	12.8	7.2	4.8	3.4	1.5	-0.1	17.2	8.0	37.2	13.5
134	Kenya	512.3	16.7	13.9	4.9	0.7	1.1	0.8	-0.6	9.3	4.6	35.4	17.3
135	Cameroon	379.9	25.5	4.0	4.3	-1.0	0.4	-0.1	-0.6	4.7	6.3	22.5	20.5
136	Congo	32.5	10.8	7.8	1.0	0.0	0.4	-3.6	0.0	19.0	1.3	35.3	1.6
137	Comoros	18.7	26.4	18.1	9.2	-0.4	0.0	0.0	0.0	0.4	1.3	2.3	5.0
Low human development													
138	Pakistan	702.8	5.0	2.8	1.1	0.6	0.5	-0.2	-0.6	4.8	4.6	23.0	26.8
139	Sudan	225.4	7.2	6.2	2.0	0.0	3.4	0.0	0.0	0.4	0.5	7.5	3.2
140	Bhutan	53.3	25.5	16.5	10.9	0.0	0.0	-0.9	0.0	1.8	1.4	5.5	4.2
141	Togo	69.8	15.4	16.0	5.7	0.0	2.5	(.)	0.0	5.3	2.4	11.9	6.1
142	Nepal	389.8	16.9	11.7	7.1	0.2	0.1	-0.4	-0.1	1.9	1.8	13.4	6.5
143	Lao People's Dem. Rep.	281.2	53.3	17.3	16.4	0.7	4.2	0.0	0.0	1.1	2.5	8.7	8.1
144	Yemen	265.0	14.4	8.4	3.1	-2.7	-2.4	3.3	0.0	3.5	2.6	5.6	3.8
145	Bangladesh	1,171.5	8.5	7.0	2.5	(.)	0.6	0.2	(.)	2.5	1.7	27.4	9.1
146	Haiti	208.3	25.6	5.7	5.1	0.3	0.3	0.0	0.0	1.2	1.0	11.0	8.0
147	Madagascar	322.3	20.2	12.9	8.3	0.7	2.1	-0.5	(.)	7.2	2.4	45.5	7.7
148	Nigeria	184.8	1.6	0.9	0.4	2.1	2.6	-0.4	-0.4	11.7	2.5	22.6	4.3
149	Djibouti	71.4	112.9	46.4	12.9	0.0	0.0	-0.1	0.0	3.6	2.4	..	5.5
150	Uganda	819.4	35.2	15.5	13.3	0.0	3.6	0.4	0.2	3.4	2.6	58.9	23.7
151	Tanzania, U. Rep. of	1,044.6	29.7	27.5	11.6	0.0	2.1	0.1	-0.1	4.2	2.4	32.9	16.2
152	Mauritania	211.9	79.5	23.3	22.7	0.7	0.5	-0.1	-0.3	14.3	10.7	29.9	25.9
153	Zambia	795.1	76.3	14.6	27.3	6.2	6.9	-0.3	-0.3	6.2	6.4	14.9	18.7
154	Senegal	423.5	45.0	14.4	9.7	1.0	2.4	-0.3	(.)	5.7	5.2	20.0	14.4
155	Congo, Dem. Rep. of the	183.5	3.6	9.6	..	-0.1	(.) [e]	-0.1	0.0	3.7	0.3 [e]	13.5	1.2 [e]
156	Côte d'Ivoire	351.8	22.0	6.4	3.8	0.4	1.1	0.1	-1.6	11.7	10.9	35.4	22.4
157	Eritrea	176.0	48.1	..	29.0	..	5.8	..	0.0	..	0.5	..	1.1
158	Benin	238.6	38.0	14.5	11.0	0.1	1.4	(.)	0.0	2.1	3.5	8.2	12.6
159	Guinea	152.7	18.7	10.4	5.1	0.6	2.1	-0.7	(.)	6.0	4.4	20.0	15.3
160	Gambia	49.1	37.7	31.3	11.6	0.0	3.3	-2.4	(.)	11.9	4.4	22.2	7.0
161	Angola	306.7	23.3	2.6	3.5	-3.3	19.2	5.6	-5.6	3.2	13.6	8.1	15.1
162	Rwanda	322.0	42.3	11.3	17.9	0.3	0.8	-0.1	0.0	0.8	2.0	14.0	24.7
163	Malawi	445.3	39.4	26.8	26.2	0.0	2.7	0.1	0.0	7.1	3.5	29.3	11.7
164	Mali	359.7	31.7	19.9	15.7	-0.3	3.3	(.)	0.0	2.8	4.2	12.3	12.1
165	Central African Republic	75.9	20.4	16.8	7.9	0.1	0.5	(.)	0.0	2.0	1.5	13.2	12.9
166	Chad	131.1	16.6	18.0	9.3	0.0	1.1	(.)	(.)	0.7	1.9	4.4	9.3
167	Guinea-Bissau	80.4	67.1	52.7	37.3	0.8	0.0	(.)	0.0	3.4	2.9	31.0	8.6
168	Ethiopia	693.0	11.0	14.8	10.8	0.2	0.8	-0.8	-0.1	3.4	2.2	34.9	13.9
169	Burkina Faso	336.0	29.1	12.0	15.3	0.0	0.5	(.)	0.0	1.2	2.5	6.8	17.3
170	Mozambique	876.2	47.9	40.7	23.3	0.4	3.7	1.0	(.)	3.2	2.3	26.2	11.4
171	Burundi	92.7	14.6	23.3	13.5	0.1	1.7	-0.5	0.0	3.7	3.1	43.4	37.2
172	Niger	211.0	19.5	16.0	11.6	(.)	0.8	0.4	-0.1	4.0	1.6	17.4	9.4
173	Sierra Leone	182.4	41.4	6.8	28.7	3.6	0.2	0.4	0.0	2.4	6.7	10.1	48.0

16 Flows of aid, private capital and debt

	Official development assistance (ODA) received (net disbursements) [a]				Net foreign direct investment inflows (as % of GDP) [b]		Other private flows (as % of GDP) [b, c]		Total debt service			
	Total (US$ millions)	Per capita (US$)	As % of GDP						As % of GDP		As % of exports of goods and services	
	2000	2000	1990	2000	1990	2000	1990	2000	1990	2000	1990	2000
Developing countries	31,652.5 T	6.7	1.4	0.5	0.9	2.5	0.5	1.0	4.3	6.3	18.6	18.6
Least developed countries	12,141.2 T	19.1	11.9	7.6	(.)	2.6	0.6	-0.4	3.1	2.9	15.6	9.6
Arab States	3,750.4 T	15.2	3.4	0.7	0.9	0.3	..	..	..	..	14.7	8.7
East Asia and the Pacific	7,687.5 T	4.1	0.7	0.3	1.7	2.8	0.8	0.7	4.3	4.6	15.7	10.8
Latin America and the Caribbean	3,813.0 T	7.4	0.4	0.2	0.7	3.9	0.3	1.1	4.0	9.2	23.5	38.7
South Asia	4,230.3 T	3.0	1.1	0.6	(.)	0.5	0.3	0.8	2.3	2.6	19.9	13.0
Sub-Saharan Africa	11,791.8 T	19.4	..	6.2	..	2.1	..	..	..	..	19.6	10.5
Central and Eastern Europe and the CIS	7,449.8 T	18.7	..	..	(.)	3.7	..	..	..	..	14.3	15.3
OECD	..	..	..	..	1.0 [f]	4.0 [f]	..	..	..	..	..	..
High-income OECD	..	..	..	..	1.0 [f]	4.1 [f]	..	..	..	..	..	..
High human development	..	..	..	..	1.0 [f]	4.1 [f]	..	..	..	..	..	..
Medium human development	23,908.3 T	5.9	0.9	0.5	0.6	2.4	0.7	1.0	3.8	6.2	18.8	18.0
Low human development	12,504.2 T	14.9	8.2	4.7	0.4	2.0	0.3	-0.5	5.1	3.6	20.5	11.7
High income	..	..	..	..	1.0 [f]	4.1 [f]	..	..	..	..	..	..
Middle income	16,725.5 T	6.3	0.7	0.3	0.7	3.0	0.5	1.2	3.8	6.7	16.9	18.4
Low income	22,242.3 T	9.3	3.0	2.1	0.3	0.6	0.7	-0.2	4.6	4.4	26.5	15.9
World	39,923.5 T	7.8	..	..	1.0 [f]	3.8 [f]	..	..	..	..	..	..

Note: This table presents data for countries included in Parts I and II of the Development Assistance Committee's (DAC) list of aid recipients (OECD, Development Assistance Committee 2002c). The denominator conventionally used when comparing official development assistance and total debt service to the size of the economy is GNP, not GDP (see the definitions of statistical terms). GDP is used here, however, to allow comparability throughout the table. With few exceptions the denominators produce similar results.

a. ODA receipts are total net ODA flows from DAC countries, other OECD countries, multilateral organizations and Arab countries as well as Estonia and Israel. A negative value indicates that the repayment of ODA loans exceeds the amount of ODA received. Aggregates include net official aid. See the definitions of statistical terms. b. A negative value indicates that the capital flowing out of the country exceeds that flowing in. c. Other private flows combine non-debt-creating portfolio equity investment flows, portfolio debt flows and bank and trade-related lending. See the definitions of statistical terms. d. Data refer to net official aid. See the definitions of statistical terms. e. Data refer to 1998. f. Data used to calculate the aggregate include countries not shown in the table.

Source: Column 1: OECD, Development Assistance Committee 2002d; *column 2:* calculated on the basis of data on ODA from OECD, Development Assistance Committee (2002d) and data on population from UN (2001); *columns 3 and 4:* calculated on the basis of data on ODA from OECD, Development Assistance Committee (2002d) and data on GDP from World Bank (2002b); *columns 5 and 6:* calculated on the basis of data on foreign direct investment and GDP from World Bank (2002b); aggregates calculated for the Human Development Report Office by the World Bank; *columns 7 and 8:* calculated on the basis of data on portfolio investment (bonds and equity), bank and trade-related lending and GDP from World Bank (2002b); *columns 9 and 10:* calculated on the basis of data on total debt service and GDP from World Bank (2002b); *columns 11 and 12:* World Bank 2002b; aggregates calculated for the Human Development Report Office by the World Bank.

17 Priorities in public spending

HDI rank	Public expenditure on education (as % of GNP)		Public expenditure on health (as % of GDP)		Military expenditure (as % of GDP) [a]		Total debt service (as % of GDP) [b]	
	1985-87 [c]	1995-97 [c]	1990	1998	1990	2000	1990	2000
High human development								
1 Norway	6.5	7.7 [d]	6.4	7.0 [e]	2.9	1.8	..	..
2 Sweden	7.3	8.3 [d]	7.6	6.6	2.6	2.1	..	..
3 Canada	6.7	6.9 [d, f]	6.8	6.6 [e]	2.0	1.2	..	..
4 Belgium	5.1 [g]	3.1 [d, h]	6.6	6.3 [e]	2.4	1.4	..	..
5 Australia	5.1	5.5 [d]	5.3	6.0	2.2	1.7	..	..
6 United States	5.0	5.4 [d, f]	4.7	5.7 [e]	5.3	3.1	..	..
7 Iceland	4.8	5.4 [d]	6.8	7.4 [e]	0.0	0.0	..	..
8 Netherlands	6.9	5.1 [d]	5.7	6.0 [e]	2.5	1.6	..	..
9 Japan	..	3.6 [f]	4.6	5.7	0.9	1.0	..	..
10 Finland	5.5	7.5 [d]	6.4	5.2 [e]	1.6	1.3	..	..
11 Switzerland	4.7	5.4 [d]	5.7	7.6	1.8	1.1	..	..
12 France	5.5	6.0 [d]	6.7	7.3 [e]	3.5	2.6	..	..
13 United Kingdom	4.8	5.3 [d]	5.1	5.8 [e]	3.9	2.5	..	..
14 Denmark	7.2	8.1 [d]	7.0	6.9 [e]	2.0	1.5	..	..
15 Austria	5.9	5.4 [d]	5.2	5.9 [e]	1.0	0.8	..	..
16 Luxembourg	4.1	4.0 [d]	5.7	5.7 [e]	0.9	0.7	..	..
17 Germany	..	4.8 [d]	5.9	7.9 [e]	2.8 [i]	1.5	..	..
18 Ireland	6.7	6.0 [d]	4.8	5.2	1.2	0.7	..	..
19 New Zealand	5.4	7.3 [d]	5.8	6.3 [e]	1.8	1.0	..	..
20 Italy	5.0	4.9 [d]	6.3	5.6 [e]	2.1	2.1	..	..
21 Spain	3.7	5.0 [d]	5.2	5.4	1.8	1.3	..	..
22 Israel	6.7	7.6 [d, f]	3.8	6.0	12.2	8.0	..	..
23 Hong Kong, China (SAR)	2.5	2.9	1.6	..	..	..	..	..
24 Greece	2.2	3.1 [d]	4.7	4.7	4.7	4.9	..	..
25 Singapore	3.9	3.0	1.0	1.1	4.8	4.8	..	..
26 Cyprus	3.6 [j]	4.5 [j]	..	..	5.0	3.2	..	..
27 Korea, Rep. of	3.8	3.7 [d]	1.8	2.4 [e]	3.7	2.8	3.3	5.1
28 Portugal	3.8 [g]	5.8 [d]	4.1	5.1	2.7	2.1	..	..
29 Slovenia	..	5.7	..	6.7	..	1.2	..	..
30 Malta	3.4	5.1	..	..	0.9	0.8	..	..
31 Barbados	6.2 [f]	7.2 [f]	5.0	4.5	..	..	..	..
32 Brunei Darussalam	..	..	1.6	..	6.7 [k]	7.6 [l]	..	..
33 Czech Republic	..	5.1 [d]	4.8	6.6 [e]	..	2.0	3.0	9.4
34 Argentina	1.4 [g]	3.5	4.2	2.4 [e]	1.3	1.3	4.4	9.6
35 Hungary	5.6	4.6 [d]	..	5.2	2.5	1.5	12.8	17.4
36 Slovakia	..	4.7	5.0	5.7	..	1.8	2.1	13.5
37 Poland	4.6	7.5 [d]	4.8	4.7 [e]	2.7	1.9	1.6	6.5
38 Chile	3.3	3.6	2.2	2.7	3.6	3.3	9.1	8.7
39 Bahrain	5.2	4.4	..	2.6	5.1	4.0	..	..
40 Uruguay	3.2	3.3	2.0	1.9	2.1	1.1	10.6	6.7
41 Bahamas	4.0	..	2.8	2.5	..	..	..	..
42 Estonia	..	7.2	1.9	5.1 [e]	..	1.6	..	8.6
43 Costa Rica	4.5	5.4	6.7	5.2	0.0	0.0	8.8	4.1
44 Saint Kitts and Nevis	3.7 [m]	3.8	2.7	3.1	..	..	1.9	6.2
45 Kuwait	4.8	5.0	4.0	..	48.5	8.2	..	..
46 United Arab Emirates	2.1	1.7	0.8	0.8	..	..	..	..
47 Seychelles	10.2	7.9	3.6	4.8	4.0	1.8	5.9	2.8
48 Croatia	..	5.3	9.5	9.5 [e]	..	3.0	..	12.8
49 Lithuania	5.3 [f]	5.9	3.0	4.7 [e]	..	1.8	..	8.0
50 Trinidad and Tobago	6.3	4.4 [f]	2.5	2.5	..	..	8.9	6.8

HDI rank	Public expenditure on education (as % of GNP)		Public expenditure on health (as % of GDP)		Military expenditure (as % of GDP) [a]		Total debt service (as % of GDP) [b]	
	1985-87 [c]	1995-97 [c]	1990	1998	1990	2000	1990	2000
51 Qatar	4.7	3.4 [f]	..	..	..	..	..	..
52 Antigua and Barbuda	2.7 [f]	..	2.8	0.4	..	..	..	..
53 Latvia	3.4	6.5	2.7	4.0 [e]	..	1.0	..	7.9
Medium human development								
54 Mexico	3.5	4.9 [d]	1.8	2.6	0.4	0.5	4.3	10.1
55 Cuba	6.8	6.7	4.9	..	..	..	..	..
56 Belarus	5.0	5.9	2.5	4.6	..	1.3	..	0.8
57 Panama	4.8	5.1	4.6	4.9	1.4	1.2 [e]	6.5	9.4
58 Belize	4.7	5.0	2.2	2.3	1.2	..	5.0	8.1
59 Malaysia	6.9	4.9	1.5	1.4	2.6	1.9	9.8	6.7
60 Russian Federation	3.4	3.5 [d]	2.5	..	12.3 [n]	4.0	2.0	4.6
61 Dominica	5.6	..	3.9	3.8	..	..	3.5	3.8
62 Bulgaria	5.4	3.2	4.1	3.9 [e]	4.2	3.0	6.6	9.9
63 Romania	2.2	3.6	2.8	3.8 [e]	3.5	2.1	(.)	6.4
64 Libyan Arab Jamahiriya	9.6	..	..	..	..	..	..	..
65 Macedonia, TFYR	..	5.1	9.2	5.3	..	2.1	..	4.5
66 Saint Lucia	5.5	9.8 [f]	2.1	2.4	..	..	1.6	5.7
67 Mauritius	3.3	4.6	..	1.8	0.3	0.2	5.9	12.6
68 Colombia	2.6 [g]	4.1 [g]	1.2	5.2	2.6	2.3	9.7	6.4
69 Venezuela	5.0	5.2 [f]	2.5	2.6	2.0	1.2	10.3	4.9
70 Thailand	3.4	4.8	0.9	1.9	2.2	1.6	6.2	11.5
71 Saudi Arabia	7.4	7.5	..	..	12.8	11.6	..	..
72 Fiji	6.0	..	2.0	2.9	2.3	1.5 [e]	7.7	2.0
73 Brazil	4.7	5.1	3.0	2.9 [e]	1.9	1.3	1.8	10.5
74 Suriname	10.2	3.5 [f]	3.5	..	..	..	..	..
75 Lebanon	..	2.5 [g]	..	2.2	5.0	3.6	3.5	11.0
76 Armenia	..	2.0	..	4.0 [e]	..	4.4	..	2.2
77 Philippines	2.1	3.4	1.5	1.6 [e]	1.4	1.2	8.1	9.0
78 Oman	4.1	4.5	2.0	2.9	18.3	9.7	7.0	7.7 [l]
79 Kazakhstan	3.4	4.4	3.2	2.7 [e]	..	0.7	..	10.1
80 Ukraine	5.3	5.6	3.0	2.9 [e]	..	3.6	..	11.5
81 Georgia	..	5.2 [f]	3.0	0.8 [e]	..	0.9	..	3.9
82 Peru	3.6	2.9	1.3	2.4	2.4	..	1.8	8.1
83 Grenada	4.5	4.7	3.3	2.9	..	..	1.9	2.9
84 Maldives	5.2	6.4	3.6	3.7	..	..	4.4	3.6
85 Turkey	1.2 [m]	2.2 [d]	2.2	3.3 [e]	3.5	4.9	4.9	10.6
86 Jamaica	4.9	7.5	2.6	3.0	..	..	15.6	8.7
87 Turkmenistan	4.1	..	4.0	4.1	..	3.8	..	10.9 [l]
88 Azerbaijan	5.8	3.0	2.7	1.0 [e]	..	2.7	..	3.4
89 Sri Lanka	2.7	3.4	1.5	1.7 [e]	2.1	4.5	4.8	4.5
90 Paraguay	1.1 [g]	4.0 [g]	0.7	1.7	1.2	1.0	6.2	4.4
91 St. Vincent & the Grenadines	6.0	6.3 [f]	4.4	4.2	..	..	2.2	4.6
92 Albania	..	..	3.3	2.0 [e]	..	1.2	0.1	0.7
93 Ecuador	3.5	3.5	1.5	1.7	1.9	..	10.1	9.4
94 Dominican Republic	1.3	2.3	1.6	1.9	..	..	3.3	2.6
95 Uzbekistan	9.2 [f]	7.7	4.6	3.4	..	1.7 [e]	..	11.7
96 China	2.3	2.3	2.2	2.1 [e]	2.7	2.1	2.0	2.0
97 Tunisia	6.2	7.7	3.0	2.2	2.0	1.7	11.6	9.8
98 Iran, Islamic Rep. of	3.7	4.0	1.5	1.7	2.7	3.8	0.5	3.3
99 Jordan	6.8	7.9	3.6	3.6	11.1	9.5	15.5	8.0
100 Cape Verde	2.9	..	..	1.8	..	1.3	1.7	2.9

	Public expenditure on education (as % of GNP)		Public expenditure on health (as % of GDP)		Military expenditure (as % of GDP) [a]		Total debt service (as % of GDP) [b]	
HDI rank	1985-87 [c]	1995-97 [c]	1990	1998	1990	2000	1990	2000
101 Samoa (Western)	..	..	2.8	4.8 [e]	..	..	2.7	3.6
102 Kyrgyzstan	9.7	5.3	4.7	2.2 [e]	..	1.9	..	13.3
103 Guyana	8.5	5.0	2.9	4.5	0.9	..	74.5	16.2
104 El Salvador	3.1 [f]	2.5	1.4	2.6	2.7	0.7	4.3	2.8
105 Moldova, Rep. of	3.6	10.6	4.4	2.9 [e]	..	0.4	..	10.5
106 Algeria	9.8	5.1 [m]	3.0	2.6	1.5	3.5	14.2	8.4
107 South Africa	6.1	7.6	3.1	3.3	3.8	1.5	..	3.1
108 Syrian Arab Republic	4.8	4.2	0.4	0.9	6.9	5.5	9.7	2.0
109 Viet Nam	..	3.0	0.9	0.8	7.9	..	2.7	4.2
110 Indonesia	0.9 [f, g]	1.4 [o]	0.6	0.8 [e]	1.3	1.1	8.7	12.2
111 Equatorial Guinea	1.7 [f]	1.7 [f]	1.0	..	..	..	3.9	0.4
112 Tajikistan	..	2.2	4.9	5.2	..	1.2	..	8.8
113 Mongolia	11.7	5.7	6.4	..	5.7	2.5	..	3.0
114 Bolivia	2.1	4.9	2.1	4.1	2.4	1.5	7.9	8.0
115 Egypt	4.5	4.8	1.8	..	3.5	2.3	7.1	1.8
116 Honduras	4.8	3.6	3.2	3.9	..	0.6 [e]	12.8	9.7
117 Gabon	5.8	2.9 [m]	2.0	2.1	..	0.3 [l]	3.0	9.5
118 Nicaragua	5.4	3.9 [m]	7.0	8.5	2.1	1.1	1.6	12.5
119 São Tomé and Principe	3.8	..	..	..	..	..	4.9	9.5
120 Guatemala	1.9 [g]	1.7 [g]	1.8	2.1	1.5	0.8	2.8	2.3
121 Solomon Islands	4.7 [f]	3.8 [f]	5.0	..	..	..	5.5	3.3
122 Namibia	..	9.1	3.7	3.3 [e]	5.7 [k]	3.3	..	..
123 Morocco	6.2 [g]	5.3 [g]	0.9	1.2	4.1	4.2	6.9	10.0
124 India	3.2	3.2	0.9	..	2.7	2.4	2.6	2.2
125 Swaziland	5.6	5.7	1.9	2.5	1.5	1.6	5.6	1.6
126 Botswana	7.3	8.6	1.7	2.5	4.1	3.7	2.8	1.3
127 Myanmar	1.9 [g]	1.2 [f, g]	1.0	0.2	3.4	1.7	..	..
128 Zimbabwe	7.7	7.1 [f]	3.2	3.0 [e]	4.5	4.8	5.4	6.4
129 Ghana	3.4	4.2	1.3	1.7 [e]	0.4	1.0	6.3	9.1
130 Cambodia	..	2.9	..	0.6	2.4	2.4	2.7	1.0
131 Vanuatu	7.4	4.8	2.6	..	..	..	1.6	1.0
132 Lesotho	4.1	8.4	2.6	..	3.9	3.1 [e]	3.8	7.3
133 Papua New Guinea	..	..	3.1	2.5	2.1	0.8	17.2	8.0
134 Kenya	7.1	6.5	2.4	2.4	2.9	1.8	9.3	4.6
135 Cameroon	2.8	..	0.9	1.0	1.5	1.3	4.7	6.3
136 Congo	4.9 [f]	6.1	1.5	2.0	..	..	19.0	1.3
137 Comoros	..	..	2.9	..	..	..	0.4	1.3
Low human development								
138 Pakistan	3.1	2.7	1.1	0.7 [e]	5.8	4.5	4.8	4.6
139 Sudan	..	1.4	0.7	..	3.6	3.0	0.4	0.5
140 Bhutan	3.7	4.1	1.7	3.2	..	..	1.8	1.4
141 Togo	4.9	4.5	1.4	1.3	3.2	..	5.3	2.4
142 Nepal	2.2	3.2	0.8	1.3	0.9	0.9	1.9	1.8
143 Lao People's Dem. Rep.	0.5	2.1	0.0	1.2	..	..	1.1	2.5
144 Yemen	..	7.0	1.1	..	8.5	5.2	3.5	2.6
145 Bangladesh	1.4 [g]	2.2 [g]	0.7	1.7	1.0	1.3	2.5	1.7
146 Haiti	1.9	..	1.2	1.4	..	..	1.2	1.0
147 Madagascar	1.9 [m]	1.9	..	1.1	1.2	1.2	7.2	2.4
148 Nigeria	1.7 [o]	0.7 [o]	1.0	0.8	0.7	0.9	11.7	2.5
149 Djibouti	..	..	..	5.4	6.3	4.4 [l]	3.6	2.4
150 Uganda	3.5 [f, g]	2.6	..	1.9	2.5	1.8	3.4	2.6

HDI rank	Public expenditure on education (as % of GNP)		Public expenditure on health (as % of GDP)		Military expenditure (as % of GDP) [a]		Total debt service (as % of GDP) [b]	
	1985-87 [c]	1995-97 [c]	1990	1998	1990	2000	1990	2000
151 Tanzania, U. Rep. of	..	..	1.6	1.3	2.0 [k]	1.3 [e]	4.2	2.4
152 Mauritania	..	5.1 [g]	..	1.4	3.8	..	14.3	10.7
153 Zambia	3.1	2.2	2.6	3.6	3.7	0.6	6.2	6.4
154 Senegal	..	3.7	0.7	2.6	2.0	1.4	5.7	5.2
155 Congo, Dem. Rep. of the	1.0	..	..	..	..	..	3.7	0.3 [i]
156 Côte d'Ivoire	..	5.0	1.5	1.2	1.5	..	11.7	10.9
157 Eritrea	..	1.8 [m]	..	..	..	22.9 [e]	..	0.5
158 Benin	..	3.2	1.6	1.6	1.8	..	2.1	3.5
159 Guinea	1.8	1.9	2.0	2.3	2.4 [k]	1.5	6.0	4.4
160 Gambia	3.7	4.9	2.2	2.3 [e]	1.1	1.1	11.9	4.4
161 Angola	6.2	..	1.4	..	5.8	21.2 [e]	3.2	13.6
162 Rwanda	3.5	..	1.7	2.0	3.7	3.0	0.8	2.0
163 Malawi	3.5	5.4	..	2.8	1.3	0.8	7.1	3.5
164 Mali	3.2	2.2	1.6	2.1	2.1	2.5	2.8	4.2
165 Central African Republic	2.6	..	..	2.0	1.6 [k]	..	2.0	1.5
166 Chad	..	2.2	..	2.3	..	1.0 [i]	0.7	1.9
167 Guinea-Bissau	1.8	..	1.1	..	..	1.3 [i]	3.4	2.9
168 Ethiopia	3.1	4.0	0.9	1.2 [e]	8.5	9.4 [e]	3.4	2.2
169 Burkina Faso	2.3	3.6 [f]	1.0	1.5 [e]	3.0	1.6	1.2	2.5
170 Mozambique	2.1	..	3.6	2.8	10.1	2.5	3.2	2.3
171 Burundi	3.1	4.0	1.1	0.6	3.4	5.4	3.7	3.1
172 Niger	..	2.3 [m]	..	1.2	..	1.4 [e]	4.0	1.6
173 Sierra Leone	1.7	..	..	0.9	0.9	1.4	2.4	6.7

Note: The denominator conventionally used when comparing expenditures and debt with the size of the economy is GNP, not GDP (see the definitions of statistical terms). GDP is used here whenever possible, however, to allow comparability throughout the table. With few exceptions the denominators produce similar results.

a. As a result of a number of limitations in the data, comparisons of military expenditure data over time and across countries should be made with caution. For detailed notes on the data see SIPRI (2001). b. For aggregates see table 16. c. Data refer to total public expenditure on education, including current and capital expenditures. See the definitions of statistical terms. Data refer to the most recent year available during the period specified. d. Data may not be strictly comparable with those for earlier years as a result of methodological changes. e. Data refer to 1999. f. Data refer to a year or period other than that specified. g. Data refer to the ministry of education only. h. Data refer to the Flemish community only. i. Data refer to the Federal Republic of Germany before reunification. j. Data refer to the Office of Greek Education only. k. Data refer to 1991. l. Data refer to 1998. m. Data do not include expenditure on tertiary education. n. Data refer to the Soviet Union. o. Data refer to the central government only.

Source: Columns 1 and 2: UNESCO 2000; *columns 3 and 4:* World Bank 2002b; *columns 5 and 6:* SIPRI 2002a; *columns 7 and 8:* calculated on the basis of data on total debt service and GDP from World Bank (2002b).

18 Unemployment in OECD countries

		Unemployment			Youth unemployment		Long-term unemployment (as % of total unemployment) [a]	
HDI rank	Unemployed people (thousands) 2000	Rate (% of labour force) 2000	Average annual rate (% of labour force) 1990-2000	Female rate as % of male rate 2000	Rate (% of labour force aged 15-24) [b] 2000	Female rate as % of male rate 2000	Female 2000	Male 2000
High human development								
1 Norway	80.8	3.4	4.7	88	10.2	114	2.9	6.7
2 Sweden	203.5	4.7	6.1	87	11.9	93	27.7	33.1
3 Canada	1,091.2	6.8	9.3	96	12.6	81	10.0	12.2
4 Belgium	300.7	7.0	8.5	156	15.2	141	56.7	55.9
5 Australia	610.8	6.3	8.4	89	12.3	87	24.0	30.6
6 United States	5,651.6	4.0	5.6	105	9.3	92	5.3	6.7
7 Iceland	2.0	1.4	3.2	158	4.7	63	14.1	8.7
8 Netherlands	187.1	2.6	5.5	161	6.6	137	33.4	31.7
9 Japan	3,200.4	4.7	3.2	91	9.2	76	17.1	30.7
10 Finland	253.0	9.8	11.7	116	21.6	104	22.4	26.9
11 Switzerland	72.0	2.0	3.3	136	4.8	70	30.2	28.0
12 France	2,503.7	9.5	10.9	140	20.7	129	40.8	38.3
13 United Kingdom	1,634.1	5.5	7.7	79	11.8	77	19.0	33.7
14 Denmark	133.3	4.7	7.1	123	6.7	107	20.0	20.1
15 Austria	198.7	4.7	5.1	97	6.3	81	27.2	29.3
16 Luxembourg	5.0	2.6	2.5	173	6.4	129	18.8 [c]	26.4 [c]
17 Germany	3,133.2	7.5	7.7	113	7.7	89	53.1	50.1
18 Ireland	76.4	4.3	11.3	97	6.4	113	47.5 [d]	59.5 [d]
19 New Zealand	113.2	6.0	7.8	95	13.2	85	14.3	23.1
20 Italy	2,494.9	10.7	10.7	180	29.7	139	60.9	60.7
21 Spain	2,370.6	14.1	19.1	212	25.5	170	46.6	36.6
24 Greece	500.8	11.4	9.7	228	29.5	170	61.0	49.4
27 Korea, Rep. of	889.4	4.1	3.3	71	10.2	66	0.7	3.1
28 Portugal	204.7	4.0	5.5	159	8.6	187	40.0	46.7
33 Czech Republic	454.5	8.9	5.7 [e]	144	17.0	104	50.7	49.2
35 Hungary	262.5	6.5	9.3 [f]	81	12.1	84	43.6	50.6
36 Slovakia	485.2	18.8	14.0 [g]	100	35.2	93	55.1	54.1
37 Poland	2,785.0	16.1	13.2 [e]	126	35.2	112	41.3	34.1
Medium human development								
54 Mexico	440.5	2.2	3.6	117	4.4	111	2.0	0.5
85 Turkey	1,451.0	6.4	7.4	99	13.2	90	28.5	17.5
OECD [h]	31,789.9 T	6.2	6.7 [i]	119	11.8	103	33.0	30.1

a. Data refer to unemployment lasting 12 months or longer. b. The age range for the labour force may be 16-24 for some countries. c. Data are based on a small sample and must be treated with caution. d. Data refer to 1999. e. Data refer to the average annual rate between 1993 and 2000. f. Data refer to the average annual rate between 1992 and 2000. g. Data refer to the average annual rate between 1994 and 2000. h. Aggregates are from OECD (2001a and 2001b). i. OECD average does not include the Czech Republic, Hungary, Poland and Slovakia.

Source: Columns 1 and 2: OECD 2001a; *column 3:* calculated on the basis of data on unemployment rates from OECD (2001a); *columns 4 and 6:* calculated on the basis of data on male and female unemployment rates from OECD (2001b); *columns 5, 7 and 8:* OECD 2001b.

19 Energy and the environment

HDI rank		Traditional fuel consumption (as % of total energy use) 1997	Electricity consumption per capita (kilowatt-hours) 1980	1999	GDP per unit of energy use (PPP US$ per kg of oil equivalent) 1980	1999	Carbon dioxide emissions Per capita (metric tons) 1980	1998	Share of world total (%) 1998	Cartagena Protocol on Biosafety	Framework Convention on Climate Change	Kyoto Protocol to the Framework Convention on Climate Change [b]	Convention on Biological Diversity
High human development													
1	Norway	1.1	18,289	24,248	2.4	4.8	9.5	7.6	0.1	●	●	○	●
2	Sweden	17.9	10,216	14,138	2.1	4.0	8.6	5.5	0.2	○	●	○	●
3	Canada	4.7	12,329	15,260	1.5	3.3	17.1	15.3	1.9	○	●	○	●
4	Belgium	1.6	4,402	7,286	2.4	4.5	13.4	10.0	0.4	○	●	○	●
5	Australia	4.4	5,393	8,884	2.1	4.4	13.9	17.9	1.4		●	○	●
6	United States	3.8	8,914	11,994	1.6	3.9	20.1	19.9	22.5		●	○	○
7	Iceland	..	12,553	23,110	1.9	2.4	8.2	7.6	(.)	○	●		●
8	Netherlands	1.1	4,057	5,993	2.2	5.2	10.8	10.5	0.7	●	●	○	●
9	Japan	1.6	4,395	7,443	3.4	6.3	7.9	9.0	4.7		●	○	●
10	Finland	6.5	7,779	14,366	1.8	3.6	11.9	10.3	0.2	○	●	○	●
11	Switzerland	6.0	5,579	7,291	4.4	7.3	6.5	5.7	0.2	○	●	○	●
12	France	5.7	3,881	6,392	2.9	5.3	9.0	6.3	1.5	○	●	○	●
13	United Kingdom	3.3	4,160	5,384	2.5	5.8	10.2	9.2	2.2	○	●	○	●
14	Denmark	5.9	4,222	6,030	3.0	6.9	12.3	10.1	0.2	○	●	○	●
15	Austria	4.7	4,371	6,176	3.5	7.2	6.9	7.9	0.3	○	●	○	●
16	Luxembourg	..	9,803	12,755	1.1	5.7	29.1	18.2	(.)	○	●	○	●
17	Germany	1.3	5,005	5,690	2.3	5.8	12.4	10.1	3.4	○	●	○	●
18	Ireland	0.2	2,528	5,011	2.3	7.0	7.4	10.4	0.2	○	●	○	●
19	New Zealand	0.8	6,269	8,426	2.9	4.0	5.7	7.9	0.1	○	●	○	●
20	Italy	1.0	2,831	4,535	3.9	7.7	6.6	7.2	1.7	○	●	○	●
21	Spain	1.3	2,401	4,497	3.8	6.1	5.3	6.2	1.0	○	●	○	●
22	Israel	0.0	2,826	5,689	3.6	6.1	5.5	10.1	0.2		●	○	●
23	Hong Kong, China (SAR)	0.7	2,167	5,178	6.4	8.4	3.2	5.4	0.1	–	–	–	–
24	Greece	4.5	2,064	3,854	4.8	6.0	5.4	8.0	0.4	○	●	○	●
25	Singapore	0.0	2,280	6,641	2.4	3.6	12.5	23.7	0.3		●		●
26	Cyprus	..	1,494	3,671	3.5	6.3	5.2	7.7	(.)		●		●
27	Korea, Rep. of	2.4	859	5,160	2.8	4.1	3.3	7.9	1.5	○	●	○	●
28	Portugal	0.9	1,469	3,616	5.6	6.9	2.8	5.5	0.2	○	●	○	●
29	Slovenia	1.5	..	5,218	..	4.9	..	7.3	0.1	○	●	○	●
30	Malta	..	1,363	3,763	3.7	6.0	3.0	4.7	(.)		●		●
31	Barbados	..	..	..	..	..	2.7	5.9	(.)		●	●	●
32	Brunei Darussalam	..	1,523	7,124	..	..	35.6	17.5	(.)				
33	Czech Republic	1.6	3,701	4,682	..	3.5	..	11.5	0.5	●	●	●	●
34	Argentina	4.0	1,170	1,938	4.7	7.1	3.8	3.8	0.6	○	●	●	●
35	Hungary	1.6	2,389	2,874	2.0	4.6	7.7	5.8	0.2		●		●
36	Slovakia	0.5	3,817	4,216	..	3.2	..	7.1	0.2	○	●	○	●
37	Poland	0.8	2,390	2,388	..	3.5	12.8	8.3	1.3	○	●	○	●
38	Chile	11.3	876	2,309	3.2	5.2	2.5	4.1	0.2	○	●	○	●
39	Bahrain	..	4,970	8,205	0.9	1.7	22.6	31.5	0.1		●		●
40	Uruguay	21.0	948	1,871	5.0	9.2	2.0	1.8	(.)	○	●	●	●
41	Bahamas	..	..	..	..	..	38.1	6.1	(.)	○	●	●	●
42	Estonia	13.8	..	3,435	..	2.6	..	11.9	0.1	○	●	○	●
43	Costa Rica	54.2	860	1,426	5.8	10.8	1.1	1.3	(.)	○	●	○	●
44	Saint Kitts and Nevis	..	..	..	..	..	1.0	2.6	(.)		●		●
45	Kuwait	0.0	5,793	14,011	1.3	1.8	18.0	27.2	0.2		●		○
46	United Arab Emirates	..	5,320	10,643	4.4	..	35.8	37.5	0.4		●		●
47	Seychelles	..	..	..	..	..	1.5	2.6	(.)	○	●	○	●
48	Croatia	3.2	..	2,674	..	4.1	..	4.4	0.1	○	●	○	●
49	Lithuania	6.3	..	1,769	..	3.1	..	4.2	0.1	○	●	○	●
50	Trinidad and Tobago	0.8	1,584	3,527	1.3	1.3	15.5	17.5	0.1		●	●	●

19 Energy and the environment

HDI rank		Traditional fuel consumption (as % of total energy use) 1997	Electricity consumption per capita (kilowatt-hours) 1980	Electricity consumption per capita 1999	GDP per unit of energy use (PPP US$ per kg of oil equivalent) 1980	GDP per unit of energy use 1999	Carbon dioxide emissions Per capita (metric tons) 1980	Carbon dioxide emissions Per capita 1998	Share of world total (%) 1998	Cartagena Protocol on Biosafety	Framework Convention on Climate Change	Kyoto Protocol to the Framework Convention on Climate Change [b]	Convention on Biological Diversity
51	Qatar	..	9,489	14,871	..	..	56.4	80.9	0.2		●		●
52	Antigua and Barbuda	..	..	..	..	..	2.3	5.0	(.)	○	●	●	●
53	Latvia	26.2	..	1,851	..	4.1	..	3.2	(.)		●	○	●
Medium human development													
54	Mexico	4.5	846	1,570	3.1	5.4	3.7	3.9	1.5	○	●	●	●
55	Cuba	30.2	823	973	..	..	3.2	2.3	0.1	○	●	○	●
56	Belarus	0.8	..	2,704	..	2.9	..	5.9	0.2		●		●
57	Panama	14.4	820	1,310	3.3	7.1	1.8	2.1	(.)	○	●		●
58	Belize	..	..	..	..	..	1.3	1.7	(.)		●		●
59	Malaysia	5.5	631	2,474	2.7	4.3	2.0	5.7	0.5	○	●	○	●
60	Russian Federation	0.8	..	4,050	..	1.9	..	9.8	5.9		●	○	●
61	Dominica	..	..	..	..	..	0.5	1.2	(.)		●		●
62	Bulgaria	1.3	3,349	2,899	0.9	2.3	8.5	5.7	0.2	●	●	○	●
63	Romania	5.7	2,434	1,511	1.6	3.8	8.7	4.1	0.4	○	●	●	●
64	Libyan Arab Jamahiriya	0.9	1,588	3,876	..	..	8.8	6.8	0.2		●		●
65	Macedonia, TFYR	6.1	..	..	..	..	..	6.2	0.1	○	○		●
66	Saint Lucia	..	..	..	..	..	1.0	1.3	(.)		●	○	●
67	Mauritius	36.1	..	..	..	..	0.6	1.5	(.)		●	●	●
68	Colombia	17.7	561	772	12.0	9.3	1.4	1.7	0.3	○	●	●	●
69	Venezuela	0.7	1,823	2,493	1.7	2.5	6.0	6.7	0.6	○	●		●
70	Thailand	24.6	279	1,352	3.0	5.2	0.8	3.2	0.8		●	○	○
71	Saudi Arabia	0.0	1,356	4,710	3.0	2.5	13.7	14.1	1.2		●		●
72	Fiji	..	..	..	..	..	1.2	0.9	(.)	●	●	●	●
73	Brazil	28.7	975	1,811	4.4	6.7	1.5	1.8	1.2		●	○	●
74	Suriname	..	..	..	..	..	6.7	5.2	(.)		●		●
75	Lebanon	2.5	789	1,778	..	3.3	2.3	5.1	0.1		●		●
76	Armenia	0.0	..	957	..	4.9	..	1.0	(.)		●		●
77	Philippines	26.9	355	454	5.6	6.9	0.8	1.0	0.3	○	●	○	●
78	Oman	..	614	2,880	..	..	5.2	8.5	0.1		●		●
79	Kazakhstan	0.2	..	2,448	..	2.1	..	7.6	0.5		●	○	●
80	Ukraine	0.5	..	2,306	..	1.2	..	7.0	1.5		●	○	●
81	Georgia	1.0	..	1,312	..	4.8	..	1.0	(.)		●	●	●
82	Peru	24.6	502	654	4.6	8.9	1.4	1.1	0.1	○	●	○	●
83	Grenada	..	..	..	..	..	0.6	2.0	(.)	○	●		●
84	Maldives	..	..	..	..	..	0.3	1.2	(.)		●	●	●
85	Turkey	3.1	439	1,396	3.6	5.9	1.7	3.2	0.8	○			●
86	Jamaica	6.0	482	2,294	1.7	2.2	4.0	4.3	(.)	○	●	●	●
87	Turkmenistan	..	..	944	..	1.2	..	6.5	0.1		●		●
88	Azerbaijan	0.0	..	1,750	..	1.6	..	5.1	0.2		●		●
89	Sri Lanka	46.5	96	255	3.5	8.1	0.2	0.4	(.)	○	●		●
90	Paraguay	49.6	245	789	4.2	5.8	0.5	0.9	(.)	○	●		●
91	St. Vincent & the Grenadines	..	..	..	..	..	0.4	1.5	(.)		●	○	●
92	Albania	7.3	1,083	783	..	10.4	1.8	0.5	(.)		●		●
93	Ecuador	17.5	361	620	3.0	4.5	1.7	2.2	0.1	○	●		●
94	Dominican Republic	14.3	433	646	3.6	6.2	1.1	2.5	0.1		●		●
95	Uzbekistan	0.0	..	1,650	..	1.1	..	4.6	0.5	○	●		●
96	China	5.7	253	758	0.8	4.2	1.5	2.5	12.8	○	●	○	●
97	Tunisia	12.4	379	911	4.0	7.4	1.5	2.4	0.1	○	●		●
98	Iran, Islamic Rep. of	0.7	495	1,407	2.9	3.4	3.0	4.4	1.2	○	●		●
99	Jordan	0.0	387	1,207	3.2	3.8	1.6	2.2	0.1	○	●		●
100	Cape Verde	..	..	..	..	..	0.4	0.3	(.)		●		●

Ratification of environmental treaties [a]

19 Energy and the environment

HDI rank		Traditional fuel consumption (as % of total energy use) 1997	Electricity consumption per capita (kilowatt-hours) 1980	Electricity consumption per capita (kilowatt-hours) 1999	GDP per unit of energy use (PPP US$ per kg of oil equivalent) 1980	GDP per unit of energy use (PPP US$ per kg of oil equivalent) 1999	Carbon dioxide emissions Per capita (metric tons) 1980	Carbon dioxide emissions Per capita (metric tons) 1998	Carbon dioxide emissions Share of world total (%) 1998	Ratification of environmental treaties [a] Cartagena Protocol on Biosafety	Framework Convention on Climate Change	Kyoto Protocol to the Framework Convention on Climate Change [b]	Convention on Biological Diversity
101	Samoa (Western)	..	..	..	..	..	0.6	0.8	(.)	○	●	●	●
102	Kyrgyzstan	0.0	..	1,512	..	5.0	..	1.4	(.)		●		●
103	Guyana	..	..	..	..	..	2.3	1.9	(.)		●		●
104	El Salvador	34.5	274	568	4.3	6.8	0.5	1.0	(.)	○	●	●	●
105	Moldova, Rep. of	0.5	..	620	..	3.2	..	2.2	(.)	○	●		●
106	Algeria	1.5	265	581	4.9	5.4	3.5	3.6	0.4	○	●		●
107	South Africa	43.4	3,213	3,776	2.7	3.5	7.7	8.7	1.4		●		●
108	Syrian Arab Republic	0.0	354	863	2.6	3.0	2.2	3.3	0.2		●		●
109	Viet Nam	37.8	50	252	..	4.1	0.3	0.6	0.2		●	○	●
110	Indonesia	29.3	44	345	2.2	4.4	0.6	1.1	1.0	○	●	○	●
111	Equatorial Guinea	..	..	..	..	..	0.3	0.6	(.)		●		●
112	Tajikistan	..	..	2,163	..	1.9	..	0.8	(.)		●		●
113	Mongolia	4.3	..	..	..	..	4.1	3.0	(.)		●		●
114	Bolivia	14.0	226	390	3.2	4.2	0.8	1.5	(.)	○	●		●
115	Egypt	3.2	380	900	3.5	4.9	1.0	1.6	0.4	○	●	○	●
116	Honduras	54.8	215	449	2.9	4.5	0.6	0.8	(.)	○	●	●	●
117	Gabon	32.9	617	700	1.9	4.5	9.0	2.4	(.)		●		●
118	Nicaragua	42.2	303	268	3.5	4.2	0.7	0.7	(.)	○	●		●
119	São Tomé and Principe	..	..	..	..	..	0.4	0.6	(.)		●		●
120	Guatemala	62.0	240	341	4.1	6.8	0.7	0.9	(.)		●	●	●
121	Solomon Islands	..	..	..	..	..	0.4	0.4	(.)		●	○	●
122	Namibia	..	..	..	..	9.6	..	0.0	(.)	○	●		●
123	Morocco	4.0	223	430	6.8	10.0	0.8	1.2	0.1	○	●	●	●
124	India	20.7	130	379	1.9	4.7	0.5	1.1	4.4	○	●		●
125	Swaziland	..	..	..	..	..	0.8	0.4	(.)		●		●
126	Botswana	..	..	..	..	..	1.1	2.4	(.)	○	●		●
127	Myanmar	60.5	31	71	..	..	0.1	0.2	(.)	○	●		●
128	Zimbabwe	25.2	973	894	1.6	3.5	1.4	1.2	0.1	○	●		●
129	Ghana	78.1	424	204	2.8	5.0	0.2	0.2	(.)		●		●
130	Cambodia	89.3	..	..	..	..	(.)	0.1	(.)		○		●
131	Vanuatu	..	..	..	..	..	0.5	0.3	(.)		●	●	●
132	Lesotho	..	..	..	..	..	..	..	..	●	●		●
133	Papua New Guinea	62.5	..	..	..	..	0.6	0.5	(.)		●	○	●
134	Kenya	80.3	92	126	1.1	2.1	0.4	0.3	(.)	●	●		●
135	Cameroon	69.2	154	184	2.8	3.8	0.4	0.1	(.)	○	●		●
136	Congo	53.0	83	48	0.8	2.8	0.2	0.7	(.)	○	●		●
137	Comoros	..	..	..	..	..	0.1	0.1	(.)		●		●
Low human development													
138	Pakistan	29.5	125	321	2.2	4.2	0.4	0.7	0.4	○	●		●
139	Sudan	75.1	34	46	1.4	3.2	0.2	0.1	(.)		●		●
140	Bhutan	..	..	..	..	..	0.0	0.2	(.)		●		●
141	Togo	71.9	..	..	4.3	4.7	0.2	0.2	(.)	○	●		●
142	Nepal	89.6	12	47	1.5	3.5	(.)	0.1	(.)	○	●		●
143	Lao People's Dem. Rep.	88.7	..	..	..	..	0.1	0.1	(.)		●		●
144	Yemen	1.4	59	110	..	4.4	0.2	0.8	0.1		●		●
145	Bangladesh	46.0	16	89	5.7	10.8	0.1	0.2	0.1	○	●	●	●
146	Haiti	74.7	41	40	3.6	5.5	0.1	0.1	(.)	○	●		●
147	Madagascar	84.3	..	..	..	..	0.2	0.1	(.)	○	●		●
148	Nigeria	67.8	68	85	0.8	1.2	1.0	0.7	0.3	○	●		●
149	Djibouti	..	..	..	..	..	1.1	0.6	(.)		●		●
150	Uganda	89.7	..	..	..	..	(.)	0.1	(.)	●	●		●

HDI rank	Traditional fuel consumption (as % of total energy use) 1997	Electricity consumption per capita (kilowatt-hours) 1980	Electricity consumption per capita (kilowatt-hours) 1999	GDP per unit of energy use (PPP US$ per kg of oil equivalent) 1980	GDP per unit of energy use (PPP US$ per kg of oil equivalent) 1999	Carbon dioxide emissions Per capita (metric tons) 1980	Carbon dioxide emissions Per capita (metric tons) 1998	Carbon dioxide emissions Share of world total (%) 1998	Ratification of environmental treaties [a] Cartagena Protocol on Biosafety	Framework Convention on Climate Change	Kyoto Protocol to the Framework Convention on Climate Change [b]	Convention on Biological Diversity
151 Tanzania, U. Rep. of	91.4	37	55	..	1.1	0.1	0.1	(.)		●		●
152 Mauritania	0.0	..	..	..	..	0.4	1.1	(.)		●		●
153 Zambia	72.7	1,016	540	0.9	1.2	0.6	0.2	(.)		●	○	●
154 Senegal	56.2	95	114	2.3	4.5	0.5	0.4	(.)	○	●	●	●
155 Congo, Dem. Rep. of the	91.7	148	43	3.3	..	0.1	(.)	(.)		●		●
156 Côte d'Ivoire	91.5	..	..	2.9	4.3	0.6	0.9	0.1		●		●
157 Eritrea	96.0	..	..	..	..	..	..	..		●		●
158 Benin	89.2	30	53	1.3	2.9	0.1	0.1	(.)	○	●		●
159 Guinea	74.2	..	..	..	..	0.2	0.2	(.)	○	●	●	●
160 Gambia	78.6	..	..	..	..	0.3	0.2	(.)	○	●	●	●
161 Angola	69.7	67	84	..	4.4	0.8	0.5	(.)		●		●
162 Rwanda	88.3	..	..	..	..	0.1	0.1	(.)	○	●		●
163 Malawi	88.6	..	..	..	..	0.1	0.1	(.)	○	●	●	●
164 Mali	88.9	..	..	..	..	0.1	(.)	(.)	○	●	○	●
165 Central African Republic	87.5	..	..	..	..	(.)	0.1	(.)	○	●		●
166 Chad	97.6	..	..	..	..	(.)	0.0	(.)	○	●		●
167 Guinea-Bissau	57.1	..	..	..	..	0.2	0.2	(.)		●		●
168 Ethiopia	95.9	16	21	..	2.2	(.)	(.)	(.)	○	●		●
169 Burkina Faso	87.1	..	..	..	..	0.1	0.1	(.)	○	●		●
170 Mozambique	91.4	34	53	0.6	2.1	0.3	0.1	(.)	○	●		●
171 Burundi	94.2	..	..	..	..	(.)	(.)	(.)		●	●	●
172 Niger	80.6	..	..	..	..	0.1	0.1	(.)	○	●	○	●
173 Sierra Leone	86.1	..	..	..	..	0.2	0.1	(.)		●		●
Developing countries	16.7	316	745	2.2	4.5	1.3	1.9	35.8	–	–	–	–
Least developed countries	75.1	59	69	..	4.0	0.1	0.2	0.4	–	–	–	–
Arab States	5.6	489	1,303	3.2	3.8	2.8	3.8	3.7	–	–	–	–
East Asia and the Pacific	9.4	253	804	1.3	4.4	1.4	2.4	17.7	–	–	–	–
Latin America and the Caribbean	15.7	845	1,450	4.1	6.0	2.4	2.6	5.3	–	–	–	–
South Asia	20.3	132	371	2.1	4.6	0.6	1.1	6.1	–	–	–	–
Sub-Saharan Africa	62.9	463	469	1.9	2.6	1.0	0.9	2.1	–	–	–	–
Central and Eastern Europe and the CIS	1.2	..	2,895	..	2.2	..	7.4	12.1	–	–	–	–
OECD	3.3	4,916	7,001	2.2	4.8	11.0	10.9	49.6	–	–	–	–
High-income OECD	3.4	5,932	8,481	2.2	4.8	12.6	12.6	43.5	–	–	–	–
High human development	3.3	5,212	7,496	2.2	4.8	11.7	11.7	50.2	–	–	–	–
Medium human development	10.8	349	928	..	3.9	1.4	2.5	40.5	–	–	–	–
Low human development	63.3	76	127	1.8	3.1	0.3	0.3	1.1	–	–	–	–
High income	3.4	5,873	8,431	2.2	4.8	12.6	12.7	45.2	–	–	–	–
Middle income	7.3	583	1,358	..	4.0	2.3	3.5	37.6	–	–	–	–
Low income	29.8	106	350	1.9	3.6	0.4	0.9	9.0	–	–	–	–
World	8.2	1,444	2,066	2.2	4.4	4.3 [c]	4.1 [c]	100.0 [c]	–	–	–	–

● Ratification, acceptance, approval, accession or succession. ○ Signature.

a. Information is as of 20 February 2002. The Cartagena Protocol on Biosafety was signed in Cartagena in 2000, the United Nations Framework Convention on Climate Change in New York in 1992, the Kyoto Protocol to the United Nations Framework Convention on Climate Change in Kyoto in 1997 and the Convention on Biological Diversity in Rio de Janeiro in 1992. b. Has not yet entered into force. c. Aggregate from CDIAC (2001). Data refer to total carbon dioxide emissions, including those of countries not shown in the main indicator tables as well as emissions not included in national totals, such as those from bunker fuels and oxidation of non-fuel hydrocarbon products.

Source: Columns 1-5: World Bank 2002b; *columns 6 and 7:* calculated on the basis of data on carbon dioxide emissions from CDIAC (2001) and data on population from UN (2001); *column 8:* calculated on the basis of data on carbon dioxide emissions from CDIAC (2001); *columns 9-12:* UN 2002b.

20 Refugees and armaments

		Internally displaced people (thousands)	Refugees [a]		Conventional arms transfers (1990 prices) [b]				Total armed forces	
			By country of asylum (thousands)	By country of origin (thousands) [d]	Imports (US$ millions)		Exports			
							US$ millions	Share (%) [e]	Thousands	Index (1985 = 100)
HDI rank		2000 [a, c]	2000	2000	1991	2001	2001	1995-2001	2000	2000
High human development										
1	Norway	–	48	..	383	109	156	0.2	27	72
2	Sweden	–	157	..	42	93	486	1.0	53	80
3	Canada	–	125	..	646	470	152	0.9	59	71
4	Belgium	–	19	..	86	33	72	0.5	39	43
5	Australia	–	58	..	130	687	(.)	0.5	51	72
6	United States	–	508	..	344	114	4,562	45.0	1,366	63
7	Iceland	–	(.)	..	..	..	(.)	(.)	..	..
8	Netherlands	–	146	(.)	189	153	225	1.8	52	49
9	Japan	–	4	..	1,502	206	(.)	(.)	237	97
10	Finland	–	13	..	56	10	3	(.)	32	87
11	Switzerland	–	58	..	283	33	36	0.3	28	138
12	France	–	103	..	1,018	(.)	1,288	8.6	294	63
13	United Kingdom	–	169	(.)	945	1,247	1,125	6.6	212	64
14	Denmark	–	71	..	119	116	(.)	(.)	22	74
15	Austria	–	17	..	2	15	61	0.1	40	74
16	Luxembourg	–	1	..	(.)	(.)	..	..	1	114
17	Germany	–	906	1	741	80	675	5.4	221	46
18	Ireland	–	3	..	10	46	(.)	(.)	12	84
19	New Zealand	–	5	..	33	60	(.)	(.)	9	74
20	Italy	–	23 [f]	..	92	428	358	1.7	251	65
21	Spain	–	7	..	90	90	4	0.7	166	33
22	Israel	–	4	(.)	1,234	45	203	0.9	172	121
23	Hong Kong, China (SAR)	–	1	..	..	..	..	..	..	..
24	Greece	–	7	(.)	459	897	11	0.1	159	79
25	Singapore	–	..	..	257	141	(.)	0.1	60	110
26	Cyprus	–	(.)	..	104	15	(.)	(.)	10	100
27	Korea, Rep. of	–	(.)	..	832	401	150	0.2	683	114
28	Portugal	–	(.) [f]	..	995	38	(.)	(.)	45	61
29	Slovenia	–	3	3	(.)	53	..	..	9	..
30	Malta	–	(.)	..	(.)	(.)	..	..	2	262
31	Barbados	–	..	..	..	..	..	..	1	60
32	Brunei Darussalam	–	..	..	2	1	..	..	5	122
33	Czech Republic	–	1	1	(.)	27	95	0.4	58	28
34	Argentina	–	2	(.)	(.)	97	3	(.)	71	66
35	Hungary	–	5	1	28	14	(.)	(.)	44	41
36	Slovakia	–	(.)	(.)	(.)	(.)	21	0.4	39	..
37	Poland	–	1	1	148	63	44	0.3	217	68
38	Chile	–	(.)	1	103	16	(.)	(.)	87	86
39	Bahrain	–	(.)	(.)	64	30	2	(.)	11	393
40	Uruguay	–	(.)	..	69	(.)	(.)	(.)	24	74
41	Bahamas	–	(.)	..	2	(.)	..	..	1	180
42	Estonia	–	(.)	(.)	(.)	(.)	(.)	(.)	5	..
43	Costa Rica	–	6	..	(.)	(.)	..	..	..	..
44	Saint Kitts and Nevis	–	..	..	..	..	..	..	..	..
45	Kuwait	–	3	1	595	34	(.)	0.1	15	128
46	United Arab Emirates	–	1	..	237	288	(.)	(.)	65	151
47	Seychelles	–	..	..	(.)	(.)	..	..	(.)	17
48	Croatia	34	22	331	(.)	59	(.)	(.)	61	..
49	Lithuania	–	(.)	(.)	(.)	19	..	..	13	..
50	Trinidad and Tobago	–	..	..	(.)	1	..	..	3	129

HDI rank	Internally displaced people (thousands) 2000 [a,c]	Refugees [a] By country of asylum (thousands) 2000	Refugees [a] By country of origin (thousands) [d] 2000	Conventional arms transfers (1990 prices) [b] Imports (US$ millions) 1991	Imports (US$ millions) 2001	Exports US$ millions 2001	Exports Share (%) [e] 1995-2001	Total armed forces Thousands 2000	Total armed forces Index (1985=100) 2000
51 Qatar	–	(.)	..	16	8	(.)	(.)	12	205
52 Antigua and Barbuda	–	..	..	..	..	..	..	(.)	200
53 Latvia	–	(.)	1	(.)	22	(.)	(.)	5	..
Medium human development									
54 Mexico	–	18	2	28	13	..	..	193	149
55 Cuba	–	1	20	96	(.)	..	..	58	36
56 Belarus	–	(.)	2	(.)	(.)	333	1.2	83	..
57 Panama	–	1	(.)	(.)	(.)	..	..	..	..
58 Belize	–	1	..	(.)	(.)	..	..	1	183
59 Malaysia	–	50	..	34	20	(.)	(.)	96	87
60 Russian Federation	491	26	39	(.)	(.)	4,979	17.0	1,520	29
61 Dominica	–	..	..	..	..	..	..	..	..
62 Bulgaria	–	1	2	335	(.)	4	0.2	80	54
63 Romania	–	2	7	39	110	(.)	(.)	207	109
64 Libyan Arab Jamahiriya	–	12	1	(.)	(.)	(.)	(.)	76	104
65 Macedonia, TFYR	–	9	4	(.)	126	..	..	16	..
66 Saint Lucia	–	..	..	..	..	..	..	..	..
67 Mauritius	–	..	..	(.)	(.)	..	..	..	..
68 Colombia	525	(.)	9	51	222	..	..	152	230
69 Venezuela	–	(.)	(.)	262	116	..	..	56	114
70 Thailand	–	105	(.)	399	162	..	..	301	128
71 Saudi Arabia	–	5	(.)	1,142	143	(.)	(.)	202	322
72 Fiji	–	..	(.)	(.)	(.)	..	..	4	130
73 Brazil	–	3	(.)	118	597	55	0.1	288	104
74 Suriname	–	..	(.)	(.)	(.)	..	..	2	100
75 Lebanon	–	3	9	(.)	1	45	(.)	64	366
76 Armenia	–	281	6	(.)	(.)	..	..	41	..
77 Philippines	–	(.)	45	43	13	..	..	106	92
78 Oman	–	0	..	(.)	30	(.)	(.)	44	149
79 Kazakhstan	–	21	2	(.)	31	9	0.2	64	..
80 Ukraine	–	3	19	..	..	430	2.1	304	..
81 Georgia	272	8	22	(.)	80	(.)	0.2	27	..
82 Peru	–	1	7	95	178	..	..	115	90
83 Grenada	–	..	..	..	..	..	..	..	..
84 Maldives	–	..	..	(.)	(.)	..	..	..	..
85 Turkey	–	3	40	777	442	2	(.)	610	97
86 Jamaica	–	(.)	..	(.)	(.)	..	..	3	133
87 Turkmenistan	–	14	(.)	..	..	..	..	14	..
88 Azerbaijan	572	(.)	284	(.)	(.)	..	..	72	..
89 Sri Lanka	707	(.)	113	108	40	..	..	115	532
90 Paraguay	–	(.)	..	3	(.)	..	..	20	140
91 St. Vincent & the Grenadines	–	..	..	..	..	..	..	..	..
92 Albania	–	1	6	(.)	(.)	..	..	54	134
93 Ecuador	–	2	(.)	180	(.)	..	..	58	135
94 Dominican Republic	–	1	..	(.)	(.)	..	..	24	110
95 Uzbekistan	–	38	4	(.)	5	..	..	59	..
96 China	–	294	110	194	3,100	588	2.2	2,810	72
97 Tunisia	–	(.)	1	4	18	..	..	35	100
98 Iran, Islamic Rep. of	–	1,868	85	1,295	335	(.)	(.)	513	84
99 Jordan	–	1	1	35	280	(.)	(.)	104	148
100 Cape Verde	–	..	..	(.)	(.)	..	..	1	14

HDI rank		Internally displaced people (thousands) 2000 [a, c]	Refugees [a] By country of asylum (thousands) 2000	By country of origin (thousands) [d] 2000	Conventional arms transfers (1990 prices) [b] Imports (US$ millions) 1991	Imports 2001	Exports US$ millions 2001	Exports Share (%) [e] 1995-2001	Total armed forces Thousands 2000	Index (1985 = 100) 2000
101	Samoa (Western)	–	..	..	..	..	..	..	..	..
102	Kyrgyzstan	–	11	1	..	..	(.)	(.)	9	..
103	Guyana	–	..	..	..	..	..	..	2	24
104	El Salvador	–	(.)	8	18	(.)	..	..	17	40
105	Moldova, Rep. of	8	(.)	3	(.)	(.)	5	0.2	10	..
106	Algeria	–	170	6	1,037	365	..	..	124	73
107	South Africa	–	15	(.)	20	17	20	0.1	63	60
108	Syrian Arab Republic	–	3	6	390	(.)	(.)	(.)	316	79
109	Viet Nam	–	16	371	(.)	74	..	..	484	47
110	Indonesia	–	123	9	8	38	20	0.1	297	107
111	Equatorial Guinea	–	..	1	..	..	..	..	1	59
112	Tajikistan	–	15	60	(.)	(.)	..	..	6	..
113	Mongolia	–	..	..	..	..	..	..	9	28
114	Bolivia	–	(.)	(.)	10	(.)	..	..	32	118
115	Egypt	–	7	4	866	486	(.)	(.)	448	101
116	Honduras	–	(.)	1	..	..	..	..	8	50
117	Gabon	–	18	..	(.)	(.)	..	..	5	196
118	Nicaragua	–	(.)	5	1	(.)	(.)	(.)	16	25
119	São Tomé and Principe	–	..	..	..	..	..	..	..	..
120	Guatemala	–	1	21	(.)	(.)	..	..	31	99
121	Solomon Islands	–	..	..	4	(.)	..	..	..	..
122	Namibia	–	27	2	(.)	25	..	..	9	..
123	Morocco	–	1	(.)	59	(.)	..	..	198	133
124	India	–	171	9	1,288	1,064	1	(.)	1,303	103
125	Swaziland	–	1	..	(.)	(.)	..	..	..	..
126	Botswana	–	4	(.)	3	32	..	..	9	225
127	Myanmar	–	0	137	185	(.)	..	..	344	185
128	Zimbabwe	–	4	..	36	7	..	..	40	98
129	Ghana	–	13	13	1	9	..	..	7	46
130	Cambodia	–	(.)	37	(.)	(.)	(.)	(.)	140	400
131	Vanuatu	–	..	..	..	..	..	..	..	..
132	Lesotho	–	..	..	4	2	..	..	2	100
133	Papua New Guinea	–	6	..	10	(.)	..	..	4	138
134	Kenya	–	206	1	13	(.)	..	..	22	162
135	Cameroon	–	44	2	(.)	1	..	..	13	179
136	Congo	–	123	28	(.)	(.)	..	..	10	115
137	Comoros	–	(.)	..	..	..	..	..	..	..
Low human development										
138	Pakistan	–	2,001	9	492	759	(.)	(.)	612	127
139	Sudan	–	415	491	39	(.)	..	..	104	185
140	Bhutan	–	..	109	..	..	..	..	6	200
141	Togo	–	12	4	10	(.)	..	..	7	194
142	Nepal	–	129	(.)	(.)	10	..	..	50	200
143	Lao People's Dem. Rep.	–	0	16	(.)	(.)	..	..	29	54
144	Yemen	–	61	2	74	33	..	..	66	103
145	Bangladesh	–	22	4	47	180	..	..	137	150
146	Haiti	–	0	7	..	..	..	..	..	..
147	Madagascar	–	(.)	..	..	..	..	..	21	100
148	Nigeria	–	7	4	20	1	(.)	(.)	76	81
149	Djibouti	–	23	2	1	1	..	..	8	280
150	Uganda	–	237	29	(.)	(.)	..	..	50	250

	Internally displaced people (thousands)	Refugees [a]		Conventional arms transfers (1990 prices) [b]					Total armed forces	
		By country of asylum (thousands)	By country of origin (thousands) [d]	Imports (US$ millions)		Exports				
						US$ millions	Share (%) [e]		Thousands	Index (1985 = 100)
HDI rank	2000 [a, c]	2000	2000	1991	2001	2001	1995-2001		2000	2000
151 Tanzania, U. Rep. of	–	681	(.)	(.)	(.)	..	..		34	84
152 Mauritania	–	(.)	30	17	(.)	..	..		16	185
153 Zambia	–	251	(.)	(.)	(.)	(.)	(.)		22	133
154 Senegal	–	21	11	(.)	(.)	..	..		9	93
155 Congo, Dem. Rep. of the	3	333	369	(.)	(.)	..	..		56	116
156 Côte d'Ivoire	–	121	(.)	(.)	(.)	..	..		8	64
157 Eritrea	1,100	2	377	(.)	60	..	..		200	..
158 Benin	–	4	..	..	..	..	..		5	107
159 Guinea	–	427	2	(.)	15	..	..		10	98
160 Gambia	–	12	1	..	..	..	..		1	160
161 Angola	258	12	433	(.)	255	(.)	(.)		108	217
162 Rwanda	–	28	118	(.)	(.)	..	..		70	1,346
163 Malawi	–	4	..	(.)	(.)	(.)	(.)		5	94
164 Mali	–	8	(.)	(.)	(.)	..	..		7	151
165 Central African Republic	–	56	(.)	(.)	(.)	..	..		3	135
166 Chad	–	18	55	(.)	(.)	..	..		30	247
167 Guinea-Bissau	–	8	1	6	(.)	..	..		7	85
168 Ethiopia	–	198	61	60	(.)	..	..		352	162
169 Burkina Faso	–	1	(.)	3	(.)	..	..		7	170
170 Mozambique	–	(.)	..	(.)	(.)	..	..		6	39
171 Burundi	56	27	568	..	..	..	..		40	769
172 Niger	–	(.)	(.)	(.)	(.)	..	..		5	241
173 Sierra Leone	300	7	401	(.)	(.)	..	..		3	97
Developing countries	..	8,460 T	..	..	..	..	..		13,226 T	97
Least developed countries	..	2,996 T	..	..	..	..	..		1,964 T	186
Arab States	..	704 T	..	..	..	..	..		1,893 T	115
East Asia and the Pacific	..	595 T	..	..	..	..	..		5,372 T	81
Latin America and the Caribbean	..	38 T	..	..	..	..	..		1,262 T	94
South Asia	..	4,191 T	..	..	..	..	..		2,736 T	110
Sub-Saharan Africa	..	2,929 T	..	..	..	..	..		1,342 T	160
Central and Eastern Europe and the CIS	..	463 T	..	..	..	..	..		..	..
OECD	..	2,476 T	..	..	..	..	..		5,217 T	72
High-income OECD	..	2,446 T	..	..	..	..	..		3,374 T	64
High human development	..	2,497 T	..	..	..	..	..		5,048 T	72
Medium human development	..	3,752 T	..	..	..	..	..		12,571 T	74
Low human development	..	5,125 T	..	..	..	..	..		2,172 T	154
High income	..	2,458 T	..	..	..	..	..		3,728 T	67
Middle income	..	2,759 T	..	..	..	..	..		10,684 T	69
Low income	..	6,157 T	..	..	..	..	..		5,379 T	123
World	..	11,374 T [g]	..	23,904 T [h]	16,231 T [h]	16,231 T [h]	..		19,791 T	78

a. Data refer to the end of 2000. They do not include Palestinian refugees. b. Figures are trend indicator values, which are an indicator only of the volume of international arms transfers, not of the actual financial value of such transfers. Published reports of arms transfers provide partial information, as not all transfers are fully reported. The estimates presented are conservative and may understate actual transfers of conventional weapons. Zero values are shown as (.). c. Includes only those to whom the United Nations High Commissioner for Refugees (UNHCR) extends assistance in pursuance to a special request by a competent organ of the United Nations. d. The country of origin for many refugees is unavailable or unreported. These data may therefore be underestimates. e. Calculated using the 1995-2001 totals for all countries and non-state actors with exports of major conventional weapons as defined in SIPRI (2002b). f. Data refer to the end of 1999. g. Aggregate from UNHCR (2002). h. Aggregate from SIPRI (2002b). It includes all countries and non-state actors with transfers of major conventional weapons as defined in SIPRI (2002b).

Source: Columns 1-3: UNHCR 2002; columns 4-6: SIPRI 2002b; column 7: calculated on the basis of data on weapons transfers from SIPRI (2002b); column 8: IISS 2001; column 9: calculated on the basis of data on armed forces from IISS (2001).

		People victimized by crime (as % of total population) [a]					
	Year [b]	Total crime [c]	Property crime [d]	Robbery	Sexual assault [e]	Assault	Bribery (corruption) [f]
National							
Australia	1999	30.1	13.9	1.2	1.0	2.4	0.3
Austria	1995	18.8	3.1	0.2	1.2	0.8	0.7
Belgium	1999	21.4	7.7	1.0	0.3	1.2	0.3
Canada	1999	23.8	10.4	0.9	0.8	2.3	0.4
Denmark	1999	23.0	7.6	0.7	0.4	1.4	0.3
England and Wales	1999	26.4	12.2	1.2	0.9	2.8	0.1
Finland	1999	19.1	4.4	0.6	1.1	2.1	0.2
France	1999	21.4	8.7	1.1	0.7	1.4	1.3
Italy	1991	24.6	12.7	1.3	0.6	0.2	..
Japan	1999	15.2	3.4	0.1	0.1	0.1	(.)
Malta	1996	23.1	10.9	0.4	0.1	1.1	4.0
Netherlands	1999	25.2	7.4	0.8	0.8	1.0	0.4
New Zealand	1991	29.4	14.8	0.7	1.3	2.4	..
Northern Ireland	1999	15.0	6.2	0.1	0.1	2.1	0.2
Poland	1999	22.7	9.0	1.8	0.2	1.1	5.1
Portugal	1999	15.5	7.5	1.1	0.2	0.4	1.4
Scotland	1999	23.2	7.6	0.7	0.3	3.0	..
Slovenia	2000	21.2	7.7	1.1	0.8	1.1	2.1
Sweden	1999	24.7	8.4	0.9	1.1	1.2	0.1
Switzerland	1999	18.2	4.5	0.7	0.6	1.0	0.2 [g]
United States	1999	21.1	10.0	0.6	0.4	1.2	0.2
Major city							
Asunción (Paraguay)	1995	34.4	16.7	6.3	1.7	0.9	13.3
Baku (Azerbaijan)	1999	8.3	2.4	1.6	0.0	0.4	20.8
Beijing (China)	1991	19.0	2.2	0.5	0.6	0.6	..
Bishkek (Kyrgyzstan)	1995	27.8	11.3	1.6	2.2	2.1	19.3
Bogotá (Colombia)	1996	54.6	27.0	11.5	4.8	2.5	19.5
Bratislava (Slovakia)	1996	36.0	20.8	1.2	0.4	0.5	13.5
Bucharest (Romania)	1999	25.4	10.8	1.8	0.4	0.6	19.2
Budapest (Hungary)	1999	32.1	15.6	1.8	9.0	0.8	9.8
Buenos Aires (Argentina)	1995	61.1	30.8	6.4	6.4	2.3	30.2
Cairo (Egypt)	1991	28.7	12.1	2.2	1.8	1.1	..
Dar es Salaam (Tanzania, U. Rep. of)	1991	..	23.1	8.2	6.1	1.7	..
Gaborone (Botswana)	1996	31.7	19.7	2.0	0.7	3.2	2.8
Jakarta (Indonesia)	1995	20.9	9.4	0.7	1.3	0.5	29.9
Johannesburg (South Africa)	1995	38.0	18.3	4.7	2.7	4.6	6.9
Kampala (Uganda)	1995	40.9	20.6	2.3	5.1	1.7	19.5
Kiev (Ukraine)	1999	29.1	8.9	2.5	1.2	1.5	16.2
La Paz (Bolivia)	1995	39.8	18.1	5.8	1.5	2.0	24.4
Manila (Philippines)	1995	10.6	3.3	1.5	0.1	0.1	4.3
Minsk (Belarus)	1999	23.6	11.1	1.4	1.4	1.3	20.6
Moscow (Russian Federation)	1999	26.3	10.9	2.4	1.2	1.1	16.6
Mumbai (India)	1995	31.8	6.7	1.3	3.5	0.8	22.9
New Delhi (India)	1995	30.5	6.1	1.0	1.7	0.8	21.0
Prague (Czech Republic)	1999	34.1	21.6	0.5	0.9	1.1	5.7
Rïga (Latvia)	1999	26.5	9.4	2.8	0.5	1.9	14.3
Rio de Janeiro (Brazil)	1995	44.0	14.7	12.2	7.5	3.4	17.1
San José (Costa Rica)	1995	40.4	21.7	8.9	3.5	1.7	9.2
Skopje (Macedonia, TFYR)	1995	21.1	9.4	1.1	0.3	0.7	7.4
Sofia (Bulgaria)	1999	27.2	16.1	1.5	0.1	0.6	16.4
Tallinn (Estonia)	1999	41.2	22.5	6.3	3.3	3.7	9.3
Tbilisi (Georgia)	1999	23.6	11.1	1.8	0.4	0.9	16.6

	Year[b]	People victimized by crime (as % of total population) [a]					
		Total crime[c]	Property crime[d]	Robbery	Sexual assault[e]	Assault	Bribery (corruption)[f]
Tirana (Albania)	1999	31.7	11.2	2.9	1.2	0.7	59.1
Tunis (Tunisia)	1991	37.5	20.1	5.4	1.5	0.4	..
Ulaanbaatar (Mongolia)	1999	41.8	20.0	4.5	1.4	2.1	21.3
Vilnius (Lithuania)	1999	31.0	17.8	3.2	2.0	1.4	22.9
Zagreb (Croatia)	1999	14.3	4.4	0.5	0.8	0.5	9.5

a. Data refer to victimization as reported in the International Crime Victims Survey. b. Surveys were conducted in 1992, 1995, 1996-97 and 2000-01. Data refer to the year preceding the survey. c. Data refer to people victimized by one or more of 11 crimes recorded in the survey: robbery, burglary, attempted burglary, car theft, car vandalism, bicycle theft, sexual assault, theft from car, theft of personal property, assault and threats and theft of motorcycle or moped. d. Includes car theft, theft from car, burglary with entry and attempted burglary. e. Data refer to female population only. f. Data refer to people who have been asked or expected to pay a bribe by a government official. g. Data refer to 1995.
Source: Columns 1-7: UNICRI 2002.

22 Gender-related development index

HDI rank		Gender-related development index (GDI)		Life expectancy at birth (years) 2000		Adult literacy rate (% age 15 and above) 2000		Combined primary, secondary and tertiary gross enrolment ratio (%)[a] 1999		Estimated earned income (PPP US$) 2000[b]		HDI rank minus GDI rank[c]
		Rank	Value	Female	Male	Female	Male	Female	Male	Female	Male	
High human development												
1	Norway	3	0.941	81.5	75.6	..[d]	..[d]	99	95	23,454[e]	36,510[e]	-2
2	Sweden	4	0.940	82.2	77.2	..[d]	..[d]	107[f]	95	19,690[e]	28,961[e]	-2
3	Canada	5	0.938	81.5	76.0	..[d]	..[d]	98	96	21,456[e]	34,349[e]	-2
4	Belgium	2	0.943	81.5	75.2	..[d]	..[d]	111[f]	107[f]	16,784	38,005	2
5	Australia	1	0.956	81.8	76.1	..[d]	..[d]	118[f]	114[f]	20,977	30,449	4
6	United States	6	0.937	79.9	74.1	..[d]	..[d]	99	91	26,259[e]	42,246[e]	0
7	Iceland	7	0.934	81.5	76.8	..[d]	..[d]	91	86	22,361	36,758	0
8	Netherlands	9	0.933	80.8	75.4	..[d]	..[d]	100	104[f]	17,635	33,822	-1
9	Japan	11	0.927	84.4	77.4	..[d]	..[d]	81	83	16,601	37,345	-2
10	Finland	8	0.933	81.1	73.9	..[d]	..[d]	108[f]	99	20,657	29,550	2
11	Switzerland	14	0.923	82.0	75.6	..[d]	..[d]	81	87	19,197	38,550	-3
12	France	12	0.926	82.4	74.7	..[d]	..[d]	96	93	18,715	30,022	0
13	United Kingdom	10	0.932	80.2	75.2	..[d]	..[d]	112[f]	100	17,931	29,264	3
14	Denmark	13	0.925	78.7	73.8	..[d]	..[d]	101[f]	94	22,835	32,518	1
15	Austria	15	0.921	81.1	74.9	..[d]	..[d]	89	90	17,914[e]	36,057[e]	0
16	Luxembourg	19	0.914	80.5	74.1	..[d]	..[d]	74[g]	71[g]	27,396	73,465[h]	-3
17	Germany	16	0.920	80.7	74.5	..[d]	..[d]	93	95	16,904	33,653	1
18	Ireland	17	0.917	79.2	74.0	..[d]	..[d]	93	89	17,078[e]	42,815[e]	1
19	New Zealand	18	0.915	80.2	74.9	..[d]	..[d]	103[f]	95	16,203	24,052	1
20	Italy	20	0.907	81.6	75.2	98.0	98.9	87	81	14,719[e]	33,084[e]	0
21	Spain	21	0.906	82.0	75.0	96.8	98.6	99	91	11,791[e]	27,503[e]	0
22	Israel	22	0.891	80.6	76.7	92.4	96.8	84	82	13,864[e]	26,565[e]	0
23	Hong Kong, China (SAR)	23	0.886	82.4	76.9	90.2	96.5	66	61	18,635	31,445	0
24	Greece	25	0.879	80.9	75.6	96.0	98.5	81	80	10,185[e]	22,998[e]	-1
25	Singapore	24	0.880	79.8	75.4	88.4	96.3	75	76	15,433	31,167	1
26	Cyprus	26	0.879	80.2	75.8	95.4	98.7	70[i]	67[i]	13,763	27,908	0
27	Korea, Rep. of	29	0.875	78.6	71.2	96.4	99.1[d]	85	95	10,791	23,884	-2
28	Portugal	28	0.876	79.2	72.1	89.9	94.7	99	94	12,134	22,850	0
29	Slovenia	27	0.877	79.1	71.7	99.6[d]	99.7[d]	85	80	13,327[e]	21,642[e]	2
30	Malta	30	0.860	80.6	75.4	92.7	91.3	79	82	7,626[e]	27,104[e]	0
31	Barbados	..	..	79.1	74.1	..	..	77	77	..	..	..
32	Brunei Darussalam	31	0.851	78.5	73.8	88.1	94.6	77	76	10,296[e,j]	22,613[e,j]	0
33	Czech Republic	32	0.846	78.2	71.5	..[d]	..[d]	70	69	10,354	17,833	0
34	Argentina	33	0.836	77.2	70.1	96.8	96.8	86	80	6,556[e]	18,424[e]	0
35	Hungary	35	0.833	75.6	67.1	99.2[d]	99.5[d]	83	79	9,243	15,893	-1
36	Slovakia	34	0.833	77.2	69.3	..[d]	..[d]	77	74	8,903[e]	13,715[e]	1
37	Poland	36	0.831	77.5	69.2	99.7[d]	99.7[d]	86	83	6,936[e]	11,288[e]	0
38	Chile	39	0.824	78.6	72.6	95.6	96.0	77	78	5,133[e]	13,786[e]	-2
39	Bahrain	40	0.822	75.8	71.6	82.6	90.9	83	77	7,010[k]	21,059[k]	-2
40	Uruguay	37	0.828	78.5	71.0	98.1	97.3	83	76	6,178[e]	12,068[e]	2
41	Bahamas	38	0.825	73.7	65.0	96.3	94.5	77	72	13,344[e]	20,779[e]	2
42	Estonia	..	..	76.0	65.1	..	..	89	84	..	..	..
43	Costa Rica	41	0.814	79.3	74.6	95.7	95.5	66	67	4,609	12,577	0
44	Saint Kitts and Nevis	..	..	..	..	..	..	..	..	..	..	..
45	Kuwait	44	0.804	78.6	74.5	79.7	84.0	61	57	6,895[e]	22,186[e]	-2
46	United Arab Emirates	47	0.798	78.0	73.7	79.3	75.0	71	65	5,320[e,j]	24,412[e,j]	-4
47	Seychelles	..	..	..	..	..	..	..	..	..	..	..
48	Croatia	43	0.806	77.7	69.8	97.3	99.3[d]	69	68	5,845[e]	10,485[e]	1
49	Lithuania	42	0.806	77.2	66.8	99.5[d]	99.7[d]	83	77	5,789	8,582	3
50	Trinidad and Tobago	45	0.798	76.7	72.0	92.1	95.5	65	65	5,532[e]	12,432[e]	1

22 Gender-related development index

HDI rank		Gender-related development index (GDI)		Life expectancy at birth (years) 2000		Adult literacy rate (% age 15 and above) 2000		Combined primary, secondary and tertiary gross enrolment ratio (%)[a] 1999		Estimated earned income (PPP US$) 2000[b]		HDI rank minus GDI rank[c]
		Rank	Value	Female	Male	Female	Male	Female	Male	Female	Male	
51	Qatar	48	0.794	71.3	68.7	83.1	80.4	75	75	6,864 [e, l]	25,277 [e, l]	-1
52	Antigua and Barbuda	..	..	..	..	..	..	..	..	..	..	..
53	Latvia	46	0.798	75.8	64.7	99.8 [d]	99.8 [d]	83	80	5,992	8,276	2
Medium human development												
54	Mexico	49	0.789	76.0	70.0	89.5	93.4	70	71	4,978	13,152	0
55	Cuba	..	..	78.4	74.5	96.6	96.8	77	76	..	..	..
56	Belarus	50	0.786	74.4	62.8	99.4 [d]	99.7 [d]	79	75	5,978 [e]	9,340 [e]	0
57	Panama	51	0.784	76.8	72.2	91.3	92.5	76	73	3,960	8,004	0
58	Belize	58	0.764	75.4	72.7	93.2	93.3	72	73	2,141 [e]	8,975 [e]	-6
59	Malaysia	54	0.776	75.0	70.1	83.4	91.4	67	64	5,711 [e]	12,338 [e]	-1
60	Russian Federation	52	0.780	72.5	60.1	99.4 [d]	99.7 [d]	82	75	6,611 [e]	10,383 [e]	2
61	Dominica	..	..	..	..	..	..	..	..	..	..	..
62	Bulgaria	53	0.778	74.8	67.1	97.9	99.0	76	69	4,587	6,898	2
63	Romania	55	0.773	73.3	66.5	97.3	99.0 [d]	70	68	4,751 [e]	8,169 [e]	1
64	Libyan Arab Jamahiriya	61	0.753	72.8	68.8	68.2	90.8	92	92	2,921 [l]	11,894 [l]	-4
65	Macedonia, TFYR	..	..	75.3	71.0	..	..	70	70	..	..	..
66	Saint Lucia	..	..	76.0	70.7	..	..	..	..	..	..	..
67	Mauritius	59	0.762	75.3	67.6	81.3	87.8	64	62	5,332 [e]	14,736 [e]	-1
68	Colombia	56	0.767	74.8	68.2	91.7	91.7	73	73	3,996 [e]	8,558 [e]	3
69	Venezuela	57	0.764	76.2	70.4	92.1	93.1	66	64	3,334 [e]	8,223 [e]	3
70	Thailand	60	0.760	73.2	67.3	93.9	97.1	61	60	4,907	7,928	1
71	Saudi Arabia	72	0.731	73.0	70.5	66.9	83.1	60	62	3,466 [e]	18,252 [e]	-10
72	Fiji	65	0.746	70.9	67.4	90.8	94.9	83	84	2,367 [e]	6,892 [e]	-2
73	Brazil	64	0.751	72.0	64.1	85.4	85.1	80	79	4,557	10,769	0
74	Suriname	..	..	73.2	68.0	..	..	86	80	..	..	..
75	Lebanon	69	0.739	74.6	71.5	80.3	92.1	81	76	2,013 [e]	6,704 [e]	-4
76	Armenia	62	0.751	75.8	69.8	97.6	99.3 [d]	77	82	2,087 [e]	3,061 [e]	4
77	Philippines	63	0.751	71.3	67.3	95.1	95.5	84	80	2,933	4,994	4
78	Oman	78	0.722	72.6	69.7	61.6	80.1	56	59	3,806 [e, l]	21,804 [e, l]	-10
79	Kazakhstan	..	..	70.3	59.1	..	..	81	73	..	..	..
80	Ukraine	66	0.744	73.5	62.7	99.5 [d]	99.7 [d]	78	77	2,716	5,085	3
81	Georgia	..	..	77.2	69.0	..	..	71	69	..	..	..
82	Peru	73	0.729	71.6	66.6	85.3	94.7	79	81	1,950	7,695	-3
83	Grenada	..	..	..	..	..	..	..	..	..	..	..
84	Maldives	68	0.739	65.8	67.3	96.8	96.6	77	77	3,329 [e]	5,582 [e]	3
85	Turkey	71	0.734	72.4	67.3	76.5	93.5	55	68	4,379 [e]	9,516 [e]	1
86	Jamaica	67	0.739	77.3	73.3	90.7	82.9	62	63	2,900 [e]	4,400 [e]	6
87	Turkmenistan	..	..	69.6	62.9	..	..	81	81	..	..	..
88	Azerbaijan	..	..	75.0	68.0	..	..	72	70	..	..	..
89	Sri Lanka	70	0.737	75.3	69.5	89.0	94.4	71	68	2,270	4,724	4
90	Paraguay	75	0.727	72.6	68.0	92.2	94.4	64	64	2,155	6,658	0
91	St. Vincent & the Grenadines	..	..	..	..	..	..	..	..	..	..	..
92	Albania	74	0.729	76.2	70.4	77.0	92.1	71	71	2,478 [e]	4,488 [e]	2
93	Ecuador	80	0.718	73.0	67.8	90.0	93.3	74	80	1,455 [e]	4,936 [e]	-3
94	Dominican Republic	79	0.718	70.0	64.8	83.6	83.6	75	69	3,125 [e]	8,849 [e]	-1
95	Uzbekistan	76	0.725	71.9	66.0	98.8	99.6 [d]	74	79	1,931 [e]	2,958 [e]	3
96	China	77	0.724	72.8	68.5	76.3	91.7	73	73	3,132 [e]	4,773 [e]	3
97	Tunisia	81	0.709	71.4	69.0	60.6	81.4	72	75	3,347 [e]	9,320 [e]	0
98	Iran, Islamic Rep. of	83	0.703	69.8	68.0	69.3	83.2	69	76	2,524 [e]	9,088 [e]	-1
99	Jordan	84	0.701	71.8	69.1	83.9	95.1	57	53	1,749	6,014	-1
100	Cape Verde	82	0.704	72.0	66.2	65.7	84.5	76	79	3,043 [e]	6,945 [e]	2

HDI rank		Gender-related development index (GDI)		Life expectancy at birth (years) 2000		Adult literacy rate (% age 15 and above) 2000		Combined primary, secondary and tertiary gross enrolment ratio (%)[a] 1999		Estimated earned income (PPP US$) 2000[b]		HDI rank minus GDI rank[c]
		Rank	Value	Female	Male	Female	Male	Female	Male	Female	Male	
101	Samoa (Western)	..	..	72.8	66.2	79.0	81.2	67	63	..	..	..
102	Kyrgyzstan	..	..	71.7	63.8	..	..	70	65	..	..	..
103	Guyana	85	0.698	67.3	58.9	98.1	98.9	66	65	2,228 [e]	5,806 [e]	0
104	El Salvador	87	0.696	73.1	67.1	76.1	81.6	64	63	2,347	6,727	-1
105	Moldova, Rep. of	86	0.698	70.3	62.8	98.3	99.5 [d]	75	70	1,680 [e]	2,577 [e]	1
106	Algeria	90	0.679	71.0	68.1	57.1	76.2	69	75	2,389 [e]	8,150 [e]	-2
107	South Africa	88	0.689	53.9	50.2	84.6	86.0	96	89	5,888 [e]	13,024 [e]	1
108	Syrian Arab Republic	92	0.669	72.4	70.0	60.5	88.3	61	65	1,537 [e]	5,522 [e]	-2
109	Viet Nam	89	0.687	70.6	65.9	91.4	95.5	64	69	1,635 [e]	2,360 [e]	2
110	Indonesia	91	0.678	68.2	64.3	82.0	91.8	61	68	2,053 [e]	4,026 [e]	1
111	Equatorial Guinea	93	0.669	52.6	49.4	74.4	92.5	59	68	8,608 [e]	21,708 [e]	0
112	Tajikistan	94	0.664	70.5	64.7	98.8	99.6 [d]	63	72	872 [e]	1,434 [e]	0
113	Mongolia	95	0.653	64.9	60.9	98.8	99.1 [d]	64	51	1,430 [e]	2,135 [e]	0
114	Bolivia	96	0.645	64.2	60.8	79.3	92.0	67	73	1,499 [e]	3,358 [e]	0
115	Egypt	99	0.628	68.8	65.7	43.8	66.6	72	80	2,003	5,227	-2
116	Honduras	98	0.628	68.9	63.2	74.5	74.7	63	60	1,295 [e]	3,596 [e]	0
117	Gabon	..	..	53.9	51.5	..	..	87	85	..	..	..
118	Nicaragua	97	0.629	71.1	66.4	66.8	66.3	65	61	1,431 [e]	3,310 [e]	2
119	São Tomé and Principe	..	..	..	..	..	..	..	..	..	..	..
120	Guatemala	100	0.617	68.0	62.2	61.2	76.1	45	53	1,836 [e]	5,772 [e]	0
121	Solomon Islands	..	..	69.7	67.2	..	..	..	..	..	..	..
122	Namibia	101	0.604	44.7	44.6	81.2	82.8	80	77	4,413 [e]	8,498 [e]	0
123	Morocco	102	0.585	69.5	65.8	36.1	61.8	46	58	2,019 [e]	5,068 [e]	0
124	India	105	0.560	63.8	62.8	45.4	68.4	49	62	1,267 [e]	3,383 [e]	-2
125	Swaziland	103	0.567	45.1	43.7	78.6	80.8	70	74	2,557 [e]	6,479 [e]	1
126	Botswana	104	0.566	40.1	40.2	79.8	74.5	70	70	5,418 [e]	9,025 [e]	1
127	Myanmar	106	0.548	58.5	53.7	80.5	89.0	55	55	747 [l]	1,311 [l]	0
128	Zimbabwe	107	0.545	42.5	43.2	84.7	92.8	63	67	1,946 [e]	3,324 [e]	0
129	Ghana	108	0.544	58.1	55.5	62.9	80.3	39	45	1,683 [e]	2,248 [e]	0
130	Cambodia	109	0.537	58.6	53.9	57.1	79.8	54	71	1,268 [e]	1,633 [e]	0
131	Vanuatu	..	..	69.8	66.7	..	..	..	..	..	..	..
132	Lesotho	111	0.521	45.6	45.8	93.6	72.5	65	57	1,223 [e]	2,853 [e]	-1
133	Papua New Guinea	110	0.530	57.7	55.8	56.8	70.6	35	42	1,670 [e]	2,840 [e]	1
134	Kenya	112	0.511	51.5	50.0	76.0	88.9	51	52	975	1,069	0
135	Cameroon	115	0.500	50.7	49.2	69.5	82.4	39	47	1,047 [e]	2,365 [e]	-2
136	Congo	113	0.506	53.4	49.2	74.4	87.5	56	69	586 [e]	1,074 [e]	1
137	Comoros	114	0.505	61.2	58.4	48.7	63.2	33	38	1,136 [e]	2,038 [e]	1
Low human development												
138	Pakistan	120	0.468	59.8	60.2	27.9	57.5	28	51	916 [e]	2,884 [e]	-4
139	Sudan	116	0.478	57.4	54.6	46.3	69.5	31	36	847 [e]	2,736 [e]	1
140	Bhutan	..	..	63.2	60.8	..	..	..	..	..	..	..
141	Togo	117	0.475	53.0	50.6	42.5	72.4	49	76	927 [e]	1,964 [e]	1
142	Nepal	119	0.470	58.3	58.8	24.0	59.6	52	67	880 [e]	1,752 [e]	0
143	Lao People's Dem. Rep.	118	0.472	54.8	52.2	33.2	64.1	52	65	1,242 [e]	1,909 [e]	2
144	Yemen	128	0.426	61.6	59.4	25.2	67.5	29	72	405 [e]	1,384 [e]	-7
145	Bangladesh	121	0.468	59.5	59.4	29.9	52.3	33	41	1,151 [e]	2,026 [e]	1
146	Haiti	122	0.467	55.7	49.7	47.8	52.0	51	53	1,049 [e]	1,902 [e]	1
147	Madagascar	123	0.463	53.8	51.5	59.7	73.6	43	46	624 [e]	1,059 [e]	1
148	Nigeria	124	0.449	51.9	51.5	55.7	72.4	41	49	532 [e]	1,254 [e]	1
149	Djibouti	..	..	44.2	41.6	54.4	75.6	18	26	..	..	..
150	Uganda	125	0.437	44.6	43.3	56.8	77.5	41	49	966 [e]	1,451 [e]	1

HDI rank		Gender-related development index (GDI)		Life expectancy at birth (years) 2000		Adult literacy rate (% age 15 and above) 2000		Combined primary, secondary and tertiary gross enrolment ratio (%) [a] 1999		Estimated earned income (PPP US$) 2000 [b]		HDI rank minus GDI rank [c]
		Rank	Value	Female	Male	Female	Male	Female	Male	Female	Male	
151	Tanzania, U. Rep. of	126	0.436	52.1	50.0	66.5	83.9	32	33	436 [e]	611 [e]	1
152	Mauritania	127	0.429	53.1	49.9	30.1	50.7	37	44	1,212 [e]	2,150 [e]	1
153	Zambia	129	0.424	40.9	41.8	71.5	85.2	46	52	562 [e]	995 [e]	0
154	Senegal	130	0.421	55.2	51.5	27.6	47.3	31	40	1,074 [e]	1,949 [e]	0
155	Congo, Dem. Rep. of the	131	0.420	52.6	50.1	50.2	73.1	26	37	548 [e,j]	986 [e,j]	0
156	Côte d'Ivoire	132	0.411	48.1	47.5	38.6	54.5	30	46	868 [e]	2,355 [e]	0
157	Eritrea	133	0.410	53.3	50.6	44.5	67.3	24	29	571	1,107	0
158	Benin	134	0.404	55.5	52.1	23.6	52.1	34	57	813 [e]	1,172 [e]	0
159	Guinea	..	..	48.0	47.0	..	..	20	37	..	..	..
160	Gambia	136	0.397	47.7	44.9	29.4	44.0	37	53	1,230 [e]	2,078 [e]	-1
161	Angola	..	..	46.6	43.9	..	..	21	25	..	..	..
162	Rwanda	135	0.398	40.9	39.4	60.2	73.7	39	41	760 [e]	1,130 [e]	1
163	Malawi	137	0.389	39.8	40.2	46.5	74.5	69	78	506 [e]	726 [e]	0
164	Mali	138	0.378	52.4	50.4	34.4	48.9	22	34	606 [e]	992 [e]	0
165	Central African Republic	139	0.364	46.0	42.7	34.9	59.7	20	29	894 [e]	1,464 [e]	0
166	Chad	140	0.353	46.9	44.5	34.0	51.6	20	42	648 [e]	1,099 [e]	0
167	Guinea-Bissau	141	0.325	46.2	43.4	23.3	54.4	27	47	495 [e]	1,023 [e]	0
168	Ethiopia	142	0.313	44.6	43.2	30.9	47.2	19	34	454 [e]	885 [e]	0
169	Burkina Faso	143	0.312	47.6	45.6	14.1	33.9	18	28	801 [e]	1,164 [e]	0
170	Mozambique	144	0.307	40.2	38.4	28.7	60.1	19	26	705 [e]	1,007 [e]	0
171	Burundi	145	0.306	41.4	39.6	40.4	56.2	16	21	490 [e]	698 [e]	0
172	Niger	146	0.263	45.5	44.9	8.4	23.8	12	20	542 [e]	947 [e]	0
173	Sierra Leone	..	..	40.2	37.6	..	..	21	32	..	..	..

a. Preliminary UNESCO estimates subject to further revision. b. Because of the lack of gender-disaggregated income data, female and male earned income are crudely estimated on the basis of data on the ratio of the female non-agricultural wage to the male non-agricultural wage, the female and male shares of the economically active population, the total female and male population and GDP per capita (PPP US$) (see technical note 1). Unless otherwise specified, estimates are based on data for the latest year available during 1991-2000. c. The HDI ranks used in this column are those recalculated for the 146 countries with a GDI value. A positive figure indicates that the GDI rank is higher than the HDI rank, a negative the opposite. d. For purposes of calculating the GDI a value of 99.0% was applied. e. No wage data available. For purposes of calculating the estimated female and male earned income an estimate of 75% was used for the ratio of the female non-agricultural wage to the male non-agricultural wage. f. For purposes of calculating the GDI a value of 100% was applied. g. The ratio is an underestimate, as many secondary and tertiary students pursue their studies in nearby countries. h. For purposes of calculating the GDI a value of $40,000 (PPP US$) was applied. i. Excludes Turkish students and population. j. Calculated on the basis of GDP per capita (PPP US$) for 1998. k. Calculated on the basis of GDP per capita (PPP US$) for 1999. l. Calculated on the basis of GDP per capita (PPP US$) for 1996 using data from Aten, Heston and Summers (2001).

Source: Column 1: determined on the basis of the GDI values in column 2; *column 2:* calculated on the basis of data in columns 3-10; see technical note 1 for details; *columns 3 and 4:* UN 2001; *columns 5 and 6:* UNESCO 2002a; *columns 7 and 8:* UNESCO 2001a; *columns 9 and 10:* unless otherwise noted, calculated on the basis of data on GDP per capita (PPP US$) from World Bank (2002b), data on wages from ILO (2002e), data on the economically active population from ILO (2002b) and data on population from UN (2001); *column 11:* determined on the basis of the recalculated HDI ranks and the GDI ranks in column 1.

GDI ranks for 146 countries			
	23 Hong Kong, China (SAR)	48 Qatar	73 Peru	98 Honduras	123 Madagascar
	24 Singapore	49 Mexico	74 Albania	99 Egypt	124 Nigeria
	25 Greece	50 Belarus	75 Paraguay	100 Guatemala	125 Uganda
1 Australia	26 Cyprus	51 Panama	76 Uzbekistan	101 Namibia	126 Tanzania, U. Rep. of
2 Belgium	27 Slovenia	52 Russian Federation	77 China	102 Morocco	127 Mauritania
3 Norway	28 Portugal	53 Bulgaria	78 Oman	103 Swaziland	128 Yemen
4 Sweden	29 Korea, Rep. of	54 Malaysia	79 Dominican Republic	104 Botswana	129 Zambia
5 Canada	30 Malta	55 Romania	80 Ecuador	105 India	130 Senegal
6 United States	31 Brunei Darussalam	56 Colombia	81 Tunisia	106 Myanmar	131 Congo, Dem. Rep. of the
7 Iceland	32 Czech Republic	57 Venezuela	82 Cape Verde	107 Zimbabwe	132 Côte d'Ivoire
8 Finland	33 Argentina	58 Belize	83 Iran, Islamic Rep. of	108 Ghana	133 Eritrea
9 Netherlands	34 Slovakia	59 Mauritius	84 Jordan	109 Cambodia	134 Benin
10 United Kingdom	35 Hungary	60 Thailand	85 Guyana	110 Papua New Guinea	135 Rwanda
11 Japan	36 Poland	61 Libyan Arab Jamahiriya	86 Moldova, Rep. of	111 Lesotho	136 Gambia
12 France	37 Uruguay	62 Armenia	87 El Salvador	112 Kenya	137 Malawi
13 Denmark	38 Bahamas	63 Philippines	88 South Africa	113 Congo	138 Mali
14 Switzerland	39 Chile	64 Brazil	89 Viet Nam	114 Comoros	139 Central African Republic
15 Austria	40 Bahrain	65 Fiji	90 Algeria	115 Cameroon	140 Chad
16 Germany	41 Costa Rica	66 Ukraine	91 Indonesia	116 Sudan	141 Guinea-Bissau
17 Ireland	42 Lithuania	67 Jamaica	92 Syrian Arab Republic	117 Togo	142 Ethiopia
18 New Zealand	43 Croatia	68 Maldives	93 Equatorial Guinea	118 Lao People's Dem. Rep.	143 Burkina Faso
19 Luxembourg	44 Kuwait	69 Lebanon	94 Tajikistan	119 Nepal	144 Mozambique
20 Italy	45 Trinidad and Tobago	70 Sri Lanka	95 Mongolia	120 Pakistan	145 Burundi
21 Spain	46 Latvia	71 Turkey	96 Bolivia	121 Bangladesh	146 Niger
22 Israel	47 United Arab Emirates	72 Saudi Arabia	97 Nicaragua	122 Haiti	

23 Gender empowerment measure

HDI rank		Gender empowerment measure (GEM)		Seats in parliament held by women (as % of total) [a]	Female legislators, senior officials and managers (as % of total) [b]	Female professional and technical workers (as % of total) [b]	Ratio of estimated female to male earned income [c]
		Rank	Value				
High human development							
1	Norway	1	0.837	36.4	25	49	0.64
2	Sweden	3	0.824	42.7	29	49	0.68
3	Canada	7	0.777	23.6	35	53	0.62
4	Belgium	14	0.706	24.9	19 [d]	50 [d]	0.44
5	Australia	10	0.759	26.5	26	48	0.69
6	United States	11	0.757	13.8	45 [d]	54 [d]	0.62
7	Iceland	2	0.833	34.9	27	53	0.61
8	Netherlands	6	0.781	32.9	27	46	0.52
9	Japan	32	0.527	10.0	9 [d]	45 [d]	0.44
10	Finland	5	0.803	36.5	27	56	0.70
11	Switzerland	13	0.718	22.4	22	42	0.50
12	France	..	..	10.9	..	..	..
13	United Kingdom	16	0.684	17.1	33	45	0.61
14	Denmark	4	0.821	38.0	23	50	0.70
15	Austria	12	0.745	25.1	28	49	0.50
16	Luxembourg	..	..	16.7	..	..	..
17	Germany	8	0.765	31.0	27	50	0.50
18	Ireland	17	0.675	13.7	34	50	0.40
19	New Zealand	9	0.765	30.8	38	54	0.67
20	Italy	31	0.539	9.1	19	44	0.44
21	Spain	15	0.702	26.6	32	45	0.43
22	Israel	22	0.596	13.3	26	55	0.52
23	Hong Kong, China (SAR)	..	..	..	25	38	..
24	Greece	41	0.512	8.7	25	47	0.44
25	Singapore	23	0.592	11.8	23	42	0.50
26	Cyprus	34	0.525	10.7	14	42	0.49
27	Korea, Rep. of	61	0.378	5.9	5	34	0.45
28	Portugal	20	0.638	18.7	32	50	0.53
29	Slovenia	25	0.585	12.2	31	51	0.62
30	Malta	..	..	9.2	..	..	..
31	Barbados	18	0.658	20.4	40 [d]	55 [d]	0.61
32	Brunei Darussalam	..	..	– [e]	..	..	..
33	Czech Republic	28	0.560	14.2	26	53	0.58
34	Argentina	..	..	31.3	..	..	..
35	Hungary	44	0.500	8.3	34	61	0.58
36	Slovakia	29	0.545	14.0	31	62	0.65
37	Poland	24	0.590	20.7	33	61	0.61
38	Chile	49	0.474	10.1	26 [d]	52 [d]	0.37
39	Bahrain	..	..	– [f]	..	..	..
40	Uruguay	36	0.519	11.5	36	54	0.51
41	Bahamas	19	0.652	19.6	31	51	0.64
42	Estonia	27	0.568	17.8	36	67	0.64
43	Costa Rica	26	0.579	19.3 [g]	33	46	0.37
44	Saint Kitts and Nevis	..	..	13.3	..	..	..
45	Kuwait	..	..	0.0	..	..	..
46	United Arab Emirates	..	..	0.0	8	25	..
47	Seychelles	..	..	23.5	..	..	..
48	Croatia	33	0.527	16.2	25	53	0.56
49	Lithuania	47	0.483	10.6	42	70	0.67
50	Trinidad and Tobago	21	0.611	20.9 [g]	42	53	0.44

HDI rank	Gender empowerment measure (GEM)		Seats in parliament held by women (as % of total) [a]	Female legislators, senior officials and managers (as % of total) [b]	Female professional and technical workers (as % of total) [b]	Ratio of estimated female to male earned income [c]
	Rank	Value				
51 Qatar	..	..	– [e]	..	..	..
52 Antigua and Barbuda	..	..	8.3	..	..	..
53 Latvia	30	0.539	17.0	37	67	0.72
Medium human development						
54 Mexico	38	0.517	15.9	24	41	0.38
55 Cuba	..	..	27.6	..	..	..
56 Belarus	..	..	18.4	..	..	..
57 Panama	48	0.475	9.9	33 [d]	46 [d]	0.49
58 Belize	45	0.499	13.5	37 [d]	39 [d]	0.24
59 Malaysia	43	0.505	14.5	20 [d]	45 [d]	0.46
60 Russian Federation	53	0.450	6.4	37	64	0.64
61 Dominica	..	..	18.8	..	..	..
62 Bulgaria	..	..	26.2	..	..	..
63 Romania	54	0.450	9.3	26	57	0.58
64 Libyan Arab Jamahiriya	..	..	..	..	..	..
65 Macedonia, TFYR	..	..	6.7	..	..	..
66 Saint Lucia	..	..	13.8	..	..	..
67 Mauritius	58	0.410	5.7	23	38	0.36
68 Colombia	42	0.509	12.2	38 [d]	49 [d]	0.47
69 Venezuela	56	0.442	9.7	24 [d]	58 [d]	0.41
70 Thailand	50	0.458	9.6	27 [d]	55 [d]	0.62
71 Saudi Arabia	..	..	– [e]	..	..	..
72 Fiji	..	..	..	..	..	..
73 Brazil	..	..	6.7	..	62 [d]	..
74 Suriname	37	0.518	17.6	28 [d]	51 [d]	0.37
75 Lebanon	..	..	2.3	..	..	..
76 Armenia	..	..	3.1	..	..	..
77 Philippines	35	0.523	17.2	35 [d]	66 [d]	0.59
78 Oman	..	..	– [e]	..	..	..
79 Kazakhstan	..	..	11.2	..	..	..
80 Ukraine	57	0.428	7.8	36	63	0.53
81 Georgia	..	..	7.2	..	..	..
82 Peru	39	0.516	18.3	28	39	0.25
83 Grenada	..	..	17.9	..	..	..
84 Maldives	62	0.361	6.0	15	40	0.60
85 Turkey	63	0.312	4.2	9 [d]	36 [d]	0.46
86 Jamaica	..	..	16.0	..	..	..
87 Turkmenistan	..	..	26.0	..	..	..
88 Azerbaijan	..	..	10.5	..	..	..
89 Sri Lanka	64	0.274	4.4	4	49	0.48
90 Paraguay	59	0.408	8.0	23 [d]	54 [d]	0.32
91 St. Vincent & the Grenadines	..	..	22.7	..	..	..
92 Albania	..	..	5.7	..	..	..
93 Ecuador	46	0.484	14.6	28 [d]	47 [d]	0.29
94 Dominican Republic	40	0.514	14.5	31	49	0.35
95 Uzbekistan	..	..	7.2	..	..	..
96 China	..	..	21.8	..	..	..
97 Tunisia	..	..	11.5	..	..	..
98 Iran, Islamic Rep. of	..	..	3.4	..	..	..
99 Jordan	..	..	3.3	..	..	..
100 Cape Verde	..	..	11.1	..	..	..

HDI rank		Gender empowerment measure (GEM)		Seats in parliament held by women (as % of total) [a]	Female legislators, senior officials and managers (as % of total) [b]	Female professional and technical workers (as % of total) [b]	Ratio of estimated female to male earned income [c]
		Rank	Value				
101	Samoa (Western)	..	..	6.1	..	..	..
102	Kyrgyzstan	..	..	6.7	..	..	..
103	Guyana	..	..	20.0	..	..	..
104	El Salvador	52	0.454	9.5	33	47	0.35
105	Moldova, Rep. of	51	0.456	12.9	33	67	0.65
106	Algeria	..	..	4.0	..	..	..
107	South Africa	..	..	29.8 [h]	..	..	..
108	Syrian Arab Republic	..	..	10.4	..	..	..
109	Viet Nam	..	..	26.0	..	..	..
110	Indonesia	..	..	8.0	..	..	..
111	Equatorial Guinea	..	..	5.0	..	..	..
112	Tajikistan	..	..	12.4	..	..	..
113	Mongolia	..	..	10.5	..	..	..
114	Bolivia	55	0.450	10.2	36	40	0.45
115	Egypt	65	0.260	2.4	10	31	0.38
116	Honduras	60	0.405	5.5	36 [d]	51 [d]	0.36
117	Gabon	..	..	11.0	..	..	..
118	Nicaragua	..	..	20.7	..	..	..
119	São Tomé and Principe	..	..	9.1	..	..	..
120	Guatemala	..	..	8.8	..	..	..
121	Solomon Islands	..	..	0.0	..	..	..
122	Namibia	..	..	20.4	..	..	..
123	Morocco	..	..	0.5	..	..	..
124	India	..	..	8.9	..	..	..
125	Swaziland	..	..	6.3	..	..	..
126	Botswana	..	..	17.0	..	..	..
127	Myanmar	..	..	– [i]	..	..	..
128	Zimbabwe	..	..	10.0	..	..	..
129	Ghana	..	..	9.0	..	..	..
130	Cambodia	..	..	9.3	..	..	..
131	Vanuatu	..	..	0.0	..	..	..
132	Lesotho	..	..	10.7	..	..	..
133	Papua New Guinea	..	..	1.8	..	..	..
134	Kenya	..	..	3.6	..	..	..
135	Cameroon	..	..	5.6	..	..	..
136	Congo	..	..	12.0	..	..	..
137	Comoros	..	..	– [i]	..	..	..
Low human development							
138	Pakistan	..	..	– [i]	9 [d]	26 [d]	..
139	Sudan	..	..	9.7	..	..	..
140	Bhutan	..	..	9.3	..	..	..
141	Togo	..	..	4.9	..	..	..
142	Nepal	..	..	7.9 [g]	..	..	..
143	Lao People's Dem. Rep.	..	..	21.2 [g]	..	..	..
144	Yemen	..	..	0.7	..	..	..
145	Bangladesh	66	0.223	2.0	5 [d]	35 [d]	0.57
146	Haiti	..	..	9.1	..	..	..
147	Madagascar	..	..	8.0 [g]	..	..	..
148	Nigeria	..	..	3.3	..	..	..
149	Djibouti	..	..	0.0	..	..	..
150	Uganda	..	..	24.7	..	..	..

HDI rank	Gender empowerment measure (GEM)		Seats in parliament held by women (as % of total) [a]	Female legislators, senior officials and managers (as % of total) [b]	Female professional and technical workers (as % of total) [b]	Ratio of estimated female to male earned income [c]
	Rank	Value				
151 Tanzania, U. Rep. of	..	..	22.3	..	..	..
152 Mauritania	..	..	3.0 [g]	..	..	..
153 Zambia	..	..	12.0	..	..	..
154 Senegal	..	..	19.2	..	..	..
155 Congo, Dem. Rep. of the	..	..	– [i]	..	..	..
156 Côte d'Ivoire	..	..	8.5	..	..	..
157 Eritrea	..	..	14.7	..	..	..
158 Benin	..	..	6.0	..	..	..
159 Guinea	..	..	8.8	..	..	..
160 Gambia	..	..	2.0 [g]	..	..	..
161 Angola	..	..	15.5	..	..	..
162 Rwanda	..	..	25.7	..	..	..
163 Malawi	..	..	9.3	..	..	..
164 Mali	..	..	12.2	..	..	..
165 Central African Republic	..	..	7.3	..	..	..
166 Chad	..	..	2.4	..	..	..
167 Guinea-Bissau	..	..	7.8	..	..	..
168 Ethiopia	..	..	7.8	..	..	..
169 Burkina Faso	..	..	11.0	..	..	..
170 Mozambique	..	..	30.0	..	..	..
171 Burundi	..	..	14.4 [g]	..	..	..
172 Niger	..	..	1.2	..	..	..
173 Sierra Leone	..	..	8.8	..	..	..

a. Data are as of 8 March 2002. Where there are lower and upper houses, data refer to the weighted average of women's shares of seats in both houses. b. Data refer to the latest year available during the period 1991-2000. Those for countries that have implemented the recent International Standard Classification of Occupations (ISCO-88) are not strictly comparable with those for countries using the previous classification (ISCO-68). c. Calculated on the basis of data in columns 9 and 10 in table 22. Estimates are based on data for the latest year available during the period 1991-2000. d. Data are based on the International Standard Classification of Occupations (ISCO-68) as defined in ILO (2001). e. The country has never had a parliament. f. The first legislature of Bahrain was dissolved by decree of the emir on 26 August 1975. g. Information for the most recent elections was not available in time for publication; data are based on previous elections. h. Calculated on the basis of the 54 permanent seats (that is, excluding the 36 special rotating delegates appointed on an ad hoc basis). i. The parliament elected in 1990 has never been convened nor authorized to sit, and many of its members were detained or forced into exile. j. Parliament has been dissolved or suspended for an indefinite period.

Source: Column 1: determined on the basis of the GEM values in column 2; *column 2:* calculated on the basis of data in columns 3-6; see technical note 1 for details; *column 3:* calculated on the basis of data on parliamentary seats from IPU (2002); *columns 4 and 5:* calculated on the basis of occupational data from ILO (2002e); *column 6:* calculated on the basis of data in columns 9 and 10 in table 22.

GEM ranks for 66 countries

1	Norway	16	United Kingdom	33	Croatia	50	Thailand
2	Iceland	17	Ireland	34	Cyprus	51	Moldova, Rep. of
3	Sweden	18	Barbados	35	Philippines	52	El Salvador
4	Denmark	19	Bahamas	36	Uruguay	53	Russian Federation
5	Finland	20	Portugal	37	Suriname	54	Romania
6	Netherlands	21	Trinidad and Tobago	38	Mexico	55	Bolivia
7	Canada	22	Israel	39	Peru	56	Venezuela
8	Germany	23	Singapore	40	Dominican Republic	57	Ukraine
9	New Zealand	24	Poland	41	Greece	58	Mauritius
10	Australia	25	Slovenia	42	Colombia	59	Paraguay
11	United States	26	Costa Rica	43	Malaysia	60	Honduras
12	Austria	27	Estonia	44	Hungary	61	Korea, Rep. of
13	Switzerland	28	Czech Republic	45	Belize	62	Maldives
14	Belgium	29	Slovakia	46	Ecuador	63	Turkey
15	Spain	30	Latvia	47	Lithuania	64	Sri Lanka
		31	Italy	48	Panama	65	Egypt
		32	Japan	49	Chile	66	Bangladesh

24 Gender inequality in education

HDI rank		Adult literacy		Youth literacy		Net primary enrolment		Net secondary enrolment		Gross tertiary enrolment [a]	
		Female rate (% age 15 and above) 2000	Female rate as % of male rate 2000	Female rate (% age 15-24) 2000	Female rate as % of male rate 2000	Female ratio (%) 1998	Female ratio as % of male ratio 1998	Female ratio (%) 1998	Female ratio as % of male ratio 1998	Female ratio (%) 1998	Female ratio as % of male ratio 1998
High human development												
1	Norway	..	..	..	..	100	100	97	101	76	140
2	Sweden	..	..	..	..	100	100	100	104	74	142
3	Canada	..	..	..	..	96	100	93	98	66	130
4	Belgium	..	..	..	..	100	100	96	102	..	..
5	Australia	..	..	..	..	..	..	..	..	..	..
6	United States	..	..	..	..	95	100	76	73	83	116
7	Iceland	..	..	..	..	98	98	88	106	51	171
8	Netherlands	..	..	..	..	100	99	93	101	49	101
9	Japan	..	..	..	..	100	100	..	..	40	85
10	Finland	..	..	..	..	98	100	95	101	92	122
11	Switzerland	..	..	..	..	93	99	80	93	30	75
12	France	..	..	..	..	100	100	95	102	57	125
13	United Kingdom	..	..	..	..	100	101	95	103	64	122
14	Denmark	..	..	..	..	100	100	91	103	63	134
15	Austria	..	..	..	..	90	103	..	..	52	108
16	Luxembourg	..	..	..	..	100	102	..	..	10 [b]	113 [b]
17	Germany	..	..	..	..	88	102	88	101	45	96
18	Ireland	..	..	..	..	100	101	78	103	50	121
19	New Zealand	..	..	..	..	100	100	..	..	..	..
20	Italy	98.0	99	99.8	100	100	100	89	102	53	128
21	Spain	96.8	98	99.8	100	100	100	93	103	60	118
22	Israel	92.4	95	99.2	100	95	100	85	101	57	142
23	Hong Kong, China (SAR)	90.2	93	99.8	101	..	..	..	..	..	..
24	Greece	96.0	97	99.8	100	95	100	88	103	52	107
25	Singapore	88.4	92	99.8	100	..	..	..	..	..	..
26	Cyprus	95.4	97	99.8	100	81	101	79	117	22 [c]	133 [c]
27	Korea, Rep. of	96.4	97	99.8	100	98	101	..	..	..	..
28	Portugal	89.9	95	99.8	100	100	95	92	109	51	130
29	Slovenia	99.6	100	99.8	100	93	99	91	104	61	134
30	Malta	92.7	102	99.8	102	100	101	78	94	21	113
31	Barbados	..	..	..	..	..	..	100	105	45	228
32	Brunei Darussalam	88.1	93	99.8	101	..	..	..	..	15	193
33	Czech Republic	..	..	..	..	90	100	81	103	27	103
34	Argentina	96.8	100	98.8	100	100	100	76	107	56	144
35	Hungary	99.2	100	99.8	100	82	101	86	102	37	124
36	Slovakia	..	..	..	..	..	..	..	..	28	111
37	Poland	99.7	100	99.8	100	96	100	59	108	..	..
38	Chile	95.6	100	99.1	100	87	99	72	105	32	88
39	Bahrain	82.6	91	98.6	100	98	102	85	112	32	156
40	Uruguay	98.1	101	99.5	100	93	101	76	136	45	184
41	Bahamas	96.3	102	98.3	102	87	100	100	97	..	..
42	Estonia	..	..	..	..	95	98	83	115	56	141
43	Costa Rica	95.7	100	98.6	101	..	..	..	..	..	..
44	Seychelles	..	..	..	..	..	..	..	..	..	..
45	Saint Kitts and Nevis	..	..	..	..	..	..	..	..	..	..
46	Kuwait	79.7	95	93.2	102	67	98	58	101	27	214
47	United Arab Emirates	79.3	106	94.4	108	82	98	73	106	..	..
48	Croatia	97.3	98	99.8	100	77	100	82	102	33	118
49	Lithuania	99.5	100	99.8	100	93	99	86	101	50	153
50	Trinidad and Tobago	92.1	96	97.2	99	93	100	75	107	7	138

HDI rank	Adult literacy Female rate (% age 15 and above) 2000	Adult literacy Female rate as % of male rate 2000	Youth literacy Female rate (% age 15-24) 2000	Youth literacy Female rate as % of male rate 2000	Net primary enrolment Female ratio (%) 1998	Net primary enrolment Female ratio as % of male ratio 1998	Net secondary enrolment Female ratio (%) 1998	Net secondary enrolment Female ratio as % of male ratio 1998	Gross tertiary enrolment[a] Female ratio (%) 1998	Gross tertiary enrolment[a] Female ratio as % of male ratio 1998
51 Qatar	83.1	103	97.1	105	85	99	69	107	39	280
52 Antigua and Barbuda	..	..	..	..	..	..	..	..	..	..
53 Latvia	99.8	100	99.8	100	92	95	83	98	62	157
Medium human development										
54 Mexico	89.5	96	96.5	99	100	101	56	100	18	93
55 Cuba	96.6	100	99.8	100	97	101	79	111	22	142
56 Belarus	99.4	100	99.8	100	..	..	..	..	53	131
57 Panama	91.3	99	96.4	99	..	..	..	..	..	..
58 Belize	93.2	100	98.7	101	99	99	43	123	..	..
59 Malaysia	83.4	91	97.7	100	98	100	97	109	..	..
60 Russian Federation	99.4	100	99.8	100	69	90	..	..	65	129
61 Dominica	..	..	..	..	..	..	..	..	..	..
62 Bulgaria	97.9	99	99.5	100	92	98	80	98	52	153
63 Romania	97.3	98	99.7	100	94	99	76	102	..	..
64 Libyan Arab Jamahiriya	68.2	75	93.1	93	..	..	76	113	57	103
65 Macedonia, TFYR	..	..	..	..	94	98	78	97	25	128
66 Saint Lucia	..	..	..	..	..	..	..	..	..	..
67 Mauritius	81.3	93	94.4	101	93	100	63	101	7	88
68 Colombia	91.7	100	97.6	101	..	..	..	..	..	..
69 Venezuela	92.1	99	98.7	101	..	..	..	..	..	..
70 Thailand	93.9	97	98.4	99	76	97	57	105	33	118
71 Saudi Arabia	66.9	81	90.3	95	57	93	..	..	22	135
72 Fiji	90.8	96	99.1	100	100	99	76	100	..	..
73 Brazil	85.4	100	94.3	104	96	95	..	..	15	122
74 Suriname	..	..	..	..	..	..	..	..	..	..
75 Lebanon	80.3	87	93.0	96	77	97	79	109	39	102
76 Armenia	97.6	98	99.7	100	..	..	..	..	..	..
77 Philippines	95.1	100	98.8	100	..	..	..	..	31	128
78 Oman	61.6	77	96.3	97	65	98	58	102	..	..
79 Kazakhstan	..	..	..	..	..	..	74	100	25	116
80 Ukraine	99.5	100	99.9	100	..	..	..	..	46	114
81 Georgia	..	..	..	..	..	..	..	..	36	112
82 Peru	85.3	90	95.3	97	100	99	61	98	15	34
83 Grenada	..	..	..	..	..	..	..	..	..	..
84 Maldives	96.8	100	99.4	101	..	..	..	..	..	..
85 Turkey	76.5	82	94.0	95	96	92	..	..	18	165
86 Jamaica	90.7	109	97.5	107	93	101	80	103	..	..
87 Turkmenistan	..	..	..	..	..	..	..	..	..	..
88 Azerbaijan	..	..	..	..	97	101	82	102	21	89
89 Sri Lanka	89.0	94	96.6	100	100	102	..	..	..	..
90 Paraguay	92.2	98	97.0	100	92	101	43	107	..	..
91 St. Vincent & the Grenadines	..	..	..	..	..	..	..	..	..	..
92 Albania	77.0	84	96.4	97	..	..	..	..	..	..
93 Ecuador	90.0	96	97.0	99	97	101	47	103	..	..
94 Dominican Republic	83.6	100	91.9	102	88	101	57	118	..	..
95 Uzbekistan	84.7	91	95.1	97	..	..	..	..	..	..
96 China	76.3	83	96.5	97	92	102	48	92	..	..
97 Tunisia	60.6	74	89.2	92	96	97	56	103	17	97
98 Iran, Islamic Rep. of	69.3	83	91.6	95	..	..	..	..	..	..
99 Jordan	83.9	88	99.3	100	65	102	62	107	..	..
100 Cape Verde	65.7	78	85.0	93	100	101	..	..	..	..

24 Gender inequality in education

HDI rank		Adult literacy — Female rate (% age 15 and above) 2000	Adult literacy — Female rate as % of male rate 2000	Youth literacy — Female rate (% age 15-24) 2000	Youth literacy — Female rate as % of male rate 2000	Net primary enrolment — Female ratio (%) 1998	Net primary enrolment — Female ratio as % of male ratio 1998	Net secondary enrolment — Female ratio (%) 1998	Net secondary enrolment — Female ratio as % of male ratio 1998	Gross tertiary enrolment[a] — Female ratio (%) 1998	Gross tertiary enrolment[a] — Female ratio as % of male ratio 1998
101	Samoa (Western)	79.0	97	87.5	101	98	102	68	110	7	93
102	Kyrgyzstan	..	..	..	..	84	99	..	..	..	..
103	Guyana	98.1	99	99.8	100	82	93	..	..	..	..
104	El Salvador	76.1	93	87.4	98	87	117	38	101	20	123
105	Moldova, Rep. of	98.3	99	99.8	100	..	..	..	..	..	..
106	Algeria	57.1	75	84.2	90	92	95	59	101	..	..
107	South Africa	84.6	98	91.3	100	100	100	..	..	18	115
108	Syrian Arab Republic	60.5	68	78.8	83	89	92	36	92	..	..
109	Viet Nam	91.4	96	97.2	100	95	95	50	104	9	79
110	Indonesia	82.0	89	97.1	99	..	..	..	..	..	..
111	Equatorial Guinea	74.4	80	95.4	97	73	79	14	36	..	..
112	Tajikistan	98.8	99	99.8	100	..	..	..	..	..	..
113	Mongolia	..	..	..	..	87	104	59	127	32	189
114	Bolivia	79.3	86	93.7	96	97	99	..	..	..	..
115	Egypt	43.8	66	62.7	82	89	94	..	..	..	..
116	Honduras	74.5	100	84.6	103	..	..	..	..	..	..
117	Gabon	..	..	..	..	..	..	..	..	6	55
118	Nicaragua	66.8	101	72.3	102	..	..	..	..	..	..
119	São Tomé and Principe	..	..	..	..	..	..	..	..	..	..
120	Guatemala	61.2	80	72.8	85	80	94	..	..	..	..
121	Solomon Islands	..	..	..	..	..	..	..	..	..	..
122	Namibia	81.2	98	93.3	104	90	108	38	148	8	115
123	Morocco	36.1	58	58.3	77	73	86	..	..	8	75
124	India	45.4	66	64.8	81	..	..	31	68	..	..
125	Swaziland	78.6	97	91.2	102	78	102	32	84	5	89
126	Botswana	79.8	107	92.1	109	82	104	61	118	3	79
127	Myanmar	80.5	91	90.5	99	..	..	..	..	..	..
128	Zimbabwe	84.7	91	95.7	97	..	..	..	..	..	..
129	Ghana	62.9	78	88.3	94	..	..	..	..	..	..
130	Cambodia	57.7	72	72.8	89	97	88	14	54	(.)	29
131	Vanuatu	..	..	..	..	100	98	..	..	(.)	63
132	Lesotho	93.6	129	98.5	119	64	115	19	194	3	178
133	Papua New Guinea	56.8	80	71.3	89	78	86	18	69	2	60
134	Kenya	76.0	86	94.2	98	..	..	..	..	1	47
135	Cameroon	69.5	84	93.0	99	..	..	..	..	..	..
136	Congo	74.4	85	96.8	99	..	..	..	..	..	..
137	Comoros	48.7	77	51.8	79	46	85	..	..	1	75
Low human development											
138	Pakistan	27.9	48	41.9	59	..	..	..	..	..	..
139	Sudan	46.3	67	71.5	86	42	83	..	..	7	89
140	Bhutan	..	..	..	..	15	89	5	101	..	..
141	Togo	42.5	59	63.7	73	78	79	14	44	1	21
142	Nepal	24.0	40	42.8	56	..	..	..	..	..	..
143	Lao People's Dem. Rep.	33.2	52	58.2	71	73	92	23	79	2	48
144	Yemen	25.2	37	45.9	55	44	58	20	40	5	29
145	Bangladesh	29.9	57	39.8	65	100	96	..	..	3	51
146	Haiti	47.8	92	64.5	100	82	106	..	..	..	..
147	Madagascar	59.7	81	76.6	92	63	102	13	107	2	85
148	Nigeria	55.7	77	83.8	93	..	..	..	..	..	..
149	Djibouti	54.4	72	79.4	90	27	72	..	..	(.)	100
150	Uganda	56.8	73	72.1	84	100	100	8	85	1	53

HDI rank		Adult literacy		Youth literacy		Net primary enrolment		Net secondary enrolment		Gross tertiary enrolment [a]	
		Female rate (% age 15 and above) 2000	Female rate as % of male rate 2000	Female rate (% age 15-24) 2000	Female rate as % of male rate 2000	Female ratio (%) 1998	Female ratio as % of male ratio 1998	Female ratio (%) 1998	Female ratio as % of male ratio 1998	Female ratio (%) 1998	Female ratio as % of male ratio 1998
151	Tanzania, U. Rep. of	66.5	79	87.9	94	49	103	3	74	(.)	26
152	Mauritania	30.1	59	40.6	71	58	94	..	..	..	..
153	Zambia	71.5	84	85.5	94	72	98	20	85	2	46
154	Senegal	27.6	58	41.7	70	54	84	..	..	..	..
155	Congo, Dem. Rep. of the	50.2	69	74.9	85	31	95	9	58	..	..
156	Côte d'Ivoire	38.6	71	59.7	85	51	75	..	..	4	36
157	Eritrea	44.5	66	60.4	75	31	86	17	80	(.)	16
158	Benin	23.6	45	36.0	51	..	..	10	46	1	25
159	Guinea	..	..	..	..	37	69	7	38	..	..
160	Gambia	29.4	67	48.8	74	57	89	20	72	..	..
161	Angola	..	..	..	..	53	87	..	..	1	69
162	Rwanda	60.2	82	81.4	95	92	102	..	..	..	..
163	Malawi	46.5	62	61.0	75	..	..	7	96	(.)	39
164	Mali	34.4	70	60.2	83	34	70	..	..	..	..
165	Central African Republic	34.9	58	58.8	77	43	68	..	..	1	18
166	Chad	34.0	66	59.9	82	42	62	3	29	..	..
167	Guinea-Bissau	23.3	43	43.4	59	..	..	..	..	..	..
168	Ethiopia	30.9	66	48.4	79	30	73	12	63	(.)	24
169	Burkina Faso	14.1	41	23.3	51	28	68	6	59	..	..
170	Mozambique	28.7	48	46.2	61	37	81	6	71	(.)	32
171	Burundi	40.4	72	62.0	94	34	84	..	..	1	41
172	Niger	8.4	35	13.7	42	20	64	5	63	..	..
173	Sierra Leone	..	..	..	..	..	..	..	..	..	..
	Developing countries	66.0	81	80.5	91	..	..	..	..	..	..
	Least developed countries	42.8	68	58.1	79	..	..	..	..	..	..
	Arab States	50.1	68	72.5	85	..	..	..	..	..	..
	East Asia and the Pacific	79.4	86	96.4	98	..	..	..	..	..	..
	Latin America and the Caribbean	87.4	98	94.4	101	..	..	..	..	..	..
	South Asia	43.8	66	61.2	79	..	..	..	..	..	..
	Sub-Saharan Africa	53.6	77	73.0	89	..	..	..	..	..	..
	Central and Eastern Europe and the CIS	98.3	99	99.4	100	..	..	..	..	..	..
	OECD	..	..	..	..	..	..	..	..	..	..
	High-income OECD	..	..	..	..	..	..	..	..	..	..
	High human development	..	..	..	..	..	..	..	..	..	..
	Medium human development	72.2	85	86.6	94	..	..	..	..	..	..
	Low human development	38.5	63	56.7	76	..	..	..	..	..	..
	High income	..	..	..	..	..	..	..	..	..	..
	Middle income	80.9	89	94.3	98	..	..	..	..	..	..
	Low income	52.8	74	68.8	84	..	..	..	..	..	..
	World	..	..	..	..	..	..	..	..	..	..

a. Tertiary enrolment is generally calculated as a gross ratio. b. The ratio is an underestimate, as many students pursue their studies in nearby countries. c. Excludes Turkish institutions.

Source: Columns 1 and 3: UNESCO 2002a; column 2: calculated on the basis of data on adult literacy rates from UNESCO (2002a); column 4: calculated on the basis of data on youth literacy rates from UNESCO (2002a); columns 5 and 7: UNESCO 2002c; column 6: calculated on the basis of data on net primary enrolment ratios from UNESCO (2002c); column 8: calculated on the basis of data on net secondary enrolment ratios from UNESCO (2002c); column 9: UNESCO 2002b; column 10: calculated on the basis of data on gross tertiary enrolment ratios from UNESCO (2002b).

25 Gender inequality in economic activity

HDI rank		Female economic activity rate (age 15 and above)			Employment by economic activity (%)						Contributing family workers	
					Agriculture		Industry		Services		Female (as % of total)	Male (as % of total)
		Rate (%)	Index (1990 = 100)	As % of male rate	Female	Male	Female	Male	Female	Male		
		2000	2000	2000	1995-2001[a]	1995-2001[a]	1995-2001[a]	1995-2001[a]	1995-2001[a]	1995-2001[a]	1995-2000[a]	1995-2000[a]
High human development												
1	Norway	59.1	108	84	2	6	9	33	88	61	62	38
2	Sweden	62.5	101	89	1	4	12	38	87	59	64	36
3	Canada	60.1	104	82	2	5	11	32	86	63	69	31
4	Belgium	39.7	105	66	2	3	13	37	86	60	85	15
5	Australia	55.8	107	77	3	6	10	31	86	63	59	41
6	United States	58.8	106	81	1	4	12	32	86	64	62	38
7	Iceland	66.6	101	83	5	12	15	34	80	53	67	33
8	Netherlands	45.4	105	66	2	4	9	31	84	63	78	22
9	Japan	50.8	103	67	6	5	22	38	72	57	82	19
10	Finland	57.0	99	86	4	8	14	40	82	52	47	53
11	Switzerland	50.7	103	66	4	5	13	36	83	59	..	..
12	France	48.5	106	76	1	2	13	35	86	63	..	..
13	United Kingdom	52.8	105	74	1	2	12	36	87	61	65	35
14	Denmark	61.7	100	84	2	5	15	37	83	58	..	..
15	Austria	43.9	102	65	7	6	14	43	79	52	67	33
16	Luxembourg	37.9	104	57	..	..	..	..	..	..	..	..
17	Germany	47.9	100	69	2	3	19	46	79	50	75	25
18	Ireland	37.1	115	52	2	12	15	38	82	50	56	44
19	New Zealand	57.2	108	79	6	11	12	32	81	56	68	32
20	Italy	38.3	106	58	4	6	21	39	74	55	55	45
21	Spain	37.5	111	56	5	8	14	41	81	51	64	36
22	Israel	48.4	113	67	1	3	12	35	86	61	77	23
23	Hong Kong, China (SAR)	50.7	104	65	(.)	(.)	12	28	88	71	..	..
24	Greece	38.0	107	58	20	16	12	29	67	54	69	31
25	Singapore	50.1	99	64	(.)	(.)	23	33	77	67	70	30
26	Cyprus	49.0	102	62	10	11	18	30	71	58	87	13
27	Korea, Rep. of	53.2	110	70	12	10	19	34	68	56	88	12
28	Portugal	51.2	104	71	14	11	24	44	62	44	66	34
29	Slovenia	54.6	98	80	11	11	28	46	61	42	58	40
30	Malta	25.8	111	37	..	..	..	..	..	..	..	..
31	Barbados	61.7	106	79	3	5	11	30	85	64	..	..
32	Brunei Darussalam	50.0	111	62	..	..	..	..	..	..	..	..
33	Czech Republic	61.2	100	83	4	6	28	49	69	48	78	22
34	Argentina	35.6	122	46	(.)	1	10	34	89	64	64	36
35	Hungary	48.5	102	71	4	9	25	42	71	48	67	33
36	Slovakia	62.7	99	84	5	10	26	49	69	42	70	33
37	Poland	57.1	100	80	19	19	21	41	60	39	60	40
38	Chile	37.6	118	49	5	19	14	31	82	49	..	..
39	Bahrain	33.5	118	39	..	..	..	..	..	..	..	..
40	Uruguay	48.0	108	66	1	6	14	34	85	61	..	..
41	Bahamas	66.6	103	83	1	6	5	24	93	69	..	..
42	Estonia	61.0	96	82	7	11	22	40	70	49	59	41
43	Costa Rica	37.1	112	46	4	22	17	27	79	51	41	59
44	Saint Kitts and Nevis	..	..	..	..	..	..	..	..	..	..	..
45	Kuwait	36.6	97	48	..	..	..	..	..	..	..	..
46	United Arab Emirates	31.7	108	37	..	..	..	..	..	..	..	..
47	Seychelles	..	..	..	..	..	..	..	..	..	..	..
48	Croatia	48.7	102	73	17	16	22	38	60	46	76	24
49	Lithuania	57.8	97	80	16	24	40	33	63	43	61	39
50	Trinidad and Tobago	44.1	113	59	3	11	13	37	83	52	70	30

HDI rank	Female economic activity rate (age 15 and above)			Employment by economic activity (%)						Contributing family workers	
	Rate (%) 2000	Index (1990 = 100) 2000	As % of male rate 2000	Agriculture		Industry		Services		Female (as % of total)	Male (as % of total)
				Female 1995-2001[a]	Male 1995-2001[a]	Female 1995-2001[a]	Male 1995-2001[a]	Female 1995-2001[a]	Male 1995-2001[a]	1995-2000[a]	1995-2000[a]
51 Qatar	41.0	124	45	..	..	..	..	..	..	..	..
52 Antigua and Barbuda	..	..	..	..	..	..	..	..	..	..	..
53 Latvia	60.0	95	80	14	17	18	35	69	49	52	48
Medium human development											
54 Mexico	39.4	116	47	7	23	22	29	71	47	49	51
55 Cuba	49.5	117	65	..	..	..	..	..	..	..	..
56 Belarus	59.3	98	82	..	..	..	..	..	..	..	..
57 Panama	43.3	112	55	2	25	10	22	88	52	27	73
58 Belize	27.1	113	32	6	37	12	19	81	44	..	..
59 Malaysia	48.4	108	61	13	21	29	33	58	46	..	..
60 Russian Federation	59.3	99	82	8	15	23	36	69	49	41	58
61 Dominica	..	..	..	14	31	10	24	72	40	..	..
62 Bulgaria	56.8	95	86	..	..	..	..	..	..	..	..
63 Romania	50.7	98	76	45	39	22	32	33	29	71	29
64 Libyan Arab Jamahiriya	25.0	122	33	..	..	..	..	..	..	..	..
65 Macedonia, TFYR	49.7	103	72	..	..	..	..	..	..	..	..
66 Saint Lucia	..	..	..	16	27	14	24	70	49	..	..
67 Mauritius	37.9	109	48	13	15	43	39	45	46	54	46
68 Colombia	48.1	113	60	0	2	20	30	80	68	69	31
69 Venezuela	43.1	114	53	2	16	13	29	85	55	..	..
70 Thailand	73.3	98	85	47	50	17	20	36	31	66	34
71 Saudi Arabia	21.2	142	27	..	..	..	..	..	..	..	..
72 Fiji	37.0	140	45	..	..	..	..	..	..	..	..
73 Brazil	43.8	98	52	19	26	10	27	71	47	..	..
74 Suriname	36.0	121	48	3	7	10	32	86	56	..	..
75 Lebanon	29.6	122	39	..	..	..	..	..	..	..	..
76 Armenia	62.4	100	88	..	..	..	..	..	..	..	..
77 Philippines	49.5	106	61	27	47	12	18	61	36	..	..
78 Oman	19.2	151	25	..	..	..	..	..	..	..	..
79 Kazakhstan	61.1	101	81	..	..	..	..	..	..	..	..
80 Ukraine	55.6	98	80	..	..	..	..	..	..	64	36
81 Georgia	55.7	100	78	..	..	..	..	..	..	..	..
82 Peru	34.5	117	43	3	8	11	25	86	67	62	38
83 Grenada	..	..	..	10	16	12	32	77	46	..	..
84 Maldives	65.4	100	80	..	..	..	..	..	..	57	43
85 Turkey	49.9	114	61	72	34	10	25	18	41	..	..
86 Jamaica	67.1	101	85	10	30	9	26	81	45	66	34
87 Turkmenistan	62.1	105	81	..	..	..	..	..	..	..	..
88 Azerbaijan	54.6	105	75	..	..	..	..	..	..	..	..
89 Sri Lanka	42.9	107	55	49	38	22	23	27	37	56	44
90 Paraguay	36.8	109	43	3	7	10	31	87	62	..	..
91 St. Vincent & the Grenadines	..	..	..	..	..	..	..	..	..	..	..
92 Albania	59.7	103	73	..	..	..	..	..	..	..	..
93 Ecuador	32.7	118	39	2	10	14	26	84	63	63	37
94 Dominican Republic	40.0	117	47	3	24	20	27	77	48	23	77
95 Uzbekistan	62.3	105	85	..	..	..	..	..	..	..	..
96 China	72.7	99	86	..	..	..	..	..	..	..	..
97 Tunisia	36.9	112	47	..	..	..	..	..	..	..	..
98 Iran, Islamic Rep. of	29.0	134	37	..	..	..	..	..	..	..	..
99 Jordan	26.6	157	34	..	..	..	..	..	..	..	..
100 Cape Verde	46.1	108	53	..	..	..	..	..	..	..	..

HDI rank	Female economic activity rate (age 15 and above)			Employment by economic activity (%)						Contributing family workers	
	Rate (%) 2000	Index (1990 = 100) 2000	As % of male rate 2000	Agriculture		Industry		Services		Female (as % of total)	Male (as % of total)
				Female 1995-2001[a]	Male 1995-2001[a]	Female 1995-2001[a]	Male 1995-2001[a]	Female 1995-2001[a]	Male 1995-2001[a]	1995-2000[a]	1995-2000[a]
101 Samoa (Western)	..	..	..	..	..	..	..	..	..	..	..
102 Kyrgyzstan	60.8	104	84	53	52	8	14	38	34	..	..
103 Guyana	40.7	113	49	..	..	..	..	..	..	..	..
104 El Salvador	45.8	123	54	6	37	25	24	69	38	42	58
105 Moldova, Rep. of	60.4	99	84	..	..	..	..	..	..	62	38
106 Algeria	29.5	154	39	..	..	..	..	..	..	..	..
107 South Africa	47.2	101	59	..	..	..	..	..	..	..	..
108 Syrian Arab Republic	28.6	121	37	..	..	..	..	..	..	..	..
109 Viet Nam	73.8	97	91	..	..	..	..	..	..	..	..
110 Indonesia	55.2	110	67	42	41	16	21	42	39	..	..
111 Equatorial Guinea	45.7	101	52	..	..	..	..	..	..	..	..
112 Tajikistan	57.6	111	79	..	..	..	..	..	..	..	..
113 Mongolia	73.5	102	88	..	..	..	..	..	..	..	..
114 Bolivia	48.0	106	58	2	2	16	40	82	58	63	37
115 Egypt	35.0	115	44	35	28	9	25	56	46	36	64
116 Honduras	40.3	119	47	9	50	25	21	66	30	40	60
117 Gabon	63.2	101	76	..	..	..	..	..	..	..	..
118 Nicaragua	47.2	117	56	..	..	..	..	..	..	..	..
119 São Tomé and Principe	..	..	..	..	..	..	..	..	..	..	..
120 Guatemala	36.0	128	42	14	36	18	26	68	38	..	..
121 Solomon Islands	81.2	97	92	..	..	..	..	..	..	..	..
122 Namibia	53.7	101	67	39	38	8	19	52	42	..	..
123 Morocco	41.4	107	52	6	6	40	32	54	63	..	..
124 India	42.1	104	50	..	..	..	..	..	..	..	..
125 Swaziland	41.5	106	52	..	..	..	..	..	..	..	..
126 Botswana	63.0	96	77	..	..	..	..	..	..	..	..
127 Myanmar	65.8	100	75	..	..	..	..	..	..	..	..
128 Zimbabwe	65.3	98	78	..	..	..	..	..	..	..	..
129 Ghana	80.1	98	98	..	..	..	..	..	..	..	..
130 Cambodia	80.4	98	97	..	..	..	..	..	..	..	..
131 Vanuatu	..	..	..	..	..	..	..	..	..	..	..
132 Lesotho	47.4	102	56	..	..	..	..	..	..	..	..
133 Papua New Guinea	67.6	100	79	..	..	..	..	..	..	..	..
134 Kenya	74.7	100	85	16	20	10	23	75	57	..	..
135 Cameroon	49.3	104	58	..	..	..	..	..	..	..	..
136 Congo	58.4	100	71	..	..	..	..	..	..	..	..
137 Comoros	62.5	99	73	..	..	..	..	..	..	..	..
Low human development											
138 Pakistan	35.3	124	42	66	41	10	20	23	39	39	61
139 Sudan	34.8	113	41	..	..	..	..	..	..	..	..
140 Bhutan	57.1	100	65	..	..	..	..	..	..	..	..
141 Togo	53.4	101	62	..	..	..	..	..	..	..	..
142 Nepal	56.7	101	66	..	..	..	..	..	..	..	..
143 Lao People's Dem. Rep.	74.4	101	84	..	..	..	..	..	..	..	..
144 Yemen	30.5	108	37	..	..	..	..	..	..	..	..
145 Bangladesh	66.3	101	76	78	54	8	11	11	34	74	26
146 Haiti	56.0	97	70	..	..	..	..	..	..	..	..
147 Madagascar	69.1	99	78	..	..	..	..	..	..	..	..
148 Nigeria	47.6	102	56	2	4	11	30	87	66	..	..
149 Djibouti	..	..	..	..	..	..	..	..	..	..	..
150 Uganda	79.5	98	88	..	..	..	..	..	..	..	..

HDI rank	Female economic activity rate (age 15 and above)			Employment by economic activity (%)						Contributing family workers	
	Rate (%) 2000	Index (1990 = 100) 2000	As % of male rate 2000	Agriculture		Industry		Services		Female (as % of total)	Male (as % of total)
				Female 1995-2001[a]	Male 1995-2001[a]	Female 1995-2001[a]	Male 1995-2001[a]	Female 1995-2001[a]	Male 1995-2001[a]	1995-2000[a]	1995-2000[a]
151 Tanzania, U. Rep. of	81.8	98	93	..	..	..	..	..	..	..	..
152 Mauritania	63.4	98	74	..	..	..	..	..	..	..	..
153 Zambia	64.2	98	75	..	..	..	..	..	..	..	..
154 Senegal	61.6	101	72	..	..	..	..	..	..	..	..
155 Congo, Dem. Rep. of the	60.6	98	72	..	..	..	..	..	..	..	..
156 Côte d'Ivoire	43.9	102	51	..	..	..	..	..	..	..	..
157 Eritrea	74.7	99	87	..	..	..	..	..	..	..	..
158 Benin	73.6	96	90	..	..	..	..	..	..	..	..
159 Guinea	77.3	98	89	..	..	..	..	..	..	..	..
160 Gambia	69.7	101	78	..	..	..	..	..	..	..	..
161 Angola	72.8	98	82	..	..	..	..	..	..	..	..
162 Rwanda	82.6	99	89	..	..	..	..	..	..	..	..
163 Malawi	77.9	98	90	..	..	..	..	..	..	..	..
164 Mali	70.1	97	79	..	..	..	..	..	..	..	..
165 Central African Republic	67.6	97	79	..	..	..	..	..	..	..	..
166 Chad	67.2	101	77	..	..	..	..	..	..	..	..
167 Guinea-Bissau	57.0	100	63	..	..	..	..	..	..	..	..
168 Ethiopia	57.3	99	67	88	89	2	2	11	9	..	..
169 Burkina Faso	75.0	97	85	..	..	..	..	..	..	..	..
170 Mozambique	82.8	99	92	..	..	..	..	..	..	..	..
171 Burundi	82.0	99	89	..	..	..	..	..	..	..	..
172 Niger	69.4	99	75	..	..	..	..	..	..	..	..
173 Sierra Leone	44.6	105	54	..	..	..	..	..	..	..	..
Developing countries	55.8	101	67	..	..	..	..	..	..	..	..
Least developed countries	64.8	100	75	..	..	..	..	..	..	..	..
Arab States	32.9	117	41	..	..	..	..	..	..	..	..
East Asia and the Pacific	68.9	99	82	..	..	..	..	..	..	..	..
Latin America and the Caribbean	42.0	108	51	..	..	..	..	..	..	..	..
South Asia	43.3	106	51	..	..	..	..	..	..	..	..
Sub-Saharan Africa	62.3	99	73	..	..	..	..	..	..	..	..
Central and Eastern Europe and the CIS	57.8	99	81	..	..	..	..	..	..	..	..
OECD	51.1	105	70	..	..	..	..	..	..	..	..
High-income OECD	51.7	105	73	..	..	..	..	..	..	..	..
High human development	51.3	105	72	..	..	..	..	..	..	..	..
Medium human development	56.3	101	68	..	..	..	..	..	..	..	..
Low human development	56.9	102	66	..	..	..	..	..	..	..	..
High income	51.6	105	73	..	..	..	..	..	..	..	..
Middle income	59.5	100	73	..	..	..	..	..	..	..	..
Low income	51.6	103	61	..	..	..	..	..	..	..	..
World	55.3	102	68	..	..	..	..	..	..	..	..

Note: As a result of a number of limitations in the data, comparisons of labour statistics over time and across countries should be made with caution. For detailed notes on the data see ILO (2002b, 2002d and 2002e). The percentage shares of employment by economic activity may not sum to 100 because of rounding or the omission of activities not classified.
a. Data refer to the most recent year available during the period specified.
Source: Columns 1-3: calculated on the basis of data on the economically active population and total population from ILO (2002b); *columns 4-9:* ILO 2002d; *columns 10 and 11:* calculated on the basis of data on contributing family workers from ILO (2002e).

26 Gender, work burden and time allocation

| | | Burden of work | | | Time allocation (%) | | | | | |
| | | Total work time (minutes per day) | | Females as | Total work time | | Market activities | | Non-market activities | |
	Year	Females	Males	% of males	Market activities	Non-market activities	Females	Males	Females	Males
Selected developing countries										
Urban areas										
Colombia	1983	399	356	112	49	51	24	77	76	23
Indonesia	1992	398	366	109	60	40	35	86	65	14
Kenya	1986	590	572	103	46	54	41	79	59	21
Nepal	1978	579	554	105	58	42	25	67	75	33
Venezuela	1983	440	416	106	59	41	30	87	70	13
Average [a]	–	481	453	107	54	46	31	79	69	21
Rural areas										
Bangladesh	1990	545	496	110	52	48	35	70	65	30
Guatemala	1977	678	579	117	59	41	37	84	63	16
Kenya	1988	676	500	135	56	44	42	76	58	24
Nepal	1978	641	547	117	56	44	46	67	54	33
Highlands	1978	692	586	118	59	41	52	66	48	34
Mountains	1978	649	534	122	56	44	48	65	52	35
Rural hills	1978	583	520	112	52	48	37	70	63	30
Philippines	1975-77	546	452	121	73	27	29	84	71	16
Average [a]	–	617	515	120	59	41	38	76	62	24
National [b]										
India	2000	457	391	117	61	39	35	92	65	8
Mongolia	2000	545	501	109	61	39	49	75	51	25
South Africa	2000	332	273	122	51	49	35	70	65	30
Average [a]	–	445	388	116	58	42	40	79	60	21
Selected OECD countries [c]										
Australia	1997	435	418	104	46	54	30	62	70	38
Austria [d]	1992	438	393	111	49	51	31	71	69	29
Canada	1998	420	429	98	53	47	41	65	59	35
Denmark [d]	1987	449	458	98	68	32	58	79	42	21
Finland [d]	1987-88	430	410	105	51	49	39	64	61	36
France	1999	391	363	108	46	54	33	60	67	40
Germany [d]	1991-92	440	441	100	44	56	30	61	70	39
Hungary	1999	432	445	97	51	49	41	60	59	40
Israel [d]	1991-92	375	377	99	51	49	29	74	71	26
Italy [d]	1988-89	470	367	128	45	55	22	77	78	23
Japan	1996	393	363	108	66	34	43	93	57	7
Korea, Rep. of	1999	431	373	116	64	36	45	88	55	12
Latvia	1996	535	481	111	46	54	35	58	65	42
Netherlands	1995	308	315	98	48	52	27	69	73	31
New Zealand	1999	420	417	101	46	54	32	60	68	40
Norway [d]	1990-91	445	412	108	50	50	38	64	62	36
United Kingdom [d]	1985	413	411	100	51	49	37	68	63	32
United States [d]	1985	453	428	106	50	50	37	63	63	37
Average [e]	–	423	403	105	52	48	37	69	64	31

Note: Data are estimates based on time use surveys available in time for publication. Time use data are also being collected in other countries, including Benin, Chad, Cuba, the Dominican Republic, Ecuador, Guatemala, the Lao People's Democratic Republic, Mali, Mexico, Morocco, Nepal, Nicaragua, Nigeria, Oman, the Philippines, Thailand and Viet Nam. Market activities refer to market-oriented production activities as defined by the 1993 revised UN System of National Accounts; surveys before 1993 are not strictly comparable with those for later years.

a. Refers to the unweighted average for the countries or areas shown above. b. Classifications of market and non-market activities are not strictly based on the 1993 revised UN System of National Accounts, so comparisons between countries and areas must be made with caution. c. Includes Israel and Latvia although they are not OECD countries. d. Harvey 1995. e. Refers to the unweighted average for the selected OECD countries above (that is, excluding Israel and Latvia).

Source: For urban and rural areas in selected developing countries, Goldschmidt-Clermont and Pagnossin Aligisakis (1995) and Harvey (1995); for national studies in selected developing countries, UN (2002a); for selected OECD countries and Latvia, unless otherwise noted, Harvey (2001).

27 Women's political participation

HDI rank	Year women received right [a] — To vote	Year women received right [a] — To stand for election	Year first woman elected (E) or appointed (A) to parliament	Women in government at ministerial level (as % of total) [b] 2000	Seats in parliament held by women (as % of total) [c] — Lower house or single house	Seats in parliament held by women (as % of total) [c] — Upper house or senate
High human development						
1 Norway	1907, 1913	1907, 1913	1911 A	42.1	36.4	–
2 Sweden	1861, 1921	1907, 1921	1921 E	55.0	42.7	–
3 Canada	1917, 1950	1920, 1960	1921 E	24.3	20.6	32.4
4 Belgium	1919, 1948	1921, 1948	1921 A	18.5	23.3	28.2
5 Australia	1902, 1962	1902, 1962	1943 E	19.5	25.3	28.9
6 United States	1920, 1960	1788 [d]	1917 E	31.8	14.0	13.0
7 Iceland	1915	1915	1922 E	33.3	34.9	–
8 Netherlands	1919	1917	1918 E	31.0	36.0	26.7
9 Japan	1945, 1947	1945, 1947	1946 E	5.7	7.3	15.4
10 Finland	1906	1906	1907 E	44.4	36.5	–
11 Switzerland	1971	1971	1971 E	28.6	23.0	19.6
12 France	1944	1944	1945 E	37.9	10.9	10.9
13 United Kingdom	1918, 1928	1918, 1928	1918 E	33.3	17.9	16.4
14 Denmark	1915	1915	1918 E	45.0	38.0	–
15 Austria	1918	1918	1919 E	31.3	26.8	20.3
16 Luxembourg	1919	1919	1919 E	28.6	16.7	–
17 Germany	1918	1918	1919 E	35.7	31.7	24.6
18 Ireland	1918, 1928	1918, 1928	1918 E	18.8	12.0	18.3
19 New Zealand	1893	1919	1933 E	44.0	30.8	–
20 Italy	1945	1945	1946 E	17.6	9.8	7.8
21 Spain	1931	1931	1931 E	17.6	28.3	24.3
22 Israel	1948	1948	1949 E	6.1	13.3	–
23 Hong Kong, China (SAR)	..	..	..	..	..	..
24 Greece	1927, 1952	1927, 1952	1952 E	7.1	8.7	–
25 Singapore	1947	1947	1963 E	5.7	11.8	–
26 Cyprus	1960	1960	1963 E	..	10.7	–
27 Korea, Rep. of	1948	1948	1948 E	6.5	5.9	–
28 Portugal	1931, 1976	1931, 1976	1934 E + A	9.7	18.7	–
29 Slovenia	1945	1945	1992 E [e]	15.0	12.2	–
30 Malta	1947	1947	1966 E	5.3	9.2	–
31 Barbados	1950	1950	1966 A	14.3	10.7	33.3
32 Brunei Darussalam	– [f]	– [f]	– [f]	0.0	– [f]	– [f]
33 Czech Republic	1920	1920	1992 E [e]	..	15.0	12.3
34 Argentina	1947	1947	1951 E	7.3	30.7	33.3
35 Hungary	1918	1918	1920 E	35.9	8.3	–
36 Slovakia	1920	1920	1992 E [e]	19.0	14.0	–
37 Poland	1918	1918	1919 E	18.7	20.2	23.0
38 Chile	1931, 1949	1931, 1949	1951 E	25.6	12.5	4.1
39 Bahrain	1973 [g]	1973	– [h]	..	– [h]	– [h]
40 Uruguay	1932	1932	1942 E	..	12.1	9.7
41 Bahamas	1961, 1964	1961, 1964	1977 A	16.7	15.0	31.3
42 Estonia	1918	1918	1919 E	14.3	17.8	–
43 Costa Rica	1949	1949	1953 E	28.6	19.3 [i]	–
44 Saint Kitts and Nevis	1951	1951	1984 E	0.0	13.3	–
45 Kuwait	– [f]	– [f]	– [f]	0.0	0.0	–
46 United Arab Emirates	– [f]	– [f]	– [f]	..	0.0	–
47 Seychelles	1948	1948	1976 E + A	23.1	23.5	–
48 Croatia	1945	1945	1992 E [e]	16.2	20.5	6.2
49 Lithuania	1921	1921	1920 E	18.9	10.6	–
50 Trinidad and Tobago	1946	1946	1962 E + A	8.7	16.7	32.3 [i]

		Year women received right[a]		Year first woman elected (E) or appointed (A) to parliament	Women in government at ministerial level (as % of total)[b] 2000	Seats in parliament held by women (as % of total)[c]	
HDI rank		To vote	To stand for election			Lower house or single house	Upper house or senate
51	Qatar	–[f]	–[f]	–[f]	0.0	–[f]	–[f]
52	Antigua and Barbuda	1951	1951	1984 A	0.0	5.3	11.8
53	Latvia	1918	1918	..	6.7	17.0	–
Medium human development							
54	Mexico	1947	1953	1952 A	11.1	16.0	15.6
55	Cuba	1934	1934	1940 E	10.7	27.6	–
56	Belarus	1919	1919	1990 E [e]	25.7	10.3	31.1
57	Panama	1941, 1946	1941, 1946	1946 E	20.0	9.9	–
58	Belize	1954	1954	1984 E + A	11.1	6.9	37.5
59	Malaysia	1957	1957	1959 E	..	10.4	26.1
60	Russian Federation	1918	1918	1993 E [e]	..	7.6	3.4
61	Dominica	1951	1951	1980 E	0.0	18.8	–
62	Bulgaria	1944	1944	1945 E	18.8	26.2	–
63	Romania	1929, 1946	1929, 1946	1946 E	20.0	10.7	5.7
64	Libyan Arab Jamahiriya	1964	1964	..	12.5	..	–
65	Macedonia, TFYR	1946	1946	1990 E [e]	10.9	6.7	–
66	Saint Lucia	1924	1924	1979 A	18.2	11.1	18.2
67	Mauritius	1956	1956	1976 E	9.1	5.7	–
68	Colombia	1954	1954	1954 A	47.4	11.8	12.7
69	Venezuela	1946	1946	1948 E	0.0	9.7	–
70	Thailand	1932	1932	1948 A	5.7	9.2	10.5
71	Saudi Arabia	–[f]	–[f]	–[f]	..	–[f]	–[f]
72	Fiji	1963	1963	1970 A	20.7	5.7	..
73	Brazil	1934	1934	1933 E	0.0	6.8	6.3
74	Suriname	1948	1948	1975 E	..	17.6	–
75	Lebanon	1952	1952	1991 A	0.0	2.3	–
76	Armenia	1921	1921	1990 E [e]	..	3.1	–
77	Philippines	1937	1937	1941 E	..	17.8	12.5
78	Oman	–[f]	–[f]	–[f]	..	–[f]	–[f]
79	Kazakhstan	1924, 1993	1924, 1993	1990 E [e]	17.5	10.4	12.8
80	Ukraine	1919	1919	1990 E [e]	..	7.8	–
81	Georgia	1918, 1921	1918, 1921	1992 E [e]	9.7	7.2	–
82	Peru	1955	1955	1956 E	16.2	17.5	–
83	Grenada	1951	1951	1976 E + A	25.0	26.7	7.7
84	Maldives	1932	1932	1979 E	..	6.0	–
85	Turkey	1930	1934	1935 A	0.0	4.2	–
86	Jamaica	1944	1944	1944 E	12.5	13.3	23.8
87	Turkmenistan	1927	1927	1990 E [e]	..	26.0	–
88	Azerbaijan	1921	1921	1990 E [e]	2.6	10.5	–
89	Sri Lanka	1931	1931	1947 E	..	4.4	–
90	Paraguay	1961	1961	1963 E	..	2.5	17.8
91	St. Vincent & the Grenadines	1951	1951	1979 E	0.0	23.0	–
92	Albania	1920	1920	1945 E	15.0	5.7	–
93	Ecuador	1929, 1967	1929, 1967	1956 E	20.0	14.6	–
94	Dominican Republic	1942	1942	1942 E	..	16.1	6.7
95	Uzbekistan	1938	1938	1990 E [e]	4.4	7.2	–
96	China	1949	1949	1954 E	5.1	21.8	–
97	Tunisia	1957, 1959	1957, 1959	1959 E	10.0	11.5	–
98	Iran, Islamic Rep. of	1963	1963	1963 E + A	9.4	3.4	–
99	Jordan	1974	1974	1989 A	0.0	1.3	7.5
100	Cape Verde	1975	1975	1975 E	35.0	11.1	–

	Year women received right [a]		Year first woman elected (E) or appointed (A) to parliament	Women in government at ministerial level (as % of total) [b] 2000	Seats in parliament held by women (as % of total) [c]	
HDI rank	To vote	To stand for election			Lower house or single house	Upper house or senate
101 Samoa (Western)	1990	1990	1976 A	7.7	6.1	–
102 Kyrgyzstan	1918	1918	1990 E [e]	..	10.0	2.2
103 Guyana	1953	1945	1968 E	..	20.0	–
104 El Salvador	1939	1961	1961 E	15.4	9.5	–
105 Moldova, Rep. of	1978, 1993	1978, 1993	1990 E	..	12.9	–
106 Algeria	1962	1962	1962 A	0.0	3.4	5.6
107 South Africa	1930, 1994	1930, 1994	1933 E	38.1	29.8	31.5 [j]
108 Syrian Arab Republic	1949, 1953	1953	1973 E	11.1	10.4	–
109 Viet Nam	1946	1946	1976 E	..	26.0	–
110 Indonesia	1945	1945	1950 A	5.9	8.0	–
111 Equatorial Guinea	1963	1963	1968 E	..	5.0	–
112 Tajikistan	1924	1924	1990 E [e]	..	12.7	11.8
113 Mongolia	1924	1924	1951 E	10.0	10.5	–
114 Bolivia	1938, 1952	1938, 1952	1966 E	..	11.5	3.7
115 Egypt	1956	1956	1957 E	6.1	2.4	–
116 Honduras	1955	1955	1957 [k]	33.3	5.5	–
117 Gabon	1956	1956	1961 E	12.1	9.2	13.2
118 Nicaragua	1955	1955	1972 E	23.1	20.7	–
119 São Tomé and Principe	1975	1975	1975 E	..	9.1	–
120 Guatemala	1946	1946	1956 E	7.1	8.8	–
121 Solomon Islands	1974	1974	1993 E	..	0.0	–
122 Namibia	1989	1989	1989 E	16.3	25.0	7.7
123 Morocco	1963	1963	1993 E	4.9	0.6	0.4
124 India	1950	1950	1952 E	10.1	8.8	9.1
125 Swaziland	1968	1968	1972 E + A	12.5	3.1	13.3
126 Botswana	1965	1965	1979 E	26.7	17.0	–
127 Myanmar	1935	1946	1947 E	..	– [l]	– [l]
128 Zimbabwe	1957	1978	1980 E + A	36.0	10.0	–
129 Ghana	1954	1954	1960 A [k]	8.6	9.0	–
130 Cambodia	1955	1955	1958 E	7.1	7.4	13.1
131 Vanuatu	1975, 1980	1975, 1980	1987 E	..	0.0	–
132 Lesotho	1965	1965	1965 A	..	3.8	27.3
133 Papua New Guinea	1964	1963	1977 E	0.0	1.8	–
134 Kenya	1919, 1963	1919, 1963	1969 E + A	1.4	3.6	–
135 Cameroon	1946	1946	1960 E	5.8	5.6	–
136 Congo	1963	1963	1963 E	..	12.0	–
137 Comoros	1956	1956	1993 E	..	– [m]	– [m]

Low human development

138 Pakistan	1947	1947	1973 E	..	– [m]	– [m]
139 Sudan	1964	1964	1964 E	5.1	9.7	–
140 Bhutan	1953	1953	1975 E	..	9.3	–
141 Togo	1945	1945	1961 E	7.4	4.9	–
142 Nepal	1951	1951	1952 A	14.8	5.9	15.0 [i]
143 Lao People's Dem. Rep.	1958	1958	1958 E	10.2	21.2 [i]	–
144 Yemen	1967 [n]	1967 [n]	1990 E [k]	..	0.7	–
145 Bangladesh	1972	1972	1973 E	9.5	2.0	–
146 Haiti	1950	1950	1961 E	18.2	3.6	25.9
147 Madagascar	1959	1959	1965 E	12.5	8.0	..
148 Nigeria	1958	1958	..	22.6	3.4	2.8
149 Djibouti	1946	1986	– [o]	5.0	0.0	–
150 Uganda	1962	1962	1962 A	27.1	24.7	

HDI rank	Year women received right[a]		Year first woman elected (E) or appointed (A) to parliament	Women in government at ministerial level (as % of total)[b] 2000	Seats in parliament held by women (as % of total)[c]	
	To vote	To stand for election			Lower house or single house	Upper house or senate
151 Tanzania, U. Rep. of	1959	1959	..	..	22.3	–
152 Mauritania	1961	1961	1975 E	13.6	3.8 [i]	1.8
153 Zambia	1962	1962	1964 E + A	6.2	12.0	–
154 Senegal	1945	1945	1963 E	15.6	19.2	–
155 Congo, Dem. Rep. of the	1967	1970	1970 E	..	– [m]	– [m]
156 Côte d'Ivoire	1952	1952	1965 E	9.1	8.5	–
157 Eritrea	1955	1955	1994 E	11.8	14.7	–
158 Benin	1956	1956	1979 E	10.5	6.0	–
159 Guinea	1958	1958	1963 E	11.1	8.8	–
160 Gambia	1960	1960	1982 E	30.8	2.0 [i]	–
161 Angola	1975	1975	1980 E	14.7	15.5	–
162 Rwanda	1961	1961	1965 [k]	13.0	25.7	–
163 Malawi	1961	1961	1964 E	11.8	9.3	–
164 Mali	1956	1956	1964 E	33.3	12.2	–
165 Central African Republic	1986	1986	1987 E	..	7.3	–
166 Chad	1958	1958	1962 E	..	2.4	–
167 Guinea-Bissau	1977	1977	1972 A	8.3	7.8	–
168 Ethiopia	1955	1955	1957 E	22.2	7.7	8.3
169 Burkina Faso	1958	1958	1978 E	8.6	8.1	13.0
170 Mozambique	1975	1975	1977 E	..	30.0	–
171 Burundi	1961	1961	1982 E	4.5	19.5	..
172 Niger	1948	1948	1989 E	10.0	1.2	–
173 Sierra Leone	1961	1961	..	8.1	8.8	–

a. Data refer to the year in which the right to vote or stand for election on a universal and equal basis was recognized. Where two years are shown, the first refers to the first partial recognition of the right to vote or stand for election. b. Data were provided by states based on their definition of national executive and may therefore include women serving as ministers and vice ministers and those holding other ministerial positions, including parliamentary secretaries. c. Data are as of 18 March 2002. d. No information is available on the year all women received the right to stand for election. However, the constitution does not mention gender with regard to this right. e. Refers to the year women were elected to the current parliamentary system. f. Women's right to vote and to stand for election has not been recognized. Brunei Darussalam, Oman, Qatar and Saudi Arabia have never had a parliament. g. According to the constitution in force (1973), all citizens are equal before the law; however, women were not able to exercise electoral rights in the only legislative elections held in Bahrain, in 1973. Women were allowed to vote in the referendum of 14-15 February 2001, however, which approved the National Action Charter. h. The first legislature of Bahrain was dissolved by decree of the emir on 26 August 1975. i. Information for the most recent elections was not available in time for publication; data refer to previous elections. j. Calculated on the basis of the 54 permanent seats (that is, excluding the 36 special rotating delegates appointed on an ad hoc basis). k. No information or confirmation available. l. The parliament elected in 1990 has never been convened nor authorized to sit, and many of its members were detained or forced into exile. m. Parliament has been dissolved or suspended for an indefinite period. n. Refers to the former People's Democratic Republic of Yemen. o. The country has not yet elected or appointed a woman to the national parliament.

Source: Columns 1-3: IPU 1995 and 2001b; *column 4:* IPU 2001a; *columns 5 and 6:* calculated on the basis of data on parliamentary seats from IPU (2002).

28 Status of major international human rights instruments

HDI rank	International Convention on the Elimination of All Forms of Racial Discrimination 1965	International Covenant on Civil and Political Rights 1966	International Covenant on Economic, Social and Cultural Rights 1966	Convention on the Elimination of All Forms of Discrimination Against Women 1979	Convention Against Torture and Other Cruel, Inhuman or Degrading Treatment or Punishment 1984	Convention on the Rights of the Child 1989
High human development						
1 Norway	●	●	●	●	●	●
2 Sweden	●	●	●	●	●	●
3 Canada	●	●	●	●	●	●
4 Belgium	●	●	●	●	●	●
5 Australia	●	●	●	●	●	●
6 United States	●	●	○	○	●	○
7 Iceland	●	●	●	●	●	●
8 Netherlands	●	●	●	●	●	●
9 Japan	●	●	●	●	●	●
10 Finland	●	●	●	●	●	●
11 Switzerland	●	●	●	●	●	●
12 France	●	●	●	●	●	●
13 United Kingdom	●	●	●	●	●	●
14 Denmark	●	●	●	●	●	●
15 Austria	●	●	●	●	●	●
16 Luxembourg	●	●	●	●	●	●
17 Germany	●	●	●	●	●	●
18 Ireland	●	●	●	●	○	●
19 New Zealand	●	●	●	●	●	●
20 Italy	●	●	●	●	●	●
21 Spain	●	●	●	●	●	●
22 Israel	●	●	●	●	●	●
23 Hong Kong, China (SAR)	–	–	–	–	–	–
24 Greece	●	●	●	●	●	●
25 Singapore				●		●
26 Cyprus	●	●	●	●	●	●
27 Korea, Rep. of	●	●	●	●	●	●
28 Portugal	●	●	●	●	●	●
29 Slovenia	●	●	●	●	●	●
30 Malta	●	●	●	●	●	●
31 Barbados	●	●	●	●		●
32 Brunei Darussalam						●
33 Czech Republic	●	●	●	●	●	●
34 Argentina	●	●	●	●	●	●
35 Hungary	●	●	●	●	●	●
36 Slovakia	●	●	●	●	●	●
37 Poland	●	●	●	●	●	●
38 Chile	●	●	●	●	●	●
39 Bahrain	●				●	●
40 Uruguay	●	●	●	●	●	●
41 Bahamas	●			●		●
42 Estonia	●	●	●	●	●	●
43 Costa Rica	●	●	●	●	●	●
44 Saint Kitts and Nevis				●		●
45 Kuwait	●	●	●	●	●	●
46 United Arab Emirates	●					●
47 Seychelles	●	●	●	●	●	●
48 Croatia	●	●	●	●	●	●
49 Lithuania	●	●	●	●	●	●
50 Trinidad and Tobago	●	●	●	●		●

HDI rank	International Convention on the Elimination of All Forms of Racial Discrimination 1965	International Covenant on Civil and Political Rights 1966	International Covenant on Economic, Social and Cultural Rights 1966	Convention on the Elimination of All Forms of Discrimination Against Women 1979	Convention Against Torture and Other Cruel, Inhuman or Degrading Treatment or Punishment 1984	Convention on the Rights of the Child 1989
51 Qatar	●				●	●
52 Antigua and Barbuda	●			●	●	●
53 Latvia	●	●	●	●	●	●
Medium human development						
54 Mexico	●	●	●	●	●	●
55 Cuba	●			●	●	●
56 Belarus	●	●	●	●	●	●
57 Panama	●	●	●	●	●	●
58 Belize	●	●	○	●	●	●
59 Malaysia				●		●
60 Russian Federation	●	●	●	●	●	●
61 Dominica		●	●	●		●
62 Bulgaria	●	●	●	●	●	●
63 Romania	●	●	●	●	●	●
64 Libyan Arab Jamahiriya	●	●	●	●	●	●
65 Macedonia, TFYR	●	●	●	●	●	●
66 Saint Lucia	●			●		●
67 Mauritius	●	●		●	●	●
68 Colombia	●	●	●	●	●	●
69 Venezuela	●	●	●	●	●	●
70 Thailand		●		●		●
71 Saudi Arabia	●			●	●	●
72 Fiji	●			●		●
73 Brazil	●	●	●	●	●	●
74 Suriname	●	●	●	●		●
75 Lebanon	●	●	●	●		●
76 Armenia	●	●	●	●	●	●
77 Philippines	●	●	●	●	●	●
78 Oman						●
79 Kazakhstan	●			●		●
80 Ukraine	●	●	●	●	●	●
81 Georgia	●	●	●	●	●	●
82 Peru	●	●	●	●	●	●
83 Grenada	○	●	●	●		●
84 Maldives	●			●		●
85 Turkey	○	○	○	●	●	●
86 Jamaica	●	●	●	●		●
87 Turkmenistan	●	●	●	●	●	●
88 Azerbaijan	●	●	●	●	●	●
89 Sri Lanka	●	●	●	●	●	●
90 Paraguay	○	●	●	●	●	●
91 St. Vincent & the Grenadines	●	●	●	●	●	●
92 Albania	●	●	●	●	●	●
93 Ecuador	●	●	●	●	●	●
94 Dominican Republic	●	●	●	●	○	●
95 Uzbekistan	●	●	●	●	●	●
96 China	●	○	●	●	●	●
97 Tunisia	●	●	●	●	●	●
98 Iran, Islamic Rep. of	●	●	●			●
99 Jordan	●	●	●	●	●	●
100 Cape Verde	●	●	●	●	●	●

28 Status of major international human rights instruments

HDI rank		International Convention on the Elimination of All Forms of Racial Discrimination 1965	International Covenant on Civil and Political Rights 1966	International Covenant on Economic, Social and Cultural Rights 1966	Convention on the Elimination of All Forms of Discrimination Against Women 1979	Convention Against Torture and Other Cruel, Inhuman or Degrading Treatment or Punishment 1984	Convention on the Rights of the Child 1989
101	Samoa (Western)				●		●
102	Kyrgyzstan	●	●	●	●	●	●
103	Guyana	●	●	●	●	●	●
104	El Salvador	●	●	●	●	●	●
105	Moldova, Rep. of	●	●	●	●	●	●
106	Algeria	●	●	●	●	●	●
107	South Africa	●	●	○	●		●
108	Syrian Arab Republic	●	●	●			●
109	Viet Nam	●	●	●	●		●
110	Indonesia	●				●	●
111	Equatorial Guinea		●	●	●		●
112	Tajikistan	●	●	●	●	●	●
113	Mongolia	●	●	●	●	●	●
114	Bolivia	●	●	●	●	●	●
115	Egypt	●	●	●	●	●	●
116	Honduras		●	●	●	●	●
117	Gabon	●	●	●	●	●	●
118	Nicaragua	●	●	●	●	○	●
119	São Tomé and Principe	○	○	○	○	○	●
120	Guatemala	●	●	●	●	●	●
121	Solomon Islands	●		●			●
122	Namibia	●	●	●	●	●	●
123	Morocco	●	●	●	●	●	●
124	India	●	●	●	●	○	●
125	Swaziland	●					●
126	Botswana	●	●		●	●	●
127	Myanmar				●		●
128	Zimbabwe	●	●	●	●		●
129	Ghana	●	●	●	●	●	●
130	Cambodia	●	●	●	●	●	●
131	Vanuatu				●		●
132	Lesotho	●	●	●	●		●
133	Papua New Guinea	●			●		●
134	Kenya	●	●	●	●	●	●
135	Cameroon	●	●	●	●	●	●
136	Congo	●	●	●	●		●
137	Comoros	○			●	○	●
Low human development							
138	Pakistan	●			●		●
139	Sudan	●	●	●		○	●
140	Bhutan	○			●		●
141	Togo	●	●	●	●	●	●
142	Nepal	●	●	●	●	●	●
143	Lao People's Dem. Rep.	●	○	○	●		●
144	Yemen	●	●	●	●	●	●
145	Bangladesh	●	●	●	●	●	●
146	Haiti	●	●		●		●
147	Madagascar	●	●	●	●	○	●
148	Nigeria	●	●	●	●	●	●
149	Djibouti				●		●
150	Uganda	●	●	●	●	●	●

28 Status of major international human rights instruments

HDI rank	International Convention on the Elimination of All Forms of Racial Discrimination 1965	International Covenant on Civil and Political Rights 1966	International Covenant on Economic, Social and Cultural Rights 1966	Convention on the Elimination of All Forms of Discrimination Against Women 1979	Convention Against Torture and Other Cruel, Inhuman or Degrading Treatment or Punishment 1984	Convention on the Rights of the Child 1989
151 Tanzania, U. Rep. of	●	●	●	●		●
152 Mauritania	●			●		●
153 Zambia	●	●	●	●	●	●
154 Senegal	●	●	●	●	●	●
155 Congo, Dem. Rep. of the	●	●	●	●	●	●
156 Côte d'Ivoire	●	●	●	●	●	●
157 Eritrea	●	●	●	●		●
158 Benin	●	●	●	●	●	●
159 Guinea	●	●	●	●	●	●
160 Gambia	●	●	●	●	○	●
161 Angola		●	●	●		●
162 Rwanda	●	●	●	●		●
163 Malawi	●	●	●	●	●	●
164 Mali	●	●	●	●	●	●
165 Central African Republic	●	●	●	●		●
166 Chad	●	●	●	●	●	●
167 Guinea-Bissau	○	○	●	●	○	●
168 Ethiopia	●	●	●	●	●	●
169 Burkina Faso	●	●	●	●	●	●
170 Mozambique	●			●	●	●
171 Burundi	●	●	●	●	●	●
172 Niger	●	●	●	●	●	●
173 Sierra Leone	●	●	●	●	●	●
Others[a]						
Afghanistan	●	●	●	○	●	●
Andorra				●		●
Bosnia and Herzegovina	●	●	●	●	●	●
Cook Islands						●
Holy See	●					●
Iraq	●	●	●	●		●
Kiribati						●
Korea, Dem. Rep. of		●	●	●		●
Liberia	●	○	○	●		●
Liechtenstein	●	●	●	●	●	●
Marshall Islands						●
Micronesia, Fed. Sts.						●
Monaco	●	●	●		●	●
Nauru	○	○			○	●
Niue						●
Palau						●
San Marino	○	●	●			●
Somalia	●	●	●		●	
Tonga	●					●
Tuvalu				●		●
Yugoslavia	●	●	●	●	●	●
Total states parties[b]	161	148	145	168	128	191
Signatures not yet followed by participation	9	7	7	3	11	1

● Ratification, accession or succession. ○ Signature not yet followed by ratification.

Note: Information is as of 20 February 2002.

a. These are the countries or areas, in addition to the 173 countries or areas included in the main indicator tables, that have signed or ratified at least one of the six human rights instruments. b. Refers to ratification, accession or succession.

Source: Columns 1-6: UN 2002b.

29 Status of fundamental labour rights conventions

HDI rank	Freedom of association and collective bargaining		Elimination of forced and compulsory labour		Elimination of discrimination in respect of employment and occupation		Abolition of child labour	
	Convention 87[a]	Convention 98[b]	Convention 29[c]	Convention 105[d]	Convention 100[e]	Convention 111[f]	Convention 138[g]	Convention 182[h]
High human development								
1 Norway	●	●	●	●	●	●	●	●
2 Sweden	●	●	●	●	●	●	●	●
3 Canada	●			●	●	●		●
4 Belgium	●	●	●	●	●	●	●	
5 Australia	●	●	●	●	●	●		
6 United States				●				●
7 Iceland	●	●	●	●	●	●	●	●
8 Netherlands	●	●	●	●	●	●	●	●
9 Japan	●	●	●		●		●	●
10 Finland	●	●	●	●	●	●	●	●
11 Switzerland	●	●	●	●	●	●	●	●
12 France	●	●	●	●	●	●	●	●
13 United Kingdom	●	●	●	●	●	●	●	●
14 Denmark	●	●	●	●	●	●	●	●
15 Austria	●	●	●	●	●	●	●	●
16 Luxembourg	●	●	●	●	●	●	●	●
17 Germany	●	●	●	●	●	●	●	●
18 Ireland	●	●	●	●	●	●	●	●
19 New Zealand			●	●	●	●		●
20 Italy	●	●	●	●	●	●	●	●
21 Spain	●	●	●	●	●	●	●	●
22 Israel	●	●	●	●	●	●	●	
23 Hong Kong, China (SAR)	−	−	−	−	−	−	−	−
24 Greece	●	●	●	●	●	●	●	●
25 Singapore		●	●	○				●
26 Cyprus	●	●	●	●	●	●	●	●
27 Korea, Rep. of					●	●	●	●
28 Portugal	●	●	●	●	●	●	●	●
29 Slovenia	●	●	●	●	●	●	●	●
30 Malta	●	●	●	●	●	●	●	●
31 Barbados	●	●	●	●	●	●	●	●
32 Brunei Darussalam								
33 Czech Republic	●	●	●	●	●	●		●
34 Argentina	●	●	●	●	●	●	●	●
35 Hungary	●	●	●	●	●	●		●
36 Slovakia	●	●	●	●	●	●		●
37 Poland	●	●	●	●	●	●	●	
38 Chile	●	●	●	●	●	●	●	●
39 Bahrain			●	●		●		●
40 Uruguay	●	●	●	●	●	●	●	●
41 Bahamas	●	●	●	●	●	●		●
42 Estonia	●	●	●	●	●	●		●
43 Costa Rica	●	●	●	●	●	●	●	●
44 Saint Kitts and Nevis	●	●	●	●	●	●		●
45 Kuwait	●		●	●		●	●	●
46 United Arab Emirates			●	●	●	●	●	●
47 Seychelles	●	●	●	●	●	●	●	●
48 Croatia	●	●	●	●	●	●	●	●
49 Lithuania	●	●	●	●	●	●	●	
50 Trinidad and Tobago	●	●	●	●	●	●		

HDI rank	Freedom of association and collective bargaining		Elimination of forced and compulsory labour		Elimination of discrimination in respect of employment and occupation		Abolition of child labour	
	Convention 87 [a]	Convention 98 [b]	Convention 29 [c]	Convention 105 [d]	Convention 100 [e]	Convention 111 [f]	Convention 138 [g]	Convention 182 [h]
51 Qatar			●			●		●
52 Antigua and Barbuda	●	●	●	●		●	●	
53 Latvia	●	●		●	●	●		
Medium human development								
54 Mexico	●		●	●	●	●		●
55 Cuba	●	●	●	●	●	●	●	
56 Belarus	●	●	●	●	●	●	●	●
57 Panama	●	●	●	●	●	●	●	●
58 Belize	●	●	●	●	●	●	●	●
59 Malaysia		●	●	○		●	●	●
60 Russian Federation	●	●	●	●	●	●	●	
61 Dominica	●	●	●	●	●	●	●	●
62 Bulgaria	●	●	●	●	●	●	●	●
63 Romania	●	●	●	●	●	●	●	●
64 Libyan Arab Jamahiriya	●	●	●	●	●	●	●	●
65 Macedonia, TFYR	●	●	●	●	●	●	●	
66 Saint Lucia	●	●	●	●	●	●		●
67 Mauritius		●	●	●		●	●	●
68 Colombia	●	●	●	●	●	●	●	
69 Venezuela	●	●	●	●	●	●	●	
70 Thailand			●	●	●			●
71 Saudi Arabia			●	●	●	●		●
72 Fiji		●	●	●				
73 Brazil		●	●	●	●	●	●	●
74 Suriname	●	●	●	●				
75 Lebanon		●	●	●	●	●		●
76 Armenia					●	●		
77 Philippines	●	●		●	●	●	●	●
78 Oman			●					●
79 Kazakhstan	●	●	●	●	●	●	●	
80 Ukraine	●	●	●	●	●	●	●	●
81 Georgia	●	●	●	●	●	●	●	
82 Peru	●	●	●	●	●	●		●
83 Grenada	●	●	●	●	●			
84 Maldives								
85 Turkey	●	●	●	●	●	●	●	●
86 Jamaica	●	●	●	●	●	●		
87 Turkmenistan	●	●	●	●	●	●		
88 Azerbaijan	●	●	●	●	●	●	●	
89 Sri Lanka	●	●	●		●	●	●	●
90 Paraguay	●	●	●	●	●	●		
91 St. Vincent & the Grenadines	●	●	●	●	●	●		●
92 Albania	●	●	●	●	●	●	●	●
93 Ecuador	●	●	●	●	●	●	●	●
94 Dominican Republic	●	●	●	●	●	●	●	●
95 Uzbekistan		●	●	●	●	●		
96 China					●		●	
97 Tunisia	●	●	●	●	●	●	●	●
98 Iran, Islamic Rep. of			●	●	●	●	●	
99 Jordan		●	●	●	●	●	●	
100 Cape Verde	●	●	●	●	●	●		●

HDI rank	Freedom of association and collective bargaining		Elimination of forced and compulsory labour		Elimination of discrimination in respect of employment and occupation		Abolition of child labour	
	Convention 87 [a]	Convention 98 [b]	Convention 29 [c]	Convention 105 [d]	Convention 100 [e]	Convention 111 [f]	Convention 138 [g]	Convention 182 [h]
101 Samoa (Western)								
102 Kyrgyzstan	●	●	●	●	●	●	●	
103 Guyana	●	●	●	●	●	●	●	●
104 El Salvador			●	●	●	●	●	●
105 Moldova, Rep. of	●	●	●	●	●	●	●	
106 Algeria	●	●	●	●	●	●	●	●
107 South Africa	●	●	●	●	●	●	●	●
108 Syrian Arab Republic	●	●	●	●	●	●	●	●
109 Viet Nam					●	●		●
110 Indonesia	●	●	●	●	●	●	●	●
111 Equatorial Guinea	●	●	●	●	●	●	●	●
112 Tajikistan	●	●	●	●	●	●	●	
113 Mongolia	●	●			●	●		●
114 Bolivia	●	●		●	●	●	●	
115 Egypt	●	●	●	●	●	●	●	
116 Honduras	●	●	●	●	●	●	●	●
117 Gabon	●	●	●	●	●	●		●
118 Nicaragua	●	●	●	●	●	●	●	●
119 São Tomé and Principe	●	●			●	●		
120 Guatemala	●	●	●	●	●	●	●	●
121 Solomon Islands			●					
122 Namibia	●	●	●	●		●	●	●
123 Morocco		●	●	●	●	●	●	●
124 India			●	●	●	●		
125 Swaziland	●	●	●	●	●	●		
126 Botswana	●	●	●	●	●	●	●	●
127 Myanmar	●		●					
128 Zimbabwe		●	●	●	●	●	●	●
129 Ghana	●	●	●	●	●	●		●
130 Cambodia	●	●	●	●	●	●	●	●
131 Vanuatu								
132 Lesotho	●	●	●	●	●	●	●	●
133 Papua New Guinea	●	●	●	●	●	●	●	●
134 Kenya		●	●	●	●	●	●	●
135 Cameroon	●	●	●	●	●	●	●	
136 Congo	●	●	●	●	●	●		
137 Comoros	●	●	●	●	●			
Low human development								
138 Pakistan	●	●	●	●	●	●		●
139 Sudan		●	●	●	●	●		
140 Bhutan								
141 Togo	●	●	●	●	●	●	●	●
142 Nepal		●	●		●	●	●	●
143 Lao People's Dem. Rep.			●					
144 Yemen	●	●	●	●	●	●	●	●
145 Bangladesh	●	●	●	●	●	●		●
146 Haiti	●	●	●	●	●	●		●
147 Madagascar	●	●	●	●	●	●	●	
148 Nigeria	●	●	●	●	●			
149 Djibouti	●	●	●	●	●			
150 Uganda		●	●		●			●

29 Status of fundamental labour rights conventions

HDI rank	Freedom of association and collective bargaining		Elimination of forced and compulsory labour		Elimination of discrimination in respect of employment and occupation		Abolition of child labour	
	Convention 87 [a]	Convention 98 [b]	Convention 29 [c]	Convention 105 [d]	Convention 100 [e]	Convention 111 [f]	Convention 138 [g]	Convention 182 [h]
151 Tanzania, U. Rep. of	●	●	●	●			●	●
152 Mauritania	●	●	●	●	●	●	●	●
153 Zambia	●	●	●	●	●	●	●	●
154 Senegal	●	●	●	●	●	●	●	●
155 Congo, Dem. Rep. of the	●	●	●	●	●	●	●	●
156 Côte d'Ivoire	●	●	●	●	●	●		
157 Eritrea	●	●	●	●	●	●	●	
158 Benin	●	●	●	●	●	●	●	●
159 Guinea	●	●	●	●	●	●		
160 Gambia	●	●	●	●	●	●	●	●
161 Angola	●	●	●	●	●	●	●	●
162 Rwanda	●	●	●	●	●	●	●	●
163 Malawi	●	●	●	●	●	●	●	●
164 Mali	●	●	●	●	●	●	●	●
165 Central African Republic	●	●	●	●	●	●	●	●
166 Chad	●	●	●	●	●	●		●
167 Guinea-Bissau		●	●	●	●	●		
168 Ethiopia	●	●		●	●	●	●	
169 Burkina Faso	●	●	●	●	●	●	●	●
170 Mozambique	●	●		●	●	●		
171 Burundi	●	●	●	●	●	●	●	
172 Niger	●	●	●	●	●	●	●	●
173 Sierra Leone	●	●	●	●	●	●		
Other countries [i]								
Afghanistan				●	●	●		
Bosnia and Herzegovina	●	●	●	●	●	●	●	●
Iraq		●	●	●	●	●	●	●
Liberia	●	●	●	●		●		
San Marino	●	●	●		●	●		●
Somalia			●	●		●		
Yugoslavia	●	●	●		●	●	●	
Total ratifications	139	151	160	155	156	154	116	116

● Convention ratified. ○ Ratification denounced.

Note: Information is as of 20 February 2002.

a. Freedom of Association and Protection of the Right to Organize Convention (1948). b. Right to Organize and Collective Bargaining Convention (1949). c. Forced Labour Convention (1930). d. Abolition of Forced Labour Convention (1957). e. Equal Remuneration Convention (1951). f. Discrimination (Employment and Occupation) Convention (1958). g. Minimum Age Convention (1973). h. Worst Forms of Child Labour Convention (1999). i. These are the countries or areas, in addition to the 173 countries or areas included in the main indicator tables, that have ratified at least one of the eight fundamental labour rights conventions.

Source: Columns 1-8: ILO 2002c.

Human development index components

	Life expectancy at birth (years) 1995-2000[a]	Adult literacy rate (% age 15 and above) 2000	Combined primary, secondary and tertiary gross enrolment ratio (%) 1999	GDP per capita (PPP US$) 2000	Total population (thousands) 2000	Total fertility rate (per woman) 1995-2000[a]	Infant mortality rate (per 1,000 live births) 2000	Under-five mortality rate (per 1,000 live births) 2000	Adults living with HIV/AIDS (% age 15-49) 2001[b]	Under-nourished people (as % of total population) 1997/99	Population using improved water sources (%) 2000
Afghanistan	42.5	..	30	..	21,765	6.9	165	257	..	58	13
Andorra	..	..	..	..	86	..	6	7	..	..	100
Bosnia and Herzegovina	73.3	..	..	..	3,977	1.4	15	18	<0.10[c]	4	..
Iraq	58.7	55.9	49	..	22,946	5.2	105	130	<0.10	14	85
Kiribati	..	..	..	..	83	..	52	70	..	..	47
Korea, Dem. Rep. of	63.1	..	..	..	22,268	2.1	23	30	..	40	100
Liberia	48.1	54.0	16	..	2,913	6.8	157	235	..	42	..
Liechtenstein	..	..	..	..	33	..	10	11	..	..	..
Marshall Islands	..	..	..	..	51	..	55	68	..	..	..
Micronesia, Fed. Sts.	..	..	..	..	123	4.3	20	24	..	..	..
Monaco	..	..	..	..	33	..	4	5	..	..	100
Nauru	..	..	..	..	12	..	25	30	..	..	..
Palau	..	..	..	..	19	..	24	29	..	..	79
San Marino	..	..	..	..	27	..	6	6	..	..	..
Somalia	46.9	..	7	..	8,778	7.2	133	225	1.00	75	..
Tonga	..	..	..	..	99	..	17	21	..	..	100
Tuvalu	..	..	..	..	10	..	38	53	..	..	100
Yugoslavia	72.2	..	52	..	10,552	1.8	17	20	0.19	5	..

Note: The table presents data for UN member countries not included in the main indicator tables.
a. Data refer to estimates for the period specified. b. Data refer to the end of 2001. c. Data refer to the end of 1999.
Source: Columns 1, 5 and 6: UN 2001; *column 2:* UNESCO 2002a; *column 3:* UNESCO 2001a; *column 4:* World Bank 2002b; *columns 7 and 8:* UNICEF 2002b; *column 9:* UNAIDS and WHO 2002; *column 10:* FAO 2001; *column 11:* WHO, UNICEF and WSSCC 2000.

CALCULATING THE HUMAN DEVELOPMENT INDICES

The diagrams here offer a clear overview of how the five human development indices
used in the *Human Development Report* are constructed, highlighting both their similarities
and their differences. The text on the following pages provides a detailed explanation.

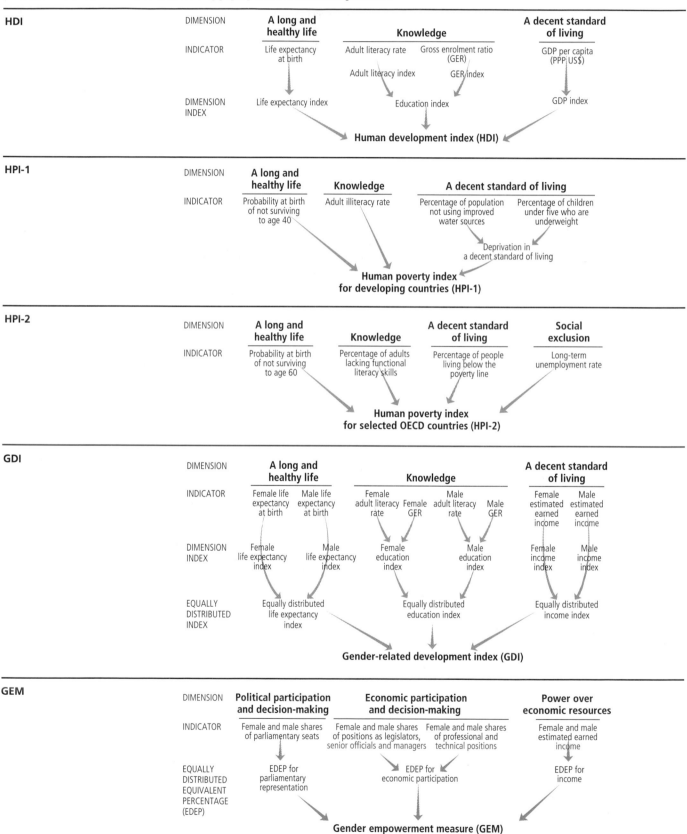

The human development index (HDI)

The HDI is a summary measure of human development. It measures the average achievements in a country in three basic dimensions of human development:

• A long and healthy life, as measured by life expectancy at birth.
• Knowledge, as measured by the adult literacy rate (with two-thirds weight) and the combined primary, secondary and tertiary gross enrolment ratio (with one-third weight).
• A decent standard of living, as measured by GDP per capita (PPP US$).

Before the HDI itself is calculated, an index needs to be created for each of these dimensions. To calculate these dimension indices —the life expectancy, education and GDP indices—minimum and maximum values (goalposts) are chosen for each underlying indicator.

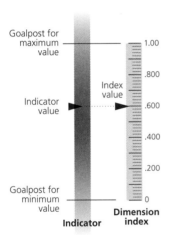

Performance in each dimension is expressed as a value between 0 and 1 by applying the following general formula:

$$\text{Dimension index} = \frac{\text{actual value} - \text{minimum value}}{\text{maximum value} - \text{minimum value}}$$

The HDI is then calculated as a simple average of the dimension indices. The box at right illustrates the calculation of the HDI for a sample country.

Goalposts for calculating the HDI

Indicator	Maximum value	Minimum value
Life expectancy at birth (years)	85	25
Adult literacy rate (%)	100	0
Combined gross enrolment ratio (%)	100	0
GDP per capita (PPP US$)	40,000	100

Calculating the HDI

This illustration of the calculation of the HDI uses data for Côte d'Ivoire.

1. Calculating the life expectancy index

The life expectancy index measures the relative achievement of a country in life expectancy at birth. For Côte d'Ivoire, with a life expectancy of 47.8 years in 2000, the life expectancy index is 0.380.

$$\text{Life expectancy index} = \frac{47.8 - 25}{85 - 25} = \textbf{0.380}$$

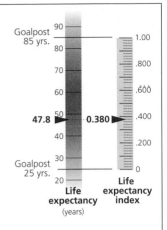

2. Calculating the education index

The education index measures a country's relative achievement in both adult literacy and combined primary, secondary and tertiary gross enrolment. First, an index for adult literacy and one for combined gross enrolment are calculated. Then these two indices are combined to create the education index, with two-thirds weight given to adult literacy and one-third weight to combined gross enrolment. For Côte d'Ivoire, with an adult literacy rate of 46.8% in 2000 and a combined gross enrolment ratio of 38% in 1999, the education index is 0.439.

$$\text{Adult literacy index} = \frac{46.8 - 0}{100 - 0} = 0.468$$

$$\text{Gross enrolment index} = \frac{38 - 0}{100 - 0} = 0.380$$

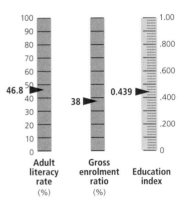

$$\text{Education index} = 2/3 \text{ (adult literacy index)} + 1/3 \text{ (gross enrolment index)}$$
$$= 2/3 \text{ (0.468)} + 1/3 \text{ (0.380)} = \textbf{0.439}$$

3. Calculating the GDP index

The GDP index is calculated using adjusted GDP per capita (PPP US$). In the HDI income serves as a surrogate for all the dimensions of human development not reflected in a long and healthy life and in knowledge. Income is adjusted because achieving a respectable level of human development does not require unlimited income. Accordingly, the logarithm of income is used. For Côte d'Ivoire, with a GDP per capita of $1,630 (PPP US$) in 2000, the GDP index is 0.466.

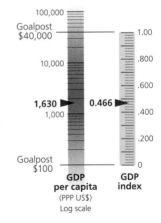

$$\text{GDP index} = \frac{\log (1,630) - \log (100)}{\log (40,000) - \log (100)} = \textbf{0.466}$$

4. Calculating the HDI

Once the dimension indices have been calculated, determining the HDI is straightforward. It is a simple average of the three dimension indices.

$$\text{HDI} = 1/3 \text{ (life expectancy index)} + 1/3 \text{ (education index)}$$
$$+ 1/3 \text{ (GDP index)}$$
$$= 1/3 \text{ (0.380)} + 1/3 \text{ (0.439)} + 1/3 \text{ (0.466)} = \textbf{0.428}$$

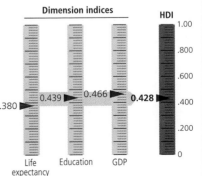

The human poverty index for developing countries (HPI-1)

While the HDI measures average achievement, the HPI-1 measures *deprivations* in the three basic dimensions of human development captured in the HDI:

- A long and healthy life—vulnerability to death at a relatively early age, as measured by the probability at birth of not surviving to age 40.
- Knowledge—exclusion from the world of reading and communications, as measured by the adult illiteracy rate.
- A decent standard of living—lack of access to overall economic provisioning, as measured by the percentage of the population not using improved water sources and the percentage of children under five who are underweight.

Calculating the HPI-1 is more straightforward than calculating the HDI. The indicators used to measure the deprivations are already normalized between 0 and 100 (because they are expressed as percentages), so there is no need to create dimension indices as for the HDI.

In this year's Report, because reliable data on access to health services are lacking for recent years, deprivation in a decent standard of living is measured by two rather than three indicators—the percentage of the population not using improved water sources and the percentage of children under five who are underweight. An unweighted average of the two is used as an input to the HPI-1.

The human poverty index for selected OECD countries (HPI-2)

The HPI-2 measures deprivations in the same dimensions as the HPI-1 and also captures social exclusion. Thus it reflects deprivations in four dimensions:

- A long and healthy life—vulnerability to death at a relatively early age, as measured by the probability at birth of not surviving to age 60.
- Knowledge—exclusion from the world of reading and communications, as measured by the percentage of adults (aged 16–65) lacking functional literacy skills.
- A decent standard of living—as measured by the percentage of people living below the income poverty line (50% of the median disposable household income).
- Social exclusion—as measured by the rate of long-term unemployment (12 months or more).

Calculating the HPI-1

1. Measuring deprivation in a decent standard of living

An unweighted average of two indicators is used to measure deprivation in a decent standard of living.

$$\text{Unweighted average} = 1/2 \text{ (population not using improved water sources)} + 1/2 \text{ (underweight children under five)}$$

A sample calculation: Central African Republic
Population not using improved water sources = 40%
Underweight children under five = 24%

$$\text{Unweighted average} = 1/2 (40) + 1/2 (24) = 32.0\%$$

2. Calculating the HPI-1

The formula for calculating the HPI-1 is as follows:

$$\text{HPI-1} = [1/3 \, (P_1^{\alpha} + P_2^{\alpha} + P_3^{\alpha})]^{1/\alpha}$$

Where:
P_1 = Probability at birth of not surviving to age 40 (times 100)
P_2 = Adult illiteracy rate
P_3 = Unweighted average of population not using improved water sources and underweight children under age five
$\alpha = 3$

A sample calculation: Central African Republic
$P_1 = 45.3\%$
$P_2 = 53.3\%$
$P_3 = 32.0\%$

$$\text{HPI-1} = [1/3 \, (45.3^3 + 53.3^3 + 32.0^3)]^{1/3} = \textbf{45.2}$$

Calculating the HPI-2

The formula for calculating the HPI-2 is as follows:

$$\text{HPI-2} = [1/4 \, (P_1^{\alpha} + P_2^{\alpha} + P_3^{\alpha} + P_4^{\alpha})]^{1/\alpha}$$

Where:
P_1 = Probability at birth of not surviving to age 60 (times 100)
P_2 = Adults lacking functional literacy skills
P_3 = Population below income poverty line (50% of median disposable household income)
P_4 = Rate of long-term unemployment (lasting 12 months or more)
$\alpha = 3$

A sample calculation: United Kingdom
$P_1 = 9.9\%$
$P_2 = 21.8\%$
$P_3 = 13.4\%$
$P_4 = 1.5\%$

$$\text{HPI-2} = [1/4 \, (9.9^3 + 21.8^3 + 13.4^3 + 1.5^3)]^{1/3} = \textbf{15.1}$$

Why $\alpha = 3$ in calculating the HPI-1 and HPI-2

The value of α has an important impact on the value of the HPI. If $\alpha = 1$, the HPI is the average of its dimensions. As α rises, greater weight is given to the dimension in which there is the most deprivation. Thus as α increases towards infinity, the HPI will tend towards the value of the dimension in which deprivation is greatest (for the Central African Republic, the example used for calculating the HPI-1, it would be 53.3%, equal to the adult illiteracy rate).

In this Report the value 3 is used to give additional but not overwhelming weight to areas of more acute deprivation. For a detailed analysis of the HPI's mathematical formulation see Sudhir Anand and Amartya Sen's "Concepts of Human Development and Poverty: A Multidimensional Perspective" and the technical note in *Human Development Report 1997* (see the list of selected readings at the end of this technical note).

The gender-related development index (GDI)

While the HDI measures average achievement, the GDI adjusts the average achievement to reflect the *inequalities* between men and women in the following dimensions:

• A long and healthy life, as measured by life expectancy at birth.
• Knowledge, as measured by the adult literacy rate and the combined primary, secondary and tertiary gross enrolment ratio.
• A decent standard of living, as measured by estimated earned income (PPP US$).

The calculation of the GDI involves three steps. First, female and male indices in each dimension are calculated according to this general formula:

$$\text{Dimension index} = \frac{\text{actual value} - \text{minimum value}}{\text{maximum value} - \text{minimum value}}$$

Second, the female and male indices in each dimension are combined in a way that penalizes differences in achievement between men and women. The resulting index, referred to as the equally distributed index, is calculated according to this general formula:

$$\text{Equally distributed index}$$
$$= \{[\text{female population share (female index}^{1-\epsilon})]$$
$$+ [\text{male population share (male index}^{1-\epsilon})]\}^{1/1-\epsilon}$$

ϵ measures the aversion to inequality. In the GDI $\epsilon = 2$. Thus the general equation becomes:

$$\text{Equally distributed index}$$
$$= \{[\text{female population share (female index}^{-1})]$$
$$+ [\text{male population share (male index}^{-1})]\}^{-1}$$

which gives the harmonic mean of the female and male indices.

Third, the GDI is calculated by combining the three equally distributed indices in an unweighted average.

Goalposts for calculating the GDI

Indicator	Maximum value	Minimum value
Female life expectancy at birth (years)	87.5	27.5
Male life expectancy at birth (years)	82.5	22.5
Adult literacy rate (%)	100	0
Combined gross enrolment ratio (%)	100	0
Estimated earned income (PPP US$)	40,000	100

Note: The maximum and minimum values (goalposts) for life expectancy are five years higher for women to take into account their longer life expectancy.

Calculating the GDI

This illustration of the calculation of the GDI uses data for Brazil.

1. Calculating the equally distributed life expectancy index
The first step is to calculate separate indices for female and male achievements in life expectancy, using the general formula for dimension indices.

FEMALE
Life expectancy: 72.0 years

$$\text{Life expectancy index} = \frac{72.0 - 27.5}{87.5 - 27.5} = 0.742$$

MALE
Life expectancy: 64.1 years

$$\text{Life expectancy index} = \frac{64.1 - 22.5}{82.5 - 22.5} = 0.693$$

Next, the female and male indices are combined to create the equally distributed life expectancy index, using the general formula for equally distributed indices.

FEMALE
Population share: 0.506
Life expectancy index: 0.742

MALE
Population share: 0.494
Life expectancy index: 0.693

$$\text{Equally distributed life expectancy index} = \{[0.506 \,(0.742^{-1})] + [0.494 \,(0.693^{-1})]\}^{-1} = \mathbf{0.717}$$

2. Calculating the equally distributed education index
First, indices for the adult literacy rate and the combined primary, secondary and tertiary gross enrolment ratio are calculated separately for females and males. Calculating these indices is straightforward, since the indicators used are already normalized between 0 and 100.

FEMALE
Adult literacy rate: 85.4%
Adult literacy index: 0.854
Gross enrolment ratio: 80.0%
Gross enrolment index: 0.800

MALE
Adult literacy rate: 85.1%
Adult literacy index: 0.851
Gross enrolment ratio: 79.3%
Gross enrolment index: 0.793

Second, the education index, which gives two-thirds weight to the adult literacy index and one-third weight to the gross enrolment index, is computed separately for females and males.

$$\text{Education index} = 2/3 \,(\text{adult literacy index}) + 1/3 \,(\text{gross enrolment index})$$

$$\text{Female education index} = 2/3 \,(0.854) + 1/3 \,(0.800) = 0.836$$

$$\text{Male education index} = 2/3 \,(0.851) + 1/3 \,(0.793) = 0.832$$

Finally, the female and male education indices are combined to create the equally distributed education index:

FEMALE
Population share: 0.506
Education index: 0.836

MALE
Population share: 0.494
Education index: 0.832

$$\text{Equally distributed education index} = \{[0.506 \,(0.836^{-1})] + [0.494 \,(0.832^{-1})]\}^{-1} = \mathbf{0.834}$$

3. Calculating the equally distributed income index
First, female and male earned income (PPP US$) are estimated (for details on this calculation see the addendum to this technical note). Then the income index is calculated for each gender. As for the HDI, income is adjusted by taking the logarithm of estimated earned income (PPP US$):

$$\text{Income index} = \frac{\log(\text{actual value}) - \log(\text{minimum value})}{\log(\text{maximum value}) - \log(\text{minimum value})}$$

FEMALE
Estimated earned income (PPP US$): 4,557

MALE
Estimated earned income (PPP US$): 10,769

$$\text{Income index} = \frac{\log(4,557) - \log(100)}{\log(40,000) - \log(100)} = 0.637$$

$$\text{Income index} = \frac{\log(10,769) - \log(100)}{\log(40,000) - \log(100)} = 0.781$$

Calculating the GDI continues on next page

Calculating the GDI (continued)

Second, the female and male income indices are combined to create the equally distributed income index:

FEMALE
Population share: 0.506
Income index: 0.637

MALE
Population share: 0.494
Income index: 0.781

Equally distributed income index = $\{[0.506\,(0.637^{-1})] + [0.494\,(0.781^{-1})]\}^{-1}$ = **0.701**

4. Calculating the GDI

Calculating the GDI is straightforward. It is simply the unweighted average of the three component indices—the equally distributed life expectancy index, the equally distributed education index and the equally distributed income index.

GDI = 1/3 (life expectancy index) + 1/3 (education index) + 1/3 (income index)
= 1/3 (0.717) + 1/3 (0.834) + 1/3 (0.701) = **0.751**

Why ϵ = 2 in calculating the GDI

The value of ϵ is the size of the penalty for gender inequality. The larger the value, the more heavily a society is penalized for having inequalities.

If $\epsilon = 0$, gender inequality is not penalized (in this case the GDI would have the same value as the HDI). As ϵ increases towards infinity, more and more weight is given to the lesser achieving group.

The value 2 is used in calculating the GDI (as well as the GEM). This value places a moderate penalty on gender inequality in achievement.

For a detailed analysis of the GDI's mathematical formulation see Sudhir Anand and Amartya Sen's "Gender Inequality in Human Development: Theories and Measurement," Kalpana Bardhan and Stephan Klasen's "UNDP's Gender-Related Indices: A Critical Review" and the technical notes in *Human Development Report 1995* and *Human Development Report 1999* (see the list of selected readings at the end of this technical note).

The gender empowerment measure (GEM)

Focusing on women's opportunities rather than their capabilities, the GEM captures gender inequality in three key areas:

• Political participation and decision-making power, as measured by women's and men's percentage shares of parliamentary seats.
• Economic participation and decision-making power, as measured by two indicators—women's and men's percentage shares of positions as legislators, senior officials and managers and women's and men's percentage shares of professional and technical positions.
• Power over economic resources, as measured by women's and men's estimated earned income (PPP US$).

For each of these three dimensions, an equally distributed equivalent percentage (EDEP) is calculated, as a population-weighted average, according to the following general formula:

EDEP = {[female population share (female index$^{1-\epsilon}$)]
+ [male population share (male index$^{1-\epsilon}$)]}$^{1/1-\epsilon}$

ϵ measures the aversion to inequality. In the GEM (as in the GDI) $\epsilon = 2$, which places a moderate penalty on inequality. The formula is thus:

EDEP = {[female population share (female index^{-1})]
+ [male population share (male index^{-1})]}$^{-1}$

For political and economic participation and decision-making, the EDEP is then indexed by dividing it by 50. The rationale for this indexation: in an ideal society, with equal empowerment of the sexes, the GEM variables would equal 50%—that is, women's share would equal men's share for each variable.

Finally, the GEM is calculated as a simple average of the three indexed EDEPs.

Calculating the GEM

This illustration of the calculation of the GEM uses data for Venezuela.

1. Calculating the EDEP for parliamentary representation

The EDEP for parliamentary representation measures the relative empowerment of women in terms of their political participation. The EDEP is calculated using the female and male shares of the population and female and male percentage shares of parliamentary seats according to the general formula.

FEMALE
Population share: 0.497
Parliamentary share: 9.7%

MALE
Population share: 0.503
Parliamentary share: 90.3%

$$\text{EDEP for parliamentary representation} = \{[0.497\,(9.7^{-1})] + [0.503\,(90.3^{-1})]\}^{-1} = 17.60$$

Then this initial EDEP is indexed to an ideal value of 50%.

$$\text{Indexed EDEP for parliamentary representation} = \frac{17.60}{50} = \mathbf{0.352}$$

2. Calculating the EDEP for economic participation

Using the general formula, an EDEP is calculated for women's and men's percentage shares of positions as legislators, senior officials and managers, and another for women's and men's percentage shares of professional and technical positions. The simple average of the two measures gives the EDEP for economic participation.

FEMALE
Population share: 0.497
Percentage share of positions as legislators, senior officials and managers: 24.3%
Percentage share of professional and technical positions: 57.6%

MALE
Population share: 0.503
Percentage share of positions as legislators, senior officials and managers: 75.7%
Percentage share of professional and technical positions: 42.4%

$$\text{EDEP for positions as legislators, senior officials and managers} = \{[0.497\,(24.3^{-1})] + [0.503\,(75.7^{-1})]\}^{-1} = 36.90$$

$$\text{Indexed EDEP for positions as legislators, senior officials and managers} = \frac{36.90}{50} = 0.738$$

$$\text{EDEP for professional and technical positions} = \{[0.497\,(57.6^{-1})] + [0.503\,(42.4^{-1})]\}^{-1} = 48.80$$

$$\text{Indexed EDEP for professional and technical positions} = \frac{48.80}{50} = 0.976$$

The two indexed EDEPs are averaged to create the EDEP for economic participation:

$$\text{EDEP for economic participation} = \frac{0.738 + 0.976}{2} = \mathbf{0.857}$$

3. Calculating the EDEP for income

Earned income (PPP US$) is estimated for women and men separately and then indexed to goalposts as for the HDI and the GDI. For the GEM, however, the income index is based on unadjusted values, not the logarithm of estimated earned income. (For details on the estimation of earned income for men and women see the addendum to this technical note.)

FEMALE
Population share: 0.497
Estimated earned income (PPP US$): 3,334

MALE
Population share: 0.503
Estimated earned income (PPP US$): 8,223

$$\text{Income index} = \frac{3,334 - 100}{40,000 - 100} = 0.081$$

$$\text{Income index} = \frac{8,223 - 100}{40,000 - 100} = 0.204$$

The female and male indices are then combined to create the equally distributed index:

$$\text{EDEP for income} = \{[0.497\,(0.081^{-1})] + [0.503\,(0.204^{-1})]\}^{-1} = \mathbf{0.116}$$

4. Calculating the GEM

Once the EDEP has been calculated for the three dimensions of the GEM, determining the GEM is straightforward. It is a simple average of the three EDEP indices.

$$\text{GEM} = \frac{0.352 + 0.857 + 0.116}{3} = \mathbf{0.442}$$

Female and male earned income

Despite the importance of having gender-disaggregated data on income, direct measures are unavailable. For this Report crude estimates of female and male earned income have therefore been derived.

Income can be seen in two ways: as a resource for consumption and as earnings by individuals. The use measure is difficult to disaggregate between men and women because they share resources within a family unit. By contrast, earnings are separable because different members of a family tend to have separate earned incomes.

The income measure used in the GDI and the GEM indicates a person's capacity to earn income. It is used in the GDI to capture the disparities between men and women in command over resources and in the GEM to capture women's economic independence. (For conceptual and methodological issues relating to this approach see Sudhir Anand and Amartya Sen's "Gender Inequality in Human Development" and, in *Human Development Report 1995,* chapter 3 and technical notes 1 and 2; see the list of selected readings at the end of this technical note.)

Female and male earned income (PPP US$) are estimated using the following data:

- Ratio of the female non-agricultural wage to the male non-agricultural wage.
- Male and female shares of the economically active population.
- Total female and male population.
- GDP per capita (PPP US$).

Key

W_f / W_m = ratio of female non-agricultural wage to male non-agricultural wage
EA_f = female share of economically active population
EA_m = male share of economically active population
S_f = female share of wage bill
Y = total GDP (PPP US$)
N_f = total female population
N_m = total male population
Y_f = estimated female earned income (PPP US$)
Y_m = estimated male earned income (PPP US$)

Note

Calculations based on data in the technical note may yield results that differ from those in the indicator tables because of rounding.

Estimating female and male earned income

This illustration of the estimation of female and male earned income uses 2000 data for Ethiopia.

1. Calculating total GDP (PPP US$)

Total GDP (PPP US$) is calculated by multiplying the total population by GDP per capita (PPP US$).

Total population: 62,908 (thousand)
GDP per capita (PPP US$): 668
Total GDP (PPP US$) = 668 (62,908) = 42,022,544 (thousand)

2. Calculating the female share of the wage bill

Because data on wages in rural areas and in the informal sector are rare, the Report has used non-agricultural wages and assumed that the ratio of female wages to male wages in the non-agricultural sector applies to the rest of the economy. The female share of the wage bill is calculated using the ratio of the female non-agricultural wage to the male non-agricultural wage and the female and male percentage shares of the economically active population. Where data on the wage ratio are not available, a value of 75% is used.

Ratio of female to male non-agricultural wage (W_f/W_m) = 0.75
Female percentage share of economically active population (EA_f) = 40.9%
Male percentage share of economically active population (EA_m) = 59.1%

$$\text{Female share of wage bill } (S_f) = \frac{W_f/W_m (EA_f)}{[W_f/W_m (EA_f)] + EA_m} = \frac{0.75 (40.9)}{[0.75 (40.9)] + 59.1} = \mathbf{0.342}$$

3. Calculating female and male earned income (PPP US$)

An assumption has to be made that the female share of the wage bill is equal to the female share of GDP.

Female share of wage bill (S_f) = 0.342
Total GDP (PPP US$) ($Y$) = 42,022,544 (thousand)
Female population (N_f) = 31,649 (thousand)

$$\text{Estimated female earned income (PPP US$) } (Y_f) = \frac{S_f(Y)}{N_f} = \frac{0.342 (42,022,544)}{31,649} = \mathbf{454}$$

Male population (N_m) = 31,259 (thousand)

$$\text{Estimated male earned income (PPP US$) } (Y_m) = \frac{Y - S_f(Y)}{N_m} = \frac{42,022,544 - [0.342 (42,022,544)]}{31,259} = \mathbf{885}$$

Selected readings

Anand, Sudhir, and Amartya Sen. 1994. "Human Development Index: Methodology and Measurement." Occasional Paper 12. United Nations Development Programme, Human Development Report Office, New York. *(HDI)*

————. 1995. "Gender Inequality in Human Development: Theories and Measurement." Occasional Paper 19. United Nations Development Programme, Human Development Report Office, New York. *(GDI, GEM)*

————. 1997. "Concepts of Human Development and Poverty: A Multidimensional Perspective." In United Nations Development Programme, *Human Development Report 1997 Papers: Poverty and Human Development.* New York. *(HPI-1, HPI-2)*

Bardhan, Kalpana, and Stephan Klasen. 1999. "UNDP's Gender-Related Indices: A Critical Review." *World Development* 27(6): 985–1010. *(GDI, GEM)*

United Nations Development Programme. 1995. *Human Development Report 1995.* New York: Oxford University Press. Technical notes 1 and 2 and chapter 3. *(GDI, GEM)*

————. 1997. *Human Development Report 1997.* New York: Oxford University Press. Technical note 1 and chapter 1. *(HPI-1, HPI-2)*

————. 1999. *Human Development Report 1999.* New York: Oxford University Press. Technical note. *(HDI, GDI)*

ASSESSING PROGRESS TOWARDS THE MILLENNIUM DEVELOPMENT GOALS

This year's *Human Development Report* assesses the progress by countries towards specific targets outlined in the Millennium Development Goals. Each target has been set for 2015, with 1990 as the reference year. So achieving a target of, say, halving a rate or ratio by 2015 would mean reducing its 1990 value by 50% by 2015. Assessing the achievements of countries between 1990 and 2000 reveals whether they are progressing fast enough to meet the targets.

Monitoring progress at the global level requires data that are comparable. Yet data are missing or unreliable for some targets and for many countries. Countries at higher levels of develop-

ment are more likely to have data, so those included in the assessment are likely to be among the better performers. High-income OECD countries have been excluded from the assessment. The number of countries whose progress has been assessed for each target ranges from 52 to 166 (technical note table 2.1).

The assessment of countries' achievements is based on the following criteria:
• *Achieved:* The country has already achieved the target.
• *On track:* The country has attained the rate of progress needed to achieve the target by 2015 or has attained 90% of that rate of progress.
• *Lagging:* The country has achieved 70–89% of the rate of progress required to achieve the target by 2015.

• *Far behind:* The country has achieved less than 70% of the required rate of progress.
• *Slipping back:* The country's level of achievement is at least 5 percentage points worse in 2000 than in 1990.

The rate of progress required to meet the target is determined by the achievement that would be required by 2000, assuming a linear path of progress. Where data are not available for 1990 or 2000, data for the closest available year have been used. To be assessed, a country must have data at least five years apart. All countries within 10 percentage points of the universal goal (such as 100% school enrolment) in 2000 are considered to be on track. For child mortality, countries with an under-five mortality rate below 15 per 1,000 are considered to be on track.

Technical note table 2.1
Indicators used in assessment of progress towards Millennium Development Goals

	Indicator	Countries assessed[a]	Source
Hunger	Percentage of people undernourished, 1990/92 and 1997/99	100 (77)	FAO 2001
Universal education	Net primary enrolment ratio, 1987–93[b] and 1994–97[c]	75 (46)	UNESCO 2001b
	Percentage of children reaching grade 5, 1990 and 1995–97[c] cohort	52 (34)	UNESCO 1999b
Gender equality	Ratio of girls to boys in school (girls' gross enrolment ratio to boys'), 1990–92[b] and 1995–98[c]		
	Primary level	104 (67)	UNESCO 1999a
	Secondary level	101 (66)	UNESCO 1999a
Child mortality	Under-five mortality rate (per 1,000 live births), 1990 and 2000	166 (86)	UNICEF 2002b
Safe water	Percentage of people with access to improved water sources, 1990 and 2000	93 (75)	WHO, UNICEF and WSSCC 2000

a. Figures in parentheses refer to the percentage of the world population covered by the assessment.
b. Data refer to year closest to 1990 during the period specified.
c. Data refer to the most recent year available during the period specified.

Statistical references

Anand, Sudhir, and Amartya Sen. 1994. "Human Development Index: Methodology and Measurement." Occasional Paper 12. United Nations Development Programme, Human Development Report Office, New York.

———. 1995. "Gender Inequality in Human Development: Theories and Measurement." Occasional Paper 19. United Nations Development Programme, Human Development Report Office, New York.

———. 1997. "Concepts of Human Development and Poverty: A Multidimensional Perspective." In United Nations Development Programme, *Human Development Report 1997 Papers: Poverty and Human Development.* New York.

Aten, Bettina, Alan Heston and Robert Summers. 2001. "Penn World Tables 6.0." University of Pennsylvania, Center for International and Interarea Comparisons, Philadelphia.

Bardhan, Kalpana, and Stephen Klasen. 1999. "UNDP's Gender-Related Indices: A Critical Review." *World Development* 27(6): 985–1010.

CDIAC (Carbon Dioxide Information Analysis Center). 2001. *Trends: A Compendium of Data on Global Change.* [http://cdiac.esd.ornl.gov/trends/trends.htm]. March 2002.

FAO (Food and Agriculture Organization of the United Nations). 2001. *The State of Food Insecurity in the World 2001.* [http://www.fao.org/SOF/sofi/index_en.htm]. February 2002.

Goldschmidt-Clermont, Luisella, and Elisabetta Pagnossin Aligisakis. 1995. "Measures of Unrecorded Economic Activities in Fourteen Countries." Background paper for *Human Development Report 1995.* United Nations Development Programme, Human Development Report Office, New York.

Harvey, Andrew S. 1995. "Market and Non-Market Productive Activity in Less Developed and Developing Countries: Lessons from Time Use." Background paper for *Human Development Report 1995.* United Nations Development Programme, Human Development Report Office, New York.

———. 2001. "National Time Use Data on Market and Non-Market Work by Both Women and Men." Background paper for *Human Development Report 2001.* United Nations Development Programme, Human Development Report Office, New York.

Hill, Kenneth, Carla AbouZahr and Tessa Wardlaw. 2001. "Estimates of Maternal Mortality for 1995." *Bulletin of the World Health Organization* 79(3): 182–93.

IISS (International Institute for Strategic Studies). 2001. *The Military Balance 2001–2002.* Oxford: Oxford University Press.

ILO (International Labour Organization). 2001. *Yearbook of Labour Statistics.* Geneva.

———. 2002a. Correspondence on underemployment. February. Geneva.

———. 2002b. *Estimates and Projections of the Economically Active Population, 1950–2010.* 4th ed., rev. 2. Database. Geneva.

———. 2002c. *ILO Database on International Labour Standards (ILOLEX).* [http://ilolex.ilo.ch:1567/english/index.htm]. February 2002.

———. 2002d. *Key Indicators of the Labour Market 2001–2002.* [http://kilm.ilo.org/kilm/]. February 2002.

———. 2002e. *Laboursta Database.* [http://laborsta.ilo.org]. February 2002.

IPU (Inter-Parliamentary Union). 1995. *Women in Parliaments 1945–1995: A World Statistical Survey.* Geneva.

———. 2001a. Correspondence on women in government at the ministerial level. March. Geneva.

———. 2001b. Correspondence on year women received the right to vote and to stand for election and year first woman was elected or appointed to parliament. March. Geneva.

———. 2002. *Parline Database.* [http://www.ipu.org/wmn-e/classif.htm]. March 2002.

ITU (International Telecommunication Union). 2002. *World Telecommunication Indicators.* Database. Geneva.

LIS (Luxembourg Income Study). 2001. "Population below Income Poverty Line." [http://www.lisproject.org/techdoc.htm]. February 2001.

———. 2002. "Population below Income Poverty Line." [http://lisweb.ceps.lu/keyfigures/povertytable.htm]. February 2002.

London Group on Environmental Accounting. 2002. "London Group on Environmental Accounting: SEEA 2000 Revision." [http://www4.statcan.ca/citygrp/london/london.htm]. March 2002.

Milanovic, Branko. 2002. Correspondence on income, inequality and poverty during the transition from planned to market economy. World Bank. March. Washington, DC.

Murray, Scott. 2001. Correspondence on functional literacy. Statistics Canada. March. Ottawa.

OECD (Organisation for Economic Co-operation and Development). 2001a. *Economic Outlook* 2(70). Paris.

———. 2001b. *Employment Outlook 2001.* Paris.

OECD (Organisation for Economic Co-operation and Development), Development Assistance Committee. 2002a. Correspondence on net grants by non-governmental organizations. January. New York.

———. 2002b. Correspondence on official development assistance disbursed. January. New York.

———. 2002c. *DAC Journal: Development Cooperation 2001 Report* 3(1). Paris.

———. 2002d. *DAC Online.* Database. Paris.

OECD (Organisation for Economic Co-operation and Development) and Statistics Canada. 2000. *Literacy in the Information Age: Final Report on the IALS.* Paris.

SIPRI (Stockholm International Peace Research Institute). 2001. *SIPRI Yearbook: Armaments, Disarmament and International Security.* Oxford: Oxford University Press.

———. 2002a. Correspondence on military expenditure data. February. Stockholm.

———. 2002b. Correspondence on weapons transfer data. March. Stockholm.

Smeeding, Timothy M., Lee Rainwater and Gary Burtless. 2000. "United States Poverty in a Cross-National Context." In Sheldon H. Danziger and Robert H. Haveman, eds., *Understanding Poverty.* New York: Russell Sage Foundation; and Cambridge, Mass.: Harvard University Press.

UN (United Nations). 1993. *System of National Accounts 1993.*

[http://esa.un.org/unsd/sna1993/introduction.asp]. April 2002.

———. 1998. *World Population Prospects 1950–2050: The 1998 Revision*. Database. Department of Economic and Social Affairs, Population Division. New York.

———. 2001. *World Population Prospects 1950–2050: The 2000 Revision*. Database. Department of Economic and Social Affairs, Population Division. New York.

———. 2002a. Correspondence on time use surveys. Department of Economic and Social Affairs, Statistics Division. February. New York.

———. 2002b. "Multilateral Treaties Deposited with the Secretary-General." [http://untreaty.un.org]. February 2002.

———. 2002c. *United Nations Population Division Database on Contraceptive Use*. Department of Economic and Social Affairs, Population Division. January. New York.

———. 2002d. *World Urbanization Prospects: The 2001 Revision*. Department of Economic and Social Affairs, Population Division. New York.

UNAIDS (Joint United Nations Programme on HIV/AIDS) and WHO (World Health Organization). 2002. *Report on the Global HIV/AIDS Epidemic 2002*. Geneva.

UNCTAD (United Nations Conference on Trade and Development). 2001. "Third United Nations Conference on the Least Developed Countries." [http://www.unctad.org/conference/]. April 2002.

UNDP (United Nations Development Programme). 1995. *Human Development Report 1995*. New York: Oxford University Press.

———. 1997. *Human Development Report 1997*. New York: Oxford University Press.

———. 1999. *Human Development Report 1999*. New York: Oxford University Press.

UNESCO (United Nations Educational, Scientific and Cultural Organization). 1997a. *International Standard Classification of Education 1997*. [http://www.uis.unesco.org/en/pub/pub0.htm]. February 2002.

———. 1997b. *Statistical Yearbook 1996*. Paris.

———. 1999a. Correspondence on gross enrolment ratios. April. Paris.

———. 1999b. *Statistical Yearbook 1999*. Paris.

———. 2000. Correspondence on education expenditure. December. Paris.

———. 2001a. Correspondence on gross enrolment ratios. March. Paris.

———. 2001b. Correspondence on net enrolment ratios. March. Paris.

———. 2002a. Correspondence on adult and youth literacy rates. January. Montreal.

———. 2002b. Correspondence on gross enrolment ratios. February. Montreal.

———. 2002c. Correspondence on net enrolment ratios. February. Montreal.

UNHCR (United Nations High Commissioner for Refugees). 2002. Correspondence on refugees and internally displaced persons. February. Geneva.

UNICEF (United Nations Children's Fund). 2000. *The State of the World's Children 2001*. New York: Oxford University Press.

———. 2002a. Correspondence on infant and under-five mortality rates. January. New York.

———. 2002b. *Official Summary: The State of the World's Children 2002*. New York: Oxford University Press.

UNICRI (United Nations Interregional Crime and Justice Research Institute). 2002. Correspondence on crime victims. March. Turin.

UNSD (United Nations Statistics Division) and UNEP (United Nations Environment Programme). 2000. "Integrated Environmental and Economic Accounting." Studies in Methods, No. 78. United Nations Sales No. E00.XVII.17. New York.

Ward, Michael. 2001. "Purchasing Power Parity and International Comparisons." Background paper for *Human Development Report 2001*. United Nations Development Programme, Human Development Report Office, New York.

WHO (World Health Organization). 2001a. Correspondence on access to essential drugs. Department of Essential Drugs and Medicines Policy. February. Geneva.

———. 2001b. *Global Tuberculosis Control: WHO Report 2001*. [http://www.who.int/gtb/publications/globrep01/index.html]. February 2002.

———. 2002a. Correspondence on births attended by skilled health staff. March. Geneva.

———. 2002b. Correspondence on cigarette consumption. March. Geneva.

———. 2002c. Correspondence on malaria data. February. Geneva.

———. 2002d. "WHO Estimates of Health Personnel." [http://www3.who.int/whosis/health_personnel/health_personnel.cfm]. February 2002.

WHO (World Health Organization), UNICEF (United Nations Children's Fund) and WSSCC (Water Supply and Sanitation Collaborative Council). 2000. *Global Water Supply and Sanitation Assessment 2000 Report*. Geneva.

WIPO (World Intellectual Property Organization). 2001. *Intellectual Property Statistics*. Publication A. Geneva.

World Bank. 2002a. Correspondence on GDP per capita annual growth rates. March. Washington, DC.

———. 2002b. *World Development Indicators 2002*. CD-ROM. Washington, DC.

Definitions of statistical terms

Armed forces, total Strategic, land, naval, air, command, administrative and support forces. Also included are paramilitary forces such as the gendarmerie, customs service and border guard, if these are trained in military tactics.

Arms transfers, conventional Refers to the voluntary transfer by the supplier (and thus excludes captured weapons and weapons obtained through defectors) of weapons with a military purpose destined for the armed forces, paramilitary forces or intelligence agencies of another country. These include major conventional weapons or systems in six categories: ships, aircraft, missiles, artillery, armoured vehicles and guidance and radar systems (excluded are trucks, services, ammunition, small arms, support items, components and component technology and towed or naval artillery under 100-millimetre calibre).

Births attended by skilled health staff The percentage of deliveries attended by a doctor (a specialist, a non-specialist or a person with midwifery skills who can diagnose and manage obstetrical complications as well as normal deliveries), nurse or midwife (a person who has successfully completed the prescribed course of midwifery and is able to give the necessary supervision, care and advice to women during pregnancy, labour and the postpartum period and to care for newborns and infants) or trained traditional birth attendant (a person who initially acquired his or her ability by delivering babies or through apprenticeship to other traditional birth attendants and who has undergone subsequent extensive training and is now integrated in the formal health care system).

Birth-weight, infants with low The percentage of infants with a birth-weight of less than 2,500 grams.

Carbon dioxide emissions Anthropogenic (human-originated) carbon dioxide emissions stemming from the burning of fossil fuels and the production of cement. Emissions are calculated from data on the consumption of solid, liquid and gaseous fuels and gas flaring.

Cellular mobile subscribers People subscribing to a communications service in which voice or data are transmitted by radio frequencies.

Children reaching grade 5 The percentage of children starting primary school who eventually attain grade 5 (grade 4 if the duration of primary school is four years). The estimates are based on the reconstructed cohort method, which uses data on enrolment and repeaters for two consecutive years.

Cigarette consumption per adult, annual average The sum of production and imports minus exports of cigarettes divided by the population aged 15 and above.

Consumer price index Reflects changes in the cost to the average consumer of acquiring a basket of goods and services that may be fixed or change at specified intervals.

Contraceptive prevalence The percentage of married women aged 15–49 who are using, or whose partners are using, any form of contraception, whether modern or traditional.

Contributing family worker Defined according to the International Classification by Status in Employment (ICSE) as a person who works without pay in an economic enterprise operated by a related person living in the same household.

Crime, people victimized by The percentage of the population who perceive that they have been victimized by certain types of crime in the preceding year, based on responses to the International Crime Victims Survey.

Debt service, total The sum of principal repayments and interest actually paid in foreign currency, goods or services on long-term debt, interest paid on short-term debt and repayments to the International Monetary Fund.

Earned income (PPP US$), estimated (female and male) Roughly derived on the basis of the ratio of the female non-agricultural wage to the male non-agricultural wage, the female and male shares of the economically active population, total female and male population and GDP per capita (PPP US$). For details on this estimation see technical note 1.

Earned income, ratio of estimated female to male The ratio of estimated female earned income to estimated male earned income. See *earned income (PPP US$), estimated (female and male)*.

Economic activity rate The proportion of the specified group supplying labour for the production of economic goods and services during a specified period.

Education expenditure, public Public spending on public education plus subsidies to private education at the primary, secondary and tertiary levels. It includes expenditure at every level of administration—central, regional and local. See *education levels*.

Education index One of the three indices on which the human development index is built. It is based on the adult literacy rate and the combined primary, secondary and tertiary gross enrolment ratio. For details on how the index is calculated see technical note 1.

Education levels Categorized as pre-primary, primary, secondary or tertiary in accordance with the International Standard Classification of Education (ISCED). *Pre-primary education* (ISCED level 0) is provided at such schools as kindergartens and nursery and infant schools and is intended for children not old enough to enter school at the primary level. *Primary education* (ISCED level 1) provides the basic elements of education at such establishments as primary and elementary schools. *Secondary education* (ISCED levels 2 and 3) is based on at least four years of previous instruction at the first level and provides general or specialized instruction, or both, at such institutions as middle school, secondary school, high school, teacher training school at this level and vocational or technical school. *Tertiary education* (ISCED levels 5–7) refers to education at such institutions as universities, teachers colleges and higher-level professional schools—requiring as a minimum condition of admission the successful completion of education at the second level or evidence of the attainment of an equivalent level of knowledge.

Electricity consumption per capita Refers to gross production, in per capita terms, which includes consumption by station auxiliaries and any losses in the transformers that are considered integral parts of the station. Also included is total electric energy produced by pumping installations without deduction of electric energy absorbed by pumping.

Employment by economic activity Employment in industry, agriculture or services as defined according to the International Standard Industrial Classification (ISIC) system (revisions 2 and 3). *Industry* refers to mining and quarrying, manufacturing, construction and public utilities (gas, water and electricity). *Agriculture* refers to agriculture, hunting, forestry and fishing. *Services* refer to wholesale and retail trade; restaurants and hotels; transport, storage and communications; finance, insurance, real estate and business services; and community, social and personal services.

Energy use, GDP per unit of The ratio of GDP (PPP US$) to commercial energy use, measured in kilograms of oil equivalent. This ratio provides a measure of energy efficiency by showing comparable and consistent estimates of real GDP across countries relative to physical inputs (units of energy use). See *GDP (gross domestic product)* and *PPP (purchasing power parity)*.

Enrolment ratio, gross The number of students enrolled in a level of education, regardless of age, as a percentage of the population of official school age for that level. See *education levels*.

Enrolment ratio, net The number of students enrolled in a level of education who are of official school age for that level, as a percentage of the population of official school age for that level. See *education levels*.

Essential drugs, population with access to The percentage of the population for whom a minimum of 20 of the most essential drugs are continuously and affordably available at public or private health facilities or drug outlets within one hour's travel from home.

Exports, high technology Exports of products with a high intensity of research and development. They include high-technology products such as in aerospace, computers, pharmaceuticals, scientific instruments and electrical machinery.

Exports, manufactured Defined according to the Standard International Trade Classification to include exports of chemicals, basic manufactures, machinery and transport equipment and other miscellaneous manufactured goods.

Exports of goods and services The value of all goods and other market services provided to the rest of the world, including the value of merchandise, freight, insurance, transport, travel, royalties, licence fees and other services. Labour and property income is excluded.

Exports, primary Defined according to the Standard International Trade Classification to include exports of food, agricultural raw materials, fuels and ores and metals.

Fertility rate, total The average number of children a woman would bear if age-specific fertility rates remained unchanged during her lifetime.

Foreign direct investment, net inflows of Net inflows of investment to acquire a lasting management interest (10% or more of voting stock) in an enterprise operating in an economy other than that of the investor. It is the sum of equity capital, reinvestment of earnings, other long-term capital and short-term capital.

Fuel consumption, traditional Estimated consumption of fuel wood, charcoal, bagasse, non-commercial energy and animal, industrial, municipal and pulp and paper waste. Traditional fuel use and commercial energy use together make up total energy use.

Functional literacy skills, people lacking The proportion of the adult population aged 16–65 scoring at level 1 on the prose literacy scale of the International Adult Literacy Survey (IALS). Most tasks at this level require the reader to locate a piece of information in the text that is identical to or synonymous with the information given in the directive.

GDP (gross domestic product) The total output of goods and services for final use produced by an economy, by both residents and non-residents, regardless of the allocation to domestic and foreign claims. It does not include deductions for depreciation of physical capital or depletion and degradation of natural resources.

GDP index One of the three indices on which the human development index is built. It is based on GDP per capita (PPP US$). For details on how the index is calculated see technical note 1.

GDP per capita (PPP US$) See *GDP (gross domestic product)* and *PPP (purchasing power parity)*.

GDP per capita (US$) GDP per capita converted to US dollars using the average official exchange rate reported by the International Monetary Fund. An alternative conversion factor is applied if the official exchange rate is judged to diverge by an exceptionally large margin from the rate effectively applied to transactions in foreign currencies and traded products. See *GDP (gross domestic product)*.

GDP per capita annual growth rate Least squares annual growth rate, calculated from constant price GDP per capita in local currency units.

Gender empowerment measure (GEM) A composite index measuring gender inequality in three basic dimensions of empowerment—economic participation and decision-making, political participation and decision-making and power over economic resources. For details on how the index is calculated see technical note 1.

Gender-related development index (GDI) A composite index measuring average achievement in the three basic dimensions captured in the human development index—a long and healthy life, knowledge and a decent standard of living—adjusted to account for inequalities between men and women. For details on how the index is calculated see technical note 1.

Gini index Measures the extent to which the distribution of income (or consumption) among individuals or households within a country deviates from a perfectly equal distribution. A value of 0 represents perfect equality, a value of 100 perfect inequality.

GNP (gross national product) Comprises GDP plus net factor income from abroad, which is the income residents receive from abroad for factor services (labour and capital), less similar payments made to non-residents who contribute to the domestic economy.

Grants by NGOs, net Resource transfers by national non-governmental organizations (private non-profit-making agencies) to developing countries or territories identified in part I of the Development Assistance Committee (DAC) list of recipient countries. They are calculated as gross outflows from NGOs minus resource transfers received from the official sector (which are already counted in official development assistance).

Health expenditure per capita (PPP US$) The sum of public and private expenditure (in PPP US$), divided by the population. Health expenditure includes the provision of health services (preventive and curative), family planning activities, nutrition activities and emergency aid designated for health (but does not include provision of water and sanitation). See *health expenditure, private; health expenditure, public;* and *PPP (purchasing power parity).*

Health expenditure, private Direct household (out of pocket) spending, private insurance, charitable donations and direct service payments by private corporations. Together with public health expenditure, it makes up total health expenditure. See *health expenditure per capita (PPP US$)* and *health expenditure, public.*

Health expenditure, public Recurrent and capital spending from government (central and local) budgets, external borrowings and grants (including donations from international agencies and non-governmental organizations) and social (or compulsory) health insurance funds. Together with private health expenditure, it makes up total health expenditure. See *health expenditure per capita (PPP US$)* and *health expenditure, private.*

HIV/AIDS, people living with The estimated number of people living with HIV/AIDS at the end of the year specified.

Human development index (HDI) A composite index measuring average achievement in three basic dimensions of human development—a long and healthy life, knowledge and a decent standard of living. For details on how the index is calculated see technical note 1.

Human poverty index (HPI-1) for developing countries A composite index measuring deprivations in the three basic dimensions captured in the human development index—longevity, knowledge and standard of living. For details on how the index is calculated see technical note 1.

Human poverty index (HPI-2) for selected OECD countries A composite index measuring deprivations in the three basic dimensions captured in the human development index—longevity, knowledge and standard of living—and also capturing social exclusion. For details on how the index is calculated see technical note 1.

Illiteracy rate, adult Calculated as 100 minus the adult literacy rate. See *literacy rate, adult.*

Imports of goods and services The value of all goods and other market services purchased from the rest of the world, including the value of merchandise, freight, insurance, transport, travel, royalties, licence

fees and other services. Labour and property income is excluded.

Income or consumption, shares of Based on national household surveys covering various years. Because data come from surveys covering different years and using different methodologies, comparisons between countries must be made with caution.

Income poverty line, population below The percentage of the population living below the specified poverty line:
• $1 a day—at 1985 international prices (equivalent to $1.08 at 1993 international prices), adjusted for purchasing power parity.
• $2 a day—at 1985 international prices (equivalent to $2.16 at 1993 international prices), adjusted for purchasing power parity.
• $4 a day—at 1990 international prices, adjusted for purchasing power parity.
• $11 a day (per person for a family of three)—at 1994 international prices, adjusted for purchasing power parity.
• National poverty line—the poverty line deemed appropriate for a country by its authorities.
• 50% of median income—50% of the median disposable household income.
See *PPP (purchasing power parity).*

Infant mortality rate The probability of dying between birth and exactly one year of age expressed per 1,000 live births.

Internally displaced people People who are displaced within their own country and to whom the United Nations High Commissioner for Refugees (UNHCR) extends protection or assistance, or both, in pursuance to a special request by a competent organ of the United Nations.

Internet host A computer system connected to the Internet—either a single terminal directly connected or a computer that allows multiple users to access network services through it.

Labour force All those employed (including people above a specified age who, during the reference period, were in paid employment, at work, self-employed or with a job but not at work) and unemployed (including people above a specified age who, during the reference period, were without work, currently available for work and seeking work).

Legislators, senior officials and managers, female Women's share of positions defined according to the International Standard Classification of Occupations

(ISCO-88) to include legislators, senior government officials, traditional chiefs and heads of villages, senior officials of special interest organizations, corporate managers, directors and chief executives, production and operations department managers and other department and general managers.

Life expectancy at birth The number of years a newborn infant would live if prevailing patterns of age-specific mortality rates at the time of birth were to stay the same throughout the child's life.

Life expectancy index One of the three indices on which the human development index is built. For details on how the index is calculated see technical note 1.

Literacy rate, adult The percentage of people aged 15 and above who can, with understanding, both read and write a short, simple statement on their everyday life.

Literacy rate, youth The percentage of people aged 15–24 who can, with understanding, both read and write a short, simple statement on their everyday life.

Malaria cases The total number of malaria cases reported to the World Health Organization by countries in which malaria is endemic. Many countries report only laboratory-confirmed cases, but many in Sub-Saharan Africa report clinically diagnosed cases as well.

Market activities Defined according to the 1993 revised UN System of National Accounts to include employment in establishments, primary production not in establishments, services for income and other production of goods not in establishments. See *non-market activities* and *work time, total.*

Maternal mortality ratio reported Reported annual number of deaths of women from pregnancy-related causes per 100,000 live births, not adjusted for the well-documented problems of underreporting and misclassification.

Military expenditure All expenditures of the defence ministry and other ministries on recruiting and training military personnel as well as on construction and purchase of military supplies and equipment. Military assistance is included in the expenditures of the donor country.

Non-market activities Defined according to the 1993 revised UN System of National Accounts to include household maintenance (cleaning, laundry and meal preparation and cleanup), management and shopping for own household; care for children, the sick, the elderly and the disabled in own household; and community services. See *market activities* and *work time, total.*

Official aid Grants or loans that meet the same standards as for official development assistance (ODA) except that recipient countries do not qualify as recipients of ODA. Part II of the Development Assistance Committee (DAC) list of recipient countries identifies these countries.

Official development assistance (ODA), net Grants or loans (net of repayments) to qualifying countries or territories, identified in part I of the Development Assistance Committee (DAC) list of recipient countries, that are undertaken by the official sector with promotion of economic development and welfare as the main objective and are made on concessional financial terms.

Official development assistance (ODA) to least developed countries See *official development assistance (ODA), net* and country classifications for least developed countries.

Oral rehydration therapy use rate The percentage of all cases of diarrhoea in children under age five treated with oral rehydration salts or recommended home fluids, or both.

Patents granted to residents Refers to documents issued by a government office that describe an invention and create a legal situation in which the patented invention can normally be exploited (made, used, sold, imported) only by or with the authorization of the patentee. The protection of inventions is generally limited to 20 years from the filing date of the application for the grant of a patent.

Physicians Includes graduates of a faculty or school of medicine who are working in any medical field (including teaching, research and administration).

Population growth rate, annual Refers to the annual exponential growth rate for the period indicated. See *population, total.*

Population, total Refers to the de facto population, which includes all people actually present in a given area at a given time.

PPP (purchasing power parity) A rate of exchange that accounts for price differences across countries, allowing international comparisons of real output and incomes. At the PPP US$ rate (as used in this

Report), PPP US$1 has the same purchasing power in the domestic economy as $1 has in the United States. For details on conceptual and practical issues relating to PPPs see box 5 in the note on statistics.

Private flows, other A category combining non-debt-creating portfolio equity investment flows (the sum of country funds, depository receipts and direct purchases of shares by foreign investors), portfolio debt flows (bond issues purchased by foreign investors) and bank and trade-related lending (commercial bank lending and other commercial credits).

Probability at birth of not surviving to a specified age Calculated as 1 minus the probability of surviving to a specified age for a given cohort. See *probability at birth of surviving to a specified age.*

Probability at birth of surviving to a specified age The probability of a newborn infant surviving to a specified age if subject to prevailing patterns of age-specific mortality rates.

Professional and technical workers, female Women's share of positions defined according to the International Standard Classification of Occupations (ISCO-88) to include physical, mathematical and engineering science professionals (and associate professionals), life science and health professionals (and associate professionals), teaching professionals (and associate professionals) and other professionals and associate professionals.

Refugees People who have fled their country because of a well-founded fear of persecution for reasons of their race, religion, nationality, political opinion or membership in a particular social group and who cannot or do not want to return.

Research and development expenditures Current and capital expenditures (including overhead) on creative, systematic activity intended to increase the stock of knowledge. Included are fundamental and applied research and experimental development work leading to new devices, products or processes.

Royalties and licence fees, receipts of Receipts by residents from non-residents for the authorized use of intangible, non-produced, non-financial assets and proprietary rights (such as patents, trademarks, copyrights, franchises and industrial processes) and for the use, through licensing agreements, of produced originals of prototypes (such as films and manuscripts). Data are based on the balance of payments.

Sanitation facilities, population using adequate The percentage of the population using adequate sanitation facilities, such as a connection to a sewer or septic tank system, a pour-flush latrine, a simple pit latrine or a ventilated improved pit latrine. An excreta disposal system is considered adequate if it is private or shared (but not public) and if it hygienically separates human excreta from human contact.

Science, math and engineering, tertiary students in The share of tertiary students enrolled in natural sciences; engineering; mathematics and computer sciences; architecture and town planning; transport and communications; trade, craft and industrial programmes; and agriculture, forestry and fisheries. See *education levels.*

Scientists and engineers in R&D People trained to work in any field of science who are engaged in professional research and development (R&D) activity. Most such jobs require the completion of tertiary education.

Seats in parliament held by women Refers to seats held by women in a lower or single house or an upper house or senate, where relevant.

Telephone mainline A telephone line connecting a subscriber to the telephone exchange equipment.

Terms of trade The ratio of the export price index to the import price index measured relative to a base year. A value of more than 100 implies that the price of exports has risen relative to the price of imports.

Tuberculosis cases The total number of tuberculosis cases reported to the World Health Organization. A tuberculosis case is defined as a patient in whom tuberculosis has been bacteriologically confirmed or diagnosed by a clinician.

Under-five mortality rate The probability of dying between birth and exactly five years of age expressed per 1,000 live births.

Under height for age, children under age five Includes moderate and severe stunting, which is defined as below two standard deviations from the median height for age of the reference population.

Undernourished people People whose food intake is insufficient to meet their minimum energy requirements on a chronic basis.

Under weight for age, children under age five Includes moderate and severe underweight, which is defined as below two standard deviations from the median weight for age of the reference population.

Unemployment Refers to all people above a specified age who are not in paid employment or self-employed, but are available for work and have taken specific steps to seek paid employment or self-employment.

Unemployment, long-term Unemployment lasting 12 months or longer. See *unemployment.*

Unemployment, youth Refers to unemployment between the ages of 15 or 16 and 24, depending on the national definition. See *unemployment.*

Urban population The midyear population of areas defined as urban in each country, as reported to the United Nations. See *population, total.*

Voter turnout The number of votes (including blank or invalid votes) as a percentage of the number of registered voters.

Water sources, population not using improved Calculated as 100 minus the percentage of the population using improved water sources. See *water sources, population using improved.*

Water sources, population using improved The proportion of the population using any of the following types of water supply for drinking: piped water, a public tap, a borehole with a pump, a protected well, a protected spring or rainwater.

Women in government at ministerial level Defined according to each state's definition of a national executive and may include women serving as ministers and vice ministers and those holding other ministerial positions, including parliamentary secretaries.

Work time, total Time spent on market and non-market activities as defined according to the 1993 revised UN System of National Accounts. See *market activities* and *non-market activities.*

Classification of countries

Countries in the human development aggregates

High human development (HDI 0.800 and above)

Antigua and Barbuda
Argentina
Australia
Austria
Bahamas
Bahrain
Barbados
Belgium
Brunei Darussalam
Canada
Chile
Costa Rica
Croatia
Cyprus
Czech Republic
Denmark
Estonia
Finland
France
Germany
Greece
Hong Kong, China (SAR)
Hungary
Iceland
Ireland
Israel
Italy
Japan
Korea, Rep. of
Kuwait
Latvia
Lithuania
Luxembourg
Malta
Netherlands
New Zealand
Norway
Poland
Portugal
Qatar
Saint Kitts and Nevis
Seychelles
Singapore
Slovakia
Slovenia
Spain
Sweden
Switzerland
Trinidad and Tobago
United Arab Emirates
United Kingdom
United States
Uruguay

(53 countries or areas)

Medium human development (HDI 0.500–0.799)

Albania
Algeria
Armenia
Azerbaijan
Belarus
Belize
Bolivia
Botswana
Brazil
Bulgaria
Cambodia
Cameroon
Cape Verde
China
Colombia
Comoros
Congo
Cuba
Dominica
Dominican Republic
Ecuador
Egypt
El Salvador
Equatorial Guinea
Fiji
Gabon
Georgia
Ghana
Grenada
Guatemala
Guyana
Honduras
India
Indonesia
Iran, Islamic Rep. of
Jamaica
Jordan
Kazakhstan
Kenya
Kyrgyzstan
Lebanon
Lesotho
Libyan Arab Jamahiriya
Macedonia, TFYR
Malaysia
Maldives
Mauritius
Mexico
Moldova, Rep. of
Mongolia
Morocco
Myanmar
Namibia
Nicaragua
Oman
Panama
Papua New Guinea
Paraguay
Peru
Philippines
Romania
Russian Federation
Saint Lucia
Saint Vincent and
    the Grenadines
Samoa (Western)
São Tomé and Principe
Saudi Arabia
Solomon Islands
South Africa
Sri Lanka
Suriname
Swaziland
Syrian Arab Republic
Tajikistan
Thailand
Tunisia
Turkey
Turkmenistan
Ukraine
Uzbekistan
Vanuatu
Venezuela
Viet Nam
Zimbabwe

(84 countries or areas)

Low human development (HDI below 0.500)

Angola
Bangladesh
Benin
Bhutan
Burkina Faso
Burundi
Central African Republic
Chad
Congo, Dem. Rep. of the
Côte d'Ivoire
Djibouti
Eritrea
Ethiopia
Gambia
Guinea
Guinea-Bissau
Haiti
Lao People's Dem. Rep.
Madagascar
Malawi
Mali
Mauritania
Mozambique
Nepal
Niger
Nigeria
Pakistan
Rwanda
Senegal
Sierra Leone
Sudan
Tanzania, U. Rep. of
Togo
Uganda
Yemen
Zambia

(36 countries or areas)

Countries in the income aggregates [a]

High income
(GNP per capita of $9,266 or more in 2000)

Australia
Austria
Bahamas
Barbados
Belgium
Brunei Darussalam
Canada
Cyprus
Denmark
Finland
France
Germany
Greece
Hong Kong, China (SAR)
Iceland
Ireland
Israel
Italy
Japan
Kuwait
Luxembourg
Malta
Netherlands
New Zealand
Norway
Portugal
Qatar
Singapore
Slovenia
Spain
Sweden
Switzerland
United Arab Emirates
United Kingdom
United States
(35 countries or areas)

Middle income
(GNP per capita of $756–9,265 in 2000)

Albania
Algeria
Antigua and Barbuda
Argentina
Bahrain
Belarus
Belize
Bolivia
Botswana
Brazil
Bulgaria
Cape Verde
Chile
China
Colombia
Costa Rica
Croatia
Cuba
Czech Republic
Djibouti
Dominica
Dominican Republic
Ecuador
Egypt
El Salvador
Equatorial Guinea
Estonia
Fiji
Gabon
Grenada
Guatemala
Guyana
Honduras
Hungary
Iran, Islamic Rep. of
Jamaica
Jordan
Kazakhstan
Korea, Rep. of
Latvia
Lebanon
Libyan Arab Jamahiriya

Lithuania
Macedonia, TFYR
Malaysia
Maldives
Mauritius
Mexico
Morocco
Namibia
Oman
Panama
Papua New Guinea
Paraguay
Peru
Philippines
Poland
Romania
Russian Federation
Saint Kitts and Nevis
Saint Lucia
Saint Vincent and
  the Grenadines
Samoa (Western)
Saudi Arabia
Seychelles
Slovakia
South Africa
Sri Lanka
Suriname
Swaziland
Syrian Arab Republic
Thailand
Trinidad and Tobago
Tunisia
Turkey
Turkmenistan
Uruguay
Vanuatu
Venezuela
(79 countries or areas)

Low income
(GNP per capita of $755 or less in 2000)

Angola
Armenia
Azerbaijan
Bangladesh
Benin
Bhutan
Burkina Faso
Burundi
Cambodia
Cameroon
Central African Republic
Chad
Comoros
Congo
Congo, Dem. Rep. of the
Côte d'Ivoire
Eritrea
Ethiopia
Gambia
Georgia
Ghana
Guinea
Guinea-Bissau
Haiti
India
Indonesia
Kenya
Kyrgyzstan
Lao People's Dem. Rep.
Lesotho
Madagascar
Malawi
Mali
Mauritania
Moldova, Rep. of
Mongolia
Mozambique
Myanmar
Nepal
Nicaragua
Niger
Nigeria

Pakistan
Rwanda
São Tomé and Principe
Senegal
Sierra Leone
Solomon Islands
Sudan
Tajikistan
Tanzania, U. Rep. of
Togo
Uganda
Ukraine
Uzbekistan
Viet Nam
Yemen
Zambia
Zimbabwe
(59 countries or areas)

a. Based on World Bank classifications (effective as of 1 July 2001).

Developing countries

Algeria	Guinea	Saint Vincent and	Djibouti	Croatia	Spain
Angola	Guinea-Bissau	the Grenadines	Equatorial Guinea	Czech Republic	Sweden
Antigua and Barbuda	Guyana	Samoa (Western)	Eritrea	Estonia	Switzerland
Argentina	Haiti	São Tomé and Principe	Ethiopia	Georgia	Turkey
Bahamas	Honduras	Saudi Arabia	Gambia	Hungary	United Kingdom
Bahrain	Hong Kong, China	Senegal	Guinea	Kazakhstan	United States
Bangladesh	(SAR)	Seychelles	Guinea-Bissau	Kyrgyzstan	*(30 countries or areas)*
Barbados	India	Sierra Leone	Haiti	Latvia	
Belize	Indonesia	Singapore	Lao People's Dem. Rep.	Lithuania	**High-income**
Benin	Iran, Islamic Rep. of	Solomon Islands	Lesotho	Macedonia, TFYR	**OECD countries** [b]
Bhutan	Jamaica	South Africa	Madagascar	Moldova, Rep. of	Australia
Bolivia	Jordan	Sri Lanka	Malawi	Poland	Austria
Botswana	Kenya	Sudan	Maldives	Romania	Belgium
Brazil	Korea, Rep. of	Suriname	Mali	Russian Federation	Canada
Brunei Darussalam	Kuwait	Swaziland	Mauritania	Slovakia	Denmark
Burkina Faso	Lao People's Dem. Rep.	Syrian Arab Republic	Mozambique	Slovenia	Finland
Burundi	Lebanon	Tanzania, U. Rep. of	Myanmar	Tajikistan	France
Cambodia	Lesotho	Thailand	Nepal	Turkmenistan	Germany
Cameroon	Libyan Arab Jamahiriya	Togo	Niger	Ukraine	Greece
Cape Verde	Madagascar	Trinidad and Tobago	Rwanda	Uzbekistan	Iceland
Central African Republic	Malawi	Tunisia	Samoa (Western)	*(25 countries or areas)*	Ireland
Chad	Malaysia	Turkey	São Tomé and Principe		Italy
Chile	Maldives	Uganda	Senegal	## OECD	Japan
China	Mali	United Arab Emirates	Sierra Leone	Australia	Luxembourg
Colombia	Mauritania	Uruguay	Solomon Islands	Austria	Netherlands
Comoros	Mauritius	Vanuatu	Sudan	Belgium	New Zealand
Congo	Mexico	Venezuela	Tanzania, U. Rep. of	Canada	Norway
Congo, Dem. Rep. of the	Mongolia	Viet Nam	Togo	Czech Republic	Portugal
Costa Rica	Morocco	Yemen	Uganda	Denmark	Spain
Côte d'Ivoire	Mozambique	Zambia	Vanuatu	Finland	Sweden
Cuba	Myanmar	Zimbabwe	Yemen	France	Switzerland
Cyprus	Namibia	*(123 countries or areas)*	Zambia	Germany	United Kingdom
Djibouti	Nepal		*(44 countries or areas)*	Greece	United States
Dominica	Nicaragua	**Least developed**		Hungary	*(23 countries or areas)*
Dominican Republic	Niger	**countries** [a]	## Central and	Iceland	
Ecuador	Nigeria	Angola	*Eastern Europe*	Ireland	
Egypt	Oman	Bangladesh	*and the*	Italy	
El Salvador	Pakistan	Benin	*Commonwealth*	Japan	
Equatorial Guinea	Panama	Bhutan	*of Independent*	Korea, Rep. of	
Eritrea	Papua New Guinea	Burkina Faso	*States (CIS)*	Luxembourg	
Ethiopia	Paraguay	Burundi		Mexico	
Fiji	Peru	Cambodia	Albania	Netherlands	
Gabon	Philippines	Cape Verde	Armenia	New Zealand	
Gambia	Qatar	Central African Republic	Azerbaijan	Norway	
Ghana	Rwanda	Chad	Belarus	Poland	
Grenada	Saint Kitts and Nevis	Comoros	Bulgaria	Portugal	
Guatemala	Saint Lucia	Congo, Dem. Rep. of the		Slovakia	

a. The United Nations currently designates 49 countries as least developed countries. The Report includes in that classification only the 44 countries that are also included in the human development index. Thus Afghanistan, Kiribati, Liberia, Somalia and Tuvalu are not included in the classification *least developed countries*.

b. Excludes the Czech Republic, Hungary, the Republic of Korea, Mexico, Poland, Slovakia and Turkey.

Arab States

Algeria
Bahrain
Djibouti
Egypt
Jordan
Kuwait
Lebanon
Libyan Arab Jamahiriya
Morocco
Oman
Qatar
Saudi Arabia
Sudan
Syrian Arab Republic
Tunisia
United Arab Emirates
Yemen
(17 countries or areas)

Asia and the Pacific

East Asia and the Pacific
Brunei Darussalam
Cambodia
China
Fiji
Hong Kong, China (SAR)
Indonesia
Korea, Rep. of
Lao People's Dem. Rep.
Malaysia
Mongolia
Myanmar
Papua New Guinea
Philippines
Samoa (Western)
Singapore
Solomon Islands
Thailand
Vanuatu
Viet Nam
(19 countries or areas)

South Asia
Bangladesh
Bhutan
India
Iran, Islamic Rep. of
Maldives
Nepal
Pakistan
Sri Lanka
(8 countries or areas)

Latin America and the Caribbean

Antigua and Barbuda
Argentina
Bahamas
Barbados
Belize
Bolivia
Brazil
Chile
Colombia
Costa Rica
Cuba
Dominica
Dominican Republic
Ecuador
El Salvador
Grenada
Guatemala
Guyana
Haiti
Honduras
Jamaica
Mexico
Nicaragua
Panama
Paraguay
Peru
Saint Kitts and Nevis
Saint Lucia
Saint Vincent and
    the Grenadines
Suriname
Trinidad and Tobago
Uruguay
Venezuela
(33 countries or areas)

Southern Europe

Cyprus
Turkey
(2 countries or areas)

Sub-Saharan Africa

Angola
Benin
Botswana
Burkina Faso
Burundi
Cameroon
Cape Verde
Central African Republic
Chad
Comoros
Congo
Congo, Dem. Rep. of the
Côte d'Ivoire
Equatorial Guinea
Eritrea
Ethiopia
Gabon
Gambia
Ghana
Guinea
Guinea-Bissau
Kenya
Lesotho
Madagascar
Malawi
Mali
Mauritania
Mauritius
Mozambique
Namibia
Niger
Nigeria
Rwanda
São Tomé and Principe
Senegal
Seychelles
Sierra Leone
South Africa
Swaziland
Tanzania, U. Rep. of
Togo
Uganda
Zambia
Zimbabwe
(44 countries or areas)

Indicator	Indicator tables
A	
Armed forces	
index	20
total	20
Arms transfers, conventional	
exports	
share of total	20
total	20
imports, total	20
B	
Births attended by skilled health staff	6
Birth-weight, infants with low	7
C	
Carbon dioxide emissions	
per capita	19
share of world total	19
Cellular mobile subscribers	11
Children reaching grade 5	10
Cigarette consumption per adult, annual average	7
Consumer price index, average annual change in	12
Contraceptive prevalence	6
Contributing family workers	
female	25
male	25
Crime, people victimized by	
assault	21
bribery (corruption)	21
property crime	21
robbery	21
sexual assault	21
total crime	21
D	
Debt service, total	
as % of exports of goods and services	16
as % of GDP	16, 17
E	
Earned income, estimated	
female	22
male	22
ratio of female to male	23
Economic activity rate, female	25
as % of male rate	25
index	25
Education expenditure, public	
as % of GNP	9, 17
as % of total government expenditure	9

Indicator	Indicator tables
pre-primary and primary	9
secondary	9
tertiary	9
Education index	1
Electricity consumption per capita	19
Employment by economic activity	
agriculture	
female	25
male	25
industry	
female	25
male	25
services	
female	25
male	25
Energy use, GDP per unit of	19
Enrolment ratio, gross	
combined primary, secondary and tertiary	1, 30
female	22
male	22
tertiary	
female	24
female as % of male	24
Enrolment ratio, net	
primary	10
female	24
female as % of male	24
secondary	10
female	24
female as % of male	24
Environmental treaties, ratification of	19
Essential drugs, population with access to	6
Exports	
of goods and services	14
high technology	14
manufactured	14
primary	14
F	
Fertility rate, total	5, 30
Foreign direct investment, net inflows of	16
Fuel consumption, traditional	19
Functional literacy skills, people lacking	4
G	
GDP index	1
GDP per capita (PPP US$)	1, 12, 30
annual growth rate	12
highest value during 1975–2000	12
year of highest value	12
GDP, total	
in PPP US$ billions	12
in US$ billions	12
Gender empowerment measure (GEM)	23

Indicator	Indicator tables
Gender-related development index (GDI)	22

H

Indicator	Indicator tables
Health expenditure	
per capita (PPP US$)	6
private	6
public	6, 17
HIV/AIDS	
adult rate of	7, 30
children living with	7
women living with	7
Human development index (HDI)	1
trends in	2
Human poverty index (HPI-1) for developing countries	3
Human poverty index (HPI-2) for selected OECD countries	4
Human rights instruments, status of major international	28

I

Indicator	Indicator tables
Illiteracy rate, adult	3
Immunization of one-year-olds	
against measles	6
against tuberculosis	6
Imports of goods and services	14
Income inequality measures	
Gini index	13
income ratio, richest 10% to poorest 10%	13
income ratio, richest 20% to poorest 20%	13
Income or consumption, share of	
poorest 10%	13
poorest 20%	13
richest 10%	13
richest 20%	13
Infant mortality rate	8, 30
Internally displaced people	20
Internet hosts	11

L

Indicator	Indicator tables
Labour rights conventions, status of fundamental	29
Life expectancy at birth	1, 8, 30
female	22
male	22
Life expectancy index	1
Literacy rate, adult	1, 10, 30
female	22, 24
female as % of male	24
male	22
Literacy rate, youth	10
female	24
female as % of male	24

M

Indicator	Indicator tables
Malaria cases	7
Maternal mortality ratio reported	8
Military expenditure	17

O

Indicator	Indicator tables
Official development assistance (ODA) disbursed, net	15
as % of GNP	15
net grants by NGOs	15
per capita of donor country	15
to least developed countries	15
total	15
Official development assistance (ODA) received (net disbursements)	
as % of GDP	16
per capita	16
total	16
Oral rehydration therapy use rate	6

P

Indicator	Indicator tables
Patents granted to residents	11
Physicians	6
Population	
aged 65 and above	5
annual growth rate	5
total	5, 30
under age 15	5
urban	5
Poverty, income	
population living below $1 a day	3
population living below $2 a day	3
population living below $4 a day	4
population living below $11 a day	4
population living below 50% of median income	4
population living below national poverty line	3
Private flows, other	16

R

Indicator	Indicator tables
Refugees	
by country of asylum	20
by country of origin	20
Research and development (R&D)	
expenditures	11
scientists and engineers in	11
Royalties and licence fees, receipts of	11

S

Indicator	Indicator tables
Sanitation, adequate facilities, population using	6
Science, math and engineering, tertiary students in	10

Indicator	Indicator tables
Survival	
probability at birth of not surviving to age 40	3
probability at birth of not surviving to age 60	4
probability at birth of surviving to age 65	
female	8
male	8

T

Telephone mainlines	11
Terms of trade	14
Tuberculosis cases	7

U

Under-five mortality rate	8, 30
Under height for age, children under age five	7
Undernourished people	7, 30
Under weight for age, children under age five	3, 7
Unemployed people	18
Unemployment rate	18
average annual	18
female as % of male	18
youth	18
youth, female as % of male	18
Unemployment, long term	4
female	18
male	18

Indicator	Indicator tables
W	
Water, improved sources	
population not using	3
population using	6, 30
Women's economic participation	
female legislators, senior officials and managers	23
female professional and technical workers	23
Women's political participation	
female legislators, senior officials and managers	23
seats in parliament held by women	23, 27
women in government at ministerial level	27
year first woman elected or appointed to parliament	27
year women received right to stand for election	27
year women received right to vote	27
Work time	
females	26
as % of males	26
market activities	26
non-market activities	26
males	26
market activities	26
non-market activities	26
total	
market activities	26
non-market activities	26

Countries and regions that have produced human development reports

Arab States
Algeria, *1998, 2001**
Bahrain, *1998*
Djibouti, *2000*
Egypt, *1994, 1995, 1996, 1997-98, 1998-99, 1999-2000, 2002**
Iraq, *1995, 2002**
Jordan, *2000, 2001**
Kuwait, *1997, 1998-99, 2000*
Lebanon, *1997, 1998, 2001**
Libyan Arab Jamahiriya, *1999*
Morocco, *1997, 1998-99, 2001**
Occupied Palestinian territory, *1996-97, 2000-01**
Saudi Arabia, *2000**
Somalia, *1998, 2001*
Syrian Arab Republic, *2000**
Tunisia, *1999*
United Arab Emirates, *1997*
Yemen, *1998, 2001**

Asia and the Pacific
Bangladesh, *1992, 1993, 1994, 1995, 1996, 1998, 2000*
Bhutan, *2000, 2002**
Cambodia, *1997, 1998, 1999, 2000, 2001**
China, *1997, 1999, 2002**
East Timor, *2001**
Fiji, *1997*
India, *1996, 1997, 1999, 2001*
India, Arunachal Pradesh, *2001**
India, Assam, *2001**
India, Himachal Pradesh, *2001**
India, Idduki, *2000*
India, Karnataka, *1999, 2001**
India, Madhya Pradesh, *1995, 1998, 2001**
India, Maharashtra, *2001**
India, Orissa, *2001**
India, Punjab, *2001**
India, Rajasthan, *1999, 2000, 2002**
India, Sikkim, *2001*
India, Tamil Nadu, *2001**
India, Uttar Pradesh, *2001**
Indonesia, *2001*
Iran, Islamic Rep. of, *1999, 2002**
Korea, Rep. of, *1998*
Lao People's Dem. Rep., *1998, 2001**
Maldives, *2000**
Mongolia, *1997, 2000*
Myanmar, *1998*
Nepal, *1998, 2001, 2002**
Pakistan, *2001**
Palau, *1999*
Papua New Guinea, *1998*
Philippines, *1994, 1997, 2000, 2002**
Samoa (Western), *2002**
Singapore, *2001**
Solomon Islands, *2001**

Sri Lanka, *1998, 2001**
Thailand, *1999, 2002**
Tuvalu, *1999*
Vanuatu, *1996*
Viet Nam, *2001, 2003**

Europe and the CIS
Albania, *1995, 1996, 1998, 2000, 2002**
Armenia, *1995, 1996, 1997, 1998, 1999, 2000, 2001, 2002**
Azerbaijan, *1995, 1996, 1997, 1998, 1999, 2000, 2001**
Belarus, *1995, 1996, 1997, 1998, 1999, 2000, 2002**
Bosnia and Herzegovina, *1998, 2000*
Bulgaria, *1995, 1996, 1997, 1998, 1999, 2000, 2001*
Bulgaria, Sofia, *1997*
Croatia, *1997, 1998, 1999, 2001**
Czech Republic, *1996, 1997, 1998, 1999, 2002**
Estonia, *1995, 1996, 1997, 1998, 1999, 2000, 2001**
Georgia, *1995, 1996, 1997, 1998, 1999, 2000, 2001-02**
Hungary, *1995, 1996, 1998, 1999, 2002**
Kazakhstan, *1995, 1996, 1997, 1998, 1999, 2000, 2002**
Kosovo, *2001-02**
Kyrgyzstan, *1995, 1996, 1997, 1998, 1999, 2000, 2001*
Latvia, *1995, 1996, 1997, 1998, 1999, 2000-01*
Lithuania, *1995, 1996, 1997, 1998, 1999, 2000, 2001*
Macedonia, TFYR, *1997, 1998, 1999, 2001**
Malta, *1996*
Moldova, Rep. of, *1995, 1996, 1997, 1998, 1999, 2000, 2002**
Poland, *1995, 1996, 1997, 1998, 1999, 2000, 2002**
Romania, *1995, 1996, 1997, 1998, 1999, 2000, 2001**
Russian Federation, *1995, 1996, 1997, 1998, 1999, 2000, 2001**
Saint Helena, *1999*
Slovakia, *1995, 1997, 1998, 1999, 2000, 2002**
Slovenia, *1998, 1999, 2000, 2002**
Tajikistan, *1995, 1996, 1997, 1998, 1999, 2000, 2001-02, 2003**
Turkey, *1995, 1996, 1997, 1998, 1999, 2001, 2002-03**
Turkmenistan, *1995, 1996, 1997, 1998, 1999, 2000*
Ukraine, *1995, 1996, 1997, 1998, 1999, 2001, 2002**
Uzbekistan, *1995, 1996, 1997, 1998, 1999, 2000*
Yugoslavia, *1996, 1997, 1998, 2002**

Latin America and the Caribbean
Argentina, *1995, 1996, 1997, 1998, 1999, 2001, 2002**
Argentina, Province of Buenos Aires, *1996, 1997, 1998, 1999*

Belize, *1997, 1998*
Bolivia, *1998, 2000, 2002*
Bolivia, Cochabamba, *1995*
Bolivia, La Paz, *1995*
Bolivia, Santa Cruz, *1995*
Brazil, *1996, 1998, 2002**
Brazil, Rio de Janeiro, *2001-02*
Chile, *1996, 1998, 2000, 2002**
Colombia, *1998, 1999, 2000, 2003**
Costa Rica, *1995, 1996, 1997, 1998, 1999, 2000, 2001*
Cuba, *1996, 1999, 2001**
Dominican Republic, *1997, 1999*
Ecuador, *1999, 2001*
El Salvador, *1997, 1999, 2001, 2002-03**
Guatemala, *1998, 1999, 2000*
Guyana, *1996, 2001**
Honduras, *1998, 1999*
Jamaica, *2000, 2001**
Nicaragua, *2000, 2001**
Panama, *2002*
Paraguay, *1995, 1996, 2002**
Peru, *1997*
Trinidad and Tobago, *2000, 2002**
Uruguay, *1999, 2001**
Venezuela, *1995, 1996, 1997, 1998, 1999, 2000*

Sub-Saharan Africa
Angola, *1997, 1998, 1999*
Benin, *1997, 1998, 1999, 2000, 2001, 2002**
Botswana, *1997, 2000, 2002**
Burkina Faso, *1997, 1998, 2000, 2001, 2002**
Burundi, *1997, 1999*
Cameroon, *1992, 1993, 1996, 1998*
Cape Verde, *1997, 1998, 1999, 2002**
Central African Republic, *1996, 2000, 2001**
Chad, *1997, 1999, 2000*
Comoros, *1997, 1998, 2001, 2002**
Congo, Dem. Rep. of the, *2000*
Côte d'Ivoire, *1997, 2000*
Equatorial Guinea, *1996, 1997*
Ethiopia, *1997, 1998*
Gabon, *1999, 2002**
Gambia, *1997, 2000*
Ghana, *1997, 1998, 1999, 2000*
Guinea, *1997, 1998, 1999*
Guinea-Bissau, *1997, 2002**
Kenya, *1999, 2001, 2002**
Lesotho, *1998, 2001**
Liberia, *1999*
Madagascar, *1997, 1999, 2000*
Madagascar, Fianarantsoa, *2002**
Madagascar, Mahajanga, *2002**
Madagascar, Tulear, *2002**
Malawi, *1997, 1998, 2001**
Mali, *1995, 1998, 1999, 2000, 2002**
Mauritania, *1996, 1997, 1998, 2001*

Mozambique, *1998, 1999, 2000, 2001*
Namibia, *1996, 1997, 1998*
Niger, *1997, 1998, 1999, 2000, 2002**
Nigeria, *1996, 1998, 2000–01*
Rwanda, *1999, 2002**
São Tomé and Principe, *1998*
Senegal, *1998*
Sierra Leone, *1996, 1998, 2001**
South Africa, *1998, 2000, 2002**
Swaziland, *1997, 1998, 2000*

Tanzania, U. Rep. of, *1997, 1999, 2001**
Togo, *1995, 1997, 1999, 2002**
Uganda, *1996, 1997, 1998, 2001, 2002**
Zambia, *1997, 1998, 1999–2000, 2002**
Zimbabwe, *1998, 1999, 2000*

Regional reports
Africa, *1995*
Arab States, *2001**
Central America, *1999, 2001**

Central and Eastern Europe and the CIS, *1995, 1996, 1997, 1998, 1999*
Latin America and the Caribbean, *2001**
Organization of Eastern Caribbean States, *2002**
Pacific Islands, *1994, 1999*
South Asia, *1997, 1998, 1999, 2000, 2001*
South-East Asia, *2001**
Southern African Development Community, *1998, 2000*
West and Central Africa, *2002**

Human development reports focusing on democratic governance

More than 270 regional, national and subnational human development reports have addressed governance-related issues as integral dimensions of human development, including reports on decentralization, participation and other topics. The following is a selection of reports with democracy or democratic governance as their core theme.

National reports
Asia and the Pacific
Human Development Report, India, 2001
Towards a New Consensus: Democracy and Human Development in Indonesia, 2001
Human Development and People's Participation in Governance, Philippines, 1994

Europe and the CIS
The Role of the State, Armenia, 1998
Citizen Participation in Governance— From Individuals to Citizens, Bulgaria, 2001
Human Development Report, Czech Republic, 1999
Human Rights, Liberties and Elections— The Quest for Democracy, Czech Republic, 1998

Democratic Governance—Alternative Approaches to Kyrgyzstan's Future Development, 2001
Democratic Governance for Human Development, Kyrgyzstan, 2000
Public Policy Process and Human Development, Latvia, 2000–01
Good Governance and Social Development, Republic of Moldova, 2002*
Human Development Report, Republic of Moldova, 1998
Human Development Report—The Power of Participation, Ukraine, 2001

Latin America and the Caribbean
Informe de Desarrollo Humano en Bolivia, 2002

Sub-Saharan Africa
Rapport National sur le Développement Humain au Bénin, 2000
Promoting Good Governance for Human Development and Poverty Eradication, Gambia, 2000

Participatory Governance for Human Development, Kenya, 2002*
Transition to Peaceful Democratic Governance, Liberia, 1999

Regional reports
The Crisis of Governance, South Asia, 1999
Governance and Human Development in Southern Africa, Southern African Development Community, 1998

* Under preparation as of March 2002.
Note: Information as of March 2002.
Source: Prepared by the National Human Development Report Unit, Human Development Report Office.

To access selected human development reports online, please visit http://www.undp.org/hdro/.

To obtain copies, contact:

United Nations Development Programme
Human Development Report Office
National Human Development Report Unit
304 East 45th Street, 12th floor
New York, NY 10017 USA
Telephone: 212 906 3674
Fax: 212 906 5161
Email: mary.ann.mwangi@undp.org